D0555599

Sofia Brown
May 1, 2016
Lakl Hazel
Bible Church
Boise ID

WHAT THE Bible IS ALL ABOUT

BIBLE HANDBOOK
REVISED & UPDATED

Dr. Henrietta C. Mears

Tyndale House Publishers, Inc.
Carol Stream, Illinois

What the Bible Is All About

Visit Tyndale online at www.tyndale.com.

Copyright © 1953, 2011 by Gospel Light. Copyright assigned to Tyndale House Publishers, Inc., 2015. All rights reserved.

All Scripture quotations, unless otherwise indicated, are taken from the Holy Bible, *New International Version,*® *NIV.*® Copyright © 1973, 1978, 1984, 2011 by Biblica, Inc.® Used by permission. All rights reserved worldwide.

Other versions used are:

AMP—Scripture taken from the *Amplified Bible,*® copyright © 1954, 1958, 1962, 1964, 1965, 1987 by The Lockman Foundation. Used by permission.

CEV—Scripture taken from the Contemporary English Version, copyright © 1991, 1992, 1995 by American Bible Society. Used by permission.

The Douay-Rheims Bible, 1899 American Edition of the John Murphy Company, Baltimore, Maryland.

KJV—Scripture quotations are taken from the *Holy Bible,* King James Version.

Moffatt—*The Bible: James Moffatt Translation* by James A. R. Moffatt. Copyright © 1922, 1924, 1925, 1926, 1935 by Harper Collins San Francisco. Copyright 1950, 1952, 1953, 1954 by James A. R. Moffatt.

NASB—Scripture taken from the New American Standard Bible,® copyright © 1960, 1962, 1963, 1968, 1971, 1972, 1973, 1975, 1977, 1995 by The Lockman Foundation. Used by permission.

TYNDALE, Tyndale's quill logo, and *What the Bible Is All About* are registered trademarks of Tyndale House Publishers, Inc.

The Library of Congress has cataloged the original edition as follows:
Mears, Henrietta C. (Henrietta Cornelia), 1890-1963
  [What the Bible is all about]
  What the Bible is all about handbook / Henrietta C. Mears.
    p. cm.
  Includes index.
  Originally published: What the Bible is all about. Ventura, Calif: Regal Books, c1999.
  ISBN 978-0-8307-5966-8 (NIV)
  1. Bible—Criticism, interpretation, etc. I. Title
BS511.3 .M43 2002
220.3—dc21

ISBN 978-1-4964-1604-9

Printed in the United States of America

21 20 19 18 17 16 15
 7   6   5   4   3   2   1

Contents

Books of the Major Prophets

Books of the Minor Prophets

PART TWO: THE NEW TESTAMENT

The Gospels

History

Letters of Paul

PART THREE: APPENDICES

Foreword

Dr. Billy Graham

Millions of people today are searching for a reliable voice of authority. The Word of God is the only real authority we have. His Word sheds light on human nature, world problems and human suffering. But beyond that, it clearly reveals the way to God.

The message of the Bible is the message of Jesus Christ, who said, "I am the way, the truth, and the life" (John 14:6, *KJV*). It is the story of salvation; the story of your redemption and mine through Christ; the story of life, of peace, of eternity.

Our faith is not dependent upon human knowledge and scientific advance but upon the unmistakable message of the Word of God.

The Bible has a great tradition and a magnificent heritage. It contains 66 books written over a period of several hundred years by many different men. Yet the message, divinely inspired by the Holy Spirit, is clear throughout. The 66 books become one.

The Bible is old, yet it is ever new. It is the most modern book in the world today. There is a false notion that a book as ancient as the Bible cannot speak to modern needs. People somehow think that in an age of scientific achievement, when knowledge has increased more in the past 25 years than in all preceding centuries put together, this ancient Book is out-of-date. But to all who read and love the Bible, it is relevant for our generation.

It is in the Holy Scriptures that we find the answers to life's ultimate questions: Where did I come from? Why am I here? Where am I going? What is the purpose of my existence?

One of the greatest needs in the Church today is to come back to the Scriptures as the basis of authority and to study them prayerfully in dependence on the Holy Spirit. When we read God's Word, we fill our hearts with His words, and God is speaking to us.

William Lyon Phelps, called the most beloved professor in America, and one-time president of Yale University, made the oft-quoted statement, "I thoroughly believe in a university education for both men and women; but I believe a knowledge of the Bible without a college course is more valuable than a college course without the Bible."

One of the greatest tragedies today is that, although the Bible is an available, open book, it is a closed book to millions—either because they leave it unread or because they read it without applying its teachings to themselves. No greater tragedy can befall a person or a nation than that of paying lip service to a Bible left unread or to a way of life not followed.

The Bible, the greatest document available for the human race, needs to be opened, read and believed. One survey indicated that only 12 percent of the people who said they believe the Bible actually read it every day; 34 percent read it only once a week, and 42 percent read it only once in a great while.

This book, *What the Bible Is All About*, will help make the reading and study of God's Word interesting, challenging and useful. We commend it to you.

Preface

William T. Greig Jr.
Former Chairman, Gospel Light

In the early 1950s my wife, Doris, and I were invited to teach the high school class in a small Baptist church in a suburb of Minneapolis, Minnesota. We were newly married and accepted the challenge with some trepidation. We agreed we would do better if we divided the group. I would teach the boys and Doris would teach the girls.

Doris and I both wanted to understand the Bible better. Doris had become a believer during a Billy Graham meeting at a Youth for Christ conference about two years earlier. I was fortunate to have been brought up in a Christian home and had been taught the Word by my parents since childhood. Yet we each hungered to know more of the Word. We also were aware that the kids in Sunday School knew precious little of Bible truth. So we decided to tackle the daunting task of teaching each of our classes through the entire Bible—all 66 books—in one year, 42 weeks. We secured a high school course then published by Gospel Light called the *Scripture Panorama Series*.

Dr. Henrietta C. Mears, founder of Gospel Light, authored this classic course. She believed firmly that no young person in her Sunday School should be able to say what a young college man had told her many years before: "If I had to pass a test in the Bible, I would absolutely flunk!" So she wrote this "crash" course for people who knew little if anything about the Bible but who wanted to know enough to understand the essential message of each of the books as they studied or read devotionally. The central theme of the entire Word of God is His dealings with His people and His provision of salvation through faith in Jesus Christ the Messiah—promised throughout the Old Testament and revealed fully in the New Testament.

Doris and I learned much that year, and so did our classes. It was intense but rewarding. Nothing of great value is ever accomplished without consistent effort invested on our part. You only get out what you put in. So it was with this course. It was a spiritual growing experience for all, and it helped us both to grow in grace and in our relationship to Jesus Christ and to each other, not to mention our class members.

In the mid-1950s, Richard Woike, president of the Christian Business Men's Committee, challenged me to read through the Bible every year. He would buy a new Bible each year on his birthday and read through it from Genesis through Revelation in one year. I liked the idea but got bogged down in Leviticus and Numbers, as many do. So I developed my own plan, which I found particularly rewarding. I began in Genesis, Job and Matthew and read a page or two of each section every day. This took me through the entire Bible in one year. It was rewarding particularly having this book, *What the Bible Is All About*, at my side, to answer hard questions and give me perspective about each book.

I decided I wanted more time each day for personal reflection and cross-referencing, so I developed a two-year plan, which also allowed me time to adopt Richard Woike's other discipline: He wrote in the head margin of every page the key message he learned from that page. This Bible reading plan is adapted in the form of bookmarks, included with this volume. You will find them at the back of the book. Keeping a copy of *What the Bible Is All About* on hand as you read through the Bible will give you an unforgettable experience. You will grow both in your knowledge of the Word of God and in your relationship to the Living Word, the Lord Jesus Christ.

In the early 1960s, a friend in the Billy Graham Association (BGA) headquarters in Minneapolis inquired about creating a book out of the *Scripture Panorama Series* teachers' books. Working together we jointly published *What the Bible Is All About*. Dr. Graham, who had a close relationship with Henrietta Mears going back to the late 1940s, wrote the foreword. A copy was given by the BGA to each person who responded to Dr. Graham's invitations in crusades, on TV or on radio. Millions of copies were given away through the years.

Dr. Mears believed firmly that the Bible is the authority of the teacher, so the teacher should teach directly from an open Bible, though some of us need outlines and personal notes to be more effective. Teachers and class members alike will grow deeper in their knowledge of the truth and their personal relationship to Jesus Christ, the Living Word, as they are taught spiritual truth directly from the Bible by the Holy Spirit. Jesus promised that His Holy Spirit would lead us to all truth (see John 16:13).

George Barna tells us that at the close of the twentieth century, the vast majority of people, including many Christians, did not believe in absolute truth. According to Barna, 71 percent of all adults said there is no such thing as absolute truth. This group of adults was further broken down: 78 percent among baby busters, 68 percent among born-again Christians, 71 percent among those who attended a mainline Protestant church, 75 percent among those who attended a Catholic church. This book can be used by the Holy Spirit to open His Word to us and teach us God's absolute truth, Jesus Christ.

HOW TO USE THIS BOOK

The purpose of this book is to familiarize the reader with the Bible through a general overview. This book contains 52 chapters, spanning the books of the Bible—Genesis to Revelation. These chapters can be studied one chapter a week for the year. At the beginning of each chapter is a list of Selected Bible Readings, a Scripture reading related to the chapter for each day of the week.

This revised and updated edition includes updates to Henrietta's original language and additional information regarding the author, date and purpose for each book of the Bible. Note that there are a number of appendices at the end of this book. Appendix A, "Teaching Suggestions," provides some general guidelines for how to use this material in a teaching setting. Appendix B, "Becoming a Member of God's Family," explains how to become a Christian and then how to live as a Christian. Appendix C, "A

Glossary of Bible Words," explains unfamiliar words that may be new to the reader, including a pronunciation guide for many of the words. Appendix D includes maps of Bible lands during the time of Scripture; and Appendix E includes a one-year and two-year Bible reading plan.

Understanding the Bible

The Bible Portrays Jesus Christ, the Savior of the World

SELECTED BIBLE READINGS

DAY OF THE WEEK		MAIN TOPIC
Sunday: 2 Timothy 3:10-17	God-Given	
Monday: Deuteronomy 11:1-9; Joshua 1:8-9	Should Be Treasured	
Tuesday: Psalm 119:9-18	Should Be Kept	
Wednesday: Psalm 119:105-117	Righteous	
Thursday: Isaiah 55:1-11; Matthew 4:4	Nourishing	
Friday: Luke 24:36-45	Alive	
Saturday: Revelation 22:8-21	Returning	

"Behind and beneath the Bible, above and beyond the Bible, is the God of the Bible."

The Bible is God's written revelation of His will to humanity. Its central theme is salvation through Jesus Christ.

The Bible contains 66 books, written by 40 authors, covering a period of approximately 1,600 years.

The Old Testament was written mostly in Hebrew (a few short passages in Aramaic). About 100 years (or more) before the Christian era, the entire Old Testament was translated into the Greek language. Remember, our English Bible is a translation from these original languages.

The word "Bible" comes from the Greek word *biblos*, meaning "book."

The word "testament" means "covenant," or "agreement." The Old Testament is the covenant God made with people about their salvation before Christ came. The New Testament is the agreement that God made with people about their salvation after Christ came.

In the Old Testament we find the covenant of law. In the New Testament we find the covenant of grace that came through Jesus Christ. One led into the other (see Galatians 3:17-25):

- The Old begins—the New completes.
- The Old gathers around Mount Sinai—the New around Mount Calvary.
- The Old is associated with Moses—the New with Christ (see John 1:17).

The authors of the Bible were kings and princes, poets and philosophers, prophets and statesmen. Some were learned in all the arts of the times and others were unschooled fishermen.

Other books soon are out-of-date, but this book spans the centuries.

Most books must be adapted to the age level of the intended reader, but old and young alike love this book.

Most books only interest the people in whose language they were written, but not this book. And no one ever stops to think it was written in what are now dead languages.

- The Old Testament begins with God (see Genesis 1:1)— the New Testament begins with Christ (see Matthew 1:1).
- From Adam to Abraham we have the history of all people—from Abraham to Christ we have the history of the Chosen People.
- From Christ on, we have the history of the Church.

A historian once noted, "Most people's knowledge of history is like a string of graduated pearls without the string." This statement seems to be especially true of Bible history. Many people know the Bible characters and the principal events but are hopelessly lost when they are called upon to connect the stories in order. Anyone who has experienced the thrill of learning to place the individual characters in their right setting in regard to place and time can realize the difference it makes in the enjoyment of God's Word.

Pick up the "pearls" in the Scriptures and string them into order from Genesis to Revelation so that you can "think through" the Bible story.

INTERESTING FACTS

Old Testament Books
The books in the Old Testament may be grouped as follows:

- Five books of Law
- Twelve books of History
- Five books of Poetry
- Seventeen books of Prophecy (5 major prophets; 12 minor prophets)

New Testament Books
The New Testament was written to reveal to us the character and teaching of Jesus Christ, the mediator of the New Covenant, by at least eight men, four of whom—Matthew, John, Peter and Paul—were apostles; two—Mark and Luke—were companions of the apostles; and two—James and Jude—were brothers of Jesus. The books were written at various times during the second half of the first century. The books in the New Testament may be grouped as follows:

- Four Gospels
- One book of History
- Twenty-one Epistles (13 Pauline; 8 general)
- One book of Prophecy

God, humanity, sin, redemption, justification, sanctification, glorification—in two words: "grace," "glory." In one word: "Jesus."

Christ quotes from 22 Old Testament books: in Matthew, 19 times; in Mark, 15 times; in Luke, 25; in John, 11. The book of Hebrews quotes (verbatim or by allusion) the Old Testament 85 times. Revelation quotes the Old Testament 245 times.

The *New International Version* of the Bible

The *New International Version* contains these interesting elements:

- Number of verses—31,173
- Number of words—727,969
- Longest chapter—Psalm 119
- Shortest chapter—Psalm 117
- Longest verse—Esther 8:9
- Shortest verse—John 11:35
- Longest book in the Old Testament—Psalms
- Longest book in the New Testament—Luke
- Most chapters in the New Testament—Matthew

Old Testament—Principal Places

There are 12 principal places around which the history of the Old Testament is written:

1. Eden (Genesis 1–3)
2. Ararat (Genesis 8:4)
3. Babel (Genesis 11:1-11)
4. Ur of the Chaldeans (Genesis 11:28–12:3)
5. Canaan (with Abraham) (Genesis 12:4-7)
6. Egypt (with Joseph) (Genesis 37–45, especially 41:41)
7. Sinai (Exodus 19:16–20:21)
8. Wilderness (Numbers 14:26-35)
9. Canaan (with Joshua) (Joshua 1:1-9)
10. Assyria (captivity of Israel) (2 Kings 18:9-12)
11. Babylon (captivity of Judah) (2 Kings 24:11-16)
12. Canaan (the land of Israel—return of the exiles) (Ezra 1:1–2:70)

As you build the story of the Bible around these places, you see the whole history in chronological order.

Old Testament—Principal Facts

Still another way to think through the Bible is by following the great facts in order:

1. Creation (Genesis 1:1–2:3)
2. Fall of man (Genesis 3)
3. Flood (Genesis 6–9)
4. Babel (Genesis 11:1–9)
5. Call of Abraham (Genesis 11:10–12:3)
6. Descent into Egypt (Genesis 46–47)
7. Exodus (Exodus 7–12)
8. Passover (Exodus 12)
9. Giving of the Law (Exodus 19–24)
10. Wilderness wanderings (Numbers 13–14)
11. Conquest of the Promised Land (Joshua 11)
12. Dark ages of the Chosen People (Judges)
13. Anointing of Saul as king (1 Samuel 9:27–10:1)
14. Golden age of Israelites under David and Solomon—united kingdom (2 Samuel 5:4-5; 1 Kings 10:6-8)
15. The divided kingdom—Israel and Judah (1 Kings 12:26-33)
16. The captivity in Assyria and Babylon (2 Kings 17; 25)
17. The return from exile (Ezra)

New Testament—Principal Facts

1. Early life of Christ (Matthew 1:18–2:23; Luke 1–2)
2. Ministry of Christ (Gospels of Matthew, Mark, Luke and John)
3. Church in Jerusalem (Acts 1–2)
4. Church extending to the Gentiles (Acts 10–11; 13–20)
5. Church in all the world (Romans 10–11,15; Ephesians 2:22-23)

Principal Biblical Periods

I. Period of the patriarchs to Moses (Genesis)
  A. The godly line—leading events
    1. Creation
    2. Fall
    3. Flood
    4. Dispersion
  B. The chosen family—leading events
    1. Call of Abraham
    2. Descent into Egypt; bondage

II. Period of great leaders: Moses to Saul (Exodus to Samuel)
  A. Exodus from Egypt
  B. Wandering in wilderness
  C. Conquest of Canaan
  D. Rule of judges

III. Period of the kings: Saul to the captivities (Samuel, Kings, Chronicles, the prophetical books)
  A. The united kingdom
    1. Saul
    2. David
    3. Solomon
  B. The divided kingdom
    1. Judah
    2. Israel

IV. Period of foreign rulers: captivities to Christ (Ezra, Nehemiah, Esther, prophecies of Daniel and Ezekiel)
  A. Captivity of Israel
  B. Captivity of Judah

V. Christ (Gospels of Matthew, Mark, Luke and John)

VI. The Church (Acts and the Epistles)
  A. In Jerusalem
  B. To the Gentiles
  C. In all the world

STUDYING THE BIBLE, THE WORD

Remember that in God's Word the foundation of Christianity is laid in the revelation of the one and only true God. God chose a people (the children of Israel) to reveal this truth and to preserve a record of Himself.

1. Regard the Bible as One Book, One History, One Story

The Bible is one book, one history, one story—His story. Behind 10,000 events stands God, the builder of history, the maker of the ages. Eternity bounds the one side, eternity bounds the other side, and time is in between: Genesis (origins) to Revelation (endings) and all the way in between, God is working things out. You can go into the minutest detail everywhere and see that there is one great purpose moving through the ages: the eternal design of the almighty God to redeem a wrecked and ruined world.

The Bible is one book, and you cannot read separate excerpts and expect to comprehend the magnificence of divine revelation. You must see it in its completeness. God has taken pains to give a progressive revelation, and we should take pains to read it from beginning to end. Don't suppose reading little scraps can ever be compensation for doing deep and systematic study of the Bible itself. We must concentrate on the Book and look at it as a whole, not treat each chapter or book piecemeal, as a stand-alone piece. One would scorn to read any other book, even the lightest novel, in this fashion.

Another way we can study the Bible is by groups—law, history, poetry, major and minor prophets, Gospels, Acts, Epistles and Revelation. Here again we find great unity, for Christ said, "It is written about me in the scroll—I have come to do your will, my God" (Hebrews 10:7). Everything points to the King!

Discover the Message

Each book has a message, and we should try to discover what that message is. Read until you discover the message of the book. For instance, in John it is easy to discover the purpose; it is stated in

John 20:31. The message is not always given so clearly, but the truth *is* there to be found.

In one sense we should treat the Bible as we treat any other book. When we get a book from the library, we would never think of reading just a paragraph, taking some 10 minutes, reading a little at night and then reading a little in the morning, and so spending weeks, perhaps months, in reading through the book. No interest could be maintained in any story by such a procedure. Take a love story, for instance. We would naturally begin at the beginning and read right through to the end (unless we turned to the finish to see how the story ended).

Do you come to the Bible with such eagerness? Do you read with that purpose and persistence? The Bible is not a book of separate, stand-alone texts; it is a story—a revelation—to be begun and pursued and ended as we start and continue other books. Don't trifle with the Bible. Don't divide it into short devotional paragraphs and think you have understood its messages. It may be excusable for those who can hardly read to open the Bible and take whatever their eyes light upon as the message of God. Many people do that, but the Bible isn't to be misused in that manner. We must come to it in a commonsense fashion. Believe that every book is about something, and read and reread until you find out what that something is.

Start with the Actual Book

First read the Book—not books about the Book or books of commentaries or even comments at the bottom of the page. They will come in good time, perhaps, but give the Book a chance to speak for itself and to make its own impression, to bear its own testimony. As the late country-music singer Johnny Cash is credited with saying, "The Bible sure does throw a lot of light on the commentaries."

Don't wish to put on colored glasses of people's opinions and then read through the interpretation put on the Bible by other minds. Let the Spirit of God Himself teach you. We all have a right to read it for ourselves. "No prophecy of Scripture came about by the prophet's own interpretation" (2 Peter 1:20). Read it seeking enlightenment. The Bible is a revelation, and God will flash light upon the page as you come humbly.

The Word of God is alive and every part is necessary to the perfection of the whole. We don't say that every part is equally important. If you were to ask me whether I would give up my finger or my eye, of course I would part with my finger; so it is with the Word of God. All is necessary to make a perfect whole, but some portions are more precious than others. You can't take away the Song of Solomon and have a perfect revelation. No one says that the Song of Solomon is comparable with John's Gospel, but both are parts of an organism, and that organism is not complete if any part is missing.

The Bible is a whole and we can't tamper with it. For example, to add anything to the book of Revelation or to take anything from it would mar its absolute perfection (see Revelation 22:18-19). The canon of Scripture is closed. Other works throw valuable light upon it, but the Book itself stands unique, alone and complete; the parts comprise the perfection of the whole.

2. Make Time for Bible Reading

Many say, "The Bible is so great, I don't know where to begin and don't know how to do it." This is often said quite earnestly and sincerely. It is true that unless we have some method, we shall assuredly lose the very best results, even though we may spend much time reading it.

G. Campbell Morgan, a well-respected Bible teacher, once stated, "The Bible can be read from Genesis 1 to Revelation 22 at pulpit rate in 78 hours." A lawyer challenged him on that. Morgan told him to go and try it before he issued a challenge. The lawyer went home and read the Bible in less than 80 hours.

Do you want to read through the Bible? Leave 80 hours for it. Schedule that time. How much time can you give each day? How many days a week? This is a highly practical proposition and should be used by the very busiest. We are all busy and must take time for it. If we are going to know the Bible, we must give time to it and arrange for it. We must adjust our lives so that time is made. Unless we do, we shall never come into any worthy knowledge of the Word, for it is impossible to acquire that needful knowledge of the Word only by listening to sermons on the Bible. The Bible reveals the will of God in order to lead us into it. Each book has a direct teaching. Find out what it is and conform to it. This is our purpose. We are going to consider the Bible, book by book.

3. Read a Book a Week

So we come to these books as complete in themselves, yet keeping in mind their vital relation to what precedes and what succeeds each one. We should read them one at a time. Read a book in a week (or use one of the reading plans provided at the back of this book). Now don't suppose that this is impossible. It is not. How much time do you spend reading books in 24 hours? How much time reading newspapers? How much time do you watch television or play video games? How much time do you spend on the Internet? Now the longest of the Bible books doesn't take longer than some of you probably devote to television or your computer in one day.

Some of the larger books in the Old Testament (such as Genesis, Exodus, Deuteronomy and Isaiah) might take some hours to read carefully; and if it is too much, divide them into seven equal parts, but put your reading into strict limits. Don't give yourself time to lose the impression made by the first reading before you get to the second, and don't suppose that you can grasp the content and intent of any book at a single reading.

Don't suppose that as you walk down the corridors of a gallery and look at the pictures you have seen the gallery. You see some pictures on the wall, but you don't know what they are about. You must sit in front of a picture and study it. So it is with the Bible.

Now the Bible, although it is a library of books, is also the Book. It is a story—a grand story—that moves from start to finish. Here surely is something that is phenomenal in literature. Suppose, for instance, you were to cover the great fields of knowledge—such as law, history, philosophy, ethics and prophecy—and you were to bring these different subjects all together in one book. What, to begin with, would you call the book? Then what unity could one possibly expect to find in such a jumble of subjects? Such an infinite number and variety of themes and styles as are found in the Bible, brought together across not a few generations in the history of people but across centuries, makes the likelihood of any unity being present amazingly small. No publisher would risk publishing such a book, and if he or she did, nobody would buy it or read it. That is, however, what is done in the Bible.

Remember, 40 different authors gave us the books of the Bible over a period of about 1,600 years. All these are brought together, bound, and are called "the Book." We can begin at Genesis and read through to the end. It is not jarring. We can pass from one style of literature to another as easily as though we were reading a story written by one hand and produced by one life, and indeed we have here a story produced by one mind though not written by one hand (see 2 Peter 1:21).

4. Look for Purpose—God's Plan for Salvation

The Bible tells us of the origin of sin and how this curse separated us all from God. We discover how utterly impossible it was for the law to bring to us the salvation we need, for by the deeds of the law could no flesh be justified, for "all have sinned" (Romans 3:20-23). Then we find the promise of a Savior, One who was to come "to seek and to save what was lost" and "give his life as a ransom for many" (Luke 19:10; Matthew 20:28). We see all through the ages that one purpose is evident—that of preparing a way for the coming of the Redeemer of the world.

5. Ask the Holy Spirit to Guide You

There is no royal road to learning and certainly there is no royal road to knowledge of the Bible. The Spirit of God will lead us into all truth, to be sure, but God's command is that we do our best to be approved, unashamed workmen (see 2 Timothy 2:15).

6. Read Attentively

Give to the Bible attention with intention, and intention will necessitate attention. Perhaps there is so little attention in Bible reading today because there is so little intention. We must come to it with a purpose and have a clearly defined object; we must know what we are about.

7. Appreciate the Bible's Uniqueness

Although divinely inspired, the Bible is human. The thought is divine, and the revelation is divine; but the expression of the communication is human. "But prophets, though human [human element], spoke from God as they were carried along by the Holy Spirit [divine element]" (2 Peter 1:21).

So we have here a book unlike all others. The Book, a divine revelation, a progressive revelation, a revelation of God to humanity communicated through men, moves on smoothly from its beginning to its great end. Way back in Genesis, we have the beginning; in Revelation we have the ending; and from Exodus to Jude we see how God carried out His purpose. We can't dispense with any part of it.

Bible history takes us back into the unknown past of eternity, and its prophecies take us into the otherwise unknown future.

The Old Testament is the foundation; the New Testament is the superstructure. A foundation is of no value unless a building is built upon it. A building is impossible unless there is a foundation. So the Old Testament and New Testament are essential to one another. As Saint Augustine, one of the most influential Christians who has ever lived, said:

The New is in the Old contained,
The Old is in the New explained.
The New is in the Old latent,
The Old is in the New patent.

The Old Testament and New Testament constitute a divine library, one sublime unity, origins in past to issues in future, processes between, connecting two eternities.

RECOGNIZING CHRIST, THE LIVING WORD

The Old Testament is an account of a nation (the Jewish nation). The New Testament is an account of a man (the Son of man). The nation was founded and nurtured of God in order to bring the man into the world (see Genesis 12:1-3).

God Himself became a man so that we might know what to think of when we think of God (see John 1:14; 14:9). His appearance on the earth is the central event of all history. The Old Testament sets the stage for it. The New Testament describes it.

As a man, Christ lived the most perfect life ever known. He was kind, tender, gentle, patient and sympathetic. He loved people. He worked marvelous miracles to feed the hungry. Multitudes—weary, pain ridden and heartsick—came to Him, and He gave them rest (see Matthew 11:28-30). It is said that if all the deeds of kindness that He did "were written down, the whole world would not have room for all the books that would be written" (John 21:25).

Then He died—to take away the sin of the world and to become the Savior of men.

Then He rose from the dead. He is alive today. He is not merely a historical character but a living person—this is the most important fact of history and the most vital force in the world today. And He promises eternal life to all who come to Him.

The whole Bible is built around the story of Christ and His promise of life everlasting to all. It was written only that we might believe and understand, know and love, and follow Him.

Apart from any theory of inspiration or any theory of how the Bible books came to their present form or how much the text may have suffered in passing through the hands of editors and copyists or what is historical and what may be poetical—assume that the Bible is just what it appears to be. Accept the books as we have them in our Bible; study them to know their contents. You will find a unity of thought that indicates that one mind inspired the writing of the whole series of books, that it bears on its face the stamp of its author, and that it is in every sense the Word of God.

MASTERING THE CONTENTS OF EACH BOOK

The following is a rhyme that will give you a clue to the contents of each book of the Bible:

Old Testament
Pentateuch

In Genesis the world was made,
  In Exodus the march was told;
Leviticus contains the law,
  In Numbers are the tribes enrolled;
In Deuteronomy again
  We're urged to keep God's law alone.
And these five books of Moses make
  The oldest writings that are known.

Historical Books

Brave Joshua to Canaan leads,
  In Judges oft the Jews rebel;
We read of David's name in Ruth,
  And First and Second Samuel;
In First and Second Kings we read
  How bad the Hebrew state became;
In First and Second Chronicles,
  Another history of the same.
In Ezra captive Jews return,
  While Nehemiah builds the wall;
Queen Esther saves her race from death.
  These books "Historical" we call.

Poetical Books

In Job we read of patient faith,
  In Psalms are David's songs of praise;
The Proverbs are to make us wise;
  Ecclesiastes next portrays
How vain fleeting earthly pleasures are;

The Song of Solomon is all
About the love of God, and these
    Five books "Poetical" we call.

Prophetical Books
Isaiah tells of Christ to come,
    While Jeremiah tells of woe,
And in his Lamentations mourns
    The Holy City's overthrow.
Ezekiel speaks of mysteries,
    While Daniel foretells kings of old;
Hosea calls men to repent;
    In Joel, judgments are foretold.
Amos tells of wrath, and Edom
    Obadiah is sent to warn,
While Jonah shows how Christ should rise,
    And Micah where He should be born;
In Nahum, Nineveh is seen;
    In Habakkuk, Chaldea's guilt;
Zephaniah, Judah's sins;
    Haggai, the temple's built.
Zechariah tells of Christ,
    And Malachi of John, his signs.
The Prophets number seventeen,
    And all the books are thirty-nine.

New Testament
Matthew, Mark, Luke and John
    Tell of Christ, His life they trace;
Acts shows the Holy Spirit's work;
    And Romans how we're saved by grace.
Corinthians instructs the church,
    Galatians shows God's grace alone;
Ephesians, how we are "in Christ,"
    Philippians, Christ's joys made known.
Colossians portrays Christ exalted.

And Thessalonians tells the end.
In Timothy and Titus both,
   Are rules for pastors to attend.
Philemon pictures charity,
   Thirteen Epistles, penned by Paul.
The Jewish law prefigured Christ;
   And Hebrews clearly shows it all.
James shows that faith by works must live,
   And Peter urges steadfastness,
While John exhorts to Christian love;
   And those who live it, God will bless.
Jude shows the end of evil men,
   While Revelation tells of heaven.
These end the whole New Testament;
   In all, they number twenty-seven.

PART ONE

The Old Testament

BOOKS OF LAW

Genesis · Exodus · Leviticus · Numbers · Deuteronomy

BOOKS OF HISTORY

Joshua · Judges · Ruth · 1 Samuel · 2 Samuel · 1 Kings · 2 Kings
1 Chronicles · 2 Chronicles · Ezra · Nehemiah · Esther

BOOKS OF POETRY

Job · Psalms · Proverbs · Ecclesiastes · Song of Solomon

BOOKS OF THE MAJOR PROPHETS

Isaiah · Jeremiah · Lamentations · Ezekiel · Daniel

BOOKS OF THE MINOR PROPHETS

Hosea · Joel · Amos · Obadiah · Jonah · Micah
Nahum · Habakkuk · Zephaniah · Haggai
Zechariah · Malachi

Books of Law

of the Old Testament

GENESIS • EXODUS • LEVITICUS

NUMBERS • DEUTERONOMY

Key Events of the Books of Law

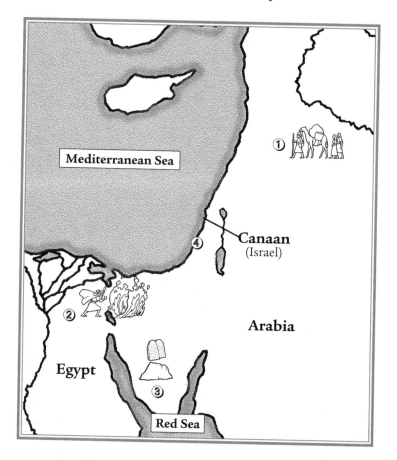

Books of Law: There Is One and Only One True God

The five books of the Law are also called "the Pentateuch," which means "five scrolls." The core of this ancient literature was written by Moses (see Luke 24:27; John 5:46). These books describe the creation of the world, God's call to the Hebrews ① to be His special people, their captivity and release ② from Egypt, the law ③ that guided them on their way to the Promised Land ④ and how God blessed the people when they obeyed and disciplined them when they disobeyed.

Understanding Genesis

Genesis Portrays Jesus Christ, Our Creator God

AUTHOR: The author of the book of Genesis is not identified. Traditionally, it has always been assumed that the author was Moses, according to the testimony of the Old Testament (see Exodus 17:14; 24:4; Numbers 33:2) and the New Testament according to the Lord Jesus and His apostles (see John 5:46).

DATE: The book of Genesis does not indicate when it was written. The date of authorship may be between 1265 and 1220 BC, between the time Moses led the Israelites out of Egypt and his death.

PURPOSE AND SUMMARY: The word "genesis" signifies "generation" or "origin" and comes from the Greek translation of Genesis 2:4. It is an appropriate title for the first book of the Bible, which contains the record of the origin of the universe, the human race,

Genesis

family life, nations, sin and redemption. The first 11 chapters, which deal with primeval or pre-patriarchal times, present the events preceding Hebrew history from Adam to Abraham. The remaining chapters (12–50) are concerned with God's dealings with the patriarchs Abraham, Isaac, Jacob and Jacob's son Joseph, all "fathers" of the people whom God has chosen to carry out His plan for the redemption of mankind. The book closes with these "Chosen People" in Egypt.

Genesis is the seed plot of the Word of God. The title "Genesis," which is Greek, means "origin," and the first Hebrew word of Genesis is translated "in the beginning"—words that indicate both the scope and the limits of the book. It tells us the beginning of everything except God. Another thing to notice is that it tells only of beginnings. There is no finality here. Upon its truths all the future revelation of God to people is built up.

Satan appears to have special enmity for the book of Genesis. No wonder the adversary has bent his attacks upon it. It exposes him as the enemy of God and the deceiver of the human race; it foretells his destruction; it depicts his doom (see Genesis 3). Without Genesis, our knowledge of a creating God would be pitifully limited; we would be woefully ignorant of the beginnings of our universe.

A BOOK OF BEGINNINGS

Genesis is the book of beginnings:

- The beginning of the world—Genesis 1:1-25
- The beginning of the human race—Genesis 1:26–2:25
- The beginning of sin in the world—Genesis 3:1-7
- The beginning of the promise of redemption—Genesis 3:8-24
- The beginning of family life—Genesis 4:1-15
- The beginning of civilization—Genesis 4:16–9:29

- The beginning of the nations of the world—
  Genesis 10–11
- The beginning of the Hebrew people—Genesis 12–50
- Adam began with God and fell through disobedience—
  Genesis 3:1-24
- Abel began with God by the blood of sacrifice—
  Genesis 4:4
- Noah began with God by way of the ark—
  Genesis 6:8,14,22
- Abraham began with God when he built altars—
  Genesis 12:8

These all made new beginnings for humankind.

Genesis is the record of the beginnings of all these things. No wonder that when people, because of spiritual blindness (see Ephesians 4:18), reject God's revelation in this peerless record of beginnings, they worship chance as the creator, beasts as their ancestors and fallen humanity as the flower of natural evolution!

A Book of History

Genesis begins with "God" (Genesis 1:1) but ends "in a coffin" (Genesis 50:26). This book is a history of human failure. But we find that God meets every failure. He is a glorious Savior. We find that "where sin increased, grace increased all the more" (Romans 5:20).

Genesis gives us a record of at least 2,000 years. It is not entirely history; it is a spiritual interpretation of history. In two chapters, God flashes on the wall an account of the creation of the world and of humanity. From there on, we see the story of redemption: God is bringing lost people back to Himself.

We have noted Satan's reasons for attacking this majestic book. Its authorship by Moses, its scientific accuracy and its literal testimony to human sin as deliberate disobedience to God have all been bitterly attacked. The Word of God, however, definitely declares Genesis to be one of the living oracles delivered to Moses. To its infallible truth and its testimony to the Messiah, our Lord Jesus testified Himself (see John 5:46-47).

If Genesis were to be discounted, a divine Creator, a divine creation, a divinely promised Redeemer and a divinely inspired Bible would also have to be discounted. But around its sacred pages is the protection of the Holy Spirit of God who inspired its words. If there were more study of Genesis instead of so much argument about it, its truth would be clearer. Many origins are recorded in the first 11 chapters: natural universe, human life, sin, death, redemption, civilization, nations and languages.

The remainder of the book—Genesis 12–50—delves into the beginnings of the Hebrew people: first in their founding through Abraham and then in their subsequent development and history through the great figures of Isaac, Jacob and Joseph. This great Hebrew nation was founded with the definite purpose that through it the whole world should be blessed.

A Book of Promises and Answers

God promised Abraham, a believer in Him, that his descendants:

1. Would inherit the land of Canaan
2. Would become a great nation
3. Would be a blessing on all nations (see Genesis 12:1-3)

God repeated these promises to Isaac and Jacob (see Genesis 26:1-5; 28:13-15).

Genesis tells us seven great names and messages:

1. Bow with Abel at the cross of the slain lamb.
2. Catch up with Enoch and walk with God.
3. Believe God and launch out with Noah on God's waters.
4. Go forth with Abraham in faith.
5. Dig wells with Isaac and get down to divine resources.
6. Climb ladders with Jacob and see God.
7. Be true like Joseph and live with God.

Genesis answers the great questions of the soul:

- What is the eternity of God?
- Where did we come from?
- Where did sin come from?
- How can sinful people get back to God (Abel's sacrifice)?
- How can we please God (Abraham's faith)?
- How can we have power with God and people (Jacob's surrender)?

Three words might give us the outline of Genesis:

1. Generation—"In the beginning God" (Genesis 1:1)
2. Degeneration—"Now the serpent" (Genesis 3:1)
3. Regeneration—"Now the LORD" (Genesis 12:1, *KJV*)

Genesis is the record of human failure: first in an ideal environment (Eden), then under the rule of conscience (from the Fall to the Flood), and finally under patriarchal rule (Noah to Joseph). In every case of human failure, however, God met human need with marvelous promises of sovereign grace. It is therefore fitting that the Bible's first book should show us the failure of humanity under every condition met by the salvation of God.

Won't you make a genesis (a beginning) of your own with a new love of our Lord in your own life?

Hints of the Messiah

Remember, Jesus Christ is the center of the Bible. He is somewhere on every page. In Genesis we see Him in type (the foreshadowing of Christian meanings in Old Testament people and events) and prophecy (supernatural knowledge given by God to holy people to reveal truth and to foretell events) in:

- Seed of woman—Genesis 3:15
- The entrance into the ark of safety—Genesis 7:1,7
- The offering up of Isaac—Genesis 22:1-24

• Jacob's ladder—Genesis 28:12
• Judah's scepter—Genesis 49:10
• Joseph lifted from pit to throne—Genesis 37:28; 41:41-44

The Period of the Patriarchs

The period of the patriarchs is the groundwork and basis of all history. It covers the time from Adam to Moses. In consequence of the failures on the part of people during this early period, God called out an individual. He put aside the nations and called a man, Abraham, who was to become the father of the Hebrew nation. We enter into this period in Genesis 12.

There are five patriarchal fathers: Abraham, Isaac, Jacob, Joseph and Job. (The book of Job must be put after the book of Genesis and before the book of Exodus. Job certainly lived before Moses, and we read of Moses in Exodus 2.)

God called Abraham and with him made a covenant, known as the Abrahamic Covenant. Become familiar with this covenant (Genesis 12:1-3). If you are not, the whole study of the Chosen People (in fact, the whole Old Testament) will have little meaning. God repeated that covenant to Abraham's son Isaac and again to his grandson Jacob (see Genesis 26:1-5; 28:13-15). He repeated it to no one else.

These three, therefore, are the covenant fathers, and that is why you read in Scripture, "I am the God of your fathers, the God of Abraham, Isaac and Jacob" (Acts 7:32). He never adds anyone else. God gave His covenant to these three and it is for them to communicate it to others. What is the covenant? Read Genesis 12:1-3, 26:1-5 and 28:13-15.

The Link Between Family and Nation

A very large portion of the story of Genesis is devoted to Joseph (see Genesis 37–48). Why? Because Joseph is the link between the family and the nation. Up till the time of Joseph, the main concern is a family, the family of Abraham, Isaac and Jacob. Some 70 souls are found at the end of the book of Genesis, constituting the family of Jacob. But still it is a family with which God is dealing. Read about this family and the blessings Jacob gave to each of his sons (see Genesis 49).

The moment we turn the page and step into Exodus, the main concern is a nation, not a family. During the long period from the end of Genesis to the opening of Exodus, the Hebrew nation has developed, and Joseph is the connection between it and the family.

Joseph is a character presented without fault—not that he didn't have any faults, but his faults are not recorded. He was a man of flesh and blood like us. God honored him, for there are at least 130 parallels between the life of Joseph and the life of Jesus. He is therefore the messianic patriarch, the patriarch who reflected the Christ Himself.

THE AUTHOR OF GENESIS

The age-long Hebrew and Christian position is that Moses, guided by the Spirit of God, wrote Genesis. The book closes approximately 300 years before Moses was born, so Moses could have received his information only by direct revelation from God or from historical records to which he had access that had been handed down from his forefathers. Read Luke 24:27 and John 7:19 to learn what Jesus said about Moses.

Every year proof is being dug up in Egypt and Israel that writing existed in Moses' day and that what is recorded in the Pentateuch is historically accurate. Moses was educated in the palace of Pharaoh and "was educated in all the wisdom of the Egyptians" (Acts 7:22), which included the literary profession; and Moses did know how to write and in fact encouraged it in others (see Exodus 34:27; Numbers 17:2; Deuteronomy 6:9; 24:1,3; Joshua 8:32).

No doubt the creation story was written long before Moses, maybe by Abraham or Noah or even by Enoch, the grandson of Adam (see Genesis 4:17). Who knows? Writing was in common use before the days of Abraham. In Ur, as in every important city in Babylonia, the libraries contained thousands of books, dictionaries, grammars, reference works, encyclopedias, and works on mathematics, astronomy, geography, religion and politics. No doubt Abraham had received traditions or records from Shem, the son of Noah (see Genesis 6:10), about the story of Creation and the Fall of humanity and of the Flood. Abraham lived in a society of culture, books and libraries. He no doubt made careful and accurate copies of all that happened to him and of the promises God had made to him. He put it down on clay tablets in cuneiform writing (the alphabet of the Babylonians) to be handed down as part of the annals of the nation he was founding.

GENESIS 1–2: CREATION

As Genesis begins, we see these words untarnished by the ages: "In the beginning God created the heavens and the earth" (Genesis 1:1). In these few simple words we have the Bible declaration of the origin of the material universe. God called all things into being by the word of His power. He spoke and worlds were framed (see Hebrews 11:3). Interpretations of the method of God may vary, but the truth of the fact remains.

God's creative work was progressive:

1. The world of matter—Genesis 1:3-19
2. The system of life—Genesis 1:20-25
3. Humanity, the crown of Creation—Genesis 1:26-27

Who was the God mentioned so many times in the first 31 verses of Genesis? Read John 1:1 and Hebrews 1:1. Here we see that the One who redeemed us by His precious blood, our Savior, was the Creator of this universe. Someone has said that God the Father is the architect; God the Son, the builder; and God the Holy Spirit, the beautifier of the universe. We find the Holy Spirit in Genesis 1:2.

In chapter 1 we have the account of Creation in outline form; in chapter 2 is part of the same in detail. The detail concerns the creation of humanity, for the Bible is the history of the redemption of humanity.

Know this: God created people in His own image to have fellowship with Himself. But we have cut ourselves off from God by sin. Only when sin is removed can we have fellowship again. This is why Jesus Christ came to this earth: that He might bear "our sins in his body on the cross" (1 Peter 2:24). Read 1 John 1 to learn how sin keeps us from fellowship not only with God but also with one another. First John 1:9 tells us what we can do to have a restored fellowship.

GENESIS 3–4: THE FALL

Adam and Eve were created in a state of innocence but with the power of choice. They were tested under the most favorable circumstances. They were endowed with clear minds and pure hearts, with the ability to do right. God gave them His own presence and fellowship (see Genesis 3:8).

Satan, the author of sin, acting through a serpent, tempted Adam and Eve to doubt God's word. They yielded to the temptation and failed the test. Here sin entered the world. Satan still influences people to disobey God. The results of Adam and Eve's sin are enumerated in Genesis 3. They were separated from God, the ground was cursed, and sorrow filled their hearts.

In mercy, God promised One who would redeem us from sin (see Genesis 3:15). The offspring of the woman (the virgin-born Jesus) would come to destroy the works of the devil (see 1 John 3:8).

Immediately after the Fall, people began to offer sacrifices to the Lord. No doubt God ordered these sacrifices. They were for the purpose of keeping before people the fact of their fall and of the coming sacrifice. It would be by the shedding of Jesus' blood that people were to be redeemed from sin and death (see Hebrews 9:22).

Two of Adam's sons, Cain and Abel, brought their sacrifices to the Lord: "Cain brought some of the fruits of the soil as an offering to the LORD. And Abel also brought an offering—fat portions from some of the firstborn of his flock" (Genesis 4:3-4). Abel's offering was accepted while Cain's was rejected. From our knowledge of the Word, it is quite evident that Cain's was not accepted because any sacrifice brought to the Lord must be done with proper motivation and through faith and obedience. Cain became angry with his brother, Abel, and in his wrath killed him.

The first writing began when God put "a mark," or sign, on Cain (Genesis 4:15). That mark stood for an idea, and the people knew what it stood for. Thus marks, signs and pictures came to be used to record ideas, words or combinations of words. These pictures were made on pottery or hard clay tablets, painted or engraved. This is the kind of writing found in the lowest levels of the prehistoric cities of Babylonia. The oldest known writings are of pictures on clay tablets.

Long before God gave the Law to Moses (see Exodus 20), we find several very definite ordinances given in the book of Genesis. At the very beginning God instituted the Sabbath (see Genesis 2:1-3) and marriage (see Genesis 2:24). And the law of the tithe was evidently observed. Read about Abraham's tithe in Genesis 14:20, and read Jacob's words in Genesis 28:22. God has evidently made people realize from the very beginning that they were only stewards of all they had.

This civilization before the Flood is called the antediluvian civilization. It perished in the judgment of the Flood. It was the civilization started by Cain. It ended in destruction.

The Bible teaches—and the archaeologist confirms—that the people of the world before the Flood were not mere savages. They had attained a considerable degree of civilization. Everything in material civilization is touched on in Genesis 4:16-22. Although not much is known about the antediluvians, some places have been discovered that could possibly be from this period. Some relics of their handwork that have been uncovered give evidence of a civilization such as the Bible describes.

In three cities—Ur, Kish and Fara—Professor Leonard Woolley, a British field archaeologist, excavated the layer of silt possibly left by the flood. Underneath the flood deposit in Ur, layers of rubbish full of stone and flint instruments, colored pottery, seals and burnt brick were found. The same is true of the other two cities.

Turn to Genesis 4:16-22 and see what is mentioned of early civilization in the Scriptures:

- Herdsmen: "Adah gave birth to Jabal; he was the father of those who live in tents and raise livestock" (4:20).
- Musicians: "His brother's name was Jubal; he was the father of all who play stringed instruments and pipes" (4:21).
- Craftsmen and manufacturers: "Zillah also had a son, Tubal-Cain, who forged all kinds of tools out of bronze and iron" (4:22).
- Builders: "Cain made love to his wife, and she became pregnant and gave birth to Enoch. Cain was then building a city, and he named it after his son Enoch" (4:17).

The civilization founded by Cain may have been equal to that of Greece or Rome, but God's judgment was upon it. Why? Read Genesis 6:5-7.

GENESIS 5–9: THE FLOOD

The account of the flood in the Bible is very plain and straightforward. The story is not told because it is startling or interesting but because it is an incident in the history of redemption that the Bible relates. After the Fall, God had given the world a new beginning, but soon the wickedness of people increased. Evil grew rampant and threatened to destroy everything that was good. Only one righteous man remained—Noah. So God sent the flood to restore good upon the earth.

Adam and Eve had yielded to an outward temptation, but now people had yielded to a temptation from within. "The LORD saw how great the wickedness of the human race had become on the earth, and that every inclination of the thoughts of the human heart was only evil all the time" (Genesis 6:5). God was going to separate the righteous from the wicked. He was taking the first step toward a chosen nation.

God had been long-suffering in His patience with people. The Holy Spirit had been in conflict with people. Noah had warned them for 120 years while he was building the ark. Even after Noah and his wife and his three sons and their wives—taking with them two of every unclean animal and 14 of every clean animal—had entered the ark, there was a respite of seven days before the flood came; but God's mercies were refused and so people had to perish (see Genesis 6–7). Noah was saved from the flood by the ark (a perfect type or Old Testament picture example of Christ, our ark, or refuge). When he came out, the first thing he did was to erect an altar and worship God (see Genesis 8:20).

Out of the fearful judgment of the earth by the Flood, God saved eight people. He gave the purified earth to these people with ample power to govern it (see Genesis 9:1-6). He gave them control of every living thing on earth and sea. For the first time God gave people human government. People were to be responsible for governing the world for God. The most solemn responsibility God gave to humans is the taking of a life for a life (see Genesis 9:6): God established capital punishment for homicide.

Sir Charles Marston was the British field archaeologist who excavated Jericho. He unearthed thousands of witnesses in stone and pottery to learn the truth concerning the Scriptures. Records of many people who scientists said never existed were brought to light, and many geographical locations the scientists said were only Bible names were unearthed.

Marston discovered that the events recorded in the first chapters of the book of Genesis appear to be centered around the Euphrates River. The surrounding country is called Shinar, Chaldea or Mesopotamia. We have known it as Babylonia; today it is called Iraq. It is a land of deserts through which the Tigris and Euphrates flow down to the Persian Gulf. But the deserts are studded with the ruins of ancient cities and scored with the channels of old irrigation canals; the silt has covered all.

Excavations revealed the ruins of a vast civilization that existed around 5000 BC. Two great peoples, the Sumerians and the Semites, created this civilization. We do not know the origin of the Sumerians, but the Semites take their name from Shem, the eldest son of Noah; and the Hebrew people, from which Abraham sprang, was a branch of this people.

Archaeological discoveries in Mesopotamia bare evidence of the Flood, both in cuneiform writings and in actual flood deposits. The cuneiform libraries have given us ample accounts of and references to this catastrophe. Also found was a clay prism on which are inscribed the names of the 10 kings who reigned before the Flood.

Dr. Stephen Herbert Langdon, an American field archaeologist, found evidence of the Flood at Kish near ancient Babylon, and his findings during the 1920s were subsequently published in his book *Excavations at Kish*. The excavations at Kish revealed two distinct flood strata, one 19 feet below the other.

Professor Woolley's discoveries of the deposits were made while excavating Ur of the Chaldeans, a good deal farther south, about halfway between Baghdad and the Persian Gulf. Dr. Langdon associated the Ur Flood deposits with the lower level of Kish. He reported that Babylonian and Assyrian scribes frequently referred to the age "before the flood." One king praised himself as one "who loved to read the writings of the age before the flood."

GENESIS 10–11: BABEL

After the Flood, the world was given a new start. But instead of spreading out and repopulating the earth as God had commanded, the main body of Noah's descendants seems to have migrated from Armenia, where Noah's family left the ark, back toward the plain of Babylonia, where they built the great tower of Babel in defiance of God. They thought they could establish a worldwide empire that would be independent of God.

The human race was then divided into nations speaking different languages, according to Noah's three sons, Shem, Ham and Japheth. Shem's sons settled in Arabia and to the east; Ham's sons settled in Africa; Japheth's sons settled in Europe.

The great Jewish historian Josephus declared that the tower of Babel was built because the people did not want to submit to God.

As we read the story in Genesis 11:1-9, the narrative seems to imply that the people were at cross purposes with God. People in their pride tried to glorify themselves, but it is God's purpose that people shall only glorify Him. In judgment, God sent a confusion of tongues and scattered the people around the world. As a result there was this confusion of tongues and worldwide dispersion of people. A difference in language tends to separate people in more ways than one and to check progress in commerce, in arts and in civilization.

GENESIS 12–38: THE CALL OF ABRAHAM

In spite of the wickedness of the human heart, God wanted to show His grace. He wanted a Chosen People:

- to whom He might entrust the Holy Scriptures
- to be His witness to the other nations
- through whom the promised Messiah would come

He called a man named Abram to leave his home in idolatrous Ur to go to an unknown land where God would make him the father of a mighty nation (see Genesis 12:1-3; Hebrews 11:8-19). This begins the history of God's Chosen People, Israel.

Wherever Abraham went, he erected an altar to God. God honored him by revealing Himself to him. "And he was called God's friend" (James 2:23). God made a covenant with him that he should be the father of a great nation and that through him the nations of the earth would be blessed (Genesis 12:1-3). His family became God's special charge. God dealt with them as with no other people. The Jews are always spoken of as God's Chosen People.

Through Isaac, Abraham's son, the promises of God were passed down to Jacob, who, despite his many faults, valued God's covenant blessing. He was enthusiastic about God's plan of founding a nation by which the whole world would be blessed. Jacob in his wanderings suffered for his sin and through chastening came out a great man. His name was changed to Israel, a prince with God (see Genesis 32:28). This is the name by which God's Chosen People were called—Israelites. And his 12 sons became the heads of the 12 tribes of Israel. Read Genesis 49.

GENESIS 39–50: DESCENT INTO EGYPT

Isaac and Rebecca made the mistake of playing favorites with their two sons. Isaac favored the hunter, Esau. Rebecca favored the quiet one, Jacob. Jacob did the same thing in the treatment of his son Joseph, which aroused jealousy in the other sons. Joseph is one of the outstanding noble characters of the Old Testament. It was through Joseph that Jacob's family was transplanted to Egypt. Joseph's life is one of the most perfect illustrations in the Bible of God's overruling providence. He was sold as a slave at 17; at 30 he became ruler in Egypt; 10 years later his father, Jacob, entered Egypt.

After Isaac's death and after Joseph had been sold into Egypt, Jacob and his sons and their children, numbering 70 in all, went down into that land because of a famine. There, the pharaoh who was reigning at that time exalted them. When he learned that they were shepherds, he permitted them to settle in the land of Goshen, where they grew in number, wealth and influence.

God knew that it was necessary for the Israelites to leave Canaan until they had developed national strength, so they could take possession of the land of Canaan. God wanted to safeguard them against mingling and intermarrying with the idolatrous peoples then in the land.

Read Genesis 49 to learn what Jacob's dying words were to his 12 sons. We see here again the promise to Judah of a descendant who is to be the coming ruler. Remember, Christ is called "the Lion of the tribe of Judah" (Revelation 5:5).

The book of Genesis ends in failure. The last words are "in a coffin in Egypt" (Genesis 50:26). Death only marks the pathway of sin; "the wages of sin is death" (Romans 6:23). The people needed a Savior!

POINTS TO REMEMBER

Eight names are mentioned in Genesis that we should remember in order:

1. God
2. Adam
3. Satan
4. Noah
5. Abraham
6. Isaac
7. Jacob
8. Joseph

Six places are of supreme importance in connection with the history of Genesis:

1. Eden
2. Ararat
3. Babel
4. Ur of the Chaldees
5. Canaan (the Promised Land)
6. Egypt

2

Understanding Exodus

Exodus Portrays Jesus Christ, Our Passover Lamb

SELECTED BIBLE READINGS

DAY OF THE WEEK		MAIN TOPIC
Sunday: Exodus 1:1-22	Bondage in Egypt	
Monday: Exodus 3–4	Call of Moses	
Tuesday: Exodus 7:20–11:10	Plagues of Egypt	
Wednesday: Exodus 12:1-51	Passover of God's Children	
Thursday: Exodus 20:1-26	Law of Moses	
Friday: Exodus 25:1-9; 28:1-14,30-43	Worship in the Tabernacle	
Saturday: Exodus 33:12–34:17	Renewal of Moses' Commission	

AUTHOR: The author of the book of Exodus is not identified. Traditionally, it has been assumed that Moses was the author of the book (see Exodus 17:14; 24:4-7; 34:27).

DATE: The book of Exodus does not indicate when it was written. The date of authorship may be between 1265 and 1220 BC, between the time Moses led the Israelites out of Egypt and his death.

PURPOSE AND SUMMARY: The name "Exodus" means "going out" or "departure." While it refers to one of the most important events of the book, the Exodus of the Israelites from Egypt, other highly significant events are also found here, such as the oppression of the Chosen People in Egypt, the flight and call of Moses, and God's covenant with the nation Israel at Sinai—an experience climaxed by

His giving of the moral law (Ten Commandments) through Moses to the people. A code of secular laws is also included, and the latter part of the book contains an elaborate description of the sacred Ark of the Covenant and its tent (tabernacle), God's place of dwelling among His people.

Exodus is connected to Genesis in much the same way that the New Testament stands in relationship to the Old Testament. Genesis tells of humanity's failure under every test and in every condition; Exodus is the thrilling epic of God rushing to the rescue. It tells of the redeeming work of a sovereign God.

Exodus is preeminently the book of redemption in the Old Testament. It begins in the darkness and gloom yet ends in glory; it begins by telling how God came down in grace to deliver an enslaved people and ends by declaring how God came down in glory to dwell in the midst of a redeemed people.

Exodus, which is Greek, means "way out." Without Genesis, the book of Exodus has no meaning. It begins with the Hebrew word *we*, which means "and" or "now." The story is just continuing. This book, like many other books of the Old Testament, begins with the word "and," even though this word does not always appear in translations. This seems to point to the fact that each author was not just recording his own story but only his part of a great drama that began in the events of the past and looked forward to that which would come. Take the five books of Moses (Genesis, Exodus, Leviticus, Numbers and Deuteronomy); each book is about something and those five things are vitally related to one another.

THREE KEY ELEMENTS

1. The Great Hero, Moses

The book gives us the story of Moses, the great hero of God. D. L. Moody, the great American evangelist, once said that Moses spent

40 years thinking he was somebody, 40 years learning he was nobody, and 40 years discovering what God can do with a nobody (see Hebrews 11:23-29).

2. The Law
The last half of the book (Exodus 19–40) teaches us that the redeemed must do the will of their Redeemer, consecrating themselves to His service and submitting to His control. Therefore, the moral law is given, followed by the ceremonial law, which was in part provision for the violator of the moral law.

3. The Tabernacle
God gave the Tabernacle as a detailed picture of the Redeemer to come, in His many offices, and as a dwelling place for His visible glory on earth. Its wonderful typology is rich in Christian truth.

EXODUS 1:1-22: BONDAGE

As this book opens, three-and-a-half centuries have passed since the closing scene of Genesis. The book of Genesis is a family history. The book of Exodus is a national history. We have no account of what happened during this long period of silence. Abraham, the patriarch, had died when his grandson Jacob was 15 years old. Jacob's favorite son, Joseph, had been sold as a slave into Egypt and had risen to great power and influence. The sons of Jacob had gained great favor because of their brother Joseph. Only 70 people went down into Egypt, but before they left Egypt, the people had grown into a nation of 3,000,000.

When Joseph died and a new dynasty came to the throne in Egypt, the wealth and great numbers of the children of Israel made them objects of suspicion in the eyes of the Egyptians. The pharaohs, wishing to break with them, reduced them to a slavery of the worst sort. This was hard for a people who had lived free, having been bestowed with every favor. They remembered the promises God had given to Abraham and his descendants (see Genesis 12:1-3), and it made this bondage doubly hard to understand.

The story told in the books of Exodus, Leviticus, Numbers and Deuteronomy shows that God did not forget the promise He had made to Abraham—"I will make you into a great nation" (Genesis 12:2).

The family records of Abraham, Isaac and Jacob no doubt had been carried into Egypt, and there they became part of Israel's national annals. Through the long years of bondage, they clung to the promise that one day Canaan would be their home.

Here in Exodus we will see God coming down to deliver the people from Egypt (see Exodus 3:7-8). Now the individuals and families had been organized into a nation. God was going to give them laws with which to govern themselves. He was going to take them back to the land He had promised them.

EXODUS 3–4: THE EXODUS

Think of the preparation that had to be made for moving so great a host, "six hundred thousand men on foot, besides women and children. Many other people went up with them, and also large droves of livestock, both flocks and herds" (Exodus 12:37-38).

No doubt it was a well-organized expedition. Moses had appealed to Pharaoh again and again to let the children of Israel go (see Exodus 5:1; 7:16). The plagues and the negotiations Moses had to make with Pharaoh must have lasted for nearly a year. This gave the children of Israel time to gather their things. The plagues taught the children of Israel some great things, besides forcing Pharaoh to let the children of Israel go.

In the construction of any great edifice, a blueprint has to be drawn and a pattern made. God designed our salvation before the foundation of the world (see Ephesians 1:4), and we find the pattern for salvation in the book of Exodus. Exodus is the historical picture of divine grace in the redemption of humanity by God to Himself by Jesus Christ, who is at once our great Apostle (Moses) and High Priest (Aaron) (see Hebrews 3:1).

Exodus

The story of Exodus is repeated in every soul that seeks deliverance from the entangling and debilitating influence of the world. From this point of view, the book is human, from the first verse to the last. The things that happened were by way of example, and they were written for our admonition (see 1 Corinthians 10:6-11). We study Exodus in order to see God's way of delivering sinful people and His gracious purposes in thus rescuing them.

EXODUS 12–19: THE PASSOVER

Exodus 12 gives us the thrilling story of the Passover, the clearest Old Testament picture of our individual salvation through faith in the shed blood of our Lord Jesus Christ. In this chapter is the basis for calling Christ the Lamb of God, Christ our Passover, and the many tender references to His crucifixion as the death of our own Passover Lamb: "For Christ, our Passover lamb, has been sacrificed" (1 Corinthians 5:7).

As the Passover chapter (12) is the heart of the book, so is the whole book a pattern of our salvation. Perhaps the children of Israel did not know the significance of this feast the night before they left Egypt, but they believed God and obeyed.

God had sent nine plagues on Egypt in order to make Pharaoh willing to let His people go. Almost a year had passed, and with each plague there was a hardening of Pharaoh's heart. Finally God said that the firstborn in all Egypt should die. This tenth plague would have fallen on the Israelites, too, had they not killed the paschal lamb and been protected by its blood of redemption (see Exodus 12:12-13).

The Order of the Passover

Every person should study the divine order of the Passover as it is given in Exodus 12:

First, "Take a lamb" (Exodus 12:3; see also Hebrews 9:28; Isaiah 53:6; John 19:14; 1 Corinthians 5:7). It was not the spotlessness of the living lamb that saved them (see Hebrews 9:22; 1 John 1:7;

Revelation 1:5). It was not Christ's sinless life that saves us, but His death on the cross.

Second, "*Put some of the blood on the top and on both sides of the door-frame*" (Exodus 12:22). It is not enough for the lamb to be slain. The blood was sufficient but not efficient unless applied. Every Israelite head of family had to apply it to his own household; notice that it was to go over the doorway, not under. What have you done with the blood, the blood of our Passover Lamb who died on Mount Calvary? (See Luke 23:33 [*Calvaria* is Latin for "skull"]; see also John 1:12.)

The hyssop—a common weed but obtainable by everyone—is typical of faith. The blood on the lintel is that which saved—not what they thought about it, but what they did with it counted: "When I see the blood, I will pass over you" (Exodus 12:13).

Not blood in the basin but blood applied that saves a soul. Not all the blood shed on Calvary's cross can save a soul from death unless it is applied; then, "When I see the blood, I will pass over you."

Not feelings, not personal worthiness, but one thing saved them: "blood" (Hebrews 9:22).

Third, "*Eat the lambs*" (Exodus 12:7). After the blood was shed and applied to the doorframe, the Israelites were instructed to eat. So it is with us: salvation first, then feeding—fellowship, worship, walk and service.

Feeding did not save them, but blood first; then nourishment was possible, for Jesus' "flesh is real food" (John 6:55). Read John 6:54-58.

Fourth, "*Remove the yeast*" (Exodus 12:15). "Search me, God. . . . See if there is any offensive way in me" (Psalm 139:23-24). Yeast (or "leaven," *KJV*) is often a type of sin: "Be on your guard against the yeast of the Pharisees and Sadducees" (Matthew 16:6); "get rid of the old yeast" (1 Corinthians 5:7).

Leaven of unrighteousness must be removed from our lives if we are to eat with God.

Fifth, "*Eat the meat . . . with bitter herbs*" (Exodus 12:8). Christ tasted the bitter cup for us; and some bitterness we, too, must suffer. "No discipline seems pleasant at the time, but painful" (Hebrews 12:11).

The lamb was to be feasted upon not raw, not unbaked, but as a suffering lamb that had passed through fire. It was to be eaten in haste with nothing left over. Not a bone was to be broken! Christ's body was broken but not His bones (see Psalm 34:20; John 19:36).

Sixth, "Be dressed and ready to travel" (Exodus 12:11, CEV). They ate the food standing, fully dressed, ready to go. All provision was made for the journey. What a contrast that night! Peaceful feasting in the houses of Israel; awful mourning in the houses of Egypt!

The Passage Through the Red Sea

We have read of the Passover. Now comes the passage. The Passover sealed them. The passage through the Red Sea steeled them. They left Egypt under the blood, a marked people. They passed through the Red Sea a directed, determined people. God led them out and shut the door behind them!

"When I came out of Egypt . . ." (Exodus 13:8). When did you come out? (Remember, Egypt represents allegiance to the world.)

EXODUS 20–24: THE GIVING OF THE LAW

In Exodus 20–24 we see the Law given, broken and restored. Up till this time in Israel's history, all has been grace and mercy. God had heard the cry of their bondage and answered them. God selected a leader and trained him. God defeated their enemies. God fed them, yet they rebelled. Now a new order of things is brought about at Sinai.

The Law demands nothing short of perfection. The psalmist says, "The law of the LORD is perfect" (Psalm 19:7; read verses 8-11). Only one man since it was given has been able to keep it perfectly. Christ not only kept the Law, but He also paid the complete penalty for the broken Law. Christ suffered that we might be spared (see Hebrews 9:13-15; 10:1-22; 1 Peter 1:18-20).

If we could not keep the Law, why was it given? That we might know our exceeding sinfulness. The Law is God's mirror to show us our exceeding sinfulness. "So then, the law is holy, and the commandment is holy, righteous and good" (Romans 7:12). The Law did not make us sin, but it showed us that we are sinners. The physician comes and looks at a child, and the symptoms reveal that she has measles. He gives her some medicine that appears to make her break out. The doctor did not make the child have measles, but he proved that measles was there. Read Galatians 4:4-5; Romans 8:1-4; 3:19-28.

Two mountain peaks stand in contrast to each other in God's Word:

1. Mount Sinai—With all of its horror thundered forth the Law (see Exodus 19).
2. Calvary—Placed opposite Sinai by God, Calvary took away all the fire and thunder and made possible a meeting place between God and the sinner.

We each have a choice about how we shall approach God, either by the Law or by blood (see Hebrews 12:18-29).

No provision was made in the Law for failure. It is all or nothing—the whole Law or a broken thing. One hole in a bowl, one crack in a pitcher, makes it unfit for its purpose. One flaw in a character mars the perfection God requires under the Law.

We are told that "God spoke all these words" (Exodus 20:1). God gave the whole testimony and the people assumed the whole responsibility of keeping it. Read what the people said in Exodus 19:8. Why did Israel accept the Law rather than cry for mercy? Human pride always makes us think that we can please God by ourselves. Before Israel even received the Law or started to keep it, they were dancing around the golden calf and worshiping a god they had made (see Exodus 32:1-10,18).

EXODUS 25–40: THE BUILDING OF THE TABERNACLE

Exodus 25–40 gives us one of the richest veins in inspiration's exhaustless mines. We must use our imagination and reason as we enter the holy precincts and gaze upon the significant furniture. God told Moses He wished a sanctuary, or holy dwelling place, that should point to Christ and tell of His person and work.

The Outer Court
Herein we see the altar on which the burnt offerings were sacrificed. Remember, Christ is our sin offering (see Exodus 27:1-8). The bronze basin was there for the cleansing of the priests before they could enter into the holy place to render their service (see Exodus 30:18).

The Holy Place
Herein was the golden lampstand (see Exodus 25:31-40), typifying Christ, the Light of the world; the Bread of the Presence (see Exodus 25:23-30), for Christ is the Bread of life; and the golden altar of incense (see Exodus 30:1-10), symbolizing Christ's intercession for us.

Holy of Holies
Now if we draw back the beautiful veil (which typifies the body of Christ), we will see the Ark of the Covenant, the symbol of God's presence. Into this holy of holies, the high priest came only once a year to sprinkle the blood of atonement. (The book of Hebrews tells us that Christ is not only our High Priest but also that He was our atonement, and so we can go into the holy of holies [the presence of God] at any time with boldness.)

The Tabernacle Itself
The Tabernacle, having the cloud of glory over it, taught the people that God was dwelling in their midst (see Exodus 25:8). The Tabernacle was the common center and rallying point that could be moved from time to time. Critics say that the account of the Tabernacle and its wonderful structure could not be true. They say that the times were too primitive, but research has given abundant evidence of great skill in such matters long before the Exodus. Fine linen was used in many ways. Fine work in gold has

been discovered in tombs dating back as early as the twelfth Egyptian dynasty, and Moses lived in the eighteenth dynasty.

POINTS TO REMEMBER

- Redemption was not an afterthought with God (see Ephesians 1:4).
- The Law was broken in the people's hearts before it was broken by Moses' hand.
- Over against Sinai is Calvary!
- God's mirror reveals but never cleanses.
- The blood of the Lamb makes us safe; our trust in God's Word makes us sure.
- God's plan will never be frustrated.

3

Understanding Leviticus

Leviticus Portrays Jesus Christ, Our Sacrifice for Sin

SELECTED BIBLE READINGS

DAY OF THE WEEK		MAIN TOPIC
Sunday: Leviticus 1		Burnt Offering
Monday: Leviticus 8		The Priests
Tuesday: Leviticus 11		Food Laws
Wednesday: Leviticus 16		Atonement
Thursday: Leviticus 23		Feasts
Friday: Leviticus 26		God's Pledge
Saturday: Leviticus 27		Dedication

AUTHOR: The author of the book of Leviticus is not identified. Traditionally, it has been assumed that Moses was the author of the book.

DATE: The book of Leviticus does not indicate when it was written. The date of authorship may be between 1265 and 1220 BC, between the time Moses led the Israelites out of Egypt and his death.

PURPOSE AND SUMMARY: This book was so named because it describes the laws of service and worship that were of special importance to the tribe of Levi. Although it has been called the Handbook of the Priests, many basic precepts of the New Testament are foreshadowed in this book, such as the seriousness of sin in God's sight, the necessity of atonement for sin, the holiness of God, and the necessity of a mediator between God and man.

"Get right," say the offerings. There are five of them:

1. Burnt offering
2. Grain offering
3. Fellowship offering
4. Sin offering
5. Guilt offering

"Keep right," say the feasts. There are 10 of them:

1. Sabbath
2. Passover
3. Unleavened Bread
4. Firstfruits
5. Weeks (or Pentecost)
6. Trumpets
7. Day of Atonement
8. Tabernacles
9. Sabbath Year
10. Year of Jubilee

Leviticus is called the Book of Atonement (see Leviticus 16:30-34). It is also called the Book of Laws. The book of Leviticus is God's picture book for the children of Israel to help them in their religious training, and every picture points forward to the work of Jesus Christ.

The title "Leviticus" suggests the subject matter of the book—the Levites and the priests and their service in the Tabernacle. We remember in the book of Exodus how at Mount Sinai God gave Moses the exact instructions about how to build the Tabernacle and about the institution of the priesthood to carry on the service in this holy place. As Leviticus opens (like Exodus, opening with the Hebrew word *we* ["and" or "now"]), the children of Israel are still at Mount Sinai, and God is continuing to give His instructions for orderly worship in the Tabernacle.

In Genesis, we see humanity ruined; in Exodus, humanity redeemed; in Leviticus, humanity worshiping.

Leviticus is a timely book, for it insists on keeping holy the body as well as the soul. It teaches that the redeemed ones must be holy because their Redeemer is holy. God says, "Be holy, because I am holy" (Leviticus 11:44-45; see also 19:2; 20:7,26). It gives us not only the key for our spiritual life and its holy walk, but it also surprises us with real lessons in hygiene and sanitation for the care of the body.

Leviticus is a divine book. The opening verse gives us the clue to the whole: "The Lord called to Moses and spoke to him from the tent of meeting." Leviticus is God speaking to us through the Tabernacle and its meaning.

Leviticus is a personal book, as the second verse implies: "When anyone among you brings an offering to the LORD." Notice that God expects each person to bring his or her own gift. The way is often as important as the gift. Have you an offering for the Lord? Then this book will appeal to you.

LEVITICUS 1:1–6:7: SACRIFICE AND SEPARATION

One of the most important questions in life is, "How may an unholy people approach a holy God?"

At the very beginning of Leviticus, we see God making provision for His people to approach Him in worship. This book shows redeemed Israel that the way to God is by sacrifice and that the walk with God is with separation (because of our sins).

Isn't it strange that deep down in every heart there is a sense of guilt and the feeling of a need to do something to secure pardon or gain the favor of the one wronged? Pagans bring their sacrifices to the altar of their gods, for they realize that they cannot do anything about their sins themselves. They must make atonement for them. Some of the mothers in India used to throw their babies into the river Ganges to appease their gods. (The British colonial government tried to put a stop to this, but the practice continued for many years.)

Pagans cannot see beyond their sacrifices. When we look at the sacrifices in this book, we find that they are only types, or symbolic representations, that point to the perfect sacrifice for our sins that was to be made on Calvary.

All the sacrifices in this book point to "the Lamb of God, who takes away the sin of the world!" (John 1:29).

Sin may be forgiven, but it must receive its penalty. "The wages of sin is death" (Romans 6:23). Sin keeps us from drawing near to God. He is "too pure to look on evil" (Habakkuk 1:13).

There can be no fellowship between God and the sinner until sin has been dealt with; the only way is sacrifice: "Without the shedding of blood there is no forgiveness" (Hebrews 9:22).

Five offerings are described in Leviticus. God wants us to understand the awful reality of sin, so He asks for a sacrifice, or an offering, each day. (Notice that bullocks, oxen, goats, sheep, turtledoves and pigeons are mentioned for sacrifice. The offering was determined by the ability of the one who brought it.) Learn the following list of the offerings, with a keyword to identify each one, to fix in your mind the first six chapters of Leviticus:

1. Burnt offering—"surrender" of Christ for the world (Leviticus 1)
2. Grain offering—"service" of Christ in life (Leviticus 2)
3. Fellowship offering—"serenity" of Christ in life (Leviticus 3)
4. Sin offering—"substitute" of Christ for sin (Leviticus 4–5:13)
5. Guilt offering—"satisfaction" by Christ for demands of God (Leviticus 5:14–6:7)

None of these five sacrifices, or offerings, forgave sins. They only pointed forward to the true sacrifice, God's very own Son (see Hebrews 10), for the sins of the world. What we bring is our sins; what Christ brings is the offering and the atonement for our sins.

1. The Burnt Offering (Leviticus 1)

This is a representation of Christ offering Himself who was without sin to God. There were daily burnt offerings. Christ offered Himself in the sinner's place (see Leviticus 1:4). This was an offering of dedication. Why first? Because sacrifice comes first. No one begins with God until all has been yielded to God (see Leviticus 1:3), and this was the most common sacrifice in the ancient Temple.

- Dedication is our part—consecration is God's part.
- We dedicate ourselves to God—He consecrates us, to His service.

As the old hymn that many Christians sing goes:

Consecrate me now to Thy service Lord,
By the power of grace divine;
Let my soul look up with a steadfast hope,
And my will be lost in Thine.

This is a burnt offering.

2. The Grain Offering (Leviticus 2)

This is the sacrifice of daily devotion. As the burnt offering typifies Christ in death, so the grain offering typifies Christ in life. The fine flour speaks of the character of Christ—His perfection in thought, in word, in action.

Let us feed on the perfect grain offering, but we must come to Him first with our whole burnt offering. Then we keep coming with our continual grain offering. It is our very best—our gift of life. Remember, though, that the slain offering *must* come first.

3. The Fellowship Offering (Leviticus 3)

This represents fellowship and communion with God. It is an offering of thanksgiving.

Christ is our peace (see Ephesians 2:14). He has reconciled all things to Himself "by making peace through his blood, shed on the cross" (Colossians 1:20).

4. The Sin Offering (Leviticus 4–5)

This shows us Christ on the cross in the sinner's place. In this offering we see an acknowledgment of sin: "When anyone sins . . . he must bring" (Leviticus 4:2-3). This offering is for expiation, or atonement. In the other offerings, the offerer comes as a worshiper; but here, the offerer comes as a convicted sinner. God holds us accountable for our sins. We are like criminals who have been tried, found guilty and sentenced to death.

Though placed last, the sin and guilt offerings are included in all that goes before. The only reason burnt offerings, grain offerings or fellowship offerings can be made is that the blood of pardon has been shed. God has accepted the one offering of His Son, which every lesser offering typified (symbolically represented).

In non-Christian religions, worshipers bring sacrifices to their god; Christians accept the sacrifice from their God.

5. The Guilt Offering (Leviticus 5:14–6:7)

This shows us that Christ has even taken care of our sins against others. The blood of the guilt offering cleanses the conscience and sends the trespasser back to the one he or she wronged, not only with the principal, but also with an additional "fifth of the value" (Leviticus 6:5). The injurer is forgiven, and the injured becomes an actual gainer.

It is a grave error to suppose that you are safe and right if you live up to your own conscience. God has scales. We can never comprehend His holiness.

LEVITICUS 8–10: THE PRIEST

We have been studying the great subject of sacrifice, but no one could bring his or her own sacrifice to God. Each person had to bring it to the priest, and he in turn would offer it to God.

God chose one tribe out of the 12 to care for the Tabernacle. This was the tribe of Levi. One family of Levites, Aaron's, would be the priests. The priests had charge of the sacrifices and were supported by the tithes of the people.

The priest offered the prayers and praises and sacrifices of the people to God on their behalf. He stood for them and pleaded their cause.

The burdened Israelites who desired to approach God brought their animals to the court of the Tabernacle. At the altar of burnt offerings they laid their hands on an animal's head to express penitence and consecration. The animal was then killed and its blood sprinkled on the altar.

The priest representing the worshiper then came to the laver, in which he washed his hands, thus indicating the clean life that should follow the forgiveness of sins. He entered the holy place, passed by the sacred furnishings, the lampstand and the table of bread, and came to the altar of incense, where prayer was offered.

One day in the year the high priest passed beyond the veil that separated the holy place and the most holy place and stood before the mercy seat, with the blood of the atonement, to intercede for the people.

The priest could not consecrate himself. Moses acted for God in this service. Each priest presented his body as a living sacrifice for service, just as Paul wants us to do (see Romans 12:1-2).

The priests had charge of the sacrifices, or offerings, we have just studied. The Levites were their assistants. They took care of the Tabernacle, formed choirs, and were guides and instructors in the later Temple.

Notice the opening of Leviticus 10. At the very beginning of the history of the work of the priesthood, there is evidence of failure. Nadab and Abihu, two sons of Aaron, offered "strange fire" (KJV) before the Lord, "contrary to his command. So fire came out from the presence of the LORD and consumed them" (Leviticus 10:1-2).

We read in Leviticus 10:3 that Aaron held his peace. He was their father, but he dared not question God. We talk too much before God. We must learn to walk softly in the divine presence. The other priests were solemnly charged to show no signs of mourning and to abide at their posts.

Animal sacrifices are no longer necessary because all sacrifices were fulfilled in Christ. Therefore priests are no longer necessary. Christ Himself is the great High Priest for humanity (see Hebrews 2:17; 4:15). He is at the right hand of the Father today, making intercession for us. We approach God by Him and Him alone (see Hebrews 10:12; 7:25; John 14:6). He is the only mediator between God and humanity. And no one else can come between God and humanity.

- When we see Christ as sacrifice, we see beauty and completeness.

- When we see Christ as priest, we see His divine perfection—"For we do not have a high priest who is unable to sympathize with our weaknesses, but we have one who has been tempted in every way, just as we are—yet was without sin" (Hebrews 4:15).

- As sacrifice, Christ establishes the relationship of His people with God; as priest, He maintains that position.

We read of this perfect and eternal priesthood in the book of Hebrews. Heaven, not earth, is the sphere of Christ's priestly ministry. He never appeared in the Temple on earth to offer sacrifice. He went there to preach and teach but not to sacrifice. Except in the sense that all believers are priests (see 1 Peter 2:5), there is no such thing as a priest on earth. The believer is a spiritual priest. It is not necessary that any child of God go before any person on earth to obtain entrance into the presence of God. Every Christian has the right to enter, because he or she knows Jesus Christ. The Lord said, "I am the way" (John 14:6). "Let us then approach God's throne of grace with confidence, so that we may receive mercy and find grace to help us in our time of need" (Hebrews 4:16).

LEVITICUS 23; 25:
TEN FEASTS

As the first part of Leviticus has to do with offerings and the offerers, so the last part of the book deals with feasts and feasters. The sacrifices spoke of the blood that saved. The feasts spoke of the food that sustains. Both are of God.

The sacrifices correspond to the cup of the Lord's Supper, which reminds us of Christ's death on the cross whereby we are redeemed. The bread of the Communion, of which we are partakers, corresponds to His life.

1. The Sabbath (Leviticus 23:1-3)

The Sabbath was given the foremost place. It was a perpetually recurring feast to be held through the whole year on every seventh day. It was a day of worship and rest, celebrating the finished work of God in creation (see Genesis 2:2-3). Christians celebrate the first day of the week, the day our Lord arose from the grave (see Luke 24:1; Acts 20:7; 1 Corinthians 16:2). Thus we celebrate the finished work of redemption.

2–3. The Passover (Leviticus 23:4-5) and Unleavened Bread (Leviticus 23:6-8)

These were the first feasts of the year. Passover, which lasted one day, was immediately followed by the Feast of Unleavened Bread, which lasted seven days.

The Passover spoke of redemption and was celebrated every spring at our Easter time. It was the Fourth of July for the children of Israel. They did not celebrate it with fireworks and parades but with a great service of worship to God. All the Israelites who could made their way to Jerusalem.

The Jewish people were still celebrating this feast when our Lord was on this earth. Read in the Word the times that He went to the Passover feast (see Luke 2:41-52; Matthew 26:19; John 13). The Jewish people today continue to celebrate this same feast. They are still looking for their Messiah.

Leviticus

4. Firstfruits (Leviticus 23:9-14)

This was observed by the Israelites during the Feast of Unleavened Bread. This Feast of Firstfruits typified Christ's resurrection and ours (see 1 Corinthians 15:20). Fifty days later Passover was observed.

5. Weeks (Leviticus 23:15-22)

This was observed 50 days after the Feast of Firstfruits. In the New Testament, the name for this feast is Pentecost. Fifty days after Christ's resurrection, the Holy Spirit descended upon the disciples, and the Church was born. Pentecost was the birthday of the Church. The death and resurrection of Christ had to be accomplished before the descent of the Holy Spirit.

6. Trumpets (Leviticus 23:23-25)

This has become the New Year's Day (Rosh Hashanah) of the Jewish people. The Israelites celebrated it in September or October, and the Jewish people still celebrate this feast. It points forward to the future gathering of the dispersed people of Israel (see Zechariah 14:16).

7. The Day of Atonement (Leviticus 23:26-32)

This followed the Feast of Trumpets by 10 days. This was the most solemn day of the year of God's Chosen People. On this day, the sins of the nation were confessed. Confession is always the first step toward righteousness. It reveals a right attitude toward sin. It leads to a desire for forgiveness. God says, "If we confess our sins, he is faithful and just and will forgive us our sins and purify us from all unrighteousness" (1 John 1:9).

On this day, Jehovah's ("Jehovah" is a form of the divine name, more properly "Yahweh") relationship to His people was established—all the nation's sins, failures and weaknesses of the people were atoned for. The blood was shed and the sins of the people were covered so that God could take up His abode in the midst of His people in spite of their uncleanness.

We learn in Leviticus 16 that God was hidden behind a veil in the Tabernacle and that the priests and the people were to remain at a distance. Read Leviticus 16:2. The way was not yet made open to approach God. Now "we may approach God with freedom and confidence" (Ephesians 3:12). We can run into God's presence at any time, for Christ has made the way possible for us. In the book of Leviticus, however, God was shut in from humanity, and humanity was shut out from God.

The Day of Atonement was the only day in the year when the high priest was permitted to enter the holy of holies. He went in with an offering for the atonement of the sins of the people. "Atonement" means "cover," so this offering "covered" (not took away) the sins of the people until the great sacrifice on Calvary was made. Read Hebrews 10:1-2,11-12.

8. Tabernacles (Leviticus 23:33-36)

This was the last required feast of the year. Also called the Feast of Booths, or Ingathering, it commemorated the time when the children of Israel lived in tents during their wilderness journey. It was celebrated in the fall of the year and lasted an entire week. The people lived in booths outdoors and listened to the reading of the Law.

The Feast of the Passover in the spring and the Feast of Tabernacles in the fall kept before the children of Israel the marvelous way in which they had been delivered from Egypt and were sustained in the wilderness. God did not want them to forget the way in which the gods of Egypt were utterly discredited and the great nation of Egypt humbled.

The Feast of Tabernacles reminded them that by their own disobedience they were compelled to wander 40 years in the wilderness, but in spite of their unbelief, God was faithful in caring for them and in bringing them to their inheritance. These special days reminded them of their dependence upon Jehovah and of the blessings that would come if they would be obedient to His will.

9. The Sabbath Year (Leviticus 25:1-7)

This was the year of meditation and devotion. It was a yearlong Sabbath celebrated every seven years. The purpose and character of the Sabbath was magnified.

God wanted to impress upon the minds of the people that the very land was holy to Him. Thus, "the land he promised them" (Deuteronomy 9:28) became "the holy land" (Zephaniah 2:5). There was to be quiet over the whole land during these days. All breathed the spirit of rest and meditation. Every day was like the Sabbath, and the minds of the people were kept on the things of the Lord. The Law was read. This time exerted a tremendous influence upon the lives of the people.

10. The Year of Jubilee (Leviticus 25:8-55)

This was celebrated every fiftieth year. It was inaugurated on the Day of Atonement with the blowing of trumpets. As in the Sabbath Year, the land was not cultivated. All slaves of Israelite blood were freed. The blowing of the trumpets that ushered in the year released every bondperson. Jewish historians tell us that the Year of Jubilee was observed at the time of the fall of Judah in 586 BC. References are made to it in Isaiah 5:7-10; 61:1-2; Ezekiel 7:12-13; 46:16-18.

Another outstanding event during this celebration was the restoration to the original owner of all land that had in any way been taken away from him. That is, it was returned to the family to whom it had been assigned in the original distribution. What a wise provision it was from an economic standpoint. But God also no doubt had a more far-reaching plan, which concerned the coming of the Messiah: Every tribal and family register must be carefully kept so that the rights of all would be protected. This would apply especially to Judah, the tribe from which the Messiah was to come. From these family registers, our Lord's genealogy can be exactly traced.

POINTS TO REMEMBER

Leviticus is a book for a redeemed people, showing how God is to be approached and worshiped. The book of Exodus is the book of redemption, but the book of Leviticus tells how the redeemed ones can worship God.

Only through the blood of Christ can we have access to God.

God demands a holiness that Christ alone can give, for we are sharers in His holiness (see Hebrews 12:10).

In Genesis we see humanity ruined; in Exodus, humanity redeemed; in Leviticus, humanity worshiping.

Seven is a significant number in Leviticus:

- Every seventh day was the Sabbath.
- Every seventh year was a Sabbath Year.
- Every seven times seven years was followed by the Year of Jubilee.
- Pentecost was seven weeks after Passover.
- In the seventh month were the Feasts of Trumpets, Tabernacles and Atonement.
- Pentecost lasted seven days.
- Passover lasted seven days.

This book, like Revelation, is built around a series of sevens.

Leviticus

Understanding Numbers

Numbers Portrays Jesus Christ, Our "Lifted-up One"

SELECTED BIBLE READINGS

AUTHOR: The author of the book of Numbers is not identified. Traditionally, it has been assumed that Moses was the author of the book.

DATE: The book of Numbers does not indicate when it was written. The date of authorship may be between 1265 and 1220 BC, between the time Moses led the Israelites out of Egypt and his death.

PURPOSE AND SUMMARY: The name of this book originated from the two numberings of the people (censuses) described in it: the first at Sinai in the second year of the Exodus and another on the plains of Moab opposite Jericho in the fortieth year. A better title is the one given the book in the Hebrew Bible, *Bemidhbar* ("In the Wilderness"), for it describes the locale of the major events of the book. In all these events, the writer sees the guiding hand of God, sustaining, delivering and keeping covenant with His people as He prepares them for entrance into the land promised first to Abraham (see Genesis 12).

The children of Israel were saved to serve. So is every child of God today.

Beware of unbelief! The apostle Paul says to us, "You were running a good race. Who cut in on you to keep you from obeying the truth?" (Galatians 5:7). Unbelief hinders blessing. God tells why we cannot enter into His blessings (see Hebrews 3:19).

Numbers might be called the Wilderness Wanderings, because it describes the journey of the Israelites from Sinai to the border of Canaan, the land of promise, covering about 40 years.

Numbers might also be called the Book of the March and the Roll Call (see Numbers 33:1-2).

It might, too, be called the Book of Murmurings, because from beginning to end it is filled with the spirit of rebellion against God. Read what God says about this in Psalm 95:10.

Numbers is indeed the book of the wilderness, recording the pitiable failure of Israel at Kadesh Barnea, and the consequent wanderings and experiences of the people in the wilderness. It records the pilgrimage, warfare, service and failure of the second generation of the nation after the Exodus from Egypt. However, there is more to Numbers than this. The first 10 chapters give us divine legislation; chapters 11–20 tell the story of the nation's failure; but the closing chapters of the book record Israel's return to Jehovah's favor and final victory, even in the wilderness.

While the annals of many powerful nations of that same time are lost to the world, these of a comparative handful of people are preserved. The reason for this is that the Messiah who would redeem the world was to come from this people. This is the reason God was so patient with them. He wanted to preserve them for Himself. In 1 Corinthians 10, we learn that the things that happened to them were "examples" for us (verse 6). In other words, their whole history was an object lesson for us, illustrating God's dealing with us today.

The key thought in Numbers, the fourth book of Moses, is discipline. In Genesis, we see humanity ruined; in Exodus, humanity redeemed; in Leviticus, humanity worshiping; in Numbers, humanity serving. This is the order the Law lays down. Only someone who is saved can serve and worship God. Remember, we are saved to serve. We are not saved by good works, but we are "created in Christ Jesus to do good works, which God prepared in advance for us to do" (Ephesians 2:10). The Law can bring us up to the land of promise, but only our divine Joshua (Christ) can bring us in. Paul says that the law is the "schoolmaster" (*KJV*) to bring us to Christ (see Galatians 3:24). The law cannot save us, for we are saved "not by works, so that no one can boast" (Ephesians 2:9).

- Leviticus deals with the believers' worship—Numbers deals with the believer's walk.
- In Leviticus we see the believers' privileges—in Numbers the wilderness is the drill field.

If you know five names, you will master the story of the book of Numbers:

1. Moses, the great leader
2. Aaron, the high priest, Moses' brother
3. Miriam, Moses' and Aaron's sister
4. Joshua, one of the two spies who dared to believe God and so lived to enter Canaan
5. Caleb, one of the two spies who dared to believe God and so lived to enter Canaan

The geography of the book takes us:

1. From Sinai to Kadesh
2. From Kadesh around and back to Kadesh
3. From Kadesh straight to the border of Canaan

The children of Israel learned three important lessons:

1. They must trust God, not people, when they face a crisis (see Psalm 37:5). Read Numbers 13:26–14:25.
2. God would supply all their needs according to His riches (see Philippians 4:19):
   • Food—Numbers 11:6-9
   • Meat—Numbers 11:31-33
   • Water—Numbers 20:8
   • Leaders—Numbers 1:1,3
   • Promised Land—Numbers 14:7-8
3. They must worship God according to His instructions.

It was God's plan that the children of Israel should go straight into the land He had promised them, the land of Canaan, but the people would not. God said that all those at Kadesh more than 20 years old, except Joshua and Caleb, would have to die. A new generation arose during the 40 years of wanderings, but at the end the nation was about as strong in numbers as the day they had left Egypt (read Numbers 26).

NUMBERS 1–12: PREPARATION FOR THE JOURNEY

As Numbers opens, we see the children of Israel in the wilderness of Sinai. The Law had been given, the Tabernacle had been built, and the priests had been assigned to their service. Now God was going to prepare the nation for its work. The teachings of this book are very applicable to the Christian life.

Order is heaven's first law. We see God numbering and arranging the tribes (see Numbers 1–2), and choosing and assigning duties to the priests and Levites (see Numbers 3–4). God is the author of order.

The thought of God numbering His people and gathering them about Himself is most precious to our hearts. He dwelt in the camp. The 12 tribes guarded the Tabernacle of the Lord. The Levites camped directly around the court, and Moses and Aaron and the priests guarded the entrance to where God was.

The circumference of the camp arranged in this way and facing the Tabernacle is supposed to have been 12 miles. What an imposing sight the camp must have been to the outward eye, in the midst of the desert, with God stretching over them in a cloud by day and fire by night (see Numbers 9:15-23)! He was their night-light and their day shade. Their shoes and their clothes did not wear out (see Deuteronomy 29:5). Think of 600,000 men, aged 20 or older, and more than 2,000,000 women, children and younger men in this great camp! But the most glorious thing was that God was in their midst.

In the first chapter, Moses is commanded to take a census. For Christians, too, there is a census, for Christ numbers His jewels and knows them: "A scroll of remembrance was written in his presence concerning those who feared the LORD and honored his name" (Malachi 3:16). The Lord knows by name all who are His (see Philippians 4:3; 2 Timothy 2:19). Even the hairs of our head are numbered (see Matthew 10:30; Luke 12:7). How wonderful to know that God cares for each of His children!

In this chapter we find the declaration of the Israelites' pedigree. Can you trace your genealogy to the risen Lord? Are you sure of your pedigree (see John 1:12)?

God's Provision

Here were about three million people on a sterile desert with very little grass, very little water and no visible means of support. How were they to be fed? God was there! How were they to trace their way through a howling wilderness where there was no path? God was there! God's presence provided everything! What? Are these three million to be fed on air? Who has charge of the commissary? Where is the baggage? Who is to attend to the clothing? God was there! In faith's arithmetic, God is the only figure that counts.

No one had gone before to blaze a trail for the children of Israel. There was not a footprint, not a landmark. It is much like our life as a Christian today. We are passing through a trackless desert—a moral wilderness. There is no trail. We would not know where to walk except for one little sentence from the lips of the Lord: "I am the way" (John 14:6). He will guide us step by step. There is no uncertainty, for He said, "Whoever follows me will never walk in darkness, but will have the light of life" (John 8:12).

God gave His children a cloud to guide them by day and a pillar of fire by night. It is interesting to see how they were guided a step at a time. They did not know when they were to go and when they were to stop, but the Ark of the Covenant (signifying God's presence) went on before, the pillar of cloud always leading (see Numbers 10:33).

The People's Sins

Sin, however, crept into this well-ordered camp life. The people began to murmur against God. God sent a judgment of fire (see Numbers 11:1-3). Then they complained about their food (see Numbers 11:4). It seemed monotonous. They longed for the garlic and onions of Egypt, and they wanted fish. As a result of their complaining, God sent them quails for 30 days. They made gluttons of themselves. "But while the meat was still between their teeth and before it could be consumed, the anger of the LORD burned against the people, and he struck them with a severe plague" (Numbers 11:33). Many became ill and died.

Then we read of the sin of Aaron, the high priest, and of Miriam, the sister of Moses. God had chosen Moses to be the leader of this great people, and Aaron and Miriam were only his assistants. Jealousy crept into their hearts. They wanted more honor. Read Numbers 12:1-16 to learn about Miriam's terrible punishment of suffering with leprosy for seven days.

God's Promises

We find the invitation of God's marching host to the people round about them: "Come with us and we will treat you well, for the LORD has promised good things to Israel" (Numbers 10:29). We, like the Israelites, are just humans making many mistakes and capable of wandering far. But God has given us heavenly attendants and blessed guides:

- The Ark of the Covenant is the Word of God in our midst.
- The sound of the silver trumpet is the witness of a faithful prophet.
- The pillar of fire and of cloud is the comfort and guidance of the Holy Spirit.
- The Tabernacle and its ordinances are for the worship of God in the sanctuary.
- Christ, the "apostle and high priest" of our faith, gives significance to it all (Hebrews 3:1).

Who does not need them? Who can make progress without them? Invite others to join our band and go with us. We should always be taking others by the hand and inviting them to go with us.

NUMBERS 13–20:21: WANDERINGS IN THE WILDERNESS

After one year at Mount Sinai, the Israelites journeyed to Kadesh—a swift and jubilant journey. They did not travel all the time but remained in some places with their flocks and herds grazing on the surrounding hills. When the cloud lifted, they marched. Just south of the Promised Land, they sent out spies to look over what they would possess.

When the spies came back and told them that the land contained giants and that the Israelites looked like grasshoppers to them, the Israelites lost heart (see Numbers 13:33). They would not listen to Joshua and Caleb, who agreed with all that was told but added, "We should go up and take possession of the land, for we can certainly do it" (Numbers 13:30). But the people would not trust God. They said, "We should choose a leader and go back to Egypt" (Numbers 14:4).

When they refused to enter Canaan, the door was closed to them. It meant wandering in the wilderness for 40 years. God said that He would not allow any of those who were more than 20 years old to enter Canaan, except Joshua and Caleb.

Think of the lost years from Kadesh back to Kadesh because people would not believe and trust God. After two years in the wilderness, the children of Israel could have gone into the land of promise immediately had it not been for the sin of unbelief. They listened to the discouraging words of most of the spies, and they doubted.

Hesitant Israel was plunged into the wasting years of wilderness wanderings. Sadly Moses reminded them of it: "Thirty-eight years passed from the time we left Kadesh Barnea until we crossed the Zered Valley. By then, that entire generation of fighting men had perished from the camp, as the LORD had sworn to them" (Deuteronomy 2:14).

Eleven days from the land of promise! But they turned back. They could have made 11 days of progress, but they chose 40 years of wandering.

God opens doors that no human can close, and He closes doors that no human can open (see Isaiah 22:22; Revelation 3:8). God opened the door and about three million souls walked out of Egypt; He closed the door when the Egyptians tried to follow. God took the children of Israel out of Egypt so that He could take them into Canaan, the land of promise. God did not want the children of Israel just to come out of Egypt. He wanted to have them come into the Promised Land. This they could have done in a relatively short time—not more than two or three weeks. Remember that the spies made the trip and returned within 40 days. But as we have already seen, the Israelites' fear disqualified them to take over the land of promise.

The Appearance of Giants

This record tells the story of many a Christian life and, in part, the story of every life. Giants of selfishness and greed, far surpassing the Anakim, or Anakites (a people the Israelites feared because they were "strong and numerous, and . . . tall" [Deuteronomy 2:21]), oppose our advance! But when the returns are all in, the fact remains that there is One with us stronger than they!

Like 10 of the spies, we can be pessimists; or like Joshua and Caleb, optimists. Like the 10, we can put difficulties between us and God and say we are not able; or like the two, we can put God between the difficulties and ourselves and say we are able!

We start out with high hope in the enthusiasm of our first love. Yonder lies the land of possibilities and achievement. Then the giants appear—giants of opposition from without; giants of fear from within. Oftentimes our fear keeps us from enjoying all that God wants to give us. We fear what others will say. We fear what might happen if we put our trust completely in Christ. Our faith fails. We forget God. We compare our difficulties with our own strength rather than committing them to the great arm of God. Then we turn back into the wilderness of half trust, half victory and whole despair.

Numbers 33 is the pitiful logbook of this journey: "They left Hazeroth and camped at Rithmah. They left Rithmah and camped at Rimmon Perez. They left Rimmon Perez and camped at Libnah" (Numbers 33:18-20). This goes on until the end of this dismal chapter! Going and going, pitching and departing, but never arriving anywhere. An endless circle of aimless wanderings with no destination reached. When we doubt God, we find this to be our experience, too. We feel defeated and discouraged. We wander around but never accomplish anything. It is like a swinging door—lots of motion but getting no place.

The Return of Murmuring

Before this scene ends, we find Israel murmuring again, this time because of the shortage of water. Chapter 20 describes how the people complained bitterly to Moses and Aaron and said they wished they had never been brought out of Egypt. The land was dry and parched and there was no water to drink. Moses and Aaron again went to God. God told Moses to take his rod and speak to the rock before the people, and the rock would give forth water.

Moses' patience, however, was at an end. The people had complained about everything. In a fit of anger, he called the people "rebels" and instead of speaking to the rock, he struck it. Water gushed out. Even though Moses had disobeyed, God was faithful and kept His promise.

Is it not sad that even children of God fail under testing? Moses' error was great, yet it showed him to be just like us. Moses put himself up as God: "Listen, you rebels, must we bring you water out of this rock?" (Numbers 20:10). This dishonored Jehovah God. Much earlier in the Israelites' journey, God had told Moses to strike a rock at Horeb to get water (see Exodus 17:5-6), but this rock at Kadesh was only to be spoken to. Because Moses struck the rock instead of speaking to it, he was not permitted to enter the Promised Land. Christ, like the rock, was to be struck once for our sins (see 1 Corinthians 10:4). He need not be struck again.

There are three ways of knowing people, a rabbi in the Talmud says:

1. In their cups
2. With their cash
3. In their wrath

How true it is that rude table manners suggest poor upbringing; bad conduct in business reveals unscrupulous inclinations; lashing out in anger exposes a disreputable commonness. Moses' lashing out in anger resulted in his not crossing over into the Promised Land.

The Question of Aaron's Priesthood

One of the important things we have not covered is an incident in Numbers 17: the questioning of Aaron's priesthood. Because it had been questioned, God Himself was to confirm it. Moses gathered 12 staffs, one from the leader of each tribe, and placed them overnight in the Tent of Meeting. God put life into Aaron's staff alone, causing it to sprout and bud. We find this reflected in the fact that all the authors of the religions of the world have died—even Christ—but only Christ was raised from the dead and exalted to be our high priest (see Hebrews 4:14; 5:4-10).

NUMBERS 20:22–36: ON TO CANAAN

When the Israelites had arrived at Kadesh this second time, all the Israelites who had left Egypt had died, except Moses, Aaron, Joshua, Caleb, Miriam and the children who were under 20 years of age when the spies had entered the land. While they camped in Kadesh, Miriam, Moses' sister, died (see Numbers 20:1), and Aaron, Moses' brother, now more than 100 years old, also died (see Numbers 20:28).

Then Israel moved on again. They started from Kadesh, this time with faces set resolutely toward the Promised Land. The way was difficult, much harder than before; but faith had been renewed, discipline had done its work, and the arm of God went forth conquering and to conquer.

Learn here the lesson of God's second best. He offers the perfect way, and if we refuse it, it is gone forever—every male more than 20 years of age who refused to go into the land of promise the first time (except Joshua and Caleb, who had believed God) died in the wilderness.

But God is kind, and He sets before us another way, a second best (it may even be a third, for His mercy is wonderful; and He forgives us 70 times 7 times). He brings us through, provides for us, never failing in His grace; but, oh, how much we miss and how many burdens we have to bear by not taking the first and the best. How costly this is!

Israel was complaining again, although over and over again God had proven to them that His way is best. Discontent and murmuring seem to have been ingrained habits of the children of Israel. Grumbling is the easiest thing in the world to learn; and as someone once said, "No talent, no self-denial, no brains, no character is required to set up the grumbling business." (What's the use of grumbling? It never makes a heavy burden light. It never subtracts from ills. Instead it always adds to them.)

The Israelites battled with the Canaanites and became discouraged. Then they grumbled because they had to march around the land of Edom instead of through it. They growled again against God and against Moses because they loathed the manna (see Numbers 21:5). They never were content.

This time God sent venomous snakes among the people, which caused suffering and death. After the people confessed their sins, Moses prayed for the deliverance of the people. God did not take away the venomous snakes, but He told Moses to make a bronze snake and fasten it to a pole so that all could see it. Then anyone who looked on it would live (see Numbers 21:6-9).

The Bible reveals that the whole human family has felt the ancient serpent's sting of sin, which means death (see 1 Corinthians 15:56; Hebrews 2:14-15). The only way people can live is by looking to the One who took upon Himself the likeness of a human and was lifted up on the cross to take the sting of death upon Himself (see Philippians 2:7-8). If we look on Him, our Savior, we shall live (see John 3:14-15).

Numbers

Understanding Deuteronomy

Deuteronomy Portrays Jesus Christ,
Our True Prophet

SELECTED BIBLE READING

DAY OF THE WEEK		MAIN TOPIC
Sunday: Deuteronomy 1:6-46	Rebellion	
Monday: Deuteronomy 5:1-33; 6:4-18	The Law	
Tuesday: Deuteronomy 18:15-22	The Messiah, Prophet	
Wednesday: Deuteronomy 30	God's Covenant	
Thursday: Deuteronomy 32:1-44	Moses' Song	
Friday: Deuteronomy 33	God's Blessings	
Saturday: Deuteronomy 34	Moses' Death	

AUTHOR: The author of the book of Deuteronomy is not identified. Traditionally, it has been assumed that Moses was the author of the book.

DATE: The book of Deuteronomy does not indicate when it was written. The date of authorship may be 1220 BC, at the time of, or just after, Moses' death.

PURPOSE AND SUMMARY: The final book of the Pentateuch derives its English name from the Greek work *deuteronomion*, meaning "second law," or "law repeated." Deuteronomy is essentially Moses' farewell addresses to a new generation. He summons them to hear the Law of God, instructs them in the application of its principles to the new circumstances awaiting them, and has them renew the covenant that God had made with their fathers—a covenant that must be faithfully observed as the condition of God's blessings upon them in the Promised Land.

"See that you do" are the words of Moses to the people (Deuteronomy 12:32). He wanted them to be "doers of the word, and not hearers only" (James 1:22, *KJV*).

This book shows the blessings of obedience and the curses of disobedience. Everything depends on obedience—life itself, possession of the Promised Land, victory over foes, prosperity and happiness. We find this book teaching the inflexibility of the Law. "You shall" and "you shall not" occur over and over again (see chapter 5). And there is "the blessing if you obey" and "the curse if you disobey" (Deuteronomy 11:27-28).

The book of Deuteronomy is a collection of the instructive speeches and songs that Moses gave as his farewell to the children of Israel. Moses delivered his addresses probably within a period of seven days, about a month before the crossing of the Jordan River as he stood on the great divide between his earthly and heavenly life (see Deuteronomy 1:1-3). From the top of Mount Nebo (sometimes called Mount Pisgah), he recalled over a century crammed full of epoch-creating events. Then he turned his gaze to the future of the people he was about to leave.

The book contains a most interesting and instructive summary of the wilderness history of Israel, and in the last chapter we find an account of Moses himself. Carefully compare Moses' review of the events with the account given in Exodus and Numbers. You will find that Deuteronomy gives the divine rather than the human view. In particular, compare Deuteronomy 1 with Numbers 13–14.

Deuteronomy is a book of remembrance. The name "Deuteronomy" means "second law," which indicates that the Law is repeated. Moses did this to remind the people what God had done for them and what they were to do to serve Him when they reached the

Promised Land. It omits the things that relate to the priests and Levites but includes the things that the people should know. And it covers only about two months, including the 30 days of mourning for Moses.

This book is the last of the five books of Moses. These five books are often called the "Pentateuch," meaning five books:

- Genesis tells of the beginnings of the chosen nation Israel.
- Exodus relates the organization of the people into a nation and the giving of the Law.
- Leviticus tells the way God's Chosen People were to worship God.
- Numbers gives a story of the wanderings of God's people.
- Deuteronomy relates the final preparation for entering the Promised Land.

Moses was the writer but not the author of the Pentateuch. More than 500 times in these first five books we find expressions such as "the Lord spoke" and "God said." Who is the divine author of the Bible? For the answer, read 2 Peter 1:20-21.

The Christian heart always beats a bit faster when it comes to Deuteronomy, for this book was a favorite with our Savior. Jesus quoted from this book when He was tempted in the wilderness by His adversary the devil (see Matthew 4:1-11; Luke 4:1-13). The following passages were the weapons with which He repelled the tempter: Deuteronomy 8:3; 6:13,16 and 10:20. Thus this book, God's book about obedience, Moses' last charge to his people, seems to have about it the peculiar blessing and protection of Christ Himself. Jesus even took Deuteronomy as His code of conduct (see Luke 4:4,8,12).

You will come to appreciate the full force and magnetic beauty of Deuteronomy only as you read its pages. Read it through in a single sitting. Nothing in literature matches the majesty of its eloquence; nothing in the Old Testament has any more powerful appeal for the spiritual life. No book in all the Word of God pictures better the life that is lived according to God's will, and the

Deuteronomy

blessings showered upon the soul who comes into the richness and fullness of spiritual living along the rugged pathway of simple obedience.

If you want a taste of heaven on earth, become familiar with Deuteronomy. Walk with Moses and then march ahead by way of the Promised Land, Canaan, the "land flowing with milk and honey" (Exodus 3:8).

"Brethren," a man once said, "when I get to the gates of heaven, if they shut me out, I'll say, 'Anyhow, I had a good time getting here.'" Are you having a good time on your way to heaven? God "has blessed us in the heavenly realms with every spiritual blessing in Christ" (Ephesians 1:3), but we must appropriate and possess those blessings by faith.

DEUTERONOMY 1–4: MOSES LOOKS BACK

As Deuteronomy opens and Moses begins his first address to God's people, we see the children of Israel on the border of the land of Canaan, in a place where an 11-days' journey, some 40 years before, could have brought them. Yet it had taken them 40 years. How slowly they covered the ground! What windings and turnings! We marvel at Israel's slowness. We should rather marvel at our own! How often *we* have to go over the same ground again and again. We, like they, are kept back by our deplorable unbelief. We should be ashamed at the time it takes us to learn our lessons!

God, however, is such a faithful teacher. He never lets us pass on to another grade until we are ready. God never fails us when we put our trust in Him. But He cannot do many mighty works because of our unbelief (see Matthew 13:58). So it was too with the Israelites.

Several hundred years before, God had promised to Abraham and his "seed" (Hebrew: *zerah,* offspring, descendant[s]) a rich and wondrous land, and they were now standing upon its borders (Genesis 17:8, *KJV*). They finally were ready to enter the land after all the years of anticipation and hope. The closing chapters of Numbers found them camped by the Jordan, waiting to go over into the Promised Land itself.

In Deuteronomy God put before the children of Israel the conditions for their entering and holding the land. We see all these conditions summed up in one great word: "obedience." The children of Israel entered the Promised Land under the conditions of the Law.

The book of Deuteronomy is one long plea for hearty obedience to God based on the grand motives of love and fear: "And now, Israel, what does the LORD your God ask of you but to fear the LORD your God, to walk in obedience to him, to love him, to serve the LORD your God with all your heart and with all your soul" (Deuteronomy 10:12). In the first four books of the Pentateuch, God is choosing Israel. Now He is letting Israel choose Him.

Besides Moses, only Caleb and Joshua were left from the generation that had come out of Egypt. All the others were dead. The younger generation who now lived had suffered hardships in the wilderness wanderings and were ready and anxious for conquest! But Moses must first repeat the Law to them.

Moses, a grand old man, is now 120 years old. He knows that his work is finished, for God had told him that another will lead the people into Canaan (see Numbers 20:12). He begins his farewell address to the people by describing how he had led them these past 40 years. As God had instructed him, he had delivered God's people from the bondage of Egypt; guided them through the many dangers that confronted them; trained them; gave them forms of government, laws and religious institutions; and molded them into a nation.

Moses gives the children of Israel this look back, recalling the history of Israel and reviewing their wanderings. He reminds them of God's faithfulness and urges them to be grateful and obedient. He likens God's care of them to a loving father who cherishes his little ones, fearing they might become lost in the wilderness or become injured by the heat of the sun. He supplied all their needs; they lacked nothing (see Deuteronomy 2:7).

The children of Israel were now at the end of their journey, in the plain east of the Jordan, overlooking the land they had come so far to possess. It lay before them in the glories of the springtime. But the impassable Jordan River roiled in front of them; and on the other side, walled cities rose up in seemingly impregnable strength. The Israelites were like young graduates leaving high school or college, about to enter upon their life's work.

Moses spoke to his beloved people in the most earnest and eloquent way and appealed to them to serve and obey God. His words still echo down the corridors of time!

DEUTERONOMY 5–26: MOSES LOOKS UP

In Deuteronomy 12:1, we see the key to this section, Moses' second address: "These are the decrees and laws you must be careful to follow in the land." Israel was going into a new land and everything would depend on their constant and intelligent obedience to God who was giving them the land. God wanted to teach Israel the love that is the real fulfilling of the law (see Matthew 22:37-40; Romans 13:8-10).

Moses now sets forth the Law simply and clearly so that it would take a living hold of the people. God says, "You are My people; I love you. I have chosen you; I am in the midst of you. I will protect you. I am only asking you to obey Me for your own good" (paraphrased from several passages). He repeatedly reminds them that they are "a people holy to the LORD" (Deuteronomy 7:6; 14:2,21; 26:19). Because God's people are His, He wants them to walk in the world in the way that befits them, and He tells them what they should do:

- Separate themselves from evil—Deuteronomy 14
- Show charity toward their fellow humans—Deuteronomy 15
- Gather together to worship—Deuteronomy 16 (see also Hebrews 10:25; today's carelessness about going to church and worshiping reflects spiritual decay)
- Be disciplined—Deuteronomy 17

In Deuteronomy 18, God tells of the great prophet, the Lord Jesus Christ. He alone knows the future. Nowadays, many people make the mistake of consulting fortune-tellers, mediums, palm readers and practitioners of astrology and sorcery to "learn" the future—spiritualism is rampant! (If you want to know what God thinks about the modern séance, look up Leviticus 19:31; 20:6 and Isaiah 8:19-20; and study the dark story in 1 Samuel 28 in the light of 1 Chronicles 10:13.)

God showed the Israelites that their highest duty was to exhibit the spirit of loving obedience. They were to be thankful, yes, really thankful. They were to be full of joy and gladness. Why shouldn't they be joyful in the best land on earth and with such a God as Jehovah? Surely they ought to be glad and love their God with all their heart.

Moses' heart, however, was burdened because he knew that Israel had a hard heart and the people were self-willed (see Deuteronomy 31:24-29). Note this: Disobedient children who are rebellious toward their parents are an abomination in God's sight! How many children today (see their description by Paul in 2 Timothy 3:1-9) would have been put to death under the solemn command of Deuteronomy 21:18-21?

If we read Deuteronomy 21:22-23 and compare it with John 19:31, we see why Christ was under a curse as He hung between heaven and earth on the cross: In Galatians 3:10-13 we read that He is cursed because He was bearing our sins (see also 2 Corinthians 5:21). What effect did this have on Paul (see 2 Corinthians 5:14-15)?

DEUTERONOMY 27–33: MOSES LOOKS OUT

In Moses' third address, we see Moses giving the people some solemn warnings. He first spoke of the blessings the children of Israel could enjoy if they would be obedient. He then told them the results of disobedience: Misfortune would follow them in everything they would undertake—in business, in farming and in health. They would suffer greatly for their disobedience to God.

Deuteronomy 28 is a most remarkable chapter. It traces what Israel might have been if they had been obedient to begin with (see verses 1-14) and is yet to be in the millennial age to come (see Deuteronomy 30:1-10; Isaiah 60–62; Jeremiah 31:1-9; Zechariah 14:8-21; Romans 11:25-31).

Verses 47-49 could refer to the Roman invasion, AD 70, under Titus. This was indeed a bloody page of history!

Verses 63-67 describe the Jewish people today:

1. "The LORD will scatter" (verse 64)—The Jewish people are scattered from one end of the earth to the other, and Jewish communities are found throughout the world.

2. "No repose, no resting place" (verse 65)—Only rarely in their history have the Jewish people found complete security.

3. "Anxious . . . despairing . . . in constant suspense, filled with dread" (verses 65-67)—Jewish history is full of persecution and tragedies. Think of the way they have been treated in many countries.

God foretold all this more than 3,000 years ago!

Deuteronomy 31 records what Moses spoke to Joshua, his personal attendant throughout the wilderness wandering. Joshua, one of the spies who had dared to believe God, was now 80 years old; and Moses committed to him the leadership of this great people! The charge that Moses gave to the people and to Joshua was built on one great fact: The Lord is with you, so be strong (see Deuteronomy 31:7-8). If God is present, fear is baseless!

Moses stood as a witness to the grace of God. He sang a song for Israel (see Deuteronomy 32). Moses had celebrated the deliverance of Israel from Egypt with a song (see Exodus 15), and now he closed his life's work with another. (He wrote a third, which we know as Psalm 90.) Christians have always had a song! And in heaven throughout the ages, everyone will sing!

DEUTERONOMY 34: MOSES LOOKS DOWN

According to Deuteronomy 34, after the song and final words of blessing, Moses went up to the top of Mount Nebo, and there God showed him the Promised Land toward which his face had so long been set. We know that he died there and that the Lord buried him. No one knows where. Someone once said, "God buried his burial." God buries the workman but carries on the work. (Why do you think Moses' grave was hidden? No doubt it would have become the object of superstitious idolatry.)

Whether Moses himself wrote Deuteronomy 34 by revelation or whether Joshua added it later is immaterial.

The horde of slaves made into a nation by Moses wept for him 30 days. Had it not been for their perversity, they might still have had him with them.

We read of Moses again in the Gospels. One day Jesus took Peter, James and John and climbed up Mount Hermon to the north of the Sea of Galilee. Then Moses and Elijah appeared and talked with Jesus about His coming death (see Matthew 17:1-3).

Deuteronomy

Books of History

of the Old Testament

JOSHUA • JUDGES • RUTH

1 SAMUEL • 2 SAMUEL

1 KINGS • 2 KINGS

1 CHRONICLES • 2 CHRONICLES

EZRA • NEHEMIAH

ESTHER

Key Events of the Books of History

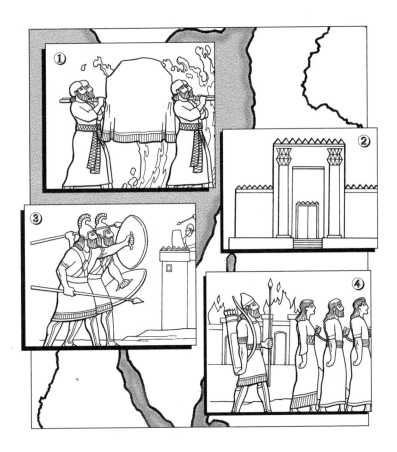

Books of History: The Rise and Fall of the Davidic Kingdom

God brought His chosen people ① into the Promised Land with miracles, military victories and treaties. Then God allowed the Israelites a brief measure of earthly glory ② during the reigns of David and Solomon. To King David, God promised an everlasting kingdom. However, the Davidic dynasty split. Assyrians ③ erased the Northern Kingdom (722 BC), and Babylonians ④ conquered the Southern Kingdom (605-586 BC). Eventually, the Persians allowed the Jewish people to resettle Judah and rebuild the Jerusalem Temple.

Understanding Joshua

Joshua Portrays Jesus Christ, Captain of Our Salvation

AUTHOR: The book of Joshua does not explicitly name its author. Possibly Joshua the son of Nun, the successor of Moses as leader over Israel, wrote much of this book. The end of the book was written by at least one other person after the death of Joshua, and it is also possible that several sections were edited or compiled following Joshua's death.

DATE: The book of Joshua was likely written between 1200 and 1170 BC.

PURPOSE AND SUMMARY: This book serves as the link between the Pentateuch and the later historical books. Its name is derived from the principal character, Joshua. Chapters 1 to 22 describe the conquest of the land and its division among the tribes of Israel. In the final chapters (23–24), Joshua exhorts the people in a series of farewell addresses to "be careful to obey all that is written in the Book of the Law of Moses" and solemnly challenges them to renew their covenant commitment to God (Joshua 23:6).

"Take possession of the land the LORD your God is giving you for your own" (Joshua 1:11). It is God's to give! It is ours to possess!

When we open the book of Joshua, we are beginning the second division of the Old Testament, the books of history. No book has more encouragement and wisdom for the soldier of the cross than does this book. It is full of spiritual truth.

Joshua is the book of conquest or the battlefield of the Canaan heritage. This book relates the settlement of the children of Israel in Canaan, proving God's faithfulness in keeping His promise with Abraham. What was the promise? Read Genesis 12:1-3.

This book bears the name of Joshua, the hero of this great conquest. "Joshua" was originally *Hoshea*, meaning salvation, or *Jehoshua*, "the Lord's salvation." Joshua is called the servant of Jehovah, one by whom God issued His orders and by whom He accomplished His purposes—God's prime minister. (For all you know, God may have decided to make you a captain in His army or to make you a standard-bearer in the legion of His cross. Are you getting ready?)

The book of Joshua starts where Deuteronomy stops. It is a continuation of the history of the Chosen People, a fulfillment of the anticipation in Deuteronomy. Moses led the Chosen People out of bondage:

- Moses passed through the Red Sea.
- Moses led Israel from bondage.
- Moses gave a vision of faith.
- Moses told of an inheritance.

Joshua led the Chosen People into the Promised Land. In this book, we see Israel not only overcome the enemy but also occupy the land God had promised them. Joshua completes what Moses began!

God never leaves His work unfinished. Remember that the great craftsman always has another tool sharpened and ready for use. Service is for everyone. You can always honor God best by taking up your task with a strong and resolute heart that trusts God.

Moses was dead, but the march must continue! God was now speaking to Joshua. Yes, God is still speaking today; and if we listen, we will hear Him speak to us.

The apostle Paul is dead, but the cross he preached remains. People may perish, but the true leader, though invisible, is on the field and will never fail!

"Moses is dead!" Then the march must be halted? Without their leader, the followers might feel abandoned, and there might be gloom in the camp. But we see *realization* in Joshua:

- Joshua passed over the Jordan River.
- Joshua led Israel into blessing.
- Joshua led the Chosen People into a life of faith.
- Joshua led the Israelites into possession.

God had been preparing Joshua for years. He was born in slavery in Egypt, but God led him out and made him a co-laborer with Moses. He was always a valiant captain. He was the one that was almost stoned to death because he had urged the children of Israel to advance into Canaan 40 years earlier (see Numbers 14:6-10). Success is readiness for opportunity!

Remember as we study this book of Joshua that God gives—people take. This book focuses on overcoming the enemy and occupying the land. God says, "Take it all."

This book seems to fall into two great parts. If you can only remember this much of an outline, you will remember the most important things:

1. Conquest of the Promised Land—Joshua 1–12
2. Occupation of the Promised Land—Joshua 13–24

Joshua

JOSHUA 1–2: ARMY MOBILIZATION

Open your Bible to the first two chapters of Joshua. We find the children of Israel right on the border of the land of promise, near the banks of the Jordan. The boundaries of the Promised Land, as given in Joshua 1:4 are the wilderness on the south, the Lebanon mountains on the north, the Euphrates River on the east, and the Mediterranean on the west.

A New Role for Joshua

Joshua is the leader of the children of Israel now. We hear God say, "Moses my servant is dead. Now then, you and all these people, get ready to cross the Jordan River" (Joshua 1:2). Joshua probably stood with bowed head and a lonely heart, for his wise counselor and friend was gone. But God said to Joshua, "As I was with Moses, so I will be with you; I will never leave you nor forsake you. . . . Be strong and courageous. Do not be afraid; do not be discouraged, for the LORD your God will be with you wherever you go" (Joshua 1:5,9). These words must have come to him in answer to a prayer for help in his great undertaking. And these words are just as true for us today.

Moses had to die before the children of Israel could go into Canaan. Moses could not enter Canaan himself, to say nothing of bringing anyone else in. Israel *had* to wait until Moses was out of the way. To the Christian, Moses represents the Law. Joshua represents Christ. Christ alone can lead us into the inheritance that is ours. Paul says, "Not by works, so that no one can boast" (Ephesians 2:9). Oh, that all Christians would simply lean on their faithful Joshua and follow Him only! Christ wants to lead us into what He has purchased on the cross for us. It takes Moses and Joshua together to present to us the finished work of Christ.

We see an anxious crowd of people all waiting to enter the land they had so long been promised. Can you picture the row upon row of tents and all the people wondering when Joshua would say "go"? Joshua sent men through the camp to tell the people that in three days they would cross the Jordan, and to be prepared for the journey (see Joshua 1:10-11).

Important Words from God

God says some very important things that are recorded in this first chapter of Joshua:

- Set your foot down—"I will give you every place where you set your foot, as I promised Moses" (Joshua 1:3).

- Take it all—"Your territory will extend from the desert to Lebanon, and from the great river, the Euphrates—all the Hittite country—to the Mediterranean Sea in the west" (Joshua 1:4). Not until Solomon's day, some 500 years later, was this fully realized (see 2 Chronicles 9:26), but it started with Joshua.

- Be on the move—"Moses my servant is dead. Now then, you and all these people, get ready to cross the Jordan River" (Joshua 1:2).

- Take the sword—"Keep this Book of the Law always on your lips" (Joshua 1:8).

- Go in for a full life—"Three days from now you will cross the Jordan here to go in and take possession of the land the LORD your God is giving you for your own" (Joshua 1:11).

The book of Law was Joshua's Bible. Our Bible is far more complete, and we know more about God's will because Christ has interpreted it for us. Do we meditate upon the Word? Do we turn from it to the right or to the left? Read God's words to Joshua, recorded in Joshua 1:7.

Ready for Service

Joshua called the officers together and gave them detailed directions. Hear what some of these men said: "Whatever you have commanded us we will do, and wherever you send us we will go" (Joshua 1:16). They were ready for any service.

We see both Joshua and the people prepared for the journey. Remember, Joshua had been one of the 12 spies who had been sent to Canaan 40 years earlier. Now he sends two scouts to bring a report of the land. Read in Joshua 2 the story of Rahab and the spies.

Joshua asked the spies especially to find out the strength of Jericho, for this was the first stronghold they would have to attack after crossing the river. The spies aroused suspicion but were saved from death by Rahab, who hid them under flax that was spread on the roof of her house. The spies learned from Rahab that all the people in the city were terrified of the Israelites, and the spies promised that they would spare her and her household when the city was taken. Rahab let them down by a rope through the window of her house, which was part of the city wall, and they returned to tell Joshua the good news that "all the people are melting in fear because of us" (Joshua 2:24).

Rahab hung a scarlet cord out of her window so that her house would be marked and spared when the city was destroyed. We find this woman's name in the genealogy of Jesus (see Matthew 1:5).

The Canaanites, the people of the land, were the descendants of Canaan, the son of Ham. They were a wicked and idolatrous people. God's destruction of Sodom and Gomorrah had been a warning for them, but they had not changed a bit (see Genesis 19:24-25). Now God was going to destroy their power and give their land to the Israelites.

JOSHUA 3–5: A FORWARD MARCH

Read Joshua 3–5. Encouraged by the report the spies had brought, the Israelites moved from their encampment at Shittim, six miles from the Jordan, to a spot near the swollen stream. At dawn the officers passed through the camp and ordered all to watch the Ark and follow it at "a distance of about two thousand cubits" (about a thousand yards); "then you will know which way to go, since you have never been this way before" (Joshua 3:4). The children of Israel had followed the cloud in the wilderness. Now they would follow the Ark of the Covenant, which represented the presence of Jehovah.

The great leader Joshua instructed the people to sanctify themselves, for on the next day the Lord would do "amazing things" in their midst (Joshua 3:5). The long journey in the desert was over, and the mystery of an unknown country and an unknown life were ahead of them. The people grew serious, impressed by the new experience to come. (Life is always opening new and unexpected things to us. There is no monotony in the life of a Christian.)

At the beginning of the Exodus from Egypt, there was a crossing of the Red Sea. Now at the close of the Exodus, there is a crossing of the Jordan River. Both were memorable events in the history of the children of Israel. But of all the great mass of people that crossed the Red Sea, only Caleb and Joshua remained of their generation. Why? (Reread Numbers 13–14 if you've forgotten.)

It was springtime, so the Jordan was overflowing, and the people of Jericho must have thought it impossible for the Israelites to cross or they would have been there to oppose them. There were no bridges and only a few fords, but these were not passable at this time of the year. The spies had crossed and recrossed by swimming, no doubt. But how could a great multitude with women and children and baggage cross?

God had a way. He gave the directions for the people to follow. Martin Luther once said, "I know not the way He [Christ] leads me, but well do I know my Guide."

The way to cross the Jordan was to cross it. Joshua told the priests to take up the Ark and step into the Jordan, even though the river was overflowing its banks. When the soles of their feet touched the waters of the Jordan, they stood on dry ground, and all Israel passed over on dry ground (see Joshua 3:9-17). With men this would be impossible, but with God all things are possible. God is always doing the impossible. God's very words are empowering. A man once said, "If God tells me to jump through a stone wall, it would be my duty to jump; it would be God's duty to remove the wall!"

Joshua

What was the Ark? The symbol of the divine Presence. And Christ is the reality of the divine Presence. He says, as God did to Moses and Joshua, "Surely I am with you always" (Matthew 28:20).

God goes before us and says, "Follow me" (Matthew 4:19; 8:22; 16:24; Luke 9:23; John 21:19); and He sends His Holy Spirit to whisper in our ear and say, "This is the way; walk in it" (Isaiah 30:21). The living Ark of the Covenant is still our guide. He will guide us in the little as well as the great things of life. Yes, "the LORD makes firm the steps of the one who delights in him" (Psalm 37:23).

The Bible tells us that after the crossing of the river, "from right where the priests [stood]" in the riverbed, 12 stones were taken and piled up on the other shore as a lasting memorial of the wonders God did for the Israelites (Joshua 4:3). No formal prayer is recorded, but memorial stones were set up. The people wanted to perpetuate the memory of their great Deliverer.

JOSHUA 6: JERICHO'S FALL

Jericho was not far from the Jordan and was only about a 20-minute walk from the encampment at Gilgal. I have stood on the site of the city of Joshua's conquest whose massive walls have been unearthed. The modern Jericho is centered around the Byzantine town of Ericha, about a mile away from the ancient stronghold that was destroyed and rebuilt in the reign of Ahab.

A man passing by a building that was being torn down stopped to look at a laborer who was pulling on a rope fastened to the top of the wall.

"Do you think that you are going to pull that thick wall down that way?" he finally asked in amazement.

Between his tugs the man answered, "It doesn't look that way to me, but I guess the boss knows what he's about."

And the boss did know, for the wall had been undermined; and after an hour of tug after tug, the great wall vibrated, swayed and fell down flat.

The walls of Jericho had to come down so that the Israelites might proceed to conquer the Promised Land, for Jericho was the key to southern Canaan. How could this be brought about? To the Israelites, God's directions seemed strange, but like that modern laborer they kept steadily at the task assigned to them. They were confident that their leader, God, knew what they did not and that they would soon enter the city. What was their task? Read Joshua 6.

The procession of priests, Ark, men and trumpets that marched daily around the city were the only visible means for its capture. How futile must such a march have seemed to the people of Jericho, yes, and to the Israelites themselves. But God knew what He would do. God gives us victories through ways that seem utterly foolish to us (see 1 Corinthians 1:17-29).

Some people have tried to explain that the fall of Jericho was no miracle but a simple scientific fact: God knew that a certain vibration would destroy the wall, so the sound of the trumpets and a shout would cause the wall to fall. Whether this is the case or not, the miracle remains that the wall fell. God accomplished the destruction with or without "scientific" means. The glory is the Lord's, not Joshua's. When the people obeyed the command of the Lord given by Joshua, they saw God's power.

The fall of Jericho before the blast of rams' horns and the great shout by the people was a miracle so stupendous that the rationalist can but *try* to discredit it. The Israelites believed they were following God's plan. The seven trumpets leading a procession for seven days (and seven times on the seventh day) showed the Israelites that this was Jehovah's plan of conquest as directly as an American flag informs people today that the property over which it waves is under the protection of the United States. God put an invisible band around the foundation of that city wall and tightened it, and when God does that to the foundation of any structure—national or personal—beware!

It is not hard work that is needed; it is the lack of vision that makes us fail (see Proverbs 29:18). It is easy to blow a trumpet, and a little thing to walk around a wall. The hard thing is to see the good in it. Say, "Lord, one step is enough for me."

Joshua

JOSHUA 7–8: AI CAMPAIGN

The capture of Jericho gave the Israelites a chance to enter central Canaan. The next place strategically important was Ai, which commanded the entrance into the valley leading into western Canaan.

As he had done in the case of Jericho, Joshua sent spies to Ai to learn the situation. Made overconfident by their recent success, the spies gave poor advice on their return, saying, "Not all the army will have to go up against Ai. Send two or three thousand men to take it and do not weary the whole army, for only a few people live there" (Joshua 7:3).

So a small force was sent up the steep slope, but when the garrison at Ai sallied forth and attacked them, the Israelites fled without striking a blow. In the disaster, all saw the withdrawal of God's guiding hand. They soon learned that they could not trust in their own strength alone. " 'Not by might nor by power, but by my Spirit,' says the LORD Almighty" (Zechariah 4:6).

One man's sin caused Israel's defeat. (Israel had become a unified nation, so no one could act alone.) Achan had hidden, among other things, a wedge of gold. Read the entire story in Joshua 7. Beware of the wedge of gold (see Joshua 7:13)! Achan alone was guilty, yet we read: "Israel has sinned; they have violated my covenant, which I commanded them to keep. They have taken some of the devoted things; they have stolen, they have lied, they have put them with their own possessions" (Joshua 7:11).

No one can sin in total isolation. None of us lives exclusively for him- or herself. One child with chicken pox can infect an entire classroom. A few influenza germs can infect a whole nation. The sin of one becomes the sin of the community.

Every sin you commit will hunt you down, find you out and make you pay. Know this: Not one sin has been committed on this earth for which the person who committed it did not suffer. You may escape the law of the land. You cannot escape the law of God.

JOSHUA 10: CENTRAL CAMPAIGN

The Israelites went out a second time to Ai. This time they were victors. The taking of Ai showed real military strategy—and obedience. In working for the Lord, there must always be a recognition of the value of the best in human reason, but strategy without obedience is worth nothing. Dwight L. Moody once said, "Work as if everything depended upon you, and pray as if everything depended upon God."

The fame of Israel began to spread far and wide. Most of the kings of central Canaan formed a league against the oncoming Israelites. But the Gibeonites played a trick on the Israelites in order to achieve a treaty with them. As a result, Joshua condemned the Gibeonites to become the "woodcutters and water carriers in the service of the whole assembly" (Joshua 9:21).

Then Joshua routed the allied army. Read about the hailstorm and the prolonged daylight God sent to help His warrior (see Joshua 10:10-13). "Sun, stand still over Gibeon" (Joshua 10:12). Ordinary things come to a standstill when God is about His work.

JOSHUA 11: NORTHERN CAMPAIGN

After all of central and southern Canaan was in Israel's possession, a new confederacy had to be faced and conquered. The northern kings had joined together and tried to break the power of the conquering Israelites. But in divine strength, Joshua routed them all. This did not all happen at once. Scripture says that it took "a long time" (Joshua 11:18). Then at last the land rested from war (see Joshua 11:23).

As an aside, Jerusalem is so named in this chapter for the first time in the Bible. To think that since then it has become possibly the most famous place in the world! The Crusaders shed rivers of blood trying to capture it from 1095 to 1291. In 1917, General Edmond Allenby led a victorious offensive against Turkish armies and took this citadel without a shot being fired! In 1948, Jewish settlers fought for and established Jerusalem as the capital of the modern state of Israel. In 1967, as a result of the Six-Day War, the city was reunited after nearly 20 years of division. It is a city with a great past history and a bright future history. Here Christ will reign when He comes again "with power and great glory" (Luke 21:27).

In Joshua 11, we see God judging these wicked people, the Canaanites. Until recently it was supposed that Canaan was at this time a country of semi-barbarians. Now we know that as early as 2500 BC, Canaan was subject to Mesopotamian rulers, whose language and civilization had been adopted there. Next came Egyptian domination, and we know for a fact the high culture Egypt had. Many of the Tell el-Amarna tablets, dating from possibly as early as 1385 BC—after the conquest of Canaan by the Israelites—are letters to the pharaoh of Egypt, written in Akkadian, a language known throughout the Near East at the time, by various rulers in Canaan. At that period Canaan had already behind it a long civilized past. The country was filled with schools and libraries, richly furnished palaces, and workshops of artisans. The cities on the coast had large fleets, partly of merchantmen and partly of warships; and an active trade was carried on with all parts of the known world.

JOSHUA 13–24: LAND DIVISION

By the time of Joshua 13, Joshua was an old man, about 90 years old, and he realized that the conquest of the land was by no means complete. There yet remained "very large areas of land to be taken over" (Joshua 13:1). In order that the children of Israel might do this, he divided it among them.

"This is Judah's. This is Asher's. This is Simeon's. This is Benjamin's." We hear the people saying these things, even while the Amorites and the Jebusites were still in possession of the Promised Land (Joshua 13–15). The division of the land, however, was the announcement by faith of certain things that under God's guidance they proposed to accomplish.

How sad it is for people whose aspirations never get a foot in advance of their present achievements. Unless we keep a vision before us and dream dreams, we will never win either materially or spiritually. This is just what the Israelites did. They reached out into a hoped-for but unknown future when they divided great stretches of country that were still in the hands of their foes!

Although all this land was allotted to the various tribes, a long struggle followed, and all of the land was not conquered until the time of David. At the time of Joshua, only the mountainous land was subdued; the cities and the plains were hardly touched.

In our reading, we need to keep in mind that when the land was divided, the strong did not take the best part of the land because they were strong, leaving the leftovers for the weak. Neither did the rich purchase the choicest spots, leaving the poor the more undesirable sites. The assignment was made by lot, so no one could be jealous. They met before the Ark of Covenant, the symbol of God's presence. Joshua's assignments were determined by God's will in the matter, for God cares about the distribution of goods.

Do you see any application of this principle today? God cares about the inequalities He sees in the condition of His children. He cares that the weak are thrust aside by the shrewd and strong. God had an interest in a worker's hours and wages, in capital and labor. God is concerned that there should be a more equal division of His blessings in this world, for He says that "everyone will sit under their own vine and under their own fig tree" (Micah 4:4).

Only one tribe was not allotted land. "Moses . . . had not granted the Levites an inheritance among the rest" (Joshua 14:3). You should remember that this tribe was set apart for the sacred service of the priesthood, therefore the Levites received no land.

JOSHUA 14: CALEB'S LAND

Caleb now was 85 years old. Joshua and he were the only spies who had dared to trust God! How many spies did Moses send into Canaan? How many of their names do you remember? No doubt these two are the only ones. Two trusted God, and these are the only names we know.

Caleb asked his friend Joshua for the high, walled cities. He added, "The LORD helping me, I will drive them out just as he said" (Joshua 14:12). He valued his inheritance because of the hard work it offered and the opportunity it gave him for conquering it! Joshua's recognition of his friend, and of his right to a choice possession, was quick and generous. He granted him the mountain and blessed his aged friend.

Caleb was old, but he gloried in the hardness of the task. One of the teachers of Helen Keller said that Helen was the happiest person she had ever met, even though she was deaf and blind. Her teacher attributed her attitude to her having had to overcome so much. Caleb was the happiest man in the camp because he had overcome so much and had more fields to conquer! Horace Mann, the nineteenth-century champion of public schools, once said, "Difficulties are things which show what men are."

The Lord has never promised His children that they will have an easy time serving Him. In fact, Christ said, "In this world you will have trouble" (John 16:33). The promise is not for ease; the promise is for victory. Christ said, "I have overcome the world" (John 16:33). We grow in adversity, for we learn to trust the Lord more. Paul said to Timothy, "Join with me in suffering, like a good soldier of Christ Jesus" (2 Timothy 2:3).

General Booth, the British evangelist who founded the Salvation Army, was once asked the secret of his success. General Booth slowly replied, "I will tell you the secret. God has had all there was of me."

Similarly, Caleb said, "I, however, followed the LORD my God wholeheartedly" (Joshua 14:8).

We might call attention to the fact that the cities of refuge that God planned, spoken of in Numbers 35:6-34 and Deuteronomy 4:41-43 and 19:4-13, are also established at this time (see Joshua 20).

JOSHUA 24: JOSHUA'S FAREWELL

Joshua had become an old man. He knew that he would not live much longer. He wanted to give the people some last words of admonition.

He called first the leaders and then all the people together and urged them to remember the power and faithfulness of God; then he admonished them to be faithful to Him: "Now fear the LORD and serve him with all faithfulness" (Joshua 24:14). He warned them against apostasy (abandoning their faith) and said, "Choose for yourselves this day whom you will serve, whether the gods your ancestors served beyond the Euphrates, or the gods of the Amorites, in whose land you are living. But as for me and my household, we will serve the LORD" (Joshua 24:15).

It is a good thing to have people make an open confession and commit themselves to a solemn promise. Caleb and Joshua, old men now, had made an open confession and were true to their promises.

Likewise, it is a great help for young people to stand and make a public confession of Christ and unite with the Church. This public commitment gives each person something to live up to. (Read Romans 10:9-10 to see what Paul says about confession.)

In response to Joshua that day, the people said, "Far be it from us to forsake the LORD to serve other gods! . . . We too will serve the LORD" (Joshua 24:16-18).

At 110 years of age, grand old Joshua died. And as a great tribute to a great leader, Joshua 24:31 tells us that "Israel served the LORD throughout the lifetime of Joshua."

The book closes with death. We see three graves:

1. Joshua's, the great leader of Israel
2. Eleazer's, the priest
3. Joseph's, whose bones the children of Israel had carried with them from Egypt

All were now buried in the Promised Land.

Joshua

POINTS TO REMEMBER

- Canaan, or the Promised Land, was 180 miles long and approximately 40 miles wide. The boundaries were the wilderness on the south, the Lebanon ranges on the north, the Euphrates on the east and the Mediterranean on the west. It was in the center of six mighty civilizations that made ancient history:

  1. Egypt—300 miles to the south
  2. Nineveh—700 miles northeast
  3. Babylon—700 miles east
  4. Persia—1,000 miles east
  5. Greece—800 miles northwest
  6. Rome—1,500 miles northwest

- Do not pray for an easy task. Pray to be stronger!

- The greatness of your power is the measure of your surrender. It is not a question of who you are or of what you are, but whether God controls you.

- "I . . . followed the LORD my God wholeheartedly" (Caleb's words, Joshua 14:8).

- Be sure—be sure—*be sure* to remember that you cannot hide your sin from God.

- God commands your complete commitment and service to Him.

- Facts do not change; feelings do.

- It is not enough to light a fire; you must put fuel on it.

7

Understanding Judges and Ruth

Judges Portrays Jesus Christ, Our Deliverer-Judge;
Ruth Portrays Jesus Christ, Our Kinsman-Redeemer

SELECTED BIBLE READINGS

DAY OF THE WEEK		MAIN TOPIC
Sunday: Judges 1–2:5	Victories Start	
Monday: Judges 2:16–3:11	Judge Deliverers	
Tuesday: Judges 4:4–5	Deborah and Barak	
Wednesday: Judges 6:1-16; 7:16-25	Gideon, the Farmer	
Thursday: Judges 11:12-40	Jephthah's Vow	
Friday: Judges 15–16	Samson, the Strong Man	
Saturday: Book of Ruth	Ruth's Story	

UNDERSTANDING JUDGES

AUTHOR: The book of Judges does not specifically name its author. Jewish and Christian traditions hold that the prophet Samuel was the author of Judges. Internal evidence indicates that the author of Judges lived shortly after the period of the Judges, and Samuel fits this qualification.

DATE: The book of Judges was likely written between 1045 and 1000 BC.

PURPOSE AND SUMMARY: Named after the judges of Israel, the heroic leaders whose deeds it records, this book covers a period of time from the death of Joshua to the birth of Samuel, an era often called the Dark Ages of Hebrew history. Judges records how the disobedience of God's people led to disaster and how God continued to intervene in His mercy and deliver them.

Judges describes a new hour in the history of Israel. Remember, Israel had come from a long era of bondage in Egypt to a period of 40 years when she lived in tents and wandered in the wilderness. Now the march was over. The nomads were to become settlers in a land of their own. The book of Judges is in a way another book of beginnings where we see a new nation adjusting to her national life. It is filled, not only with struggles and disasters, but also with the moral courage of a select few.

Someone has called the book of Judges the account of the Dark Ages of the Israelite people. The change from being nomads to being a nation was not as easy for them as they had expected it to be. The people turned away from God, and God turned away from the people (see Judges 2:13,23). The book begins with compromise and ends with confusion. This is what happens in every unsurrendered life!

One particular phrase runs through the last five chapters of the book: "Everyone did as they saw fit" (Judges 17:6; the modern equivalent is "doing your own thing"). Mark this phrase every time you find it. We find the people falling away from Jehovah and worshiping the gods of the nations round about them (see Judges 2:13). They forgot that God had chosen them for a purpose—to tell the world the truth that there is but one true God. In punishment for their sins God would deliver them into the hand of a different nation. Then under the oppression of their enemies, they would cry to God for mercy and He would hear them and send a judge to deliver them. So the book is full of rebellion, punishment, misery and deliverance. It has a discordant key throughout.

Judges covers the period after the death of the people's great leader Joshua to just before the ascension of Saul to the throne of Israel. During this time, judges rule the people. These were individuals whom God raised up as deliverers on different occasions in different parts of the land to rescue His oppressed people. We read, "In those days Israel had no king" (Judges 17:6). It covers about the first 350 years in the land of promise. The judges were

Judges

not just one governor after another. The times of their rule could have overlapped.

There is a decided monotony in the description of each successive stage of sin in Israel, but there is an equally remarkable variety in the instruments and methods of deliverance God used. There is something different in the story of each judge, and the book gives us a record of great exploits.

There were 14 judges: Othniel, Ehud, Shamgar, Deborah, Gideon, Tola, Jair, Jephthah, Ibzan, Elon, Abdon, Samson, Eli and Samuel. (The stories of Eli and Samuel appear in 1 Samuel.) Abimelech, a petty ruler, was not called by God to judge.

There were three types of judges:

1. The warrior-judges such as Gideon and Samson
2. Priest-judges such as Eli
3. Prophet-judges such as Deborah and Samuel

The chief judges were Deborah, Gideon, Samson and Samuel.

After reading Judges, you may think that the whole of these 350 years or so was spent in rebellion and sin. But if you read it carefully, you will see that only about 100 out of these possibly 350 years were spent in disloyalty to God.

One thing we learn from the book of Judges is that a people who spend much of their time in disobedience to God make little progress during their lifetime. The book of Numbers recounts the 40 years of wandering in the wilderness, but this book repeats again and again a record of wandering away from God.

This book is in sharpest contrast to Joshua:

In Joshua	In Judges
Joy	Sobs
Heavenly vision	Earthly emphasis
Victory	Defeat
Progress	Decline
Faith	Unbelief
Freedom	Servitude

Here is a summary of Judges that is easy to remember: "Seven apostasies, seven servitudes to seven idolatrous and cruel nations, and seven deliverances!"

Read this book through in a week. It can be done in an hour or two. To learn just the great facts of the Bible, however necessary this is, will never satisfy or make Christians real blessings to others. We must know what God is teaching us. So as you read Judges, carefully study the following three things:

1. The wickedness of the human heart (see Judges 2:11-13,17,19; 8:33-35; 10:6; 13:1)

2. God's delight in using the weak things (see 1 Corinthians 1:26-29)—Note the stories of Ehud, an assassin with a homemade dagger (see Judges 3); Deborah, a woman (see Judges 4; see also Judges 9:53); Gideon, a man from an obscure family in the smallest tribe (see Judges 6); Shamgar, a rustic with an ox goad (see Judges 3:31); Gideon's little pitcher-armed band (see Judges 7); the jaw bone used by Samson (see Judges 15:14-19).

3. The Holy Spirit in Judges—Othniel: "The Spirit of the LORD came on him" (Judges 3:10); Gideon: "The Spirit of the LORD came on Gideon" (Judges 6:34); Jephthah: "The Spirit of the LORD came on Jephthah" (Judges 11:29); Samson: "The Spirit of the LORD began to stir him" (Judges 13:25; see also 14:6 and 15:14, among other passages). Zechariah's words, " 'Not by might nor by power, but by my Spirit,' says the LORD Almighty," might be written as a guide to the spiritual interpretation of Judges (Zechariah 4:6).

The critics of the Bible would have the history of God's Chosen People start here in these dark days of the judges as a wild, lawless, nomadic people before eventually developing into a higher civilization. But just because Israel failed to keep God's Law does not mean that there was no law. Similarly today, just because the people of this world disregard the Ten Commandments and put aside the teachings of Christ does not prove that these words were never spoken.

Human pride would love to believe that humanity's trend is upward. But God's Word shows us that the natural course is downward.

JUDGES 1–3:4: ISRAEL'S FAILURE

Joshua had died (see Judges 1:1). Much of the Promised Land was still to be conquered. The first act of the children of Israel was to seek God's will about how they should start the final conquest. They began well. They consulted God.

God appointed Judah, the kingly tribe, as the lead group in occupying the Promised Land (see Judges 1:2). The work began in earnest, but it ended in weakness. The people did not obey God. And Israel's troubles were due directly to her disobedience to God. They did not exterminate the enemies in the land, as directed by God; rather, they worshiped the idols of the peoples and became morally corrupt: "But Manasseh did not drive out the people of Beth Shan or Taanach or Dor. . . . Nor did Ephraim. . . . Neither did Zebulun. . . . Nor did Asher. . . . Neither did Naphtali. . . . The Amorites confined the Danites"—six nonfulfillments in succession (Judges 1:27-36). Chapter 1 is a chapter of failures.

The children of Israel went into the land and settled where they wanted and began to raise enough for their living. Soon enemies from the outside came along, caught the tribe off guard and took people captive. But their enemies also included traitors from within. God had told His people to do away with them. But did they?

Since chapter 1 records a series of disobediences, of course chapter 2 is a chapter of defeat and failure. God gave them up to their own will. He said, " 'You shall not make a covenant with the people of this land, but you shall break down their altars.' Yet you have disobeyed me. Why have you done this? And I have also said, 'I will not drive them out before you; they will become traps for you, and their gods will become snares to you' " (Judges 2:2-3). The children of Israel brought their judgment upon themselves and became their own executioners. Several times Israel was on the verge of being exterminated, but we can thank God that He intervened.

Sometimes we wonder why God didn't remove all the enemies from the Promised Land before He let the children of Israel go in. But God had a definite reason for not doing this. Read Judges 3:1-4. God uses the results of our lack of faith in Him to prove to us our sin and weakness. He does not forget His covenant, but He allows our very weakness, our guilty weakness, to drive us back to Him.

God wanted the Chosen People to realize that they were a holy people. They must not mix with the wicked nations around them. They must continually separate themselves. God knew that separation makes a people strong. Christians today must remember the same thing: Do not mix with the world. We must keep close to God and must war against sin and unrighteousness. God wants us to be good warriors. (Read Ephesians 6:10-18 and see the armor He provides.)

In the beginning of Judges, then, we see that an uncritical toleration toward an utterly corrupt people resulted in the undoing of God's Chosen People. Read Judges 2:20-22 to learn the result of this disobedience.

JUDGES 3:5–16: THE JUDGES

Beginning in Judges 3, we have a picture of seven failures of faith (or apostasies), seven oppressions (or punishments) and seven deliverances. The Israelites' sin usually involved their intermarrying with the surrounding idolatrous peoples, worshiping at their shrines and practicing their values.

First Apostasy—Judges 3:7-11
    Sin—Idolatry
    Punishment—Mesopotamians; eight years
    Deliverer and Judge—Othniel

Second Apostasy—Judges 3:12-31
    Sins—Immorality and idolatry
    Punishment—Moabites; 18 years
    Deliverers and Judges—Ehud and Shamgar

Third Apostasy—Judges 4–5
     Sin—Departed from God
     Punishment—Canaanites; 20 years
     Deliverer and Judge—Deborah (and Barak)

Fourth Apostasy—Judges 6–8:32
     Sin—Departed from God
     Punishment—Midianites; seven years
     Deliverer and Judge—Gideon

Fifth Apostasy—Judges 8:33–10:5
     Sin—Departed from God
     Punishment—Civil war and rebellion
     Deliverers and Judges—Tola and Jair

Sixth Apostasy—Judges 10:6–12:15
     Sin—Idolatry increased
     Punishment—Philistines and Ammonites; 18 years
     Deliverers and Judges—Jephthah, Ibzan, Elon and Abdon

Seventh Apostasy—13–16
     Sin—Departed from God
     Punishment—Philistines; 40 years
     Deliverer and Judge—Samson

Joshua had no successor. After his death, each tribe acted independently. There was no capital city for the nation and no fixed government.

There also was no unity of action, except in times of danger when the tribes combined for their own good. When the people sinned against God, their enemies defeated them and ruled them. When in their distress they sought the Lord, He sent great leaders, called judges, who delivered them.

But this scene is not only filled with punishment and servitude; it also contains deliverances, for God was always near His people, and when they cried, He answered. God is always brooding over His disobedient children. He promises us that He will never leave us nor forsake us (see Hebrews 13:5). We see defeat on our part but deliverance on God's part: "Where sin increased, grace increased all the more" (Romans 5:20).

In these 14 chapters of Judges, we see God's dealings with His rebellious Chosen People—people whom He had crowned with His best blessings and upon whom He had lavished His tender love. We also see the patience of God and His constant readiness to respond to the least sign of penitence in His people (see Judges 3:9,15; 4:3-7; 6:6-12; 10:15-16). He repeated His mercy again and again, although it was never appreciated. (Think about these things, and you will draw nearer to this God of mercy and love and grace. Look up, repent, and trust God.)

God fulfilled His purpose for Israel by leaving around them in Canaan a circle of strong tribes unlike each other. It is said, "These are the nations the LORD left to test all those Israelites who had not experienced any of the wars in Canaan. . . . They were left to test the Israelites to see whether they would obey the LORD's commands, which he had given their ancestors through Moses" (Judges 3:1-4).

One of the best-known nations whom the Lord used to test Israel was the Philistines, who had settled on the coastal plain. They were a maritime people, ready for any fray that promised land and gain. In wealth and civilization, they no doubt presented a real contrast to the Israelites, and their equipment gave them great advantage in war. Even in the period of the judges there were imposing temples in the Philistine cities. The Israelites feared the Philistines and did not mix freely with them.

JUDGES 3:7-11: FIRST APOSTASY

The Israelites settled among the Syrian nations and seemed too ready to yield for the sake of living at peace with these other nations. Read Judges 3:5-8. They intermarried to make their position safer. They traded with the Amorites, Hivites and Perizzites. They established boundary lines to make things run smoothly. Next they accepted their neighbors' religion and then their bad customs (see Judges 3:6-7).

Soon the Mesopotamians began to oppress them (see Judges 3:8). The Israelites then realized that they had a God from whom they had departed. Israel was a prodigal people—they had left the God whose presence had before assured them victory. For eight years they were under the oppression of these northern nations, and year by year, conditions grew worse.

It was from the far south that God sent help in answer to their pitiful cry (see Judges 3:9). The deliverer was Othniel, who was Caleb's nephew. No doubt he had had frequent skirmishes with the Arab marauders from the wilderness. "The Spirit of the LORD came on him, so that he became Israel's judge and went to war" (Judges 3:10). First he prayed; then they went out to battle. When we see an army bow in prayer, we have faith in their spirit and courage, for they recognize their dependence on God!

Othniel's concerns were to put away the idolatry of Israel, to teach them the Law of the Lord and to remind them of their calling as a nation. Soon success and victory were theirs (see Judges 3:10-11).

Othniel, the first of the judges, was one of the best. He pointed Israel to a higher level of reverence for God and His plans. Forty years of rest followed.

By Othniel's example, we see that only a person who fears God and loves righteousness more than country can do real service for his or her country.

JUDGES 3:12-31: SECOND APOSTASY

Israel's second judge, Ehud, is in marked contrast to Othniel, the judge without reproach. By Ehud's example, we see that God used different kinds of personalities to deliver His people.

The long peace the country enjoyed after the Mesopotamian army had been driven out let the people fall into prosperity and to lapse again into spiritual weakness (see Judges 3:12). This time the Moabites led the attack. The punishment lasted for 18 years.

Judges

Once again the people cried to God. This time, Ehud, with whom
Shamgar's name is associated, was the deliverer (see Judges 3:15).
This Benjamite chose his own method of action, and he assassinated the Moabite king. Eighty years of rest for Israel followed
(see Judges 3:30).

Shamgar, the man with an ox goad, followed Ehud as judge
and deliverer (see Judges 3:31).

JUDGES 4–5: THIRD APOSTASY

After Shamgar, a prophetess arose in Israel (see Judges 4:4). She
was one of those rare women whose heart burns with enthusiasm
when people's hearts are despondent. Many a queen has reigned
with honor and wisdom (England's Elizabeth II, for example),
and often a woman's voice has struck a deep note that has roused
nations. (Remember, we still live during a time when men hold
most positions of authority.)

Israel had been terribly oppressed by Sisera for 20 years (see
Judges 4:3). Again the people cried out, and God heard. This time
the story of deliverance is filled with romance and song. Deborah, a daughter of the people, had gained the confidence of the
people to such a degree that they had appointed her as judge.

Deborah called Barak to help her. The land had been so
filled with Canaanite spoilers that the highways could not be
used. War was everywhere, and the Israelites were defenseless and
crushed; but God delivered them from their oppression through
the joint efforts of Deborah and Barak.

After Jabin, king of Canaan, and his 900 chariots were defeated, we might expect that Israel would at last make a real
start to accomplish her true career. The tribes had had their
third lesson and should have known by then the danger of leaving God: Without God they were as weak as babes. Would they
not now bend themselves to Him? Not yet. The true reformer
had not yet come.

Deborah's work, however, was not in vain. She destroyed the
pagan altars and improved the land. Everywhere the people

plowed new ground, built houses and repaired roads. But they were also falling again into the old habit of friendly association with the Canaanites.

Following deliverance from this servitude, the land rested for 40 years.

JUDGES 6–8:32: FOURTH APOSTASY

Then the fourth apostasy came (see Judges 6:1). This time the deliverer was Gideon, a humble farmer. The Midianites had held the Israelites under bondage for seven years, and there was no organized defense against the Midianites who made constant raids upon the Israelites. So terrible was it that the Israelites hid in caves (see Judges 6:2). Again they cried to the Lord. God answered by calling Gideon to act as deliverer. He broke down the altar of Baal and restored the worship of God. The story of the conflict is one of the most fascinating in history. Everyone should know the story of Gideon and his band of 300 with their jars and horns. Refresh yourself with this story by reading Judges 7:7-24.

After the great victory over the Midianites, the Israelites sought to make Gideon king, but he refused. Gideon was not perfect. We find in the record some things that he should not have done, but he did have a faith in Jehovah that God could honor, and God gave his name a place in the Hall of Faith (see Hebrews 11:32).

Consider what constitutes a missionary call. How does God call men and women today? The angel of Jehovah generally comes when a person is busy (see Judges 6:11-12), and history is full of examples of this:

- Deborah was an Ephramite housewife.
- Saul was out hunting livestock.
- David was tending sheep.
- The disciples were fishing.
- Martin Luther, Reformation leader, was a busy pastor and professor.

- William Carey, the founder of modern missions, was a cobbler.
- George Washington, the first president of the United States, was a farmer-surveyor.
- Abraham Lincoln, the sixteenth president of the United States, was a country lawyer.
- Frances Willard, the social reformer and temperance leader, was a schoolteacher.
- Dwight L. Moody, evangelist and visionary, was a shoe salesman.

You say, "Those people outside the Bible never saw an angel!" How do you know they didn't? God speaks to men and women in many different ways and surprises us as much as He surprised the young Jewish farmer Gideon.

JUDGES 8:33–10:5: FIFTH APOSTASY

Although Gideon was one of the most successful judges to maintain order, and the country was in quietness 40 years, almost immediately after Gideon died, we see the people falling into the sin of idolatry by worshiping the Baals: "No sooner had Gideon died than the Israelites again prostituted themselves to the Baals" (Judges 8:33). How often the personal influence of the hero is everything while he is alive, but confusion follows his death.

No sooner was Gideon's funeral over than discord began. After Gideon, there was no rightful ruler to follow. Gideon left many sons, but not one of them could take his place. Abimelech, a son of Gideon, unprincipled and brutal, secured the allegiance of the men at Shechem and usurped the position of king. He ruled three years in tyranny. He was slain by a woman, and a period of 45 years of quiet followed under the judgeships of Tola and Jair.

Those who are busy for the Lord are those who move the world upward!

Judges

JUDGES 10:6–12:15: SIXTH APOSTASY

During the sixth apostasy, we find the people almost entirely given over to idolatry. Their condition was appalling. God sent judgment this time from the Philistines for 18 years. At last, sorely distressed, they cried to God. For the first time, it is recorded that He refused to hear them and reminded them of how repeatedly He had delivered them (see Judges 10:13). The true attitude of Jehovah toward them is found in this statement: "And he could bear Israel's misery no longer" (Judges 10:16).

Deliverance came through Jephthah. Jephthah's history is very interesting. He was a man of heroic daring and impetuous foolishness. Read the story of his vows and victories, especially the vow he made concerning his only child (see Judges 11:30-40). After his great victory, Jephthah judged Israel for only six years.

JUDGES 13–16: SEVENTH APOSTASY

The seventh apostasy opens with, "Again the Israelites did evil in the eyes of the LORD" (Judges 13:1). This time they were disciplined by the Philistines, under whose awful oppression they lived for 40 years. Here we read the story of Samson. It is a story filled with opportunity and failure.

In those days, everything was dependent upon physical strength. That was what made a leader great. In this case, God used it to begin the deliverance from the Philistines. Before his birth, Samson was appointed by God to deliver Israel from the Philistines (see Judges 13:5). Everything should have been in Samson's favor, but he entered into an unholy alliance, which meant his downfall. The final fall occurred at Gaza (see Judges 16). Nothing is more pathetic than Samson, blind and bound, grinding in the house of the Philistines, when he ought to have been delivering his nation from them (see Judges 16:20-21).

For the Israelites, the story of the judges ends here with Samson, and though it is not taken up again until 1 Samuel, the remaining chapters in Judges (and the book of Ruth) are thematically placed after Samson.

JUDGES 17–21: THE APPENDIX

The last chapters of Judges give us a picture of disorder and confusion:

1. In the religious life of the nation—Judges 17–18
2. In the moral life of the nation—Judges 19
3. In the political life of the nation—Judges 21

Israel had forsaken God and now we see the depths into which they had sunk. Read Judges 17:6, and you will find the reason for it all.

These events probably took place soon after Joshua's death, and they give us a picture of the internal condition of the Chosen People. The story of the backsliding of individuals is followed by the backsliding of the nation.

The last chapter proves that the children of Israel had lost the way to God's house, so low had they sunk. We find faithlessness, failure and forfeiture! But God still loves His own.

The history of the Church through the ages has been similar—with Martin Luther, leader of the Protestant Reformation; John Knox, Scottish reformer; and John Wesley, founder of the Methodists as deliverers. The biography of many an everyday Christian is just like this as well. God opens doors and gives us grace for great tasks. Then we forget Him and begin to focus our interests on the world. This brings loss and defeat. But God will hear our cry of repentance and will restore us to favor again.

UNDERSTANDING RUTH

AUTHOR: The book of Ruth does not specifically name its author. Jewish and Christian traditions hold that the prophet Samuel wrote the book of Ruth.

DATE: The exact date the book was written is uncertain. However, the prevalent view is a date between 1011 and 931 BC.

PURPOSE AND SUMMARY: The book is from the same period as the book of Judges. Though national sin and corruption portray a dark picture in Judges, the story of Ruth, the Moabitess, and her loyalty and devotion to Naomi, her Hebrew mother-in-law, reflects the faithfulness of the Lord to His people in the days of the judges.

This delightful story should be read in connection with the first chapters of Judges, as no doubt it gives us an idea of the domestic life of Israel at that period of oppression. Samuel may have been the author of this book, but no one knows for sure where or when it was written. This book, written on a separate scroll, was read at Pentecost, the harvest festival.

Ruth was the great-grandmother of David, the ancestor of Christ; and her story is about the beginning of the messianic family within the messianic nation into which, more than a thousand years later, the Messiah would be born.

There are some interesting things to notice in this book:

- Ruth was a Moabitess. The Moabites were descendants of Lot. They were pagans, worshiping many gods and goddesses. Of course we know that although Ruth was born a pagan, it was either through her first husband or through Naomi that she learned of the one true God. God, in establishing the family that was to produce the world's Savior, chose a beautiful pagan girl and led her to Bethlehem where she met Boaz.

- Boaz was the son of Rahab, the prostitute who helped Joshua's spies in Jericho (see Joshua 2), so he was half-Canaanite. He was Ruth and Naomi's kinsman-redeemer, a relative of Naomi who first made Ruth a family member and then made her his bride.

Ruth

- The story is one of God's grace. God adopted the Gentiles into Christ's family by making Christ's great-grandmother a Moabitess and His great-grandfather a half-Canaanite.

8

Understanding First Samuel

First Samuel Portrays Jesus Christ, Our King

AUTHOR: The author of 1 and 2 Samuel is anonymous. First Samuel 10:25 indicates that Samuel wrote a book, and this suggests that he may have written part of 1 and 2 Samuel. Other possible authors of 1 and 2 Samuel include the prophets Nathan and Gad (see 1 Chronicles 29:29).

DATE: Originally, 1 and 2 Samuel were one book. The translators of the Septuagint, the 3rd-to-2nd-century BC Greek translation of the Hebrew Old Testament, separated the book of Samuel into two books; and Bible translations have preserved the separate books to this day. The events of 1 Samuel span approximately 100 years, from about 1100 BC to about 1000 BC. The events of 2 Samuel cover another 40 years. The date of writing 1 and 2 Samuel, then, would be sometime after 960 BC.

PURPOSE AND SUMMARY: These books were named after Samuel, not only because he is the principal figure in the first part, but also because he anointed the two other principal characters, Saul and David. The books of Samuel cover a period of time in Israel's history from the birth of Samuel to the close of the reign of David. First Samuel presents the transition from Israel's judges to the monarchy under Saul. Second Samuel deals almost exclusively with the history of David as king and presents a vivid picture of a theocratic monarchy in which the king represents God's rule over God's people.

We enter now our study of the royal history. Let us look at the six books before us:

- 1 Samuel—Saul, the people's choice
- 2 Samuel—David, God's choice
- 1 Kings—Solomon and Israel
- 2 Kings—Israel's kings
- 1 Chronicles—Solomon and the Temple
- 2 Chronicles—The kings and the Temple

Royal history begins with the book of Samuel. The long period of the rule of the judges ends with Samuel. When Samuel came into power the people were in an awful state. They had practically rejected God, and they were clamoring for an earthly king (see 1 Samuel 8:4-7). This book describes the beginning of the 500-year period of the kings of Israel (approximately 1050-586 BC).

The events recorded in 1 Samuel cover a period of about 100 years from the childhood of Samuel through the turbulent times of Saul to the beginning of the reign of the king whom God chose—David. The description given in 1 and 2 Samuel of the personal lives of these three men gives us an exceedingly graphic picture of these times. Samuel was the last of the judges; Saul was the first of the kings. The record brings us up to the time when

David is ready to permanently establish the monarchy, and God is ready to permanently establish David's throne (see Psalm 89).

The book may be divided under the names of its three chief characters: Samuel (see 1 Samuel 1–7); Saul (see 1 Samuel 8–15); and David (see 1 Samuel 16–31). The history of this book is presented to us in the attractive cloak of biography. Everyone likes a true story.

Many of us have known and loved the stories that are recorded in 1 Samuel. From the time we were little children, who does not know the story of the boy Samuel being called by God (see 1 Samuel 3), of the young David defeating the giant Goliath (see 1 Samuel 17), and of the friendship between David and Jonathan (see 1 Samuel 18)?

1 SAMUEL 1–7: SAMUEL, THE KING MAKER

The meaning of "Samuel" is "name of God." This book opens with the record of Hannah, Samuel's mother, praying for a son whom God could use. Samuel, the last of the judges, was God's answer to this prayer: "Samuel was ministering before the LORD— a boy wearing a linen ephod" (1 Samuel 2:18).

Samuel was the last of the judges, the first of the prophets and the founder of the monarchy. The record of this great man's life is beyond reproach. It is hard to find a single mistake that Samuel made.

Throughout Samuel's long and useful life he was God's man. He was preeminently a man of prayer. This first book that bears his name is a marvelous study of the place and power of prayer, illustrated from life. Samuel was a child of prayer (see 1 Samuel 3:1-19); he brought victory to his people through prayer (see 1 Samuel 7:5-10); when the nation wanted a king, Samuel prayed to the Lord (see 1 Samuel 8:6); intercessory prayer was the keynote of his life (see 1 Samuel 12:19-23).

In the dark and turbulent times of Israel, we hear the prayer of faith from the lips of a simple trusting woman, Hannah. She asked God for a son whom she could dedicate to Him for service (see 1 Samuel 1:9-19).

When Samuel was born, Hannah brought him to the Tabernacle at Shiloh. Although the corruption of the priesthood was appalling, Samuel was protected and grew as a boy in the fear of the Lord (see 1 Samuel 1:24-28; 2:12-26; 3:1-21).

Eli was both judge and priest at this time. He had ruled for 40 years. He was an indulgent father and as a result his two sons, Hophni and Phinehas, also priests, were allowed to act in a most disgraceful manner. As a result there was moral corruption, and God warned Eli of the downfall of his house.

Fungus growth in a tree usually is not detected for a long time. Everything seems fine on the outside; but when the crash suddenly comes, the true state of the tree can be seen. Israel had been sinning for a long time, and eventually a catastrophe came and the corruption was exposed.

Invasion by the Philistines

During the next invasion of their enemies the Philistines, Israel was defeated, the Ark was taken and Eli's sons were killed. When Eli, then an old man of 98, heard all this, he died of the shock (see 1 Samuel 4:18). Read all of 1 Samuel 4–6 to learn the history of the Philistines' possession of the Ark.

This mention of the Philistines is the first since Judges 13–16. The 40-year bondage of the Israelites (see Judges 13:1) seems to have come to a close in the days of Samuel (see 1 Samuel 7:13-14), during his twentieth year as judge (see 1 Samuel 7:2).

The Philistines were Israel's powerful enemy and lived to the southwest on the coast. Perhaps this renewed action on their part was due to the death of Samson. The battle, probably fought about four miles northwest of Jerusalem, soon went against Israel. They wondered why God had deserted them. While warring against God, they asked God to war for them. Read the account of the revival at Mizpah recorded in 1 Samuel 7.

We cannot win while we war against God! Apart from the immediate causes, rebellion against God is the root reason for tragic wars even today. Civilization in general has not been seeking first and always the glory and will of God. The United States has failed to meet this test, as well as all other nations. Civilized nations have failed, as they were bound to do, and they always will fail as long as God is left out.

Though this life is bound to be a fight against evil, it may always be a winning fight if we enlist under the banner of the captain of our salvation and make His will our will. "We are more than conquerors" (Romans 8:37).

After Israel's first defeat by the Philistines, did they look to the Ark of God for protection or did they look to the God of the Ark (see 1 Samuel 4:3-7,10)?

Mercy from God

The Ark of God was a poor substitute for the God of the Ark. Many people today think that when they wear religious symbols or perform religious rituals or give money to charitable causes, they will be safe. They think that these things are charms, or talismans, to bring them victory. (Can you give some illustrations of this?)

It has been said, "Man's extremity is God's opportunity!" Although at the time the loss was terrible, God overruled for good. Through Samuel God provided:

1. Deliverance from the Philistines
2. Preparation for the kingdom
3. A permanent sanctuary instead of a tabernacle at Shiloh
4. A better priesthood

What brought about this timely revival? Three things:

1. A praying mother—1 Samuel 1
2. A chastened people—1 Samuel 2
3. A faithful prophet—1 Samuel 3

God always gives us the best we will take, for His mercy endures forever. We are free human agents. We can choose for ourselves, but we may well tremble at the consequences. We must choose God's best or our own way.

A Sense of Need

Israel needed a praying band of Christians—a people brought to a sense of their need, and a consecrated preacher to bring about revival. (The same is true today!) Under the Philistine rule, Israel had no definite center of worship; but Samuel grew into manhood and assumed the leadership for which he had been born. The first hopeful sign after Israel's long rebellion and defeat was that they had a sense of need. They began to want God. They "turned back to the LORD" (1 Samuel 7:2). The Jews are going to do this again some day when Christ, "the one they have pierced," returns to this earth and reveals Himself to His own people (see Zechariah 12:10-11).

God cannot do much for people who do not feel they need anything. There are those who think they are all right. God pities those people.

"Well," said Samuel, "if you really mean business, you've got to show me. Do something. Prove it. How? Put away your strange gods" (see 1 Samuel 7:3). "Put away" might be reworded "cut it out." If you mean business, God will mean business.

Religion is not just a matter of emotion but also of will. It is often easy for us to talk big, but it is another thing to live up to what we say. We often make promises to God that we never keep. How sad that sometimes our lives shout "Lie!" to what our lips say.

The people began to lament, and Samuel took advantage of this and called on them to return to their God and put away their idols. Samuel erected an altar and called it Ebenezer (see 1 Samuel 7:12). "Ebenezer" means "stone of help." Christ our victory is called "the rock" or "the stone" in both the Old Testament and the New Testament (Daniel 2:35; Psalm 118:22; Matthew 21:42).

The Ministry of Samuel

In just one brief paragraph—1 Samuel 7:15-17—we find the actual story of Samuel's judgeship. His home was at Ramah. From here he was a sort of circuit rider covering his territory (Bethel, Gilgal and Mizpah) once a year, and overseeing and administering the affairs of the people. (We find missionaries still doing this today. They choose some place as home and then move out through the surrounding country.)

Beginning with Samuel, God introduced a new way of dealing with Israel. He called prophets through whom He would speak; and starting with Samuel, prophecy became a definite part of the life of Israel. "Indeed, beginning with Samuel, all the prophets who have spoken have foretold these days" (Acts 3:24).

Samuel's greatest ministry was the organization of the kingdom. The independent tribes were now going to be formed into a nation. In order to survive among other strong nations, Israel had to become powerful. The Israelites had refused to take God seriously and obey Him as He had commanded them, so He permitted Samuel to find a king for them. The people wanted to "be like all the other nations" (1 Samuel 8:20). God wanted them to be unlike the other nations. In Deuteronomy 17:14-20, God had prophesied that Israel should have a king, but He did not want them to become independent of Him.

1 SAMUEL 8–15: SAUL, THE CHOSEN KING

God never intended for Israel to have any king but Himself. He would send them great leaders and these in turn would receive their orders directly from Him. But Israel, in her falling away, had become restless. The people wanted a king like the other surrounding nations. We find that God granted their request, but here is a great lesson: We can have either God's best or His second best—His directive will or His permissive will.

Saul, the Israelites' first king, was a failure. He was handsome to look at—he was tall and had a noble bearing. He started out splendidly. He proved to be an able military leader. He defeated the enemies about him—the Philistines, the Amalekites and the Ammonites.

Saul was humble at first, but he became proud and disobedient to God. No man had a greater opportunity than Saul and no man ever was a greater failure. His jealousy of David bordered on insanity.

Inasmuch as Saul was granted to Israel as king in response to Israel's sinful demand for a king—contrary to God's will—did Saul ever really have a chance to "make good" in God's sight? Could he possibly have succeeded under such circumstances? Was he not condemned by God to failure even before he started as king?

We find the answer clearly in God's Word. In 1 Samuel 12:12-15, the prophet of God told Israel that, although they had demanded their king in defiance of God, if both they and their king would fear Jehovah and serve Him, all would be well (see verse 12). Note what follows this word of Samuel (see verses 16-18). Then we see the fact that Israel confessed her sin in asking for a king, and Samuel reassured Israel, promising blessing if they served God (see verse 19).

The only reason any soul is ever rejected by God is that that soul has first rejected God. God takes the initiative in love: "We love because he first loved us" (1 John 4:19). People take the initiative in sin (see 1 Samuel 15:23).

Note four things that describe Saul's ordination:

1. Divine (see 1 Samuel 9:3-20)—He went out with a bridle and came back with a scepter.

2. Prophetic (see 1 Samuel 10:1)—Samuel was his tutor and friend. What an advantage, but it was thrown away. (How often we do this today!)

3. Spiritual—"The Spirit of God came powerfully upon him" (1 Samuel 10:10). He *grieved* this Spirit; then he *quenched* Him. If the Holy Spirit is to remain, He must be loved and obeyed.

4. Popular—"Then the people shouted, 'Long live the king!'" (1 Samuel 10:24).

Saul failed God in several ways:

1. Presumption at God's altar—1 Samuel 13:11-13
2. Cruelty to his son Jonathan—1 Samuel 14:44
3. Disobedience in the matter of Amalek—1 Samuel 15:23

4. Jealousy and hatred of David—1 Samuel 18:29
5. Sinful appeal to the witch of Endor—1 Samuel 28:7

Saul waged six campaigns:

1. Against the Ammonites—Beginning of reign; against insurmountable obstacles; army mobilized with great haste; Ammonites completely ruined; Saul's prestige as king strengthened (see 1 Samuel 11).

2. Against the Philistines—Saul sinned in assuming the function of priest; God rejected Saul; bravery of Jonathan and single companion created panic among Philistines; enemy routed (see 1 Samuel 13).

3. Against the Amalekites—Saul drove the enemy into the desert; marred success by disobedience; seized valuable property; lied to Samuel; prophet repeated that God had rejected him (see 1 Samuel 15).

4. Against the Philistines—Saul in constant warfare with Philistines; David as a child appeared after Saul's anointing; David met Goliath, giant of Philistines, and slew him; panic resulted; David won distinction (see 1 Samuel 14; 17).

5. Against David—Blind jealousy drove Saul to seek David's life; David became an outcast; David was repeatedly delivered; Saul was David's enemy till his own death; David had an unshakable friendship with Saul's son Jonathan (see beginning 1 Samuel 18).

6. Against the Philistines—Battlefield was the plains of Jazreel; dark Saul made his visit to the witch of Endor; Samuel was called up; Samuel prophesized Saul's defeat and death; Israel completely defeated; Saul and three sons slain (see 1 Samuel 28–31).

All through the years, Samuel mourned for Saul (see 1 Samuel 15:35). When Saul failed, Samuel was faithful in warning him; then in loneliness he mourned over him.

In a battle with the Philistines, Saul and his three sons met death. Here a life so full of promise ended in defeat and failure. Saul had not obeyed God absolutely. If I sold 1,000 acres of land and reserved for myself one acre in the center, I would make sure I had the right to go over those 1,000 acres to get to mine. One trouble with us is that we reserve a room for Satan in our hearts and he knows he has a right-of-way. This was the trouble with Saul.

Think of the difference between the end of Saul of Tarsus (Paul) and Saul the king! One put God first; the other put himself first!

God is showing in this book that He must be all in all, that His children have no blessing apart from Him.

The morning of Saul's life was bright, but soon the sky became overcast. Then his sun set in the blackest storm clouds. Follow carefully his rise, his reign and his ruin.

1 SAMUEL 16–31: DAVID, THE KING PROVEN

As the third division of the book opens, we see Samuel mourning for Saul. God rebukes him and tells him to arise and anoint the new king (see 1 Samuel 16:1).

David, the apple of God's eye, was one of the greatest characters of all times. He made great contributions to the history of Israel both spiritually and nationally.

In this book we see David as a shepherd lad, a minstrel, an armor bearer, a captain, the king's son-in-law, a writer of psalms and a fugitive. He was anointed three times and was the founder of the royal line from which the King of kings came.

David, Jesse's son and the great-grandson of Ruth and Boaz, was born in Bethlehem. He was the youngest of eight sons. When David was only 18, God told Samuel to anoint him king to succeed Saul. Even after his anointing, he continued to tend his father's sheep, and we read of his brave deeds in defending them from wild beasts.

As a harpist, David's fame reached the king. Saul's melancholy led to David being called to the royal court to play music. One of the most charming stories of real love in friendship is found between David and Jonathan, Saul's son.

When David was promoted to a high command in the army, his great success roused the jealousy of Saul who determined to kill him. He made five attacks on David's life (see 1 Samuel 19:10,15,20-21,23-24). But God preserved David. "If God is for us, who can be against us?" (Romans 8:31). David was delivered from all these dangers. Read David's words in Psalms 37 and 59.

These were trying days for David, the young man who had been appointed to the kingly office. It was natural that he should initially go to Samuel for protection. All this was training for the one whom God was preparing for the throne. He learned to be a warrior; and he learned not only how to handle men, but also how to handle himself. He became independent and courageous. He learned, too, in those trying days, to trust God, not men. He always awaited God's time.

David was an outcast for no wrong that he had done but because of the insane jealousy of Saul. With each trial and affliction, David grew; and instead of letting Saul's hatred harden his heart, he returned love for hate.

Finally David took refuge in flight. During this time Samuel died. Twice was Saul's life in David's hand, but both times he spared Saul. Feeling that he should perish one day by the hand of Saul, he took refuge among the Philistines. (Psalm 56 was written then.) After the Philistines killed Saul and his sons, David's exile ended.

The closing chapter of our book is draped in black. It gives the final picture of one of the most disastrous failures in Israel's history. Saul died on the field of battle by his own hand. Advantages and opportunities in youth never guarantee success in manhood. One must keep true to God. Saul's undoing was not so much disobedience as half-hearted obedience (see 1 Samuel 15). He was a victim of human pride and jealousy.

9

Understanding Second Samuel

Second Samuel Portrays Jesus Christ, Our King

SELECTED BIBLE READINGS

DAY OF THE WEEK		MAIN TOPIC
Sunday: 2 Samuel 1	David, Mourner for Jonathan and Saul	
Monday: 2 Samuel 2–3:1	David, King of Judah	
Tuesday: 2 Samuel 5	David, King of All Israel	
Wednesday: 2 Samuel 7	David, a House Established	
Thursday: 2 Samuel 11	David, the Sinner	
Friday: 2 Samuel 12:1-23; Psalm 51	David, the Repenter	
Saturday: 2 Samuel 24	David, the Census Taker	

AUTHOR: The author of 1 and 2 Samuel is unknown. First Samuel 10:25 indicates that Samuel wrote a book, and this suggests that he may have written part of 1 and 2 Samuel. Other possible authors of 1 and 2 Samuel are the prophets Nathan and Gad (see 1 Chron. 29:29).

DATE: Originally, 1 and 2 Samuel were one book. The translators of the Septuagint, the 3rd-to-2nd-century BC Greek translation of the Hebrew Old Testament, separated the book of Samuel into two books; and Bible translations have preserved the separate books to this day. The events of 1 Samuel span approximately 100 years, from about 1100 BC to about 1000 BC. The events of 2 Samuel cover another 40 years. The date of writing 1 and 2 Samuel, then, would be sometime after 960 BC.

PURPOSE AND SUMMARY: These books were named after Samuel, not only because he is the principal figure in the first part, but also because he anointed the two other principal characters, Saul and David. The books of Samuel cover a period of time in Israel's history from the birth of Samuel to the close of the reign of David. First Samuel presents the transition from Israel's judges to the monarchy under Saul. Second Samuel deals almost exclusively with the history of David as king and presents a vivid picture of a theocratic monarchy in which the king represents God's rule over God's people.

We must not only crown Christ as King of our lives, but we must also set Him on His rightful throne.

First Samuel records the failure of the people's king, Saul. Second Samuel describes the enthronement of God's king, David, and the establishment of the house of David through which the Messiah, Jesus Christ, would later come. When Christ comes again, He will sit upon the throne of David (see Isaiah 9:7; Luke 1:32).

Second Samuel is occupied with the story of David as king (see 2 Samuel 5:3). It does not tell the whole story, for the story actually begins in 1 Samuel and continues in 1 Kings. First Chronicles deals with it also but from another point of view.

The contents of 2 Samuel will be easier to remember if we study it as a continuation of a biography. David occupies the field of view. He comes into his own. Let us begin with David's preparation and discipline, his testing days:

1. Called from the sheepfold—1 Samuel 16:11-13
2. Given victory over Goliath—1 Samuel 17
3. Persecuted by Saul—1 Samuel 18–31

The children of Israel had clamored for a king. God first gave them one after their own heart, Saul. Then He gave them one after His own heart, David. This is the substance of 2 Samuel:

1. David was made king over Judah—2 Samuel 1-4.
2. David was made king over all Israel—2 Samuel 5-24.

Notice the blessedness of the life that recognizes the "Lord's anointed" and puts the true King on the throne of the heart (1 Samuel 24:6,10; 26:9,11,16,23):

- Such a life is sheltered—"You were the one who led Israel on their military campaigns" (2 Samuel 5:2).

- Such a life is nurtured—"You will shepherd my people Israel" (2 Samuel 5:2; see also Psalm 23:1-2).

- Such a life is victorious, with Christ's own victory—"And you will become their ruler" (2 Samuel 5:2).

Jesus says, "Follow me." If we obey, He will shield us and shepherd us and make our victory sure!

The story of David begins with his being a shepherd (see 1 Samuel 16-17); then we see him as a prince in the court (see 1 Samuel 18-20); and finally he becomes an exile from the court (see 1 Samuel 21-31).

No one found anywhere in God's Word is as multifaceted as David—the shepherd boy, the court musician, the soldier, the true friend, the outcast captain, the king, the great general, the loving father, the poet, the sinner, the brokenhearted old man, but always the lover of God. David was a man after God's own heart—not because of boasted perfection, but because of confessed imperfections. He hid himself in God. (Read 1 John 1:9 to learn what God tells us to do when we sin.)

If we read 2 Samuel 7:18-22 and 8:14-15, we find David at his very best, when he was at the height of his prosperity. It shows what he had become and what he might have continued to be if only he had remained faithful to God.

We find David as a sort of Robin Hood of the Bible. We love the stories of his daring courage and his encounters with lions and bears and even a giant. He was a man of wonderful personal power and charm. Can you find, as you read this book, where David clearly portrays the following outstanding qualities?

1. Faithfulness
2. Modesty
3. Patience
4. Courage
5. Bigheartedness
6. Trustfulness
7. Penitence

It would be well to compare Saul and David and roughly measure their stature one against the other. Both were kings of Israel. Both reigned about the same length of time, 40 years. Both had the loyal support of the people, and both had the promise of God's power to back them. Yet Saul was a failure and David was a success. Saul's name is a blot on Israel's history, and David's name is honored today both by Jew and Gentile.

What is the reason for the differences? It would be in our best interest to find out, for these same factors may work in our own lives, and knowing them may help us to correctly choose the forces that will carry us on a godly course.

Saul had a brilliant start and for a while made good. But with success came pride. (Read Proverbs 16:18.) Thirty-five years of his reign were spent in insecurity and failure. He had lost his hold on God. Pride and jealousy were his undoing. He finally died a suicide in a lost battle, and he left his kingdom at war with its neighbors and divided in its loyalty (see 1 Samuel 31).

Similar to Saul, David lost his hold on God. After David had spared Saul, David seemed every inch a king, and he was willing to wait for God to tell him that he would surely prevail (see 1 Samuel 26:9-11). He was at a high point, and his training seemed complete. However, when David realized that his life was in danger, he made the great mistake of associating himself with the Philistines instead of continuing to trust God (see 1 Samuel 27).

The devil would rather throw a man when he is on the heights; he falls farther and harder. And he threw David. For it was at that time that David passed into one of the worst periods of his life and stayed there for almost a year and a half (see 1 Samuel 27:1). David fell from a mountain peak of spiritual victory and privilege to a black valley of defeat; and he deliberately chose to stay there, weak and discouraged, for a long time.

David's faith had collapsed. Without God's counsel, he left the country of God's people and went to live in the land of the enemy, hopelessly certain of dying at Saul's hand unless he escaped. He joined Achish, king of Gath, who gave him Ziklag in which to live (see 1 Samuel 27:1-7).

David lied to Achish to win his favor, saying that he had raided the people of Judah when he had not. David met calamity. At last he flung himself upon God: "But David found strength in the LORD his God" (1 Samuel 30:6). He asked God what to do. God answered; and under His guidance, David had a real victory over his enemies (see 1 Samuel 30).

Notice what happened at almost exactly the same time in the lives of Saul and David. Saul, an unrepentant sinner, went down to death, dragging his family and his country with him (see 1 Samuel 31:3-7). David, a repentant sinner, was given a glorious victory over the enemy and many were saved with him (see 1 Samuel 30:17-20). We are all sinners of one kind or another. Which ending do we want for our lives?

Read David's sorrowful lament over Saul and Jonathan, found in 2 Samuel 1:17-27. Then consider the following questions:

- How did Saul meet his death? (Read 1 Samuel 31:4.)
- Why is suicide wrong?
- Can suicide ever be justified?
- What motive prompts suicide?
- Who fell in the same battle with Saul? (Read 1 Samuel 31:2.)
- What was David's attitude when he heard of their deaths?
- Might one not expect David to have been glad to hear of Saul's death?

David's lament about Saul's death showed his attitude. Every-thing was clear now for David to fulfill the divine purpose and be-come king of Israel.

There is no parallel account to that in 2 Samuel 2 of David's succession to the kingdom of Judah, but 1 Chronicles 11 and 12 give a vivid picture of the men of Israel as they came to make David king over the whole land.

After the death of both King Saul and Jonathan, his beloved friend, David naturally wanted to know what was to be the next step. So David sought guidance from God (see 2 Samuel 2:1). David did not ask about being a king but only about the place where he should go. The nation of Israel needed a leader and the divine answer was that he should go up to the city of Hebron (see 2 Samuel 2:3).

Hebron was one of the most ancient cities (see Numbers 13:22). It was in existence in Abraham's day. When Canaan was conquered, it became the possession of Caleb and was one of the cities of refuge (see Joshua 14:13-15; 21:11-13). This was David's capital for the first seven years of his reign. This made the city still more important. It was 15 miles south of Jerusalem, in the center of Judah, and a strong place. It was especially suitable as a capital of the new kingdom, with the Philistines on the one side and the followers of Saul on the other.

Study the facts of 2 Samuel 2:8–4:12. Amid fighting and civil war and intrigue, David did not lift a finger to secure the kingdom of Israel; he made no effort to seize the kingdom by force. The op-position steadily weakened itself, and David's cause steadily grew stronger. David knew that it was God's plan that he should be king of Israel, but again he was willing to wait. Seven and a half years after ascending Judah's throne, David was made king of Israel.

Why was David's success assured when he was made king? Saul chose the way of self; David chose God's way. Because of this, God called him "a man after his own heart" (1 Samuel 13:14).

Some people grow under responsibility; others swell. We learn from Saul's failures and David's accomplishments that the sur-rendered life is the only secure and truly successful life.

2 SAMUEL 1–10: DAVID'S RISE, SUPREMACY AND RULE

As 2 Samuel opens, we find David just returning to Ziklag after his great victory over the Amalekites. He had come back weary in body but refreshed in spirit because of his great success. No doubt he was wondering what had been the outcome of that great battle at Mount Gilboa. His dearest friend, Jonathan, and King Saul, were in that battle.

David was not kept in suspense for long. An Amalekite from the camp of Israel came running that great distance to tell David of the disaster. Because the Amalekite claimed to have killed Saul, the Lord's anointed, David dealt severely with him. Read 2 Samuel 1:1-16.

David was 30 years old, and never did a man of that age—or any age—act in a nobler way. His generous heart not only forgot all that Saul had done but also remembered all that was favorable in Saul's character. (Recall some of the things Saul had done against David.)

How beautiful is this spirit of forgiveness! See that same spirit when men nailed Christ to the cross (see Luke 23:34) and when men stoned the martyr Stephen to death (see Acts 7:60). David wrote a song for this occasion called "The Song of the Bow." It is filled with extreme tenderness, especially when it speaks of his beloved friend (2 Samuel 1:19-27).

The death of Saul did not end David's troubles. He had formed an alliance with Achish. He had gone as near to the position of a traitor to his country as he could without actually fighting against it.

His own tribe, Judah, was by far the friendliest to him. They knew better how cruelly Saul had hunted him down and why he had thrown himself into the hands of Achish.

King of Judah

After God directed him to Hebron, no sooner had David gone up to the city than the men of Judah came and anointed him king over the house of Judah. Although it was not all that God had promised David, it was a large installment, for Judah was the royal tribe.

The men of Judah who came to meet David were probably the elders of his own tribe. They came to elect him as king, and although he had been anointed privately by Samuel to indicate that God had chosen him, it was natural and necessary to repeat the anointing in public as the outward and visible inauguration of his reign.

Remember that Saul was anointed privately, too (see 1 Samuel 10:1). Anointing with oil meant a divine appointment. Saul was set apart for the service of king. He was given the right to rule the people.

David's kingship, however, was not acknowledged by all of the people. Abner, the captain of Saul's army, at once took steps to appoint Saul's son to take his place.

The earnest efforts of David to ward off strife and bring the people together in recognizing him as king were all in vain. The spirit of Saul, which was so antagonistic to David, was perpetuated in Abner, who was determined to center the kingdom of Israel around the house of Saul, not of David (see 2 Samuel 2:8-10). The followers of Saul did not consult Jehovah but merely tried to stem the popular tide in David's direction.

Civil war followed, and "the war between the house of Saul and the house of David lasted a long time. David grew stronger and stronger, while the house of Saul grew weaker and weaker" (2 Samuel 3:1). The cause of its weakness was that God was against it.

King of Israel

After seven and one-half years of opposition, David finally won the heart of all Israel by his justice and great spirit. He was left now without a rival. Representatives of all the tribes came to Hebron to anoint him king of the whole nation (see 2 Samuel 5). The monarchy in Israel was, however, never an absolute autocracy (see 1 Samuel 10:25; 1 Kings 12:3).

In the prime of his life, David came into his complete inheritance. This was the task God intended him to do. He reigned 40 years in all: seven and a half years in Hebron over Judah and 33 years in Jerusalem over the whole land.

One of the great results of David's kingship was the unity of the whole nation under him as leader. He brought the various conflicting elements into one group. We find a united people under a young leader united to God. In order to go from greatness to greatness, the Israelites needed only to have kept on following David's leading down the years. They had only to follow David's greater Son to have gone on from glory to glory!

David trusted God with all his heart and leaned not to his own understanding; he acknowledged God in all his ways, and God did direct his path (see Proverbs 3:5-6). How did David obtain guidance? By asking for it. Just how God gave the answer we are not told. But God has assured us that if we ask, He will answer (see 1 John 5:14-15; Jeremiah 33:3). And God never breaks His word. We have to make decisions almost every hour of our lives. Should I continue in this direction in my life? Should my vacation be spent at home or should I travel? Would we take false steps if God made the decisions for us? Could we fail?

Conquest of Jerusalem

From the anointing of David as king at Hebron, we go with him to the field of battle.

The first thing that engaged David was the capture of Jerusalem, the stronghold of Zion. Since the days of Joshua, Jerusalem alone had defied the attack of Israel. It was an impregnable fortress still in the hands of the Jebusites. David thought it was best suited to be his nation's capital, and after its capture, it became the residence of David and the capital of his kingdom (see 2 Samuel 5:6-9; 1 Chronicles 11:4-8).

After David had established the capital at Jerusalem, he wished to bring the Ark of God into the new ruling center. He realized the people's need for God, but we are not told that he consulted with God. A real tragedy followed. What was it? Read 2 Samuel 6:1-19. What do you know of God's directions for carrying the Ark?

It is not what we think but what God says that is important. Uzzah's human opinion was that it was all right to take hold of the Ark to keep it from falling. He was sincere, but it was directly contrary to what God had said. So Uzzah died. We can always know what God has said if we are willing to pay the price of knowing by studying His Word and trusting what He says (see John 7:17).

After three months, the Ark was duly placed in the Tabernacle. Read the story in 2 Samuel 6.

What were the greatest things David did for his people?

1. Captured Jerusalem and built it bigger and stronger
2. Conquered the Philistines
3. Unified the people

But all this would be of little use without putting God at the center. This is really what gave the nation unity and power. Neither a nation nor an individual can be great without Christ in his or her heart.

Man of God

All the events in David's reign that followed the capture of Jerusalem may be summed up in these words: "And David became more and more powerful, because the LORD Almighty was with him" (1 Chronicles 11:9). God had been getting David ready for this reign. The training was difficult. But it is good to receive such training while young. Many a great person can testify to this.

David was an active man. He was fond of work. His wars with outside nations had ceased. Now he sought to find what he could do to improve and beautify his kingdom. He compared the elegance of his own palace with the Tabernacle where Jehovah dwelt. He thought that there should not be such a difference, so he called Nathan the prophet and consulted him about building a temple for Jehovah. At first it seemed as though God would let him do this, but God had a different purpose for David. Read 2 Samuel 7:4-17 to learn what God told Nathan to tell David.

David's spirit is again revealed in his submission to God's plan for him. God allowed him to gather materials for his son Solomon to use to build the Temple. God's servants do not think it a misfortune that the Lord thwarts their plans and desires. Real servants learn what God's will is and yield their will to the Master's!

Don't pass over the sweet story of David's treatment of crippled young Mephibosheth when he learned that Mephibosheth was his best friend's son (see 2 Samuel 9).

Although his heart was inclined to peace, David was powerful in every art of war, and chapter 10 recounts some of his perilous undertakings. This closing account of David's rise to power prepares for the terrible story of his fall.

David's start was slow and discouraging. But David had faith in God. He was patient and was willing to wait for God to lead. He was humble before God and the people. He was humble in his success; and when he sinned, he genuinely repented. David's was a great career. He used every talent God gave him for the glory of his Creator and to build up the people of God's choice. He brought Israel to the height of her glory, extending by conquest her boundaries from the Mediterranean to the Euphrates. He left a rich heritage to his race—a heritage that included power, wealth, honor and songs and psalms. But above all, he left an example of loyalty to God.

Will we not all adopt David's plan of life? He started right! He began with God. He committed every plan into His keeping (see Psalm 37:5). David never forgot that God was supreme. When he sinned, he bowed in penitence and sorrow, and God forgave him.

2 SAMUEL 11–20: DAVID'S FALL

We wish the life of David could have ended before chapter 11 was written. But the golden era passed away and what was left is a checkered tale of sin and punishment. In all of God's Word, no chapter is more tragic or more full of warning for the child of

God. It tells the story of David's fall. It is like an eclipse of the sun. His sins of adultery and virtual murder were a terrible blot on David's life. He became a broken man. God forgave him, but the Word says, "The sword will never depart from your house" (2 Samuel 12:10). He reaped just what he had sown. We see the harvest in his own house and in the nation.

Look over the steps in David's fall. You will find the steps downward in rapid succession.

First, he was idle (see 2 Samuel 11:1-2). It was the time for a king to go to war, but he was not there. He remained in Jerusalem, in the place of temptation. At evening time he arose from his bed and walked on the roof of his house. He was in that idle, listless mood that opens one to temptation. He saw the beautiful Bathsheba and he wanted her. His first sin was in the fact that he saw. Don't look on evil. Ask God to control your eyes. Don't let sin enter your mind. If David had nipped the temptation in the bud, he would have saved himself a world of agony and awful sin. Instead of driving it out of his mind, however, he cherished it.

Next, "David sent someone to find out about her" (2 Samuel 11:3). He asked about this woman and then he took her (see verse 4). He brought her to his house. He forgot what was due to the faithful soldier whose wife she was.

But the next step was far worse—his sin against Uriah, one of the bravest of his soldiers. He decided that he must get rid of him. He made Joab his confidant in sin, his partner in murder.

This sin was the more terrible because the head of the nation had committed it. God had singled this man out for favor. He was no longer a young man. He had passed through many experiences. Then, too, the excellent service of Uriah entitled him to rewards, not death.

Why do you suppose this tragic story is given in the Bible? It bears the character of a beacon, warning the mariner against some of the most perilous rocks that are to be found in the sea of life. Never neglect watching and praying. An hour's sleep left Samson at the mercy of Delilah. Don't fool with any sin, even in thought. The door may be opened to a dangerous brood. It doesn't take a whole box of matches to start a fire. One will do it!

A year later, the prophet Nathan visited David and charged him with his sin. We can imagine the anguish of David's heart that year. We read of David's sincere repentance (see also Psalm 51). God told David that his child would die because of his sin. Read 2 Samuel 12:13-32 to learn how David accepted this punishment. When his child died, David rose and worshiped God.

"A living sorrow is worse than a dead one," says a proverb. The death of his child was a grievous sorrow to David, but the living sorrow he endured through his beloved son Absalom we cannot imagine. The rebellion of this young man is full of tragedy. Absalom was a handsome young man, but he was treacherous. He weaned away his father's subjects by treachery. He sat at the city gate and told the farmers what he would do if he were their ruler. When men bowed in his honor, he kissed their hands. He drove a beautiful chariot drawn by prancing horses. He became a favorite.

Through a spy system, he stole the kingdom from his father. When David left Jerusalem, Absalom gathered his army in Hebron and marched triumphantly into the city. Finally David prepared for battle with Absalom. During the fray, apparently Absalom's long hair was snagged in the trees of the forest, and Absalom was caught.

Absalom was heartless and cruel. David suffered because of both Absalom's victory and his defeat and slaying. Read 2 Samuel 18:19–19:4, David's lament over Absalom when he heard the news of his death.

2 SAMUEL 20–24: DAVID'S LAST DAYS

After the rebellion was crushed, King David returned to his kingdom. New officers were installed and reconstruction began everywhere. But David's next to last act was to sin again, this time by taking a census of the fighting men, which God had not told him to do. The land was punished with a three-day pestilence.

The last verses of 2 Samuel tell of King David's last act, his buying Araunah's threshing floor and erecting an altar there (see 2 Samuel 24:18-25). This has special significance, for on this site the great Temple of Solomon was later built. (On this sacred spot today stands the Dome of the Rock, one of the most important Islamic mosques in the world.) David was only 70 years old when he died.

POINTS TO REMEMBER

David was a mighty king and warrior. He is ranked with Abraham, Moses and Paul. His great spirit is revealed to us in the psalms that he wrote, and we need to understand David's life in order to understand and use the psalms. We must know, too, why Christ was called the Son of David (see Acts 13:22-23). David stands halfway between Abraham and Christ.

David had his faults. He did much that was very wrong, but he kept his nation from going into idolatry. Although his private sins were grievous, he stood like a rock for Jehovah. He sinned, but he repented and gave God a chance to forgive and cleanse him. He illustrates the conflict Paul describes in Romans 7: He was a great saint even though he was a great sinner.

David took a chaotic nation and established a dynasty that was to last until the time of the captivity, a period of more than 450 years. There never was a greater warrior or statesman than David. He made Israel the dominant power of western Asia.

Under David's rule, Israel reached its high-water mark. It has been called Israel's golden age. No idol worship and no worldly functions occurred when the sweet psalmist, the shepherd boy of Bethlehem, commanded the ship of state. His merchant caravans crossed the deserts, traveling routes from the Nile to the Tigris and Euphrates, and Israel prospered in those days. When Israel was right with God, she was invincible against all odds.

Do not pray for an easy task. Pray to be stronger! The greatness of your spiritual power is the measure of your surrender. It is not a question of who you are or of what you are but whether God controls you.

10

Understanding First Kings, Second Kings, First Chronicles and Second Chronicles

First and Second Kings and First and Second Chronicles Portray Jesus Christ, Our King

SELECTED BIBLE READINGS

UNDERSTANDING FIRST AND SECOND KINGS

AUTHOR: The books of 1 and 2 Kings do not specifically name their author. Jewish and Christian traditions maintain that the prophet Jeremiah wrote the books.

DATE: The books were likely written between 560 and 540 BC, less than 30 years after the destruction of Jerusalem in 586 BC.

PURPOSE AND SUMMARY: First and 2 Kings are the sequel to 1 and 2 Samuel and should be read as a continuation of the history of Israel that started in 1 and 2 Samuel. Originally one book, 1 and 2 Kings relate the history of Israel from the end of David's reign, through Solomon's reign, through the division of Solomon's kingdom into northern and southern kingdoms, to the destruction of the northern kingdom (Israel) in 722 BC and the fall of Jerusalem and the southern kingdom (Judah) in 586 BC. This was the period of Israel's glory, division, decline and fall.

If we reject God, He will reject us. If we obey God, He will bless us. "In those days the Lord began to reduce the size of Israel" (2 Kings 10:32).

In the Hebrew, the language in which these books were originally written, 1 and 2 Kings formed one book, 1 and 2 Samuel another, and 1 and 2 Chronicles a third. When they were translated into the Greek language, the translators divided them because Greek required one third more space than Hebrew, and the scrolls on which they were written were limited in length.

The books of Kings were written while the first Temple was standing. First and 2 Kings are just a continuation of the books of Samuel. As their name suggests, they record the events of the reign of Solomon and then of the succeeding kings of Judah and Israel. They cover a period of 400 years and tell the story of the growth and then decay of the kingdom. We see the kingdom divided. We see both Israel and Judah led into captivity. The southern kingdom (Judah) had 20 kings, and the northern kingdom (Israel) had 19 kings.

These are two of the most important books of history in the world. Even today, artifacts unearthed by archaeologists prove that the history written in the books of Kings is accurate and complete. At first they may seem dry to you, but the lives of the kings and the stories in these books prove several noteworthy things:

1. "God does not show favoritism" (Acts 10:34; "is no respecter of persons," *KJV*).

2. When our all is on the altar, God never keeps us waiting for the fire (see 1 Kings 18:38). (What is the spiritual meaning of this?)

3. The final captivity was because of disobedience to God. It was prophesied (see Deuteronomy 28:49). (What has God said about the individual who forgets Him?)

These books also have several "bookends":

1. They begin with King David and end with the king of Babylon.

2. They open with the building of the Temple and end with the burning of the Temple.

3. They open with David's first successor to the throne, Solomon, and end with David's last successor, Jehoiachin, released from captivity by the king of Babylon.

Remember that these books of Kings cover practically the whole rule of the kings over God's Chosen People. During Solomon's reign, the kingdom reached the height of its grandeur. With the death of Solomon, the kingship really ceased to be the medium through which God governed His people. The great Elijah then introduced the period of the prophets. First Kings ends with the story of this prophet, while 2 Kings centers around Elisha. The decline of the kingdoms continued until we see both Israel and Judah led into captivity.

1 KINGS 1–10: THE SPLENDID REIGN OF SOLOMON

As the scene opens, we find that "when King David was very old, he could not keep warm even when they put covers over him" (1 Kings 1:1). He was prematurely aged, for he was only 70. Because of David's feebleness, however, a rebellion started against him. Adonijah's attempt to get his father's throne was natural, because he was the oldest surviving son (see 2 Samuel 3:4). This rebellion called for prompt action, which Nathan the prophet took. David had seen that his son Solomon was the most fit to succeed him. Solomon was also God's choice (see 1 Chronicles 22:9; 1 Kings 2:15). And it was clear that the choice of Solomon was popular (see 1 Kings 1:39-40). Adonijah soon saw that opposition was useless. Because of this rebellion, Solomon, who was but 19, was crowned before David's death (see 1 Kings 1:30,39,53).

Solomon received his religious training from Nathan the prophet. This wise prophet loved Solomon and gave him the name Jedidiah, which means "loved by the LORD" (see 2 Samuel 12:25). Solomon's reign began in a blaze of glory. It was splendor without surrender. As with Saul, however, Solomon's life ended in an anticlimax: "His heart was not fully devoted to the LORD his God, as the heart of David his father had been" (1 Kings 11:4). Remember, God wants our hearts!

Yet Solomon was a magnificent king; his throne was the grandest the world had ever seen and his life was filled with happenings of marvelous significance. His kingdom of 60,000 square miles was 10 times as great as that which his father had inherited.

Solomon Was a Great and Good Man

- His rearing was under the religious and wise Nathan.
- His kingship was clear. All the city rang with the glad cry, "Solomon has taken his seat on the royal throne" (1 Kings 1:46).
- His charge from his father was full of promise (see 1 Kings 2:1-9).
- His choice of wisdom from God was a divine choice (see 1 Kings 3).
- His cabinet was greater than any king of Israel ever had (see 1 Kings 4).
- His lifework was building the Temple. The equivalent today of several million dollars was spent to erect it. Its

service of dedication went down on record because of its sublimity.

- The kingdom he established realized at last, after 400 years, the broad dimensions outlined to Joshua (see Joshua 1:4).
- The wealth and glory of Solomon's reign fairly took away the breath of the Queen of Sheba: "There was no more spirit [breath] in her" (1 Kings 10:5, *KJV*).
- His handsomeness is hinted at in Psalm 45.
- His ardent affection is seen in song (see Song of Solomon).

After David's final words of admonition to his son to be absolutely loyal to Jehovah, the king died, having reigned for 40 years.

As a young man, Solomon realized that governing is a serious business, so he began his reign with prayer. God appeared to Solomon in a dream early in his reign and asked him to make a choice of anything that he might wish. The young king's wise choice revealed his feeling of being unable to do all that he had been called to do. What was his request of the Lord? The youth had not been swept off his feet by his father's praise when David twice called him a wise man (see 1 Kings 2:6-9), so Solomon asked for "a discerning heart" (1 Kings 3:9). God gave him the wisdom he asked for.

What is God's promise to us (see James 1:5)? "Ask for whatever you want me to give you" (1 Kings 3:5). This is an important privilege that belongs to each one of us. Each of our lives reveals what we have asked for. (What is your choice? And do you have a heart that listens to the Spirit's voice?)

Solomon was the wisest man the world ever saw until the coming of Him who could say of Himself, "And now something greater than Solomon is here" (Matthew 12:42). All the earth acknowledged Solomon, but when the "something greater than Solomon" came, "his own did not receive him" (John 1:11). That was a tragedy. (Have you received Him?)

First, Solomon organized his leaders. He gathered around him a wise company of officers of state, each responsible for his own department. This led to days of tremendous prosperity in the kingdom.

The greatest undertaking of Solomon's reign was building the Temple. This was what his father, David, had longed to do. The immense foundation of great hewn stones upon which Solomon's Temple was built remains to this day, now under the Dome of the Rock. One stone alone is 38 feet, 9 inches long. Such huge stones, the fragrant cedar wood and the copper-covered dome gave the Temple unusual splendor.

The Temple was built on a historic spot. On Mount Moriah, Abraham had offered up Isaac (see Genesis 22:2). And we saw how David secured Araunah's threshing floor on this same spot.

The Israelites used to have to make pilgrimages to the Temple to meet God. But now we know the wonderful truth that our bodies are the temples of God (see 1 Corinthians 3:16; 6:19). (Is your body a real temple? God wishes to live in you, but He cannot if you are defiled with sin.)

Solomon's Temple is the first of three earthly temples mentioned in Scripture. The Babylonians destroyed it in about 587 BC (see 2 Kings 25:8-9). The second was Zerubbabel's (see Ezra 5:2; 6:15-18). This one was not comparable in elegance to Solomon's. The third was Herod's temple, an expansion of Zerubbabel's, erected on a grander scale in 20 BC and completed in AD 64. The emperor Titus destroyed this temple in AD 70.

Solomon Was a Weak and Erring Man

Solomon was a great and glorious king, but we soon find the note of decline:

- Unlike his father, David, Solomon dealt cruelly with his brother Adonijah (see 1 Kings 2:24-25).
- Like Saul, his heart was lifted up in pride (see 1 Kings 10:18-29).
- Led by his heathen wives, he fell into idolatry (see 1 Kings 11).

Solomon did not display spiritual wisdom. The book of Ecclesiastes, with its note of despair, is a confession of it. He did not have a heart at peace with God.

Read 1 Kings 9; 10:14-29 to find the possible, not to say the probable, dangers to Solomon. Note his high position, his great wisdom, his countless riches. It is hard not to forget God in the hour of such wonderful prosperity, thinking only of possessions. It was this very glory that led to Solomon's downfall.

Because of Solomon's backsliding, God raised up enemies to vex him. In the book of Ecclesiastes, Solomon describes the futility of his life at this time.

But before that happened, the Queen of Sheba witnessed Solomon's reign at its zenith and saw the fulfillment of David's prayer for his son, offered about a year before his death.

Solomon's reputation probably had spread through the voyages of his navy (see 1 Kings 9:21-28). The fame of Solomon was associated with Jehovah, and it was Solomon's fame concerning the name of the Lord that was the thing that interested Her Majesty, the Queen of Sheba. Three things impressed her:

1. Solomon himself, and his wisdom and wealth—
    1 Kings 10:1,7
2. Solomon's servants—1 Kings 10:8
3. Solomon's God—1 Kings 10:9

1 KINGS 11–16: THE DIVISION OF THE KINGDOM

Solomon reigned 40 years, the second great period of the united kingdom (see 1 Kings 11). Note that Saul, David and Solomon each reigned 40 years (see Acts 13:21; 2 Samuel 5:4; 1 Kings 11:42). At first all went well, but later there was serious trouble.

Solomon set up a great establishment in Jerusalem. He built his famous Temple, bringing in foreign workmen and materials to do it, and then he built himself a palace that dazzled his own subjects and his foreign visitors.

A rise to such prosperity and power as Solomon enjoyed has its dangers, though. Such a life costs money to maintain and meant increased taxation, which grew into burdens that were unbearable for the people, and that bred the seeds of unrest and revolution. Luxury and idolatry had broken down the people's morale, and there was much corruption, so the kingdom now was to be divided.

Consider the events leading up to the division. For years there had been jealousy between the northern kingdom (Israel) and the southern kingdom (Judah). The cause went back 300 years and mainly consisted of the jealousy between the tribes of Ephraim and Judah. Note the blessings Jacob gave to Ephraim (see Genesis 48:17-22; 49:22-26). And from the time of Joshua, who was of that tribe, Ephraim took a leading place. The transfer of authority to Judah came under David, who was of the tribe of Judah. All this tribal jealousy was intensified by the hardships felt by the people through Solomon's high-handed actions. His demands created oppression, and his unfaithfulness to God demanded judgment (see 1 Kings 11:26-43; 12:4).

When Solomon's son Rehoboam threatened to levy heavier burdens upon the people, his unwise headstrong action added fuel to a fire that had been gathering and burning for nearly 300 years, from the time of the judges.

The revolt of the 10 tribes immediately followed, and only one tribe, that of Benjamin, remained loyal (see 1 Kings 12:16-17). This tension led to the appointment of Jeroboam as king of the northern kingdom (see 1 Kings 12:20), while Rehoboam ruled the two tribes, Judah and Benjamin, in the south.

The Division Foreseen

A new name of great importance appears in the pages of this story: Jeroboam. This young man of low origin had risen to notice because of faithful service and fine accomplishments. The prophet Ahijah made a startling revelation to Jeroboam. Using a symbolic gesture, he took off his new coat and tore it into 12 strips and then he said to Jeroboam, "Take ten pieces for yourself, for this is what the LORD, the God of Israel, says: 'See, I am going to tear the kingdom out of Solomon's hand and give you ten tribes'" (1 Kings 11:31).

The judgment was upon Solomon for his long years of luxury and pride and power.

Every ruler should look ahead and see toward what rocks he may be steering his kingdom, and whether or not he is heading toward the day when his power shall be taken out of his hand. Have we not seen men in our day, rising to great wealth and power, stripped to nothing and fleeing from outraged justice?

Things do not happen by accident. There is a cause at the root of every revolution. The event that sparks the uprising may come as suddenly as an explosion, but somewhere something was at work undermining the structure. The French Revolution had at its root centuries of oppression.

Religious apostasy had been gnawing like a deadly worm at the root of Israel's life. One day the tree fell. Nothing destroys a nation like religious decline. Take the sun out of the sky, and there will be no grass or flowers or orchards. Take God out of our nation, and there will be no homes or schools or social life.

God's Purpose Carried Out

Though they didn't know it, the people, by their revolution, were carrying out the divine purpose (see 1 Kings 12:15; 11:29-33). God could not overlook Solomon's disobedience to His clearest commands.

So the kingdom of God's Chosen People was divided. It has now been divided for almost 3,000 years. Because of sin, this kingdom went to pieces and finally into captivity (see 2 Kings 17 and 25). It is part of the gospel, the good news, that those two great sections of divided Israel are going to be united again on this earth at Christ's return in glory. (Read the wonderful passages in Isaiah 11:10-13 and Ezekiel 37:15-28.)

1 KINGS 17–22; 2 KINGS 1:1–2:2: THE MINISTRY OF ELIJAH

Elijah was a bolt of fire God let loose upon wicked Ahab and idolatrous Israel. He flashed across the pages of history as suddenly and terribly as a flash of lightning. "Elijah the Tishbite, from Tishbe in Gilead" is the brief biography by which he is

1 Kings

introduced (1 Kings 17:1). "Elijah" means "Jehovah is my God."
It fit him perfectly. He was the most outstanding of the prophets. Follow his sudden appearance, his undaunted courage, his
zeal, the heights of his triumph on Mount Carmel, the depths
of his despondence, his glorious rapture into heaven in the
whirlwind, and his reappearance on the Mount of Transfiguration (see Matthew 17:1-8).

He was a striking character from the highlands of Gilead.
His long thick hair hung over a cloak of sheepskin. Jehovah sent
him to do away with the awful worship of Baal during the reign
of Ahab, who had married the wicked foreign princess Jezebel.
Suddenly emerging from the desert and standing before the corrupt king in the splendor of his court, the stern prophet boldly
said, "As the LORD, the God of Israel, lives, whom I serve, there
will be neither dew nor rain in the next few years except at my
word" (1 Kings 17:1). He was given power to shut up the heavens,
so there would be no rain for three and a half years. He called
down fire from heaven before the prophets of Baal at Mount
Carmel. He was the evangelist of his day, thundering out warnings to this idolatrous people. The events in his great career will
fascinate you. Read them carefully.

2 KINGS 1–9: THE MINISTRY OF ELISHA

Elisha succeeded Elijah. He was almost shy and retiring in contrast to the fiery Elijah. Elijah trained Elisha as his successor,
but they are in marked contrast to each other: Elijah was the
prophet of judgment, law and severity. Elisha was the prophet
of grace, love and tenderness. Elisha's ministry lasted 50 years.
Most of his miracles were deeds of kindness and mercy. Elisha
had a great influence upon the kings of the day, and although
he did not approve of what they did, he was always coming to
their rescue.

Baal worship was introduced by the wicked Jezebel; and after
30 years was exterminated by Elijah, Elisha and Jehu.

2 KINGS 1–17: THE CORRUPTION OF ISRAEL

Jeroboam, the ruler of the northern kingdom, Israel, made Shechem his capital. It seemed the natural place because it was in the center of the land.

It was the custom required by the Law to go up to Jerusalem regularly to worship (see Deuteronomy 12:11,14; 16:6,15-16; 1 Samuel 1:3,7). Because Jeroboam was afraid to have his 10 tribes journey to Jerusalem, the capital of Rehoboam's kingdom, to worship God, he made two golden calves and placed them in convenient spots—Bethel (see Genesis 28:11-19) in the southern end of the kingdom and Dan (see Judges 18:29-30) in the northern end—so the people would not have to go to Jerusalem.

Close to 20 times he is described as being the reason that Israel sinned. Beware of man-made religion. We must worship where and how God tells us!

God says, "Let us . . . not [give] up meeting together, as some are in the habit of doing" (Hebrews 10:24-25). God knows we need fellowship in worship to keep the spiritual coals alive, but we constantly hear people say that they can worship better alone in the woods or by the sea. Learn now to do what God asks you to do. Remember, a request from a king is a command!

After 200 years, the people were carried into captivity by the king of Assyria in 732 BC (see 2 Kings 17). Many of God's prophets had warned Israel of their looming captivity, but they would not turn from their idolatry and worship only Jehovah.

The Assyrians were great and cruel warriors. They built their kingdom with their pillage from other countries. Their practices were horrible. They skinned men alive, cut out their tongues, put out their eyes, dismembered their bodies and then made mounds of the skulls of men to instill fear! For 300 years Assyria was a world empire.

2 KINGS 13–25: THE CAPTIVITY OF JUDAH

The southern kingdom tried to conquer the northern kingdom. For 80 years there was continuous war between them. But these wars failed. Then there was a period of 80 years of peace between these two kingdoms, following the marriage of the son of Jehoshaphat (southern king) to the daughter of Ahab (northern king). Finally there was a period of 50 years when the kingdoms intermittently warred with each other until the captivity.

In the southern kingdom, there was only one dynasty (Davidic) from King Rehoboam to King Zedekiah. The great prophets of that day were Nathan, Isaiah, Micah, Jeremiah, Joel and Zephaniah.

About 136 years after Assyria had taken the northern kingdom into captivity, Nebuchadnezzar, the king of Babylon, took the southern kingdom captive. Jerusalem was destroyed, the Temple burned and the princes led away. The people had forgotten God and refused to listen to the warnings of the prophets. God wanted His people to learn the lesson of obedience and dependence upon Him.

POINTS TO REMEMBER

In 1 Kings we see the kingdom of Israel, filled with pride and arrogance, falling apart. In 2 Kings, sinning even more, Israel goes into captivity. Surely the way of the transgressor is hard. The history of the Jews is a record of God's dealings with disobedient children. But in all God's punishments, He is kind and merciful, for He loves them still.

The secret of the downfall of the Jewish people is found in 2 Kings 3:2: "He did evil in the eyes of the LORD." Be loyal and true to God. It does not pay to do evil.

The moving figures and powerful factors of those days were the prophets Elijah and Elisha. Elijah was the strength of Israel. Jezebel and Ahab had frightened the people into submission. But Elijah stood. Read 1 Kings 17:1, where Elijah said, "As the LORD God of Israel liveth, before whom I stand" (*KJV*). And there he stood for God, like a rock, in the face of all the weakness of Israel. We ask today, "Where now is the LORD, the God of Elijah?"

(2 Kings 2:14). We would be mightily blessed if we could see some of this old-time power.

Elijah was the champion of the Most High. He brought God to the people. He was the pastor-evangelist of Israel's day.

There is a great difference between the fall of Israel and Judah. Israel was scattered throughout the nations for an indefinite period, but God specified the length of Judah's captivity to be 70 years. Judah was to return to Jerusalem, which she did later. The Messiah was to come out of Judah; and God was preparing the way for Him to come there and not to Babylon or Assyria.

God was using even the rulers of foreign nations to work out His plan. Cyrus, king of Persia, for example, was going to issue a decree that would allow the Jews to return to their homeland, the land of Israel.

UNDERSTANDING
FIRST AND SECOND CHRONICLES

AUTHOR: The books of 1 and 2 Chronicles do not name their author. Jewish and Christian traditions hold that Ezra, the priest, wrote 1 and 2 Chronicles.

DATE: The books of 1 and 2 Chronicles may have been written between 450 and 425 BC, during the time of Ezra and Nehemiah, when the Jewish people were restored to Jerusalem after the Babylonian captivity and when they rebuilt the wall surrounding Jerusalem under Nehemiah's leadership.

PURPOSE AND SUMMARY: In the Hebrew canon of Scripture, 1 and 2 Chronicles formed a single volume called "The matters of the days [of the kings of Judah and Israel]" (i.e., "The annals of the kings of Judah and Israel"). The translators of the Greek Septuagint, the 3rd-to-2nd-century BC Greek translation of the Hebrew Old Testament, gave Chronicles the title *Paraleipomena*, meaning "things left over," implying their use as a supplement to Samuel and Kings. Jerome (c. AD 340-420) called them "a chronicle of the whole and sacred history" from Adam to Cyrus (539 BC), hence their English name. Chronicles is a summary of Hebrew history that duplicates much of the books of Samuel and of Kings, but it focuses more on the spiritual deeds and misdeeds of the kings and on the importance of worshiping the Lord properly through the ministry of the priests and the Temple.

Through such books as the Chronicles we get the history of the Jewish nation. Through this nation our Lord came to earth. God chose this people for the fulfillment of His great promises and purposes. He is still their God (see Romans 11:1), and His purposes are still to be fulfilled in them. In light of this truth, books such as the Chronicles take on new meaning and power.

The first book of Chronicles is a review of the genealogy of the Israelites and the story of David's reign.

Second Chronicles first describes Solomon's reign and then moves on to cover the history of the division of the kingdom and the history of the kings of Judah (the southern kingdom). It is a book of great revivals that occurred while five different kings reigned:

1. Asa—2 Chronicles 15
2. Jehoshaphat—2 Chronicles 20
3. Joash—2 Chronicles 23-24
4. Hezekiah—2 Chronicles 29-31
5. Josiah—2 Chronicles 35

Jesus Christ is portrayed as King in the books of both Kings and Chronicles.

Understanding Ezra
and Nehemiah

Ezra and Nehemiah Portray Jesus Christ,
Our Restorer

SELECTED BIBLE READINGS

DAY OF THE WEEK		MAIN TOPIC
Sunday: Ezra 1–3	Jerusalem's Exiles Return	
Monday: Ezra 4–6	The Temple Is Rebuilt	
Tuesday: Ezra 7–10	Ezra Returns	
Wednesday: Nehemiah 1–3	Nehemiah Rebuilds the Wall	
Thursday: Nehemiah 4–6	Nehemiah Overcomes Opposition	
Friday: Nehemiah 7–9	Ezra Reads the Law	
Saturday: Nehemiah 11–13	Nehemiah Establishes Reforms	

AUTHOR: The books of Ezra and Nehemiah do not specifically name their author. Jewish and Christian traditions hold that the prophet Ezra wrote both Ezra and Nehemiah, which were originally one book in the Hebrew canon of the Old Testament. It is interesting to note that once Ezra appears on the scene in Ezra 7, the author of the book of Ezra switches from writing in the third person to first person. This also suggests that Ezra may have been the author of both books.

DATE: The books of Ezra and Nehemiah may have been written between 458 and 420 BC, during or just after the time of the events recorded in these books.

PURPOSE AND SUMMARY: Written originally as one book, these two books describe the return in 539 BC of the Jewish exiles to Jerusalem, after 70 years of living in exile in Babylon, and the subsequent restoration of the Jerusalem Temple in 516 BC and the rebuilding of the wall around Jerusalem under Nehemiah's leadership in 445 BC. Since they contain nearly all of the direct information known of the post-exilic period of Jewish history, the books of Ezra and Nehemiah are of special importance.

As with Samuel, Kings and Chronicles, we find that Ezra and Nehemiah were one book in the earliest Hebrew Bible. These books tell the story of one of the most important events in Jewish history—the return of God's Chosen People from exile in Babylon.

The purposes of God may sometimes seem delayed, but they are never abandoned. "Remember the instruction you gave your servant Moses," prayed Nehemiah (Nehemiah 1:8). The books of Ezra and Nehemiah tell the story of how God remembered and how He brought back His people from exile. Read Jeremiah 29:10-13, which tells us of this remembrance.

During the captivity, the prophets Jeremiah and Ezekiel told the Jews that they would be restored, and the prophets predicted that the people would return to their own land and rebuild Jerusalem. Jeremiah told them that this would happen at the end of 70 years: "When seventy years are completed for Babylon, I will come to you and fulfill my good promise to bring you back to this place" (Jeremiah 29:10; see also Jeremiah 25:11-12). Remember that the books of Kings ended with the story of the captivity of first the northern kingdom of Israel and then the southern kingdom of Judah.

Daniel was carried away captive to Babylon at the time of the captivity of Judah. The last incident in the book of Daniel is the story of Daniel in the lions' den (see Daniel 6:16-24). This happened about 10 years before Cyrus became king over Babylon, so Daniel was an old man when the events described in Ezra and Nehemiah took place.

Ezra

Rebuilding the national life of the Jewish people is covered in the 100 years described in these two books, and two particular periods of time are very important:

1. 537–517 BC: The 20 years from the first year of Cyrus to the sixth year of Darius when the people under Zerubbabel, the governor, and Joshua, the priest, rebuilt the Temple. (Read Ezra 1–6; Zechariah and Haggai; the genealogies of 1 Chronicles 1:1–9:44; the last two verses of 2 Chronicles; Psalms 126 and 137; and the reference to Cyrus in Isaiah 44:23–45.)

2. 458–433 BC: The 25 years when Nehemiah, the governor, and Ezra, the priest, rebuilt the wall of Jerusalem and restored the city. (Malachi was the prophet of this day.)

Ezra gives the record of both of these periods. Nehemiah tells of the second period, building the wall.

Although the keynote for each book is different (Ezra's is Ezra 7:10; Nehemiah's is Nehemiah 6:3), the two books do have many similarities:

- Both begin at Persia and end at Jerusalem.
- Both center around the man of God who wrote them.
- Both stories begin with a Persian king's decree.
- Both tell of building as their chief theme.
- Both contain a long prayer of humiliation and confession in the ninth chapter.
- Both end with the purification of the people.

Old Testament history closes about 100 years after the Jews returned from their captivity. Then Alexander the Great broke the Persian hold, and world power passed from Persia to Greece. (The historical record indicates that Alexander showed consideration to the Jews.)

UNDERSTANDING EZRA

The book of Ezra has both a backward and a forward look.

The backward look involves a second exodus for captive Israel. The first exodus was out of Egypt. This second exodus was from Babylon. This time Ezra was leader in place of Moses. He, like Moses, was an inspired writer and leader. Both men were great organizers, lawgivers and teachers raised up to fulfill God's gracious purpose and bring captive Israel out of bondage. Both of these great leaders dealt with Israel in a strong and merciful way.

The forward look involves the Israelites' return to Jerusalem in timid, struggling relays. But God gave them a foothold. It was His city and it is His city still. He will again bring back His own; He will raise up Zion out of ruins.

To review, first the 10 northern tribes (the northern kingdom) were taken captive by Assyria (see 2 Kings 17), and then the two southern tribes (Benjamin and Judah, the southern kingdom) were taken captive by Babylon (see 2 Kings 25). The 10 northern tribes never returned to Jerusalem. The southern tribes were restored to their own land under the Persian Empire, after the Medes and Persians had conquered the Babylonians.

A Brief Time Line

- 537 BC—The first Jews returned to Jerusalem from Babylon.
- 516 BC—The Temple was restored.
- 479 BC—Esther, the wife of Xerxes, became queen of Persia.
- 458 BC—Ezra led the second expedition from Babylon.
- 445 BC—Nehemiah rebuilt the wall of Jerusalem.

EZRA 1–6: EXILES RETURN AND REBUILD THE TEMPLE

As the book of Ezra opens, we find Cyrus, king of Persia, making throughout his kingdom a proclamation permitting the Jews who were captives in his kingdom to return to Jerusalem (see Ezra 1:1-4). Cyrus even gave back to the Israelites the golden vessels Nebuchadnezzar had taken from the Temple in Jerusalem (see Ezra 1:7-11).

Two hundred years before, God had prophesied that He would do this, and He named Cyrus as the one He would use. The record of this remarkable prophecy, which calls a king by his name 200 years before his time, is found in Isaiah 44:28; 45:1-4. No doubt this proclamation by Cyrus was made in part due to the fact that he saw these words of Isaiah.

Daniel's influence in this court was very powerful. One of the princes carried away by Nebuchadnezzar to his court, Daniel had been the ancient equivalent of a great prime minister in the court in Babylon. Now he was an old man.

At the time of the captivity 70 years before, only people from the higher classes were taken to Babylon. The rest were left in their own land to suffer (see Jeremiah 24:5-8; 44:15). Now at Cyrus's first call in 537 BC, no more than 50,000 Jews availed themselves of the opportunity to return to Jerusalem under Zerubbabel (see Ezra 1:1-4). Everyone did not return; only the earnest and pious Jews went back. It was a time of real sifting among the people. After 70 years, most of them had built homes and established themselves and were content to remain in Babylon. They did not care to face the dangers and hardships of returning across more than 700 miles of barren desert and arriving in a city that had been destroyed.

Although the leaders were from the tribe of Judah, no doubt there were representatives from the whole of Israel. Only those who loved God were ready to make the attempt. Many of the returning Jews had been born in Babylon during the 70 years. These were not considered captives but exiles. Notice that beginning at this time the Israelites are called Jews because most of them were of the tribe of Judah, and the name "Jews" comes from Judah.

Everything is taken care of when God is in charge. Not only money for rebuilding the Temple in Jerusalem, but also traveling expenses and all the other needs were provided by God at Cyrus's

direction (see Ezra 1:4,6). Someone has said that God used Babylon as the safety-deposit vault for the silver and gold vessels of
the Temple.

The names of those who returned are given in chapter 2. They
laid the foundation of the Temple the first thing upon returning. It was a time of great rejoicing. It is interesting to notice that
before they built homes for themselves, they first thought of a
house for the Lord. And they did not build the Temple first but
the altar (see Ezra 3:2).

The place where sin must be dealt with must come first in
every life. The heart must be right if God is to bless. The altar
was the center of the Jews' religion; the cross is the center of the
Christian faith.

Read Ezra 4:1-22 to learn about the hindrances to the work.
Hindrances to all real work for God are to be expected. (The
Church must not have the help of the world.) And the opposition disheartened them. They needed Haggai's message. (Refer to
the book of Haggai.) Haggai and Zechariah, the prophets, encouraged the people from within the ranks (see Ezra 4:23–5:17),
and within four years the Temple was completed and dedicated
(see Ezra 6).

Zerubbabel's Temple was very plain and simple. It was not
the sumptuous edifice that Solomon's had been. In fact, it was
in such contrast to the elegance of the first Temple that the old
men who had seen Solomon's Temple wept aloud. But it was
God's house, so the people thanked God and took courage.

EZRA 7–10: EZRA RETURNS AND THE JEWS REFORM

Ezra appears in person in the seventh chapter of the book. At least
60 years after the Jews had first returned to Jerusalem, he led a
second expedition from Babylon to reinforce the struggling
colonists in Judah (458 BC). Ezra received a commission from Artaxerxes, the king who half-blindly aided in accomplishing God's
plans for His people (see Ezra 7:11–8:14). Read Ezra 7:25 and find

how impressed the king was with Ezra's love of God's Word. Oh, that we might live in such a way that others would learn to have respect for God's Book!

This contingent under Ezra consisted of 1,700 Jews. It took them four months to make the journey, and King Artaxerxes financed it (see Ezra 7:12-26). Thirteen years later, this same king authorized Nehemiah to build the wall of Jerusalem (see Nehemiah 2). Cyrus, Darius and Artaxerxes, the three Persian kings, were very friendly to the Jews.

When Ezra returned to Jerusalem, he found things even worse than he had expected. Although the people had not returned to idolatry, they had intermarried with the people of the land and had done everything the pagans had taught them (see Ezra 9:1-4). The princes and rulers were the worst offenders. Ezra tore his garments and literally pulled out his hair in grief! Read Ezra 9:5-15, Ezra's touching prayer and confession.

As Ezra was praying and weeping before God, a great congregation assembled. What happened? Read Ezra 10. The people who had gathered about him through the long hours of the day eventually recognized the greatness of their sin as they saw how it affected Ezra. Finally one of their number spoke and acknowledged the sin. (Read what God says about confession of sin in 1 John 1:9.) At once, Ezra led them into a sacred covenant with God.

POINTS TO REMEMBER

Founder of Synagogue Worship

Tradition tells us that Ezra was the founder of the synagogue worship that started during the days of the captivity. Because the Temple had been destroyed and the people were scattered, they needed some place to worship God, so Ezra helped each Jewish community have its own place of worship and instruction. After the Jews returned to their homeland, the synagogues were started in homes as well as in other lands where the people were scattered. Under Ezra we also see the great revival of Bible study.

Ezra

The synagogue worship that Ezra instituted is the parent of our own form of worship.

Recorder and Keeper of Canon

Of Ezra it is said that he "had devoted himself to the study and observance of the Law of the LORD, and to teaching its decrees and laws in Israel" (Ezra 7:10). His name means "help." He belongs to the great triumvirate of the Old Testament law—Moses, Samuel and Ezra. He wrote and worked to keep the canon intact and to hold Israel, God's Chosen People, to her divinely appointed mission. We are indebted to Ezra for the literary and ecclesiastical renaissance of that day.

According to tradition, he, assisted by the great synagogue of which he was president, settled the canon of Old Testament Scripture, a task that God appointed him to do. Tradition makes him the president of a council of 120 men who formed the Old Testament canon.

In addition to Ezra's outstanding ministry of the Word, he probably wrote portions of 1 and 2 Chronicles, and Psalm 119, which is a wonderful poem about the Word of God.

Ezra was the Thomas Jefferson of his time, laying the constitutional foundations for the future.

Prayer of Confession—with Nehemiah

Prayer is the most important privilege of a Christian. Turn to Nehemiah 9, and you will find the prayer of Nehemiah. Nehemiah's prayer began where Ezra's ended—with utter surrender to God. (Compare Nehemiah 9:1-2 with Ezra 9:15 and 10:1.)

God had definitely promised to bring the Jews back after 70 years in Babylon. We read in the very first verse of Ezra that it was to fulfill this word that "the LORD moved the heart of Cyrus king of Persia" to proclaim the restoration. (Look this up!) But it is through prayer that God wished (and still wishes!) to have His will brought to pass. The restoration was wholly undeserved by Israel, but it was the goal of God's heart of mercy.

See the three main results of this restoration of God's people to their land again:

1. Through the rebuilding of the Temple, God opened the door of fellowship with Himself—after the 70 years of suffering, the Chosen People were ready to return and build and wait until He, the true Servant, would come.

2. God renewed His promise of a coming Redeemer—it was prophesied that the Redeemer would be associated with Judah.

3. "The set time" when Christ would come was made ready—this was what Paul wrote about in Galatians 4:4.

UNDERSTANDING NEHEMIAH

NEHEMIAH 1–7: REPAIRING THE CITY'S WALL

Nehemiah was the cupbearer at the court of King Artaxerxes. This was a position of high honor. But in this position of familiarity with the king, he had not forgotten his people. The news brought to him about Jerusalem made him very sad. This sadness could not be wholly hidden, and the king detected it. The Jews had been back home for almost a hundred years but had made no attempt to rebuild Jerusalem beyond the restoration of the Temple, because their enemies made it almost impossible.

Artaxerxes' stepmother was Esther, the Jewess, who no doubt was still alive. It may have been that Nehemiah received his appointment through her influence. Whatever the case, he was loyal enough to his people to ask permission to leave the luxury of the king's court and go back to rebuild Jerusalem, the capital of his homeland. The king gave his consent. (Even today, Jews everywhere long to see Jerusalem flourish, and they turn their faces to that place as their homeland.)

When Nehemiah reached Jerusalem in 445 BC, Ezra had already been there for 13 years. Ezra was a priest and had been

Nehemiah

teaching the people the Word of God. But Nehemiah was a civil governor. He had come with the authority of the king of Persia to build the wall of Jerusalem. After he had been there only three days, he went up and viewed the wall at night. When he saw its dilapidated condition, he encouraged the people to begin building immediately. Nehemiah was a real engineer, and the work was accomplished in 42 days by each family working on an assigned portion of the wall. Their attitude was expressed in this sentence: "The people worked with all their heart" (Nehemiah 4:6). The people did, however, encounter a few problems.

First the Samaritans, the enemies of the Jews, derided them. The Samaritans hindered the work so much that the Jews had to keep watch night and day. The derision then turned to anger, and Nehemiah decided to divide the men into two groups—one keeping watch while the other worked.

Then opposition rose within the ranks. Some of the Jews became tired and complained that there was so much rubbish that the wall could not be built. (All the rubble had to be removed in a thick canvas pad on a carrier's back; there were, of course, no wheelbarrows or trucks to convey the material.) Then there were complaints that the rich were demanding usury that the poor were unable to pay.

After this, enemies of the Jews tried to trick Nehemiah into stopping the building, but Nehemiah only prayed, and again he foiled the enemies. The Persian kings were always the friends of the Jews.

After the wall was completed, Nehemiah put his brother Hanani in charge of the city of Jerusalem (see Nehemiah 7:1-4). When Ezra took a census, the whole number of Jews was 42,360, besides 7,337 servants and 245 singing men and women (see Nehemiah 7:5-73).

NEHEMIAH 8–13: REPAIRING THE PEOPLE'S MORALS

All the people gathered in the street before the water gate in the city of Jerusalem and requested Ezra the scribe to bring out the book of the Law of Moses. He stood upon a pulpit of wood and read and explained the Law to the people (see Nehemiah 8:1-13). This public reading brought true repentance to the people and a great revival broke out. The same thing had happened before: When Josiah found the book of the Law, a great reformation started (see 2 Kings 22–23; 2 Chronicles 34–35). When Martin Luther read the Bible, the Protestant Reformation began. We need to have the Word read today!

Their captivity in Babylon cured the Jewish people of idolatry. Remember, up to that time, in spite of all the warnings of the prophets, the people would worship the idols of the peoples around them. The Jews had intermarried with the idolatrous neighbors, and this was one of the reasons for their sin. But from the days of the captivity to the present (about 2,500 years), the Jewish people have never again been guilty of this sin.

Intermarriage of Christians with those who do not believe is also a dangerous thing, even today. Paul said, "Do not be yoked together with unbelievers" (2 Corinthians 6:14).

POINTS TO REMEMBER

- Nehemiah left a life of ease and luxury and security for a life of toil and danger and heartbreaks.

- Nehemiah was a reformer! And no one being reformed truly appreciates the person who is doing the reforming.

- Nehemiah was a man of prayer, and he was fearless and courageous. We do not find a blot on his character.

Nehemiah

A Quick Look at

The Old Testament: Genesis Through Nehemiah

PORTRAYAL OF JESUS

Because the Bible portrays Jesus Christ as the Savior of the world, the important thing in the study of the Bible is to find how Jesus Christ is portrayed in each book. From Genesis through Nehemiah, the following portrayals need to be remembered:

- Genesis portrays Jesus Christ as our Creator-God.
- Exodus portrays Jesus Christ as our Passover Lamb.
- Leviticus portrays Jesus Christ as our sacrifice for sin.
- Numbers portrays Jesus Christ as our lifted-up One.
- Deuteronomy portrays Jesus Christ as our true prophet.
- Joshua portrays Jesus Christ as captain of our salvation.
- Judges portrays Jesus Christ as our Deliverer-Judge.
- Ruth portrays Jesus Christ as our Kinsman-Redeemer.
- First and Second Samuel, First and Second Kings, and First and Second Chronicles portray Jesus Christ as our King.
- Ezra and Nehemiah portray Jesus Christ as our Restorer.

TIME LINE FROM THE BEGINNING TO NEHEMIAH

???–2000 BC (Genesis 1–11)
Period: The world before Abram (Creation, Sin, Flood, Babel)
People: Adam, Eve, Cain, Seth, Noah, Shem, Ham, Japheth

2000–1700 BC (Genesis 12–50)
Period: Age of the patriarchs (Call of Abraham, Migration to Egypt, Growth of Israel)
People: Abraham, Isaac, Jacob, Joseph

1700–1450 BC (Exodus–Deuteronomy)
Period: Oppression in Egypt (Exodus, The Law, Worship, Wilderness)
People: Moses, Miriam, Aaron, Joshua

1450–1100 BC (Joshua–1 Samuel 7)
Period: Conquest of Canaan and time of the judges (Invasion of Canaan, Bondage and deliverance)
People: Joshua, Caleb, Othniel, Ehud, Shamgar, Deborah, Barak, Gideon, Jephthah, Samson, Eli, Samuel

1100–600 BC (1 Samuel 8–2 Chronicles)
Period: Monarchy united, divided, and declining (Kingdom established, Temple built, Kingdom divided, Destruction of Samaria, Discovery of the Law, Destruction of Jerusalem)
People: Saul, David, Solomon, Jeroboam, Rehoboam, Ahab, Asa, Jehu, Elijah, Elisha, Jehoshaphat, Joab, Amaziah, Jeroboam II, Hoshea, Uzziah, Jotham, Ahaz, Hezekiah, Manasseh, Josiah, Jehoiakim, Zedekiah

500–400 BC (Ezra–Nehemiah)
Period: Return from exile (Decree of Cyrus, Close of Old Testament history)
People: Zerubbabel, Ezra, Nehemiah

OUTLINE OF OLD TESTAMENT HISTORY

I. Period of Patriarchs: Adam to Moses (Genesis)
   A. God's Chosen Men
     In the beginning we find no nations. God chose men who made Him known, but the earth became more and more wicked (see Genesis 6:5).

       1. Adam, created in God's image
       2. Seth, Adam's godly son
       3. Enoch, who walked with God
       4. Noah, who built the ark
       5. Shem (Noah's son) and his descendants

      Important Events
       1. Creation (Genesis 1–2)
       2. Fall (Genesis 3)
       3. Flood (Genesis 6–8)
       4. Babel and the Dispersion (Genesis 11)

      Great Nations Established
       1. Egypt in North Africa
       2. Canaan on the Mediterranean
       3. Babylonia between the Tigris and Euphrates Rivers
       4. Assyria, north of Babylonia

  B. God's Chosen Family
     Humankind as a whole had failed (see Genesis 6:5), so God limited His promises to a single family. He called Abraham to become the father of God's nation.

     Important Events
      1. Abraham called (Genesis 12:1–25:11)
      2. Jacob chosen (Genesis 25:19–36:43)
      3. Joseph cherished (Genesis 45–46)

  C. God's Chosen People
     The 12 tribes became the nation of Israel.

II. Period of Great Leaders: Moses to Saul (Exodus–1 Samuel)
  A. The Exodus (Exodus)
  B. The Wilderness Wanderings (Exodus, Leviticus, Numbers, Deuteronomy)
  C. Conquest of Canaan (Joshua)
  D. The Rule of the Judges (Judges)

III. Period of Kings: Saul to the Babylonian Captivity (1 and 2 Samuel–2 Chronicles; prophetical books)
Tribal life developed into national life.

A. The United Kingdom—Saul, David, Solomon

B. The Divided Kingdom
   1. Kings of Israel (northern kingdom)
   2. Kings of Judah (southern kingdom)
   3. The fall of the northern kingdom
   4. The fall of the southern kingdom

IV. Period of Foreign Kings: Captivity to Christ (Ezra–Esther; Ezekiel–Daniel)
God was preparing the land, the people and the world for the coming Christ.
A. Preparation for the Coming Messiah
B. Restoration Under Persian Kings

QUIZ FOR REVIEW

1. Review the books of the Bible by stating how Christ is portrayed in each one.

2. Answer the following questions:

   A. What was Solomon's greatest work? Describe it.
   B. What books of the Bible did Solomon write?
   C. Why was the kingdom divided after Solomon's death?
   D. What were the kings of Israel like? How did this kingdom end? Who were her conquerors? (You need to know this.) Who were Israel's prophets?
   E. What were the kings of Judah like? Who took Judah captive and where was she taken?

3. Tell who is described in the following:

A. This man (a) was never born; (b) never had a birthday; (c) owned a great estate; (d) was perfect physically; (e) was a great zoologist, gave every animal a name.
(Adam)

B. This man (a) was father of the oldest man in the world; (b) lived a godly life in one of the most wicked generations in the world; (c) was the only man in 3,000 years who did not die; (d) walked into heaven.
(Enoch)

C. This man (a) was radiant with righteousness in the midst of moral darkness, and saved his family of seven by his faith in God; (b) was a great ship builder, but built a huge ship on a desert, miles from the sea; (c) never had to launch his ship into the sea—the sea came to it and lifted it to the top of a mountain; (d) gathered the greatest collection of animals the world has ever known; (e) had sons who were the fathers of the nations of the world.
(Noah)

D. This man was akin to a covered wagon pioneer: (a) he left a great city of culture at God's request and traveled across a trackless desert; (b) he left a beautiful home and lived in a tent for 100 years; (c) he was called "a friend of God"; (d) he was the father of a great nation; (e) his son was born after he was a hundred years old; (f) angels visited him.
(Abraham)

E. This man (a) and his young friend believed God when no one else would; (b) was a great general; (c) did not have to build a bridge to transport his army into the land that he wanted to conquer; (d) used trumpets instead of bombers and priests instead of trained soldiers to destroy a city.
(Joshua)

F. This man (a) was an adopted child; (b) lived amidst the wealth of the day; (c) enjoyed unlimited education; (d) in spite of this, chose to identify himself with the poor people from whom he came rather than with the rulers with whom he lived; (e) was forced to live in a desert for 40 years; (f) was chosen as the leader of three million people and led them out from under the bondage of the strongest ruler of his day without firing a shot; (g) made slaves become rich overnight; (h) was the meekest man on earth and yet he lost his temper; (i) talked with God; (j) died an unknown death; (k) was buried by no man.

(Moses)

INTERESTING FACTS

- Between chapters 6 and 7 of Ezra, three great world battles (Salamis, Thermopylae and Marathon) were fought; and two great world leaders (Confucius and Buddha) died! Time elapsed: 58 years!

- In the Old Testament, the book of Esther follows the book of Nehemiah; in history, the events in Esther occur 30 years before Nehemiah!

- The purposes of God are sometimes delayed; but they are never abandoned!

Understanding Esther

Esther Portrays Jesus Christ, Our Advocate

SELECTED BIBLE READINGS

AUTHOR: The book of Esther does not name its author. Jewish and Christian traditions attribute the book to Mordecai (a major character in the book of Esther), or to Ezra and Nehemiah (who would have been familiar with this period of Persian history).

DATE: The book may have been written between 460 and 350 BC.

PURPOSE AND SUMMARY: The book of Esther, in the form of a short story similar to the book of Ruth, has its setting in the palace at Susa, one of the three capitals of the Persian empire. The book of Esther describes the Jewish community living in exile in the Persian empire and gives a view of the hostility of their non-Jewish enemies in Persia. The book describes how Esther, a Jewish woman, became the queen of Ahasuerus (Xerxes), subsequently risking her life in order to save her people, the Jewish people, from total destruction.

Though the word "God" never appears in the book, God's providential care of His people is clearly implied in the language of the book: "And who knows but that you have come to your royal position for such a time as this?" (Esther 4:14).

You may have heard of the great Xerxes (485-465 BC), king of Persia, and of his famous expedition against Greece and how the Greeks defeated his tremendous fleet at the battle of Salamis in 480 BC. Historians tell us that this was one of the world's most important battles. From parallel passages written by the Greek historian Herodotus (485-425 BC), we find that the feast described in the first chapter of Esther was the occasion for planning the campaign against Greece (the third year of Xerxes' reign). Esther replaced Vashti as queen in the seventh year of Xerxes' reign, when he was seeking comfort after his disastrous defeat (see Esther 2:16-17).

In the midst of this famous chapter in world history occurs the beautiful and charming Bible story of Esther. Although God's name is not mentioned in the book of Esther, every page is full of God, who hides Himself behind every word. Matthew Henry, a famous British Bible commentator, said of the book, "If the name of God is not here, His finger is." And Dr. Arthur Pierson, an American missionary statesman and pastor, called it "The Romance of Providence." God has a part in all the events of human life.

Although Yuri Gagarin, the first man to travel in space, once scoffed that he did not see God in outer space, the world today cannot get rid of God; neither could Israel. He never let His people go in the past, and He will never let them go in the future. He followed them to their captivity in Babylon. When the prophets were silent and the Temple closed, God was still standing guard. When the kings of earth feasted and forgot, God remembered; and with His hand He wrote their doom or moved their hand to work His glory.

The book of Esther opens with the feast of the world's prince Xerxes; it closes with the feast of God's prince Mordecai. For a while, Haman is exalted; at last, Mordecai. As you read this story, note the upsets in human history and the final triumph of God's Chosen People.

Esther is like Joseph and David. God had each one hidden away for His purpose. When the day came, He brought each to the front to work out His plan. God hid Joseph away in a dungeon in Egypt, but when God was ready, He placed Joseph in the position of prime minister of that country. God always has someone in reserve to fulfill His purposes. Sometimes it is a man like Joseph or Moses. Sometimes it is a woman like Hannah, Esther or Mary. Think of some men in more recent history, such as Martin Luther and Abraham Lincoln and Billy Graham, whom God seems to have prepared and kept "hidden" until they were needed.

Esther stands out as one of God's chosen ones. She is a sweet and winsome person. She came to the kingdom for just "such a time as this" (Esther 4:14). We see her taking her life in her hand. As she goes in for her people's sake unto the king, she says, "And if I perish, I perish" (Esther 4:16).

Two beautiful girls acted on behalf of God's people: Ruth and Esther. Ruth became the ancestress of the Deliverer of Israel, and Esther saved the people so that the Deliverer might come. God carefully protected the Jewish nation through the centuries for the purpose of blessing the whole world. They could not be wiped out before they brought the Savior into the world. God's Chosen People had to fulfill God's plan. Therefore God kept this nation according to His promise to Abraham.

Although when this story was written and who its author was are not known for certain, it is generally believed to have happened between the events described in chapters six and seven of the book of Ezra, when not more than 50,000 of the captive Jews had returned to Jerusalem from Babylon under the edict of Cyrus. If they had all returned to Jerusalem, the book of Esther would not have been written.

The book is named for a Jewish orphan who became a Persian queen. The name "Esther" means "star." This book and the book of Ruth are the only books in the Bible that bear the names of women.

Someone has said that all the events of this book center around three feasts:

1. Feast of King Ahasuerus—Esther 1-2
2. Feast of Esther—Esther 7
3. Feast of Purim—Esther 9

ESTHER 1: REJECTION OF VASHTI

The great feast to which Vashti refused to come, as has been learned from inscriptions uncovered by archaeologists, was held to consider the expedition against Greece, for which Xerxes spent four years in preparation.

As this book opens, the king was entertaining all the nobles and princes of his kingdom in the royal palace at Susa. The gathering was planned on a colossal scale, and it lasted 180 days (see Esther 1:4). Then the men feasted for seven days in the gorgeous palace gardens, and the beautiful Queen Vashti entertained the women in her private apartment.

Susa was the winter residence of the Persian kings. Remember, Nehemiah was in the palace in Susa (see Nehemiah 1:1). Excavations at Susa, started in the mid-1800s, have located several of the places mentioned in the book of Esther—the inner court, the outer court, the king's gate and the palace garden. Even a die, or *pur*, which was used to cast lots, was found (see Esther 3:7).

When the king and princes were in the midst of their drunken revelry, the king called for Vashti so that he could show off her beauty. Of course, no Persian woman would permit this, because it was considered an affront to her womanhood. But the men's drunkenness had caused the most sacred rules of Oriental etiquette to be broken: The seclusion of the harem was to be violated for the amusement of the dissolute king and his boon companions. Vashti refused. This made the king a laughingstock. To defend himself, he deposed the queen. Read Esther 1:12-22 to learn the details.

(Remember, modesty is the crown jewel of womanhood. Never be false to your pure ideals. Men are bound to protect this crown jewel in womanhood. Modesty is seldom displayed, however, by a female who does not also possess nobler virtues.)

ESTHER 2: CROWNING OF ESTHER

Between chapters 1 and 2, Xerxes made his historic attack on Greece with an army of five million men, suffering a terrible defeat in the famous naval battle of Salamis (480 BC).

Two years later, Xerxes married Esther and made her his queen. The little Jewish orphan girl, raised by her cousin Mordecai, was lifted to the Persian throne. (According to Herodotus, at this time the Persian Empire comprised more than half the then-known world.)

Esther was Xerxes' queen for 13 years. She, no doubt, lived for many years into the reign of her stepson, Artaxerxes. Under this king, Nehemiah rebuilt Jerusalem. Esther's marriage to Xerxes gave the Jews prestige at this court and made it possible for Nehemiah to rebuild Jerusalem (see Nehemiah 2:1-8).

The great palace of Xerxes at Persepolis, where Esther no doubt spent much of her time, has been excavated. The description of it, even in its ruin, is magnificent. The city itself was destroyed by fire by Alexander the Great in 331 BC and was buried in the sands of the desert. Ever since the 1800s, archaeologists of many nations have been working to excavate and restore the palace as completely as possible.

To make the story of this Jewish girl more real and interesting, let us give you a little description of this palace. The foundation of the palace was a platform 50 feet high and covered an area of two and a half acres. Underneath it was a vast sewer system, miles in length, through which one may walk today. The walls of the palace were covered with the most magnificent carvings and reliefs and sculptures. Two large rooms in the Louvre display this artwork. When archaeologists finally cleared away the rubbish, they found this artwork preserved and as fresh and beautiful as it was when Queen Esther walked through the corridors and looked upon it.

The second chapter of Esther describes the scene in this palace. Richly colored awnings were stretched across from marble pillars to silver rods, shading the exalted guests as they reclined on gold and silver seats while they feasted gluttonously and drank heavily.

There was a grand audience hall where men came from the four corners of the earth to pay their honor to the great king, Esther's husband. The giant columns still rise in their grandeur, speaking of the former glory of the palace.

It should be noted here that while Esther was being prepared to be Xerxes' queen, we learn the story of Mordecai's saving the king's life (see Esther 2:21-23). This account figures prominently later in the book.

ESTHER 3–4: PLOTTING OF HAMAN

After the grand scenes in Esther 1–2, we see a form casting a shadow across the picture. In Esther 3, we read about the ascendancy of a man by the name of Haman. He was a wicked man whose day of triumph was short and whose joy endured but for a moment. (See the description of this in Job 20:4-5.)

Haman was the Judas of Israel. He was a wicked monster in the life of God's Chosen People. During the reading of the book of Esther in a Jewish synagogue at the Feast of Purim, the congregation might be found taking part in a chorus at every mention of the name of Haman: "May his name be blotted out," while boys pound stones and bits of wood on which his hated name is written.

When Haman appears in the story of Esther, he had just been exalted to the highest position under the king of Persia (see Esther 3:1), becoming the chief minister to the king. The high honor turned his head. He swelled with vanity and was bitterly humiliated when Mordecai, at the king's gate, did not pay homage to him as had been commanded by the king (see Esther 3:2).

Inflated with pride, he could not endure the indifference of any subject. The little fault of Mordecai was magnified into a capital offense. Mordecai, a Jew, would not give honor to this Amalekite, a Jewish enemy. Haman became so enraged that he wanted to have a wholesale massacre of all the Jews in the kingdom (see Esther 3:6). To determine the month his enemies would be destroyed, lots were cast; and March, just 11 months away, was identified (see Esther 3:7,12). Haman tried to prove to the king that all the Jews were disloyal subjects. He even offered to pay the king a bribe of millions of dollars (see Esther 3:9). The king signed a royal decree that meant that every Jewish man, woman and child was to be killed and all their property was to be taken. (Compare this treatment with that used by the Nazi regime.)

Imagine the fasting and the praying and the weeping in sackcloth that took place among the Jews (see Esther 4:1-3).

Queen Esther saw it all and asked Mordecai what it meant. He gave her a copy of the king's decree that told the sad story. Then he added, "And who knows but that you have come to your royal position for such a time as this?" (Esther 4:14).

It would do well for all of us to pause and ask ourselves this same question: *Why has God allowed me to live at this particular hour?* To do what is right may mean that we must jeopardize our lives. Then we must face the issue and answer as this young queen did: "And if I perish, I perish" (Esther 4:16).

ESTHER 5-7: RISK BY ESTHER

Queen Esther answered the challenge of Mordecai. She who had been placed in the palace on beds of ease had not succumbed to the luxury of her surroundings. For the sake of her oppressed people, the Jews, she chose a course that was terribly dangerous for herself.

There is one thing to do always: Do what is right and leave the rest to God. God prepares people for emergencies. Failure is not sin; faithlessness is. There is a time to act. As Brutus says in Shakespeare's *Julius Caesar,* "There is a tide in the affairs of men which taken at the flood leads on to fortune" (act 4, scene 3, lines 218-219). Act when God speaks.

The beauty of Esther was that she was not spoiled by her great rise in prominence. Though she became the queen of a great king, she did not forget the kind porter who raised her from childhood. Once she accepted her dreaded task, she proceeded to carry it out with courage. It was a daring act for her to enter the presence of the king without first being summoned. Who could tell what this fickle monarch would do? Think what he had done to Vashti!

When the king had received her, Esther used all the resources available to her. She knew the king's weakness for good living, so she invited him to a banquet. Read Esther 6:1-11 to learn what happened that night when the king could not sleep. How was Haman trapped? Read Esther 6:6. At the second banquet, Esther pleaded for her own life. She had Haman on the spot.

The king granted Esther's wish. Haman was hung on the very scaffold he had prepared for Mordecai, and Mordecai was elevated to the place of honor next to the king.

As you study God's Word, you will find that through the ages, Satan has tried to destroy, first God's people, the Jews; next Christ Himself; then the Church. But God has thwarted his plans. Even "the gates of Hades will not overcome" His Church (Matthew 16:18). God will triumph! Christ has won the victory!

ESTHER 8–10: DELIVERANCE OF THE JEWS

The book of Esther closes with the account of Mordecai being promoted to take the place made vacant by Haman's death (see

Esther 10:3). The Jewish porter became the second man of the Persian Empire, just under the king.

The Feast of Purim, celebrated annually, was inspired by the dramatic story of Esther. The feast does not celebrate the downfall of Haman so much as the deliverance of the people.

This feast celebrating the deliverance of the Jewish people from a fearful danger is a sort of Thanksgiving Day for the Chosen People. Although they had forsaken God, He had spared them. Deliverance seems to be the keynote of Jewish history. God has always delivered this nation from danger and servitude. God will always deliver His people in the hour of their trouble.

This book of Esther is an important link in a chain of events that tell of reestablishing the Hebrew nation in their own land in preparation for the coming of the Messiah into the world. The Jewish people had escaped extermination. It was God's purpose that they should be preserved to bring forth the Savior of the world.

The character of Xerxes illustrates how unlimited power often is crushed and dissolved beneath the weight of its own immensity. Those who are exalted to the pedestal of a god are made dizzy by their own altitude.

King Xerxes' defeat by the Greeks was the beginning of the decline of the Persian Empire; and Xerxes was dead by the age of 54, assassinated by the head of his royal bodyguard.

POINTS TO REMEMBER

- Esther is a sweet and attractive character:
    Beautiful and modest—Esther 2:15
    Winsome—Esther 2:9-17; 5:1-3
    Obedient—Esther 2:10
    Humble—Esther 4:16
    Courageous—Esther 7:6
    Loyal and constant—Esther 2:22; 8:1-2; 7:3-4

- There is always only one thing to do: Do what is right and leave the rest to God.

- "I will go to the king, even though it is against the law. And if I perish, I perish" (Esther 4:16). God meets emergencies with human lives He has redeemed and prepared.

- "And who knows but that you have come to your royal position for such a time as this?" (Esther 4:14). Prayer moves the hand that moves the world. A devoted woman moved a determined monarch.

- "Surely your wrath against mankind brings you praise" (Psalm 76:10). Those who walk in holy sincerity with Christ may walk in holy security among humanity.

- God's pioneers leave all to gain all.

Books of Poetry

of the Old Testament

JOB • PSALMS • PROVERBS

ECCLESIASTES

SONG OF SOLOMON

Key Events of the Books of Poetry

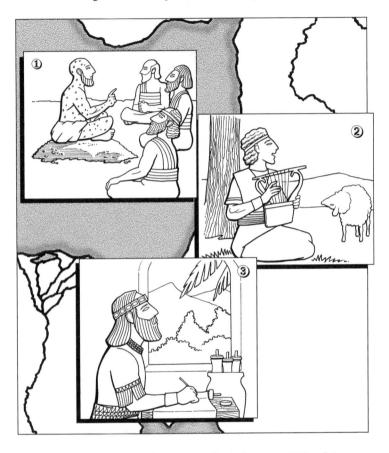

Books of Poetry: The Heart of Wisdom and Worship

Biblical poetry teaches that true worship and wisdom can only come from appropriate fear and affection for God. Coming in the form of a cosmic struggle between the Lord and His angelic enemies (Job) ①, the full range of emotions in verse (Psalms) ②, a father's and mother's wisdom sayings to their son (Proverbs), musings about the human condition (Ecclesiastes) ③, and the love song of a bride and groom (Song of Solomon), the books of poetry also teach us how to anticipate a hopeful end to history through the coming of the Messiah.

14

Understanding Job

Job Portrays Jesus Christ, Our Redeemer

AUTHOR: The book of Job does not specifically name its author. The most likely candidates are Job, Elihu, Moses or Solomon.

DATE: The date of the authorship of the book would be determined by the author of the book. If Moses were the author, the date would be around 1240 BC. If Solomon were the author, the date would be around 950 BC.

PURPOSE AND SUMMARY: The book is named after Job, its chief character. The book deals with the ageless question concerning human suffering, particularly the affliction of the righteous. The book shows that the suffering of righteous Job came from the Lord, who allowed Satan to attack him in order to purge and prepare him for greater blessing and influence from the hand of the Lord (see Job 33:14-19; 42). The arguments about the cause of Job's sufferings, carried on between Job and his friends, refute the popular view that all suffering is the result of sin in the life of the sufferer.

We have finished reading the historical books of the Old Testament—Joshua through Esther. Now we open the books of poetry—Job, Psalms, Proverbs, Ecclesiastes and Song of Solomon. These books tell about the experiences of the heart.

Job's keyword is "tested": "But he knows the way that I take; when he has tested me, I will come forth as gold" (Job 23:10).

Trials and suffering are for our education and training. The athlete is not put under strict discipline for punishment but merely to make him ready for the race. Christ is continuously preparing us for the race that is set before us (see Hebrews 12:1-2).

Job is no doubt one of the most wonderful poems ever written (only the prologue and epilogue are prose). The English poet Alfred Lord Tennyson called it "the greatest poem, whether of ancient or modern literature." The story in this amazing book takes place in the days of the patriarchs. For all we know, this book may be one of the most ancient complete pieces of literature in existence. It is one of the oldest, if not the oldest, books in the Bible. The Word of God settles the fact that Job was a real person. God speaks through the prophet Ezekiel and says, "Even if these three men—Noah, Daniel and Job—were in it, they could save only themselves by their righteousness" (Ezekiel 14:14; see also 14:20). If you doubt Job's existence, you will have to refute Noah and Daniel.

It is fitting that the oldest book should deal with one of the oldest questions: "Why do godly people suffer?" This is the subject of the book (although it also deals with a wide scope of knowledge—the power of Satan, telling of his might and the limit of his authority; the fact of the Resurrection; and why a person should serve God). People have always asked why God permits good people to suffer. Haven't you wondered yourself why some good person has to die of an awful disease or has to be confined to a bed of pain? The drama of Job offers an answer to this question. I believe it gives God's answer.

It is easy to become confused about this problem of suffering. Remember, the disciples of Christ thought that suffering was the result of sin in a life (see John 9:2). The book of Job gives an entirely different reason for suffering. In Job's case, God was honoring him. It was true that God could trust Job to remain faithful to God in spite of everything. How wonderful it would be if you and I learned to thank God in all that happens to us.

THE STORY OF JOB

This book should first be read as a narrative. The story of Job is a simple one. It opens with a scene in heaven and then tells of Job's fall from prosperity to poverty. This is followed by the great discussion between Job and his four friends: Eliphaz, the religious dogmatist, much like an ancient Pharisee; Bildad, who sought to comfort Job with worn-out platitudes; Zophar, who thought he had a corner on all religious wisdom; and Elihu, the impetuous youth. Finally, the climax of the book is reached when God speaks. Job responds to God, at last in a humble spirit, and the question about suffering is answered. This is the story of the book.

Different Views of Suffering

Next, we should read the book for its subject—suffering. We find that each story character looks at suffering differently:

1. The shallow view of Satan—The children of God love and serve Him because it pays in riches and honor (see Job 1–2:8). Satan said that Job's godliness was selfishness; that he served God for profit; that when prosperity ended, he would be godly no more. In effect, Satan was saying, "Who wouldn't serve God for a sizable income every year? Watch

him when his prosperity ends." He received permission to test Job (see Job 2:6).

2. The scarcely-less-false view of Eliphaz, Bildad and, for the most part, Zophar—The unrighteous suffer because of their sins, and the righteous are rewarded. Hence, they reasoned that Job must have sinned, and this suffering was his punishment. Job's suffering was great; therefore, he must have been a great sinner. They said, "Who, being innocent, has ever perished?" (Job 4:7).

3. Elihu's far-more-just answer to the question (but his eloquent discourse was marred by conceit)—He defended God and believed that affliction was the punishment God inflicted as a loving Father. But this did not explain to Job the reason for suffering. Elihu argued that suffering was God's discipline to bring His sons back into fellowship with Himself. He believed that suffering was sent to keep us from sinning.

4. Jehovah's view (by revealing Himself to Job)—When men see God, something always happens. The godly are allowed to suffer so that they may see themselves first. Read Isaiah 6:1-5; Genesis 17:1-3; Daniel 10:4-8. When we come to the end of ourselves, God can lift us up. Job was a good man, but he was self-righteous. Read Job 29:1-25, and you will find the personal pronouns "I," "my" and "me" 42 times. It reminds one of Romans 7.

God has a wise purpose in all of our suffering. God wants to show His "manifold wisdom" (Ephesians 3:10). He wants the trial of our faith to work patience. He wants to bring us out of the fire as pure gold, all the dross burned up. God, the great metallurgist of heaven, puts us in the fire; then He watches us and removes our impurities before He pulls us out of the fire. He wants to reveal real character. Furthermore, we have an unseen "cloud of witnesses" gathered in the great stadium of heaven to watch us as we are tested (Hebrews 12:1).

How little did Job realize that so much depended on his steadfastness and trust in God when he said, "Though he slay me, yet will I hope in him" (Job 13:15). I wonder if we realize today the issues that depend on our faithfulness to God. If God could only find more of us who would trust Him, how much we would encourage others to trust!

What was Job's attitude toward God? He first had access to God through the blood of sacrifice (see Job 1:5). Then with an undivided and incorruptible heart, he walked with God.

Job had a conscience that was right with God. He knew that his heart was true, so he could accept the accusations of his friends. And he finally could show them that their conclusion was wrong and that the wicked often prosper in this world (see Job 24:6).

Light from the New Testament

The problem of suffering has had much light thrown on it from the New Testament—especially from the cross of Christ (see also Luke 22:31-32; 1 Corinthians 5:5; 11:31-32; Hebrews 12:7-11). Here we see the world's most righteous Man, the world's greatest sufferer. We know now that the righteous suffer with the wicked because of sin that fills the world with misery. We also know that there are natural consequences of sin—for the godly as well as for the sinner. And we know as well, as has already been noted, that disciplining is sometimes done for training and sometimes for correction. There is a suffering that Christians must endure for Christ's sake and the gospel's.

Do you know of any good person today who is suffering? Of course you do. Everyone does. One of the greatest saints I ever knew was blind; another was so poor that we, as children, carried things to him to eat and saved our money to buy clothes for him. We gave material things to him, but he gave spiritual blessings to us. God allowed Stephen to be stoned (see Acts 7:59) and Paul to have "a thorn" in his flesh to "torment" him (2 Corinthians 12:7). Even Jesus knew suffering.

God's Dealings with Job

God trusted Job; therefore, He assigned to him this great problem of suffering. Because He loved Job, He allowed him to suffer, "because the Lord disciplines the one he loves" (Hebrews 12:6). When Job was in the midst of his anguish, he realized that it is only the gold that is worth putting into the fire. Anything else would be consumed. James said, "Consider it pure joy, my brothers and sisters, whenever you face trials of many kinds, because you know that the testing of your faith develops perseverance" (James 1:2-3).

When Job was prosperous and upright and benevolent, he was in danger of becoming self-confident and could easily forget that he was only the steward of the power and place in this world that God had given him. God does not give us great gifts just to please ourselves. The *Westminster Shorter Confession* tells us that the chief end of man is "to glorify God." "For even Christ did not please himself" (Romans 15:3); He came to glorify the Father.

God dealt with Job in three ways:

1. He was broken (see Job 16:12,14; 17:11).
2. He was melted (see Job 23:10).
3. He was softened, so he could say, "The hand of God hath touched me. God maketh my heart soft" (Job 19:21; 23:16, *KJV*).

Do you ever sing, "Spirit of the living God, fall fresh on me. Melt me, mold me, fill me, use me"? Do you know what that really would mean for you? This is what happened to Job.

Job never really saw himself until he saw God. This is true of every life. Read Isaiah 6:1-9 to see how it affected Isaiah when he, as a young man, saw God.

Job was all ready to reason with God, as many do today, about His dealings with him. He could not understand God.

Read what God asked Job: "Will the one who contends with the Almighty correct him?" (Job 40:2). Think of trying to correct the God of this universe! The wisdom of people is only foolishness with God. Read Job's answer: "I am unworthy—how can I reply to you? I put my hand over my mouth" (Job 40:4).

God kept dealing with Job until he came to the very end of himself! Read Job's words: "Surely I spoke of things I did not understand, things too wonderful for me to know.... My ears had heard of you but now my eyes have seen you. Therefore I despise myself and repent in dust and ashes" (Job 42:3-6).

A vision of God Himself completed the work in Job and brought him to his knees. We find Job a disciplined, softened servant. God turned the tide, and a double measure of Job's prosperity was given back to him—twice as many sheep, oxen, donkeys and camels! He rejoiced again in his sons and daughters, the same number as before.

Job no longer asked a question but made a statement: "I know that my redeemer lives, and that in the end he will stand on the earth. And after my skin has been destroyed, yet in my flesh I will see God" (Job 19:25-26).

Job's vision of a future life, which had been uncertain before, was clear now. We read about him asking a question so many others have asked: "If someone dies, will they live again?" (Job 14:14). Paul answered this question in the great resurrection chapter of the Bible, 1 Corinthians 15; and Jesus answered it in His statement, "The one who believes in me will live, even though they die" (John 11:25). What a wonderful vision of the future life we have in these words! What a prophecy of the coming of the Savior!

The Life of Job

Remember as you read this book that Job was a wealthy and righteous man:

- Blameless (Job 1:1,8)—He was undivided in his loyalty to high principles ("perfect," *KJV*).

- Upright (Job 1:1,8)—He was "straight" (in the original Hebrew).
- Feared God (Job 1:1; see also 1:8)—He had the beginning of wisdom.
- Shunned evil (Job 1:1; see also 1:8)—His moral conduct was above reproach.
- Prosperous (see Job 1:2-4)—He had large herds of animals and many servants.
- Praying (see Job 1:5)—He regularly offered glory to God.
- Popular (see Job 29:21-25)—He was consulted in many matters and his opinion was valued.
- Proven (see Job 42:10-12)—Job prayed for others and he was restored.

Job was right with man and with God. Remember that it was God who described him and then added, "There is no one on earth like him" (Job 1:8). What an honor God gave to Job to use these words to describe him!

As the book opens, we see Job surrounded by wealth, family, position and friends. We see this man visited by Satan. A swift succession of calamities followed. Remember, these things did not come about because of anything wrong in Job, but all of Job's friends thought the reason for his troubles lay in himself. God, however, made it very plain in the opening of the book that this was not true.

Watch this man stripped of his wealth and reduced to poverty! His children taken! His health gone! Then he lost the confidence of his wife! Finally his friends went! Let us watch this man whom God said was perfect!

JOB 1:6–2:10: SATAN AND THE SAINT

In Job 1:6, "the angels" ("the sons of God," *KJV*) presented themselves before the Lord. These angelic beings are the messengers of God. The mystery is that Satan was among them. He was angelic, but he had fallen. Here, however, there is no hint that he is out of place or that he had forced himself into the audience chamber.

The Figure of Satan

Let us stop and study this person for a while, this figure of the adversary, or Satan, who is in such sharp contrast to the Almighty. Satan is depicted with great clarity—a real being, not an imaginary one. The Bible tells us that Satan comes "as an angel of light" to deceive and to tempt (2 Corinthians 11:14). We cannot help but contrast the Satan depicted in the book of Job with the grotesque, gigantic, awful figure usually depicted by poets.

Our strange distorted picture of the devil is derived for the most part from Dante's *Divine Comedy*. In part one, *The Inferno*, Dante attempted to paint a picture of this monster of hell. In Dante's depiction, Satan's enormous size is matched by his hideousness. We also find a portrayal of Satan in Milton's *Paradise Lost* and *Paradise Regained*. Milton's description of Satan is magnificent, but Milton's regal archfiend does not even seem related to the Satan of the book of Job. Neither does Goethe's Mephistopheles in *Faust* offer us a true picture, although, no doubt, Goethe's depiction of a cynical devil, nonchalantly damning someone, is based on the book of Job.

Satan could call up the Sabean and Chaldean raiders and have them carry away Job's oxen and donkeys and camels (see Job 1:13-17). He could use lightning to kill Job's sheep, could cause the wind to kill Job's children and could even cause Job to have boils. Remember, he is "the ruler of the kingdom of the air" (Ephesians 2:2).

But know this also: There are limits to Satan's great power. Satan is mighty, but God is almighty! Satan can break through only where God allows him to (see Job 1:10). What a comfort it is to know that no calamity can come to us that the Father does not allow. He who has "shut up the sea behind doors" and said, "This far you may come and no farther; here is where your proud waves halt" (Job 38:8,11), "will not let [us] be tempted beyond what [we] can bear" (1 Corinthians 10:13).

Remember, the Almighty holds Satan in check so that he can only strike where he is given permission (see Job 1:12).

Satan's Conflict with God

God asked Satan, "Where have you come from?" (Job 1:7). What a tragedy is in the answer! "From roaming throughout the earth, going back and forth on it," said Satan (Job 1:7). Remember, this reveals the endless restlessness of evil: "Be alert and of sober mind. Your enemy the devil prowls around like a roaring lion looking for someone to devour" (1 Peter 5:8).

God spoke again and asked, "Have you considered my servant Job?" (Job 1:8).

What do you think God meant by "considered"? It is a strong word, as if God knew that Satan had been watching Job's every act. In other words, God asked Satan, "Have you been trying to find a flaw?"

Satan said, "Does Job fear God for nothing?" (Job 1:9). He seemed to imply that he, Satan, was trying to find out why this fellow is so perfect. "Have you not put a hedge around him and his household and everything he has?" (Job 1:10). That was the truth, of course. Then he added, "You have blessed the work of his hands" (Job 1:10). This was true also. "So that his flocks and herds are spread throughout the land" (Job 1:10). Yes, all this was correct.

But Satan went on, "But stretch out your hand and strike everything he has, and he will surely curse you to your face" (Job 1:11). Satan's charge against Job was that a man only serves God for what he can get out of it. Really, Job is not so much on trial here as is God. It is less a question of Job's loyalty than it is of God's power. Is God able "to guard what I have entrusted to him until that day" (2 Timothy 1:12)?

(This same thing is being said today! Some say that some ministers are preaching the gospel only for the reward they can get for doing the preaching, and that poor non-Christians in other lands are professing a belief in Christ only because in return they will be given food and shelter.)

So God told the devil, "All right, try it out! Take everything away from Job and see what happens!" (see Job 1:12).

Do you see that the real conflict here was between God and Satan? God was proving the truth about His statement of Job's integrity in following Him. Job proved that Satan's statement concerning God's children was a lie; that is, they only serve Him for what they can get out of it. God never allowed the devil to prove that, because if humans only serve God for what they can get out of Him, God had blundered when He made humans.

The Reason for Suffering

When the trials came, Job did not understand the meaning of all his suffering. He knew it was not because he had sinned, as his friends had said. But he did wonder what God was doing. Like Job, we will not always understand what God is working out on the battleground of our hearts. But know this: There is a reason and value to everything God allows and that "in all things God works for the good of those who love him, who have been called according to his purpose" (Romans 8:28).

Don't always try to find an immediate answer for why you have to suffer painful trials and saddening experiences. It's natural to wonder why, for example, God takes away a faithful young man in the prime of his life but allows a cruel and brutal tyrant to live. Sometimes we have to wait for the answer.

Sometimes, however, we never find the answer. We may be honest and sincere, as were Job's friends, but God's ways are past our finding out and beyond our understanding.

Remember, you can never walk before God and try to lead a godly life without Satan coming to walk with you—accusing you, finding fault in and with you, and vexing you.

Satan comes to do mischief to saints. He distracts our attention. He gets us to start criticizing each other. He sows dissension in the congregation. He excites the pride of preachers and singers, of generous donors and of those who pray out loud. He chills our spirit and freezes our prayers. Yes, when the Word is being sown, the fowls of the air come to pluck it away (see Matthew

13:3-23), so do not be surprised to find hypocrites in every congregation of God's children.

JOB 2:11–37:24: JOB AND HIS FRIENDS

Get acquainted with Job's friends. Let me introduce you to them. First there is courtly Eliphaz, then argumentative Bildad, then blunt Zophar and finally youthful Elihu. The scene should be a familiar one. Everyone has a reason that explains someone else's experiences and problems. So Job's four friends came to his home.

True Friends

There are things we can say in favor of these four men, although their words of "comfort" were anything but that (Job 2:11). The first is that they came at all. They were friends who stuck through adversity. When all of his many friends and acquaintances had forgotten Job, these four came. (Generally when a man loses his wealth and position and health, he has no friends left.)

The second thing in their favor is that they kept still for seven days. This is good! They seemed to be trying to find out the reason for all of Job's troubles before they spoke. (Someone has said that instead of talking with Job, they came and talked at him.)

They all did come up with a reason, and they proceeded to tell Job why they thought he was suffering as he did: They all agreed that he must have sinned miserably to have caused this suffering.

Eliphaz backed his argument by a dream (see Job 4–5); Bildad, by some old proverbs (see Job 8); Zophar, by experience and reason (see Job 11). Elihu came nearest the truth when he argued that suffering was God's discipline to bring the soul back into fellowship with God; but it was not the whole truth (see Job 32–37).

God called Job "blameless and upright" (Job 1:1). His friends were wrong in charging him with sin as the only possible cause of his calamities.

Wretched Comforters

Job received different "comforting" words after he cried from the ashes, "I cannot understand it. It doesn't seem right" (see Job 3).

Job's wife, discouraged, said, "Something is wrong. Your religion is a failure. You should curse God and go ahead and die" (see Job 2:9). This means nothing other than "Say goodbye to God." It is the voice of despair.

Eliphaz basically said, "God never makes a mistake. What have you done to bring this on yourself?"

Bildad essentially said, "God is just. Confess your sin."

Zophar suggested, "God is all-wise. He knows man."

Elihu, God's man, said the wisest thing: "God is good; look up, and trust Him, for He is God."

JOB 38–42: JEHOVAH AND JOB

The scene begins with God gloriously revealing Himself. Jehovah is heard from the whirlwind: "Brace yourself like a man; I will question you, and you shall answer me" (Job 40:7). In a series of about 60 questions, God said, in effect, "Who can do all these things but Myself?" God is thus revealed to Job, and Job to himself.

The Righteous Comforter

As so often is true with us, when Job came into the presence of God, he forgot the speech he thought he would make (see Job 40:4-5)! There was no arguing with God. Finally, Job went flat down on his face and answered God: "I know that you can do all things; no purpose of yours can be thwarted" (Job 42:2). Then comes the great confession: "My ears had heard of you but now my eyes have seen you. Therefore I despise myself and repent in dust and ashes" (Job 42:5-6). This is the only place to learn God's lessons—on your face, with your mouth shut!

This is the victory of submissive faith. When we bow to God's will, we find God's way. Stoop to conquer. Bend to obey. This is the lesson of Job.

The philosophy of Job's friends was wrong. Job was glad to see them and he could pour out his troubles to them, but they did not understand him. Job had tried to explain, but he was misunderstood. Only God understands!

A True Servant

Jehovah explained to Job (by revealing Himself to him) that when men see God, something always happens. The godly are allowed to suffer so they may see themselves. Read Isaiah 6:1-5. When Isaiah saw himself as he really was, he cried out, "I am a man of unclean lips" (Isaiah 6:5). God allows His children to suffer in order to reveal character, to set forth an object lesson and to bring to light some hidden sin. In Job's case, that hidden sin was self-righteousness.

Did you ever think you looked all right until some friend dropped in to invite you to go some place? When you saw how nice your friend looked, you immediately realized you needed to work on improving your appearance. So often this is true in the presence of Christ. The very purity of His Person makes us feel sinful. Measure your life by His life, and you will feel as Job did.

In Job 42, we find three important points:

1. The consciousness of God (verse 5)
2. The collapse of Job (verse 6)
3. The commission to serve (verse 7)

POINTS TO REMEMBER

This book well illustrates the text of Romans 8:28. How wonderful to hear of the patience of Job and to have seen that in the end, the Lord is a God of pity and mercy. A morning of joy always follows a night of sorrow.

In his trouble, Job found God. Many know God as Creator and believe in His greatness, but they do not really *know* God. The more we understand His ways, however, the more we will love Him and put our trust in Him.

Job "tore his robe" (Job 1:20). It is worthwhile for us to learn that we are meant to feel grief. Sorrow has its use in our lives. We are told, "Do not make light of the Lord's discipline" but be "trained by it" (Hebrews 12:5,11). "Jesus wept" (John 11:35)! Christ does not destroy our natural emotions. Jesus told the women of Jerusalem to weep for themselves and for their children (see Luke 23:28).

Job recognized that loss and sorrow are the laws of life. We have to learn that all possessions are transient. We are losing something every moment. We cannot stop and weep about everything that is taken from us. We have to learn a hard lesson: We can continue to live in spite of all our losses. Begin to learn while you are young that nothing is necessary but Christ.

The book of Job is rich:

- In philosophy—Ancient as the book is, it is filled with a divine record of human philosophy and our vain attempts to display wisdom. Human reason has never been able to go beyond the attempts made by Job's friends to explain the great mysteries of human experience (see 1 Corinthians 2:14; Colossians 2:8).

- In gems of spiritual truth—Be sure to make note of the following references: Job 1:21; 5:17; 13:15; 14:14; 16:21; 19:23-27; 23:10; 26:7-14; 28:12-28; 42:1-6. These are some of the most frequently quoted and best-loved passages in the Bible.

15

Understanding Psalms

Psalms Portrays Jesus Christ, Our All in All

SELECTED BIBLE READINGS

DAY OF THE WEEK		MAIN TOPIC
Sunday: Psalms 1; 19	Psalms of Law	
Monday: Psalms 29; 104	Psalms of Creation	
Tuesday: Psalms 52–53	Psalms of Judgment	
Wednesday: Psalms 22; 40–41	Psalms of Christ	
Thursday: Psalms 3; 31	Psalms of Life	
Friday: Psalms 37; 42	Psalms of the Heart	
Saturday: Psalms 90; 139	Psalms of God	

AUTHOR: The brief descriptions that introduce the psalms ascribe 73 psalms to David. David's personality and identity are clearly reflected in many of these psalms. While it is clear that David wrote many of the individual psalms, he is not the author of the entire collection. Two of the psalms are attributed to David's son, Solomon (see Psalms 72; 127). Psalm 90 is a prayer assigned to Moses. Another group of 12 psalms is ascribed to the family of Asaph (see Psalms 50; 73–83). The sons of Korah are named as authors of 11 psalms (see Psalms 42, 44–49, 84–85, 87–88). Psalm 88 is attributed to Heman, while Psalm 89 is assigned to Ethan the Ezrahite. With the exception of Solomon and Moses, all these additional authors were priests or Levites who were responsible for providing music for sanctuary worship during David's reign. Fifty of the psalms designate no specific person as author.

DATE: The psalms span a period of many centuries. The oldest psalm in the collection is probably the prayer of Moses, Psalm 90; it is a reflection on the frailty of humanity compared to the eternal nature and power of the Lord. The latest psalm may be Psalm 137, a song of lament clearly written during the days when the Jewish people were being held captive by the Babylonians, from about 605 to 539 BC.

PURPOSE AND SUMMARY: The book of Psalms is a collection of 150 psalms. The Hebrew name is translated "The Book of Praises." In the canon of the Hebrew Old Testament, the book is divided into five books matching the fivefold structure of the Torah, the first five books of Moses from Genesis to Deuteronomy. The book of Psalms was the worship book and the prayer book of ancient Israel. Israel prayed their worship songs and sang their prayers. The variety and unity of psalms have given this book a unique place in the devotional life of the individual and the Church. Almost every aspect of humanity's relation to God is depicted in the psalms: simple trust, the sense of sin, appeals to the Lord in time of trouble, and the conviction that the world is in the hands of a loving God.

"Come, let us sing for joy to the LORD; let us shout aloud to the Rock of our salvation" (Psalm 95:1). Here we see the panoramic nature of the book of Psalms. The sights that catch and hold our attention are so numerous that they defy exhaustive treatment in one short chapter.

"Ascribe to the LORD the glory due his name; worship the LORD in the splendor of his holiness" (Psalm 29:2). This is the key verse to the book of Psalms. The door into the temple of praise and prayer is open. Go in with the psalmist to rest and pray. It is a real privilege to be alone with God, away from the rush and busyness of everyday life.

No doubt Psalms is the best-loved book in the Old Testament. Someone has called it the solid gold of Christian experience. Dip into anywhere you choose and you will find a treasure.

Every psalm is a direct expression of the soul's consciousness of God. (Which psalms are you familiar with? Pause a moment to recall those psalms.)

The Hebrew title of this book is translated "The Book of Praises," which indicates that the contents of the book are praise, prayer and worship. The name "Psalms" comes from the Greek. We find that the early Christian fathers called this book the Psalter.

The book of Psalms is the national hymnbook of Israel. It contains 150 poems to be set to music for worship. Worship is the central idea. The psalms magnify and praise the Lord, exalting His attributes, His names, His Word and His goodness. Every human experience is related to Him.

We see the life of the believer pictured in all of life's experiences: joy and sorrow, victory and failure.

The psalms are full of Christ. They describe the whole program of His suffering and death. We even have Christ's own words to justify our looking for Him in the psalms. He said, "Everything must be fulfilled that is written about me in the Law of Moses, the Prophets and the Psalms" (Luke 24:44). So let us look and see what we can find:

- His prophetic office—Psalm 22:22
- His priestly office—Psalms 40:6,8; 22; 49; 110
- His kingly office—Psalms 2; 21; 45; 72
- His sufferings—Psalms 22; 69
- His resurrection—Psalm 16

Many quotations from the book of Psalms are found in the New Testament, and at least 20 of these directly refer to Christ and His life and death.

Another extremely useful classification of the psalms may be made according to the subjects of the individual psalms:

- Instruction—Psalms 1; 19; 39
- Praise—Psalms 8; 29; 93; 100
- Thanksgiving—Psalms 30; 65; 103; 107; 116

Psalms

- Penitence—Psalms 6; 32; 38; 51; 102; 130; 143
- Trust—Psalms 3; 27; 31; 46; 56; 62; 86
- Distress—Psalms 4; 13; 55; 64; 88
- Aspiration—Psalms 42; 63; 80; 84; 137
- History—Psalms 78; 105; 106
- Prophecy (psalms of the Messiah)—Psalms 2; 16; 22; 24; 40; 45; 68-69; 72; 97; 110; 118

We often speak of the psalms as the psalms of David, because he is considered the principal writer of them. He gives the keynote, and his voice rises highest in the sacred choir. Seventy-three of the 150 psalms are assigned to him. But there were other authors besides him. Moses wrote psalm 90. Solomon wrote two (72; 127). Besides these, Asaph (David's choir leader), the sons of Korah (a family of official musicians), and Jeduthun wrote some. Fifty are anonymous.

But we do not need be that concerned with finding out who wrote them. Let us rather read and enjoy these grand expressions of praise. They are about God and they are for you. Sing them and make them your own. Catch David's note and spirit. He wrote marching songs, prayer songs, rally songs, hilltop songs and confession songs. Sing as you march. Keep step with David and David's Lord all the way.

PSALMS 1–41: HUMANKIND

Psalms 1–41 are a collection of psalms that tell about the state of humankind—our blessedness, fall and recovery:

1. Humankind blessed—Psalm 1
2. Humankind fallen from our high position and at enmity with God—Psalms 2; 14
3. Humankind restored by our blessed Redeemer, Jesus—Psalms 16–41

Psalm 1 tells us of the road to success. Everyone wants to prosper. No one wishes to fail. The psalmist says that everyone may prosper. Think of it! It will be well for every young person to master the rules for success laid down here.

Things Not to Do (Psalm 1:1)

1. "Walk in step with the wicked"—Do not take advice from the ungodly or follow the pattern of their lives.

2. "Stand in the way that sinners take"—Standing in sin shows that you have been brought under the spell of evil.

3. "Sit in the company of mockers"—The scorner sits in the most despicable place possible, idly watching the struggles of others and does not care that many are losing the fight. You ask the scorner, "Isn't there great need in this world?" "I suppose," the scorner answers but just sits and plays the cynic. The scorner is sure that every minister, missionary or Christian worker is either a fool or a hypocrite.

Things to Do (Psalm 1:2)

1. Read the Bible.
2. "Delight" in the Bible.
3. Meditate on the Bible.

The more you read the Word, the more you want to. As one great Christian leader has said, "The gospel feeds you; then it makes you hungry." It never grows stale. You cannot read the Bible too often or too much.

Results of Obeying (Psalm 1:3)

When the Christian has followed the don'ts and dos, what is the result? Three things:

1. Planted—"That person is like a tree planted by streams of water." The Christian has a settled and steadfast life in luxuriant soil.

2. Purposeful—"which yields its fruit in season." The Christian has a productive life.

3. Prosperous—"and whose leaf does not wither." The Christian has an abiding, happy life.

Blessings from Christ's Work (Psalms 22–24)

Other psalms in this group show the final blessings of humankind because of the glorious work of Jesus:

- Psalm 22 tells of the Good Shepherd giving His life for His sheep. We see the cross and hear the cries of our dying Savior. As you read this psalm, you will recognize the facts.

- Psalm 23 tells of the great Shepherd keeping His sheep. We read, "The LORD is my shepherd, I lack nothing" (verse 1). He promises to guide us and provide for and keep us.

- Psalm 24 tells of the chief Shepherd, in His glory, rewarding His sheep. He is our King and He is coming to reign in power and great glory.

The Portrayal of Calvary (Psalm 22)

Psalm 22 gives a picture of Calvary. We see the crucifixion portrayed here more clearly than in any other part of the Old Testament. The psalm opens with the cry from our Lord in the darkest hour of His life: "My God, my God, why have you forsaken me?" (verse 1). It closes with, "He has done it!" (verse 31). The original Hebrew means "It is finished"—the last cry of the Savior (John 19:30).

Psalm 22:6 says, "But I am a worm and not a man, scorned by everyone, despised by the people." This tells us of the offense of the cross! Read and compare these verses:

- Psalm 22:1 with Matthew 27:46
- Psalm 22:6-7 with Luke 23:35-36
- Psalm 22:6-8 with Matthew 27:39,41,43
- Psalm 22:12-13 with Matthew 27:36,44
- Psalm 22:28 with 1 Corinthians 15:23-24

"I am poured out like water, and all my bones are out of joint. My heart has turned to wax; it has melted within me" (Psalm 22:14). This depicts excessive perspiration because of physical torture. It also indicates the breaking of Jesus' heart.

Jesus tells us why His heart was broken: "Scorn has broken my heart" (Psalm 69:20). In John 19:34-35, we read that not only to confirm His death but also as another sign of scorn, "one of the soldiers pierced Jesus' side with a spear, bringing a sudden flow of blood and water. The man who saw it has given testimony, and his testimony is true. He knows that he tells the truth, and he testifies so that you also may believe."

Death by a broken heart, caused by intense agony of suffering, is very rare. But Jesus bore reproach and shame for others. Bearing our sins hid Him from His Father's face—this is what really broke His heart.

"My tongue sticks to the roof of my mouth" (Psalm 22:15). This verse describes intense thirst. According to the account in the New Testament, "knowing that everything had now been finished, and so that the Scripture would be fulfilled, Jesus said, 'I am thirsty'" (John 19:28). Psalm 69:21 says, "They put gall in my food and gave me vinegar for my thirst." Read John 19:28-29.

"They pierce my hands and my feet" (Psalm 22:16). Crucifixion! The Roman method of death by crucifixion is described here: hands and feet nailed to the cross; bones of hands, arms, shoulders out of joint as a result of hanging from the cross, straining bone and muscle. Jewish law did not prescribe this method of punishment.

"They divide my clothes among them and cast lots for my garment" (Psalm 22:18). Even the act of the soldiers is described here. Read Matthew 27:35.

PSALMS 42–72: ISRAEL

Psalms 42-72 describe Israel:

1. Her ruin—Psalms 42–49
2. Her Redeemer—Psalms 50–60
3. Her redemption—Psalms 61–72

This collection of psalms opens with a cry from the depth of oppression, described in Psalm 42. It ends with the King reigning over the redeemed nation: "May he rule from sea to sea and from the River to the ends of the earth" (Psalm 72:8). Read this glorious psalm.

Several psalms speak of penitence, but the chief one is Psalm 51. It is a psalm of David. If you turn again to 2 Samuel 11–12, you will find the story of David's sin. After Nathan the prophet told David the story of the despicable fellow who took the only lamb belonging to a poor man, we hear him say to David, "You are the man!" (2 Samuel 12:7). David did not try to dodge the issue but said, "I have sinned against the LORD" (2 Samuel 12:13). Then Nathan reassured him, saying, "The LORD has taken away your sin" (2 Samuel 12:13).

We think it strange when we read that David, "a man after his [God's] own heart," would have broken God's law as he did (1 Samuel 13:14). But when we compare what other kings would have done under the same circumstances, we shouldn't be so surprised. At least David confessed and said, "I have sinned against the Lord." That is what sin is—breaking God's law.

Notice in Psalm 51:4 these words: "Against you, you only, have I sinned and done what is evil in your sight." This psalm is a prayer of contrition and confession. David cries for mercy from a God whom he knows is merciful and full of lovingkindness.

We learn from this psalm that we must confess our sins to God and that when we do, God will fulfill His gracious promise to forgive us (see also 1 John 1:9). Whenever we are sincere in our confession to God, He will cleanse us of our sins.

PSALMS 73–89: THE SANCTUARY

In this third section of the book of Psalms, we see that in almost every one, the sanctuary is mentioned or referred to. Here we learn what God's plans for the sanctuary are. The sanctuary is seen from its ruin to its restoration in the fullness of blessing.

PSALMS 90–106: THE EARTH

The first of this group of psalms was written during the wanderings in the wilderness, but the rest of the psalms are not arranged in chronological order.

- Blessing needed—Psalms 90–94
- Blessing anticipated—Psalms 95–100
- Blessing enjoyed—Psalms 101–106

Read the opening verses of Psalms 90 and 91 together: "Lord, you have been our dwelling place throughout all generations. Whoever dwells in the shelter of the Most High will rest in the shadow of the Almighty" (Psalms 90:1; 91:1). If God is our dwelling place on this earth, we shall live in confidence, sheltered by the Almighty. Christ says, "If you remain in me and my words remain in you, ask whatever you wish, and it will be done for you" (John 15:7). The secret of a godly life is to "remain in," or "abide in" (*KJV*), the Almighty.

When the devil attacked Him, the Lord quoted Psalm 91:11-12 (see Matthew 4:6). But Christ was victorious because He lived in the place described in this same psalm. We are told that there is a point of perfect calm at the center of a hurricane. There may be storms, snares, pestilences, terrors by night, darkness and destruction; but when the soul remains, or abides, under the shadow of the Almighty, it is safe.

If you wish to praise the Lord for His goodness, read Psalm 103. It is full of worship, adoration, praise and thanksgiving. This is great exercise for the soul.

PSALMS 107–150: GOD'S WORD

All the teaching in Psalms 107–150 focuses on the Word of God. The opening psalm of this section gives the key: "He sent out his word and healed them" (Psalm 107:20).

Psalm 119 is the greatest psalm of the whole book. It extols the Word of God, which is the great revelation of the heart and mind of the Lord. This book is "more desirable than gold, yes, than much fine gold; sweeter also than honey and the drippings of the honeycomb" (Psalm 19:10, *NASB*). Almost every verse speaks of God's Word or His law, precepts or statutes. And there are many reasons to value His Word:

1. It blesses little children—Matthew 19:14.
2. It strengthens young men—1 John 2:14.
3. It sanctifies and cleanses all who read it—Ephesians 5:26.
4. It protects the widows—Exodus 22:22-23.
5. It honors the elderly—Leviticus 19:32.
6. It offers eternal life to everyone—John 3:36.

Praise is the highest duty that any creature can perform. And this is man's chief end—to glorify God. There is no heaven either here or in the world to come for people who do not praise God. If you do not enter into the spirit and worship of God in heaven, the spirit and joy of heaven cannot enter you!

POINTS TO REMEMBER

The book of Psalms begins with the word "blessed." This word is multiplied many times over in this book. The book seems to be built around this first word.

Probably no other book has so largely influenced turning points in people's lives, given expression to their deepest experiences and woven itself into every fiber of their characters.

Hold your Bible in your hand and turn to the middle of the book. Most often you will open to the book of Psalms. Not merely is this true physically, but it also signifies a deeper truth: The psalms are central in human experience.

This book has been and still is used by Hebrews and Christians alike. Many of the psalms were, in fact, specifically meant to be used in the Temple. They were all written to reflect the heart of the worshiper of God; and they are for all who are in need: the sick and suffering, the poor and needy, the prisoner and exile, the person in danger, the persecuted. Or, if you have an abounding joy, the words are there for you, too. When you find yourself in deep need, you can always find a psalm that expresses your inner-most feeling.

The book of Psalms is for the sinner, telling him or her of God's great mercy and forgiveness. It is a book for the child of God, leading him or her into new experiences with the Lord. It is a book that tells of God's perfect law and pronounces blessings upon the one who will keep it.

Psalms

Understanding Proverbs, Ecclesiastes and Song of Solomon

Proverbs Portrays Jesus Christ, Our Wisdom; Ecclesiastes Portrays Jesus Christ, the End of All Living; Song of Solomon Portrays Jesus Christ, the Lover of Our Souls

SELECTED BIBLE READINGS

DAY OF THE WEEK		MAIN TOPIC
Sunday: Proverbs 1–4	Get Wisdom	
Monday: Proverbs 5–7	Avoid Adultery and Folly	
Tuesday: Proverbs 15–17	Follow Right Actions	
Wednesday: Proverbs 20; 22; 31	Heed Wise Words	
Thursday: Ecclesiastes 1–3	Accept Your Limitations	
Friday: Ecclesiastes 11–12	Find Meaning in God	
Saturday: Song of Solomon 1:1-7; 2:1-7	Value Love	

UNDERSTANDING PROVERBS

AUTHOR: King Solomon was the principal writer of Proverbs. Solomon's name appears in Proverbs 1:1; 10:1; 25:1. We may also assume that Solomon collected and edited proverbs other than his own, since Ecclesiastes 12:9 says, "Not only was the Teacher wise, but he also imparted knowledge to the people. He pondered and searched out and set in order many proverbs." The Hebrew title of the book, *Mishle Shlomoh,* is translated "Proverbs of Solomon."

DATE: Solomon's proverbs were penned around 950 BC. During his reign as king, the nation of Israel experienced a golden age—spiritually, politically, culturally and economically. Foreign rulers from distant countries traveled great distances to listen to Solomon's wisdom (see 1 Kings 4:34).

PURPOSE AND SUMMARY: This book is a collection of proverbs and wisdom teachings. Although Solomon inspired the development of the book, its entire content was completed after Solomon's lifetime (see Proverbs 25:1). A proverb is a short, wisdom saying with practical implications. The ones included in the book of Proverbs cover a variety of subjects: listening to God's voice for wisdom; chastity; control of the tongue; laziness; knowledge; relations with others; and justice, among others. Perhaps above everything else in the book, there is the reiterated assertion that true wisdom comes from seeking the Lord and turning away from evil ("the fear of the LORD is the beginning of knowledge" [Proverbs 1:7]).

The books identified as poetical (Job, Psalms, Proverbs, Ecclesiastes and Song of Solomon) are poetical in their form only, not in the sense that they are fanciful or unreal. And although there is no meter or rhyme, there is, rather, the expression of a parallel thought rhyme—repeating the same thought in different words:

- In Psalms we find Christians on their knees—in Proverbs we find Christians on their feet.
- The Psalms are for the Christian's devotions—the proverbs are for the Christian's walk.
- The Psalms are for the prayer closet—the proverbs are for the business place, the home and the playground.

We find in Proverbs that godliness is practical. Every relationship in life is mentioned. We find our duty to God and to our neighbors, the duty of parents and children, our obligations as citizens.

The Jewish people likened the book of Proverbs to the outer court of the Temple, Ecclesiastes to the holy place, and the Song of Solomon to the holy of holies. Remember that the altar of burnt offering and the laver of cleansing were in the outer court. If we come to the book of Proverbs with a cleansed and surrendered heart and mind, we will get the most out of the book.

Rules for Everyday Living

The book of Proverbs takes us to the outer court of the congregation where the people are. Here they live their daily lives and jostle each other on the highways of life. This is a book for everyday instruction. It deals with the practical affairs of life. The author, Solomon, wrote more wisely than he lived. The wise give heed to the commands of God and obey them. The foolish ignore God's will. This book divides people into two classes—wise and foolish.

Notice how the book opens: "The proverbs of Solomon" (Proverbs 1:1). Solomon was a great king, famous for his wisdom and riches. He wrote 3,000 proverbs and 1,005 songs (see 1 Kings 4:31-32). Solomon was peculiarly qualified to write this book. God had given Solomon "wisdom and very great insight, and a breadth of understanding as measureless as the sand on the seashore" (1 Kings 4:29). Solomon was a philosopher; he was a scientist of no mean ability. He was an architect of a temple that was one of the wonders of the world; and, of course, he was also a king.

That Solomon was the author of this book implies no more than that he took the lead in gathering these sayings, which were probably already current among the people, given by the Holy Spirit through the centuries, and put them into the orderly arrangement we have today. See what Solomon said about this in Ecclesiastes 12:9: "He pondered and searched out and set in order many proverbs."

There are actually several names given in the book regarding authorship:

- Solomon—Proverbs 1:1; 25:1
- The wise—Proverbs 22:17
- Men of Hezekiah—Proverbs 25:1

Proverbs

- Agur—Proverbs 30:1
- King Lemuel and his mother—Proverbs 31:1

Proverbs is divided into three sections:

1. Advice for young people—Proverbs 1–10
2. Advice for all people—Proverbs 11–20
3. Advice for all rulers—Proverbs 21–31

The book closes with one of the most beautiful chapters in the Word: Proverbs 31, a chapter about women's rights. "Honor her for all that her hands have done, and let her works bring her praise at the city gate" (verse 31). Wherever Christ goes, womanhood is lifted up. In non-Christian countries, where Christ is not known, a woman is rarely more than a chattel or a slave. In Christian lands, a woman is equal to a man.

Rules for Righteousness

This book presents a system of conduct for life. You cannot find any agnosticism here. The existence of God is assumed. Be wise and find God's way for your life! This book is to provide rules for the righteous life. "Blessed are those who find wisdom, those who gain understanding" (Proverbs 3:13).

The real power and beauty in this book are in the true meaning of the word "wisdom." It is evident that this word means more than mere knowledge. In fact, the wisdom of Proverbs is embodied in the Incarnate Word of the New Testament. Christ Himself is in this book (see Luke 24:27).

Wisdom is represented as dwelling with God from all eternity: "I was formed long ago, at the very beginning, when the world came to be. . . . I was there when he set the heavens in place, when he marked out the horizon on the face of the deep . . . and when he marked out the foundations of the earth. Then I was constantly at his side" (Proverbs 8:23-30). Compare these verses with John 1:1-2; Hebrews 1:2; Colossians 1:15-16; 2:3. Jesus was the designer of the universe.

When you read the book of Proverbs, put "Christ" in place of "wisdom" in the verse (see 1 Corinthians 1:30). You will then begin to understand the wonderful power that is in this book. "We know also that the Son of God has come and has given us understanding, so that we may know him who is true" (1 John 5:20).

Some of God's Wisdom

The purpose of the book of Proverbs is stated clearly at the beginning, in Proverbs 1:2-3: "For gaining wisdom and instruction; for understanding words of insight; for receiving instruction in prudent behavior, doing what is right and just and fair." This book is the true college of spirit education of the self—God wants to give us instruction "for giving prudence to those who are simple, knowledge and discretion to the young" (Proverbs 1:4). God wants us to have and to use in life plain common sense. The most uncommon thing in the world today is common sense. Don't be a fool!

God wants to give us some of His wisdom—the wisdom that created the heavens and the earth—so that we can use it as a guide for all of life (see James 1:5). Everyone practicing what the proverbs say to do would put an end to all the confusion and evil in this world, wouldn't it? Human wisdom can never solve life's problems, but God's wisdom can, for only God knows the ways of people.

How do we start to gain God's wisdom? "The fear of the Lord is the beginning of wisdom" (Proverbs 9:10; Psalm 111:10; see also Proverbs 1:7). The fear of the Lord spoken of here is not a fear of fright but a fear like that of a son who is afraid he might cause his loving father pain. It is the fear that comes from love, the fear of displeasing the Lord, that leads to godliness. We shall not begin to be wise until our lives are in right relation with Christ, the source of all wisdom. "The beginning of wisdom is this: Get wisdom. Though it cost all you have, get understanding" (Proverbs 4:7).

PROVERBS 1–10: ADVICE FOR YOUNG PEOPLE

The whole book of Proverbs is extremely practical. It would be well for us all to give it closer study for our guidance in daily life:

"In all your ways submit to him, and he will make your paths straight" (Proverbs 3:6). This is the Lord's rule for our feet. We need to turn away from the way of evil: "Avoid it, do not travel on it; turn from it and go on your way" (Proverbs 4:15). This is God's "Stop! Look! Listen!"

- Wise up! Worship is the first step to wisdom (Proverbs 1:7).
- Walk straight! The straight and narrow has the lowest accident rate (Proverbs 2:20).
- Ask God for directions! Ask God about everything: He knows every road (Proverbs 3:6).
- Watch your step! Every step helps mold character; step well (Proverbs 4:26).
- Avoid God's blacklist! At all costs, do not ever be guilty of pride, lying, murder, deceit, mischief, betrayal or discord (Proverbs 6:17-19).
- Avoid bad women! Read carefully Proverbs 7:15-27.
- Seek wisdom rather than riches! Rubies of wisdom command the highest prices on the market of character values (Proverbs 8:11).
- Let good sense prevail! Nothing you should not do is ever more fun than what you should do. Wait until you see what results from doing wrong (Proverbs 9:17-18).
- Silence wanted! Wordy people seldom are wise people (Proverbs 10:19).

In Proverbs 4:23-26, we find that the whole body is to be controlled:

- "Guard your heart" (verse 23).
- "Keep your mouth free of perversity" (verse 24).
- "Let your eyes look straight ahead" (verse 25).
- "Give careful thought to the paths for your feet" (verse 26).

Young people are also advised to not resent discipline (see Proverbs 3:11-12). One of the duties of parents is to discipline their children and is based upon *God's* disciplining *His* children (see Hebrews 12:7-11). One of the signs of the last wicked days upon the earth is given by Paul as "people will be . . . disobedient to their parents" (2 Timothy 3:2). What happened to Eli and his boys because he allowed his sons to sin? Read 1 Samuel 4:11-22.

The young are also warned against the influence of bad companions, against impurity and intoxication, against anger, and against participating in quarrels and bitter struggles (see Proverbs 1:10-19; 4:14-19; 19; see also Proverbs 3; 10; 13; 15–16; 18).

Much is said about guarding the tongue, for "the tongue has the power of life and death" (Proverbs 18:21; see also Proverbs 12:22). There are many sins of the tongue. We use it too freely. Too many people lie and are deceitful in their dealings with others.

Read about pride and its consequences in Proverbs 8; 11; 16:18; 19. The Lord wants us always to be humble before Him and not to esteem ourselves better than others. Every truly great person is humble. Remember that the only way that it will be possible to follow all of these wise instructions is to have Christ, the wisdom of God, within us.

PROVERBS 11–20: ADVICE FOR ALL PEOPLE

There has never been a time when people did as well as they knew how. People have simply never lived up to the instructions they've been given, but the last thing a person could complain of is a lack of good advice about a great many subjects:

- False economy—A gift is never lost; only what is selfishly kept impoverishes (Proverbs 11:24).

- Fools—You cannot convince a fool of his or her folly; only a wise person will accept a rebuke for foolhardiness (Proverbs 12:15).

- Lying—Righteousness and lying are enemies; to a wicked person they are synonymous (Proverbs 13:5).

- Arguing—Two people ought not to get angry at the same time (Proverbs 15:1).

Proverbs

- Sin—A person deep in wickedness will invent other names for his or her wickedness, but a sin by any other name is still a sin (Proverbs 16:2).

- Friends—Companions must be chosen for their reliability to do good (Proverbs 18:24).

- Alcohol—When you decide for strong drink, don't be surprised when it decides against you (Proverbs 20:1). In Scripture, drunkenness is roundly condemned with other severe sins: "Do you not know that wrongdoers will not inherit the kingdom of God? Do not be deceived: Neither the sexually immoral nor idolaters nor adulterers nor men who have sex with men nor thieves nor the greedy nor drunkards nor slanderers nor swindlers will inherit the kingdom of God" (1 Corinthians 6:9-10).

- Profiteering—Holding something back so that a higher price can be exacted during a time of need is unethical (Proverbs 11:26).

- Legacy—"The righteous lead blameless lives; blessed are their children after them" (Proverbs 20:7). The *Douay-Rheims* version of the Bible reads: "The just that walketh in his simplicity, shall leave behind him blessed children." This is a good man's legacy to the world. Godly parents are also a blessing to their children and should instruct them in the right way (see Proverbs 22:6).

PROVERBS 21–31: ADVICE FOR ALL RULERS

- Self-Control—A guarded mouth makes for an untroubled soul (Proverbs 21:23).

- Reputation—Choose a good name rather than great riches. Your name goes on; your wealth stops at death (Proverbs 22:1).

- Sobriety—Red wine (and various pills and powders) are colorful but calamitous (Proverbs 23:31).

Proverbs

- Advice—The sober judgment of a sane-thinking group is more reliable than your own opinion (Proverbs 24:6).

- Women—Solitude is better than being in a house with a nagging woman (Proverbs 25:24).

- Gossip—A fire will go out when the fuel for it is gone; rumors stop when mouths are stopped (Proverbs 26:20).

- Future—There is never a guaranteed tomorrow, only today. Get what needs to be done now, for today soon becomes yesterday (Proverbs 27:1).

- Understanding—Wealth does not guarantee an understanding heart (Proverbs 28:11).

- Bribes—When those in power seek justice, our land will stand; when they accept bribes, our land will fall (Proverbs 29:4).

- Security—A trust in God is the only safe soul armor (Proverbs 30:5).

POINTS TO REMEMBER

The words in Proverbs are "like apples of gold in settings of silver" (Proverbs 25:11). Study the picture, but do not miss the apples of gold depicted here.

Proverbs is an intensely practical book, exposing a series of traps that would ensnare us. "There is no wisdom, no insight, no plan that can succeed against the LORD" (Proverbs 21:30). At last we see God's will and God's way! Hasten it, O Lord!

UNDERSTANDING ECCLESIASTES

AUTHOR: The book of Ecclesiastes does not directly identify its author. There are quite a few verses that imply Solomon wrote this book. There are also, however, some clues in the text that may suggest that a different person wrote the book after Solomon's death, possibly several hundred years later, but wrote it as a commentary on Solomon's wisdom and Solomon's falling away from obedience to the Lord at the end of his life. In any case, Jewish and Christian traditions hold that the author was Solomon.

DATE: Solomon's reign as king of Israel lasted from 970 BC to 930 BC. The book of Ecclesiastes may have been written toward the end of Solomon's reign, possibly 935 BC, or possibly later by a leader writing a commentary on Solomon's wisdom and his failures.

PURPOSE AND SUMMARY: In English, the Hebrew title of the book, *Qohelet*, means "Preacher." Traditionally held to have been written by Solomon, this book is now almost universally recognized as a commentary *about* him rather than *by* him. The author's purpose is to prove that everything "under the sun" by itself, apart from God, is vain and empty and that the only true good comes from doing all we do conscious of God's eternal goodness (Ecclesiastes 3:16; see also verses 11-14). The vanity of all things apart from God is first announced as a fact and then proved from Preacher's experience and observations. Finally, the author shows that the fullness of life is a gift from God and is not the result of man's striving or working for it (see Ecclesiastes 3:13; 5:19).

Jesus is the beginning of all in Proverbs—He is the end of all in Ecclesiastes; He is the supreme good from whom everything of life comes.

Wisdom in Proverbs is piety—wisdom in Ecclesiastes is prudence and sagacity.

Ecclesiastes is the soul's autobiography, or the book of experience. The book's key word is "vanity" (Ecclesiastes 2:11, *KJV*), or "meaningless" (*NIV*).

You do not have to go outside the Bible to find the human philosophy of life. God has given us in the book of Ecclesiastes the record of all that human thinking and natural religion have ever been able to discover concerning the meaning and goal of life. The arguments in the book, therefore, are not God's arguments, but God's record of people's arguments. This explains why such passages as 1:15; 2:24; 3:3-4,8,11,19-20 and 8:15 are in stark contrast to the rest of the Bible.

The writer, for the most part, is Solomon; and the book is a dramatic autobiography of his experiences and reflections while he was out of fellowship with God. The name "Ecclesiastes" means "Preacher," and the book is so named because it contains the meditations and sermons of the wise man, Solomon.

Solomon may have been wise, but he did not follow his own wisdom. Ecclesiastes has its origin in his tragic sin of forsaking God and seeking satisfaction in philosophy and science "under the sun"; that is, based only on speculation and thought. The inference of the book that "all was vanity and vexation of spirit" (Ecclesiastes 2:11, *KJV*), or "meaningless, a chasing after the wind" (*NIV*) is inevitable. The message of Ecclesiastes is that, apart from God, life is full of weariness and disappointment.

The problem that faced Solomon was how he could find happiness and satisfaction apart from God (see Ecclesiastes 1:1-3). He sought satisfaction in science (see Ecclesiastes 1:4-11) but could get no answer. He sought it in philosophy (see Ecclesiastes 1:12-18) but in vain; he found pleasure in mirth (see Ecclesiastes 2:1), drinking (see Ecclesiastes 2:3), building (see Ecclesiastes 2:4), possessions (see Ecclesiastes 2:5-7), wealth and music (see Ecclesiastes 2:8); but they were all empty.

He tried materialism (see Ecclesiastes 2:12-26), fatalism (see Ecclesiastes 3:1-15) and deism (see Ecclesiastes 3–4), but these likewise were vain pursuits. Natural religion (see Ecclesiastes 5:1-8), wealth (see Ecclesiastes 5:9-6) and even morality (see Ecclesiastes 7–12:12) proved equally fruitless.

The conclusion is found in Ecclesiastes 12:13 and is the best thing possible for people under the Law: "Fear God and keep his commandments." It is interesting to notice the place of youth in the argument (see Ecclesiastes 11:9–12:1). We must begin to know God when we are young, if we are to find life worth living.

Remember, Ecclesiastes only shows us the best that people can do apart from God's gospel of grace.

ECCLESIASTES 1–7: CONFESSION

The great question "Is life worth living?" is presented at the very beginning of the book of Ecclesiastes. Solomon tested a wide range of answers to that question. No man could have better done the testing or told about it—and the answer he ultimately found is reassuring for us even today.

Try wisdom (see Ecclesiastes 1)! What better thing is there in all the world? Solomon declared, "I applied myself to the understanding of wisdom" (Ecclesiastes 1:17). Yet even here he was forced to cry out that he had been "chasing after the wind. For with much wisdom comes much sorrow; the more knowledge, the more grief" (Ecclesiastes 1:17-18). This is always true of mere earthly wisdom. But "The fear of the LORD is the beginning of wisdom" (Psalm 111:10).

Try pleasure (see Ecclesiastes 2)! "I said to myself, 'Come now, I will test you with pleasure to find out what is good.' But that also proved to be meaningless" (verse 1). This was *his* deliberate conclusion. God made us all to be joyful and has given us a thousand avenues of enjoyment. Let us not sacrifice true happiness for questionable pleasure. Always make your recreation a re-creation.

Try amusements (see Ecclesiastes 2:2,8)! Philosophy failed, said the preacher, so let merriment be tried. Music, dance, wine (not to excess), the funny story, the clever repartee—these were cultivated. (On television, *Monday Night Football* will outdraw *Masterpiece Theatre* every time.) Clowns were now welcomed to the court, where only grave philosophy had been. The halls of the palace echoed with laughter and gaiety. Yet after a while, all this palled on the king's taste. He even went so far as to say that "laughter . . . is madness" (Ecclesiastes 2:2). Cheerfulness, however, *is* admirable. A hearty laugh in its proper place is delightful. It is the person who is always giggling who is a bore.

Try architecture (see Ecclesiastes 2:4)! Then he became practical. He attended to great works of state. Aqueducts, pools, palaces and other public buildings occupied his thoughts and actions. He now frowned upon court fools and welcomed great architects to the palace. But the excitement in building soon faded away.

Try gardening (see Ecclesiastes 2:5-6)! Vineyards, gardens, orchards, rare flowers, tropical plants became all the rage. Jerusalem and the surrounding areas bloomed like the Garden of Eden. But, like a new toy for a child, it pleased for a while but was soon tossed away.

Try livestock and artwork (see Ecclesiastes 2:7-8)! Then the king tried cattle breeding, art collecting and even music. Choruses and orchestras gathered in the royal palace. But even though "music has charms," it is powerless to charm with permanent happiness.

Try just typical day-to-day living—with discretion (see Ecclesiastes 3)! But again, "What benefit or gain is there?" (see verse 9; compare with 1:3; 2:11; 5:11,16; 6:11). Vanity of vanities!

Try the stoic's philosophy (see Ecclesiastes 4)! Surely this also is meaningless. He wailed, "This too is meaningless, a chasing after the wind" (verse 16)!

Try ritualism, or formal religion (see Ecclesiastes 5)! Be sure that "when you make a vow to God, do not delay to fulfill it" (verse 4). But this, too, was found to be meaningless.

Try wealth (see Ecclesiastes 6)! Solomon had it. He was a man to whom God had given "wealth, possessions and honor . . . but God does not grant them the ability to enjoy them, and strangers enjoy them instead. This is meaningless, a grievous evil" (verse 2). Many agree with Solomon in the emptiness of pleasures, but they still make money their supreme goal in life. Jesus told us to seek first the kingdom of God and His righteousness, and all these things would be added (see Matthew 6:33).

Try reputation (see Ecclesiastes 7)! "A good name is better than fine perfume, and the day of death better than the day of birth" (verse 1). It doesn't last long in this world. People are soon forgotten when they die. Vanity still!

Ecclesiastes

ECCLESIASTES 8–12: ADMONITION

Now comes the turning point. Ecclesiastes 8:12 says, "I know that it will go better with those who fear God, who are reverent before him." The full meaning of this is found in the last chapter: "Fear God and keep his commandments, for this is the duty of mankind" (Ecclesiastes 12:13).

The preacher had been looking out and back and around. In the end, he looked up and he saw God and was satisfied.

POINTS TO REMEMBER

The phrase "under the sun" (Ecclesiastes 1:3) is found 28 times in this little book. The under-the-sun life is hardly worth living; but above the sun, and in the heavenlies that Paul describes, life is glorious (see Ephesians 1).

Dr. Arthur Pierson, an American missionary statesman and pastor, once well said, "The key to Ecclesiastes is that a man is too big for this world." Dissatisfaction exists among the poor and rich alike, among the ignorant and learned, among people and kings. We find that according to this book, we can never find satisfaction and happiness in this world. True happiness apart from Christ is impossible.

The last chapter of Ecclesiastes is a call to the young to lay the foundations of faith early: "Remember your Creator in the days of your youth" (Ecclesiastes 12:1). The greatest proportion of men and women who are living to serve God chose Him in childhood.

This book is given as a danger sign so that we may be spared having to learn the bitter truth about life: Seeking happiness in earthly things is an empty pursuit.

UNDERSTANDING SONG OF SOLOMON

AUTHOR: Solomon may have written the Song of Solomon, or someone else may have written the book about Solomon's falling into sexual sin and amassing a large harem of wives at the end of his life. According to the first verse in the Hebrew text, where the title of the book is "Solomon's Song of Songs," the book was written by Solomon or regarding him ("The Song of Songs which is by Solomon" or "The Song of Songs which is about Solomon"). The title "Song of Songs" is a superlative, meaning this is the best song out of all songs.

DATE: Solomon may have written this song during the early part of his reign, around 965 BC; or it may have been written later than Solomon's reign, if someone else wrote it.

PURPOSE AND SUMMARY: This book, the only one in the Bible that has love as its sole theme, is actually a collection of sequential marriage songs. The song is didactic and moral in its purpose, showing that marriage and sexual faithfulness to one's spouse is God's highest call for men and women. The song has also been traditionally interpreted as showing God's love for His Chosen People and as showing Christ's love for His Bride, the Church.

The Song of Solomon has been called the Christian's love song. The key text is Song of Solomon 6:3.

This is a song of love in marriage in Middle Eastern language and imagery. The characters in the song are Solomon, the Shulammite maid and the daughters of Jerusalem. The love of Solomon and the maid illustrates the love between Jehovah and His people. This is seen in many passages in the Bible. Moreover, Solomon as a lover was a type of Christ (see Ephesians 5). Personal love of Christ is the greatest need of the Church today. The knowledge of sin forgiven and of Christ's redeeming work continues to draw us to Him.

Song of Solomon

Books of the Major Prophets

of the Old Testament

ISAIAH • JEREMIAH

LAMENTATIONS • EZEKIEL

DANIEL

Key Events of the Books of the Major Prophets

Books of the Major Prophets: God Is the Sovereign of History

The major prophets wrote from the eighth to the sixth centuries before Christ, as nations were rising and falling ① around Israel, and idolatry ② and injustice were endemic in Israel. The major prophets teach us that God has a plan for history and that through the coming Messiah He will eventually subdue all His enemies under His feet and bring peace ③ to the Earth. The major prophets also vividly teach us that God is deeply concerned with moral integrity and justice in our daily lives.

Understanding Isaiah

Isaiah Portrays Jesus Christ, the Messiah

AUTHOR: Isaiah 1:1 identifies the author of the book of Isaiah as the prophet Isaiah.

DATE: The book of Isaiah was written between 739 and 681 BC, the dates of Isaiah's prophetic ministry.

PURPOSE AND SUMMARY: This book, as is true of all the prophetical books, derives its name from the prophet whose messages it records. The unity of Isaiah, a problem related to authorship and contents, has been the subject of much debate. The message of the book is twofold: judgment upon Judah for her sins (see Isaiah 1–39), and comfort and hope for an exiled people (see Isaiah 40–66). In these messages of encouragement are found some of the most graphic portrayals of the Messiah in the Old Testament.

INTRODUCTION TO THE PROPHETICAL BOOKS

The poetical books belong to the golden age of the nation of Israel—the prophetical books belong to the dark ages of God's Chosen People.

Let us find the scriptural definition of a prophet. Read Deuteronomy 18:18: "I will raise up for them a prophet like you [Moses] from among their fellow Israelites, and I will put my words in his mouth. He will tell them everything I command him." Also note verse 19: "I myself will call him to account anyone who does not listen to my words that the prophet speaks in my name."

Prophecy is God's revelation of His plans to His children. So important is prophecy in God's Word that it occupies about one third of the whole Bible.

The office of prophet was instituted in Samuel's time. When the kingdom was divided and Judah and Israel were established as separate monarchies, the great prophets appeared.

The prophets were men whom God raised up during the dark days of Israel's history. They were the evangelists of the day, the religious patriots of the hour. These prophets spoke fearlessly to kings and people alike of their sins and failures. Read what God said about them in 2 Kings 17:13: "The Lord warned Israel and Judah through all his prophets and seers: 'Turn from your evil ways. Observe my commands and decrees, in accordance with the entire Law that I commanded your ancestors to obey and that I delivered to you through my servants the prophets.'"

The period of the prophets in Israel covered 500 years, from the tenth to the fifth century BC. Then the voices of the prophets were silenced until John the Baptist.

The 500-year time period during which the prophets spoke encompassed the Assyrian captivity of Israel (the northern kingdom) and the Babylonian captivity of Judah (the southern kingdom). The record of these is found in 2 Kings 17:1-23; 24:11–25:21.

Isaiah

Some of the prophets served before the exile (pre-exilic), some during (exilic) and some afterwards (post-exilic).

The prophets before the exile (or pre-exilic prophets), in chronological order of their writings, were Obadiah, Joel, Jonah, Amos, Hosea, Isaiah, Micah, Nahum, Habakkuk, Zephaniah and Jeremiah. The pre-exilic prophets to Israel were Jonah, Amos and Hosea. The pre-exilic prophets to Judah were Obadiah, Joel, Isaiah, Micah, Nahum, Habakkuk, Zephaniah and Jeremiah.

The exilic prophets (during the exile, or captivity, in Babylon) were Ezekiel and Daniel. They prophesied to all the Israelites. Jeremiah's lifetime also extended into this period. The post-exilic prophets (those who prophesied after the exile) were Haggai, Zechariah and Malachi.

The intended hearers of the prophets were as follows:

- Israel—Amos, Hosea and Ezekiel
- Nineveh—Jonah and Nahum
- Babylon—Daniel
- Edom—Obadiah
- Judah—Joel, Isaiah, Micah, Jeremiah, Habakkuk, Zephaniah, Haggai, Zechariah and Malachi

There are 17 prophetical books in the Old Testament (including Lamentations). They are subdivided into 4 major and 12 minor prophets. This classification is made not because of their importance but because of the length of their writings.

THE MESSAGE OF EACH PROPHET

Although each prophet stated some timeless general principles, the prophet's chief duty was to deal with the moral and religious life of his own people during his day. A prophet was never sent while the nation was walking in obedience to God. All the writings include rebukes, because of the bad conditions that existed at the time the prophecies were given. Nothing was general about the prophet's denunciations and reprimands. The prophet's remarks were always very pointed and were meant for the particular people the prophet addressed.

The prophet was always an Israelite. He not only spoke of judgment that would come to pass to the people because of their sin, but he also was a foreteller of future events. The events of which he spoke mainly concerned the nation of Israel. Other peoples were mentioned only as they came in contact with Israel.

Let us note some of the prophecies of the future that are recounted. Keep these in mind as you study the prophetical books:

1. The dispersion and captivity of God's Chosen People—The Jews are to be scattered among the nations of the world.

2. The coming of the Messiah—Most religious Jews were and are still looking for their Messiah.

3. The restoration of the Chosen People to their own land under the coming Messiah, David's greater Son—Millions of Jewish people from the four corners of the earth have returned to Israel to dwell in the Promised Land, and it seems as if almost all Jewish people have a longing in their hearts to be a part of Israel as a nation.

4. The reign of the Messiah over the whole earth—Even though we see the collapse of God's people in the Old Testament—first Israel and then Judah being led into captivity—God revealed that the ending of His nation did not end His plans for His people. There is yet to be a glorious future when the Prince of Peace will reign over His people and sway His scepter "from sea to sea and from the River to the ends of the earth" (Psalm 72:8).

The prophets foretold the failure and the restoration of the Chosen People and the coming of the Messiah. Each prophet showed how God was going to bring to pass His purposes through the Messiah. Most religious leaders during Christ's time on earth failed to recognize Jesus as the promised Messiah: "He came to that

Isaiah

which was his own, but his own did not receive him" (John 1:11). The Messiah came to establish His kingdom, but the religious leaders rejected Him (see John 19:15). However, His kingdom will be established over the whole earth some time in the future.

G. Campbell Morgan said that there were three elements in the message of the prophets:

1. A message to their own age, directly from God
2. A message of predicted future events
   (a) The failure of God's Chosen People and God's judgment upon them and the nations around them
   (b) The coming of the Messiah and His rejection and final glory
   (c) The Messianic Kingdom ultimately to be established on the earth
3. A living message to our own age (eternal principles of right and wrong)

When you read the Gospels, you constantly find phrases such as "so was fulfilled what the Lord had said" and "to fulfill what was spoken through the prophet." After examining these passages, we find that God fulfills prophecy literally. Learn to interpret the meaning of the words of the prophets in a literal, natural way. Do not force a spiritual interpretation and thus miss the real meaning. There are, of course, figurative passages also. But you will find that as soon as you determine the meaning of the imagery, they, too, will have been fulfilled literally. This method makes the study of the prophets a simple one.

THE CHARACTER OF THE PROPHETS

The prophets were fearless men. They denounced the sins of their day. They called people away from idols and back to God. It is true that the prophets were concerned about the moral and political corruption of the nation, but the fact that the people were

Isaiah

worshiping idols was their greatest concern. The nation had a wrong attitude toward God. Christ gave us a succinct statement of what our attitude should be: "Love the Lord your God with all your heart and with all your soul and with all your strength and with all your mind" (Luke 10:27).

The prophets were the most unpopular men in their day, for they dealt with the sinful conditions of the people. Prophets were sent when the nation was out of step with God—when they were walking in disobedience. Truth is seldom popular with the sinner.

God knows that what someone's attitude is toward God will affect that person's whole moral life. Creed always determines conduct. This is true not only of individuals but also of nations. The adage "It makes no difference what a man believes as long as he is sincere" is completely refuted by the prophets.

The prophets exposed the cold formalism of their religion. They constantly reminded the people that Jehovah was the only true God. They pointed the people to the Law. The prophets were statesmen of the highest order. They were prophets in that they came to tell forth what God said. They were not only forth-tellers but also fore-tellers.

The Spirit of God spoke through the prophets: "as he said through his holy prophets of long ago" (Luke 1:70). Read 2 Peter 1:21; Jeremiah 1:9; Ezekiel 2:7 to find how the message was given. Read Luke 24:25-27 to learn what Christ said of the prophets.

The prophecies concerning Christ Himself are so definite that it gives great assurance to us that the Bible is the Word of God.

UNDERSTANDING ISAIAH

God puts a telescope before the eyes of the prophets and lets them look far into the future. We find that this spirit of expectation is especially prevalent in Isaiah, where the keynote is salvation. We hear the prophet cry, "He is coming!" Isaiah was truly a man of vision; in fact, his name means "Jehovah saves." Read the

Isaiah

opening words: "The vision concerning Judah and Jerusalem that Isaiah son of Amoz saw" (Isaiah 1:1).

Isaiah was a man who certainly spoke boldly during his own time, but as a prophet, he spoke of the future as well; hence, he is the prophet for all times. We sit at his feet today, and following his index finger as it points into the future, we hear him say, "Lo, your King!"

This great statesman was the prophet of Judah, the southern kingdom. He lived at the time that Israel, the northern kingdom, was destroyed by Assyria. Isaiah was the one whose voice saved the kingdom of Judah during those trying times.

It is interesting to note that this is also the time of Romulus and Remus and the founding of Rome. The traditional date of the building of Rome is 753 BC, just a few years after the birth of the prophet Isaiah. About this time Sparta and Athens in Greece were also founded.

Isaiah told of the judgment that must fall on Judah because she would not fulfill her mission in the world. But throughout the book, we find the ultimate triumph of God's plan through His appointed Servant, the Lord Jesus Christ, who would win final victory through suffering and death (see Isaiah 53).

Two Emphases

The book of Isaiah is written with two distinct emphases. Because of this, some Bible scholars believe that there was more than one author. This need not be the case. Rather, it is the work of one man with two messages. In the first part of the book, Isaiah pictured Israel. In the last part of the book, the prophet described seeing Jesus bearing our load of sin and then Christ exalted and glorified; and then Isaiah loudly proclaimed his vision from the housetop. It is the same prophet all the time, but he adapted his language to the theme at hand.

The only way to understand Isaiah is to understand the prophet's Christ. It is far more important that we be familiar with the truths of the book than the theories of its authorship. Don't let anyone interpret the book for you who does not know its author.

Isaiah

The divisions of the book of Isaiah are an interesting coincidence. In structure, Isaiah is a miniature Bible. Isaiah has 66 chapters, just as the Bible has 66 books. Isaiah has two great divisions, just as there are in the Bible, with 39 chapters in the first (like the Old Testament) and 27 chapters in the second (like the New Testament).

The Old Testament opens with God's case against humans because of their sin. Isaiah opens the same way (see Isaiah 1:18). The first section of Isaiah closes with the prophecy of the coming King of Righteousness and the redemption of Israel, just as the prophets close the Old Testament with the prediction of His coming kingdom (see Isaiah 34–35). The second part of Isaiah (beginning with chapter 40) opens with "the voice of him that crieth in the wilderness" (Isaiah 40:3, *KJV*) and is concerned with the person and work of Jesus Christ. The New Testament opens in the exact same way: John the Baptist, the forerunner of Jesus, is announced as "the voice of one crying in the wilderness" (John 1:6,23, *KJV*). The book of Isaiah ends with the vision of new heavens and a new earth in which righteousness dwells (see Isaiah 62:1-2; 65:17; 66:22). The New Testament closes with this same view in Revelation 21. This striking similarity between Isaiah and Revelation is unforgettable once both books are studied.

The book of Isaiah is like a jewelry box, and its most precious gem is the fifty-third chapter. This chapter is at the center of the second part of Isaiah, or the last 27 chapters. This is the chapter that tells about the Savior who "took up our infirmities and bore our diseases" (Matthew 8:17). Chapter 53 is a wonderful one to store in your memory. Each verse is a nugget of golden truth. This is the chapter that pictures Christ, our suffering Redeemer.

Two Comings of Christ

We see Christ in this book and hear the prophet crying, "He is coming!" and "He is coming again!" He is coming as Savior, as Isaiah depicted in chapter 53, in humiliation as our sin-bearer. He is coming again in power and great glory, as Isaiah depicted in chapter 34.

If we were to look through a telescope, we would see two mountain peaks with a valley in between. One mountain would be called Calvary; on its hilltop, a cross. But as we looked farther we would see the other peak, radiant with the light of a crown! This hill would be Olivet, where Christ will return. The eye of the ancient seer went farther than the sufferings of Calvary; his eye caught the kingdom and the glory that will follow!

Isaiah spoke of Christ's death when he said, "Though your sins are like scarlet, they shall be as white as snow; though they are red as crimson, they shall be like wool" (Isaiah 1:18). And Isaiah said, "He was despised and rejected by mankind" (Isaiah 53:3). This describes the time when Christ came to dwell among His people, but not all of His people accepted Him. When He comes again, we will hear, "Arise, shine, for your light has come, and the glory of the LORD rises upon you" (Isaiah 60:1). Then Isaiah told of His coming kingdom "in the last days" (Isaiah 2:2; see also verses 3-5).

The entire life of Christ is portrayed in Isaiah:

- Birth—Isaiah 7:14; 9:6
- Family—Isaiah 11:1
- Anointing—Isaiah 11:2
- Character—Isaiah 11:3-4
- Simple life—Isaiah 7:15
- Gentleness—Isaiah 42:1-4
- Death—Isaiah 53
- Resurrection—Isaiah 25:8
- Glorious reign—Isaiah 11:3-16; 32

The Ministry of Isaiah

Isaiah was a man of royal blood. He was a young aristocrat from a princely line. He was brought up in the court and had high standing with the people of Jerusalem. He not only was a prophet, but he also married a prophetess (see Isaiah 8:3,18). His training was the best. After his labor of 60 years, tradition tells us that at the age of 120, he died a martyr during the reign of Manasseh.

Isaiah was a special messenger to Judah. Look over 2 Kings 15–20 and note the moral and political rottenness of Judah and Israel, and the danger from the surrounding Gentile nations. Assyria was strong and aggressive, striving for world power. Egypt was on the south, and Judah and Israel lay on the road between these two enemies. Both Assyria and Egypt aimed at a world empire. Therefore, the Holy Land became the battleground of the ages.

Isaiah did not fail in his ministry. He laid bare the sins of his people and called them to repent and turn to God or face punishment (see Isaiah 1; 2:6–3). "Come back to God," he cried. But his chief theme was the coming One: Jesus. He saw Christ's near first coming and he saw Christ's faraway Second Coming. In all, he saw Christ. A glorious future is in store for Judah when Christ comes again. Jerusalem is to be the capital of the coming kingdom (see Isaiah 2:1-5; 4).

When the German astronomer Johannes Kepler failed to explain the motion of heavenly bodies by assigning each an orbit that was a circle, he realized that if each planet had an orbit that was an ellipse with two foci, the motion of the planets could be explained. So when in our reverent study of God's Word we note the two points of Christ on the cross and Christ on the throne, the Word shines clear and we begin to see what the prophet saw: the world's Redeemer, coming first in humiliation and then again in power and great glory.

Isaiah concentrated on four particular concerns:

1. Rebellion—"Woe to the sinful nation" (1:4; see also 1:2-3,10-15,21-23).
2. Retribution—"You will be devoured" (1:20; see also 1:5-8,15,28).
3. Repentance—"If you are willing and obedient, you will eat the good things" (1:19; see also 1:16-17,27).
4. Restoration—"Zion will be delivered" (1:27; see also 1:9,18,24-26, 28-31).

The people of Judah thought that if they kept up all outward observances of their religious service, all would be well. Isaiah denounced their hypocrisy (see Isaiah 1:15). He told them of forgiveness if they would repent, but he promised them a sword if they continued in their rebellion against God.

God's truths of redemption go beyond our reasoning, but they do not insult our reasoning; they rather appeal to it. For our worship to be right in the presence of God, we must be right in the presence of people.

ISAIAH 1–6: UNDER UZZIAH AND JOTHAM

Read Isaiah 1:1 and you will discover that Isaiah was a prophet "during the reigns of Uzziah [also called Azariah], Jotham, Ahaz and Hezekiah." During this time, the statesman prophet preached in Jerusalem.

Now turn to Isaiah 6 and you will see that Isaiah received his real commission in the year King Uzziah died. No doubt he had written chapters 1–5 before this time. Uzziah's long reign of 42 years was glorious for the most part; however, it ended in gloom. For the last four years of his life, Uzziah was a leper. He was shut off from all the business of state, and the kingdom was under the regency of his son Jotham (see 2 Kings 15:5). The early chapters of Isaiah fit the situation perfectly.

Isaiah's preaching that God was about to abandon Judah may have seemed extremely cruel, but the Lord is infinitely more concerned with the purity of His people than with their prosperity.

Jotham, Uzziah's successor, is only mentioned twice in the book (see Isaiah 1:1; 7:1). It does not seem that Isaiah was active during his reign. It is the reign of the next two kings, Ahaz and Hezekiah, with which Isaiah's prophecy mainly deals.

Ahaz reigned 16 years and Hezekiah reigned 29 years. Ahaz was a wicked king and, even worse, he was an idolater. Hezekiah was for the most part a good king, and he did much to remove idolatry from the people.

Isaiah's Commission

God called Isaiah just as He had called Moses, Joshua and Gideon and as He would call Paul. Isaiah's commission came at the tragic

Isaiah

death of the grand old King Uzziah (see Isaiah 6:1). His call was a never-to-be-forgotten experience. It taught him his own unworthiness and gave him his real commission to a sinning, needy world crying out for help. It came to him in the form of a "vision" (Isaiah 1:1).

This experience of Isaiah's should be every disciple's experience. The secret of all Isaiah's power lay in this vision in the Temple: "I saw the Lord" (Isaiah 1:1). Let us look at the steps leading from the opening of the vision to his final commission:

1. Conviction—"Woe to me! . . . I am ruined!" was the cry brought on by the sense of sinfulness before God's holiness (6:5).
2. Confession—"I am a man of unclean lips" (6:5). A broken heart and a contrite heart are precious to the Lord.
3. Cleansing—"Your guilt is taken away and your sin atoned for" (6:7). After confession, a flying seraphim (an angel) cleansed his lips with a hot coal from the altar.
4. Consecration—"Here am I. Send me!" (6:8).
5. Commission—"Go and tell this people" was God's command (6:9).

Hardship and peril awaited Isaiah, but God gave him a victorious strength. He was the man of the hour.

Isaiah's Message

Isaiah warned Judah of her folly and rebellion (see Isaiah 1:2-9). The people had separated themselves from God by the sins of greed, foreign alliances and idolatry (see Isaiah 2:6-9). For years Isaiah preached and told of doom. God had even called them a fruitless vine. God had tried patience and then punishment; now they would be destroyed by foreign kings.

ISAIAH 7–14: UNDER AHAZ

Ahaz, Jotham's son, was the next ruler of Judah (see Isaiah 7:1). Ahaz was utterly bad. He was an open idolater. For this sin, God allowed Rezin, king of Syria, and Pekah, king of Israel, to invade Judah. Isaiah had been silent under Jotham, but this invasion brought him to the front in his ministry. "Then the Lord said to Isaiah, 'Go out . . . to meet Ahaz' " (Isaiah 7:3).

God sent the prophet to encourage Ahaz. Isaiah appealed to him to put his trust in God for help rather than call on Tiglath-Pileser from Assyria. But Ahaz chose his own way. Besides predicting the Assyrian invasion (see Isaiah 8), the prophet saw an end to all of Israel's troubles through the birth of the Christ child who will rule over the kingdom of David in righteousness forever. He gave Ahaz this as a sign that Judah was not to perish: "Therefore the Lord himself will give you a sign: The virgin will be with child and will give birth to a son, and will call him Immanuel" (Isaiah 7:14). Read all of the prophecy of Immanuel, the virgin's Son, Jesus Christ, in Isaiah 7:10-16.

Ahaz refused the evidence upon which his faith might have been established. Instead he pursued idolatry and his own plans with Assyria, and that nation on which the king and his people leaned became the means of their punishment (see Isaiah 7:17-20).

Then Isaiah pronounced the sentence of doom upon king and land (see Isaiah 8:6-22). With nations, this is God's policy: doom for idolatry.

Prophecy Concerning Christ

In Isaiah 9:6-7 we find another great prophecy concerning Christ: "For to us a child is born, to us a son is given, and the government will be on his shoulders. And he will be called Wonderful Counselor, Mighty God, Everlasting Father, Prince of Peace. Of the increase of his government and peace there will be no end. He will reign on David's throne and over his kingdom, establishing and upholding it with justice and righteousness from that time on and forever. The zeal of the LORD Almighty will accomplish this." The Son to be given, the child to be born, was to sit on David's throne. Remember the throne of David is as real as the throne of the Caesars. Yes, Christ will sit on the throne of David. Read the angel's words to Mary: "He will be great and will be

Isaiah

called the Son of the Most High. The Lord God will give him the throne of his father David, and he will reign over Jacob's descendants forever; his kingdom will never end" (Luke 1:32-33).

We find then-present troubles and future glory strangely mixed in Isaiah 10. But in Isaiah 11, we see the picture of the glory of the future kingdom that Christ will establish on this earth. Some day He will come to Jerusalem to sit upon the throne of David, and peace will cover the earth "as the waters cover the sea" (Isaiah 11:9).

In this kingdom, the people will worship the Lord Jehovah: "Sing to the LORD, for he has done glorious things" (Isaiah 12:5). Read every word of Isaiah 11 and 12 so that you have a complete picture of this coming King and kingdom:

- The King Himself—Isaiah 11:1
- His anointing—Isaiah 11:2
- His righteous reign—Isaiah 11:3-5
- His glorious Kingdom—Isaiah 11:6-9
- His gathering together of His people from the four corners of the earth—Isaiah 11:10-16
- His kingdom worship—Isaiah 12

Prophecy Concerning Babylon

In Isaiah 13 we see great Babylon's doom. She was to carry Judah away captive, but the prophet also sees her destruction. God, of course, was carrying out His promise to Abraham: "I will bless those who bless you, and whoever curses you I will curse; and all peoples on earth will be blessed through you" (Genesis 12:3). God always brings a curse on any nation that afflicts Israel. You can follow this truth throughout history. God often allows nations to punish Israel for her national sins, but retribution is inevitable (see Deuteronomy 30:5-7; Isaiah 14:1-2; Joel 3:1-8).

When it was my privilege to drive out to old Babylon and look over the ruins of that once-magnificent city and see its absolute devastation, I thought of Isaiah's prophecy concerning this city: "Babylon, the jewel of kingdoms, the pride and glory of the Babylonians, will be overthrown by God like Sodom and Gomorrah.

She will never be inhabited or lived in through all generations; there no nomads will pitch their tents, there no shepherds will rest their flocks. But desert creatures will lie there, jackals will fill her houses; there the owls will dwell, and there the wild goats will leap about. Hyenas will inhabit her strongholds, jackals her luxurious palaces. Her time is at hand, and her days will not be prolonged" (Isaiah 13:19-22).

This is true today. Not even the tent of a nomad is pitched there. Only bats and owls make their home in its ruins. Not a shepherd is seen on the plains. There is only desolation. Yes, God's Word is true!

In Isaiah 14:28 we read that King Ahaz died. But Isaiah warned the people that the death of Ahaz must not be hailed as the end of their burdens. Even worse oppressors than Ahaz were yet to come (see Isaiah 14:28-32).

ISAIAH 15–39: UNDER HEZEKIAH

The reign of Hezekiah, a godly king, occupied one of the most important periods in all of Israel's history. The Assyrian forces, like a dark storm cloud, were threatening the northern frontiers. Before Hezekiah had completed his sixth year, Samaria had fallen beneath this invader. This success only whetted the Assyrian appetite for further conquest. Eight years later, Judah was invaded. The first invasion was by Sargon and the second by his son Sennacherib. Assyrian history confirms this. The critical year in Hezekiah's reign was the fourteenth (see Isaiah 36:1). That was the time of the Assyrian invasion, the king's deadly sickness and his recovery, and the final withdrawal of Assyrians from the land. This covered a period of about four years.

The Assyrian Invasion

The stonehearted Assyrian warriors came year after year, blazing with steel and banners. The watchmen on the wall of Jerusalem could see them advance by the smoke of the burning towns and cities the Assyrians left behind as they moved on.

King Hezekiah stripped the Temple of its treasures and took the gold from its doors and pillars in order to send the Assyrians 300 talents of silver and 30 talents of gold to buy them off (see 2 Kings 18:13-16). In desperation, help from Egypt was sought. But in the face of the fury of these Assyrians, nothing helped.

Finally the Assyrians built their campfires around the city of Jerusalem and demanded its surrender. Read the intensely dramatic account of the negotiations between the Assyrian general and the officials of Jerusalem.

Then read Isaiah 37:36-38 for the account of the swift and terrible disaster that fell upon the Assyrians as they were slain by a mysterious visitation in their camp.

Misplaced National Trust

Isaiah had denounced the alliance with Egypt and said that Judah was relying "on horses" and trusting "in the multitude of their chariots and in the great strength of their horsemen, but . . . not . . . the Holy One of Israel" (Isaiah 31:1).

Today, haven't we also put our trust in the "horses and chariots" of war's machinery? Haven't we multiplied our "horses and chariots" beyond the wildest dreams of Assyria, Egypt and Babylon? We have hitched all the forces of nature to our "chariots." We have armored tanks, stealth bombers, battleships, aircraft carriers and nuclear submarines. We have ICBMs and other weapons of mass destruction. War continues to be a hideous prospect of devastation and death.

We need to hear the prophet say today, "Woe to those who go down to Egypt for help, who rely on horses, who trust in the multitude of their chariots" (Isaiah 31:1). How great a need there is today for those who will "trust in the name of the LORD our God" (Psalm 20:7), who know the "victorious power of his right hand" (Psalm 20:6)!

History reveals a graveyard of the nations that have gone down to death through their own moral rottenness. Egypt, Babylon and Rome are memorable examples of this.

God wants us to recognize Him in national affairs. He calls, "Return, you Israelites, to the One you have so greatly revolted against" (Isaiah 31:6). As a people, we must get right with God before we can get right with other nations.

The kingdoms of Judah and Israel had become so weakened by idolatry and corruption that their enemies swept down upon them from the north like a wolf on the fold. First, the terrible Assyrian hosts trampled Israel (722 BC), and then Judah fell with the Babylonians thundering at her gate and breaking down her wall (586 BC). Both kingdoms ended, and the people were carried away into captivity.

Isaiah spent his life trying to get Judah to become reacquainted with God and His Word. He wanted them to trust wholly in God's guidance. Isn't this a worthy aim for any minister today?

ISAIAH 40–66: UNDER RESTORATION

This last part of the book of Isaiah is called "The Book of Consolation" because Isaiah tells in glowing terms, not only of the restoration of Judah but also of the coming of Jehovah's Servant to be the Messiah King.

The restoration is assured, for the Chosen People must return to their own land to prepare the way for the coming Messiah, the Servant of Jehovah, who is to redeem His people.

Isaiah 53 gives us a perfect picture of our suffering Redeemer: "Surely he took up our pain and bore our suffering" (verse 4). "We all, like sheep, have gone astray . . . and the LORD has laid on him the iniquity of us all" (verse 6). He was the substitute for the sinner.

Can you repeat verse 5 and say, "But he was pierced for [my] transgressions, he was crushed for [my] iniquities; the punishment that brought [my] peace was on him, and by his wounds [I am] healed"? Accepting this great fact makes you a child of God. He was wounded, bruised and pierced—not for His own sins, but for ours.

Isaiah 60–66 tells of the coming Kingdom—the future glory of Israel. God's goodness to redeemed Israel is described in chapters 61-62. God's promises of an era of prosperity are described in chapters 63-65.

Isaiah

Understanding Jeremiah and Lamentations

Jeremiah and Lamentations Portray Jesus Christ, the Righteous Branch

SELECTED BIBLE READINGS

UNDERSTANDING JEREMIAH

AUTHOR: Jeremiah 1:1 identifies the prophet Jeremiah as the author of the book of Jeremiah.

DATE: The book was written between 627 and 580 BC.

PURPOSE AND SUMMARY: The book of Jeremiah is the longest book in the Old Testament. Jeremiah was God's spokesman during the decline and fall of the southern kingdom, Judah, and Jerusalem. Among the prophets, not one had a more difficult task than that of

Jeremiah, who stood alone for God in the midst of the apostasy of his own people. No other prophet bares his soul to his readers as does Jeremiah. Although Jeremiah announced the coming destruction of Judah, he looked beyond this judgment to a day when everyone would know the Lord personally through the forgiveness of his or her sins (see Jeremiah 31:31-34). This new kind of relationship with the Lord would be a part of the "new covenant" the Lord would establish with His people (Jeremiah 31:31).

Here is the story of a diffident, sensitive lad who was called from the obscurity of his native town to assume at a critical hour in his nation's life the overwhelming responsibilities of a prophet. Jeremiah came from the village of Anathoth, some three miles from Jerusalem. This gave him access to the benefits the city had to offer. His father, Hilkiah, was a priest. (Some think that this was "Hilkiah the high priest" mentioned in 2 Kings 22:4, who brought the book of the Law to the notice of King Josiah, who started the great revival in the kingdom.) Jeremiah inherited the traditions of an illustrious ancestry. His early life was, no doubt, molded by strong religious influences. But God had something better for Jeremiah to do than to spend his life as a priest serving at the altar. God appointed this young man to be a prophet of the Lord in this most trying hour in the history of the Chosen People.

God often chooses unlikely instruments to do His work. He chose the sensitive, shrinking Jeremiah for what seemed a hopeless mission, with the words "Do not say, 'I am too young.' You must go to everyone I send you to and say whatever I command you. Do not be afraid of them, for I am with you and will rescue you,' declares the LORD" (Jeremiah 1:7-8).

LIFE OF JEREMIAH

Jeremiah, unlike many of the other prophets, had much to say concerning himself. He told us that he was a priest by birth (see Jeremiah 1:1). He was called by the Lord to be a prophet at an early age (see Jeremiah 1:6). He pleaded, first, his youth (only 21); second, his inexperience; and third, his lack of eloquence (see Jeremiah 1:6) as reasons for not accepting the call. (Aren't these the same excuses that young people today make for not obeying Christ?)

Jeremiah was assured that Jehovah ordained him to this work before his birth (see Jeremiah 1:5). (God tells us in Ephesians 2:10 that we were created to do good works before God even laid the foundation of the world.) He was not allowed to marry, for God had a special mission for him in life (see Jeremiah 16:1-2). Jeremiah prophesied during the time when Israel had been taken into captivity and Judah was in her decline.

Soon after Josiah's death, the kingdom of Judah was practically reduced to being a servant of Egypt. About 12 years later, Nebuchadnezzar, king of Babylon, captured Jerusalem and began deporting all the aristocracy to Babylon; this ended in the complete captivity of Judah 11 years afterward. Only a few of the poorest people were left in the Promised Land. Jeremiah continued his ministry among this remnant until they went to Egypt. He followed them (or was taken by them) to Egypt, and the last we hear of him, he was still rebuking his people. There are conflicting traditions concerning his death. Tertullian says that the Jews in Egypt stoned him to death. Others believe that he escaped (or was taken) to Babylon and died there.

Jeremiah was called to be a prophet in the thirteenth year of the reign of King Josiah (see Jeremiah 1:2). No doubt his early ministry and that of the prophet Zephaniah were among the influences that led to the reforms under the young King Josiah. Jeremiah prophesied for more than 40 years. He began his ministry 60 years after the death of Isaiah, the great evangelical prophet.

Jeremiah was contemporary with the prophetess Huldah, and with Habakkuk, Zephaniah, Ezekiel and Daniel, and perhaps even Nahum.

Jeremiah was the ninth of the prophets. He prophesied to the southern kingdom of Judah, before the exile and during the trying days of the captivity. He saw five kings upon the throne of Judah: Josiah, Jehoahaz, Jehoiakim, Jehoiachin and Zedekiah. He

Jeremiah

was to Josiah what Isaiah had been to Hezekiah. Read 2 Kings 21:1-25 to find the history of Jeremiah's time.

There were three great events in Jeremiah's life:

1. Battle of Megiddo (609 BC), between Judah and Pharaoh Neco of Egypt—Good King Josiah was killed.

2. Battle of Carchemish (605 BC), during Jehoiakim's reign, when Judah had essentially become a servant of Egypt—In this battle, the Egyptians were defeated by Babylon under Nebuchadnezzar. The first deportation of Jews followed.

3. Capture of Jerusalem by Nebuchadnezzar (587-6 BC)—The city and the Temple were destroyed, and most of those who had been left were now taken to Babylon.

There was a great contest for world supremacy in the day of Jeremiah. Assyria had been in the place of leadership for 300 years. Now she was growing weak, and Babylon was becoming more powerful. Egypt, too, was striving for supremacy. In 607 BC, Assyria was defeated by Babylon. In 605 BC, Egypt was crushed in the battle of Carchemish, and Babylon became the world's master. A few years after that battle, Babylon invaded Jerusalem and took the Jews captive. False prophets swarmed the city of Jerusalem in those days. They flattered the king and prophesied to him whatever they thought he wanted to hear.

Jeremiah's message, however, was never a popular one. At one time he barely escaped with his life (see Jeremiah 26:7-16). At another time his enemies beat him and put him in prison. People have always mistreated God's witnesses to His truth.

ANALYSIS OF JEREMIAH

It is almost impossible to outline this book chronologically. Some of the first messages are found later in the book, and some of the messages delivered later appear first in the book. No doubt

Jeremiah had given his messages many times to the people and had repeated them often before he began to have his faithful scribe, Baruch, write them down. After Baruch had written one of Jeremiah's discourses, some other message given years before might have come to Jeremiah's mind and he would have Baruch record it, possibly without dating it. Baruch would fill up his scroll as he unrolled it. Later on, when he wished to write down another incident or record another message, he would have to begin on the scroll where he left off, whether it fitted in chronologically or not. This is important to remember.

Because the book of Jeremiah is not arranged chronologically, a division of the book is difficult, and any analysis of it is more thematic than structural.

Jeremiah's prophecies had four main concerns:

1. Judah—captivity and restoration
2. Cities—Jerusalem, Babylon and Damascus
3. Gentile nations—Egypt, Philistia, Moab, Ammon, Edom, Elam and Babylon
4. Messiah

During 605 BC, the year of the first deportation of the Jews to Babylon, Jeremiah was ordered to write the predictions he had made and to have them read to the people. In the Bible, these predictions are scattered throughout chapters 24–49 and concern the future of the Jews, the Babylonian captivity and the coming Messiah:

1. God's future dealings with Judah—Jeremiah 23; 31
2. Conquest of the land by Nebuchadnezzar, king of Babylon—Jeremiah 20:4
3. Judah's exile and captivity in Babylon, and return after 70 years—Jeremiah 25–26
4. The Messiah—Jeremiah 23:6; 30:4-11; 33:14-26
5. Israel being scattered—Jeremiah 24
6. Final recovery of Israel—Jeremiah 23; 32:37-41; Ezekiel 37:21-22

In order to teach the people, Jeremiah used many symbols and symbolic gestures given to him by Jehovah. On one occasion he wore a rotted girdle; another time he put a yoke on his neck, like an ox; on another occasion, he broke a bottle in the presence of the ruler; another time he bought a field and buried the deed. (The interpretation of these is given in the text.)

There are many object lessons found in the book:

- The almond rod—Jeremiah 1:11-12
- The boiling caldron—Jeremiah 1:13-14
- The marred girdle—Jeremiah 13:1-11
- The full bottle—Jeremiah 13:12-14
- The drought—Jeremiah 14:1-12
- The potter's vessel—Jeremiah 18:1-6
- The broken bottle—Jeremiah 19:1-2
- Two baskets of figs—Jeremiah 24:1-10
- Bonds and bars—Jeremiah 27:1-12
- Buying a field—Jeremiah 32:6-15
- The hidden stones—Jeremiah 43:9-13
- Book sunk in the Euphrates—Jeremiah 51:59-64

There are many different ways that Christ is pictured in the book of Jeremiah:

- Spring of living water—Jeremiah 2:13
- Great physician—Jeremiah 8:22
- Good Shepherd—Jeremiah 23:4; 31:10
- A righteous Branch—Jeremiah 23:5
- David their king—Jeremiah 30:9
- Their Redeemer—Jeremiah 50:34
- The Lord Our Righteous Savior—Jeremiah 23:6

JEREMIAH 1: CALL AND COMMISSION OF JEREMIAH

The tragedy recorded in Jeremiah opens in the little village of Anathoth. At 21, Jeremiah was becoming aware that God had ordained him before his birth to be a prophet (see Jeremiah 1:5). God has a plan for the life of every person (see Jeremiah 29:11). Some see clearly how they are to be used. Many learn to wait upon God and trust Him for the outcome. This latter group cannot understand the ways of the Lord, but they believe His promises. Jeremiah must have been one of these. He must have wondered what God had planned for him. But because he let the Lord have His way, his life affected all of Israel.

We hear Jeremiah speak, " 'Alas, Sovereign LORD,' I said, 'I do not know how to speak; I am too young' " (Jeremiah 1:6). Like a young man, he protested and shrank from the task God gave him, and he begged to be excused. Take note of Jeremiah's reluctance to undertake the task. Jeremiah was saying, in effect, "I have not yet reached the years of maturity." In Middle Eastern society at the time, until a young man became of age, he played no role in society.

A prophet is simply God's messenger delivering not his or her own ideas but conveying to the last detail God's thoughts. (Compare Jeremiah's call with Moses' call, Exodus 4:10-12.) God had called Jeremiah to be a prophet, and Jeremiah bravely accepted the task, but he was overwhelmed at the thought of hurting anyone. He would rather live at peace with them. His prophetic message would not be happily received. Wouldn't those he provoked cut his career short? Wouldn't they try to kill him?

The young man was only too conscious of his inexperience and he almost refused God. But God knew how to overcome his hesitancy. He made the young Jeremiah conscious of a divine call. He made him see that the work to which he was commissioned was not his own.

The path of duty is the path of safety! While Jeremiah was thinking things over, a hand touched his mouth and a voice said, "I have put my words in your mouth" (Jeremiah 1:9). No longer could he complain of an inability to speak. God promises to put His message into the mouth of His prophets. (See what Christ said to His disciples in Matthew 10:20.) Then Jeremiah heard the voice add, "See, today I appoint you over nations and kingdoms to uproot and tear down, to destroy and overthrow, to build and to plant" (Jeremiah 1:10).

The Nature of Jeremiah's Commission

What God asks us to do, He fits us for; and what He fits us for, He asks us to do. A prophet was quite a change in position for Jeremiah, just a poor country preacher, but God also empowered him for the commission.

Like Jeremiah, the Church and the minister who have answered God's call today are still in a place of power. They need no other weapons than the promise of God, and they really control the building and the breaking, the planting and the pruning of the community.

Jeremiah's commission included not only his own country, but also the nations of Egypt, Ammon and Moab and the cities of Tyre and Sidon. His commission was to root out and to pull down, to destroy and to throw down. He was to root out the idolatry and pride, *and* he must finally build and plant. Jeremiah was to go only to those persons or peoples to whom the Lord sent him. And he was to say only what the Lord commanded him to say. This must be true of us also if we are to be true workers together with God.

The Reluctance of Jeremiah

Jeremiah, like people today, was engaged in the Lord's work because God said he must. He had heard the "You shall" of heaven. Although at first the cost may be great, the future gain cannot be estimated. Jeremiah tried to shrink away and offered every excuse for his unfitness, but the task was forced upon him. "You must go" (Jeremiah 1:7). Jeremiah hated the limelight. He loved the simple life. He wanted to live in the country, but the Lord had work for him in the cities. Jeremiah had to choose between his desires and God's will.

Because Jeremiah was forced into a task that was so distasteful to him, in later years he cried, "Alas, my mother, that you gave me birth, a man with whom the whole land strives and contends!"

(Jeremiah 15:10). God told Jeremiah, "Do not be afraid of them, for I am with you and will rescue you" (Jeremiah 1:8). Jeremiah was not a public speaker, and he shrank from bearing such an unwelcome message to so undisciplined a people. How often he must have thought of God's promise when he was hauled before officials and rulers. We like to announce good news; to have to tell bad news is always hard. We are afraid of how people will react, what the faces of people will show. When they register pleasure, we feel safe. When they show disgust, we want to turn away and hide.

The Touch of God's Hand

"Then the LORD reached out his hand" (Jeremiah 1:9). Compare Jeremiah's call with that of Isaiah (see Isaiah 6:7). Paul says that prophecy is a spiritual gift (see 1 Corinthians 14:1). The touch of God's hand was a tangible pledge for Jeremiah that God was with him. He could not get away from it.

The Word of the Lord is a power that carries out His will and accomplishes what He wishes (see Isaiah 55:11; Hebrews 4:12). Against this power, nothing can stand. It is a hammer that breaks rocks into pieces (see Jeremiah 23:29). God's Word shows its power in two ways—in destruction and in construction. We see this in God's words to Jeremiah. And we see its power in another way: If people accept God's Word, it will give life; if they reject it, it will bring condemnation (see John 3:36).

JEREMIAH 2–38: MINISTRY BEFORE THE FALL OF JERUSALEM

The prophecies of Jeremiah before the fall of Jerusalem were made in this order (long silences divide these):

1. Prophecies in the reign of Josiah—Jeremiah 2–12
2. Prophecies in the reign of Jehoiakim—Jeremiah 13–20; 25–27:11
3. Prophecies in the reign of Zedekiah—Jeremiah 21–24; 27:12–39

Reign of Josiah

"During the reign of King Josiah, the LORD said to me" (Jeremiah 3:6). The first 12 chapters of Jeremiah cover the prophecy of this period:

- Jeremiah 2–6—Here we read about Judah's sin and God's call to repentance. Judgments are predicted.
- Jeremiah 7–9—Here we read more warnings. We see the prophet's grief.
- Jeremiah 10–12—Here we see that the people continued to practice idolatry and to disobey God. The Lord's disappointment in His people is shown.

In the early years of his ministry, during the reign of Josiah, Jeremiah's message for the most part was a warning to Judah and a call to her to repent (see Jeremiah 3:6,12-13,22-23). He spared nothing in exposing the moral rottenness of the people (see Jeremiah 7:1-26). He warned them of coming judgments if they would not return to God. He especially told them of the danger from the north (see Jeremiah 4:6). He said that the avengers would come like "a lion . . . out of his lair" (Jeremiah 4:7). They would sweep over the land with "chariots . . . like a whirlwind" and with "horses . . . swifter than eagles"; they would spread terror before them and leave ruin behind them (Jeremiah 4:13).

In chapter 26, we see Jeremiah taking a stand on the same spot as in Jeremiah 7. On this occasion he nearly lost his life. The address in chapter 7 was probably given during the reign of Josiah himself.

It is probable that for some time after his call, Jeremiah continued to reside in Anathoth, but before long he was compelled to leave the home of his birth and make his home in Jerusalem. The men of his hometown had made a conspiracy to put him to death (see Jeremiah 11:18-23). The disloyalty of his neighbors, and especially of his own relatives, came as a painful shock to the unsuspecting prophet. But Jehovah told him that this was only the beginning of his troubles, and it was a time of preparation for still greater trials in the days to come (see Jeremiah 12:5-6).

Jeremiah's chief enemies were the priests and the prophets (see Jeremiah 26:7-8). They had a large following among the people.

It is sad to note that the principal opposition to the message of God came from the professedly religious people. It was the same in our Lord's case—remember that the Pharisees and Sadducees were always conspiring to decide how they might kill Jesus—and it is often the same today. Jesus said that if we live godly lives, we will suffer persecution. Many people hate God, and those same people will hate His children.

We do not know much about Jeremiah's work during the later years of Josiah's reign. No doubt he was in great sympathy with this young reformer, but he realized that his work did not go deep enough. When King Josiah died at the battle of Megiddo, Judah suffered a calamity from which she never recovered. During this battle, Judah made a noble attempt to withstand the Egyptian army advancing against Assyria under Pharaoh Neco.

King Josiah's younger brother Jehoahaz succeeded him, whom "the people of the land" placed on the throne instead of the older brother Eliakim (2 Chronicles 36:1). But Jehoahaz was allowed to reign for only three months. He was deposed by Neco and carried off in chains to Egypt, where he died. Neco was now virtually an overlord of Judah. He appointed Eliakim to be ruler and changed his name to Jehoiakim.

The reformation that Josiah had started only touched the surface, and the work was abandoned after his death. During Jehoiakim's reign, the nation fell back into the worst form of idolatry.

Reign of Jehoiakim

Dr. W. Graham Scroggie, an English theologian and author, said that Jeremiah's prophecies during Jehoiakim's reign recount events in this order:

1. Jeremiah 26
2. Jeremiah 46–49
3. Jeremiah 25
4. Jeremiah 36:1-8

5. Jeremiah 45
6. Jeremiah 36:9-32
7. Jeremiah 14
8. Jeremiah 15
9. Jeremiah 16
10. Jeremiah 17
11. Jeremiah 18–19:13
12. Jeremiah 19:14–20:1
13. Jeremiah 35
14. Jeremiah 22–23:8
15. Jeremiah 23:9-40
16. Jeremiah 13

In substance, Jeremiah predicted the judgment of the nations and Judah. He corrected the false prophets. He foretold the Babylonian captivity. And he suffered for his message.

It was a sad day for Judah when Jehoiakim ascended to power. It was a bad day for Jeremiah, too. Read Jeremiah 26:1-7 to learn what God said to Jeremiah at the beginning of Jehoiakim's reign. Jehoiakim was a bad ruler. He was proud, selfish, covetous and vindictive. He weighed the land down with taxes to meet the demands of his Egyptian conqueror (see 2 Kings 23:35). He was indifferent to the suffering of his people. He devoted most of his time to enlarging and adorning his palace and carried out his costly schemes with incredible meanness.

Jeremiah did not hesitate to denounce the king in his shameless wrongdoing. In Jeremiah 22:13-19, he verbally put Jehoiakim in stocks and then released the lash of a righteous scorn, predicting that he would die without being mourned and would "have the burial of a donkey" (Jeremiah 22:19).

Jeremiah's predictions upset the people. Standing in the Temple, Jeremiah told the people that the Temple would be destroyed and Jerusalem itself would become a ruin. Jeremiah's listeners were shocked (see Jeremiah 26:7-9). They called his words blasphemy. They said, "This man should be sentenced to death because he has prophesied against this city" (Jeremiah 26:11).

The Jewish people always remembered that they were the Chosen People of God. God had given them privileges, so they concluded that God would not do to them the things Jeremiah had said He would do against the people whom He had chosen (see Amos 3:2). God had consecrated the Temple as the dwelling place for His name; therefore, the people thought He would not let it be destroyed by their enemies. This was quite false. Let us not entertain this spirit ourselves: We think we are God's children; therefore, He must forgive us, He must make us win in battle, and He must rout our enemies.

Jeremiah was charged with being unpatriotic. The cry at that time would have been "Un-Judaistic!" as today it would be "Un-American!" For Jeremiah's opponents it was "My country, right or wrong." For Jeremiah it was "God's will in my country" (see Jeremiah 26:12-15). It is not so much a question of what we think is right as it is that we learn what God considers to be the best for us and our country. Remember that God had said to Jeremiah, "Do not be afraid of them, for I am with you" (Jeremiah 1:8). We may have to endure ostracism and ridicule for Christ's sake, but His promise is sufficient.

The priests and prophets, aided by the people, laid hold of Jeremiah and threatened him with death. But Jeremiah was delivered from the hand of his enemies (see Jeremiah 26:16-24).

The fourth year of Jehoiakim's reign was one to be remembered because in that year, Jeremiah first put his prophecies in writing on a scroll (see Jeremiah 36:1-2). Baruch, Jeremiah's intimate friend who was such a comfort to him through his trials, took down the prophet's words.

We next see the prophet in a dimly lit dungeon. What happened? The rulers had bound him, so they would no longer be troubled by the word of the Lord. But the Lord told Jeremiah to write the words down. There he was, with his loyal friend Baruch at his side busily writing on a scroll the words as the prophet spoke them: "So Jeremiah called Baruch son of Neriah, and while Jeremiah dictated all the words the Lord had spoken to him, Baruch wrote them on the scroll. Then Jeremiah told Baruch, 'I am restricted; I am not allowed go to the LORD's temple. So you go to the house of the LORD on a day of fasting and read to the people from the scroll the words of the LORD that you wrote as I dictated'" (Jeremiah 36:4-6). So Baruch read the words of the Lord in the Temple (see Jeremiah 36:8).

Jeremiah's predictions upset the king. Royal officials immediately sent for Baruch and commanded him to read the scroll again (see Jeremiah 36:14-15). They decided the scroll must be brought to the king: "We must report all these words to the king" (Jeremiah 36:16). Knowing full well the character of this ruler, they advised Jeremiah and Baruch to go into hiding before the scroll was read in the royal presence (see Jeremiah 36:19).

They asked Baruch, "'Tell us, how did you come to write all this? Did Jeremiah dictate it?' 'Yes,' Baruch replied, 'he dictated all these words to me, and I wrote them in ink on the scroll'" (Jeremiah 36:17-18). Then the officials went to report to the king.

The scene changes. We are now in the winter palace of Jehoiakim, surrounded by all the luxury of an Eastern court. The king is sitting before his hearth. A fire is burning. Jehudi is reading the scroll of Jeremiah. All are listening intently. When three or four columns had been read, Jehoiakim could stand no more. With a knife, he angrily cut the scroll to pieces and threw it into the fire. This act of Jehoiakim's seemed to symbolize the doom of the city, the Temple and all the people of Judah. They had heard God's Word and rejected it (see Jeremiah 36:20-26).

Of course, Jehoiakim gave the order to seize Jeremiah and Baruch, but God "had hidden them" (Jeremiah 36:26). How often God does this for His children. He hides us under His wings and in the hollow of His hand, far from harm.

Now the Lord commanded Jeremiah to take another scroll and to write again. "So Jeremiah took another scroll and gave it to the scribe Baruch son of Neriah, and as Jeremiah dictated, Baruch wrote. . . . And many similar words were added to them" (Jeremiah 36:32).

Jehoiakim reigned 11 years. In the fourth year of Jehoiakim's reign, Nebuchadnezzar invaded Judah (605 BC), and it was then that Daniel and his companions were carried away to Babylon, and Jehoiakim himself was put into chains. After his death, his son Jehoiachin, a youth of 18, came to the throne. But Jehoiachin's reign was short (about three months and 10 days), because Nebuchadnezzar's army soon appeared at the gates of Jerusalem; and after a three-month siege, the city was captured. Nebuchadnezzar took with him back to Babylon many of the aristocrats and the brightest of the people. Among them was Jehoiachin and the queen mother. "Only the poorest people of the land were left" (2 Kings 24:14).

It was then that Jeremiah first mentioned the 70 years' captivity (see Jeremiah 25:1-14; see also Daniel 9:2). God told them just how long they must remain in exile.

Jeremiah stood in the Temple gate and spoke boldly for righteousness and God. He had uttered a series of accusations against Judah and warnings of God's inevitable judgment because of the people's sins. But he had also made an appeal to the people for them to turn back to God and receive forgiveness. We see him standing in the gate, hurling thunderbolts into the faces of the false worshipers but always holding up the pardon of God.

Jeremiah's was a moral battle, and a moral battle is harder than any other to fight and keep fighting.

JEREMIAH 39–52: MINISTRY AFTER THE FALL OF JERUSALEM

Reign of Zedediah

After Jehoiachin was taken to Babylon, Nebuchadnezzar placed Zedekiah, Jehoiakim's brother, on the throne. Only the poor were left in Jerusalem. Jeremiah likened them to bad, worthless figs, in contrast to those who had gone who were good figs (see Jeremiah 24, which is one of the first discourses of Jeremiah in Zedekiah's reign). The brightest men of the nation had been carried away. (Remember that Daniel afterward became prime minister of Babylon.) The men who were left were so weak and degenerate that the prophet could see nothing but doom for Jerusalem.

Dr. W. Graham Scroggie said that prophecies during Zedekiah's reign recount the events in this order:

1. Jeremiah 24
2. Jeremiah 27
3. Jeremiah 28
4. Jeremiah 29
5. Jeremiah 49:34
6. Jeremiah 51:1
7. Jeremiah 21
8. Jeremiah 34
9. Jeremiah 37
10. Jeremiah 38
11. Jeremiah 39:15-18
12. Jeremiah 32
13. Jeremiah 33
14. Jeremiah 30
15. Jeremiah 31
16. Jeremiah 39:1-14

Zedekiah was disposed to be friendly to Jeremiah, but he was a weak man and had no courage to make decisions of his own. He was like clay in the hands of the officials who surrounded his throne. The remnant of men who were left were not qualified to govern. They had taken the places of the real nobility of the nation, but they were in great contrast to those who had been carried into captivity.

Jeremiah incurred the displeasure of the prophets who had been taken to Babylon because, in a letter to the exiles, he directly opposed the prophets' prediction of an early return from captivity (see Jeremiah 29:1-14). The prophets in Jerusalem didn't like it, either, because they thought that they could soon throw off the yoke of Nebuchadnezzar.

Zedekiah's advisers were in favor of throwing off the Babylonian yoke and looking to Egypt for help, but Jeremiah kept insisting that the Babylonians would certainly capture the city (see

Jeremiah 37:3-10). We have seen the bitter opposition he had to meet. Now we have to watch the hatred of his enemies reach a climax in a savage demand for his death. "This man should be put to death" (see Jeremiah 38:4). This came from the officials.

Confined in the court of the guard attached to the royal palace, Jeremiah had opportunities to talk to the soldiers on duty as well as to the citizens who came along (see Jeremiah 37:21). To every one he declared the word of the Lord (see Jeremiah 37:6-10). That message was that it was foolish to resist the Babylonians. It would only result in destruction. This was so galling to the national pride of the officials named in Jeremiah 38:1 that they resolved to kill Jeremiah.

Jeremiah did, in fact, discourage the soldiers and people (see Jeremiah 38:4). And the people became convinced that resistance was useless, because God had said that Jerusalem would be captured and burned by the Babylonians. The people and the soldiers were no longer willing to jeopardize their lives by defending the city.

Jeremiah had urged Judah to submit to Babylon, in accordance with God's will, but without effect (see Jeremiah 21:1-10). Even though King Zedekiah was convinced that Jeremiah was right, Zedekiah broke his covenant with the king of Babylon. Nebuchadnezzar swiftly marched against Jerusalem and the final siege began.

The Final Siege

As the siege proceeded, the hostility of Jeremiah's enemies became more intense. The officials charged him with demoralizing the soldiers. They even petitioned the king to put him to death (see Jeremiah 38:4). Weakling that he was, Zedekiah gave Jeremiah over into the hands of the officials. Then for some reason, the officials shrank from killing him. But they chose a worse thing for Jeremiah; they lowered him with ropes into a muddy cistern and left him to die of starvation and exposure.

But God was with Jeremiah and raised up a friend to deliver him. An Ethiopian, Ebed-Melek, heard of Jeremiah's plight and made his way to the king. Gaining permission, he rushed to the cistern and lowered a quantity of "old rags and worn-out clothes" for the prophet to put under his armpits "to pad the ropes" so that Jeremiah could be pulled from the mud in the cistern (Jeremiah 38:11-13).

After Jeremiah's deliverance, Zedekiah, driven by fear, visited Jeremiah to find out what was in store for him. Jeremiah could only promise him doom for the city. Jeremiah still insisted that the king should surrender to Nebuchadnezzar, but Zedekiah was afraid of his own officials and of the Jews who were already in Babylon (see Jeremiah 38:14-28).

After 18 months of siege, Jerusalem was taken (587 BC). Zedekiah's sons were put to death before his eyes, and he himself was blinded and carried in chains to Babylon (see Jeremiah 39:1-7).

Because King Nebuchadnezzar of Babylon looked with favor on Jeremiah having never ceased urging Judah to submit to Babylon, the king spared his life and offered him anything he wanted (see Jeremiah 21:1-10; 39:11-12). Jeremiah also was given the choice of going to Babylon where freedom and honor awaited him, or staying with the Jewish remnant in Judah; he chose to cast his lot with the remnant left in the land (see Jeremiah 39:11-12; 40:1-16).

The Last Remnant

The few Jews left in Jerusalem during the Babylonian captivity all fled to Egypt, in spite of God's warning against it (see Jeremiah 43). They asked Jeremiah to pray for guidance, but when it was given, they refused to obey it. The prophet and Baruch were compelled to accompany them. Even in Egypt we find that the prophet carried out his commission. He prophesied the conquest of Egypt by Nebuchadnezzar (see Jeremiah 43:8-13). The Jews who dwelt in the Nile Valley were practicing idolatry, and Jeremiah warned them against this wickedness. When they refused to listen to his warning and continued to worship other gods, Jeremiah told them the judgment of God would fall on them (see Jeremiah 44:26-28).

We find, in chapters 40–44, two prophecies given by Jeremiah after the fall of Jerusalem:

1. To the remnant in Judah—Jeremiah 40–43:3
2. To the remnant in Egypt—Jeremiah 43:4–44

A bit of history recorded in chapter 52 gives the facts about the captivity of Judah.

This is the last we hear of Jeremiah. How long he lived in Egypt afterward we do not know. Other prophets had at least occasional successes to cheer their hearts in the midst of difficulties, but Jeremiah seemed to be fighting a losing battle to the very end. Disaster, failure and hostility were his rewards for his work. He preached to deaf ears and seemed to reap only hate in return for his love for his people. In life he seemed to accomplish little. He was brokenhearted. But God has given us a record that makes him one of the greatest of all prophets.

POINTS TO REMEMBER

We can see how close Jeremiah was to the affairs of Judah during her captivity. He had seen the condition of Judah's decline from Josiah's good reign to the day of Zedekiah. He had seen the people taken captive and carried away, and he had witnessed the destruction of Jerusalem and the Temple.

Babylon's Fall

At the same time Jeremiah was crying out against Babylon for her heinous crime in destroying God's children, he told them Babylon would be demolished and would be in ruins forever (see Jeremiah 51:37-43). This is literally true of this once-great city of the ancient world. Read again Isaiah 13:17-22, along with Jeremiah 51:37-43.

By the time of Christ, Babylon's power had gone, and in the first century AD Babylon was mostly in ruins. Its bricks were used in building Baghdad and repairing canals. For centuries it has lain in desolation. Only beasts of the desert inhabit it. This is a remarkable fulfillment of prophecy. When I stood and looked over its ruins, it was hard to believe that once this was a city of wonder and beauty, filled with luxury and gross extravagance unsurpassed in the history of the world, for today it is only a lot of scattered stones.

Judah's History

- "Chosen"—Jeremiah prophesied to God's Chosen People in Judah before their exile to Babylon.

- "Captured"—He warned the Jews of their pending captivity if they would not listen to Jehovah.

- "Carried away"—They continued to sin, so God allowed them to be carried away to Babylon by Nebuchadnezzar. God told them that they must remain captive 70 years (see Jeremiah 25:1-14; Daniel 9:2).

- "Coming Messiah"—God will not allow His children to remain scattered throughout the nations of the world forever. Someday the Jews will be gathered to their own land, and the Good Shepherd will appear (see Jeremiah 33:14-17).

Israel's Future

Jeremiah got his messages to the people by speaking to them at the Temple and as they thronged to feasts. Often he did symbolic things to attract their attention. When he was shut up in prison, he dictated his messages to Baruch, the scribe, who wrote them down and read them to the people. The scroll of Jeremiah that Jehoiakim burned no doubt took Jeremiah and Baruch about one and a half years to prepare. (Writing in those days was not like it is now. It was a long and laborious task.)

In the days when David's throne was tottering and Judah was going into captivity, the prophet announced the coming Christ, King of the house of David, "a righteous Branch" (Jeremiah 23:5). "In his days Judah will be saved and Israel will live in safety. This is the name by which he will be called: the LORD Our Righteous Savior" (Jeremiah 23:6).

Jeremiah 23 is dear to the Jews, God's Chosen People, and dear to the heart of God. It tells of the future of Judah, redeemed through the work of their Messiah. Jesus, the Good Shepherd, is promised. He will gather His sheep from every corner of the earth and they will return to their own country, the Promised Land (see Jeremiah 23:1,3). This will take place when the King comes again and sits upon the throne of David (see verse 5).

Judah's future redemption through Christ is given in chapters 30–31. The Jews are scattered today, but God is bringing them back (see Jeremiah 30:10-11; 31:10).

Jeremiah's Life

Jeremiah's life was one of deepening sadness and frustration. He had to watch the people and the city that he loved sin and sin again. And all the time, he had no hope that things might soon change. How deeply he felt all this can be seen in his Lamentations. Hudson Taylor, the founder of China Inland Mission (now Overseas Missionary Fellowship), once wrote, "God delights to trust a trustworthy child with a trial." How God must have trusted Jeremiah!

Jeremiah's Prophecies

The prophecies of Jeremiah came out of the turmoil in Judah preceding and during the Babylonian captivity like a beautiful symphony of sorrow—God's oratorio of tears and consolation as His great heart of love wept over the people He was chastening. The message of the book deals with the certainty of God's judgment because of sin, yet the tenderness and eternity of His boundless love is also certain.

The prophecies are not chronological, but each prophecy is bound up with the history of when Judah was ruled by five kings: Josiah, Jehoahaz, Jehoiakim, Jehoiachin, Zedekiah. The period ended with the captivity in Babylon. Jeremiah was concerned with backsliding. Judah had forsaken the Lord; and through Jeremiah, God sent warnings of impending judgments, beseeching His people to return to His commandments.

Jeremiah was God's prophet, speaking God's words. Read Jeremiah 1:4-10 again, which describes his marvelous call. Many times Jeremiah cried, "This is what the Lord, the Lord Almighty says." In Jeremiah 22:29 he added, "O land, land, land, hear the word of the LORD!" The book abounds in golden passages: 6:16; 9:23-24; 10:10-13; 17:7-8; 18:1-6; 20:9; 22:29; 23:5-6.

Christ appears in Jeremiah. He is wonderfully pictured in Jeremiah 23:5-6. His future kingdom is lavishly described in the golden chapters 31 and 33, and it is hard to find, in any language, words of more touching beauty than those written in these two chapters.

The whole book is a series of messages, each of which was spoken to fit the need of the moment. Therefore these messages, like the Proverbs, are "like apples of gold in settings of silver" (Proverbs 25:11), and when we apply them to ourselves, we discover that they meet our needs just as they met the needs of Jehovah's wandering people.

Understanding Lamentations

AUTHOR: The book of Lamentations does not explicitly identify its author. The tradition is that the prophet Jeremiah wrote Lamentations. This view is highly likely considering that the author witnessed the Babylonians destroying Jerusalem, as Jeremiah did (see 2 Chronicles 35:25; 36:21-22).

DATE: The book was likely written between 586 and 575 BC, soon after Jerusalem's fall to the Babylonian army.

PURPOSE AND SUMMARY: Entitled in most English versions "The Lamentations of Jeremiah," this book is placed immediately after Jeremiah in the Septuagint, the Vulgate and most modern Bibles. In the Hebrew text, it is found among "Writings." The book of Lamentations is composed of five poems lamenting the siege and destruction of Jerusalem (586 BC). The poet also makes sincere confession of sin on behalf of the people and leaders, acknowledges complete submission to the will of God, and finally prays that God will once again restore His people to their homeland.

Here is another of the Bible's exquisite books of poetry. It is commonly attributed to Jeremiah. Five beautiful, distinct poems are bound together in the book. It is not all sorrow. Above the clouds of the poet's weeping over the sins of his people, God's sun is shining. In Lamentations 3:22-27, the light breaks through to throw a shining rainbow across the murky sky. God's grace always shines above the clouds of sin (see Romans 5:20), and it will always shine in the hearts that trust in God through faith in the Lord Jesus Christ, who desires "to bestow on them a crown of beauty instead of ashes, the oil of joy instead of mourning, and a garment of praise instead of a spirit of despair" (Isaiah 61:3).

Understanding Ezekiel

Ezekiel Portrays Jesus Christ, the Son of Man

AUTHOR: The prophet Ezekiel is the author of the book of Ezekiel, according to Ezekiel 1:3. He was a contemporary of both Jeremiah and Daniel.

DATE: The book was likely written between 592 and 571 BC, during the Babylonian captivity of the Jews.

PURPOSE AND SUMMARY: Ezekiel was carried into exile in Babylon, where he received his call and exercised his prophetic ministry. Ezekiel had a dual role: prophet-priest to his people and intercessory watchman over his people. Like all other prophets from Abraham and Moses onward, Ezekiel was a prophet as well as an intercessor who stood before the Lord in prayer as a representative of God's people. The book of Ezekiel contains 48 chapters, divided at the halfway point by the fall of Jerusalem. Ezekiel's prophecies before this event are chiefly messages of judgment upon Judah for her sins; following Jerusalem's fall to the Babylonian army, Ezekiel speaks to helpless people of the hope and certainty that the Lord would restore them to their homeland and they would worship again in a rebuilt temple.

Ezekiel, the faithful preacher to the exiles in Babylon, is the author of this book.

Soon after Ezekiel was born, a great reformation of popular worship and social life took place. This was inspired by the book of Deuteronomy, which had just been published (621 BC). But this reformation was only superficial and was followed by a religious decline crowned by political disaster; Jerusalem was taken after an 18-month siege amid innumerable horrors. The Temple, on which such passionate love had been lavished, was reduced to ashes; and the people were deported to Babylon.

Jeremiah, the great prophet whom we have just finished studying, was the last of the prophets in Jerusalem before the final exile. His ministry was still going on when the end came. Recall the story.

Like Jeremiah, Ezekiel was not only a prophet, but he was a priest as well. When he was 25 years old, he was carried as a captive to Babylon in 597 BC, with the upper class of people, 11 years before the destruction of Jerusalem. This means that for 11 years, 10,000 exiles were living in Babylon, while Jeremiah and the folks at home tried to carry on in Jerusalem. For five years the captives had no preacher. Then Ezekiel began to serve them.

Ezekiel lived at the same time as Jeremiah. He also lived at the same time as Daniel, who with a few other Jewish boys had been taken to Babylon in 606 BC. Both Ezekiel and Daniel were young men about the same age. Jeremiah was older. He had been prophesying for about 30 years in Jerusalem when Ezekiel was taken away to Babylon nine years after Daniel. No doubt Ezekiel had been Jeremiah's pupil while he was in Jerusalem, and we find him preaching to the captives in Babylon the same things Jeremiah had preached. He told them of their sins and their certain judgment. He reiterated their folly in relying on Egypt. He tried to remove their false hopes of an early return to their homeland. He tried to prepare them for the news of the tragic destruction of their beloved Jerusalem.

When Ezekiel reached Babylon, he found that Daniel had attained a high position in the palace of Nebuchadnezzar, although he was only a youth. Daniel probably helped ease the lot of the captives because of his station.

A Book for Ezekiel's Time

The young prophet Ezekiel was prepared by God to be His witness to the people in their captivity. God had needed a voice to warn the people and to remind them of the reason all these calamities had happened to them. For 22 years Ezekiel dealt with the discouraged captives to whom God had sent him.

The pivot of the book is the destruction of Jerusalem:

1. Pre-siege (Ezekiel 1–24)—Six years before the destruction of Jerusalem, Ezekiel began his prophecies, and he kept predicting its certainty until it occurred.

2. Siege (Ezekiel 25–32)—After the fall of Jerusalem, Ezekiel's prophecies dealt with Judah's enemies and the overthrow of these heathen nations.

3. Post-siege (Ezekiel 33–48)—Finally, Ezekiel prophesized about the restoration and reestablishment of Judah.

"The word of the LORD came to me" (Ezekiel 24:15). This phrase occurs 49 times in Ezekiel. God's greatest communications can only be made by His servants whose own hearts have been broken. The instrument in God's hands must personally be ready to share in suffering with others, just as Jesus' body was broken for us.

A Book for Today

The book of Ezekiel is for the Jewish people today. It tells them that God will fulfill His sure promises. Their land, their city, their

Temple will be restored to them. It reveals God's plan for them.

Ezekiel is for the Christian today. It is a book of the times, for God's time is always revealed by His dealing with the Jews. When the Jews move, we know God is getting ready to act. The State of Israel has now existed officially for more than half a century, and it continues to see the return of Jews to the Promised Land. Divine history continues to be made.

A Book for the Future

You find little of Ezekiel in the Gospels or Epistles. But look in Revelation. Ezekiel and John seem to lock arms across the centuries, and looking into the future they see the unfolding of a new heaven and a new earth. Ezekiel, the prophet, peering forward with rapt gaze, half whispering, says, "Above the vault over their heads was what looked like a throne of lapis lazuli, and high above on the throne was a figure like that of a man" (Ezekiel 1:26). And John, a little nearer, revealing God's vision to him, says in clearer tones these thrilling words: "At once I was in the Spirit, and there before me was a throne in heaven with someone sitting on it. And the one who sat there had the appearance of jasper and ruby. A rainbow that shown like an emerald encircled the throne" (Revelation 4:2-3).

THE LIFE OF EZEKIEL

The northern kingdom of Israel had been taken captive 120 years before by the king of Assyria (722 BC). Then God brought judgment upon the southern kingdom of Judah. Nebuchadnezzar had come to Jerusalem and carried away 10,000 of the chief men of the southern kingdom; the captives included some of the royal line and Daniel and Ezekiel (see 2 Kings 24:14-16; 2 Chronicles 36:6-7; Daniel 1:1-3).

The people of Israel had been living with constant troubles. It took Nebuchadnezzar 20 years to completely destroy Jerusalem. He could have done it sooner, but he wanted tribute

Ezekiel

money. Then, too, Daniel was his court favorite, and his young prime minister may have influenced him. He was finally forced to devastate Jerusalem because the city persisted in allying herself with Egypt. It was a tragic hour for Jerusalem when her wall was laid flat, her houses burned, the Temple destroyed and her people dragged away as captives.

God had told of Judah's captivity by Babylon more than 100 years before the event happened (see Isaiah 39:6; Micah 4:10), and Jeremiah had foretold that the captivity would last 70 years (see Jeremiah 25:11-12). It is interesting to note that God told them the exact time of their exile. But the captivity did not bring the people of Judah back to God. This judgment of God only seemed to drive the people into greater wickedness. They worshiped idols, set up shrines in the hills and defiled the sanctuary of Jehovah (see Ezekiel 5:11). Then Ezekiel began to tell his prophecies to them.

Ezekiel's Babylonian home was by the Chebar River. This river was actually an irrigation canal that branched off from the Euphrates River above Babylon, the most beautiful city of the world. Babylon was filled with palaces, gardens, temples and bridges, making it an outstanding showplace of the East. Chebar was probably one of many canals we know of that the Babylonian monarchs had dug. Ezekiel might have been one of the captives who helped dig the canals. Tradition tells us that the little village of Kifil was the town where Ezekiel lived, died and was buried. Tel Aviv, where a colony of captive Jews dwelt, was nearby. He was 50 miles from Babylon. No doubt he often visited Daniel in the palace. The Jewish people presented a pitiable picture—no temple, national life gone, little opportunity for business. To such an audience Ezekiel devoted the best years of his life.

Ezekiel had a style and method of preaching all his own. He used symbols (see Ezekiel 4), visions (see Ezekiel 8), parables (see Ezekiel 17), poems (see Ezekiel 19), proverbs (see Ezekiel 12:22-23; 18:2) and prophecies (see Ezekiel 6; 20; 40–48).

Ezekiel was an artist. He painted strange pictures for us. They are mystifying and full of terror and sometimes hard to decipher.

They glow with life and action. He talked of sin and punishment, of repentance and blessing.

God told Ezekiel to speak to the captives "whether they listen or fail to listen" (Ezekiel 3:11). We must get alongside people to help them. This was our Lord's way. Ezekiel's responsibility was to deliver God's message. The results were not in his hands.

THE GLORY OF THE LORD

"The glory of the LORD" seems to be the key phrase in the book of Ezekiel. It occurs over and over again in the first 11 chapters. Then it does not occur again until chapter 43.

In the Old Testament, "the glory of the LORD" refers to the light that shone between the cherubim in the holy of holies—it was evidence of the presence of God. Ezekiel opens with this heavenly glory in a vision (see Ezekiel 1). The book ends with earthly glory (see Ezekiel 40–48). Ezekiel's visions given in between tell how "the glory of the LORD" was forced from the Temple at Jerusalem by the idolatry of the people.

God said, "Because you have defiled my sanctuary with all your vile images and detestable practices, I myself will shave you; I will not look on you with pity or spare you" (Ezekiel 5:11). In Ezekiel 8, we see Ezekiel in a vision transported to Jerusalem, where he sees four kinds of idolatry that were practiced in the courts of the Lord's house—even worshiping the sun, with the worshipers' backs to the sanctuary while their faces were to the east.

First "the glory of the LORD" left the cherubim for the threshold of God's house (see Ezekiel 10:4), then it moved to the east gate (see Ezekiel 10:18-19), and finally it moved clear away from the Temple and city to the Mount of Olives (see Ezekiel 11:22-23). Thus gradually, reluctantly, majestically, "the glory of the LORD" left the Temple and the holy city. Then captivity came.

This vision was Ezekiel's message to the nation. Their captivity was a result of their sins, and before they could hope for return to their land, they must return to their Lord. This message reached its climax in the impassioned cry of Ezekiel found in Ezekiel 18:30-32.

God's judgment on sin is certain and severe. His redemption is equally certain when the human heart welcomes it. Ezekiel's message closes with the promise of future glory. Ezekiel 37 is the great classic chapter describing Israel's hope. The closing vision of the Temple is equally significant. The glory of the Lord returns and fills the house of the Lord (see Ezekiel 43:2-6; 44:4).

Application for Individuals

Young Christians, this is just what can happen to us. We can grieve, or distress, the Holy Spirit and resist Him until He is forced to leave; and our heart becomes like a ruined temple deprived of its glory (see Ephesians 4:30; 1 Thessalonians 5:19). There are so many blighted Christian lives from which the radiance has gone because of disobedience.

We grieve the Spirit when we do not allow ourselves time to read the Word or to pray. We limit the Spirit when we refuse to be clean vessels through which He can work. We resist Him by allowing idols to be in our hearts. Remember, your body is the temple of the Holy Spirit (see 1 Corinthians 6:19). Does His presence glow in your life?

Application for Nation and Church

Ezekiel's prophecy is intensely practical for both a nation and the Church. As Israel's captivity was the result of sin, so we must remember that sin is a reproach to any people. A nation's troubles are the result of national apostasy, a falling away from God.

The same is true of the Church of Christ. "The glory of the Lord" left the house of the Lord because of the sins of God's people. It is also true of each individual Christian experience. God's blessing returns to His people when His people return to Him.

THE CALL OF EZEKIEL

It seems God called Ezekiel so that He could explain and justify His action in allowing His children to be taken into captivity. They had been wicked and stiff-necked; they were guilty of unspeakable sins and abominations. When other nations did what Israel had done, God wiped them out. But all of God's dealings with Israel were for correction. They should say, "I know, LORD, that your laws are righteous, and that in faithfulness you have afflicted me" (Psalm 119:75). He was punishing His children for their sins and was teaching them great lessons. He said a remnant would survive. "They shall know that I am God" was His purpose. After the captivity, the Jews were cured of their polytheism; they no longer worshiped the many gods of the surrounding peoples. They had insisted upon it before, in spite of the warnings of God; but after the Chosen People came out of Babylon, the names of other gods were banished from their lips.

God had placed Jeremiah as a tower of strength in the land of Judah. In the same way, He placed Ezekiel as a tower of strength among his captive people in the land of the Babylonians. He told Ezekiel, "I will make your forehead like the hardest stone, harder than flint" (Ezekiel 3:9). Strength characterized the ministry of the prophet whose name means "God will strengthen."

As a Home Missionary

Ezekiel was sent to his own people. It is sometimes easier to go as a missionary to another culture like China or India than to speak to the members of your own household or your own friends.

Perhaps God is speaking to us as He spoke to Ezekiel: "You are not being sent to a people of obscure speech and strange language, but to the people of Israel. Go now to your people in exile and speak to them. Say to them, 'This is what the Sovereign LORD says,' whether they listen or fail to listen" (Ezekiel 3:5,11). It was difficult for Ezekiel to speak to false prophets, elders, shepherds and princes, but God commanded it.

As a Watchman

God told Ezekiel to be a watchman. He told the prophet not to fear the people but to give them warning; and that if he did not do it, He would require their blood at his hands (see Ezekiel 3:18;

33:8). Chapters 3 and 33 in Ezekiel state plainly our personal responsibility in spreading the gospel message. Paul was so faithful in doing this that he could say, "I am innocent of the blood of any of you" (Acts 20:26).

As a Sign

To be God's sign to the people, Ezekiel underwent the loss of all personal interests. He stood ready to do anything God asked of him in order to demonstrate the plan of God for His people, and God asked some extraordinary things of him. Ezekiel shut himself up in his house (see Ezekiel 3:24). He was placed in weird positions (see Ezekiel 4:4-8). He ate his food by weight (see Ezekiel 4:10). He sacrificed personal appearance (see Ezekiel 5:1) and even moved personal and domestic goods out of his house to show the removal of Israel into captivity (see Ezekiel 12:2-7). He was told to clap his hands and stamp his feet (see Ezekiel 6:11).

God may never ask such things of us, but He may ask us to do things that are at odds with our wills and desires. Will He find us as obedient as Ezekiel? Christ seeks such followers: "I looked for someone among them who would build up the wall and stand before me in the gap on behalf of the land so I would not have to destroy it, but I found no one" (Ezekiel 22:30).

VISIONS OF EZEKIEL

Ezekiel is a prophet of visions. The key text of the book shows this: "While I was among the exiles by the Kebar River, the heavens were opened and I saw visions of God" (Ezekiel 1:1). It is urgent that you scan all these visions before you begin a detailed study of this book.

Cherubim (1—3:13)

In this vision, "four living creatures" appeared; each had an unusual face but each had the general appearance of a man (Ezekiel 1:5). The main purpose of the vision was twofold: (1) to commission

Ezekiel for service, and (2) to impress upon him the need for assimilating the words God speaks to him and giving them to the people. Note "the scroll" he ate in his vision (Ezekiel 3:1). The creatures' unswerving obedience to God's will symbolized the obedience expected of Ezekiel. Their movement as a single unit is the picture of God's will perfectly executed.

Ezekiel and Revelation are often alike in symbolism. The "figure like that of a man" upon the throne (Ezekiel 1:26) is the Son of God. "The appearance of a rainbow in the clouds on a rainy day" symbolizes the covenant God made with Noah (Ezekiel 1:28). The "fire" (Ezekiel 1:4,13,27) is God's Spirit. In Revelation, all these appear. And Christ figures prominently in all the symbolism of both books.

Godlessness and Glory (8–11)

Before the siege of Jerusalem, Ezekiel was given an extended vision that showed the people's abominations by defiling the sanctuary. "Detestable things" occur all the way through the section (Ezekiel 8:6,9,17). The "glory" of God stands in sharp contrast to the awful things (Ezekiel 8:4). God was trying to show why Israel was to be led into captivity (see Ezekiel 8:17-18).

Burning Vine (15)

The vine becomes a symbol of Judah, and the burning of a useless vine that bears no fruit is the destruction of the people of God. The abominations of Jerusalem were so great that they warranted the most severe punishment. This vision of doom was followed by the parable of the unfaithful wife. Israel was Jehovah's "bride" who had forsaken God to go whoring after other gods. Love of idols, rather than the love of God, caused Israel's downfall (see Ezekiel 16).

Dry Bones (37:1-14)

In this vision, Ezekiel saw a great valley filled with dry bones, said to be "the people of Israel" (Ezekiel 37:11). The main message of the vision is the restoration of God's people. God will gather them from around the heathen countries through which, as bones without flesh, they have been scattered. It is a picture also of the power of God to raise those who have not only been scattered but who are also "dead" in sins. This "new birth" was explained to Nicodemus (see John 3:1-21). God promised it here to Israel. The Chosen People are to be brought forth, filled with God's Spirit and brought to their land.

PARABLES AND SIGNS IN EZEKIEL

Parables and signs, as well as visions, abound in Ezekiel. The more outstanding ones command great interest.

Parable of the Two Eagles (Ezekiel 17)

The parable of the two eagles reveals "the king of Babylon" and the king of Egypt (verse 12; see also verse 15). "The top of the cedar" corresponds to Jehoiachin carried captive to Babylon (verse 3). "One of the seedlings of the land" was Zedekiah (verse 5). The "tender sprig" that Jehovah will plant is the Messiah, the future King of David's line through whom all nations will learn to know God (verse 22). Jeremiah also told of the "righteous Branch" (23:5; see also Isaiah 11:1; Zechariah 3:8; Isaiah 53). The Lord's "holy mountain, the high mountain of Israel" refers to Jerusalem (Ezekiel 20:40; see also Ezekiel 17:22-23; Micah 4:1-2; Isaiah 2:2-3).

Parable of the Two Sisters (Ezekiel 23)

The parable of the two sisters Oholah and Oholibah describes Israel's and Judah's deterioration into idolatry. (Chapters 20–23 include several parables, but this one is predominant.)

Parable of the Boiling Cauldron (Ezekiel 24:1-14)

The parable of the boiling caldron reveals the holocaust in Jerusalem at the hands of the invading Babylonians. The many descriptions of fuel, hot fire, boiled flesh and burnt bones show the intensity of the siege (see Ezekiel 24:5,10).

Parable of the Two Sticks (Ezekiel 37:15-28)

The parable of the two sticks—one Judah, the other Israel—describes how Judah and Israel will ultimately be reunited under the Shepherd King of God's people—Christ (see Ezekiel 37:24). (This was also one of the ways that Ezekiel was an important sign to the people.)

EZEKIEL 1–24: BEFORE THE SIEGE OF JERUSALEM

First Vision from God

As the book of Ezekiel opens, we see Ezekiel, a young man of about 30, captive yet being commissioned by God for great service.

Like the prophets generally, Ezekiel began his ministry only after he had had a vision and a call from God. Turn to Isaiah 6 and review the facts of Isaiah's commission; then review Jeremiah's call (see Jeremiah 1:4-10). Ezekiel opens with a similar description of when he was called.

Ezekiel gives us a dramatic picture of his vision and call to service. The Holy Being who appeared to him could go everywhere. He was all-powerful, could see everything and could rule the entire universe by His mighty hand.

The vision Ezekiel saw was unusually complicated and elaborate. Notice how many times Ezekiel uses the words "appearance" and "likeness." He knows he is trying to describe things impossible to picture.

The prophet saw a fiery cloud approaching. From out of the glow were four living creatures, suggested by the cherubim of the Temple (see 1 Kings 6:23-28; Genesis 3:24; Psalm 18:10). Each had four wings and four faces: that of a man, a lion, an ox and an eagle, symbolizing, respectively, intelligence, dignity, strength and speed. They faced east, west, north and south, suggesting that God sees all things in the universe. Wings indicated that no spot is inaccessible to divine power. There were eyes in the wheels—such wheels cannot miss their way. We see a symbol of the omnipotence (all power), omnipresence (all present) and omniscience (all knowledge) of God.

Ezekiel

The mysterious whir of the mighty wings was followed by an equally mysterious silence. The wings dropped. The chariots stopped. Above the heads of the creatures was a crystal floor on which rested a sapphire throne, and on the throne sat Almighty God Himself, a figure of supernatural brilliance and glory. The sight of a lovely rainbow around the throne softened the terror of divine majesty. Little wonder that when Ezekiel saw this vision he fell facedown. The vision was meant to destroy all self-confidence the prophet might have had.

Prophet for God

Following the vision, the Almighty upon the throne broke the awful silence. The prophet then received his call. God told the prophet to rise and accept his commission for service. God wants more than simple submission. He wants loving service. God called Ezekiel "son of man" close to 100 times in this book. Ezekiel was called to declare the message of God—a message of doom to the people. Read Ezekiel 2:1-10. This doom was justified by their rebellion. Ezekiel himself might have been tempted to rebel, but he went without flinching to speak the word.

The prophet's authority is suggested by the symbolic swallowing of a scroll. He must make the message his own. He must eat it (see Ezekiel 3:3). As bitter as the message was on the scroll—the words that Ezekiel was to speak—the scroll was sweet as honey, for it is sweet to do the will of God and to be trusted with tasks for Him.

Then Ezekiel heard the whir of the wings and the roar of the wheels when the glory of Jehovah rose from the place and the chariot departed, leaving the prophet feeling bitter and angry with his own people. In this mood he found his way to Tel Aviv and for a week remained there dazed and in a state of utter astonishment.

Watchman for God

At the end of the week, Ezekiel received another message from God. This time it was more explicit. He was called to be a watchman: "I have made you a watchman . . . give them warning from me. . . . [If] you do not warn them . . . I will hold you accountable for their blood. But if you do warn the wicked person . . . you will have saved yourself" (Ezekiel 3:17-19).

God places a great responsibility on His watchmen. How can we be so careless in the light of such words as these? How can we go to sleep and fail to warn others of their sins? Let us answer this challenge and heed this warning.

God repeated His message to Ezekiel: "I have made you a watchman" (Ezekiel 33:7).

As a watchman, Ezekiel had to warn individual people of the coming catastrophe he so clearly saw. It was not enough to warn the crowd. He was to deal with individuals, good or bad, who compose the crowd; and he was to tell them to turn from their evil ways.

God impressed Ezekiel with the idea of the responsibility each individual has. Each one must repent. Each one must hear the Word. How true this is today of every person. Each person must accept Christ personally. No one can do it for another. "Yet to all who receive him, to those who believed in his name, he gave the right to become children of God" (John 1:12; see also John 3:16; 5:24; 3:36).

Symbols of Coming Doom

In this section of the book of Ezekiel, Ezekiel cannot speak, but he is a prophet still and he can preach, if not by word, then by symbol (see Ezekiel 3:22-27). There are four symbolic acts that represent the doom Jerusalem was facing:

1. The siege of Jerusalem (4:1-3)—Ezekiel used a clay tablet and an iron pan to symbolize Jerusalem under strong attack.

2. The duration of the exile (4:4-8)—This section is curious. Here Ezekiel acted out what was to happen. He lay upon his side to symbolize the years of punishment the Jews were to suffer in exile—one day for each year.

3. The hardships of the exiles (4:9-17)—The horrors of famine due to the siege were symbolized by the

prophet's food and drink carefully measured out—about a half-pound of food and a pint of water each day.

4. The fate of the besieged (5:1-17)—The last symbols, the sword and razor, are the most terrible of them all. They suggest the completeness of the destruction.

All of these visions and symbols reveal the method of Ezekiel's prophecy. This is also the method used in Daniel and Revelation.

Justification of Punishment

The prophet was shown the way the people profaned the Temple of Jehovah. This justified to the new generation the national punishment (see Ezekiel 8–11:12).

The prophet begged Jehovah to spare a remnant, and Jehovah promised to be "a sanctuary" to them in the land of their exile (Ezekiel 11:16). He promised to finally restore them (see Ezekiel 11:13-21).

The remaining chapters in this section of Ezekiel reveal the past sins of both Samaria and Jerusalem, and the punishment and instructions in righteousness for the elders of Israel (see Ezekiel 11:22-24). God said, "I will give them an undivided heart and put a new spirit in them. . . . They will be my people, and I will be their God" (Ezekiel 11:19-20). God wanted His people to have a heartfelt religious transformation with a new spirit to worship only Him. God will give His people a new spirit (see Ezekiel 18:31; 36:26).

EZEKIEL 25–32: DURING THE SIEGE OF JERUSALEM

In Ezekiel 25–32, we hear pronouncements of doom on surrounding nations. We remember that Isaiah gave similar prophecies (see Isaiah 13–23). Jeremiah also gave similar prophecies (see Jeremiah 46–51). Each prophet mentioned different nations. Ezekiel prophesied about Ammon, Moab, Edom, Philistia, Tyre, Sidon and Egypt—Israel's enemies who must be put out of the way before Israel is restored to her land.

So at this point we hear of the future doom of these foreign powers. First we hear of Israel's near neighbors who have insulted and harassed her, and then of the more distant and more powerful ones. God pronounced His judgment upon them for their sins against Israel. All of these powers were ancient enemies of Israel. The animosity dated back to before the days of the monarchy. From Israel's petty neighbors—Ammon, Moab, Edom and Philistia—with their petty spite, Ezekiel turned to the large cities of Tyre and Sidon and to the great empire of Egypt. They, too, must go. In a passage of great literary power, Ezekiel described the brilliance of Tyre, the extent of her commerce and the pity and terror inspired by her fall.

Ezekiel 29–32 tells of the collapse of Egypt. The mighty Nebuchadnezzar with his terrible army will deliver a crushing blow, and Egypt will be devastated.

The remarkable thing about these prophecies is that they were given at a time when these cities and nations were strong and powerful. Since that time, all but one have passed into a state of utter desolation (as Babylon did) or was reduced to a place of insignificance among world powers and was absorbed by a mightier country. Many of the specific prophecies have already been fulfilled to the minutest detail. "Righteousness exalts a nation, but sin condemns any people" (Proverbs 14:34).

EZEKIEL 33–48: AFTER THE SIEGE OF JERUSALEM

Immediately after the prophecies about Israel's enemies, Ezekiel began to prophesy about the future restoration of Israel. God often reveals a bright picture of Israel's future against the backdrop of divine judgment. We can now look into the future and see the final restoration and glory of Israel. God will gather together His scattered people. God said over and over, "I will . . . I will . . ."

Shepherds of Israel had proven faithless to the people, and the flock had been scattered; but now Jehovah will set up a Shepherd, "my servant David" (Ezekiel 34:23-24). This, no doubt, refers to the Davidic covenant and to the seed of David, the Messiah. Look up this series of passages: 2 Samuel 7:16; Psalm 89:20-36; Isaiah 7:13-14; 9:6-7; 11:1-12; Jeremiah 23:2-7; Ezekiel 37:21-28; Hosea 3:4-5; Luke 1:30-33; Acts 2:29-31; 15:14-17. All of these reveal that the future blessing of Israel will come with the Messiah, David's Son. When most of the Jews rejected Jesus, they did not thwart God's plan or defeat His purpose; for in Acts we read that Jesus was raised from the dead to sit on David's throne, and Jesus will return to bless Israel (see Acts 2:30).

The Restoration of Israel

The restoration Ezekiel told about does not refer to the feeble remnant that returned to Jerusalem after the 70 years of captivity (see Ezra and Nehemiah), for it is a restoration from all nations (see Ezekiel 36:24).

Ezekiel sees a vision of all this. There is a valley of dry bones (see Ezekiel 37:1-14). The "bones" are the Jews who will be alive at the restoration of the nation (verse 11). The "graves" are the nations where they are dwelling but "buried" (verse 13). God first will bring them into their own land. Then they will be converted—a new nation will be born in a day. The Spirit will give them life. The revival of national life is possible! It is not beyond the power of God. Even dry bones, without sinew and flesh, can be made to live. The Holy Spirit can bring life. This truth is seen everywhere when the Spirit comes with His quickening power (see Genesis 2:7; Revelation 11:11).

Israel will multiply as the Chosen People return to their own land. This restoration of Israel will be a national one. They will look on Him whom they pierced, and they will mourn because of Him. And a nation will be born in a day (see Zechariah 12:10; John 19:37; Romans 11:26). The resurrection in this chapter is not of the individual Jew but of the whole nation.

Ezekiel 38 opens with the doom of "Gog, of the land of Magog, the chief prince of Meshek and Tubal." The reference is to the northern European powers that will join together to fight against the restoration of Israel, perhaps headed up by Russia.

(Read these related passages: Zechariah 14:1-9; 12:1-4; Matthew 24:14-30; Revelation 14:14-20; 19:17-21.)

Before the curtain falls, we read the description of the kingdom during the coming millennial age. (This is what the thousand-year reign of Christ on earth is called when He will sit upon the throne of David, in Jerusalem [see Revelation 20:6].) All the prophets tell us what a glorious day this will be for both Jew and Gentile. We read about the Temple; the worship there; the final possession of the land promised to Abraham and to his descendants, according to the covenant God gave to him (see Genesis 12:1-3; 13:14-15; 15:18; 17:3-8); and the many nations that will know that God alone is Lord of all (see Ezekiel 38:23).

The Golden Truth About the Golden Age

Back here in the Old Testament, while the Jews were in what seemed hopeless captivity, God declared constantly that He will restore the Jews to their own land and set up the throne and the kingdom of David through David's greater Son. With His reign will come such earthly and spiritual blessings as have not been known since the world began. This is the golden truth about the golden age that is coming to pass here on this earth (see Ezekiel 34:22-31).

Gabriel's prophecy at Jesus' birth will be literally fulfilled through David's Son, the Lord Jesus Christ (see Luke 1:30-33). This promise of a messianic King and His kingdom must be carefully distinguished from our Lord's spiritual rule over hearts and lives. The words of Gabriel to Mary still await complete, literal fulfillment (see 1 Kings 14:8; Jeremiah 30:9; Ezekiel 34:23-24; 37:24).

The appearance of the Messiah will usher in a glorious future. God will make a covenant of peace (see Leviticus 26:6; Jeremiah 31:31; Ezekiel 37:26). Wonderful blessings will be bestowed on His people. They will be assured of absolute protection from idolatrous nations, the evil beasts of Ezekiel 34:25, because they are possessed by none other than God Himself (see Ezekiel 34:31).

Understanding Daniel

Daniel Portrays Jesus Christ, the Striking Stone

SELECTED BIBLE READINGS

DAY OF THE WEEK		MAIN TOPIC
Sunday: Daniel 1–2	The Captive Daniel	
Monday: Daniel 3–4	The Proud King	
Tuesday: Daniel 5; 7–8	Belshazzar's Reign	
Wednesday: Daniel 6–9	Darius's Reign	
Thursday: Daniel 10	God's Glory	
Friday: Daniel 11	Kings' Conflict	
Saturday: Daniel 12	Daniel's Last Message	

AUTHOR: Daniel 9:2 and 10:2 identify the author of the book of Daniel as the prophet Daniel. Jesus also mentioned Daniel as the author of the book (see Matthew 24:15).

DATE: The book was most likely written between 540 and 530 BC.

PURPOSE AND SUMMARY: The book of Daniel records the life and work of the prophet Daniel in exile in Babylon from 605 BC to 536 BC. The first half of the book of Daniel shows how those who trust and obey God—like Daniel and his friends—will be vindicated by God's power—like Daniel and his friends were with signs and wonders, prophetic revelation, and angelic deliverance. In the second half of the book, a series of apocalyptic visions that Daniel received from the Lord present a view of history in which the God of Israel rules and prevails over the nations to bring about ultimate victory for the kingdom of God and the people of God.

"Young men without any physical defect, handsome, showing aptitude for every kind of learning, well informed, quick to understand, and qualified to serve in the king's palace" (Daniel 1:4)—these are some of the men with whom this book deals. They were skilled in God's wisdom as opposed to human wisdom. They had an understanding of God's revelation that unlocks the mysteries of human science. They had ability in them such as God gives to live the overcoming life!

Chief among these princely young men was the incomparable Daniel. He stands out in God's Word as the man who dared to keep a clean heart and body, and the man, therefore, through whom God chose to give His message to the Gentile nations of the world (see Daniel 1:8). A large part of this book is concerned with the thrilling personal life of this peerless captive noble of Judah, and the book is packed with heart-touching devotional passages for the personal Christian life:

- The value of a surrendered life—Daniel 1
- Light even in darkness—Daniel 2:20-22
- Triumph through trial—Daniel 3:17-25
- The reward of service—Daniel 5:17
- Prayer and confidence in God—Daniel 6:10-24
- Confession of sin—Daniel 9:3-19
- The wisdom of soul winning—Daniel 12:3

Daniel was in the palace in Babylon at the same time that Ezekiel was toiling in a slave gang. If Daniel's was the easier life in many of its material aspects, it may also be considered by far the more perilous. Ezekiel's work during these dreary exile years was to proclaim to his people God's truth and to explain the real meaning of the miseries that had befallen them. Daniel's task was to share in the actual government of Babylon.

Daniel has been called the prophet of dreams. God revealed to him His secrets. "During the night the mystery was revealed to Daniel in a vision" (Daniel 2:19). Daniel, like Ezekiel, looked far into the future. He is quoted most in Revelation. One cannot understand the great signs of Revelation without looking at their meaning in Daniel.

The book of Daniel is divided into two great sections:

1. History—narration (Daniel 1–6)
2. Prophecy—revelation (Daniel 7–12)

DANIEL'S LIFE

Daniel belonged to a family of high rank. During the first invasion by Nebuchadnezzar, when Daniel was about the age of 18, he was taken captive to Babylon. Ezekiel was taken captive nine years later during the second invasion. Daniel lived to be more than 90 years of age. He saw the Babylonian kingdom fall (539 BC) and the Medo-Persian Empire established. He held high positions under kings Nebuchadnezzar, Belshazzar, Darius (550-486 BC, king of Persia from 522-486 BC) and Cyrus (585-529 BC, called "the Great").

Model of Righteousness

Daniel's whole time in captivity was spent in the great and glamorous city of Babylon, the ancient Hollywood. He spent 69 years in a vile court. There he lived a life without blame and well favored. Daniel was among the great men of history. The historical portions of his own book prove the truth of that statement. Ezekiel, nearest to him in his own day and therefore one who knew him best, even ranked him as one of the world's triumvirate of virtue—Noah, Daniel and Job (see Ezekiel 14:14-20; 28:3). He was a model of righteousness.

Although Daniel was a captive, he rose to be prime minister of Babylon. The wonderful thing is that he always remained true to Jehovah God. Daniel was also great in heaven. God broke the silence of the skies twice to cry out, "Daniel, you who are highly esteemed" (Daniel 10:11,19). Furthermore, no position, no matter how difficult, found him without trust in God. God is able, in all temptations, to keep us from falling, unless we have deliberately placed ourselves, with Peter, at the fire of the enemy (see Jude 24).

God even honored Daniel in his prayers. Marvelous in power that Daniel's prayers were, God sent a special embassy of angels from the throne with the thrilling words, "I have come in response to [your words]" (Daniel 10:12). God exhibited His power in a remarkable way in Daniel's life, and Daniel never introduced himself or his own actions except as illustrations of that power.

Companion of Kings

Daniel was the companion of kings. He was a leader of men. He was a pioneer in reform (see Daniel 1:12). Daniel was, like Joseph, God's candle shining in pagan darkness. He was chief statesman in the first empire of the world, chief adviser of a great monarch and a great protector of his own people. God gave him favor and love in the sight of the court official, Ashpenaz. Even proud Nebuchadnezzar seemed to have had real affection for Daniel.

The feelings of Darius toward Daniel are revealed when he finds that a trap has been set for him. The king "was greatly distressed; he was determined to rescue Daniel and made every effort until sundown to save him" (6:14).

No doubt Cyrus was greatly influenced by the aged statesman. Daniel may have shown him the prophecy Isaiah had written concerning him 100 years before he was born. This might have made Cyrus issue the decree for rebuilding the Temple at Jerusalem (see 2 Chronicles 36:22-23; Ezra 1).

Prophet of God

In the book Daniel wrote, we see him preeminently as a prophet of God. He drew back the curtain and unveiled, as no one had ever done before, the hidden things of the future. Indeed, we see more and more that his great prophecies are only history written before it occurred. The book of Daniel is one of the world's great annals of anticipation.

This book reveals the power of God and His universal sovereignty:

- God the keeper (Daniel 1)—God's power kept Daniel and his companions safe. They were given understanding and wisdom above all the wise men of Babylon.

- God the revealer of secrets (Daniel 2)—God's power revealed the dream of Nebuchadnezzar to Daniel. None of the wise men of Babylon could do this.

- God the Deliverer (Daniel 3)—God's power delivered Daniel's three companions from the fiery furnace. These young men stood up alone, against a nation, with the calm assurance that God would deliver them, adding, "But even if he does not, we want you to know, Your Majesty, that we will not serve your gods or worship the image of gold you have set up" (verse 18). This occurred after they had been in Babylon about 20 years, and God was demonstrating in this most dramatic way His power over all the gods of this country.

- God the potentate (Daniel 4)—God's power dealt with the mighty Babylonian monarch Nebuchadnezzar. God struck him while the proud king was boasting of his power as he was strolling on the roof of his magnificent palace. He was driven from his kingdom to dwell among beasts—victim of a strange form of insanity.

- God the judge (Daniel 5)—God's power was shown in the awful judgment revealed to Belshazzar, son of Nabonidus, by the handwriting on the wall. That night the king was slain by the Persian army and his city was captured.

- God the All Powerful (Daniel 6)—God's power delivered Daniel from the lions' den. Remember, Daniel was an old man. He had been honored by the highest office in the whole empire when he was a young man of about 20. Now, at 90, he was thrown into the den of lions. It seems that even the lions honored him.

God used the times of captivity to reveal His power among the nations of the world. When the Chosen People were captives in Egypt, He worked miracles and wonders by the hand of Moses and showed, not only to the Israelites, but also to the Egyptians, that the Lord God is almighty. Now, during the Babylonian captivity, God manifested His power until the great world monarchs confessed that He is the living God, the Most High, the King of heaven. He visited His children even in exile and showed them again that He is "mighty to save" (Isaiah 63:1).

Unlike the other prophets, Daniel dealt more fully with the Gentile nations than with his own Jewish nation. The other prophets only mention the Gentiles as incidental to something concerning Israel. But Daniel gave us the history of the Gentile powers from Babylon to the end. The prophecies are considered among the most remarkable in all the Scriptures.

DANIEL 1–4: REIGN OF NEBUCHADNEZZAR

When the book of Daniel opens, we see a little company of four young men: Daniel, Hananiah, Mishael and Azariah (also called Shadrach, Meshach, Abednego). They had been taken captive from Jerusalem by Nebuchadnezzar and carried away to his palace in Babylon. Daniel was only about 16 years old; Nebuchadnezzar, a little older. Nebuchadnezzar came to the throne about the time Daniel was taken captive to Babylon, and he had a distinguished career as the most powerful king of the Babylonian empire. Daniel's career was marked by its extent in time and its greatness in accomplishment.

Daniel was carried to Babylon during the first deportation of the captives. He gained a high position in the kingdom and was influential throughout the 70 years of his captivity. He saw many of the captive people return to Jerusalem under the decree of Cyrus. He saw world-ruling Babylon pass away and a new empire arise. Even at the age of 90 he received a position of high distinction in the court of Persia.

Even though they were in a palace, Daniel and his friends lived in an atmosphere of loose morals and low standards. Yet we read that they kept themselves apart from the evil of that court—true to God in a day when everything was against them. Evils much like those of today were rampant everywhere in the courts of royalty.

Notice that these brave youths stood with Daniel when they faced their first temptation in the court of the Babylonian king: "Daniel resolved not to defile himself with the royal food and wine, and he asked the chief official for permission not to defile himself this way" (Daniel 1:8). To young men like these, God could tell His secrets and demonstrate His power. Remember, "The LORD confides in those who fear him" (Psalm 25:14).

These youths were confronted with three difficult positions, each of which they emerged from victorious:

1. The court of a powerful emperor
2. The fiery furnace
3. The den of lions

The Court of a Powerful Emperor

In this first scene we find the four captives in the luxurious royal court. The youths were brought very quickly face to face with a serious practical difficulty. This was a real test for these young men. As favored members of the royal court, they had been put into one of the apartments in the palace and were to be trained in state affairs and equipped for high positions. They were offered many of the delicacies from the king's table. It must have been hard indeed to refuse the king's meat and ask for simpler fare. They probably could have pleaded that they had no choice in the matter. Many of us would have argued that way. But they asked to be able to prove that their appearance would be satisfactory even without eating the royal fare. And God gave them favor in the eyes of their captors. Remember, we ought always to obey God rather than people. The king's food had probably been offered to idols (see Exodus 34:15; 1 Corinthians 10:20), and the animals used would have been killed with the blood left in, which would have made them unclean for the Israelites (see Leviticus 3:17; 7:26).

There was nothing priggish about Daniel. Making a man like Ashpenaz love him was impressive. And notice how loyal his companions were to him. This is a fine trait. Success did not turn Daniel's head. He was a man to whom, early in his career, men turned.

We are told that God gave these young men knowledge and skill in all learning and wisdom; and Daniel had understanding in all visions and dreams. This was God's reward. God's power is shown through His dealing with Daniel and his three companions in all the wisdom and understanding He gave them.

The Dream of World Empires

Then a disturbing incident happened at the palace. Nebuchadnezzar had dreamed a dream and not one of the wise men of the kingdom could tell him what it meant. So a decree had been sent forth that all the wise men should be slain, including Daniel and his friends. But Daniel was not afraid. God would tell him the dream and give him the meaning of it.

Daniel called his prayer partners and they presented their problem before God (see Daniel 2:17). "During the night the mystery was revealed to Daniel in a vision" (Daniel 2:19). God never disappoints faith.

Nebuchadnezzar's dream and its interpretation teach us some interesting things about the history of the world from that time till the end of this age. In the Bible, this period is called "the times of the Gentiles" (Luke 21:24; see also Romans 11:25) because God has put aside His own people, the Jews, for a time and has turned over the government of the world to the Gentiles.

Daniel 2 has been called the *ABC* of prophecy. It stretches out before us the most complete picture in all the Scriptures of what is to happen in the future. God revealed His plan of the future to King Nebuchadnezzar in a dream (see Daniel 2:29), which he forgot! But it worried him. No one could tell him his dream but one who knew "the God of heaven" (Daniel 2:18-19,37,44). Master the outline of history given in this second chapter.

Picture the large statue King Nebuchadnezzar dreamed of: The head was of gold, its breast and arms of silver, the belly and thighs of bronze, and its legs of iron, with its feet and toes of iron and clay. Then a rock cut out without hands struck the image and broke it to pieces; and the rock "became a huge mountain and filled the whole earth" (Daniel 2:35).

God first reveals the Gentile powers. Four great empires were to succeed one another in the government of the world from Nebuchadnezzar to the end. God said, "You [Babylon] are that head of gold" (Daniel 2:38).

The breast and arms of silver represented the Medo-Persian empire, which overthrew Babylon and became its successor (see Daniel 2:39; see also 8:20). Its power began with Cyrus under whom the Jews returned to Jerusalem (see Ezra 1:1-2).

The belly and thighs of bronze represented Greece, which conquered the Medo-Persians and ruled "over the whole earth" (Daniel 2:39; see also 8:21) under Alexander the Great (356-323 BC). The legs of iron represent Rome, the fourth world power (Daniel 2:40; see also 9:26). In Daniel 8, more is said of the fourth Gentile government than of the others. Perhaps this is because it is the last.

The feet and toes of iron and clay that cannot hold together indicate deterioration, a divided kingdom and a government weakened in its power. This last government will be the weakest. It will not be completely unified. There will be a division into many kingdoms, as there are many toes. And all will finally end in chaos.

The rock was no other than Jesus Christ.

The Kingdom of Christ

In the rock cut out without hands, we see Christ, whose kingdom will never be destroyed and who will bring to an end all the other kingdoms. Christ will come and set up a kingdom that will last forever (see Daniel 2:44-45). (To further your study, see what the Word says about the Rock and the Stone in Psalm 118:22; Isaiah 8:14; 28:16; Zechariah 3:9.)

Remember, at the time Nebuchadnezzar dreamed his dream, the Persian kingdom did not exist. It was merely a Babylonian satrapy. It would have seemed impossible that a strong Grecian empire would rise. Only wandering tribes inhabited the Hellenic states. The city of Rome was only a little town on the banks of the Tiber River. Yet God told Daniel what would come to pass.

Notice that the metals in the image deteriorate in value—gold, silver, bronze and iron. This reveals the weakening in the power of each succeeding empire. Finally we find iron mixed with brittle clay, suggesting unions attempted between incompatible partners. Name the forms of government that exist today. Do these resemble the toes of clay, "brittle" and not holding together (Daniel 2:42)?

Many ask, "When will the Rock break the iron, the bronze, the clay, the silver and the gold to pieces?" We don't know the day or hour, but the King *is* coming with power and great glory with all His holy angels to establish His kingdom.

The great King Nebuchadnezzar fell on his face and worshiped Daniel, and declared that his God was the God of all gods (see Daniel 2:46-47). But we find as we go on in the story that this wonderful revelation of God had little real effect upon Nebuchadnezzar. It did not bring him to his knees before God.

The Fiery Furnace of Nebuchadnezzar

As the curtain is pulled back again, we see in Daniel 3 that Daniel's friends faced a very tense moment. Nebuchadnezzar had set up a golden image on the plain of Dura and had commanded all peoples to fall down and worship it. If any refused, they would be cast into a fiery furnace.

But three of the people refused to obey the king. Yes, here they are again after 20 years: Shadrach, Meshach and Abednego. Spies reported their disobedience. These three knew what God had said: "You shall not make for yourself an image. . . . You shall not bow down to them or worship them" (Exodus 20:4-5). They were fearless in the presence of this eastern despot.

The story of the fiery furnace is a familiar one. What was the wonderful thing about that scene? Yes, the Son of God was with them. What effect did this have on Nebuchadnezzar? He was filled with great admiration for the miraculous power of the God of these men. But still he did not bow to worship God in humility. He called Jehovah "their own God" (Daniel 3:28). Remember, God wants us to say, "My Lord, and my God." Christ said, "When ye pray, say, our Father" (Luke 11:2, *KJV*). This scene demonstrated in a most dramatic way, before the dignitaries of the far-flung empire, the power of the Most High God. Erecting an image will be repeated by the beast—the Antichrist, the last head of Gentile world domination (see Revelation 13:11-15; 19:20).

The Dream of a Tree
In the next scene, we find that the king had another dream. Job 33:14-17 says, "For God does speak—now one way, now another—though no one perceives it. In a dream, in a vision of the night, when deep sleep falls on people as they slumber in their beds, he may speak in their ears and terrify them with warnings, to turn them from wrongdoing and keep them from pride."

God has often spoken to men in dreams to reveal His will when the Bible was not open to them. God spoke to Nebuchadnezzar once and gave him the image representing the Gentile kingdoms and showed him his doom. But the king did not repent. Then God spoke to him again from the fiery furnace where He revealed His power to him. But still Nebuchadnezzar's proud heart felt no repentance.

Now we find that God spoke to Nebuchadnezzar for a third time in the dream of the great tree that was cut down (see Daniel 4:4-27). This was a warning to Nebuchadnezzar of his coming madness. God was trying to bring this proud king to the end of himself. A year later we see him a madman, his mind gone. He fancied himself a beast (see Daniel 4:28-34). All this because he had set himself up as a rival of Almighty God. Note what Nebuchadnezzar said: "Is not this the great Babylon I have built as the royal residence, by my mighty power and for the glory of my majesty?" (Daniel 4:30).

Through his insanity, Nebuchadnezzar's eyes were opened and his conscience was touched. He confessed the greatness of God and testified about the goodness of God (see Daniel 4:34). He had learned that man is not the architect of his own fortune.

DANIEL 5; 7-8: REIGN OF BELSHAZZAR

The following points may help you know who Belshazzar was and where he came from:

- Nebuchadnezzar—He reigned to 562 BC.
- Merodach—This dissolute son of Nebuchadnezzar reigned two years.
- Neriglissar—This brother-in-law and murderer of Merodach followed with a four-year reign. He had no successor.
- Nabonidus—This son of Nebuchadnezzar's second wife ascended the throne in 556 BC. (He is also known by the name "Labyretus.")
- Belshazzar—This son of Nabonidus was a co-regent with him. The Medes imprisoned Nabonidus and captured reveling Belshazzar and Babylon.

As Daniel 5 opens, we see a great banquet hall with a thousand lords sitting about the tables. It was "ladies' night." All the king's sweethearts were there in addition to the thousand lords. Often the presence of ladies seems to inspire a man to do something spectacular. So as an extra banquet feature, Belshazzar sent for the sacred gold and silver vessels his grandfather Nebuchad-

Daniel

nezzar had stripped from the Temple in Jerusalem. He showed the revelers just how little he regarded the God of Israel. The last prince of Babylon, Belshazzar, used these sacred vessels to drink wine in honor of idols.

The Writing on the Wall

God showed His power in the awful handwriting on the wall. Daniel was called in to explain the meaning. The prophet fearlessly condemned this foolish and sensual young king. Read the details of the divine interruption in Daniel 5.

A bad reign came to a sudden end. "That very night Belshazzar, king of the Babylonians, was slain" (Daniel 5:30). We are not told in the Scriptures how the end came, but we learn from historians Xenophon, Herodotus and Berosus the strange story of the fall of the great city.

Many of the tablets from Babylon tell us that the Persian army took Babylon without a battle. Four months later, Cyrus entered the city. Darius probably received the kingdom from Cyrus as his vice-regent over some part of it.

The Vision of Four Beasts

During the first year of Belshazzar's reign, Daniel had a vision of four wild beasts (see Daniel 7), which symbolized the four kingdoms that Nebuchadnezzar had pictured in his dream (see Daniel 2). Compare them carefully. Picturing them as beasts gives us a hint about the moral character of these empires, for they are represented by ferocious wild beasts. How history's wars reveal the true heart of nations!

In Nebuchadnezzar's dream, we had a human view of the magnificence of these kingdoms. In Daniel's dream, we have God's view of the same kingdoms. Read Daniel 7:17-23 to see who Daniel says these four beasts are.

The first—Babylon—was like a lion with eagle's wings. Jeremiah likened Nebuchadnezzar both to the lion and eagle (see Jeremiah 49:19-22). Persia was the second beast—the bear—the cruel animal who delights in killing for the sake of killing. The third was a leopard or panther, a beast of prey. Its four wings connote swiftness, symbolizing the rapid marches of Alexander's army and his insatiable love of conquest. In 13 short years he had conquered the world. The fourth beast was different from all the rest. He was "terrifying and frightening and very powerful. It had large iron teeth" (Daniel 7:7).

The little horn coming up among the 10 is the Antichrist yet to come (see Daniel 7:8). We see him represented in Revelation as "a beast coming out of the sea" (Revelation 13:1; see also Daniel 7:15-25). The saints will be oppressed by the Antichrist, the last world ruler before Christ comes. The rule of today's world dictators only hints at the possible extent of the power and authority that this last great dictator, the Antichrist, will have. This period ends the great tribulation, the period during which the judgments of God are to come upon the earth for the rejection of Jesus Christ (see Revelation 5–18).

The Vision of a Ram and a Goat

Two years later, we find that Daniel had another vision, this time of a ram and a goat (see Daniel 8). Belshazzar was still on the throne. This vision includes only two of the four kingdoms envisioned earlier: Persia and Greece (see Daniel 8:20-21).

According to this vision, the kingdom of Medo-Persia would be overthrown by the king of Greece. This vision also contained the prophecy of the division of Greece, on the death of Alexander, between his four generals. Daniel had this vision at Susa, the capital of Persia, where 70 years later the events recorded in the book of Esther took place.

One of the most difficult questions in the Old Testament concerns the identity of "Darius the Mede" (Daniel 5:31). He must have been someone appointed by Cyrus, and the statement that he "took over the kingdom" confirms this. Some people think that he was better known as Astyages and was the father or grandfather of Cyrus and thus allowed to act as king until his death. Others think he was a commander in the army of Cyrus, named Gobryas, and the difference between this and "Darius" in the original would be slight.

DANIEL 6; 9: REIGN OF DARIUS

Twenty-three years after the death of Nebuchadnezzar, his great city, Babylon, fell into the hands of the Medes.

Even under these new rulers, however, Daniel remained in a place of power. But the jealousy of the other officials was aroused by the preference given to Daniel, and a plot to destroy him was quickly formed. "The administrators and the satraps tried to find grounds for charges against Daniel" (Daniel 6:4). Of course they did. He approved all their tax receipts, and they soon found that Daniel would not allow any graft. If Daniel didn't let them get away with anything, how were they going to get along with the high cost of living in Babylon? So Daniel had trouble because he would not go along with the corrupt crowd.

The Den of Lions

The group of officials used Daniel's religion to set their trap, with the same result that always happens when men are foolish enough to try to trip the Lord's faithful children (see 1 Peter 3:12-13; Deuteronomy 9:3). Remember there is always access to God through prayer in Christ. We may speak to God, not just three times a day, but whenever the need arises. The Lord Jesus invites us to pray. (Read John 14:13-14.)

The officials knew that the king would not lift a finger against Daniel, so in order to trap the king, what was their bait? Notice the subtle appeal to the king's pride.

The king was persuaded to pass a permanent decree—the laws of Medes and Persians were unchangeable (see Esther 1:19; 8:8)—without being aware of what the true consequence would be: Daniel's destruction. Just imagine, if you can, a David, an Alexander, a Caesar, a Peter the Great, a Napoleon, a Queen Victoria—any strong ruler—being tricked by a group of court officials into sacrificing a favorite if he or she did not want to! Signing that law without finding out what was behind it was inexcusable. When he found the trap he had walked into, he should have broken the promise. A bad promise is better broken than kept.

When the king saw that he had been deceived and he realized the injustice of putting Daniel to death, he did his best to avoid carrying out the law, but he finally had to obey it and had Daniel placed in the lions' den.

The envy of these officials no doubt was due to Daniel's ability and his Jewish blood. This spirit of anti-Semitism is in fulfillment of God's prophecies that the Jewish people would be hated. It continues even in modern times.

Daniel's conduct in the face of danger was quite deliberate. He knew he had to deny his religion or be prepared to die for it. There was nothing different in his actions: He prayed, as was his custom. Notice that Daniel prayed with thanksgiving (see Daniel 6:10; see also Philippians 4:6-7). When Daniel found out about the decree, he did not fall down in terror and agony, but he praised God. "Commit your way to the LORD; trust in him and he will do this" (Psalm 37:5).

His example probably influenced the other Jews. And his action, drawing attention to himself, might have reduced the danger for others. Daniel's faith during this ordeal was glorious and just what we would expect from a man mature in his faith in God.

Contrast Darius's first decree with the decree he issued after Daniel's deliverance from the den of lions (see Daniel 6:7-8,26-27). Over the vast realm went a proclamation declaring the power and greatness of Daniel's God. This scene closes with a note that "Daniel prospered during the reign of Darius and the reign of Cyrus" (Daniel 6:28).

Daniel was thrown into the den of lions, but he fell into the hands of the living God. The world cannot breed a lion that God cannot tame. Shutting lions' mouths of difficulty and temptation is God's specialty.

The Prophecy of Seventy Sevens

In Daniel 9:24-27, we read the following prophecy:

> Seventy "sevens" are decreed for your people and your holy city to finish transgression, to put an end to sin, to

atone for wickedness, to bring in everlasting righteousness, to seal up vision and prophecy and to anoint the Most Holy Place.

Know and understand this: From the time the word goes out to restore and rebuild Jerusalem until the Anointed One, the ruler, comes, there will be seven "sevens," and sixty-two "sevens." It will be rebuilt with streets and a trench, but in times of trouble. After the sixty-two "sevens," the Anointed One will be put to death and will have nothing. The people of the ruler who will come will destroy the city and the sanctuary. The end will come like a flood: War will continue until the end, and desolations have been decreed. He will confirm a covenant with many for one "seven." In the middle of the "seven" he will put an end to sacrifice and offering. And at the temple he will set up an abomination that causes desolation, until the end that is decreed is poured out on him.

"Seventy sevens" is translated "seventy weeks" in the *KJV*, which is a poor English equivalent. The term probably means 70 periods of seven years. If there are 70 seven-year periods, this is 70 × 7, or 490 years. Scripture divides these 70 sevens into three divisions with a parenthetic time lapse for the present "Gentile rule":

1. The first "seven weeks"—These 49 years began at the command to build and restore Jerusalem under Ezra and Nehemiah.

2. The second "sixty-two weeks"—These 434 years began at the building of the wall of Jerusalem and continued to the Crucifixion. Christ is "put to death and will have nothing" (Daniel 9:26). At this point, after 483 years, the clock of Israel's national life stops.

3. ("Gentile rule"—This period, lasting an unknown number of years, intervenes after the sixty-ninth week. We are in this period now, awaiting the coming of Christ.)

4. The last, or seventieth week—These seven years have not yet begun. They are years during which God deals with Israel exclusively. Beginning after the coming of Christ, the Antichrist takes power, makes a covenant with the Jews, and then breaks the covenant after half the week is up. This ushers in the time of troubles mentioned in Daniel 12:1, which is the great tribulation of Revelation. When will the seventieth week begin?

DANIEL 10–12: REIGN OF CYRUS

During the reign of Cyrus, the decree was sent out for the captives to return and rebuild the wall of Jerusalem (see Ezra 1:2-4). Daniel, now nearly 90 years old, was too elderly to return. No doubt he was also needed among the exiles in Babylon. Daniel had outlived all the friends and companions of his youth. Now he saw the Israelites gathering in the streets of Babylon, and the old man probably watched the last caravan leave the west gate of the city to return to Jerusalem. Daniel was concerned about his people. We will see how he was comforted in his perplexity. In Daniel 10, we see the vision of the glory of God.

Vision of God's Glory

In Daniel 11, we find the vision that concerns the near future of the kingdom in which Daniel was so great a personage. Three kings were yet to come in the Medo-Persian Empire. Then Alexander, the mighty king of Greece, would appear (see Daniel 11:2-3). His empire would be divided among his four generals, as had already been predicted.

Then we see the course of history down to Antiochus Epiphanes, the little horn of Daniel 8 (see verses 9-12). His desecration of the sanctuary is mentioned in Daniel 11:28 and 12:11. Beginning with Daniel 11:36, we see the description of the final "little horn" of Daniel 7—the Antichrist.

Vision of Tribulation and Resurrections

The great tribulation follows. How is it described in Daniel 12:1? This is a time of unparalleled troubles. Our Lord spoke of it in Matthew 24:21. What did He say? Mention is made of two resurrections: "Multitudes who sleep in the dust of the earth will awake: some to everlasting life, others to shame and everlasting contempt" (Daniel 12:2). These two will be 1,000 years apart (see Revelation 20:1-6). The first is the resurrection of the saints at Christ's coming to life everlasting. This is followed by 1,000 years, called the millennium. Then there will be a resurrection of the wicked to shame everlasting. Those that now "lead many to righteousness" are given significant rewards, showing us the necessity of being diligent to win souls during our wait for Christ's return (Daniel 12:3).

Daniel

Books of the Minor Prophets

of the Old Testament

HOSEA • JOEL • AMOS • OBADIAH

JONAH • MICAH • NAHUM

HABAKKUK • ZEPHANIAH • HAGGAI

ZECHARIAH • MALACHI

Key Events of the Books of the Minor Prophets

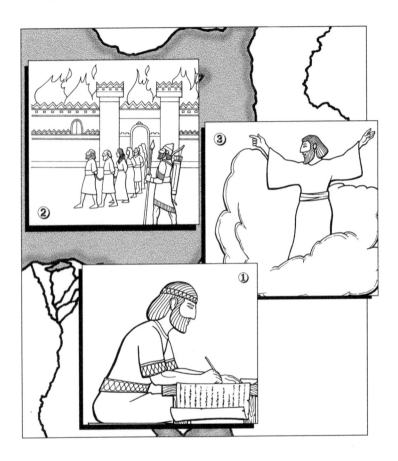

Books of the Minor Prophets: A Future Hope

By the time most of the minor prophets were writing ① (the seventh to the fifth centuries before Christ), the promise God had made to David of an everlasting kingdom was already at least 300 years old. These prophets foresaw tremendous destruction ② and sorrow for God's chosen people and for nations that would not humble themselves before God. Even so, they had faith that God would make good on His promises and send a Deliverer ③ for His people and for those nations who would bow before Him.

21

Understanding Hosea, Joel and Amos

Hosea Portrays Jesus Christ, Healer of the Backslider;
Joel Portrays Jesus Christ, Restorer; Amos Portrays Jesus Christ,
Heavenly Husbandman

SELECTED BIBLE READINGS

DAY OF THE WEEK		MAIN TOPIC
	Sunday: Hosea 4	Israel's Sins
	Monday: Hosea 3; 14	Israel's Future
	Tuesday: Joel 2	God's Repayment
	Wednesday: Joel 3	Israel's Restoration
	Thursday: Amos 3:1-7; 4:6-12	Personal Admonitions
	Friday: Amos 7–8:1-7	Prophet's Intercession
	Saturday: Amos 9	Future Blessings

UNDERSTANDING HOSEA

AUTHOR: Hosea 1:1 identifies Hosea, son of Beeri, as the author of the book of Hosea. It is Hosea's personal account of his prophetic messages to the Israelites in the northern kingdom of Israel in the 8th century BC. Hosea is the only prophet of Israel who left any written prophecies that were recorded during the later years of his life.

DATE: Hosea, the son of Beeri, prophesied for quite some time, from 750 to 715 BC, in the northern kingdom of Israel.

PURPOSE AND SUMMARY: Sometimes called the prophet of divine love, Hosea was a native of the northern kingdom of Israel and was called to be God's spokesman during that kingdom's darkest hour. The apostasy of his own people was enough to break Hosea's heart, but he also bore a heavy burden in his own life—his wife, Gomer, had become unfaithful and hired herself out as a prostitute. This mirrors how the Israelites had become unfaithful to the Lord and prostituted themselves to Canaanite gods. In this bitter experience, Hosea came to fathom God's love for His people; and Hosea pleaded with his people to repent and return to praising God's divine compassion and a love that will not let Israel go. Through Hosea, the Lord promised His people that if they return to Him, He will restore their broken lives.

With the study of Hosea's prophecy, we enter upon 12 books known as the minor prophets. Remember that the difference between the major and minor prophets is not a matter of importance but of the amount of material written.

Hosea was sent to the 10 northern tribes called Israel. He prophesied in the reign of Jeroboam II of Israel. He lived in this northern kingdom when the splendors of Jeroboam's brilliant reign of 41 years were beginning to fade into the black midnight of Israel's captivity. He prophesied during the eighth century BC.

This was a stirring time in the history of the world. Rome was founded during this period, as was Carthage, which was founded by the Phoenicians. The big Phoenician westbound ships went as far as Tarshish, a Phoenician colony in southern Spain. And during the time of Hosea, they ran as far north as the tin mines of Cornwall.

Another important event during this period was the religious reformation that Siddhartha Gautama (563-483 BC) introduced in India, which gave birth to Buddhism. This time of expansion and change presented many things similar to those of the sixteenth century after Christ.

Hosea's contemporaries were Amos, Isaiah and Micah. He has been called the Jeremiah of the northern kingdom. Remember, Jeremiah prophesied to Judah (the tribes of Judah and Benjamin that formed the southern kingdom). Hosea prophesied to Israel, the 10 tribes that formed the northern kingdom. Hosea was not trained in a seminary (school of the prophets), but he was a layman called by God to give to Israel the important message that God loved them.

HOSEA 1–3: ISRAEL'S UNFAITHFULNESS

The hero of this book, Hosea, is one of the greatest lovers in all literature. His love was so strong that even the worst actions of an unfaithful wife could not kill it. Read Hosea 1:1 for a bit of the personal history of the prophet. Then God Himself speaks His first words to Hosea (see Hosea 1:2). The people had given no heed to Amos. Hosea knew that the country was due for a downfall, but they were not disposed to listen to him.

Turn to 2 Kings 15–17, and read the page of history that covers the period of this prophet. As already stated, it was a very unsettled time. Sin was rampant. The golden age of Jeroboam II was passing and a dark cloud hung over Israel. On the death of Jeroboam, six kings followed in quick succession. Within 20 years, four were assassinated. At about the middle of Hosea's ministry, the Assyrians carried away a large part of the nation. At the end of Hosea's life, the kingdom of Israel came to an end with the fall of Samaria. The prophet lived to see his prophecies fulfilled.

We know little about Hosea other than that he had a very sad home life. The book pictures this man as gentle, frank and affectionate. He reveals himself to have a deep loving nature that enabled him to be faithful to his home and family despite his difficulties.

Hosea's Wife

As chapter 1 opens, we see a young man being told by God to do something that would naturally have been very repulsive to him.

What was it? Read Hosea 1:2-3. It was a severe test. But as in the case of Isaiah, Hosea was to be a sign for Israel.

Hosea was told to marry a woman of little worth in society, a prostitute. But Hosea truly loved her. God was using this for a sign to His people of how they remained the object of Jehovah's love in spite of their sinfulness. This may all seem very strange to us. However, God was using this to picture for us His redeeming grace. Grace is unmerited favor. Here we see Israel so undeserving of Jehovah's love, yet still He is lavishing it upon them. God has not chosen the righteous but the sinners: "But God demonstrates his own love for us in this: While we were still sinners, Christ died for us" (Romans 5:8). God's dealings with Israel picture His dealings with us now: "These things happened to them as examples and were written down as warnings for us, on whom the culmination of the ages has come" (1 Corinthians 10:11).

Hosea obeyed God and married Gomer (see Hosea 1:3). His name was hers. Home, reputation, God's favor, comfort—all were Gomer's. All that Hosea had, he gave to her. In return, Hosea's name, domestic reputation and love were all sacrificed on the altar of a shameful and worthless woman. How like our Lord Jesus this is! He not only came to us while we were yet in sin, but He also died the death of shame on Calvary for us so that all He had would be ours (see Titus 2:14).

Gomer ran away from home and left her young husband, Hosea, with two young sons and a daughter to care for. Lured away by the sin she saw around her, she fell into the moral cesspool of the day and finally was carried off as a slave. Through it all, Hosea was true to her. Still loving her, he tried everything to win her back to a happy family life. But she would not return home. What a sad picture of a person's stubbornness! What a wonderful picture of God's love!

Just as Hosea was married to an unfaithful bride, so too God was married to unfaithful Israel. This experience of Hosea's helped him to understand God's heart of love as God yearned to have wayward Israel come home to Him. No doubt there were tears in Hosea's voice, for there was tragedy in his life. He had thrown himself wholly into his mission.

As John Milton stated in *Paradise Regained,* "Who best can suffer, best can do."

God's Bride

God frequently uses marriage to symbolize His relation to Israel: "As a bridegroom rejoices over his bride, so will your God rejoice over you" (Isaiah 62:5). "For I am your husband" (Jeremiah 3:14). Israel is Jehovah's bride, while the Church is the Lamb's bride. God said of Israel, "I will betroth you to me forever" (Hosea 2:19). God had been true to His bride, the Jews. He had loved them and protected them and lavished every gift upon them. But they left God and went after other gods. They disobeyed His laws. Like Hosea's wife, they broke their marriage vows and strayed into sin and shame, eventually becoming slaves. Israel, like Gomer, had forgotten who in the past had given her blessings in abundance (see Hosea 2:8).

In his book *Whatever Became of Sin?* Karl Menninger, the world-famous psychiatrist, defined sin in a rather penetrating manner: "a refusal of the love of others." Most important of all, sin is a refusal of the love of God (see Psalm 51:4).

There are differing interpretations of this first part of the book of Hosea. Some believe that Hosea was told by God to marry a sinful woman, which he did; others, that God told Hosea to marry a woman who did not begin to sin until after the marriage; still others, that this experience of Hosea's was only a vision, not an actual experience. In any case, the undefeatable love of a true husband, to whom God likens Himself, is shown; and Israel's strange, sad, persistent backsliding is revealed.

Israel's Backsliding

Why should Israel's backsliding seem strange to us? Isn't it exactly what we all know about from personal experience? The history of people has been a history of backsliding and will continue to be so:

- Creation of people (see Genesis 1:28)—People started at the top, but soon they were moving toward the bottom.

- Fall of people (see Genesis 3:23)—People went steadily downhill from their expulsion from Eden to the time of the flood.

- Human government (see Genesis 8:20)—People went downhill until they ignored God and exalted themselves (see Genesis 11:4); then God judged them by confusing their languages.

- Promise to Abraham (see Genesis 12:1)—Israel, God's Chosen People, went downward, until they found themselves at the bottom of the hill, in bondage in Egypt.

- Mosaic Law (see Exodus 19:8)—Israel, during its entire national history, had its ups and downs. Hosea's day reflects this.

- The Word (see Old and New Testaments)—Until the end, people will sin and will break God's heart of love; but a wonderful and patient God has endured this through the centuries.

In Hosea 3:4, the then-present state of the Jewish people is described. Read it! Read it! Ever since the destruction of Jerusalem by Titus (AD 70), this description given by Hosea has fit the Jewish people. They have been a nation of wanderers over the face of the earth, going from nation to nation and from city to city. They have been a scattered, sometimes despised and often hated people (see Deuteronomy 28:63-65). But notice what is happening to them today. Hosea 3:5 describes the Jewish people's glorious future. King, prince, sacrifice and ephod—all will be restored in Christ.

HOSEA 4–10: ISRAEL'S NATIONAL SIN AND CHASTISEMENT

The second section of Hosea opens with Hosea announcing God's charges against Israel (see Hosea 4:1). Two hundred years before, the 10 tribes had seceded from Judah and set up an independent kingdom called Israel. They began immediately worshiping idols. God had sent Elijah and then Elisha to warn the people about what would happen if they continued to sin, but it was all in vain. The people refused to return to God. Now we hear a new voice. It is Hosea! "Come, let us return to the LORD" (Hosea 6:1) is the much-needed cry of the prophet. His message is "Return to God and He will return to you."

Hosea, whose name means "salvation," was poet laureate to the king. But he was more than that. He was God's voice to the people. They did not care to hear his message, for his appeal on behalf of a God grieved by His children's sins was to a nation of backsliders. It is well to remember that the names of Israel and Ephraim are closely associated with sin and backsliding. Both names are used 37 times in this book. "I know all about Ephraim; Israel is not hidden from me. Ephraim, you have now turned to prostitution; Israel is corrupt" (Hosea 5:3).

It is not more liberty we need today but more loyalty. Do not give God ready-made plans for Him to bless. Do not make your plans and then come to Him for approval. Let Him make the plans. Israel had foolishly made their own decisions. The people had become stiff necked. God will not do anything with a rebellious spirit and a defiant will.

God's Word is a mirror. What is a mirror really for? Is it to see how well you look? No! I believe it is to see your flaws—to see what is wrong so that you may correct them. "How can a young person stay on the path of purity? By living according to your word" (Psalm 119:9). "Hear the word of the LORD, you Israelites, because the LORD has a charge to bring against you who live in the land" (Hosea 4:1).

Israel's Blacklist of Sins:

- No faithfulness, no love, no acknowledgment of God—Hosea 4:1
- Prostitution and drunkenness—Hosea 4:11

- Murder—Hosea 5:2
- Deceit and robbery—Hosea 7:1
- Cheating and defrauding—Hosea 12:7

God's Symbols for Sin:

- An adulterous wife—Hosea 3:1
- A patron of prostitutes and a drunkard—Hosea 4:11
- A stubborn ("backsliding," *KJV*) heifer—Hosea 4:16
- Marauders/robbers—Hosea 6:9
- Adulterers—Hosea 7:4
- An oven—Hosea 7:7
- A half-baked cake—7:8
- An easily deceived dove—Hosea 7:11
- A faulty bow—Hosea 7:16
- Something swallowed—8:8
- A worthless thing—Hosea 8:8
- A wild donkey—Hosea 8:9

HOSEA 11–14: ISRAEL'S HOPE

Light breaks over the last chapters of Hosea. They give us a picture of Israel's ultimate blessings in the future Kingdom. We get a glimpse into God's heart of love when He, as a father, says, "When Israel was a child, I loved him, and out of Egypt I called my son" (Hosea 11:1).

God's Choice

As God looked over the vast and glittering expanse of the world, He did not choose Israel to be His people because they were the greatest or richest of the nations of the world (see Deuteronomy 7:6-8). Rather, He chose a weak, unattractive slave child to be the object of His love and care and blessings (see Hosea 11:1).

There lay Babylon in all her glory. She was then a strong and mighty nation and held great promise of a powerful future. To the south was the glory of Egypt, wrapped in the rich and jeweled web of centuries that archaeologists are still unwrapping. Even today our eyes are dazzled as we look on their splendors. The Hittites, to the north, also had a great culture and wielded much power, and the ships of the Phoenicians were sailing the seas beyond the Mediterranean. But God did not choose these peoples. He chose a slave child in Egypt—one who was making bricks without straw while in an awful bondage—upon whom He would lavish His love and blessings (see Exodus 3).

We can never understand God's choices. He chooses the weak things of the world to confound the things that are mighty (see 1 Corinthians 1:27). Whenever people love God, it is because He loved them first (see 1 John 4:19).

Israel's Sin

But Israel, the child so obviously adopted at the time of the Exodus from Egypt, began to grow persistently disobedient and rebellious. The more the prophets warned the people, the farther they went away from God. They showed no gratitude to God for all the blessings of their land. But in their freedom, they forgot God and began to sin and practice idolatry, while they plunged headlong into captivity (see Hosea 11:2). Israel, the child, had to finished her training in the slave markets of Assyria and Babylon (see Hosea 4:6-7).

God's Attitude

God has been good to us and wholeheartedly loves us. He has sent us prophets and teachers and put us in the midst of untold resources and luxury. But the more the prophets and teachers warn us, the more we are prone to turn away; and the greater our education and learning, the more self-sufficient we become. Nations today are educating themselves away from God. So did Israel. But God taught Israel that when people refuse light, the light is withdrawn (see Hosea 5:6).

We must understand God's attitude toward sin. He says, "The wages of sin is death" (Romans 6:23). "Do not be deceived: God cannot be mocked. A man reaps what he sows" (Galatians 6:7).

Hosea

Through the prophet Hosea, God revealed to His children that knowledge always creates responsibility. This truth was taught also by the apostle Peter: "It would have been better for them not to have known the way of righteousness, than to have known it and then to turn their backs on the sacred command that was passed on to them" (2 Peter 2:21). It is a dangerous thing to play with God's grace.

God's Grace

We find grace abounding in the Old Testament as well as in the New Testament.

Through Hosea, Jehovah said to Israel, "I led them with cords of human kindness, with ties of love" (Hosea 11:4). Christ drew us with cords of a man when He became a man and died for us: "And I, when I am lifted up from the earth, will draw all people to myself" (John 12:32).

God has agonized over His rebellious people and will not give them up. His mercy was aroused: "I will heal their waywardness and love them freely" (Hosea 14:4). "Where sin increased, grace increased all the more" (Romans 5:20). God had threatened Israel with His wrath, but now God offered her grace. God appealed to Israel to return and repent (see Hosea 14:1-3). Then He gave her a promised blessing (see Hosea 14:4-8).

In Hosea 1:11, God told Israel that one day Judah and Israel will be gathered and have one head, a Messiah to come and be their ruler. God again promised this in Hosea 3. Read Hosea 9:17 to see the condition of the Jewish people today—"wanderers among the nations." God will do more than forgive their backsliding; He will cure them and remove the cause.

Hosea 14 is the best chapter in the Bible for backsliders. Read the wonderful words of the Lord to backsliding Israel: "I will heal their waywardness and love them freely" (Hosea 14:4). God's great heart is bursting with love, but our sins keep Him from telling us all that He has for us. As with Israel, you may know the joy that comes when barriers have been broken down and you've been shown nothing but love. "I will be like the dew to Israel; he

Hosea

will blossom like a lily" (Hosea 14:5). The dew symbolizes the presence of the Holy Spirit. See how God pictured His abiding joy in His people after they are healed.

UNDERSTANDING JOEL

AUTHOR: The book of Joel states in Joel 1:1 that its author was the prophet Joel.

DATE: The book was likely written between 535 and 500 BC.

PURPOSE AND SUMMARY: Traditionally, Joel is called the prophet of Pentecost, since his prophecy of the outpouring of the Spirit (see Joel 2:28-32) is quoted by Peter in Acts 2:16-21 to explain the outpouring of the Holy Spirit at Pentecost. The occasion of his prophetic message was a devastating locust plague, which he interpreted as being a foreboding about the Day of the Lord, when God would act directly to punish His people for their sins. Joel calls upon the people of Judah to repent, promising that repentance will cause the Lord to pour out His Spirit and His blessings upon His people.

Joel is considered by some to be one of the earliest of all the prophets whose writings have come down to us. He possibly could have known both Elijah and Elisha in his youth. Joel appeared just a little before Hosea, but while Hosea spoke to the northern tribes in Israel, Joel spoke only to the southern kingdom of Judah. His message is to us all today.

Joel's personal history is stated in one verse: "The word of the Lord that came to Joel son of Pethuel" (Joel 1:1). His name means "Jehovah is God." Joel has been called the prophet of religious revival. He knew that revival must follow repentance. As Robert Lee, the author of *The Bible at a Glance*, wrote, "A rent heart is followed by a rent veil and heaven." Joel tried to bring his people to that place. We will find access to the throne of grace and know the presence of the Holy Spirit when we truly repent.

The land of Israel had just suffered a terrible plague of locusts that had devoured every green thing and left only desolation. Joel believed that this had been a judgment sent by God because of the sins of His people. Joel was the first to prophesy the outpouring of the Holy Spirit upon all flesh (see Joel 2:28).

JOEL 1: THE WARNING

Appalling famine, caused by an awful plague of locusts, followed by a prolonged drought, devastated the land. People and flocks were dying for lack of food and water.

Describing the plague of locusts as a judgment from God, Joel called his people in Judah to repentance. He wanted to spare them from greater judgments at the hands of hostile armies. He told the people that the locusts were just a taste of the devastation that their enemies would bring.

Joel graphically described the plague, calling the old men to confirm the fact that there had never been one like it before (see Joel 1:2). Drunkards felt the effect of it, for the vines had been destroyed (see Joel 1:5). Priests had no meat offering or drink offering (see Joel 1:9). Even cattle and sheep in the fields suffered (see Joel 1:20). Joel urged the people to hold a fast (see Joel 1:13). Then he continued to describe the plague.

Joel told the people to think about what had caused the calamity. They must mourn with true penitence if they wished to be spared further judgment (see Joel 2:12-17). Desperate, they were ready to listen to anyone who could explain their plight. It was a great hour for the preacher, for now, in their desperation, the people would turn to God.

JOEL 2: THE PROMISE

The blast of the ram's horn calling an assembly for a great fast opens Joel 2 (see verse 1). Everyone was there—old and young alike. Even brides and bridegrooms on their wedding day attended (see

Joel 2:16). The priests came in black sackcloth and bowed to the ground and cried to God within the sanctuary. "Rend your heart and not your garments. Return to the LORD your God, for he is gracious and compassionate" (Joel 2:13). It was an event to bring the people back to God.

The locusts had made an Eden into a desolate wilderness (see Joel 2:3). For anyone who has not seen what locusts can do, an army of locusts is truly an incredible thing. They fill the air and darken the sun like an eclipse (see Joel 2:2). Their flight can be heard for miles, much like a roaring fire (see Joel 2:5). They spread for miles over the land. Armies of these insects advance, destroying everything that is green. In a few minutes every leaf and blade is destroyed. Others strip the bark from the trees (see Joel 1:6-7). People dig trenches and light trees on fire; they beat and burn to death thousands of insects, but the effort is utterly useless. The land over which the locusts pass looks as if it had been swept by fire (see Joel 2:3). After the country is stripped, the insects go into cities and, like knights of old, they march into houses and consume everything that can be consumed (see Joel 2:4,7-9). A land that has been devastated by locusts takes years to recover (see Joel 1:17-20). God's promise to "repay you for the years the locusts have eaten" becomes more understandable when one sees the desolation wrought by these voracious insects (Joel 2:25).

The Prophecy of Pentecost

The prophet assured the people that God will indeed send both earthly mercies (see Joel 2:18-27) and spiritual blessings (see Joel 2:28-32). Yes, and God will send deliverance from the sky! "And afterward, I will pour out my Spirit on all people. Your sons and daughters will prophesy, your old men will dream dreams, your young men will see visions. Even on my servants, both men and women, I will pour out my Spirit in those days" (Joel 2:28-29). This is the prophecy of Pentecost.

Spiritual deliverance is the great central promise of the book of Joel. Other prophets foretold details concerning the Lord's life on earth and even of His future reign. But Joel was entrusted with the privilege of telling that God would pour out His Spirit on all people. He also said that the blessing will flow forth from Jerusalem (see Joel 2:32; 3:18). We are definitely told that this prophecy was fulfilled at Pentecost: "This is what was spoken by the prophet Joel" (Acts 2:16). Read all of Acts 2.

The Lesson for Today

In Joel, there is a lesson for us today. The Church is in a desolate condition. It has been laid waste by many spiritual foes, well described in Joel 1:4. Famine and drought are on all sides. The call goes out to today's Christians to go in true, heartfelt repentance into the dust before the Lord. This repentance must begin with ministers and elders. If we will return to the Lord, He will fulfill His promise to pour out His Holy Spirit on us, thus repaying us "for the years the locusts have eaten" (Joel 2:25). The great outpouring on Israel that Joel described is for the future (see Ezekiel 36:23-33). The great need in pulpit and pew is in the power of the Holy Spirit today.

The Day of the Lord

"The day of the Lord" mentioned five times in this short book refers to judgment (Joel 1:15; 2:1,11,31; 3:14). The book of Joel actually tells of a series of judgments—the present locusts, the invading armies about to come as a scourge of God upon the land, and the final Day of the Lord described in the third chapter of Joel. The Day of the Lord is the period of time from the return of the Lord in glory until the new heavens and the new earth appear (see Isaiah 2:17-20; 3:7-18; 4:1-2; 13:6-9; Jeremiah 46:10; Malachi 4:5; 1 Corinthians 5:5; 1 Thessalonians 5:2; 2 Thessalonians 2:2; 2 Peter 3:10). The Day of the Lord is at least 1,000 years in length (see Revelation 20:4).

JOEL 3: JUDGMENTS AND BLESSINGS

The final portion of Joel covers the following prophecies:

- Israel's enemies overthrown (Joel 3:1-15)
- Jerusalem delivered (Joel 3:16-17)

- Land blessed (Joel 3:18)
- Judah restored (Joel 3:19-21)

Only God could have told Joel of the return of the Jews from captivity. But Joel saw not only the return from Babylon, but also the Jews' return to the Promised Land from among the Gentile nations. He also told about the judgment of the nations that would take place after the battle of Armageddon (see Joel 3:2-7; see also Matthew 25:32; Revelation 19:17-21). The people's day of decision is over. God's hour of destiny has arrived.

After Israel is restored and the nations of the earth are judged (see Joel 3:1-2) then the everlasting kingdom will be set up (see Joel 3:20). Once again the Holy Land, the land of promise, will be the center of power and the gathering place of the nations for judgment. Christ will return to establish His rule as sovereign, and God will dwell in Zion (see Joel 3:17).

UNDERSTANDING AMOS

AUTHOR: Amos 1:1 identifies the author of the book of Amos as the prophet Amos.

DATE: The book was likely written between 793 and 740 BC.

PURPOSE AND SUMMARY: Among the "writing" prophets, Amos was the first of a new school of prophets. Like Elijah and John the Baptist, he spoke of how offended the Lord was by sins common in the daily life of the northern kingdom of Israel—sins of oppressing the poor, idolatry, and empty ritualistic worship of the Lord. Amos was an unschooled shepherd and a native of Judah, but he was called by God to prophesy to the northern kingdom of Israel during the reign of Jeroboam II, king of Israel (793-753 BC), and Uzziah, king of Judah (791-740 BC). Sparing no one, the prophet fearlessly announced the impending judgment of the Day of the Lord. Although

Amos

the dominant note of the book is judgment, the final words promise the restoration of a righteous remnant of God's people.

Amos was from Tekoa, a small town about 12 miles south of Jerusalem. He "was neither a prophet nor the son of a prophet" (Amos 7:14). He was not a priest or a member of the prophet's school. He was a sheepherder and took care of sycamore-fig trees. He must have been educated, for his book shows literary skill. Perhaps he traveled extensively selling his wool. The places he mentions may have been places he visited.

In Amos, we find one of many instances in the Bible of God calling a man when he was in the middle of doing his daily job (see Amos 1:1). Amos was just an ordinary working man. But God called him and sent him on his way, shepherd's crook in hand, to gather God's straying people. (Remember that when they received their commissions, David was caring for his sheep, and Gideon was in the middle of threshing wheat.)

On the wild uplands of Judah, beyond Tekoa, Amos received his training as a prophet straight from the hand of God. His beautiful writing is filled with illustrations from his mountain home. Like David, he had gazed on the stars and looked beyond to their Creator.

Amos was not the only prophet of his day. God had sent a great galaxy of messengers to save His people from the destruction they were inevitably facing. Amos (though a native of Judah) and Hosea were prophets to Israel (northern kingdom); Isaiah and Micah, to the southern kingdom of Judah. No doubt, as a boy Amos had known Jonah and possibly Elisha. These men surely knew each other well. Maybe they had gone on evangelistic campaigns together. When Amos's work was coming to a close, Isaiah and Micah appeared. These men, when boys, might have heard Amos preach. These younger prophets would have received much from this champion of Jehovah.

Amos prophesied while Uzziah was on the throne of Judah and Jeroboam II was king of Israel. This was a time of great prosperity (see 2 Chronicles 26 and 2 Kings 14:25). The old boundaries of the kingdom of David were gained back. Money poured in and armies were victorious. They were enjoying a period of peace, and all they thought about was pleasure and having a good time (see Amos 2:6-8; 5:11-12; 6:4-6).

The idea of the approaching doom of their kingdoms seemed utterly improbable to Israel. The surrounding nations were not strong enough to give them trouble (see Amos 6:1-13). Assyria had not yet risen as a conquering world power. God tried to arouse His people to a sense of their danger, so He sent two witnesses, Hosea and Amos, but to no avail.

A Man Ahead of His Time

Amos feared God so much that he feared no one else at all. Someone once said that "Amos proclaimed a message so far ahead of his time that most of the human race, and a large part of all Christendom, have not yet caught up with it." The daring words of that simple herdsman of Tekoa date back some 800 years before our Lord, yet we are still not listening!

Such courage was no more heeded in Israel's time than it is today. Of course, we will find among the evils Amos denounced some of the same evils that prevail today. Amos's voice was raised against the lack of moderation when drinking, but Amos's intent went beyond the mere excessive use of wine. Were he speaking today, he would raise his voice in thundering tones against the abuse of drugs and alcohol that has surpassed what the Israelites of Amos's time could even have dreamed of. But Amos reveals the root of all such sins: The children of Israel rejected the law of Jehovah and have not kept His statutes. As we have not. The laws of our beloved country will be kept when we learn to keep the law of God. The law of God is fulfilled in love.

A Man of Many Traits

This raw young herdsman, Amos, had a certain rugged frankness about him that was refreshing. He always hit straight from the shoulder (see Amos 1:2). He didn't fail to tell even King Jeroboam II what he should do. God wanted someone to bear His message courageously, and Amos did not fail Him. Israel needed a prophet who would tear the scales from their eyes and let them know what the consequences of their idolatry were sure to be, and Amos fearlessly did just that.

- Amos was humble—He didn't hide where he came from.
- Amos was wise—He didn't preach over the heads of the people.
- Amos was clever—He didn't catch people's interest by judging their enemies first.
- Amos was fearless—He told the truth.
- Amos was faithful—His message was always, "This is what the LORD says."

God abhors sin. The horrible cruelty of sin must be punished.

Because the kingdom was flourishing and was at peace, Amos knew that he would be unpopular and that he would be likened to, in today's terms, a man who cried wolf if he delivered God's message. David before Goliath could not have been more courageous than Amos was before Jeroboam II, who continued in the idolatry of Jeroboam I, son of Nebat (see 2 Kings 14:23-24). Read some of Amos's unique figures of speech found in Amos 2:15:

- "The archer will not stand his ground"—Jeroboam's stalwart archers were accustomed to press forward on the enemy. They never gave in. What foolishness to talk of such archers failing to stand anywhere at any time!

- "The fleet-footed soldier will not get away"—What? Will Israel's fleet-footed runners be using their speed to run away from battle? Has this insolent prophet gone crazy?

- "And the horseman will not save his life"—There were no horsemen in all the world like Jeroboam's invincible cavalry. Surely the prophet was worried about nothing!

But the climax was reached in these words of Amos: "This is what the LORD says: 'As a shepherd rescues from the lion's mouth only two leg bones or a piece of an ear, so will the Israelites living in Samaria be rescued, with only the head of a bed and a piece of fabric from a couch'" (Amos 3:12). This sounded like mockery! The idea of powerful Israel being likened to a poor sheep or, rather, the fragments of a partially eaten sheep!

Yet this is what came to pass! In less than 50 years, Israel was utterly destroyed, and the pitiful remnant of her people did not even equal the leg of a sheep taken from the jaw of a lion. Such is the picture of God's abhorrence of sin. The answer to every question about why great empires have fallen is sin. The secret of a great person's undoing is sin. Let Amos help you see sin in its true light.

If a ship at sea accidentally follows a wrong course, what happens? Yes, some sort of trouble and possibly wreckage in the end. But what if a captain knowingly follows a wrong course? Do you think the outcome would be different? No wonder prophets like Amos spoke plainly in warning people about the wrong course of sin.

AMOS 1–2: JUDGMENT AGAINST NEIGHBORING PEOPLES

Amos, a simple country preacher, left his home in Judah and traveled 22 miles to Bethel in the northern kingdom to preach to the kingdom of Israel. Why did God send him to Bethel? Surely Jerusalem needed his ministry. But God wanted the kingdom of Israel to have a strong word of warning. Bethel was the religious capital of the northern kingdom. Idolatry was there. The people had substituted calf worship for Jehovah. The people felt no need of preaching (see 1 Kings 12:25-33).

Amos started his preaching to the assembled crowds at Bethel, on a sacred feast day, by proclaiming the Lord's judgment upon six neighbors; then he moved on to include the Chosen People:

- Damascus (in Syria) because it had invaded Israel (see Amos 1:3; 2 Kings 10:32-33)
- Gaza (in Philistia) and Tyre (in Phoenicia) for conspiring with Edom in its invasion of Judah (see Amos 1:6,9; 2 Chronicles 21:16-17; 28:18)

Amos

- Edom for continuing hostility (see Amos 1:11; compare Obadiah 10-12)
- Ammon for attacking Gilead (see Amos 1:13)
- Moab for pagan practices (see Amos 2:1; 2 Kings 3:27)
- Judah for neglect and contempt of God's law, expressed in her idolatry (see Amos 2:4; 2 Chronicles 3–19; 2 Kings 25:9)
- Israel for her unrighteousness (see Amos 2:6; 2 Kings 17:17-23)
- Whole nation for her apostasy (see Amos 3:12)

The nations of the world, no matter how powerful they may be, cannot withstand the judgments of God. God sets up kingdoms and brings them down. The mighty power of the pharaohs has come to nothing. Napoleon thought he could rule the world, but he languished on Saint Helena. During World War II, there were tyrants who thought they could stamp out God's Chosen People and set themselves up as rulers of the earth, but people who try to hinder God's ultimate plan are always brought low (see Psalm 2).

When the people doubted Amos's authority, Amos gave a series of seven questions to show that because the Lord revealed His secret to him, he must prophesy (see Amos 3:3-8).

AMOS 3–6: JUDGMENT AGAINST ISRAEL

Amos denounced the sin of Israel more graphically than Hosea (see Amos 2). He spoke of Israel's careless ease and luxury, their oppression of the poor, their lying and cheating, and, worst of all, their hypocrisy in worship. Amos told the people of Israel that they were greedy, unjust, unclean and profane (see Amos 2:6-12), and that they defended and excused themselves on the grounds that they were God's Chosen People (see Amos 3:2). He reminded them that this only made their sin greater.

The Israelites, however, looked at their relationship to God differently. They saw it as merely an outward and formal thing.

They boasted that they were the chosen nation, so no real evil could befall them. We see many professing Christians today in the same danger. They imagine that their salvation is assured simply because they are members of a church. They assume that because of their church membership, God will not condemn them. Read Amos 5:21,23-24.

The Lord was greatly saddened because His people had not heeded His warnings: " 'Yet you have not returned to me,' declares the LORD" (Amos 4:6). Then God said that if the people continued to reject His repeated warnings, they would be punished (see Amos 5). God had extended an invitation: "Seek me and live" (Amos 5:4); but the people chose to ignore it.

So Amos condemned Israel. Israel was a chosen nation. She knew God's law; therefore, her sin was greater than that of any other nation. Amos told the people about their injustice in the administration of the law. They "sell the innocent for silver, and the needy for a pair of sandals" (Amos 2:6). He listed examples of their evil oppression, especially of the poor. They had forgotten righteousness. The rich were cruel. (Even among Christians today we find that wealth often counts more than character. Nothing is more dangerous in the Church than influence and power given to those who have wealth but no Christian scruples.)

Amos called the women of his day "cows of Bashan," because they only cared for luxury and worldly pleasures (Amos 4:1). This is the prophet's picture of cruel, heartless, unthinking women: a herd of cows, heavy and heedless animals treading on all in their way as they seek to gratify their appetites.

Even the religious sacrifices and feasts of the people had become an abomination. God said, "I hate . . . your religious festivals" (Amos 5:21). When they made their pilgrimages from Gilgal to Bethel, their sin only increased, for their worship was merely for show and it was mixed with idolatry (see Amos 5:4-6). God demands conduct worthy of Himself, not just empty sacrifices. Amos called attention to how God had sent drought, plagues and earthquakes as judgments on unbelieving people, but they still did not repent.

God always warns before a punishment, yes, and offers a way of escape. God denounces sin, but He offers a remedy for sin. Israel's rejection of repeated warnings should have led her to prepare for God's judgment (see Amos 5). If Israel had sought the Lord, she would not have had to experience "the day of the LORD" (Amos 5:20). She did not seek Him, however, and Assyrian fighters ushered in that day.

AMOS 7–8: VISIONS ABOUT ISRAEL'S JUDGMENT

Amos tells of Israel's coming judgment in five visions:

1. The devouring locusts (Amos 7:1-3)—In the first vision, the prophet saw that "the Sovereign LORD . . . was preparing swarms of locusts after the king's share had been harvested and just as the late crops were coming up. When they had stripped the land clean, I cried out, 'Sovereign LORD, forgive! How can Jacob survive? He is so small!' So the LORD relented. 'This will not happen,' the LORD said."

2. The consuming fire (Amos 7:4-6)—In this vision, fire so terrible as to consume the waters and the land was seen. Amos prayed, " 'Sovereign LORD, I beg you, stop! How can Jacob survive? He is so small!' So the LORD relented. 'This will not happen either,' the Sovereign LORD said" (verses 5-6).

3. The searching plumb line (Amos 7:7-11)—In this vision, Amos saw God measuring the city for destruction. The measuring revealed how far out of line Israel was. This time Amos did not have the heart even to pray. Israel's judgment was certain—"I will spare them no longer" (verse 8).

4. The basket of ripe fruit (Amos 8:1-14)—The Lord said, "The time is ripe for my people Israel; I will spare

Amos

them no longer" (verse 2). The basket revealed the sad truth that Israel, like a basket of overripe fruit, looked fine outwardly but was rotting at its core. The guilty nation was "ripe" for judgment.

5. The Lord at the altar (Amos 9:1-10)—The last vision showed God standing on the altar, ordering Amos to break the doorposts and shower the fragments over the people's heads. All the worshipers would be scattered and slain by the sword. This symbolized the final scattering of the people.

The visions end with judgment, but God closes the book with a bright outlook.

We do not know how long Amos preached in Bethel, but we know that crowds of people heard his message. When he fearlessly spoke of the doom of the surrounding peoples, the Chosen People were drawn to him and they cheered him.

Then Amaziah, the priest of Bethel, could not stand to hear any more of Amos's preaching. So, backed by the king, the priest rebuked Amos. Listen to the report he sent to the king: "Amos is raising a conspiracy against you in the very heart of Israel. The land cannot bear all his words. For this is what Amos is saying: 'Jeroboam will die by the sword, and Israel will surely go into exile, away from their native land'" (Amos 7:10-11). Amaziah told Amos to go back to Judah and to mind his own business.

The false prophet silenced Amos. He was driven from Israel. Freedom of speech was not given to the true prophet of God. Neither Elijah nor Amos was safe in Israel. When Amos found that Israel would not listen to him, he returned to Judah and recorded his experiences in a book, so all the people could read and understand them.

AMOS 9: VISIONS ABOUT THE FUTURE

Amos, like most of the prophets, told us of a bright future for God's Chosen People. The whole land will once more be a kingdom under the house of David (see Amos 9:11-12). The Tabernacle of David, now gone, will be rebuilt (see Acts 15:16-17). Israel will be restored to her land and will prosper. A happy people will dwell in a happy land.

Always keep in mind that the Jewish people who have been scattered over the face of the world are being gathered back to their land of promise. National prosperity will again flourish. Jerusalem will be the capital of a mighty kingdom. Converted Israel will be God's witnesses (see Amos 9:13-15).

During times when sin abounds, people need to hear the same things Amos spoke. We've become too tenderhearted and gentle toward the common sins of people. We've forgotten how to denounce; we've lost the power of righteous indignation.

Not so with Amos, plumb-line prophet that he was. The crooked wall always hates the straight line. So people hated Amos. They will hate us, too, if we speak out. Nevertheless, learn to speak, no matter what it costs. Always remember the Man who used a small whip to purge the Temple (see John 2:13-16).

Repentance is not just turning to God and lightheartedly saying, "I'm sorry." Not even the truest repentance can remit sin. Redemption is costly. Christ paid the price. Salvation is the establishment of a personal relationship between the individual person and God. Nothing can take the place of that (see John 1:12).

22

Understanding Obadiah, Jonah and Micah

Obadiah Portrays Jesus Christ, Our Savior; Jonah Portrays Jesus Christ, Our Resurrection and Life; Micah Portrays Jesus Christ, Our Witness Against Rebellious Nations

SELECTED BIBLE READINGS

DAY OF THE WEEK		MAIN TOPIC
Sunday: Obadiah	Doom of Edom and Deliverance of Israel	
Monday: Jonah 1–2	Jonah's Encounter with a Fish	
Tuesday: Jonah 3–4	The Obedience of the Prophet	
Wednesday: Micah 1–2	A Message to the People	
Thursday: Micah 3–4	A Message to the Rulers	
Friday: Micah 5	The Birth of the King	
Saturday: Micah 6–7	A Message to the Chosen People	

UNDERSTANDING OBADIAH

AUTHOR: Obadiah 1 identifies the author of the book of Obadiah as the prophet Obadiah.

DATE: The book was written after the 586 BC destruction of Jerusalem.

PURPOSE AND SUMMARY: Obadiah is the shortest of the prophetic books, containing only 21 verses. It is a scathing denunciation of the Edomites, descendants of Esau, Jacob's brother, who from the beginning had been hostile to Jacob's descendants, Israel. Its message is primarily one of destruction and doom for Edom, because of her treachery against Israel. The latter part of the prophecy is concerned with the Day of the Lord when God's judgment will be on other nations as well as Edom and concludes with the promise that "the kingdom will be the LORD's" (Obadiah 21).

Petra is one of the wonders of the world. It was a city unique among the works of humans. It perched like an eagle's nest (see Obadiah 4), enclosed by towering rocks. Its only approach is through a deep rock cleft more than a mile long with massive cliffs more than 700 feet high rising on either side. The city was able to withstand any invasion. We are told that its temples numbered a thousand. They were cut in and out of the pink rock of the massive cliffs. The dwellings were mostly caves cut out of the soft red sandstone (see Obadiah 3,6) and placed where you can hardly believe it possible for a human foot to climb.

South of the Dead Sea and on the western border of the Arabian plateau lies a range of precipitous red sandstone heights known as Mount Seir. Here Esau settled after he sold his birthright to his brother Jacob. Having driven out the Horites (see Genesis 14:5-6; Deuteronomy 2:12), he occupied the whole mountain. Sela, or Petra, "Rock," was their capital. Today it is called the silent city of the forgotten past.

The descendants of Esau were called Edomites. They would go out on raiding expeditions and then retreat to their impregnable fortress where they kept alive in their hearts a bitter enmity toward the Jews, which began with Jacob and Esau. They never failed to help any army who attacked the Jews. And in the time of Christ, through Herod, they obtained control of a portion of Judea. They disappear from the pages of history after the destruction of Jerusalem by Titus in AD 70.

This book is the shortest in the Old Testament. It contains only 21 verses, but it includes two important themes:

1. The doom of the proud and rebellious
2. The deliverance of the meek and humble

Obadiah spoke directly to Edom and Zion, which represent Esau and Jacob, the two sons of Isaac. But what Obadiah had to say appeals to us all with our two natures:

1. The earthly—represented by Esau—so proud and bold
2. The spiritual—represented by Jacob—chosen and set apart by God

The story of the bitter family feud that takes us back to the days of the two brothers, Jacob and Esau, unfolds before us.

OBADIAH 1-16: EDOM'S DOOM

Of the prophet who wrote this book we know nothing. We only know that his contemporary was Jeremiah. This prophecy about Edom was written because of the confederacy that Edom formed with Babylonia against Jerusalem (see Obadiah 7-14). We find the occasion of this prophecy mentioned in Obadiah 11: "On the day you stood aloof while strangers carried off his wealth and foreigners entered his gates and cast lots for Jerusalem, you were like one of them." No doubt, it was the awful day when Nebuchadnezzar captured Jerusalem and reduced it to a desolate heap.

The Edomites had helped the Babylonian marauders by catching the fleeing Israelites, treating them with cruelty and selling them as slaves. They seemed to manifest fiendish delight in the calamity that overtook Jerusalem's inhabitants.

Obadiah denounced the selfish, indifferent and presently hostile spirit of nearby Edom. She, holding the attitude of Esau, had remained aloof and had allowed Jerusalem to be captured. She had even become party in the destruction and had gone in for her part of the spoils.

God had commanded Israel, "Do not despise an Edomite, for the Edomites are related to you" (Deuteronomy 23:7). But Edom had shown an implacable hatred toward Israel from the time Israel was refused passage through Edom on the way to Canaan (see Numbers 20:14-21) to the day of the destruction of Jerusalem by the Babylonians, when Edom cried, "Tear it down . . . tear it down to its foundations!" (Psalm 137:7).

Because of Edom's pride and cruel hatred, her utter destruction was decreed (see Obadiah 3-4,10). Nothing could save the guilty nation. The people were driven from their rocky home five years after the destruction of Jerusalem when Nebuchadnezzar, passing down the valley of Arabah that formed the military road to Egypt, crushed the Edomites. They lost their existence as a nation about 150 BC, and their name perished with the capture of Jerusalem by the Romans. "As you have done, it will be done to you" (Obadiah 15).

OBADIAH 17-21: ZION'S DELIVERANCE

The book closes with the promise of deliverance for Zion: "But on Mount Zion will be deliverance; it will be holy, and Jacob will possess his inheritance" (Obadiah 17). The first step in the future reestablishment of the Jewish nation is the recovery of what was previously their own.

God's Chosen People had just been carried into captivity by Nebuchadnezzar, the holy land was deserted, and God had told Edom of her doom. Jeremiah gave this same prophecy in chapter 49. Both Jeremiah and Obadiah had probably said these things many times. Five years later Edom fell, vanquished by the same Babylon she had helped. She would be as though she had never been, swallowed up forever. This was the prophecy against Edom.

But Israel will rise again from her fall. She will possess not only her own land, but also Philistia and Edom. She will finally rejoice in the holy reign of the promised Messiah. God's Chosen People, the Jews, will regain the possessions they once had, and among the dearest to them is their Holy Land. Obadiah, as the other prophets had, predicted the coming of the Day of the Lord and the establishment of the Messiah's kingdom. Remember, a Christian, too, is an heir to the promises to be fulfilled when Christ comes. The believer possesses all things in Christ (see 2 Corinthians 6:10).

God's judgment on Edom as Israel's notable enemy should warn nations today that God has not cast off His people, and the nations that oppress them will surely bring down His judgments (see Genesis 12:3).

Jonah

UNDERSTANDING JONAH

AUTHOR: Jonah 1:1 specifically identifies the content of the book as the prophetic word that the Lord gave Jonah, whether Jonah wrote the account about himself or someone else wrote the account about Jonah.

DATE: The book was likely written around 750 BC.

PURPOSE AND SUMMARY: The book of Jonah declares the universality of God's love embracing not only Israel but also pagan nations. The book's realism is disputed. But if one is willing to accept the miraculous power of God, there is no compelling reason to deny the actuality of the miracles in Jonah. Jesus Himself mentioned Jonah and the whale as a genuine historical event, when speaking of His own death and resurrection (see Matthew 12:39-41; 16:4; Luke 11:29-32). Because he did not want to see the Ninevites repent and be spared from God's judgment, Jonah refused God's call to prophesy to the people of Nineveh about God's impending judgment. God used a storm and a whale to correct Jonah's disobedience, after which he finally obeyed. But when the people of Nineveh repented of their sins and sought God, Jonah bitterly complained to God for showing mercy to Israel's enemies.

Jonah was a native of Gath Hepher, a town about an hour's distance from Nazareth. Jewish legend tells us that he was the son of the widow of Sarepta, whom Elijah brought to life. Whether this is true or not, we don't know, but he probably was a disciple of the great Elisha and succeeded him as a prophet.

Jonah lived during the reign of Jeroboam II and aided him in making the northern kingdom of Israel very powerful and prosperous (see 2 Kings 14:25). Jonah was a famous statesman.

In the recent past, there has been a particular interest in the book of Jonah—centering on the fish! People have been so busy with tape measures and fish studies, trying to figure out the dimensions of the fish's belly and what type of fish it was, that they seem to have had no time to explore the depths of the teaching of the book. Be sure to read through this short book. Many stumble over this book. Few know it.

God is in this book. He was taking care of His prophet. God was working. He provided Jonah with four things:

- A huge fish—Jonah 1:17
- A leafy plant—Jonah 4:6
- A worm—Jonah 4:7
- A scorching east wind—Jonah 4:8

Jonah is the test book of the Bible. It challenges our faith. Our attitude toward Jonah reveals our attitude toward God and His Word. Is the story of Jonah mere naturalism or is it supernaturalism? Right here we stand or fall.

Jesus Christ Himself made the book of Jonah important. When the Pharisees and teachers of the Law asked Christ for a sign to prove His claims, He gave them only the sign of the prophet Jonah (see Matthew 12:39-41).

Two events in Jonah are of particular importance. One is the great fish swallowing Jonah, and the other is the possibility of such a large heathen city as Nineveh being converted by an obscure foreign missionary in just a few days. Read Matthew 12:41 to learn what Jesus said about it.

JONAH 1–2: AN OBSTINATE PROPHET

As the book opens, God is speaking to Jonah, giving him his commission: "Go to the great city of Nineveh and preach against it, because its wickedness has come up before me" (Jonah 1:2).

God is very definite with His orders. He told Jonah to arise and go. "But Jonah ran away from the LORD and headed for Tarshish. He went down to Joppa" (verse 3). He said no to God. Why did he flee? Read Jonah 4:2. Jonah knew that Assyria was Israel's dreaded enemy. At this time in history, Assyria seems to have been somewhat weakened in power. It was then that God told Jonah to go to the capital of that hostile country and pronounce judgment against it for its great wickedness. Jonah feared that Nineveh may repent and be spared impending doom. If, however, Assyria fell under God's judgment, Jonah's own beloved Israel may escape judgment at Assyria's hands. Jonah had the spirit of a national hero. He decided to sacrifice himself in order to save his people, but his heroism was sadly misguided.

Nineveh was one of the greatest cities of the world, situated on the east bank of the Tigris River, 400 miles from the Mediterranean. It was the capital of Assyria (see Genesis 10:11-12). The stronghold of the city was about 30 miles long and 10 miles wide. Five 100-foot-high walls and three moats (canals) surrounded it. The streets were wide enough for four chariots to be driven abreast. The palaces were large and beautiful, with the finest of gardens. Fifteen gates guarded by colossal lions and bulls allowed entry into the city. Seventy halls were decorated magnificently in alabaster and with sculptures. The temple in the city was in the form of a great pyramid that glittered in the sun. Intellectual accomplishments were incredible. But the city was as great in wickedness as it was in wealth and power.

As soon as Jonah fled, God began to act. "Then the LORD sent a great wind on the sea, and such a violent storm arose that the ship threatened to break up" (Jonah 1:4). God loved Jonah too much to let him succeed at failing to do God's task. Failure never relieves us of responsibility to serve.

Read about the events that took place before Jonah was thrown into the sea (see Jonah 1:3-15). When Jonah was thrown into the sea, he was gripped by the hand of God (see Jonah 1:17). God's way is best. If we don't accept it, He forces strange things on us.

Jonah 2 tells us how Jonah came to the end of himself. After much praying, he confessed that he could do nothing by himself: "Salvation comes from the LORD" (Jonah 2:9). Then God set him free (see Jonah 2:10).

No doubt, two things hindered Jonah when God told him to go to Nineveh—his scorn for the rest of the world and his pride. God took this out of him when he was in the fish's belly.

JONAH 3-4: AN OBEDIENT PEOPLE

God gave Jonah another chance to be of service: "Then the word of the LORD came to Jonah a second time" (Jonah 3:1). How foolish he was to make the Lord repeat His call! How much better to obey at once!

God said again, "Go to the great city of Nineveh and proclaim to it the message I give you" (Jonah 3:2).

It was not easy for Jonah to go through the streets and cry, "Forty more days and Nineveh will be overthrown" (Jonah 3:4). There was no mercy in his message. There was no tear in the prophet's voice. He was obeying God, but his heart was unchanged (see Jonah 4:1-3). The common people of Nineveh repented first. The nobles followed. This is always true. Revival starts among the common people. Think of a city like Chicago repenting and turning to God in one day because of the preaching of a modern prophet. It would be a miracle of the ages. But this is what happened when Jonah preached.

Jonah 4 describes Jonah as he sat on a hill on the east side of the city, under a plant that God provided for shade; he was sulking because he hadn't agreed with what God had had him do (see Jonah 4:6). And the book ends—abruptly!

Jonah as a Symbol of Christ

We must notice two things in this book. First, Jonah is a symbol of Christ in His death, burial and resurrection: "For as Jonah was three days and three nights in the belly of a huge fish, so the Son of Man will be three days and three nights in the heart of the earth" (Matthew 12:40).

Jonah as a Symbol of Israel

Second, Jonah is also a symbol of Israel—disobedient to God, swallowed by the nations of the world, but "given up" to return to the Promised Land. When Christ comes, Israel will be a witness of and for God everywhere.

- Jonah was called to a world mission—so was Israel.
- Jonah refused to fulfill his mission by obeying God—so did Israel.
- Jonah was punished by being cast into the sea—Israel, by being scattered among the nations.
- Jonah was preserved—so was Israel.
- Jonah repented and was cast out of the fish and restored to life—Israel will be cast out by all the nations and restored to her former position.
- Jonah, obedient to God, goes on his mission—Israel, in obedience, will become a witness to all the earth.
- Jonah was blessed because Nineveh was brought to salvation—Israel will be blessed because of the conversion of the whole world.

UNDERSTANDING MICAH

AUTHOR: The author of the book of Micah was the prophet Micah, according to Micah 1:1.

DATE: The book was likely written between 750 and 700 BC.

PURPOSE AND SUMMARY: The prophet Micah was a contemporary of the prophet Isaiah in the late eighth century BC, and he spoke at a time when conditions in Judah paralleled those in the northern kingdom of Israel during Amos's day in the early eighth century BC. Micah's messages are strikingly similar to those of Amos: Many of the same sins are denounced; and the same bold, direct language is used to show how offended God is by idolatry and oppression of the poor. While announcing God's certain judgment upon sin, he also spoke of a sure deliverance to come through the Messiah who would come from Bethlehem, whose nature would be divine and whose origins would be "from of old, from ancient times" (Micah 5:2).

Micah was a country preacher who lived in the days of Isaiah and Hosea. His home was about 20 miles south of Jerusalem in the town of Moresheth on the Philistine border. He was preaching there at the same time Isaiah was preaching in Jerusalem and Hosea was in Israel. Micah was a prophet of the common people and country life; Isaiah preached to the court in the city of Jerusalem. Micah knew his fellow country people well. Read what he says his real equipment is: "But as for me, I am filled with power, with the Spirit of the Lord, and with justice and might, to declare to Jacob his transgression, to Israel his sin" (Micah 3:8).

Micah prophesied concerning Samaria (the capital of Israel) and Jerusalem (the capital of Judah); and although the conditions were the same in both kingdoms, the burden of his prophecy was for Judah. The times in which he lived were difficult. Oppression was present within the kingdom, and foes were threatening from without. The kings Jotham, Ahaz and Hezekiah reigned during Micah's day.

The prophet denounced the social sins of his day (see Micah 2:2). Micah keenly felt these social evils. He saw the unfair treatment of the poor by the rich. He felt that these sins cried to heaven. No class was free from corrupting influences; princes, priests and people alike were all affected (see Micah 2:2,8-9,11; 3:1-3,5,11). Micah made them all sting from the lash of his words. Micah wanted the people to know that every cruel act to one's fellow citizen was an insult to God. God was offended by the unjust conduct of the people and the rulers. In spite of the state of things, however, the people tried to carry on their religious observances. Micah showed the uselessness of that (see Micah 6:7-8).

The northern kingdom of Israel was taken into captivity during Micah's lifetime—Israel would not heed the warning of the prophets. Judah did, and it was spared for 150 years. Micah knew that national sins would lead to national downfall. "Righteousness exalts a nation, but sin condemns any people" (Proverbs 14:34).

The book of Micah seems to be divided into three parts, each beginning with "Hear" (Micah 1:2) or "Listen" (Micah 3:1; 6:1). And each closes with a promise:

1. A promise to deliver Israel—Micah 2:12-13
2. A promise to overthrow the enemies in the land—Micah 5:10,15
3. A promise to fulfill the promise to Abraham—Micah 7:20

Throughout Micah, Judah's national sins are enumerated:

- Idolatry—Micah 1:7; 6:16
- Covetousness—Micah 2:2
- Oppression—Micah 2:2
- Violence—Micah 2:2; 3:10; 6:12; 7:2
- Encouragement of false prophets—Micah 2:6,11
- Corruption of princes—Micah 3:1-3
- Corruption of prophets—Micah 3:5-7
- Corruption of priests—Micah 3:11
- Bribery—Micah 3:9,11; 7:3
- Dishonesty—Micah 6:10-11

Micah contains several passages concerning Christ:

- Bethlehem will produce the ultimate Ruler—Micah 5:2
- Christ will be the King—Micah 2:12-13

- Christ will reign in righteousness over the whole earth—Micah 4:1,7

Three different people quoted Micah:

1. Judah's elders—Jeremiah 26:18 (quoting Micah 3:12)
2. The magi—Matthew 2:5-6 (quoting Micah 5:2)
3. Jesus—Matthew 10:35-36 (quoting Micah 7:6)

See also Isaiah 2:2-4; 41:15; Ezekiel 22:27; Zephaniah 3:19.
Micah also describes several characteristics of God's government:

- Jerusalem (capital of Christ's kingdom)—Micah 4:1-2
- Universalness (extent of Christ's kingdom)—Micah 4:2
- Peace (keynote of Christ's kingdom)—Micah 4:3
- Prosperity (blessing of Christ's kingdom)—Micah 4:4
- Righteousness (basis of Christ's kingdom)—Micah 4:5; 4:2

The prophets often use the word "remnant." What does it mean? "Remnant" means the small part of the nation that God always preserves for Himself (see Micah 2:12; 4:7; 5:3,7-8; 7:18).

MICAH 1–2: A MESSAGE TO THE PEOPLE CONCERNING ISRAEL'S SIN

As the book opens, we hear the cry, "Hear, you peoples, all of you, listen, earth and all who live in it, that the Sovereign LORD may bear witness against you" (Micah 1:2).

God is not asleep. He knows the sad condition of His people. He will sit in judgment of His people. Yes, the Lord was coming to call Israel to judgment because of her wrongs. Samaria and Jerusalem were pronounced guilty before the great Judge of the universe. Captivity and exile were their fate. The sins of the people are stated with blunt frankness in Micah 2:1-11, and God rebuked them especially for social injustice, unfaithfulness, dishonesty and idolatry.

Micah told them that Samaria, the capital of Israel, would fall (see Micah 1:6-7). A similar judgment would come upon Judah. Judah's sin is described as an incurable disease (see Micah 1:9). Some kinds of disease are cured only by destruction. Micah's pronouncement was that Judah's people will be taken captive, for God finds that they have incurable oppression, violence and injustice. Notice the towns of Judah mentioned in the last verses of chapter 1. Look at a good Bible atlas, and you will see that they all surround the prophet's hometown.

The idolatry of Israel spread rapidly to Jerusalem and the strong city of Lachish (see Micah 1:13). Micah especially denounced the awful spread of idolatry, and all its terrible evils, to Judah under King Ahaz. The prophet also rebuked the oppression of the poor and women and little children being driven from their homes (see Micah 2:2,9). God will bring suffering and shame upon them for their unscrupulous use of power.

More and more, we are becoming aware of the social value of the gospel of the Lord Jesus Christ. Wherever this gospel goes, we find that living conditions improve and that a brotherhood that is based on Sonship grows. Sincere worship of God always results in practical demonstrations of changed lives. Missionaries all attest to the wonderful truth of this.

MICAH 3–5: A MESSAGE TO THE RULERS CONCERNING THE COMING CHRIST

"Listen, you leaders of Jacob, you rulers of Israel" (Micah 3:1). What does God say of them? Read Micah 3:1-4. God likens their covetousness and self-aggrandizement to cannibalism. The leaders are figuratively devouring the poor, defenseless people (see Micah 3:2-3).

The nation was ready to collapse, and the princes and priests were responsible for its fall. God denounced the sin of the rulers (see Micah 3:9), the bribery among the judges (see Micah 3:11), the use of false weights and balances (see Micah 6:11). God describes these men in Micah 3:5: "As for the prophets who lead my people astray, they proclaim 'peace' if they have something to eat."

Micah, brokenhearted, told of God's judgment upon Judah for her sins. Jerusalem and its Temple will be destroyed (see Micah 3:12; 7:13). The people of Judah will be taken captive to Babylon (see Micah 4:10). But Micah seemed to speed through the words of judgment so that he could linger over the message of God's love and mercy. God will bring His people back from captivity (see Micah 4:1-8; 7:11,14-17).

Micah was a prophet of hope. He always looked beyond doom and punishment to the day of glory when Christ Himself will reign, when peace will cover the earth. God gives the promise: The Messiah will come. He will be born in Bethlehem (see Micah 4:8; 5:2-4). Then Israel will be gathered from the nations into which she has been scattered (see Micah 4:6).

Oh, that the Prince of Peace might come soon and make all these things come to pass. We pray with John on the isle of Patmos, "Amen. Come, Lord Jesus" (Revelation 22:20).

Micah told how Bethlehem, smallest among the towns in Judah, would be singled out for honor by the birth of God's Messiah, Jesus Christ, our Lord. He will not win His victories by might or by power but by His Spirit. He will come as a little babe to bring salvation to a world so in need of a Redeemer. This 700-year-old prophecy from Micah 5:2-5, together with the star, led the wise men to Jerusalem to seek the new King.

MICAH 6–7: A MESSAGE TO THE CHOSEN PEOPLE CONCERNING GOD'S ACCUSATION

"Hear, you mountains, the LORD's accusation; listen, you everlasting foundations of the earth. For the LORD has a case against his people; he is lodging a charge against Israel" (Micah 6:2). God appears to be suing His people.

God's Chosen People had ignored Him. So He told them to remember how good He had been to them and how He had kept His covenant with them (see Micah 6:3). The people, suffering from a guilty conscience, asked how they could please God. Frantically they asked if burnt offerings would do (see Micah 6:6-7).

Men and women are always trying to get back into the good graces of God with some outward religious service or some worldly rather than spiritual thing. But remember, "My sacrifice, O God, is a broken spirit; a broken and contrite heart you, God, will not despise" (Psalm 51:17). God wants righteous conduct and a real personal experience of Him in each life. Because of unrighteous conduct, the people had to suffer unbelievable consequences. God is a righteous Judge (see Micah 1:3,5; 3:12).

What does the apostle Paul tell us to do in return for God's mercies? Read Romans 12:1-2. The best way to get back into God's graces is to accept God's grace.

POINTS TO REMEMBER

The Old Testament, in Micah, gives us a definition of religion and at the same time gives us the essentials of real religion. What does God require of you? Read Micah 6:8.

- "Act justly"—be ethical in all that you do in life.
- "Love mercy"—always be considerate of others, especially when justice has not been done.
- "Walk humbly with your God"—have a personal relationship with God.

How does this compare with people's present-day definitions of "religion"?

Paul called this "the mind of Christ" (1 Corinthians 2:16); "in your relationships with one another, have the same mindset as Christ Jesus" (Philippians 2:5). If our religion is only a spiritually true creed, a huge house of worship and an elaborate ritual, then we have nothing. All must be filled with the mind of Christ. We must "worship in the Spirit and in truth" (John 4:24). God wants this spirit of Christ to be lived out through our daily lives and to be exhibited in all our conduct, in our homes and in our businesses. Can our religion stand this test?

It is interesting that when Christ summed up the same matter, He used the words "justice, mercy and faithfulness" (Matthew 23:23). He thus pointed out that equating faith with walking humbly with our God is appropriate.

Micah

23

Understanding Nahum, Habakkuk and Zephaniah

Nahum Portrays Jesus Christ, a Stronghold in the Day of Trouble;
Habakkuk Portrays Jesus Christ, the God of Our Salvation; Zepha-
niah Portrays Jesus Christ, a Jealous Lord

SELECTED BIBLE READINGS

DAY OF THE WEEK		MAIN TOPIC
Sunday: Nahum 1	The Judge and the Verdict	
Monday: Nahum 2–3	The Execution	
Tuesday: Habakkuk 1	Habakkuk's Complaint	
Wednesday: Habakkuk 2	God's Reply	
Thursday: Habakkuk 3	Habakkuk's Song	
Friday: Zephaniah 1–2	Coming Judgments	
Saturday: Zephaniah 3	The Kingdom Blessings	

UNDERSTANDING NAHUM

AUTHOR: The author of the book of Nahum is identified as "Nahum the Elkoshite" (Nahum 1:1). There are many theories as to where the town of Elkosh was located, but there is no conclusive evidence to prove any of the theories. One possibility is that "Elkosh" refers to the city later called Capernaum (which literally means "the village of Nahum") near the Sea of Galilee.

DATE: Events mentioned in the book of Nahum suggest that the book was written between 663 and 612 BC. Two events are mentioned that can help us to determine these dates. First, Nahum mentions the city of Thebes in Egypt falling to the Assyrians (663 BC) in the past tense, so the event had already happened (see Nahum 3:8). Second, the remainder of Nahum's prophecies came true in 612 BC, when the Assyrian capital, Nineveh (mentioned in Nahum 1:1), was destroyed by the Babylonians.

PURPOSE AND SUMMARY: This book is a vivid prediction of the approaching downfall of Nineveh, the capital city of the Assyrian Empire at the end of the seventh century BC. The Assyrians practiced some of the most brutal forms of warfare in the ancient Near East, including impaling their enemies, skinning them alive, and burying them alive inside the mud brick walls that surrounded cities. Nahum, whose name means "consolation" or "comfort," spoke God's comfort to His people, long harassed by Assyria, with the promise that this cruel and oppressing people would soon meet destruction at God's hand.

Nahum, the writer of this book, was a native of Elkosh. In Assyria, near the ruins of Nineveh, the natives point to a tomb as Nahum's. But most authorities think that this Elkosh was in Galilee. In name and in message, "Nahum" means "comfort" for Judah: "The LORD is good, a refuge in times of trouble. He cares for those who trust in him" (Nahum 1:7). Deliverance for Judah and destruction of her enemy Assyria were God's great themes for His people.

Nahum was probably a native of Galilee and lived during the time of good King Hezekiah and the great prophet Isaiah. No doubt, when the cruel Assyrians invaded his country and carried away the 10 tribes of Israel, he escaped into the southern kingdom of Judah. He probably lived in Jerusalem, where he later witnessed the siege of that city by Sennacherib, which ended with the miraculous destruction of the Assyrian armies. Remember, 185,000 perished in one night (see 2 Kings 19:35). It may be that Nahum 1:2 refers to this. Shortly after this event, Nahum wrote his book.

The main event prophesied in this book is the destruction of Nineveh, the city Jonah had warned. Nineveh was again guilty of sin, and God sent Nahum to declare His righteous judgment on her. In the judgment of Nineveh, God was in effect judging a sinning world. The book of Nahum was written about 150 years after the revival that occurred during Jonah's day when the city of Nineveh was brought to repentance.

No doubt the Ninevites were sincere then, at the time of Jonah, but their sincerity did not last. They were again guilty of the very sins of which they had repented. Nineveh, the glory of the Assyrians, was again completely and deliberately defiant of the living God. The people were not just backsliders! They intentionally rejected the God they had accepted (see 2 Kings 18:25,30,35; 19:10-13). Mercy given little regard finally brings judgment.

God sent Nahum to predict the final doom of such wicked and rebellious people and the complete, violent destruction of Nineveh and the empire of which she was the capital. (This city had one more rebuke, given a few years later by Zephaniah [see Zephaniah 2:13].) Assyria had enjoyed 300 years as a world empire. In 722 BC, she had destroyed Israel and threatened Judah. The Assyrians were great warriors and had built up the Assyrian Empire through the use of force and by looting other people. They were always out on raiding expeditions and did everything to inspire terror. Read Nahum 2:11-12 to learn about their beastlike violence and cruelty. They said that they did this in obedience to their god, Asshur. But the true God was going to cause Nineveh to perish in a violent and extraordinary way.

The doom of the city was delayed some 150 years after Jonah preached, but it fell at last. Nahum's prophecy was not a call to repentance but the statement of certain and final doom. Read Nahum 1:9; 3:18-19. Nineveh's name would cease to exist, and God would dig her grave (see Nahum 1:14).

NAHUM 1:1-7: THE JUDGE

In Nahum 1, we see God the holy Judge on the bench of the court of heaven, judging wicked Nineveh. The case is presented. This

God is a just God; therefore, He must avenge all crimes. God as Judge exhibits the following attributes:

- Is jealous—verse 2
- Is avenging—verse 2
- Is filled with wrath at evildoers—verse 2
- Maintains wrath against His enemies—verse 2
- Is "great in power"—verse 3
- "Will not leave the guilty unpunished"—verse 3
- Is indignant—verse 6

The following attributes are exhibited by God as Father:

- "Is slow to anger"—verse 3
- "Is good"—verse 7
- "Is . . . a refuge in times of trouble"—verse 7
- "Cares for those who trust in him"—verse 7

These attributes of God constitute the basis of all God's actions toward people, and this book gives us an excellent opportunity to see the attributes of God in action.

The first eight words of Nahum's prophecy are awe-inspiring: "The Lord is a jealous and avenging God" (Nahum 1:2). To think of a God like this makes us examine ourselves. We find that there is no righteousness in us. How this thought drives us into the loving arms of a Savior who "covers" and clothes us with the robes of His righteousness!

Notice that God did not bring judgment on Assyria in a fit of temper. He had been patient for a long time. He is "slow to anger," but He is a God of absolute justice. He is the Lord God, merciful and gracious, long-suffering and forgiving, yet He will by no means clear the guilty. Jonah acted out the first side of God's character, love (see Jonah 4:2). Nahum brought out the second side, the holiness of God that must deal with sin in judgment (see Nahum 1:2,6). This holy Judge is "just and the one who justifies those who have faith in Jesus" (Romans 3:26), because His holy law has been vindicated by the cross of Christ.

NAHUM 1:8-14: THE VERDICT

Nahum 1:8-14 details the battle-and-destruction sentence conferred on corrupt Nineveh by the Judge, God. She was weighed in the balance and found wanting, so God pronounced her sentence:

- Condemned to utter destruction—verses 8-9
- Captured while defenders were drunk—verse 1:10
- Name blotted out—verse 1:14
- Will lie in a grave—verse 1:14

We cannot read this without being struck by the solemnity of it all. Nahum told of this destruction as prophecy. We look at it today as history. Yes, the Judge brought everything to pass. Today the traveler finds the great city of Nineveh a thing of the past, still lying in ruins.

NAHUM 2–3: THE EXECUTION

Read what God says in Nahum 2–3, two short chapters. We find a picture of Nineveh's siege, fall and desolation described with graphic eloquence. All God can do with a rebellious and defiant nation is to destroy it.

The mustering of armies around Nineveh and the marshaling of forces within the city are pictured in such a way that the prophet makes his listeners graphically envision all the horrid sights of the tragic scene.

Outside the walls, the Medes have gathered. Shields are brilliantly painted. Robes are purple. Terrible spears glitter in the sun. Knives on their chariot wheels flash in the light. Inside the city, pandemonium reigns! Too late, the king tries to rally his drunken nobles to defend the beloved city. But the Tigris River has flooded and washed away most of the wall that had seemed to them an impregnable barrier (see Nahum 2:6). Their enemies take advantage of this. Part of the city is destroyed by fire (Nahum 3:13,15).

The queen is taken captive; and her maidens, like a flock of doves, moan around her.

The cries of the Medes are heard as they shout to one another, "Plunder the silver! Plunder the gold! The supply is endless, the wealth from all its treasures!" (Nahum 2:9). The city is looted while the people stand with their knees shaking in fear. Nineveh will no longer terrify the nations, because God has made an end of her. This will happen to all wicked nations of the earth.

The Medes and Babylonians completely destroyed Nineveh in 612 BC, at the zenith of her power. Nahum's prophecy came true: A sudden rise of the Tigris carried away a great part of the wall, and this aided the attacking Medes and Babylonians in their overthrow of the city.

So deep and effectively did God dig Nineveh's grave that every trace of its existence disappeared for ages and its site was not known. When Alexander the Great fought the battle of Arbela nearby in 331 BC, he did not even know that there had ever been a city there. When the Greek historian Xenophon and his army of 10,000 passed by 200 years later, he thought the mounds were the ruins of some Parthian city. When Napoleon camped near its site, he, too, was not aware that there had ever been anything of significance at the site.

Many scholars used to think that the references to Nineveh in the Bible were to a mythical place. It seemed that no such city ever existed. In 1845, however, the British archaeologist Sir Austen Layard confirmed the suspicions of his compatriot Claudius Rich that the mounds across the Tigris River from Mosul were the ruins of Nineveh. The ruins of the magnificent palaces of the Assyrian kings have been unearthed, and thousands of inscriptions have confirmed the Bible account.

POINTS TO REMEMBER

Our God Is a God of Wrath
This book is a graphic reminder that our God is a God of wrath, as well as of love, and it gives us a picture of God acting in wrath.

Read the second verse of the book again: "The LORD is a jealous and avenging God; the LORD takes vengeance and is filled with wrath. The LORD takes vengeance on his foes and vents his wrath against his enemies." It is not pleasant to be reminded that God is a God of anger as well as a God of love. But remember both attributes are His. He is a holy God. He hates sin. He will bring judgment on anyone who sins.

What We Sow, We Will Reap

As Nineveh had sowed, so must she reap. This is God's law. The Ninevites had fortified themselves so that nothing could harm them. But they had reckoned without Jehovah. What are bricks and mortar to God! The mighty empire that Shalmaneser, Sargon and Sennacherib had built up the Lord threw down with a stroke. The inventions of civilization are powerless against heaven's artillery.

Nineveh is an example for us of a nation that turned her back on God. In our day, proud civilizations are staking everything upon the strength of their people and their earthly power and machines, and there is a terrible disregard of God. Nineveh was overthrown because of her sins (see Nahum 3:1-7), and her great wealth and strength were not sufficient to save her (see Nahum 3:8-19).

Oftentimes, nations depend upon might and power to survive. They forget that it is " 'not by might nor by power, but by my Spirit,' says the LORD Almighty" (Zechariah 4:6). The person or nation that deliberately and finally rejects God, deliberately and finally and fatally elects doom. Beware of this!

Hear the apostle Peter's words of warning spoken hundreds of years after these events: "The Lord is not slow in keeping his promise, as some understand slowness. Instead he is patient with you, not wanting anyone to perish, but everyone to come to repentance. But the day of the Lord will come like a thief. The heavens will disappear with a roar; the elements will be destroyed by fire, and the earth and everything in it will be laid bare" (2 Peter 3:9-10).

UNDERSTANDING HABAKKUK

AUTHOR: Habakkuk 1:1 identifies the book of Habakkuk as an oracle from the prophet Habakkuk.

DATE: The book was likely written between 627 and 605 BC.

PURPOSE AND SUMMARY: Habakkuk is written in the form of a dialogue between the prophet and the Lord. It starts with Habakkuk's complaints questioning the Lord's allowing evildoers among God's people to go unpunished. The Lord replies that He is sending overwhelming judgment on them by bringing the Babylonian army against His people. Habakkuk is stunned by the Lord's response, but he affirms that even in overwhelming judgment, "I will rejoice in the LORD. . . . The Sovereign LORD is my strength" (Habakkuk 3:18-19).

We know little about this prophet of faith except that he asked God questions and received answers. He, like many people today, could not reconcile his belief in a good and righteous God with the facts of life as he saw them. He was troubled by an eternal Why? Why do the wicked prosper? Why is God silent in times of disaster? Even today, people of faith find themselves bewildered by many of the things that they see going on round about them. We ask, "Why does God allow such awful crimes to go unchecked? Why doesn't God stop people in their mad rush if He is all powerful?"

Habakkuk, in all his difficulties, went to God in prayer and waited patiently for His answer (see Habakkuk 2:1). He stood on the watchtower and listened to God. G. Campbell Morgan said that when Habakkuk looked at his circumstances, he was confused (see Habakkuk 1:3); but when he waited for God and listened to Him, he sang (see Habakkuk 3:18-19):

- Watch and see—Habakkuk 1
- Stand and see—Habakkuk 2
- Kneel and see—Habakkuk 3

Habakkuk was a prophet (see Habakkuk 1:1), but we find something else of interest about him. He may have been one of the Levitical choristers in the temple (see Habakkuk 3:19) or he may have helped arrange the services.

We learn much about him as a thinker and a man of faith from his own words. He was a contemporary with Jeremiah at home and with Daniel in Babylon.

The world empire of Assyria had fallen just as Nahum had prophesied. Egypt and Babylon had then contended for the top place of power. At the battle of Carchemish (605 BC), in which King Josiah was killed, the Babylonians were conquerors and the great kingdoms of the Babylonians and Chaldeans were united under Nebuchadnezzar. Habakkuk knew only too well that Judah must fall before this great rising power. But one question rose in his mind and troubled him greatly: *Why should any nation as wicked as Babylon conquer a nation like Judah, which was less evil?* It seemed to him that it was just a matter of evil triumphing over evil (see Habakkuk 1:13). What good could come of this? God had to show him His ultimate plan. Judah needed punishment. God was using Babylon to correct Judah, but Babylon's turn would come. Babylon would be utterly blotted out. For God's people, there was yet to be a glorious future and a kingdom where Jehovah Himself would prevail.

This book seems to be a dialogue between Jehovah and the prophet. Two conversations are recorded and the book closes with a hymn and doxology, which reveal that all the questions have been answered and there is a new confidence in God.

HABAKKUK 1: HABAKKUK'S COMPLAINT

This book opens with the cry of a man who has a problem he cannot solve: "How long, LORD, must I call for help, but you do not listen? Or cry out to you, 'Violence!' but you do not save" (Habakkuk 1:2)!

Habakkuk was confused and bewildered. It seemed to him that God was doing nothing to straighten out the conditions in the world. He had lived during the days of the great reformation under good King Josiah. He had seen Assyria fading in power and Babylon, under Nebuchadnezzar, rising to a place of supremacy. The world about him was in an upheaval. Violence was prevalent, and God was doing nothing about it.

But worse, he saw his own land, Judah, full of lawlessness and tyranny. The righteous were oppressed (see Habakkuk 1:4,13). The people were living in open sin. They were worshiping idols (see Habakkuk 2:18-19). They were oppressing the poor. Habakkuk knew that the day was dark. He knew that these sins were leading to an invasion of Jerusalem by a strong enemy.

Habakkuk asked God his questions. He did not call a committee or form a society to solve the problem of the day. He went straight to Jehovah and stated his problem. Then God answered, "Look at the nations and watch—and be utterly amazed. For I am going to do something in your days that you would not believe, even if you were told" (Habakkuk 1:5). God told Habakkuk that He was not indifferent to His people, but He wanted Habakkuk to look beyond the present. He was already working. God called the Babylonians to do the work of punishing Judah. They were a cruel scourge that would sweep over the land to destroy it (see Habakkuk 1:5-11).

God's answer horrified Habakkuk. He could not understand why God would use such awful means to punish His people, Judah. How was it possible for God to use such an enemy to punish His own people when He Himself is so pure and holy? Read Habakkuk 1:13, which is Habakkuk's challenge to God to defend His actions.

The nations have always been God's object lessons, illustrating His moral laws (see Habakkuk 1:12).

HABAKKUK 2: GOD'S REPLY

As Habakkuk 2 opens, we see Habakkuk facing the greatest moment of his life. Watch him as he climbs up on the watchtower to wait for God. Everything lies in ruins around the prophet.

Chaldea is coming up to destroy what is left. There is only One to whom he can turn, so he waits expectantly for God to answer (see Habakkuk 2:1).

God gives an answer (read Habakkuk 2:2-20). God admits that the Babylonians are wicked, but He declares that they will destroy themselves finally by their own evil. Pride and cruelty always bring destruction. People sometimes have to wait to know what the final outcome will be. God sometimes takes ages to show His plans. "With the Lord a day is like a thousand years, and a thousand years are like a day" (2 Peter 3:8). God's testing always reveals what people are. He removes their impurities. It may seem that the Babylonians prosper for a time, but they are doomed. "The righteous will live by his faith" (Habakkuk 2:4) is the heart of the book.

Five "woes" are mentioned in Habakkuk 2. Find what they are. Remember that evil will perish. Only righteousness will remain before God.

HABAKKUK 3: HABAKKUK'S SONG

Habakkuk is the prophet who sang in the night. Listen to the magnificent melody with which his prophecy closes: "Though the fig tree does not bud and there are no grapes on the vines, though the olive crop fails and the fields produce no food, though there are no sheep in the pen and no cattle in the stalls, yet I will rejoice in the LORD, I will be joyful in God my Savior" (Habakkuk 3:17-18). This ode was set to music and sung by the Jews at public worship.

After a sincere prayer (see Habakkuk 3:1-16), God's glory appeared. God always responds to His people's cries to Him for help. Habakkuk realized that God is in control of this universe and that He is working out His own purpose in His own time. Habakkuk learned that he can trust God implicitly. He realized that we can see only a small part of God's plan at one time. We must wait for God to reveal His entire program. We must know that God's way is best.

God cannot always give us a satisfactory answer, because our finite minds cannot grasp the thoughts of the infinite. His thoughts are high above our thoughts, and His ways above our ways (see Isaiah 55:9), but we can trust God, always! "In all things God works for the good of those who love him, who have been called according to his purpose" (Romans 8:28).

Remember, God does not promise that He will explain everything that He does, but He does assure us that we can put our absolute trust in Him (see Psalm 37:5; 2 Timothy 1:12).

One of the texts in Habakkuk had great significance for the Reformation. Do you know the story of the young Catholic monk Martin Luther, who was the leader of the Reformation in Germany? As he rose to his feet on the steps of the Scala Sancta in Rome, he remembered these words: "The just shall live by his faith" (Habakkuk 2:4, *KJV*). Not by works! This started him on his great crusade that brought about the Reformation.

Find where Habakkuk 2:4 is quoted in the New Testament and mark the passages: Romans 1:17, Galatians 3:11 and Hebrews 10:38.

UNDERSTANDING ZEPHANIAH

AUTHOR: Zephaniah 1:1 identifies the author of the book of Zephaniah as the prophet Zephaniah.

DATE: The book was likely written between 735 and 725 BC.

PURPOSE AND SUMMARY: This book, though brief, is comprehensive, embracing the two great themes of prophetic teaching: judgment and salvation—both extending to all nations. In apocalyptic terms, on the Day of the Lord—perhaps partly fulfilled in the Scythian invasion of the Near East in the late seventh century BC—Zephaniah saw God's decisive judgment upon the nations, including Judah. He exhorted the people to turn away from sin and back to the Lord, and he assured them that God would dwell in the midst of a righteous remnant, following judgment.

Little is known of Zephaniah, the writer of this book. Two facts of his personal history appear in the first verse of the prophecy: (1) We learn that very likely he was a prince of the royal house of Judah, because he was a descendant of Hezekiah. He was in a position to denounce the sins of the princes, for he himself was an aristocrat; (2) He lived during the reign of good King Josiah. His name means "the Lord hides."

Zephaniah began his ministry as a prophet in the early days of the reign of Josiah (641-610 BC). Fifty years had elapsed since the prophecy of Nahum. Three of Hezekiah's descendants had succeeded him (see 2 Kings 20–21). Two wicked and idol-worshiping kings had preceded Josiah on the throne, and the land was overrun with evil practices of every kind. Social injustice and moral corruption were rampant on every hand. The rich had amassed great fortunes by oppressing the poor. The conditions were as bad as it could be when King Josiah, only 16 years of age, started a religious revival. He became one of the most beloved of the kings of Judah. He got rid of the pagan altars and images. How the words of Zephaniah must have encouraged the reformers!

Zephaniah depicted God as both loving and severe (see Zephaniah 1:2; 3:17). He foretold the doom of Nineveh (see Zephaniah 2:13). Who else had prophesied her doom?

We hear Zephaniah denouncing the various forms of idolatry—Baal and Molek both are condemned (see Zephaniah 1–2:3). This idol worship was destroyed during Josiah's reign. No doubt Zephaniah, a pioneer in this reform movement, was mainly responsible for the revival under Josiah. Tradition tells us that Jeremiah was his colleague.

As you start reading this book, you will be appalled by its contents. There is nothing but accusations, threats and divine chastisements. The poet William Cowper said that punishment and chastisement are "the graver countenance of love." "The Lord disciplines the one he loves, and he chastens everyone he accepts as his son" (Hebrews 12:6). In all of this is proof of God's love. The book begins with sorrow and is full of sadness and gloom, but it ends with the singing of one of the sweetest songs of love in the Old Testament.

Zephaniah prophesied several important things:

1. A faithful remnant will be delivered from captivity.
2. The Gentile nations will be converted.
3. One day people everywhere, not only in Jerusalem, will worship God (see Zephaniah 2:11; see John 4:21).

God will search the people: "At that time I will search Jerusalem with lamps and punish those who are complacent, who are like wine left on its dregs, who think, 'The LORD will do nothing, either good or bad'" (Zephaniah 1:12).

ZEPHANIAH 1: JUDAH SEARCHED

Zephaniah envisioned Jehovah judging the land (see Zephaniah 1:17; 3:5). He first searched Judah and pronounced doom on all those who worshiped idols. The land must be freed from idolatry. Jehovah cannot allow such abomination to remain. We see the rulers denounced, as is every class of sinner (see Zephaniah 1:7-13):

- The idol worshipers—verses 4-5
- Those who one time swear by God and another time swear by Molek—verse 5
- Those who turned away from the Lord—verse 6

Upon all these sinners God will bring a blast of fire. It will strike the whole earth, but it will be especially hot for the inhabitants of Jerusalem. The "day of the LORD" will be a day of dread (Zephaniah 1:1,7-8,14,18). Zephaniah called the people to tremble at God's presence.

Zephaniah

The "day of the LORD" is mentioned seven times in the prophecy. Almost without exception, when "day" is used in Scripture, it means a period of time. If a number is used before it, such as "forty days," or "three days," then it is a day of 24 hours. But when "day" is used alone, it means the time in which the people lived. So when the Word says, "the day of the LORD," it means a time of the Lord's special working. To the Jews of Zephaniah's day, it meant the time when there would be a special reckoning for Judah, a time when God would deal with His people in punishment and captivity. The future Day of the Lord is the period of the great tribulation and the millennium (see Revelation 6:1-17).

ZEPHANIAH 2: THE NATIONS SEARCHED

After the prophet called the people to seek God, hoping that "perhaps [they] will be sheltered on the day of the LORD's anger" (Zephaniah 2:3), he declared that nothing can save the nation from doom but real repentance. "Seek the LORD. . . . Seek righteousness, seek humility" (Zephaniah 2:3). After this admonition to God's people, Zephaniah turned to the five heathen nations Philistia, Moab, Ammon, Ethiopia and Assyria (see Zephaniah 2:4-15). They will be visited with the wrath of God because of their pride and scorn toward the Lord's people (see Zephaniah 2:10). The desolation of Nineveh is described in wonderfully accurate terms (see Zephaniah 2:13-15). These prophecies began to be fulfilled with the conquests of Nebuchadnezzar.

Although the judgment on Israel's neighboring enemies of that time were literally fulfilled, the judgment on Israel's enemies from around the world has not yet been fulfilled. Read Zephaniah 2:10-11; 3:8 to learn what God says about how the idols of their enemies will be broken up and how the Gentiles will worship God, everyone in their own country (see Zephaniah 2:11). Instead of people having to make a pilgrimage to Jerusalem to worship God, they will be able to worship God anywhere they are.

People have always tried to establish sacred places and shrines, and people have undergone every hardship to worship at these spots. The Jews taught that Jerusalem was the only true place of worship. The Samaritans declared that Mount Gerizim ought to be the religious center. Rome and Mecca have been the goals of pilgrimages for years. In India, thousands make a pilgrimage to Benares, the Hindus' most sacred spot, to worship and bathe in the Ganges and to carry back with them its sacred water.

But Zephaniah taught that spiritual worship did not depend on a place but on the presence of God.

ZEPHANIAH 3: ISRAEL RESTORED

The prophet concluded with the wonderful promises of Israel's future restoration and of the happy state of the purified people of God in the latter days. The redeemed remnant—cleansed, humbled, trusting and rejoicing with their offerings—will return to Zion. They will be established in their land, and God will be with them (see Zephaniah 3:15,17). Zion will then be a delight among nations and a blessing to the whole earth, as was foretold in the promise God originally made to Abraham (see Genesis 12:1-3).

The rejoicing of Zephaniah 3:14-20 must refer to something besides the day when the remnant will return after the captivity of Babylon. Judah's worst judgment followed that return. She has seen little but misery ever since. Neither did anything like this occur at Christ's first coming. It must refer to the day when the Lord Himself shall sit on the throne of David, when His people shall be gathered from the four corners of the earth (see Zephaniah 3:19). This prophecy will be blessedly fulfilled in the Kingdom age, when Christ comes to this earth to reign in power and great glory.

Zephaniah

24

Understanding Haggai, Zechariah and Malachi

Haggai Portrays Jesus Christ, the Desire of All Nations; Zechariah Portrays Jesus Christ, the Righteous Branch; Malachi Portrays Jesus Christ, Son of Righteousness

SELECTED BIBLE READINGS

DAY OF THE WEEK		MAIN TOPIC
Sunday: Haggai 1–2	Challenge and Encouragement	
Monday: Zechariah 1–6	Visions	
Tuesday: Zechariah 7–8	Fasts	
Wednesday: Zechariah 9–11	Restoration	
Thursday: Zechariah 12–14	The Messiah	
Friday: Malachi 1–2	Sin and Apostasy	
Saturday: Malachi 3–4	Hope	

NOTE: Most Old Testament prophets spoke before the captivity. During the captivity in Babylon, Ezekiel and Daniel prophesied. After the return from Babylonian exile, Haggai, Zechariah and Malachi prophesied. This makes it easy to remember. Of the 16 prophets, just 2 prophesied during the exile, while 3 prophesied after and 11 before.

Haggai, Zechariah and Malachi are the last of the prophetic books. They prophesied to the Jews after they returned to Jerusalem. Nebuchadnezzar had captured Jerusalem and had completely destroyed the Temple. This, however, did not bring the Jews to national repentance. In reading Ezra, we find that when

Cyrus, king of Persia, issued a decree permitting all the captives to return to Jerusalem and rebuild their Temple, only about 50,000 returned. Most of these were priests and Levites and the pious among the people. Although the Jews increased in power and in numbers, they never established their political independence. They were a subject people under Gentile rulers from that time on.

Before Haggai's time, the Jews had returned to their own land under Zerubbabel and began to build the Temple (see Nehemiah 12). But their enthusiasm soon waned. They made no progress beyond laying the foundation. The Samaritans and their enemy neighbors were determined that Jerusalem should not be rebuilt, and they managed to stop the work for 15 years. During these years, each person became interested in building a private house. It was then that Haggai rose and gave his message. He encouraged the people to rebuild the Temple. This time it was finished in four years. It seemed incredible that God's people should have waited so long to do the very thing they had come back to do.

UNDERSTANDING HAGGAI

AUTHOR: Haggai 1:1 identifies the author of the book of Haggai as the prophet Haggai.

DATE: The book was written in approximately 520 BC.

PURPOSE AND SUMMARY: This book consists of four prophecies delivered within the space of four months, some 16 years after the return of the first exiles to Jerusalem. Work on the second Temple had begun in 536 BC, shortly after the exiles' arrival home, but after a few years the work had ceased. Haggai, a contemporary of the prophet Zechariah, challenged the people to wholeheartedly take up the task again of rebuilding the house of God.

We know little of Haggai except that he worked with Zechariah during the days following the exile. He prophesied two months before Zechariah. Zechariah prophesied for three years and Haggai prophesied for four months.

Haggai is the first voice to be heard after the exile. His name means "my feast." His book is a collection of four brief messages written between August and December.

Each of Haggai's messages is specifically dated. These dates, rather than places and characters, dominate the scenes. These were given "in the second year of King Darius," 520 BC (Haggai 1:1). The book is dominated by one central purpose: Haggai is determined to persuade the people to rebuild the Temple. It is no easy task to move a discouraged nation to rise up and build a temple. But he did it.

HAGGAI 1:1-11: A MESSAGE OF REBUKE

When 50,000 Jews returned to Jerusalem from Babylon where they had lived in captivity, they were met with a colossal task: rebuilding the Temple and restoring the worship of Jehovah. Unfortunately, the Jews labored under the same old sins—idolatry and intermarrying with idolatrous neighbors. Enemies also harassed them; and worse, they had lost the inner strength that comes from a joy in the Lord. Read Nehemiah 8:10.

Because of all this, the work dragged and the people lost heart and became selfish. Neglecting the Lord's house, they became more interested in building homes for themselves than for God (see Haggai 1:4). God would not allow this to go on, so He sent punishment. Poor crops, droughts, scanty trade, misery and turmoil made the people's spirits fail (see Haggai 1:6). They were working and slaving but not experiencing any real joy (see Haggai 1:6,9-11).

We see the effect of Haggai's challenge. His stern call to duty restored the people's sense of purpose. Zerubbabel (the governor

Haggai

of Jerusalem), Joshua (the high priest) and the people were encouraged to finish the work of rebuilding the Temple (see Haggai 1:12-15). Read Haggai 1:13 to learn how God responded to their repentance.

God sometimes allows hardships because of our indifference to Him. In Haggai's time, crops failed and business was off because the Jews had sinned by not restoring God's house. But God wants us to keep our churches looking good. Without churches, sin and vice will grow. When people forget to love God, they forget to love their fellow citizens, too. We should keep God's house in good repair (see 2 Samuel 7:2). We are not to live in fine homes and allow the church building to be in ruins.

HAGGAI 2:1-9: A MESSAGE OF ENCOURAGEMENT

How long after the first message was the second one given (see Haggai 1:1; 2:1)? For the history of this period, read Ezra 3:8-13.

As the people were building, many of them experienced a new wave of discouragement. The older people, remembering the splendor of the Temple of Solomon, were greatly disappointed in the new Temple. They thought that the new Temple did not measure up in any way to the original. How inferior in the size of the stones! How much smaller in extent was the foundation itself! How limited were their means! And besides, this second Temple would not have the things that had made the first one so glorious—the Ark, the Tabernacle furnishings and all that went with the service of the high priest (see Exodus 25–27). These pessimists dampened the enthusiasm of all the builders.

But Haggai came with a word of cheer: God was going to pour His resources into the new building. The living God was to be in the midst of this new Temple: " 'I will shake all nations, and what is desired by all nations will come, and I will fill this house with glory,' says the LORD Almighty" (Haggai 2:7). " 'The glory of this present house will be greater than the glory of the former house,' says the LORD Almighty. 'And in this place I will grant

Haggai

peace,' declares the LORD Almighty" (Haggai 2:9). What a comfort this must have been to the Jews.

HAGGAI 2:10-23: A MESSAGE OF ASSURANCE

The third and fourth messages of Haggai, concerning cleansing and blessing, were delivered three months after the Temple was started. By the use of questions and answers, Haggai showed the people their impurity. He made them realize their sinfulness. He showed them that the reason their prayers were not answered was that they had delayed completing the Temple for so long. They had spoiled all that they had done, because of their guilt. If they would renew their zeal, they would find that God would bless them.

Haggai understood why the people complained about not seeing any visible signs of blessings, although they had been working for three full months. But Haggai told them that God was working as they were working, so it would be different now, for God had said, "From this day on I will bless you" (Haggai 2:19). God has begun even before we begin.

UNDERSTANDING ZECHARIAH

AUTHOR: Zechariah 1:1 identifies the author of the book of Zechariah as the prophet Zechariah.

DATE: The book was likely written in two primary segments, between 520 and 516 BC.

PURPOSE AND SUMMARY: Sometimes called "The Apocalypse of the Old Testament," this book contains the messages of the prophet Zechariah, a contemporary of Haggai. The main divisions of the book (1-8 and 9-14) are noticeably dissimilar in both style and subject matter. The first eight chapters are primarily concerned with the rebuilding of the Temple, although the language used is highly symbolic. Chapters 9 through 14 deal with "last things," or the End Times. Many messianic prophecies are found in this book, and Zechariah prophesies the Day of the Lord, when Israel will be restored fully to the Promised Land of Israel, the nations will be judged, and God's kingdom will be established on earth by the Messiah ruling in Jerusalem.

Zechariah is a book of the future. It is the book of revelation of the Old Testament.

ZECHARIAH 1–8: THE CHOSEN PEOPLE AND THE TEMPLE

We now find Judah still a remnant, Jerusalem far from restored, and the surrounding Gentile nations feeling secure (see Zechariah 1:14-16). Zechariah, a young prophet who had stood alongside the aged Haggai, strengthened the children of Israel as they rebuilt the Temple; and he warned them not to disappoint God as their fathers had done. He pictured God's love and care for His people. He revived their hopes by painting in glowing colors the time of perpetual blessings that would come to Israel in the future.

Zechariah, like Haggai, was a prophet to the remnant of the Jews who returned from Babylon after the 70 years of captivity. Remember that the Jews, once a powerful nation as God had planned them to be, were now a pitiful and insignificant remnant, dwelling in their Promised Land only because of the courtesy of a foreign ruler. Both Haggai and Zechariah tried to tell the people that their situation would eventually change. One day the Messiah would come, and God's Chosen People would rise to power.

Zechariah was the prophet of restoration and glory, and he seemed to let the glory of Christ glow in all of his teaching and his preaching.

Born in Babylon, Zechariah was priest as well as prophet. He prophesied for three years, and his name means "Jehovah remembers." The glorious future rather than the sad present was his message. He was a poet; Haggai, on the other hand, was a plain, practical preacher.

Zechariah's keen enthusiasm for rebuilding the Temple kept the people at the task of finishing the work. Serious crop failures and an economic depression among the Jewish people had made them so discouraged that only Haggai's blunt and consistent hammering kept them at the work. Then they needed a new voice, and Zechariah's was it. He threw himself into the work of helping his great friend Haggai.

Zechariah did not condemn the people but presented in glowing terms the fact that God was present and available to strengthen and help them. He especially encouraged the governor, Zerubbabel, who was conscious of his own weakness. Zechariah said, "'Not by might nor by power, but by my Spirit,' says the LORD Almighty" (Zechariah 4:6). Zechariah promised that the seemingly insurmountable mountains of difficulty would be removed. How marvelously this truth was fulfilled at Pentecost, when God filled people with His power.

Two Aspects of One Person

Someone has said that to correctly read the visions of this book, you must shine two lights on them—the light of the cross and the light of the crown. Otherwise, you will find that you don't have the proper perspective or background to understand Zechariah's visions. The prophet, looking far into the future, saw two aspects of the future Messiah—one Person, but two appearances. First, he saw Him in humiliation and suffering; then he saw Him in majesty and great glory. Jewish people who do not believe that Jesus is the Messiah ignore the Christ of the cross. Christians too often ignore the Christ of the crown. Both are wrong!

Visions of Israel and the Future

Of the minor prophets, Zechariah alone had visions. "During the night I had a vision" (Zechariah 1:8):

- Angelic horseman (see Zechariah 1:7-17)—Here is a picture of Israel today, outcast but not forgotten by God.

- Horns and craftsmen (see Zechariah 1:18-21)—The overthrow of Israel by her enemies is foreseen.

- A measuring line (see Zechariah 2)—The coming prosperity of Jerusalem is seen. The city, walled in by the presence of God, will be restored and will be blessed by His grace.

- Joshua, the high priest (see Zechariah 3)—Filthy garments clothing the priest and representing Israel's sin will be removed and replaced; and the Branch, Christ, will come.

- A golden lampstand and two olive trees (see Zechariah 4)—Israel will be God's future light bearer. Two olive trees, anointed by God, represent Zerubbabel (the ruler) and Joshua (the priest).

- A flying scroll (see Zechariah 5:1-4)—Wicked governments will receive God's curse.

- A basket with a woman in it (see Zechariah 5:5-11)—Carried away on divine wings, wickedness will be removed.

- Four chariots (see Zechariah 6:1-8)—Dr. G. Campbell Morgan, a leading Bible scholar of the early twentieth century, described these as the "administrative forces of righteousness."

The Crowning of the High Priest

The visions are followed by a symbolic act of crowning the high priest (see Zechariah 6:9-15). Gold and silver brought from Babylon were fashioned into a crown and placed on the head of Joshua, the high priest. By this act, the two great offices of priest and king will be united. This is a symbol of Christ the King who will sit on His throne of glory as a priest when He returns to earth to set up His millennial kingdom.

The Matter of Fasting

Two years later, we find that a committee from Bethel met with Zechariah to ask him if the national fasts should be kept (see Zechariah 7–8). The Jews themselves had instituted fasting on their great anniversary days. Zechariah warned them against cold formalism in their religious observances. He urged them to change their fasts into feasts of joy and be practical in their righteousness. God says, "To obey is better than sacrifice, and to heed is better than the fat of rams" (1 Samuel 15:22).

Fasting is only profitable as an outward sign of an inward confession of sin. Merely refraining from eating will never bring a blessing. God wants a humble and contrite heart.

ZECHARIAH 9–14: THE MESSIAH AND THE KINGDOM

The last chapters of Zechariah are full of promises of the coming Messiah and a worldwide kingdom. The prophet no longer pictured a city rebuilt on its old foundations but a glorious city whose wall is the Lord. It will not be armed for war but will be a city filled with peace, for the Prince of Peace will reign.

Zechariah foretold the Savior more than any other prophet except Isaiah:

- Christ, "the Branch"—Zechariah 3:8
- Christ, "my servant"—Zechariah 3:8
- Christ's entering Jerusalem on "a colt"—Zechariah 9:9
- Christ, the good Shepherd—Zechariah 9:16; 11:11
- Christ, the stricken Shepherd—Zechariah 13:7
- Christ betrayed for "thirty pieces of silver"—Zechariah 11:12-13

- Christ's hands "pierced"—Zechariah 12:10
- Christ's people saved—Zechariah 12:10; 13:1
- Christ wounded "at the house of [His] friends"—Zechariah 13:6
- Christ's coming on the Mount of Olives—Zechariah 14:3-8
- Christ, as King—Zechariah 14:9

Christ will come the first time as the lowly One, riding upon a colt, the foal of a donkey (see Zechariah 9:9). But we see that this lowly One will become a mighty Sovereign (see Zechariah 14:8-11). The Messiah in all His glory and might will destroy all of Israel's enemies, and He will establish His kingdom in Jerusalem and sit upon the throne of David. "His rule will extend from sea to sea and from the River to the ends of the earth" (Zechariah 9:10).

Chapter 12 gives us the prophecy of the siege of Jerusalem by the Antichrist and his armies in the last days. Then we see the repentance of the Jews when they see "the one they have pierced" (Zechariah 12:10). "A fountain will be opened to the house of David and the inhabitants of Jerusalem, to cleanse them from sin and impurity" (Zechariah 13:1). Then the Messiah will return and appear on the Mount of Olives, which will be split in two by an earthquake (see Zechariah 14:4); this is reminiscent of the day when He left the earth at that same spot but promised to return (see Acts 1:11). Finally He will be King over the whole earth, and all people "will be holy to the LORD" (Zechariah 14:20-21).

The blessings of this future kingdom of Christ will be many:

- The entire world will be His kingdom—Zechariah 4:9
- There will be an abundance of rain—Zechariah 10:1
- There will be an outpouring of the Spirit on Israel—Zechariah 12:10
- The "pierced" Messiah will be recognized for who He is—Zechariah 12:10
- The geography of the land of Israel will change—Zechariah 14:4-5,10-11

· Jerusalem will be the center of worship—Zechariah 14:16-17

UNDERSTANDING MALACHI

AUTHOR: Malachi 1:1 identifies the author of the book of Malachi as the prophet Malachi.

DATE: The book was likely written between 490 and 450 BC.

PURPOSE AND SUMMARY: Malachi's name means "my messenger." The book of Malachi is an invaluable source concerning the restored Jewish community in Jerusalem during the Persian period, the fifth century BC. Two themes are predominant: the sin and apostasy of God's people (see Malachi 1-2); and the coming judgment upon the faithless, with blessings promised for those who seek the Lord and turn away from evil (see Malachi 3-4). The growing messianic expectation in the Old Testament becomes apparent in Malachi by the announcement of God's "messenger of the covenant," by whose coming God's people will be purified and judged (Malachi 3:1). The coming of the Messiah is linked to the return of the prophet Elijah who will proclaim the "day of the LORD" (Malachi 4:5).

We have now come to the last book in the Old Testament. It sums up much of the history of the Old Testament. Martin Luther called John 3:16 "the little gospel." In the same way, we might speak of Malachi as the "little Old Testament."

Malachi is the bridge between the Old and New Testaments. To understand this, read Malachi 3:1. Who is "my messenger"? Read John 1:23 and Luke 3:3-4. "Malachi" means "my messenger" (that is, "of the Lord"). Like John the Baptist, about whom he prophesied, Malachi was but a voice. There were 400 years of silence between the voice of Malachi and the voice of one crying in the wilderness, "Prepare the way for the Lord" (Matthew 3:3; Mark 1:3; Luke 3:4).

The Old Testament closes with the word "destruction" (Malachi 4:6). The New Testament closes with blessing: "The grace of the Lord Jesus be with God's people. Amen" (Revelation 22:21).

By the time of Malachi, a hundred years or more had passed since the Jews had returned to Jerusalem after the captivity in Babylon. Malachi is the last prophet to speak to Israel in her own land. "Israel" here refers to the entire remnant of Israel and Judah who returned after the exile. The initial enthusiasm after the return from Babylon had dissipated. Following a period of revival, described in Nehemiah 10:28-39, the people had become religiously cold and morally lax.

The prophet Malachi came as a reformer, but he encouraged while he rebuked. He dealt with a confused and discouraged people, whose faith in God seemed to be in danger of collapse. If they had not already become hostile to Jehovah, they were in real danger of becoming thoroughly skeptical.

MALACHI 1–2:9: THE SINS OF THE PRIESTS

The people's skepticism about God was exhibited in their indifferent attitude toward worship and in their social laxity. This is always true. The priests became irreverent and neglectful. Read Malachi 1:6: "'Where is the honor due me? . . . Where is the respect due me?' says the LORD Almighty. 'It is you priests who show contempt for my name.'" The prophet rebuked these careless priests for offering worthless animals in sacrifice to God that they would not offer to the governor. These priests stood in marked contrast to God's ideal for the priesthood. They had completely lost sight of their high calling and deserved the disgrace heaped on them. They refused to work except for money. God's condemnation of the Israelites began with these leaders (see Malachi 2:1-9).

MALACHI 2:10-3: THE SINS OF THE PEOPLE

As long as the priests were openly unfit, what could be expected from the general populace? The result was carelessness among God's people, and they no longer kept themselves separate from the heathen nations. Mixed marriages with women from outside tribes became common. Some men did not even hesitate to divorce their Jewish wives to make this possible (see Malachi 2:10-16).

The people had also robbed God of their tithes and offerings. They had become so selfish and covetous that Malachi dared to boldly challenge them with these words: "Will a mere mortal rob God?" (Malachi 3:8).

Another result of the people's carelessness was in the growing prevalence of social sin (see Malachi 3:5). Malachi 3:7 reveals the extent of the people's religious indifference and skepticism.

What would you think of a man who deliberately held something before his eyes and then complained that he could see nothing? What would you suggest might quickly solve the difficulty? Well, this is just what Malachi had to do. The people of Israel declared that Jehovah did not love them (see Malachi 1:2). They could not see that His love had been of any special advantage to them.

The sins Malachi rebuked included:

- Worshiping carelessly—Malachi 1:6-8
- Marrying idol worshipers—Malachi 2:10-12
- Questioning Jehovah's justice—Malachi 2:17–3:6
- Robbing God—Malachi 3:7-12
- Waiting impatiently—Malachi 3:17–4:3

Are any of these your sins, too? If you find some of these sins in your daily life, what should you do? Confess them to Jehovah. Israel was troubled about the result of her confession. Malachi had to encourage the people by assuring them of Jehovah's wonderful love and reminding them of His beautiful promise: "Return to me, and I will return to you" (Malachi 3:7). Turn to Malachi 3:7, and mark it in your Bible.

The children of Israel could depend on Jehovah to forgive. It was this same picture of the Father that Jesus gave when He told of the prodigal son's return. The father, seeing the boy while he was still a great way off, ran out to meet him. This is always God's attitude.

The key that opens God's big blessings is your recognition of His ownership by giving back to Him a proper share of the money or the property He permits you to acquire. "Bring the whole tithe into the storehouse" (Malachi 3:10). The tenth (or tithe) is the outward recognition that everything belongs to God. We are to bring Him our whole selves—body, soul and spirit. Then He will accept us and open the windows of heaven to pour out His blessings.

MALACHI 3–4: THE VISION OF THINGS TO COME

Why does God permit indifferent worship, moral laxity and skepticism? This attitude of the people was probably because they had not seen the glowing promises of Haggai, Zechariah and the other prophets come to fruition. The people also said that Jehovah did not seem to distinguish between good people and bad people (see Malachi 2:17). He blesses all alike, and evil people often flourish at the expense of their fellow citizens (see Malachi 3:14-15). So what's the use of being good?

Isn't this one of the standing complaints of those who think they are good? They say, "Why does God permit such things to happen?" The answer to such a complaint is that Jehovah *does* care. " 'I have loved you,' says the LORD" (Malachi 1:2). What a message to a people who had sinned as Israel had and had spurned the love of Jehovah God. He showed the Israelites how much He cares by saying that one day He will send His messenger (John the Baptist) to prepare His way; then He will come in person "suddenly" and sit in judgment and separate the evil from the good (Malachi 3:1). His judgment will be effective, "like a refiner's fire or a launderer's soap" (Malachi 3:2-3). When God really gets ready to act, what will He do? His action will be final (see Malachi 3:1-3).

God is always sending His messenger before Him to prepare His way (see Malachi 3:1). He wants all His children to honor and adore Him. He longs to have us obey and worship Him. But who is pure and clean enough to stand in His presence? And who can endure His purifying fire (see Malachi 3:2)? God's messenger will be a witness revealing our cruelty, our lies, our injustices, our double-dealing—just as of the Jews of old. Jehovah's representative will come and find us robbing Him of His due (see Malachi 3:2-5). Yet God is unchanging. He never forgets His promises of undying love and everlasting mercy.

Oh, how we need a Malachi today to prepare His way so that God's people may honor and adore Him. Malachi could cry again, "Back to God's house! Back to God's Word! Back to God's work! Back to God's grace!"

Think of the needs of this day, the needs of the Church and the needs of the world. Isn't formalism—an outward observance without a wholehearted love—a just charge against today's Church? Aren't we, too, offering gifts that cost nothing? Aren't we robbing God of His tithes?

Amid all the hypocrisy of Malachi's day, there were those in the Jewish community (a remnant) who still feared God and remained faithful to God (see Malachi 3:16). Malachi longed to develop a strong body of enthusiastic believers who could influence his people's future. It is interesting to note that God "listened and heard" what His people said about Him (Malachi 3:16).

Every believer has the ability to be like Malachi, a herald of the Christ whose coming we now wait for. We who love God and look for Him may help prepare His way by modeling Christ in the way we conduct our everyday lives.

Close by reading aloud Malachi 3:16–4:3, Malachi's solemn declaration concerning the second advent of Christ for which we wait. Yes, the Son of Righteousness will come with healing in His wings.

25

A Quick Look at
The Old Testament: Esther Through Malachi

 THEMES AND LESSONS

In the Old Testament books of Esther through Malachi, we find the following themes and lessons:

Esther
Theme: Jesus Christ is portrayed as our Advocate.
Outstanding Lesson: God will deliver His children!

Job
Theme: Jesus Christ is portrayed as our Redeemer.
Outstanding Lesson: Why do the righteous suffer?

Psalms
Theme: Jesus Christ is portrayed as our all in all.
Outstanding Lesson: Praise God!

Proverbs
Theme: Jesus Christ is portrayed as our wisdom.
Outstanding Lesson: Get wisdom!

Ecclesiastes
Theme: Jesus Christ is portrayed as the end of all living.
Outstanding Lesson: Try wisdom!

Song of Solomon

Theme: Jesus Christ is portrayed as the lover of our souls.
Outstanding Lesson: Love God!

Isaiah

Theme: Jesus Christ is portrayed as the Messiah.
Outstanding Lesson: Salvation is of God!

Jeremiah

Theme: Jesus Christ is portrayed as the righteous branch.
Outstanding Lesson: Go and tell!

Lamentations

Theme: Jesus Christ is portrayed as the righteous branch.
Outstanding Lesson: God's grace always shines!

Ezekiel

Theme: Jesus Christ is portrayed as the Son of Man.
Outstanding Lesson: Judgment and restoration will come!

Daniel

Theme: Jesus Christ is portrayed as the striking stone.
Outstanding Lesson: God is sovereign!

Hosea

Theme: Jesus Christ is portrayed as the healer of the backslider.
Outstanding Lesson: Return to God!

Joel

Theme: Jesus Christ is portrayed as the Restorer.
Outstanding Lesson: Repent, for "the day of the LORD" is coming.

Amos

Theme: Jesus Christ is portrayed as the heavenly husbandman.
Outstanding Lesson: Prepare to meet your God!

Obadiah

Theme: Jesus Christ is portrayed as our Savior.
Outstanding Lesson: Possess your possessions!

Jonah

Theme: Jesus Christ is portrayed as our resurrection and life.
Outstanding Lesson: Arise and go!

Micah

Theme: Jesus Christ is portrayed as our witness against rebellious nations.
Outstanding Lesson: Listen to God!

Nahum

Theme: Jesus Christ is portrayed as a stronghold in the day of trouble.
Outstanding Lesson: Beware, the Lord avenges!

Habakkuk

Theme: Jesus Christ is portrayed as the God of our salvation.
Outstanding Lesson: Live by faith!

Zephaniah

Theme: Jesus Christ is portrayed as a jealous Lord.
Outstanding Lesson: God is mighty to save!

Haggai

Theme: Jesus Christ is portrayed as the desire of all nations.
Outstanding Lesson: Build for God!

Zechariah

Theme: Jesus Christ is portrayed as the righteous Branch.
Outstanding Lesson: Turn to God!

Malachi

Theme: Jesus Christ is portrayed as the Son of Righteousness.
Outstanding Lesson: Repent and return to God!

FOUR HUNDRED YEARS OF SILENCE

By the time Old Testament history ends, a remnant of the Jewish exiles, chiefly of the tribe of Judah, had returned from Babylonia to the land under Zerubbabel; and about 80 years later another company had returned with Ezra. They were living peaceably in their own land with the Temple rebuilt and religious ceremonies reinstituted.

The last three books of history in the Old Testament—Ezra, Nehemiah and Esther—give us the story of this time. They cover the 100 years following the decree of Cyrus the king, allowing the Jewish people to return to their land.

From Nehemiah to the beginning of the New Testament, 400 years passed by. During this period, no biblical prophet spoke or wrote. In fact, it is called the period of silence. But as we come to the year when Jesus was born, it is important that we know some of the things that happened during that span of 400 years.

The Septuagint Is Written

Before Alexander the Great died, he divided his empire among his four generals, for he had no heirs to his throne. Egypt and all of the eastern Mediterranean, including Judah, went to his general Ptolemy. Great numbers of Jews at this time settled in Egypt, as well as other centers of culture, spreading everywhere the knowledge of their God and their hope of a Messiah.

During this time, about 285 BC, the Old Testament began to be translated into Greek. This Greek version of the Scriptures is called the Septuagint, meaning "seventy," because about 70 noted Hebrew scholars did this great work. You will sometimes find that the Septuagint is referred to by Roman numerals LXX.

The Jewish People Are Persecuted

During this 400 years, the Syrian kingdom rose. During the conflicts between Syria and Egypt, Antiochus Epiphanes, king of Syria, seized Judea. He began a bitter persecution of the Jewish people. The Jews were forbidden to worship in the Temple and were compelled to eat the flesh of swine, which God, through Moses, had forbidden (see Leviticus 11:1-8). Many Jews courageously refused to follow the king's laws, and a period of martyrdom began.

The terrible cruelties of Antiochus Epiphanes brought about the revolt of the Maccabees under the leadership of Mattathias. Encouraged by the patriotism and religious ardor of Mattathias, a group of patriotic freedom fighters gathered around him and began an insurrection that spread rapidly. When Mattathias died, his son Judas took his place. In an attempt to crush this rebellion under the Maccabees, Antiochus was defeated in three deadly conflicts. The cause of Mattathias and his family had seemed hopeless because his followers were untrained and without equipment, and they were opposed by the trained soldiers of a powerful king. But this band of ragged but loyal Jewish patriots, inspired by an undying faith in God, came out victorious!

Unfortunately, Judah enjoyed freedom for only a relatively short time, and eventually the entire area was taken over by Rome.

Rome Demands Tribute

In 63 BC, Rome gained possession of Judea, and at the time of Jesus' birth, Rome still controlled the area. The Jews had some political liberty, but they were required to pay a yearly tax to the Roman government.

PART TWO

The New Testament

THE GOSPELS
Matthew · Mark · Luke · John

HISTORY
Acts

LETTERS OF PAUL
Romans · 1 Corinthians · 2 Corinthians · Galatians
Ephesians · Philippians · Colossians · 1 Thessalonians
2 Thessalonians · 1 Timothy · 2 Timothy
Titus · Philemon

GENERAL LETTERS
Hebrews · James · 1 Peter · 2 Peter
1 John · 2 John · 3 John · Jude

PROPHECY
Revelation

The Gospels

of the New Testament

MATTHEW • MARK • LUKE • JOHN

Key Events of the Gospels

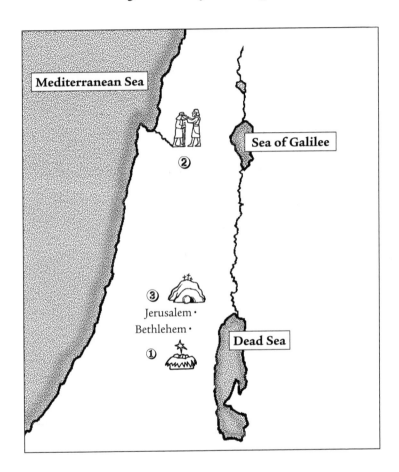

The Gospels: The Person of Jesus Christ

The Gospels record the ① birth, life, miracles, healing ministry ② , teachings, death and resurrection ③ of Jesus Christ. Each Gospel has a slightly different purpose and audience, but together they give us an amazingly clear picture of who Jesus Christ was in His earthly ministry, and they invite us to believe in the Savior of the world (see John 4:42) who conquered sin, Satan and death on the cross.

Understanding
the Gospels

The Gospels Portray Jesus Christ,
Our Savior and Lord

Dr. Henry Van Dyke, a turn-of-the-twentieth-century minister and professor of English literature at Princeton, once said:

> If four witnesses should appear before a judge to give an account of a certain event, and each should tell exactly the same story in the same words, the judge would probably conclude, not that their testimony was exceptionally valuable, but that the only event which was certain beyond a doubt was that they had agreed to tell the same story. But if each man had told what he had seen, as he had seen it, then the evidence would be credible. And when we read the four Gospels, is not that exactly what

we find? The four men tell the same story each in his own way.

The word "gospel" is derived from the two Anglo-Saxon words "God," meaning "good," and "spell," meaning "tidings" or "history." The four writers of the Gospels are called "evangelists," from a Greek word meaning "bringer of good tidings." The first three Gospels—Matthew, Mark and Luke—are called the Synoptic Gospels, because, unlike John's Gospel, they give a synopsis of Christ's life. The word "synopsis" is derived from two Greek words meaning "a view together, a collective view." So these three Gospels may be viewed together.

The Synoptic Gospels are striking in their similarities: He is here! The promised One has come! The One whom all the prophets have foretold, Jesus Christ, the Lord. They are equally striking in their differences:

- The Synoptics chiefly tell about Christ's ministry in Galilee—John's Gospel tells of Christ's ministry in Judea.

- The Synoptics tell about Christ's miracles, parables and addresses to the multitudes—John's Gospel relates Christ's deeper and more abstract discourses, His conversations and His prayers.

- The Synoptics portray Christ in action—John's Gospel portrays Christ in meditation and communion.

Every prophet in the Old Testament assured God's Chosen People again and again that a Messiah would come who would be the King of the Jews. They therefore looked forward with passionate longing and patriotism to the coming of that King in pomp and power. Expect to find this King in the Gospels "the one Moses wrote about in the Law, and about whom the prophets also wrote—Jesus" (John 1:45). But know that you will find Him infinitely more beautiful in person than any prophet's vision of Him.

We read in Isaiah 7:14: "Therefore the Lord himself will give you a sign: The virgin will conceive and give birth to a son, and will call him Immanuel" (the name "Immanuel" means "God with us"). This is the One the evangelists tell us about—Jesus who lived with us. John says, "The Word became flesh and made his dwelling among us" (John 1:14). Think of God coming down to live with people! It seems the Gospels are the center of the whole Bible. All that the prophets said leads us to our Lord's earthly life and work, and all that follows in the Epistles proceeds from them. They tell us *when* and *how* Christ came; the Epistles tell us *why* and *for what* Christ came. Notice where the four Gospels are placed in the Bible—they stand at the close of the Old Testament and before the Epistles. The Gospels are at the center of everything.

Dr. William H. Griffith Thomas, a turn-of-the-twentieth-century American New Testament scholar, suggested that we remember four words to help us link together the whole of God's revelation:

- "Preparation"—In the Old Testament, God makes ready for the coming of the Messiah.
- "Manifestation"—In the four Gospels, Christ enters the world, dies for the world and founds His Church.
- "Appropriation"—In the Acts and Epistles, the ways are revealed in which the Lord Jesus was received, appropriated and applied in individual lives.
- "Consummation"—In the book of Revelation, the outcome of God's perfect plan through Christ is revealed.

THE MEANING OF "GOSPEL"

"Gospel" means "good news." The good news concerning Jesus, the Son of God, is given to us by four writers—Matthew, Mark, Luke and John. There is only one gospel—the glad story of salvation through Jesus Christ our Lord. But we are given four pictures of Christ. The combined Gospels present a personality rather than a connected story of a life.

The word "gospel" is never used in the New Testament as a reference to a book. It always means "good news." When we speak of the Gospel of Luke, we ought to understand that it means the good news of Jesus Christ as recorded by Luke. Nevertheless, from the earliest times, the term "gospel" has been applied to each of the four narratives that record the life of Christ.

No doubt, originally the good news was oral. Men went from one place to another, telling the glad story by word of mouth. After a while, a written record was necessary. Evidently, more than one person attempted to write everything down, but nothing was successfully completed. See what Luke says in Luke 1:1-4:

> Many have undertaken to draw up an account of the things that have been fulfilled among us, just as they were handed down to us by those who from the first were eyewitnesses and servants of the word. With this in mind, since I myself have carefully investigated everything from the beginning, I too decided to write an orderly account for you, most excellent Theophilus, so that you may know the certainty of the things you have been taught.

FOUR GOSPELS INSTEAD OF ONE

As everyone knows, there are four Gospels, but this fact has given rise to several questions: Why four? Why wouldn't one straightforward, continuous narrative have been enough? Wouldn't this have been simpler and clearer? Wouldn't this have saved us from some of the difficulties that have arisen because of what some have said are conflicting accounts?

A Complete Picture of Christ

The answer seems plain: Because one or two would not have given us a well-rounded and complete picture of the life of Christ. It is true that each of the four Gospels has much in common with the others: Each deals with Christ's earthly ministry, His death and resurrection, His teachings and miracles; but each Gospel is also different because four distinct offices of Christ are portrayed in the Gospels:

1. King in Matthew
2. Servant in Mark
3. Son of man in Luke
4. Son of God in John

There are deliberate gaps that none of the evangelists attempts to fill in. For instance, all omit any account of the 18 years of Christ's life between the ages of 12 and 30. And although each Gospel is complete in itself, each author was very selective: Only a few of Christ's miracles are described and only a portion of His teachings are given in each. Each evangelist has recorded that which is relevant and pertinent to his particular theme. For example, Matthew deliberately adds to his account what Mark omits. Read what John says in 21:25: "Jesus did many other things as well. If every one of them were written down, I suppose that even the whole world would not have room for the books that would be written."

In the National Gallery in London, on a single canvas there are three portraits of Charles I. In one, his head is turned to the right; in another, to the left; and in the center is a full-face view. This odd "portrait" was painted by the Flemish painter Anthony Van Dyck for the Roman sculptor Giovanni Lorenzo Bernini, who planned to make a bust of the king. By combining the impressions he received, Bernini was better able to produce a faithful likeness. One view would not have been enough.

It may be true that the Gospels were intended to serve a purpose similar to that of those portraits. Each presents a different aspect of our Lord's life on earth. When the Gospels are viewed together, we have the complete picture. He was a King, but He was the perfect Servant, too. He was the Son of man, but we must not forget that He was the Son of God.

There are four Gospels with one Christ, four accounts with one purpose, and four sketches of one person.

The Significance of Four Gospels

Let us present another explanation for why there are four Gospels instead of one: Four is an earthly number. Scriptures explain many things for us, and many people believe that the Scriptures use numbers with precision, accuracy and real meaning:

- Seven is the perfect number.
- Three is the number of the Godhead.
- Forty is the number of testing.
- Four is the number of the earth. There are four points of the compass—north, east, south and west. There are four seasons of the year—spring, summer, autumn and winter. In the parable of the sower, our Lord divided the field into four kinds of soil. Later He said, "The field is the world" (Matthew 13:38).

If four is the earth number, how fitting that the Holy Spirit should have given us four Gospels in which to depict the earthly ministry of the heavenly One.

The Fulfillment of Prophecy

All the Gospels are bound up with the promises of the Messiah in the Old Testament. We cannot explain the Gospels apart from the great messianic prophecies in the Old Testament.

The prophets portrayed a magnificent picture of the Messiah. They told of His offices, mission, birth, suffering, death, resurrection and glory. Let us consider the four names and/or titles the prophets bestowed upon Him:

- King (see Psalm 72; Isaiah 9:6-7; 32:1; Jeremiah 23:5; Zechariah 9:9; 14:9)—These passages, among many others, tell of the kingly office of the Messiah. The prophets told much of His kingdom and its extent, and of Christ's ultimate triumph.
- The servant of Jehovah (see Isaiah 42:1-7; 52:13-15; 53)
- The man, the Son of man (see Genesis 3:15; 22:18; Isaiah 7:14-16; 9:6)
- God (see Isaiah 9:6; 40:3-5; 47:4; Jeremiah 23:6)

As these four, Jesus is set forth in the Gospels.

JESUS IN THE FOUR GOSPELS

Master this outline and you will be familiar with the contents of the Gospels for life:

1. King—Matthew presents Jesus as King. This Gospel was written primarily for the Jew, for Jesus is the Son of David. His royal genealogy is given in Matthew 1. In Matthew 5–7, in the Sermon on the Mount, we have the King's manifesto, containing the laws of His kingdom.

2. Servant—Mark depicts Jesus as Servant. Written for the Romans, this gospel contains no genealogy. Why? People are not interested in the genealogy of a servant. More miracles are found here than in any other Gospel. Romans cared little for words and were far more interested in deeds.

3. Son of man—Luke portrays Jesus as the Son of man, the perfect man. This Gospel was written for the Greeks. Christ's genealogy is given as far back as Adam (the first man) instead of to Abraham. As a perfect Man, Christ is very often seen in prayer and with angels ministering to Him.

4. Son of God—John portrays Jesus as the Son of God. Written to all who will believe, with the purpose of leading people to Christ, this Gospel illustrates and demonstrates Christ's relationship to God and as God (see John 20:31). The opening verse causes us to go back to "the beginning" (John 1:1).

Dr. W. H. Griffith Thomas gave the pictures of the Gospels in this way:

1. Matthew is concerned with the coming of a *promised Savior.*
2. Mark is concerned with the life of a *powerful Savior.*
3. Luke is concerned with the grace of a *perfect Savior.*
4. John is concerned with the possession of a *personal Savior.*

INTENDED AUDIENCES OF THE GOSPELS

In the Gospels, Christ was going to be presented to widely different groups of people who made up the world. Each group was capable of appreciating one particular kind of presentation more than another. The four groups of people in Jesus' day also represent the four types of people today.

1. The Jewish People Had Special Training

They were steeped in the Old Testament Scripture and the prophets. Matthew writes the story of Jesus' life on earth especially for these people. If Jewish people were to be impressed with Jesus, they would need to be taught by somebody who understood their customs and way of thinking. Jewish people needed to know that this Jesus came to fulfill the prophecies of the Old Testament. Over and over again we read in Matthew that an action or some words of Christ "fulfilled" what the Lord had said through a prophet.

We have the same type of people today. They revel in prophecies fulfilled and unfulfilled. They want to know what the prophets spoke and how prophecies are being fulfilled.

2. The Romans Were Masters of the World at that Time

Mark wrote especially for Romans. The Romans knew nothing about Old Testament Scriptures. They were not interested in prophecy being fulfilled. But they were vitally concerned about a remarkable leader who had appeared in Judea. He had claimed more than ordinary authority and had possessed extraordinary powers. They wanted to hear more about this Jesus—what sort of a person He really was, what He had said and what He had done.

The Romans liked Mark's straightforward message. The word "and" is used in Mark 1,375 times (in the *KJV*); and its use helps to smoothly move this narrative along. Mark's Gospel is filled with deeds, not words. Clearly it is the Gospel of the ministry of Christ.

The Romans of Jesus' day were like average businesspeople are today. They are not concerned about the genealogy of a king but with a God "who is able," a God who can *do* things and meet a person's every need. Mark is the businessperson's Gospel.

3. The Greeks Were Lovers of Beauty, Poetry and Culture

The Greeks lived in a world of large ideas. Their tastes were fastidious. The Gospel of Luke (the Greek doctor who wrote to his own countrymen) tells of the birth and childhood of Jesus. It gives the inspired songs connected with the life of Christ. We find Elizabeth's greeting when Mary visited her (see Luke 1:42-45). We can almost hear the song of the virgin mother and Zacharias's burst into praise when speech was restored to him (see Luke 1:46-55,68-79). At the Savior's birth, a chorus of angel voices ring out (see Luke 2:13-14), and then the shepherd's song of praise to God is heard (see Luke 2:20).

The Greeks of Jesus' day are like the students and idealists today who seek truth, because they believe that truth is the means to happiness.

4. All the Other People in the World Made up the Fourth Group

John's Gospel is written to all people everywhere so that they might believe that Jesus is the Christ. Christ is portrayed as the Son of God. This Gospel is filled with extraordinary claims that prove Jesus' divine character and mission.

The "all people everywhere" of John's day are like the masses today who need Christ. They include the "whoever" who will believe in the Lord Jesus because they have a sense of need and want to receive the gift of eternal life through Jesus Christ the Lord (John 3:16).

KEYS TO THE GOSPELS

Front-Door Keys

God has hung the key to the Gospel of Matthew right over the entrance. The book opens with: "This is the genealogy of Jesus the Messiah the son of David, the son of Abraham" (Matthew 1:1). This shows Jesus' covenant position as the Son of Abraham (see Genesis 12:1-3; Galatians 3:16) and His royal position as Son of David. Matthew presents Christ as King; he gives the royal genealogy in the first 17 verses. A king is not chosen by popular ballot but by birth.

Turn now to Mark. See how this book opens. No genealogy is given. The reason is that Jesus is portrayed as a Servant, and no one is interested in the pedigree of a servant.

Turn to Luke. Is a genealogy given? See Luke 3:23. Matthew traces Christ's line back to Abraham and David to show that Jesus was a Jew and of the royal line. Luke traces Jesus' line back to Adam, the first man. Christ is presented as the ideal man. He was of the line of Adam.

Turn to John. How does this book open? No genealogy but "in the beginning was the Word, and the Word was with God, and the Word was God" (John 1:1). John portrays Christ as God.

Back-Door Keys

Now let us see how the Gospels close. Turn to Matthew 28:18-20, the King's command and commission to His disciples: "All authority in heaven and on earth has been given to me. Therefore go and make disciples of all nations, baptizing them in the name of the Father and of the Son and of the Holy Spirit, and teaching them to obey everything I have commanded you. And surely I am with you always, to the very end of the age." The Messiah is still on earth, for it is on earth and not in heaven that the Son of David will reign in glory.

Now look at the close of Mark: "Then the disciples went out and preached everywhere, and the Lord worked with them and confirmed his word by the signs that accompanied it" (Mark

16:20). This is very significant and appropriate. Jesus, the Servant, is pictured as still laboring with His disciples.

Luke ends in a different way. Notice what Luke says in 24:51: "While he was blessing them, he left them and was taken up into heaven." Jesus, the perfect man, is ascending to the Father.

The closing verse of John is also significant: "Jesus did many other things as well. If every one of them were written down, I suppose that even the whole world would not have room for the books that would be written" (John 21:25). Truly, "No one ever spoke the way this man does," for He was the true Son of God (John 7:46).

27

Understanding Matthew

Matthew Portrays Jesus Christ, the Promised Messiah

SELECTED BIBLE READINGS

DAY OF THE WEEK		MAIN TOPIC
Sunday: Matthew 1:18–2:23		The King Is Born
Monday: Matthew 4		The King Begins Work
Tuesday: Matthew 5:1-17,41-48; 6:19-34		The King States Kingdom Laws
Wednesday: Matthew 10:1-33		The King Commissions His Followers
Thursday: Matthew 13:1-52		The King Explains the Kingdom
Friday: Matthew 21:1-11		The King Offers Himself as King
Saturday: Matthew 25:14-16		The King Will Return

AUTHOR: This gospel is known as the Gospel of Matthew because, according to Church tradition from at least the second century AD, the apostle Matthew wrote it. The style of the book is exactly what would be expected of a man who was once a tax collector. Matthew has a keen interest in accounting, and the book is very orderly and concise (see Matthew 18:23-24; 25:14-15).

DATE: As an apostle, Matthew wrote this book during the early period of the Church, possibly AD 50 or earlier, when the gospel was only preached to Jewish people and not yet to Gentiles (see Acts 11:19). This was a time when most Christians were Jewish messianic believers, so Matthew's focus is on the Jewish perspective of Jesus as the Messiah promised to the Jewish people.

PURPOSE AND SUMMARY: This Gospel is the most complete account of Jesus' teachings and was written to convince the writer's Jewish audience that Jesus was the Messiah descended from David, the One promised by the Old Testament prophets. The most significant teaching passages in the Gospel of Matthew are the Sermon on the Mount (5–7) and the parable sections of the book (especially chapter 13).

GENERAL CHARACTERISTICS OF MATTHEW'S GOSPEL

Matthew has a special goal in his Gospel: to show the Jews that Jesus is the long-expected Messiah, the Son of David, and that His life fulfilled the Old Testament prophecies. The purpose is given in the first verse: "This is the genealogy of Jesus the Messiah the son of David, the son of Abraham." This statement links Christ to the two great covenants God made with David and Abraham. God's covenant with David consisted of the promise of a King to sit upon his throne forever (see 2 Samuel 7:8-13). God's covenant with Abraham promised that through him all families of the earth would be blessed (see Genesis 12:3). David's son was a King. Abraham's son was a Sacrifice. Matthew opens with the birth of a King and closes with the offering of a Sacrifice.

From the beginning, Jesus is associated with the Jewish nation. Matthew was wise not to alienate the Jews who might read the story. He wants to convince them that Jesus fulfilled every prophecy concerning their promised Messiah. He quotes freely from the Old Testament more than any of the other evangelists. Twenty-nine such quotations are given. Thirteen times he says that this or that event "took place to fulfill what the Lord had said through the prophet" (Matthew 1:22).

It is difficult for us to appreciate what the Jews thought Matthew was actually asking them to do. It seemed to the Jews that according to Matthew, they must give up their traditions and orthodoxy and accept another creed. But Matthew (and Paul, especially in Galatians) shows the Jewish believers in Jesus that they were not being told to give up their old faith; rather, they only had to give up symbols and shadows for real substance.

Matthew was well acquainted with Jewish history and customs. He speaks of farming and fishing and the housekeeping of his people in the seven parables in chapter 13. He knew this intimate record would strike responsive chords in the hearts of the Jewish people.

As you read Matthew, get a clear and comprehensive view of the entire Gospel. Keep in mind the messianic character of this Gospel. Note the balance between Jesus' ministry and teaching. We find the genealogy of the King; His birth in Bethlehem, the city of David, according to Micah's prophecy (see Micah 5:2); the coming of the forerunner, John the Baptist, as Malachi had predicted (see Malachi 3:1); the ministry of the King; His rejection by Israel; and the promise of His coming again in power and glory.

The Author

The author is no doubt a Jewish believer in Jesus (see Matthew 9:9; 10:3). Matthew, whose name means "gift of the Lord," was a tax collector at Capernaum when Jesus chose him as one of the 12 disciples. His name is found in all the lists of the 12, though Mark and Luke give his other name, Levi. The only word the author speaks about himself is that he was a "publican" (*KJV*), which was then a derogatory term, similar to the word "politician" as it is sometimes used today. The other evangelists tell about the great feast Matthew gave Jesus, and they record the significant fact that Matthew left behind all he had and followed Jesus. No doubt he was a man of means.

Matthew breaks the silence of 400 years between Malachi's prophecy and the announcement of the birth of Jesus. Israel was under the domination of the Roman Empire. No man of "the house of David" had been allowed to sit upon the throne for 600 years.

Matthew

The Royal Line

Herod was not the king of Israel but a governor of Judea, appointed by the emperor of Rome. The man who really had the right to the throne of the house of David was Joseph, the carpenter, who became the husband of Mary. See the genealogy of Joseph in Matthew 1, and notice especially one name, Jeconiah, in verse 11. If Joseph had been Jesus' father according to the flesh, Jesus could never have occupied the throne, because what God's Word says made that impossible: There had been a curse on this royal line since the days of Jeconiah. In Jeremiah 22:30 we read, "This is what the LORD says: 'Record this man as if childless, a man who will not prosper in his lifetime, for none of his offspring will prosper, none will sit on the throne of David or rule anymore in Judah.'" Joseph was in the line of this curse. Therefore, if Christ had been Joseph's son, He could not have sat on David's throne.

But we find another genealogy in Luke 3. This is Mary's line back to David through Nathan, not Jeconiah (see Luke 3:31). There was no curse on this line. To Mary, God said, "Do not be afraid, Mary; you have found favor with God. You will conceive and give birth to a son, and you are to call him Jesus. He will be great and will be called the Son of the Most High. The Lord God will give him the throne of his father David, and he will reign over Jacob's descendants forever; his kingdom will never end" (Luke 1:30-33).

The Book

The book of Matthew follows after the Old Testament and is the beginning of the New. It is the connecting link between the two parts of the Bible. It is written for the Jews and it is fittingly placed. It takes for granted that the course of events up to this point is known to its readers. The Old Testament had closed with the chosen nation looking for their long-promised King, their Messiah. Now the silence is broken and the coming of the Messiah declared. Matthew's Gospel shows that Jesus was that King. It is the Gospel of fulfillment.

Matthew emphasizes the Jewish side of Lord Jesus. Only in this Gospel do we find a record of the Messiah's declaration, "I was sent only to the lost sheep of Israel" (Matthew 15:24). What did His own people do with Him? Read John 1:11.

In numerical position, the book of Matthew is the fortieth in the canon. Forty is always a number of testing, or evaluation, in Scripture:

- Jesus was tempted by the devil for 40 days.
- Israel was in the wilderness for 40 years.
- David was king for 40 years.
- Moses was in a palace for 40 years, and then he was in a desert for 40 years.

Matthew

What other instances of this number 40 do you remember in Scripture? Look the number up in your concordance.

In this fortieth book of the Bible, Israel's response to the presence of the Messiah is being tested. Christ is presented as King to the Jews, but most of the religious leaders rejected Him—not only as their Messiah, but also as their Savior (see Matthew 16:21).

MATTHEW 1–2: BIRTH OF THE KING

Matthew is the Gospel of the Messiah, God's anointed One. The main purpose of the Spirit in this book is to show that Jesus of Nazareth is the predicted Messiah, the Deliverer of whom Moses and the prophets wrote, "whose origins are from of old, from ancient times" (Micah 5:2). He is the child that was to be born, the Son given, of whom Isaiah said, "will be called Wonderful Counselor, Mighty God, Everlasting Father, Prince of Peace" (Isaiah 9:6).

The Record of Jesus' Birth

Jesus "was born in Bethlehem of Judea, during the time of King Herod" (Matthew 2:1; see also Micah 5:2). We know this place and this king. We don't have to pretend that this place or this person existed. Christianity is a historical religion. The Gospel does not begin with "Once upon a time" but starts with "Bethlehem in Judea" (Matthew 2:1). The town is there, so we can visit the actual place where Jesus was born. Herod was a real person, because ancient historians wrote about him and archaeologists have found proof of him. There is nothing mythical about this monster of iniquity.

Matthew's statements are facts and no critic or unbeliever can doubt them. The Gospel narrative sets its record in the solid foundation of history. We are not building our faith on a myth but on substantial fact. These events did not happen in a dark corner but in the broad daylight, and the entire book is not afraid of the geographer's map and the historian's pen.

The story of the birth of Jesus in Matthew differs from the record in Luke, but they complement each other. While there is much untold, God *has* told us all that we need to know. Jesus' earthly life began in a stable. His cradle was a manger. His family and friends were humble people. He was born as a helpless babe. How human was our Lord! But Jesus was announced by an archangel, welcomed by an angel choir and worshiped by earth's wisest philosophers (the Magi)! How divine was our Lord!

The History of Jesus' Line

When you begin reading Matthew and Luke, the repetition of "the father of" (Matthew 1:1-17) and "the son of" (Luke 3:23-38) may make you wonder if these lists are worth reading. You need to realize that if they were included in Scripture, they were put there for a purpose. At this point, we want to look at these two genealogies.

A genealogy is the history of the descent of an individual or family from an ancestor. The two genealogies of Christ given by Matthew and Luke are not alike, however, because each author has a different goal in mind as he traces the descent of Christ:

- Matthew traces Jesus' line back to Abraham and David to show that He was a Jew (coming from David)—Luke traces Jesus' line back to Adam to show that He belonged to the human race.

- Matthew shows Jesus as of royal descent, the King, the Messiah, the lion of the tribe of Judah, the promised ruler of Israel—Luke shows that Jesus has a human lineage; He is the ideal man, born of woman.

You will find that these pictures of Jesus are maintained all through each Gospel—Matthew portraying Jesus as the Messiah; Luke, as the man.

Why are we concerned about these genealogies? Because they give us the key to the whole life of Christ. They show us from the very start that He was not just another man but that He was descended from a royal family, and there was a king's blood in His veins. If He were not a King, He could not claim the rulership of our lives. If He were not a man, He could not know "our pain" and be acquainted with "our suffering" (Isaiah 53:4).

Go through Matthew and follow this trail of the King:

1. The King's name—"They will call him Immanuel" (Matthew 1:23).
2. The King's position—"For out of you will come a ruler who will shepherd my people Israel" (Matthew 2:6).
3. The King's announcement—"Prepare the way for the Lord, make straight paths for him" (Matthew 3:3).
4. The King's coronation—"This is my Son, whom I love; with him I am well pleased" (Matthew 3:17).
5. The King's due respect—"Worship the Lord your God, and serve him only" (Matthew 4:10).
6. The King's proclamation—"And he began to teach them" (Matthew 5:2). "He taught as one who had authority" (Matthew 7:29).
7. The King's loyalty—"Whoever is not with me is against me, and whoever does not gather with me scatters" (Matthew 12:30).
8. The King's enemies—"From that time on Jesus began to explain to his disciples that he must go to Jerusalem and suffer many things at the hands of

the elders, the chief priests and the teachers of the law" (Matthew 16:21).

9. The King's love—"The Son of Man did not come to be served, but to serve, and to give his life as a ransom for many" (Matthew 20:28).

10. The King's glory—"When the Son of Man comes . . . then the King will say . . . 'Come, you who are blessed by my Father; take your inheritance'" (Matthew 25:31-34).

11. The King's sacrifice—"When they had crucified him . . . they placed the written charge against him: THIS IS JESUS, THE KING OF THE JEWS" (Matthew 27:35-37).

12. The King's victory—"He is not here; he has risen, just as he said" (Matthew 28:6).

The Visit by the Magi

Matthew alone tells of the visit of the wise men from the East, because he alone was interested in recording the birth of a king. The wise men were Persian Magi—scholars and students of the stars. They came to worship and honor the King, not a creed. These wise men did not come asking, "Where is the one who has been born the Savior of the world?" but, "Where is the one who has been born king of the Jews?" (Matthew 2:2). This was the question on every lip. With all the prophecies that had been made to Israel, neither the world nor Israel could be criticized for expecting a king who would rule the earth from David's throne (see Jeremiah 23:3-6; 30:8-10; 33:14-16,25-26; Ezekiel 37:21; Isaiah 9:7; Hosea 3:4-5).

The adoration of the wise men foreshadowed Christ's universal dominion. Some day "every knee should bow . . . and every tongue confess that Jesus Christ is Lord, to the glory of God the Father" (Philippians 2:10-11). "May he rule from sea to sea and from the River to the ends of the earth" (Psalm 72:8).

Paul tells us in Galatians 4:4-5, "When the set time had fully come, God sent his Son, born of a woman, born under the law, to redeem those under the law, that we might receive adoption to sonship." Jesus came to be the world's Savior.

The birth of Jesus was followed by 12 years of silence until His visit with the doctors in Jerusalem. Then the Gospels are silent again, with only the words "carpenter's son" (Matthew 13:55) or "carpenter" (Mark 6:3) to throw any light on the next 18 years and to let us know what He was doing. Jesus took 30 years of preparation for three years of ministry.

MATTHEW 3–16:20: PROCLAMATION OF THE KINGDOM

John the Baptist had another name. As the prophet Isaiah began to unfold the real message of his book—the coming of the Messiah, servant of Jehovah—he introduced a character known simply as "a voice": "a voice of one calling: 'In the wilderness prepare the way for the LORD; make straight in the desert a highway for our God'" (Isaiah 40:3). This voice, although unnamed in Isaiah, is to announce the coming of Jesus Christ. His two functions—that of voice and that of messenger—are all that the Old Testament tells us of John the Baptist (see Malachi 3:1). But it actually tells us a lot. It is indeed wonderful, not only that Christ should have been foretold all through the Scriptures, but also that His forerunner, John the Baptist, also is described.

In Matthew we hear the "voice": "Repent, for the kingdom of heaven has come near." This is he who was spoken of through the prophet Isaiah: "A voice of one calling in the wilderness, 'Prepare the way for the Lord, make straight paths for him'" (Matthew 3:2-3).

The King must be announced! It was the duty of this herald to go before the King, as a Roman officer before his ruler, and command that the roads be repaired over which his master would travel. John the Baptist did this. He showed that the spiritual roads of the lives of men and women and nations were full of the potholes of sin and sharp turns of sinfulness, and they needed repairing and straightening.

We see the King stepping from His personal and private life into His public ministry (see Matthew 4). He is facing a crisis. Satan met Him after He received His Father's blessing at His baptism: "This is my Son, whom I love; with him I am well pleased" (Matthew 3:17). Jesus then begins to carry out the plans for which He came into the world. He was led into the wilderness to face the first major conflict of His public ministry.

Notice that Satan offered Jesus a shortcut to the universal Kingdom He had come to gain through the long and painful way of the cross; but Christ came to be a Savior first and then a King. How strong is the temptation to take a shortcut to our ambitions! Jesus stood victorious, His shield undented and untarnished. He went forth to conquer all other temptations, until His final victory and ascension to heaven as Lord of all (see 1 Corinthians 10:13).

The Kingdom Laws

Every kingdom or country has laws and standards by which it exercises authority over its subjects. The kingdom of heaven is no exception. Jesus declared that He came not to destroy the Law but to fulfill it. The old Law was good in its day. Moses and the prophets were far in advance of their time. They were pioneers. Jesus did not destroy this old Law, but He treated it as rudimentary and not as perfect and final.

Jesus says any reform that starts on the outside and works inward is beginning at the wrong place. Christ starts on the inside and works outward. The only way to get a good life is first to get a good heart.

From the lofty pulpit of a mountain, Jesus preached the sermon that contains the laws of His kingdom (Matthew 5–7). Read through these chapters and refresh your memory about this most wonderful of Jesus' discourses. It is filled with lessons to be learned. After more than 1,900 years, this Sermon on the Mount has lost none of its majesty or power, far surpassing any human teaching. The world has not yet caught up with its simple ideals and requirements.

Jesus spoke choice words here to His disciples. The Beatitudes describe the Christian. "Blessed are" begins each one (Matthew 5:3-11). It is not what you are striving to be but what you are in Christ that brings you joy. The Beatitudes provide a picture of Christ. They give a picture of the face of Jesus Himself, not boastingly, but truly describing the perfect Christian.

Even many people who are not Christians claim that the Sermon on the Mount outlines their religion. How little those people understand the depth of the sermon's meaning. It is important that we do not simply praise the rules outlined in the sermon but that we actually practice them in our own lives. If we live by these rules, all our personal relationships will improve, our social wounds will be healed, every dispute between nations will be solved and, yes, the whole world will be a place of order.

The root of these laws is kindness. One day filled with kindness would be a bit of heaven. Love would reign instead of lawlessness. Christ shows us that sin lies, not just in committing the act, but also in the motive behind it (see Matthew 5:21-22,27-28). No one can expect forgiveness who does not forgive (see Matthew 6:12,14-15). Has anyone yet ever fathomed the depth of Matthew 7:12? It is easy to read; it is hard to put into practice.

Jesus preached that the kingdom of heaven is "near" (Matthew 3:2; "at hand," *KJV*); and in the Sermon on the Mount, He sets forth the constitution of the Kingdom—the condition for entrance, its laws, its privileges and rewards. Fourteen times in the sermon, the King says, "I tell you." Mark those 14 times in your Bible. This reveals Jesus' authority as He deals with the law of Moses. People must not only keep the law outwardly but in spirit as well. Notice the effect upon the people: "When Jesus had finished saying these things, the crowds were amazed at his teaching, because he taught as one who had authority, and not as their teachers of the law" (Matthew 7:28-29).

The King's Power

We find the King worked amazing special miracles (Matthew 8–9). He met human needs. There are 12 astonishing miracles in these two chapters. What are they? After Jesus had performed the miracles recorded in chapter 12, "all the people were astonished and said, 'Could this be the Son of David?'" (Matthew 12:23).

The critical teachers of the law now thrust themselves into the scene and pass their hostile judgment on the actions of Jesus (see Matthew 9:3).

The King's Cabinet

Jesus not only preached Himself, but He also gathered others around Him to preach. It was necessary to organize His kingdom in order to reach a wider audience and establish it on a more permanent basis. A king must have subjects who would reflect His light. He told His disciples, "You are the light of the world" (Matthew 5:14).

Jesus still has a great message for the world, and He needs us to carry it. Spiritual ideas are of little value until they are shared by men and women and institutions who will serve as hearts and brains, hands and feet to carry them out. This is what Jesus was doing. He was calling men and women to be His companions so that He could train them to carry on His work.

Where did Jesus find His helpers? Not in the Temple among the doctors and priests and men studying Scripture. He found them on the seashore, mending their nets. Jesus did not call many mighty or noble men but rather "chose the foolish things of the world to shame the wise" (1 Corinthians 1:27).

A list of the disciples is given in Matthew 10:2-4. This is probably the most important catalogue of names in the world. These men were given work to do that would make winning battles and founding empires seem of little consequence in comparison. We find their great message was the kingdom of heaven: "As you go, proclaim this message: 'The kingdom of heaven has come near'" (Matthew 10:7). Their tremendous mission was to start it.

Note some of the warnings and instructions for the disciples Jesus stated in Matthew 10. What were they? If these requirements of discipleship hold true today, could you call yourself a disciple? Read Matthew 10:32-33, and thoughtfully consider Christ's words.

The Kingdom of Heaven

The word "kingdom" occurs more than 55 times in Matthew, for this is the Gospel of the King. The expression "kingdom of heaven" is found more than 30 times here and nowhere else in the Gospels. Most of the 15 parables recorded in Matthew begin with the phrase "The kingdom of heaven is like."

Jewish people understood the phrase "kingdom of heaven." Neither Jesus nor John needed to define it. At Sinai, God said to Israel, "You will be for me a kingdom of priests and a holy nation" (Exodus 19:6). Israel was a theocracy: God was their King; they were His subjects. The prophets had referred to the messianic kingdom again and again.

Read Matthew 13, where Jesus compared the kingdom of heaven to several different things:

- A harvest of wheat separated from weeds
- A mustard seed that grew into a tree
- Yeast worked through the dough
- A treasure hidden in a field
- A pearl of great value
- A net full of fish from which the bad have been thrown away

These parables, often called the secrets of the kingdom of heaven, describe what the result of the presence of the gospel of Christ in the world will be during this present age until the time of His return when He will gather the harvest (see Matthew 13:11; see also Matthew 13:40-43). Initially there will be growth like that of a mustard seed into a tree large enough to let "birds come and perch in its branches" (Matthew 13:32). This is Christendom, which will grow and grow, well beyond its small beginning.

But we see no bright picture of a converted world. Weeds will be mixed with the wheat, good fish will be found with the bad, and there will be yeast in what should be an unleavened loaf. (Yeast, or leaven, is often a symbol of sin. The Spirit never uses yeast as a symbol of anything good. Look this up in your concordance and determine this for yourself.)

Only Christ can determine what is good and what is bad, and at the final harvest, He will divide the two. If we are to have a kingdom on this earth, with the laws that Christ established, then we must have the King. Someday Christ will come in power and great glory and establish His throne on this earth. We will have peace when the Prince of Peace reigns!

MATTHEW 16:21–20: REJECTION OF THE KING

The sad story reads that Christ "came to that which was his own, but his own did not receive him" (John 1:11). The gospel of the Kingdom was first preached to those who should have been most prepared, the children of Israel. And although many came to believe in Jesus as the Messiah, the majority of the people rejected their King. From Matthew 12 on we see much controversy among the leaders concerning Jesus.

Jesus announced that the kingdom would be taken away from the Jewish people and given to another nation: "Therefore I tell you that the kingdom of God will be taken away from you and given to a people who will produce its fruit" (Matthew 21:43). The announcement offended the rulers, and "they looked for a way to arrest him" (Matthew 21:46).

Our Lord told Nicodemus the requirement for entrance into the kingdom of heaven (see John 3:3-7). "Whoever" believes may enjoy its privileges and blessings (John 3:16). The kingdom is for the Gentile as well as the Jew.

Why did the Jewish leaders and many of the people refuse the Kingdom? The world today still longs for the golden age; a time of peace is the greatest desire of diplomats and rulers. But they want it in their own way and on their own terms. They want to bring it about by their own efforts. They have no longing for an age brought about by the personal return of the Lord Jesus Christ. It was the same with the people in the day of John the Baptist.

Have you put Christ on the throne of your life? Have you the peace you long for? Have you accepted Christ's terms for your life?

The Church's Universal Call

In Matthew 16, we find Jesus with His disciples in Caesarea Philippi. Apparently Jesus wanted to have a private time with His disciples so that He could tell them about something important: His Church.

Only in Matthew's Gospel is the Church named. When the Kingdom was rejected, we find a change in the teachings of Jesus. He began to talk about the Church instead of the Kingdom (see Matthew 16:18). "Church" comes from the word *ecclesia*, which means "called-out ones." Because all people would not believe in Him, Christ said He was calling out everyone, Jew or Gentile, to belong to His Church, which is His Body. He began to build a new edifice, a new united body of people (see Ephesians 2:14-18).

Life's Most Important Question

When they were far away from the busy scene in which they lived, Jesus asked His disciples, "Who do people say the Son of Man is?" (Matthew 16:13).

This is the important question today! First asked by an obscure Galilean at the foot of Mount Hermon, it has come thundering down through the centuries and has become the mightiest question in the world. What do you think of Christ? What we think determines what we do and are. The ideas we hold about industry, wealth, government, morals and religion mold society and alter lives. So what we think of Christ is the determining force in the world and more than anything else influences our lives and our thoughts.

The disciples gave the answers other people were giving. The answers then were as varied as they are now. All agreed that Jesus was an extraordinary person, at least a prophet or a person who had an element of the supernatural.

Jesus then turned the general question into a sharp personal inquiry. " 'But what about you?' he asked. 'Who do you say I am?' " (Matthew 16:15). Ask yourself this question. Important as the general question is, far more important to each one of us is this personal question. No one can escape it. A neutral answer is impossible. Jesus is either God or an impostor.

Life's Most Important Answer

"You are the Messiah, the Son of the living God!" exclaimed the impulsive, fervent Peter (Matthew 16:16). This answer claims that Christ is the Messiah, the fulfillment of the prophecies of the old Hebrew prophets. This confession is great because it exalts Christ as the Son of God and lifts Him above humanity and crowns Him with deity. From now on He reveals to this handful of disciples new truths about His teachings. After this answer concerning who He was, He said to Peter and the disciples, "On this rock I will build my church" (Matthew 16:18). This is what Christ was going to do—build a Church of which He Himself was to be the chief cornerstone (see Ephesians 2:20). This Church was born on Pentecost (see Acts 2).

For the first time, the fateful shadow of the cross fell across the path of the disciples. From this time on, Jesus drew back the curtain that veiled the future, and He began to show His disciples the things that would happen in the future. He revealed that His path lay toward Jerusalem, where He would face the awful hatred of the priests and Pharisees and then the terrible cross; but He also told them about the glory of His resurrection (see Matthew 16:21).

Jesus did not reveal these things in detail until His disciples were ready to accept them. God often in His mercy hides the future from us.

MATTHEW 21–28: TRIUMPH OF THE KING

On the morning of Palm Sunday, there was a stir in Bethany and along the road leading to Jerusalem. It was understood that Jesus was to enter the city that day. Crowds of people were gathering.

A colt was procured; and the disciples, having thrown their robes over it, placed Jesus upon it, and the procession started. This little parade could not compare in magnificence with any procession at the coronation of a king or the inauguration of a president; but it meant much more for the world. Jesus for the first time permitted a public recognition and celebration of His rights as Messiah-King. The end was approaching with awful swiftness, and He must offer Himself as the Messiah, even if only to be rejected.

In their enthusiasm, the people tore off branches from the palm and olive trees and carpeted the highway, while shouts rang through the air. They believed in Jesus, and their warm enthusiasm reflected their pride in their King. In answer to the crowds who asked, "Who is this?" they boldly answered, "This is Jesus, the prophet from Nazareth of Galilee" (Matthew 21:10-11). It took courage to say that in Jerusalem. Jesus was not entering the city as a triumphant conqueror as the Romans had done. No sword was in His hand. Over Him floated no bloodstained banner. His mission was salvation!

Christ's authority was brought into question as He went into the Temple and ordered the merchants out, overturning their tables and telling them that they had made the house of God a den of thieves (see Matthew 21:12-13). A bitter controversy followed. "Then the Pharisees went out and laid plans to trap him in his words" (Matthew 22:15).

In the evening the crowds dispersed, and Jesus quietly returned to Bethany. Apparently nothing in the way of making Jesus King had been accomplished. His hour had not yet come. Christ must be Savior first; then He would come again as King of kings and Lord of lords.

The Future of the Kingdom

When Jesus delivered His Mount Olivet discourse, He foretold the condition of the world after His ascension until He comes back in glory to judge the nations, according to their treatment of "brothers and sisters of mine," the Jewish people (Matthew

25:40). This is not the judgment of the "great white throne," which is the judgment of the wicked dead (Revelation 20:11). Neither is it the judgment seat of Christ, which is the judgment of saints according to their works (see 2 Corinthians 5:10). It is the judgment of Gentile nations concerning their attitude toward God's people.

Much of Jesus' discourse in Matthew 24 and 25 is devoted to Christ's second coming. He exhorts us to be ready in the parables of the faithful servant (see Matthew 24:45-51), the 10 virgins (see Matthew 25:1-13) and the talents (see Matthew 25:14-30).

The Death and Resurrection of the King

Up until this point, we have learned about some of the highlights in the life of Jesus; now we step into the shadows as we enter Gethsemane. We see the Son of Abraham, the sacrifice, dying so that all the nations of the earth will be blessed by Him. Jesus was slain because He was named "the King of Israel" (Matthew 27:42). He was raised from the dead because He was the King of all (see Acts 2:30-36). Although a large number of disciples believed in Jesus and followed Him, the opposition of the religious leaders was bitter and they determined to put Him to death. On the grounds of blasphemy and of claiming to be the King of the Jews (the latter making Himself the enemy of the Roman emperor), Jesus was condemned by Pilate to be crucified.

Matthew is not alone in his record of the terrible circumstances of the Savior's last hours; but he makes us feel as if the mock regal trappings—the crown of thorns, the sceptre, the title over the cross—are evidence, though their purpose was only to scorn, of the kingly claim.

After hanging on the cross for six hours, the Savior died—not from physical suffering alone but also of a broken heart, for He bore the sins of the whole world to become the world's Redeemer!

The Great Price of Redemption

Jesus was put in Joseph's tomb, and on the third day He rose, as He had said He would. This is the supreme test of His kingship.

People thought He was dead and His kingdom had failed. But by His resurrection, Christ assured His disciples that the King still lived and that one day He will come back to establish His kingdom on earth.

The ascension of Jesus is not recorded in Matthew. The curtain falls with the Messiah still on earth, for it is on earth that the Son of David is yet to reign in glory. The last time the Jews saw Christ, He was on the Mount of Olives. The next time they see Him, He will again be on the Mount of Olives (see Zechariah 14:4; Acts 1:11).

The Commission for All Disciples

Matthew closes his Gospel with Jesus' climactic announcement of His great commission: "All authority in heaven and on earth has been given to me. Therefore go and make disciples of all nations, baptizing them in the name of the Father and of the Son and of the Holy Spirit, and teaching them to obey everything I have commanded you. And surely I am with you always, to the very end of the age" (Matthew 28:18-20).

On what mission were they sent? To overrun the world with armies and use weapons to force people to submit to them? No, they were to "make disciples of all nations."

From the mountaintop of Jesus' ascension, Jesus' disciples began this mission, radiating from that center out into the world; and Jesus' disciples will continue "to make disciples" until they have reached everywhere in the world. Christian faith is not a national or racial religion, and it has no natural boundaries. It is meant to reach around the globe.

Matthew

28

Understanding Mark

Mark Portrays Jesus Christ, the Servant of God

AUTHOR: Although the Gospel of Mark does not name its author, a tradition dating from the second century ascribes this book to John Mark (see Acts 12:12), a companion and spiritual son of Peter (see 1 Peter 5:13), and also an associate of Paul and Barnabas in their missionary endeavors. The early Church fathers also unanimously testified that the apostle Mark was the author.

DATE: The Gospel of Mark was likely one of the first books written in the New Testament, possibly in the late 50s or early 60s AD.

PURPOSE AND SUMMARY: Scholars generally agree that Mark wrote his Gospel in Rome for the Gentile believers. Mark accounts for the ministry of Jesus from His baptism to His ascension into heaven. Most scholars agree that Mark's purpose was neither biographical nor historical but theological: to present Jesus as the Christ, the mighty worker rather than the great teacher. Hence, Mark makes fewer references to the parables and discourses of Jesus, but he meticulously records each of Jesus' healings and miracles—20 specific miracles and allusions to others—as evidence of the fact that Jesus was the Messiah sent from God.

John, whose surname was Mark, is the author of the Gospel of Mark (see Acts 12:12,25). He was the son of Mary and cousin of Barnabas (see Colossians 4:10), and he likely was a native of Jerusalem. It is believed that the Upper Room of Mark's mother's house in Jerusalem is where the disciples met. He accompanied Paul and Barnabas to Antioch and was the cause of a serious disagreement between them (see Acts 12:25; 13:5). Then he left them, probably on account of hardships (see Acts 13:13). Finally he became a great help to Paul (see Colossians 4:10-11; 2 Timothy 4:11). Peter was the means of Mark's conversion and affectionately speaks of him as "my son" (1 Peter 5:13). We see the influence of Peter's teaching in this Gospel.

If we turn to Mark 10:45, we can quite easily determine Mark's object in writing his Gospel: "For even the Son of Man did not come to be served, but to serve, and to give his life as a ransom for many." Unlike Matthew, Mark was not trying to prove certain statements and prophecies concerning Jesus. His only object in writing was to tell clearly certain facts about Jesus—His deeds more than His words. That Jesus is the Son of God he proves, not by declaring how He came to earth, but by showing what He accomplished during His brief life on this earth, how His coming changed the world.

There is a general agreement that Mark's Gospel was written for Roman readers. The Roman culture differed from the Jewish culture in many ways. The Romans highly valued common sense. Their religion had to be practical. They had no interest in tracing beliefs back into the past. Legal genealogies and fulfillments of prophecy would leave them cold. Arguing fine points of Scripture interpretation held no interest for them. They might have said, "I know nothing of your Scriptures and care nothing for your peculiar notions; but I would be glad to hear a plain story of the life this man Jesus lived. Tell me what He did. Let me see Him just as He was."

The Gospel of Mark differs widely from Matthew in length, character and scope. Matthew has 28 chapters, abounds in parables and portrays Christ as the Son of David with kingly dignity and authority (see Matthew 28:18). Mark has 16 chapters (it is the shortest Gospel), relates only four parables and portrays Christ as the humble but perfect servant of Jehovah. Angels minister to Him.

GENERAL CHARACTERISTICS OF MARK'S GOSPEL

The skill of a gifted artist may lie in what he or she leaves out. An amateur crowds everything in. In keeping with Mark's central purpose of emphasizing Jesus as the servant, many points covered in Matthew are omitted in Mark:

- There is nothing about the virgin birth. No reference to Jesus' birth is made in the whole Gospel. This is significant. No one is interested in the pedigree of a servant.

- There is no visit of wise men. A servant does not receive homage.

- No account of Jesus as the boy in the Temple is given. During Mark's day (as it is today) people demanded a Christ who can do things. They were not interested in Jesus the boy but Christ the man who was able and willing to accomplish things.

- There is no Sermon on the Mount. Matthew devoted three whole chapters to this sermon, but Mark presents Christ as a perfect workman; such a servant has no kingdom and frames no laws.

- No quotations from the prophets are recalled. Mark's one direct quotation from the prophets is found in Mark 1:2. Matthew quotes the prophets on every page.

- No divine titles are used. Jesus is never called a king in Mark, except in derision. Matthew says, " 'They will call him Immanuel' (which means 'God with us')" (Matthew 1:23). Not so in Mark. Mark calls Him "Teacher" ("Master," *KJV*). Other evangelists call Him "Lord." Matthew 8:25 says, "Lord, save us! We're going to drown!" Mark 4:38 says, "Teacher, don't you care if we drown?"

- Matthew records 14 parables; Mark only four—the sower, the seed growing secretly (peculiar to Mark), the mustard seed and the wicked husbandmen.

- Miracles have a leading place in Mark, as parables have in Matthew. A servant works; a king speaks. Twenty miracles are detailed in Mark.

- There is no statement that Jesus' work was finished at His death. In John 19:30, Jesus said, "It is finished." This is not found in Mark. It is not for a servant to say when his work is done.

- There is no introduction in Mark. The other Gospels have lengthy openings, but the opening verse in Mark simply says, "The beginning of the good news about Jesus the Messiah," and then Mark adds, "Son of God," to guard His divine glory. How different this is from Matthew, where the focus is the King.

The word "gospel" is used eight times in Matthew, Mark, Luke and John together, and five of those times are in Mark. Yes, the servant is to bear good news! Another term that predominates Mark is the Greek word *eutheos*, which is translated as "immediately," "at once," "as soon as" and "without delay." In all, this expression is found no fewer than 20 times in Mark's Gospel. This is a servant's word.

In the *King James Version*, 12 out of 16 chapters in Mark open with the little word "and." Jesus' service was one complete, perfect whole, with no pause or breaks in it; it was continuous. We may slack off but not our Lord.

MARK 1:1-13: THE SERVANT PREPARED

The book of Mark skips over the first 30 years of Jesus' life, but these years were all needed for His human preparation for His life's work. Jesus must have grown to sympathize with a human's daily toil. Surely, He wrestled, like Jacob, with life's problems and fought many battles in the arena of His heart. Certainly, He meditated on the needs of His nation until His mental anguish almost consumed Him.

Preparation in life is always needed. Jesus' life illustrated this. The foundations of a lighthouse are necessary, though they are unseen beneath the surface. A plant sends its roots into the dark soil before it can bring forth a flower and leaf. Look at the 40 years Moses spent in the desert before he started his great work; the long period Elijah spent before he appeared before King Ahab; the early years Amos spent on a farm; the 30 years of training that John the Baptist went through. So it was with Jesus! He spent 30 years in obscurity in Nazareth before He appeared for three years of public ministry.

Getting ready for our life's work is of tremendous importance. Don't become impatient if Christ uses time to prepare you for life.

Preparation by a Messenger

This Gospel begins with John the Baptist making people ready for the coming of the Messiah. John's coming was in fulfillment of a messianic prophecy: "I will send my messenger ahead of you, who will prepare your way" (Mark 1:2). This quotation refers to Malachi 3:1 and Isaiah 40:3. In Isaiah, the messenger is known simply as "a voice": "A voice of one calling: 'In the wilderness prepare the way for the LORD; make straight in the desert a highway for our God'" (Isaiah 40:3). It is this "voice" that was to announce Jesus Christ.

We see this strange man appear on the scene in an almost sensational way: "John wore clothing made of camel's hair, with a leather belt around his waist, and he ate locusts and wild honey" (Mark 1:6).

There is a lesson here for us. God does not always choose the kind of person we would select. He often picks "the foolish things of the world to shame the wise . . . the weak things of the world to shame the strong" (1 Corinthians 1:27). No doubt, if we were to select someone to announce Christ's arrival, we would choose someone of superior birth, well educated, with a sterling reputation. This person would have to be eloquent and a fearless champion of great causes. Not so with God. Of humble birth, probably only slightly educated, not well known, and dressed like a desert hermit, John the Baptist was approved by God (see Matthew 11:11).

John's message was as startling as his appearance: "Prepare the way for the Lord, make straight paths for him" (Mark 1:3). A true revival is always a revival of righteousness.

Preparation by Baptism

John and Jesus met one day. John recognized immediately that this Man was not someone who needed the baptism of repentance that he was preaching. There was in this face a purity and majesty that struck John's heart with a sense of his own unworthiness. This man was the Son of God. John hesitated before he said, "I need to be baptized by you, and do you come to me?" (Matthew 3:14).

Jesus was, however, baptized with John's baptism in order to obey a divine order: "Let it be so now; it is proper for us to do this to fulfill all righteousness" (Matthew 3:15). Jesus set a seal of approval on John's message and work, and acknowledged him as His own true forerunner. The baptism by John was ordered by God and therefore was necessary for all those who acknowledged God and meant to keep His commandments.

Because Christ was the standard for and an example of righteousness, He would fulfill every duty that He required of others, including being baptized (see 1 Corinthians 10:13).

Preparation by Receiving the Holy Spirit

"Just as Jesus was coming up out of the water, he saw heaven being torn open and the Spirit descending on him like a dove" (Mark

1:10). The Spirit descended, not only in the manner of a dove, but also in the bodily shape of a dove (see Luke 3:22). This was a symbol; the coming of the Spirit Himself was a reality. In any service for God, the Spirit always aids the preparation by giving power and equipment. He is God's great agent for spiritual warfare.

Because Jesus went down into the baptismal water of obedience to God, He came up under an opened sky with the Holy Spirit descending upon Him; and He could hear the voice of His Father, declaring Him to be His beloved Son.

Jesus came up out of that water a new man into a new world. His relationship to His Father and His mission were proclaimed.

Preparation by a Divine Call

"A voice came from heaven" (Mark 1:11). God endorsed Jesus and His mission, and showed to the Jewish nation that Jesus was the Messiah: "God anointed Jesus of Nazareth with the Holy Spirit and power, and . . . he went around doing good and healing all who were under the power of the devil, because God was with him" (Acts 10:38). Mark 1:11 has been called Mark's Gospel in a nutshell. Later we hear this same voice at the Transfiguration: "This is my Son, whom I love. Listen to him!" (Mark 9:7).

Preparation by Testing

Baptism and temptation are here crowded together. Hardly had the voice from heaven died away then we hear a whisper from hell. Out of the baptismal benediction of the Father, Jesus stepped into a desperate struggle with the devil.

Mark says, "At once the Spirit sent him out into the wilderness," which shows how quickly the Spirit moves (Mark 1:12). "At once" indicates continuity, showing that temptation was as much a part of the preparation of the servant for His work as His baptism. Suffering and trials are as much God's plan as thrills and triumphs. Jesus was "sent" to be tempted. It was no accident or evil fate but a divine appointment.

Temptation has its place in this world. We could never develop without it. There is nothing wrong in being tempted. The wrong begins when we consent to it. We are not to run into temptation of our own accord. Jesus did not go by His own choice but was sent by the Spirit. We will find that the path of duty often takes us through temptations, but "no temptation has overtaken you except what is common to mankind. And God is faithful; he will not let you be tempted beyond what you can bear. But when you are tempted, he will also provide a way out so that you can endure it" (1 Corinthians 10:13). He always makes a way of escape! This subject is of great importance. Be sure you understand it.

MARK 1:14-8:30—THE SERVANT WORKING

As mentioned earlier, there is a continuous, unbroken service of the servant recorded in this Gospel. We read, "And He did this. And He said that." He must teach people; they were in darkness. He must cheer people; they were without hope. He must heal people; they were sick and suffering. He must free people; they were under the power of Satan. He must pardon and cleanse people; they were sinful.

We see Jesus preaching by the seashore and selecting four of the fishermen to become His first disciples to learn under His guidance how to become "fishers of men" (Mark 1:26, *KJV*). Who were they? Read Mark 1:16-20. They were to take all their practical knowledge and skill used to catch fish and use them to catch men and women. Which disciple was called in Mark 2?

It is interesting to note that Jesus never called any idle person. He called busy and successful people to follow Him. Any business can be adapted to be used in service for Christ. How was Christ's call received? "At once they left their nets and followed him" (Mark 1:18). Too often there is time lost between our call and our coming; our doing lags far behind our duty.

The action in Mark is rapid, and events appear to be happening before our very eyes. Mark's descriptions are short and direct, but he preserves many things for us that would otherwise have been lost. It is only in the Gospel of Mark that we are told, for example, that Jesus was a carpenter (see Mark 6:3).

Mark tells us that Jesus took little children "in his arms" (Mark 9:36; 10:16). Mark tells us that Jesus was "grieved" (Mark 3:5, *KJV*); that He "sighed" (Mark 8:12). He "wondered" (Mark 6:51, *KJV*). He "loved" (Mark 10:21).

The Servant Observes Sabbath

Let us spend with Jesus the Sabbath that is recorded in Mark 1:21-34, going with Him to synagogue, listening to His preaching, watching Him when interrupted by a maniac, casting out the unclean spirit and making the healing a powerful aid to His teaching. Then, after service, let us go with Him to Peter's house and see Him heal Peter's wife's mother of a severe fever; and then let us spend the Sabbath afternoon in quiet rest and friendly conversation.

Toward evening we will look out in the beautiful twilight and see men and women coming toward the house, bringing great numbers of people, sick with every kind of disease, and watch them as Jesus lays His tender hands on them and heals them. The lame jump from their stretchers and leap for joy; the blind open their eyes and see their healer; faces lined by suffering suddenly express unbelievable happiness as painful diseases are cured.

Mark records a wonderful statement concerning the Sabbath: "The Sabbath was made for man, not man for the Sabbath" (Mark 2:27). This great saying by Jesus is the central principle of Sabbath observance. The Sabbath is not made to annoy humankind, to confine them, to impoverish them, but to enrich and bless them! Try spending one Lord's day as Jesus did. I believe you will like it, and the Lord will be pleased.

Christ answers a question about what is proper to do on the Sabbath with a practical illustration (see Mark 3:1-5). His conclusion is that whatever deed is really helpful to people is proper for the Sabbath and is in perfect accord with what God meant the day to be. He illustrated this truth with this miracle of healing. Seven of Jesus' recorded miracles were performed on the Sabbath. The Sabbath was "made." It is God's gift to people.

Mark

The Servant Heals

In Mark, Jesus appears at once as one "anointed . . . with power" and as fully engaged in His work (Acts 10:38). You will find no long discussions in these next chapters, but you will find many mighty deeds. Demons were cast out (see Mark 1:21-28); fever banished (see Mark 1:29-31); different diseases healed (see Mark 1:32-34); lepers made whole (see Mark 1:40-45); a paralytic man made to walk (see Mark 2:1-12); a withered hand cured (see Mark 3:1-5); multitudes healed (see Mark 3:6-12); storm at sea quelled (see Mark 4:35-41); maniac's mind restored (see Mark 5:1-15); woman's hemorrhage stopped (see Mark 5:21-34); Jairus's daughter brought back to life (see Mark 5:35-43); five thousand fed (see Mark 6:32-44); the sea made into His sidewalk (see Mark 6:45-51); all that touched Him were made whole (see Mark 6:53-56); the deaf heard and the dumb spoke (see Mark 7:31-37); four thousand fed (see Mark 8:1-9); a blind man healed (see Mark 8:22-26).

The miracles of Jesus were proof of His mission from God. They showed that He was the promised Redeemer and King, the One we all need. Because Jesus was God, miracles were as natural to Him as acts of will are to us! Through His miracles, Jesus inspired faith in many of those who saw and heard Him.

The servant is always found working: "As long as it is day, we must do the works of him who sent me. Night is coming, when no one can work" (John 9:4). This brief description of our Lord's ministry shows how full His days were. How empty our own lives seem in comparison!

The Servant Prays

The morning following the great Sabbath day of preaching and healing, Jesus rose very early and went out of the city to a lonely place and prayed (see Mark 1:35). His work was growing rapidly, and Jesus needed communion with heaven, an intimate conversation with God. It seems as if during His prayer He was told to do a larger work, for He soon leaves on His first Galilean tour of healing and preaching (see Mark 1:37-39). Only one healing event of this tour, which lasted several days, is recorded—that of a leper whose disease was incurable (see Mark 1:40-45).

If the Son of God needed to pray before He undertook His work, how much more should we pray. Perhaps if we lack success in life, it is because we fail to pray. In other words, we have not because we ask not (see James 4:2).

The Servant Forgives Sin

"A few days later . . . the people heard that he had come home" (Mark 2:1). It is remarkable how rapidly news spread in Jesus' time, without newspapers, television, phones or the Internet. But in another part of the city, a paralytic man and his friends had heard of this new servant and His gospel of healing. His four friends brought him to Jesus and let him down into the presence of the teacher. We find in this healing the test and proof of Jesus' power, not only as a healer of the body, but also as a healer of the soul. "Who can forgive sins but God alone?" (Mark 2:7), the people said. Sins are against God and, therefore, He only can forgive. Jesus said, " 'But I want you to know that the Son of Man has authority on earth to forgive sins.' So he said to the man, 'I tell you, get up, take your mat and go home' " (Mark 2:10-11).

Through this miracle, God endorsed Jesus' claim to be the Messiah. The man got up, took up his mat and, in front of everyone, walked as a living witness to Jesus' power over sin, a visible illustration of the work Jesus came to do. Jesus came to give His life as a ransom for many so that people's sins would be forgiven: "All have sinned," and all need a Savior (Romans 3:23).

The Servant Teaches

We find the account of choosing the 12 apostles in Mark 3:13-21. Notice the fourteenth verse; it tells why Jesus chose these men: "that they might be with him." Mark it in your Bible. This is what Jesus wants of His disciples today—that they will take time to be in His presence and communicate with Him. In John 15:15, He says, "I no longer call you servants. . . . I have called you friends."

As you turn to Mark 4, notice once again that the opening word is "And" (*KJV*). "And he began again to teach" (*KJV*) as on former occasions (see Mark 4:1). What a wonderful teacher is Jesus!

Everyone should master the parables of the Kingdom in Mark 4. They were a special teaching technique used by Christ. Jesus used this method of instruction because of the growing hostility to Him and His message. He was surrounded by enemies who tried to find fault with what He had to say, but no one could object to a simple story. Besides, stories are easy to remember by almost everyone.

A parable is an analogy. It assumes a likeness between heavenly and earthly things. "Parable" comes from the Greek word meaning "beside" and "to throw." A parable, then, is a form of teaching in which one thing is thrown beside another to make a comparison.

The parable of the sower, for example, is actually about the obstacles that people have to accepting and understanding the gospel (see Mark 4:3-20). Besides the parable of the sower, our Lord told other parables as recorded by Mark in this chapter:

- The parable of the lamp—Mark 4:21-25
- The parable of the sprouting seed—Mark 4:26-29
- The parable of the mustard seed—Mark 4:30-33

After interpreting the parables, Jesus took a boat to cross the Sea of Galilee to escape the crowd. On the way, as the weary servant fell asleep, a violent storm came up on the Sea of Galilee. About to perish, the frantic disciples woke up Jesus. At a word from His lips, the sea became calm. He had power over the elements (see Mark 4:35-41).

The Servant Tests the People

Mark 5 begins again with "and" (*KJV*). Jesus is still working. What does He do now? Read parallel accounts in Matthew 8:28-34; Luke 8:26-39. Compare this miracle with other recorded cures of people possessed by demons (see Matthew 9:32-33; Mark 1:23-26; Matthew 17:14-18; Luke 9:38-42).

Mark

The miracle recorded in Mark 5, like all others, tested the character of people. It surprised them and disclosed their true natures. Notice the contrast in the way people receive the work of Christ.

Some shunned the Savior: "Those tending the pigs ran off" (Mark 5:14). Others "were afraid" and "pleaded with him to leave their region" (Mark 5:15,17). Doubtless there were other herds of swine, and they feared the loss of them. What a true picture of the attitude of many toward Christ! There is some sort of lucrative business that each does not want to give up. There are some sins that lie close to their hearts. For these reasons people push Christ away.

Some seek the Savior. The healed man "begged to go with him" (Mark 5:18). It is the same with people today. People either ask Jesus to "leave," because they want to keep their sins, or they ask Him to remain "with" them because they want to lose their sins. Do you want to keep or lose your sin?

The Servant Sends the Disciples

Jesus started out on a third preaching tour of Galilee (see Mark 6). He sent forth the 12 disciples, two by two, on independent missions (see Mark 6:7-13). Matthew 10 records the instructions they received. As they preached, Herod heard about them, and we read about his uneasy conscience, thinking that the man he had murdered was back to haunt him (see Mark 6:14-29). How much people recklessly give away in order to enjoy fleeting pleasures. For a glass of wine, a moment of passion, a little more money, a position of honor, they give away half—no, *all*—the kingdom of their souls. Gone are their health, homes, friendships, peace, happiness and eternal lives. Like Esau, they sell their birthright for a bit of stew. Like Judas, they sell their Savior for 30 bits of metal.

After the apostles were trained, Jesus sent them out on an extensive missionary tour among the villages of Galilee (see Mark 6:12-13). On returning they "gathered around Jesus" (Mark 6:30), probably at their regular rendezvous, Capernaum. They reported on their sermons, the number of conversions and the miracles that they had performed. No Christian work can be carried on for any length of time without frequent talks with Christ. We need His sympathy, approval, guidance and strength.

MARK 8:31–15—THE SERVANT REJECTED

Even before Mark sets forth Christ's direct claim to be King of the kingdom, he reveals the way the King is to be received. Jesus said, "The Son of Man must suffer many things" (Mark 8:31):

- He is to be rejected by the elders, chief priests and scribes (see Mark 8:31).
- He is to be delivered by treachery (see Mark 9:31).
- He is to be put to death by the Romans (see Mark 10:32-45).
- He is to rise again the third day (see Mark 9:31).

Jesus claimed the kingdom by presenting Himself as the heir of David (according to the prophecy of Zechariah 9:9) when He arrived in Jerusalem (see Mark 11:1-11).

How did the people accept this King? At first they welcomed Him because they hoped He would free them from servitude to Rome and from the poverty they endured. But when He entered the Temple and showed that His mission was a spiritual one, He was hated by the religious leaders with a satanic hatred that led to the plot to put Him to death (see Mark 14:1).

The Last Conflict

After Christ's public ministry, described in Mark 10:46–11:26, we read of His last conflict with the Jewish authorities and of His triumph over the leaders (see Mark 11:27-12:12).

Jesus sought to persuade the Jews to receive Him as the Messiah (see Mark 11:15-12:36). It was a busy Tuesday. Jesus was occupied from morning till night in one great and powerful effort to induce the Jewish nation to acknowledge Him and thus become that glorious nation for which it had been set apart to bless the world.

In the beautiful Temple courts, the simple Galilean met the religious authorities, arrayed in all the pomp of their official regalia. There are four sharp controversies:

1. The scribes and chief priests ask Him, "By what authority are you doing these things? . . . And who gave you authority to do this?" (Mark 11:28).
2. The Pharisees and Herodians try to catch Him in His words and ask, "Is it right to pay the imperial tax?" (Mark 12:14).
3. The Sadducees, who say there is no resurrection, ask Him, "At the resurrection whose wife will she be, since the seven were married to her?" (Mark 12:23).
4. The scribes ask Him, "Of all the commandments, which is the most important?" (Mark 12:28).

After Jesus answered them all, "from then on no one dared ask him any more questions" (Mark 12:34).

It would seem that by answering the questions, Jesus could not escape being treasonous to the Roman government, but He came away untouched. Hour by hour Jesus met the attacks, and He silenced His enemies, but they still refused to believe Him. Then He exposed all their hypocritical practices in words that fell like bombs. He tried to break through their walls of prejudice and get them to repent before it was too late, but all seemed to be in vain.

Before He goes to the cross, Jesus reveals the future to His troubled disciples (see the Olivet discourse, Mark 13). He tells them about the end of this age and about the great tribulation, and He ends with the promise of His return in power and glory.

The scheming of the chief priests to put Jesus to death, and the anointing of His body in preparation for burial, opens chapter 14 (see verse 8). Then the sad story of His betrayal at the hand of His own disciple, the celebration of the Passover and the institution of the Lord's Supper all are crowded into 25 short verses. Adding insult to injury is Peter's denial of his Lord (see Mark 14:10-11,26-31,66-71).

Mark

Then Mark records how the sufferings of Jesus in Gethsemane and on Calvary fulfilled the prophecies of Isaiah and Isaiah's great message that the Son of God would become the servant of God in order to redeem the world (see Isaiah 53).

MARK 16: THE SERVANT EXALTED

After the servant had given His life as a ransom for many, He rose from the dead. Compare the two versions of the Great Commission (see Mark 16:15; see also Matthew 28:19-20). In Mark we do not hear a King say, "All authority in heaven and on earth has been given to me," as in Matthew (Matthew 28:18). In Mark we see in Jesus' words that His disciples are to take His place, and He will serve in and through them. He is still the servant, though risen (see Mark 16:20). The command for service resounds with urgency. Not a corner of the world is to be left unvisited, not a soul to be left out!

Finally Jesus was received into heaven to sit at the right hand of God (see Mark 16:19). He who had taken on Himself the form of a servant is now highly exalted (see Philippians 2:7-9). He is in the place of power, always interceding for us. He is our Advocate.

But Christ is with us. The servant is always working in us and through us. We are laborers together with Him (see 1 Corinthians 3:9). He is still working with us (see Mark 16:20). Let us, being redeemed, follow our model and go forth to serve also! "Therefore, my dear brothers and sisters, stand firm. Let nothing move you. Always give yourselves fully to the work of the Lord, because you know that your labor in the Lord is not in vain" (1 Corinthians 15:58).

POINTS TO REMEMBER

All the way through, the perfect servant of God was dogged by His enemies. The enemy is not dead! God's servants today are called to tread a similar path.

Feeding the five thousand is one of the most important miracles performed by Jesus (see Mark 6:30-44). Evidently it made a special impression on the writers of the Gospels, as it is the only one of the 35 miracles that is recorded by all four. Review this miracle carefully. Notice that Jesus served in an orderly way.

Jesus was sold for 30 pieces of silver, the price of a slave. He was executed as only slaves were! Yes, Christ was the suffering servant and died for me! He bore my sins in His own body on the tree.

No reference is made by Mark that in the garden of Gethsemane, Jesus had the right to summon 12 legions of angels if He wanted to. No promise of the Kingdom is given to the dying thief on the cross. These claims are made by a king (in Matthew), but they are not mentioned by a servant.

A Confession of Faith

Peter's confession of faith should be on everyone's lips (see Mark 8:29). Jesus did not tell His disciples who He was. He waited for them to tell Him. When He asked, "Who do you say I am?" the climax of His ministry was reached. He was testing the chosen 12 to determine whether His teaching had been effective. Peter's answer gave Him the assurance that His goal had been attained.

What did the Pharisees think of Jesus? They had agreed to put Him to death.

What did the multitude think of Him? They deserted Him.

What did the disciples think of Him? Peter gave the answer.

What do you think of Christ?

The Greatest Sin

The greatest sin of this age, as of every age, is the rejection of Jesus Christ. Everyone who has heard the gospel must either accept the Lord as Savior or reject Him. The people of Jesus' day made their choice, and the people of our day must make theirs.

The wonderful servant who shines in the Gospels—this vision of God in the flesh—are you to look and then pass by as though you had only seen a work of art? This voice that has continued to speak throughout the centuries, are you to listen as though it were just the voice of a gifted speaker? What is Jesus to you? A name or your master? If you cannot answer the question as Peter did, will you sign this covenant:

> I promise to examine carefully the evidence that the Bible is God's book and that Jesus Christ is God's Son and man's Savior; and if I find reason to believe that this book is true and He is man's Savior, I will accept Him, confess Him before men and follow Him.

_____

(Signed)

Mark

29

Understanding Luke

Luke Portrays Jesus Christ, the Son of Man

SELECTED BIBLE READINGS

DAY OF THE WEEK		MAIN TOPIC
Sunday: Luke 1–3	The Man Made Like His Brothers	
Monday: Luke 4–8:3	The Man Tempted as We Are	
Tuesday: Luke 8:4–12:48	The Man Able to Sympathize	
Wednesday: Luke 12:49–16	The Man Going About His Father's Business	
Thursday: Luke 17–19:27	The Man Whose Speech Is Unique	
Friday: Luke 19:28–23	The Man Who Is Our Kinsman-Redeemer	
Saturday: Luke 24	The Man Who Showed Resurrection Glory	

AUTHOR: The Gospel of Luke does not identify its author, but it is clear that the same author wrote both Luke and Acts, addressing both to Theophilus, possibly a Roman dignitary (see Luke 1:3; Acts 1:1). The tradition from the earliest days of the Church has been that Luke, a physician and a close companion of the apostle Paul, wrote both Luke and Acts (see Colossians 4:14; 2 Timothy 4:11). This would make Luke the only Gentile to have written any books of the New Testament.

DATE: The Gospel of Luke was likely written between AD 59 and 63.

PURPOSE AND SUMMARY: Luke wrote to present Jesus as the Savior of the world, the compassionate healer and teacher. His careful historical approach is revealed in the preface, which states that the author has "carefully investigated everything from the beginning" (Luke 1:3). Unlike Mark, Luke includes an account of the virgin birth; and unlike Matthew, he extensively describes the Perean ministry of Jesus (see Luke 9–18).

The writer of this third Gospel was Doctor Luke, Paul's companion (see Acts 16:10-24; Colossians 4:14; 2 Timothy 4:11). He was a native of Syria and apparently was not a Jew, for Colossians 4:14 places him with other Gentile Christians. If this is true, he was the only Gentile writer of the New Testament books.

Luke's Gospel was written for the Greeks. Besides the Jews and the Romans, the Greeks were another people who had been preparing for Christ's coming. They differed from the other two groups, though, in that they possessed a wider culture and loved beauty, rhetoric and philosophy. Luke, an educated Greek himself and a keen observer, would be well suited for this task. Luke presents Jesus as the ideal of perfect manliness.

Notice that inspiration does not destroy individuality. In the introduction, Luke 1:1-4, the human element is seen in connection with God's revelation. Luke addressed his Gospel to a man named Theophilus. It is thought he was an influential Christian layman in Greece.

- Matthew presents Christ as King, to the Jews.
- Mark presents Christ as the servant of Jehovah, to the Romans.
- Luke presents Christ as the perfect man, to the Greeks.

Luke is the Gospel for the sinner. It brings out Christ's compassionate love in becoming Man to save humankind.

GENERAL CHARACTERISTICS OF LUKE'S GOSPEL

In Luke, we see God manifest in the flesh. Luke deals with the humanity of our Lord. He reveals the Savior as a man with all His sym-

Luke

pathies, feelings and growing powers—a Savior suited to all. In this Gospel, we see the God of glory coming down to our level, experiencing how we live and subject to the same circumstances.

Luke's Gospel is the Gospel of Christ's manhood. This we must know, however: Although Jesus mingles with humanity, He is in sharp contrast to people. He was the solitary God-Man. There was as great a difference between Christ as the Son of man and we as the sons and daughters of men, as Christ as the Son of God and we as the sons and daughters of God. The difference is not merely relative but absolute. Let me make this fact clear: Read the words of the angel to Mary: "So the holy one to be born" (Luke 1:35); this refers to our Lord's humanity. It is in contrast to ours. Our human nature is unclean (see Isaiah 64:6), but the Son of God, when He became incarnate (took bodily form), was "holy." Adam in his unfallen state was innocent, but Christ was holy.

Distinctions

In keeping with the theme of his Gospel, Doctor Luke has given us the most complete details concerning the miraculous birth of Jesus. We are grateful that our chief testimony concerning this fact comes from a physician. Christ, the Creator of this universe, entered this world like any other person. It is a mystery of mysteries, but enough facts are given to let us see that the predictions came true.

Luke alone tells the story of the visit from the shepherds (see Luke 2:8-20).

We learn from this Gospel that as a boy, Jesus developed normally (see Luke 2:40,52). There is no mention of unhealthy or supernatural growth. As a child, He was to obey His earthly parents, Joseph and Mary (see Luke 2:51). Only Luke tells of Jesus' visit to the Temple when He was 12 years old.

As a man, Jesus toiled with His hands, wept over the city, kneeled in prayer and knew agony in suffering. All of these actions are strikingly human. Five out of six of the miracles were miracles of healing. Luke alone tells of Jesus healing Malchus's ear (see Luke 22:51).

Luke is the Gospel for the outcast on the earth. It is Luke who tells of the good Samaritan (see Luke 10:33), the publican (see Luke 18:13), the prodigal son (see Luke 15:11-24), Zacchaeus (see Luke 19:2) and the thief on the cross (see Luke 23:43). He is the writer who has the most to say for womanhood (see Luke 1-2). Luke records Jesus' compassion for the woman of Nain and the depths of His mercy for the woman who was a sinner. His regard for women and children is shown repeatedly (see Luke 7:46; 8:3; 8:42; 9:38; 10:38-42; 11:27; 23:27).

Luke alone tells us about the bloody sweat in Gethsemane; the walk with two disciples to Emmaus; Jesus' leading His disciples out as far as Bethany and that as He lifted up His hands and blessed them, He was parted from them.

Poetry

Luke is a poetic book. It opens with a song, "Glory to God" (Luke 2:14). It closes with a song, "Praising God" (Luke 24:53). The world has been singing ever since. Thank God for such a Gospel! It preserves the precious gems of Christian hymnology:

- The Magnificat—Mary's hymn of rejoicing—Luke 1:46-55
- Song of Zacharias—Luke 1:68-79
- Song of the angels—Luke 2:8-14

Prayers

Luke tells us more of the prayers of our Lord than any other Gospel writer. Prayer is the expression of human dependence on God. Why do so many in the Church appear to be working, yet so few people appear to be reached for God? Why does there appear to be so much activity, but so few are brought to Christ? The answer is simple: There is not enough private prayer. The cause of Christ does not need less working but more praying.

Universality

The hardest thing the Early Church had to learn was that the Gentiles would have full and free admission into the Kingdom and into the Church. Simeon taught this. Read Luke 2:32. Christ sent the 70 disciples not to the lost sheep of the house of Israel alone, as Matthew says, who wrote especially for the Jews, but "to every town and place" (Luke 10:1). All of Jesus' ministry over the eastern side of Jordan was to the Gentiles.

LUKE 1–4:13: THE PREPARATION OF THE SON OF MAN

The opening of this beautiful book is significant. A man is to be described, and the writer, Luke, will teach his good friend Theophilus about Him. He tells Theophilus about his own personal knowledge of his subject: "since I myself have carefully investigated everything from the beginning" (Luke 1:3). He seems to bring something warmly human to his task of presenting the man Christ Jesus.

The opening chapter is characteristic of Luke's theme. John, as befits his theme, begins, "In the beginning was the Word, and the Word was with God, and the Word was God" (John 1:1). His tone throughout is not of this world, for he is presenting the story of the Son of God. But Luke, so different, begins his touching story about a man simply with, "In the time of Herod king of Judea there was a priest" (Luke 1:5). As the story progresses, we are introduced to human sympathies and relationships that none of the other Gospels tells us. We learn all about the circumstances that accompanied the birth and childhood of the holy babe and about the one who was sent as His forerunner. The birth of John the Baptist (see Luke 1:57-80), the angels' song to the shepherds (see Luke 2:8-20), the circumcision (see Luke 2:21), the presentation in the Temple (see Luke 2:22-38), and then the story of 12-year-old Jesus (see Luke 2:41-52) are all recorded here.

In chapter 2, Luke notes that "in those days Caesar Augustus issued a decree that a census should be taken of the entire Roman world" (Luke 2:1). Then comes a fact that we would never find in Matthew: Joseph and Mary "went to [Joseph's] own town to register" (Luke 2:3). Luke is not showing here One who has

Luke

come to rule but One who has come in humility to be fully involved in human affairs.

God brings to pass what the prophets had spoken. Micah had said that Bethlehem was to be the birthplace of Jesus, for He was part of the family of David (see Micah 5:2-5). But Mary lived in Nazareth, a town 100 miles away. God saw to it that Imperial Rome issued a decree to compel Mary and Joseph to go to Bethlehem just as the child was to be born. Isn't it wonderful how God uses the decree of a pagan monarch to bring to pass His prophecy! God still moves the hand of rulers to do His bidding.

Now keep reading! Here's the message of the angels to the watching shepherds, but we do not find the kings of the East asking for One "who has been born king" (Matthew 2:2). The angel tells the poor shepherds, "I bring you good news that will cause great joy for all the people. Today in the town of David a Savior [not a King] has been born to you" (Luke 2:10-11).

Why did the Father allow His blessed Son to be born in this lowly place? Luke is the only one of the four evangelists who mentions this point about Jesus' humanity.

Boyhood

"The child grew . . . and the grace of God was on him" (Luke 2:40). When Jesus was 12 years old, He went with His parents to Jerusalem to the Passover feast, as every Jewish boy did at that age. "The boy Jesus stayed behind in Jerusalem, but they were unaware of it" (Luke 2:43). How characteristic of a boy this is! He was found sitting among teachers, both listening to them and asking them questions (see Luke 2:46). How intensely human this is! Yet we read, "Everyone who heard him was amazed at his understanding and his answers" (Luke 2:47). Luke says that Jesus was filled with wisdom. Side by side with humans, He was always more than a man. We find Jesus' first words here: "Didn't you know I had to be in my Father's house?" (Luke 2:49). This is the first self-witness to His deity.

Then we read, "Then he went down to Nazareth with them and was obedient to them," His earthly parents (Luke 2:51). "And Jesus grew in wisdom and stature, and in favor with God and man" (Luke 2:52). All of these things are peculiar to Jesus as a man, and Luke alone records them. It is important that we notice that Jesus was a favorite ("in favor") in Nazareth. It is not a sign that we are in God's grace when we are out of favor with others.

Eighteen years of silence followed. We read of John the Baptist preaching "a baptism of repentance for the forgiveness of sins" (Luke 3:3). Then Jesus came to be baptized. Luke tells us, "When all the people were being baptized, Jesus was baptized too. And as he was praying, heaven was opened" (Luke 3:21). Jesus is linked with "all the people." He came down to the level of humans. Here only do we read of the age at which our Lord entered His public ministry (see Luke 3:23).

Genealogy

The genealogy of Jesus in Luke is given at the time of His baptism and not at His birth (see Luke 3:23). There are noticeable differences between the genealogy in Luke and the one found in Matthew 1. Each is significant!

- In Matthew we have the royal genealogy of the Son of David through Joseph—in Luke we have a strictly personal genealogy through Mary.

- Matthew establishes Jesus' legal line of descent through Joseph; Luke establishes Jesus' lineal descent through Mary.

- In Matthew Jesus' genealogy is traced forward from Abraham; in Luke it is followed backward to Adam.

- Matthew shows us Jesus' relation to the Jewish people; hence, he goes back no further than to Abraham, father of the Jewish nation—Luke shows us Jesus' connection to the human race; hence, he goes back to Adam, the father of the human family.

In Luke our Lord's line is traced back to Adam and is, no doubt, His mother's line. Notice that Luke 3:23 does not say that Jesus was the son of Joseph. What are the words? "So it was thought." In Matthew 1:16, where Joseph's genealogy is given, we learn that Joseph was the son of Jacob. Luke says that Joseph was the son of Heli. Joseph could not be the natural son of two men. But note that Luke's record does not state that Heli sired Joseph, so it is supposed that Joseph was the son by law (or son-in-law) of Heli. Heli is believed to have been Mary's father.

In Luke, the Davidic genealogy goes through Nathan, not Solomon. This too is important. The Messiah must be David's son and heir, "a descendant of David" (Romans 1:3; see also 2 Samuel 7:12-13; Acts 2:30-31). He must literally be a flesh-and-blood descendant. Hence Mary must be a member of David's house as well as Joseph's (see Luke 1:32).

"Jesus, full of the Holy Spirit, left the Jordan and was led by the Spirit into the wilderness, where for forty days he was tempted by the devil" (Luke 4:1-2). Only in Luke do we learn that the Savior was "full of the Holy Spirit" as He returned from His baptism. Then the account of His temptation is given. Notice that Luke is the only one to tell us that "Jesus returned to Galilee in the power of the Spirit" (Luke 4:14), showing that the old serpent (Satan) had utterly failed to break the fellowship between the Son of man on earth and His Father in heaven.

Just as Jesus came forth from the fire of testing in the unquenchable "power of the Spirit," so too can we. Only as we are filled with His Spirit can we overcome temptation with the power of the Spirit.

The purpose of the temptation was not to discover whether Jesus would give in to Satan but to demonstrate that He could not; the temptation illustrates the fact that there was nothing in Jesus to which Satan could appeal (see John 14:30). Christ could be tried and proven. The more you crush a rose, the more its fragrance is recognized. So the more the devil assaulted Christ, the more His perfections were revealed.

LUKE 4:14–19: THE MINISTRY OF THE SON OF MAN

Scan Luke 4:14–19, and find the events in Jesus' life as they are recorded in succession.

Jesus' Ministries

Jesus' ministry around Galilee is recorded in 4:14 to 9:50:

- Ministry in Nazareth, His hometown—Luke 4:16-30
- Preaching in Capernaum—Luke 4:31-44
- Call of Peter, James and John—Luke 5:1-11
- Call of Matthew—Luke 5:27-39
- Dealings with the Pharisees—Luke 6:1-11
- The choosing of the 12 apostles—Luke 6:12-16
- Teaching of the disciples—Luke 6:17-49
- Performance of miracles—Luke 7:1-17
- Discourses of the teacher—Luke 7:18-50
- Parables of the teacher—Luke 8:4-18
- Relatives of Jesus—Luke 8:19-21
- Calming of the sea—Luke 8:22-25
- Healing of the demon-possessed man—Luke 8:26-40
- Healing of the bleeding woman—Luke 8:43-48
- Restoration of Jairus's daughter—Luke 8:49-56
- Commissioning of the Twelve—Luke 9:1-10
- Feeding of the five thousand—Luke 9:10-17
- Confession by Peter—Luke 9:18-21
- Transfiguration of Jesus—Luke 9:27-36
- Healing of a lunatic—Luke 9:37-43

Jesus' ministry in Judea is recorded in 9:51–19:27:

- Commissioning of the 72—Luke 10:1-24
- Question of the lawyer—Luke 10:25-37
- Martha and Mary at home—Luke 10:38-42
- Teaching about praying—Luke 11:1-13
- Seeking signs from heaven—Luke 11:14-36
- Warnings about the Pharisees—Luke 12:1-12
- The sin of greed—Luke 12:13-59
- Teaching about repentance—Luke 13:1-9
- The kingdom of heaven—Luke 13:18-30
- Talks on hospitality—Luke 14:1-24

Luke

- Talks on self-denial—Luke 14:25-35
- Love of the lost—Luke 15
- Planning for the future—Luke 16:1-30
- Jesus' journey to Jerusalem—Luke 16:31–19:27

Jesus' Jerusalem ministry is found in Luke 19:28–24:

- Entry into Jerusalem—Luke 19:28-38
- Explanation of His authority—Luke 20–21:4
- Discussion of future things—Luke 21:5-38
- Eating of the last Passover—Luke 22:1-38
- Betrayal by Judas—Luke 22:39-53
- Trial before the high priest—Luke 22:54-71
- Trial before Pilate—Luke 23:1-26
- Crucifixion with two criminals—Luke 23:27-49
- Burial in the tomb—Luke 23:50-56
- Resurrection from the dead—Luke 24:1-48
- Ascension into heaven—Luke 24:49-53

This list is not complete, of course, but it gives a bird's-eye view of the busy life of the Son of man on earth. The keyword of His ministry is "compassion."

The Upbringing of a Man

Following the temptation, Jesus "went to Nazareth, where he had been brought up, and on the Sabbath day he went into the synagogue, as was his custom. And he stood up to read" (Luke 4:16). He went to the place where He had been "brought up." Upbringing is an important experience in life. We find that Jesus was accustomed to going to the synagogue on the Sabbath day, which implies that He had been reared in a godly home.

At the synagogue, Jesus stated that God had anointed Him to preach deliverance to the captives and to bring good tidings to the poor and brokenhearted (see Luke 4:18-19). He selected a text from Isaiah 61:1-2, which announced the object of His whole mission on earth. He was commissioned and sent by God, and He was divinely qualified for His work. He is our Kinsman-Redeemer. He was made like us so that He could save us. He became a man so that He could bring humankind close to God.

At this very early point in Jesus' ministry, we see that people in His hometown synagogue decided to kill Him (see Luke 4:28-30). They said, "Isn't this Joseph's son?" (Luke 4:22). This is the first hint of His future rejection. He proclaimed Himself to be the Messiah (see Luke 4:21). But they were angered because He hinted that their Messiah would also be sent to the Gentiles (see Luke 4:24-30). They believed God's grace was to be confined only to their own kind of people, so they were ready to kill Him. He refused to work miracles for them because of their unbelief. They attempted to throw Him off a cliff, but He escaped and went to Capernaum (see Luke 4:29-31). (By comparing Luke 4:16 with Matthew 13:54, it would seem that Jesus made another visit to Nazareth some months later, but He again met with opposition.)

A Gospel for the World

The Jewish people hated the Gentiles for their treatment of them when they were captives in Babylon. They regarded Gentiles with contempt and considered them unclean and enemies of God. Luke pictures Jesus as tearing down these barriers between Jew and Gentile, making repentance and faith the only conditions of admission to the Kingdom: "And repentance for the forgiveness of sins will be preached in his name to all nations, beginning at Jerusalem" (Luke 24:47). The gospel of Jesus Christ is not just one of the religions of the world. It is the living truth of God, adapted to all nations and to all classes. Read Romans 1:16.

As the Son of man, Christ looked at the needs of the Gentiles just as He looked at the needs of all people. In Luke 6, which in substance is the same as the Sermon on the Mount in Matthew, we find simple broad moral teachings, suited to the needs and wants of all people. Luke condenses into a few verses what Matthew puts into chapters 5 through 7 (see Luke 6:20-49). He makes only a passing reference to "the Law and the Prophets" (Luke 16:16), whereas Matthew emphasizes them (Matthew 7:12; 22:40).

Service of the Self

When the Twelve are commissioned, a broader field of ministry begins (see Luke 9). In Matthew we hear the Lord saying, "Do not go among the Gentiles or enter any town of the Samaritans. Go rather to the lost sheep of Israel" (Matthew 10:5-6). Luke omits this and says, "He sent them out to proclaim the kingdom of God and to heal the sick. So they set out . . . proclaiming the good news and healing people everywhere" (Luke 9:2,6).

Wherever this man Christ Jesus went, a multitude followed Him and "tried to touch him, because power was coming from him and healing them all" (Luke 6:19). He gave of Himself. Our service must be the same.

We find Jesus' power over disease and death (see Luke 7:1-17); we find Him the sinner's friend; we find that He had come "to seek and to save the lost" (Luke 19:10). He is called "a friend of tax collectors and sinners" (Luke 7:34).

The School of the Lord

The scholars of the Lord's school are His disciples, taught and trained by Jesus to carry on His message (see Luke 6:12-16).

Graduation from the school is not necessarily easy. Requirements must be fulfilled. *The entrance requirement is easy.* There is no barrier of age, sex, race or color. "And whoever does not carry their cross and follow me cannot be my disciple" (Luke 14:27). "Those of you who do not give up everything you have cannot be my disciples" (Luke 14:33). Read Luke 14:25-33.

The examinations are not the same for everyone. Jesus knows the ability and weakness of each student in His school, and He gives individual tests.

It is easy to follow Jesus' tests with Peter. In Luke 5, He tested Peter on obedience (see Luke 5:5). In Luke 9:18, Jesus gave a surprise quiz, and Peter gave a startling answer (see Luke 9:18-20).

There are a set of rules to be observed, and a right relationship with the teacher must be maintained at all times. Many people think that simply having established a relationship with the great teacher is all that is necessary, but this is not true. There must be a constant study of

Luke

His Word, a laboratory time of prayer (see Luke 11:1-4), and time spent in the gym for spiritual exercises (see Luke 5:27; 9:59).

There is a practice school, where students show off the skills they have learned. Jesus not only taught His disciples, but He also made them try out the lessons He had taught them (see Luke 10:1-12,28,36-37; 11:35; 12:8-9; 14:25-33; 18:18-26).

The course work is always the same. All classes focus on a study of the Kingdom and the King (see Luke 7:28; 8:1; 9:2,11,62; 12:32; 13:20-21,28-29; 17:20; 18:29; 19:12,15; 22:29).

LUKE 20–23: THE SUFFERING OF THE SON OF MAN

Jesus is sitting with His disciples around the table, celebrating the feast of the Passover. At this time, He institutes what we call the Lord's Supper. Listen to His words: "This is my body given for you . . . the new covenant in my blood, which is poured out for you" (Luke 22:19-20). This is different from the account in Matthew and Mark. They say, "My blood . . . which is poured out for many" (Matthew 26:28; Mark 14:24). His love is expressed in such a personal way in Luke. The evangelist adds: "Do this in remembrance of me" (Luke 22:19).

Read about the sad record of events in connection with Jesus' death. We find the disciples arguing over which one of them would be counted greatest in the Kingdom (see Luke 22:24-27). We follow Peter and we read a lamentable story—one that ends in Peter's denial of his Lord and Master (see Luke 22:54-62).

Look into the Garden of Gethsemane. Jesus is praying; and "as it were" (*KJV*), great drops of blood were on His holy brow (see Luke 22:44). Luke tells us that the angels came to minister to Him, the Son of man (see Luke 22:43). Matthew and Mark don't mention the ministering angels.

In the shadows of the garden, a contingent of soldiers approaches; leading them is Judas (see Luke 22:47). He steps up to kiss Jesus. Why, yes, he was a disciple. But the Scriptures had said that Jesus would be betrayed by a friend and sold for 30 pieces of silver (see Luke 22:47-62; Psalm 41:9; Zechariah 11:12).

Worst of all for Jesus, all but one of His friends desert Him. All flee, except John the beloved. Luke alone tells us that Jesus looks on Peter, the denier, and broke Peter's heart with His look of love (see Luke 23:61).

We follow Jesus into Pilate's hall and then before Herod (see Luke 23:1-12). We follow along the Via Dolorosa ("way of suffering") to the cross (see Luke 23:27-38). Only Luke mentions the name "Calvary" (*KJV*), which is the Latin name for "Golgotha" ("place of a skull").

There were three crosses on the hill. On one of them was a thief, dying for his crimes. Luke tells us this story, too (see Luke 23:39-45). The way this thief was saved is the way every sinner must be saved. He believed in the Lamb of God who died on the cross that day to pay the penalty for our sins.

The scene closes with the Son of man crying with a loud voice, "Father, into your hands I commit my spirit" (Luke 23:46). The centurion, in keeping with this Gospel, vindicates Jesus: "Surely this was a righteous man" (Luke 23:47).

LUKE 24: THE VICTORY OF THE SON OF MAN

We turn with great relief from the sorrow and death associated with the cross, and the darkness and gloom of the tomb, to the brightness and glory of the resurrection morning. Luke gives us a part of the scene the other authors don't mention. It is the story of the walk to Emmaus.

Luke shows that Jesus, as the disciples' resurrected Lord, is just the same loving, understanding friend He had been before His death. After Jesus' walk and conversation with them, these disciples urged Him to come in and spend the night with them. He revealed who He was when He broke the bread. Then they recognized who He was, but He vanished out of their sight. After they returned to Jerusalem, they found abundant proof of His resurrection and of His being a real man with flesh and bones.

Eleven appearances of Jesus following His resurrection are recorded—not only to individuals, but also to small groups and crowds. First, to the women, to Mary and then to the others (see Mark 16; John 20:14): to Peter alone (see Luke 24:34); to two men walking to Emmaus (see Luke 24:13); to 10 apostles in Jerusalem (see John 20:19; Thomas was absent); to the 11 remaining disciples (see John 20:26,29); to seven men at the sea of Tiberias (see John 21:1); to all of the apostles on a mountain in Galilee (see Matthew 28:16); to 500 brethren at once (see 1 Corinthians 15:6); to James (see 1 Corinthians 15:7); and finally to the little group on the Mount of Olives at His ascension (see Luke 24:51).

Three times, we are told, His disciples touched Him when He appeared to them (see Matthew 28:9; Luke 24:39; John 20:27). He ate with them, too (see Luke 24:42; John 21:12-13). Finally, as Jesus raised His hands to bless them, "he . . . was taken up into heaven" (Luke 24:51).

Jesus is no longer a local Christ, confined to Jerusalem; He is a universal Christ. He could say to His disciples who mourned for Him and who thought that because He had died, He could no longer be with them, "And surely I am with you always" (Matthew 28:20). How different was the hope and joy of those chosen followers from their despair and shame at the Crucifixion! They returned to Jerusalem with great joy.

Luke

30

Understanding John

John Portrays Jesus Christ, the Son of God

SELECTED BIBLE READINGS

DAY OF THE WEEK		MAIN TOPIC
Sunday: John 1	Christ, the Word Made Flesh	
Monday: John 3	Christ, the One from Above	
Tuesday: John 4	Christ, the One Who Satisfies	
Wednesday: John 6:1-59	Christ, the Bread of Life	
Thursday: John 9	Christ, the Light of the World	
Friday: John 10:1-39	Christ, Our Shepherd	
Saturday: John 14	Christ, the One Who Promises the Comforter	

AUTHOR: John 21:20 describes the author as "the disciple whom Jesus loved," and for both historical and internal reasons, this is understood to be John the apostle, one of the sons of Zebedee (see Luke 5:10).

DATE: Discovery of certain papyrus fragments dated around AD 135 require the Gospel of John to have been written, copied and circulated before then. And while some think the Gospel of John was written before Jerusalem was destroyed (AD 70), AD 85-90 is a more accepted date for its writing.

PURPOSE AND SUMMARY: The Gospel of John explains the mystery of the person of Christ by the use of the term *Logos* ("Word") and was written to convince readers that Jesus was the Christ, the Son of God (see John 20:31). John not only records events in Jesus' life and ministry, as do the other Gospels, but John also uniquely interprets the events by showing their deeper, spiritual meaning. The author makes significant use of such images as light, water, life, love and bread to describe the life and presence of God that Jesus brings to every believer.

The purpose of this book is stated by the author in the book's opening 18 verses, the prologue, and he states it very plainly in John 20:31. John wrote to prove that Jesus was the Christ, the promised Messiah (for the Jews) and the Son of God (for the Gentiles), and to lead believers into a life of divine friendship with Him. "Messiah" means "anointed One, who comes as divine King." The keyword is "believe." We find this word in one form or another more than 90 times in this book.

The theme of John's Gospel is the deity of Jesus Christ. More here than anywhere else Jesus' divine Sonship is set forth. In this Gospel, we are shown that the baby of Bethlehem was none other than "the one and only Son, who came from the Father" (John 1:14). John reveals the great deal of evidence that proves this truth. Although "all things were made" by Him (John 1:3) and although "in him was life" (John 1:4), He "became flesh and made his dwelling among us" (John 1:14). No person can see God; therefore, Christ came to declare Him—to be living proof of His existence. John leaves out of his story many things that are found in the other Gospels:

- No genealogy—neither Jesus' legal lineage through Joseph (as given by Matthew), nor His personal descent through Mary (as given by Luke)
- No account of Jesus' birth—because He was "in the beginning" (John 1:1)
- Nothing about Jesus' boyhood
- Nothing about Jesus' temptation
- No Transfiguration

John

- No appointing of Jesus' disciples
- No parables
- No account of the Ascension
- No Great Commission

Yet only in John is Jesus called:

- "The Word" (John 1:1)
- The Creator (see John 1:3)
- "The only begotten of the Father" (John 1:14, *KJV*)
- "The Lamb of God" (John 1:29,36)
- "I am" (John 8:58)—the revelation of the great "I AM" (Exodus 3:14)

The author of this Gospel was John, "son of thunder," "the disciple whom Jesus loved" (John 13:23; 21:7,20). His father was Zebedee, a successful fisherman; his mother was Salome, a devout follower of the Lord who may have been a sister of Mary, the mother of Jesus (see Mark 15:40; John 19:25). His brother was James. His position was probably somewhat better than that of an ordinary fisherman.

John may have been about 25 years of age when Jesus called him. He had been a follower of John the Baptist. During the reign of the Roman Emperor Domitian, John the disciple was banished to Patmos, but afterward he returned to Ephesus and became the pastor of the wonderful church there. He lived to an extreme old age in that city, the last of the 12 apostles. During this time, he wrote his Gospel concerning the deity of the Christ, co-eternal with the Father.

John wrote nearly a generation after the other evangelists, somewhere between AD 80 and 100, at the end of the first century when all of the New Testament was complete except for his own writings. The life and work of Jesus were well known at this time. The gospel had been preached, Paul and Peter had suffered martyrdom, and all the other apostles had died. Jerusalem had been destroyed by the Roman legions under Titus, AD 70.

John

All the Synoptic Gospels (Matthew, Mark and Luke) were written before AD 70, the fateful year of the overthrow of Jerusalem. By then, false teachers had begun to deny that Jesus Christ was the Son of God who had come in the form of a man. John, therefore, wrote to prove those facts, recording eyewitness accounts and the words and works of Jesus that reveal His divine power and glory.

GENERAL CHARACTERISTICS OF JOHN'S GOSPEL

John's Gospel is more elevated in tone and more exalted in view than the other Gospels. In each of the first three Gospels, Christ is viewed in human relationship with an earthly people, but in John we find spiritual relationships with a heavenly people.

In Matthew and Luke, "Son of David" and "Son of man" link Christ to the earth. In John, "Son of God" connects Him with the Father in heaven.

Luke takes care to guard our Lord's divine perfection in His humanity; John takes care to guard Jesus' divine perfection in His deity. In these days of widespread departure from the truth, the deity of Christ Jesus must be emphasized.

In John, Jesus is shown dwelling with God before any creature was formed (see John 1:1-2). He is distinguished as "the glory of the one and only" (John 1:14). "This is God's Chosen One" (John 1:34).

More than 20 times, Jesus speaks of God as "my Father." Twenty-five times He says, "Verily, verily" (*KJV*)—speaking with authority. Besides His own affirmation, six different witnesses attest to His deity.

JESUS' DEITY

In every chapter of the book of John, we see Jesus' deity:

- John 1—In his confession, Nathanael said, "You are the Son of God" (verse 49).

- John 2—In the miracle of Cana, "he revealed his glory" (verse 11).
- John 3—In His word to Nicodemus, He said that He was "his one and only Son" (the "only begotten Son," *KJV*) (verse 16).
- John 4—In His conversation with the woman of Samaria, He stated, "I, the one speaking to you—I am [the Messiah]" (verse 26).
- John 5—To the impotent man, He disclosed that "the voice of the Son of God" will call the dead to life (verse 25).
- John 6—He admitted, "I am the bread of life" (verse 35).
- John 7—He proclaimed, "Let anyone who is thirsty come to me and drink" (verse 37).
- John 8—To the unbelieving Jews, He disclosed, "Before Abraham was born, I am!" (verse 58).
- John 9—The blind man was told, "You have now seen [the Son of man]; in fact, he is the one speaking with you"—Jesus' unique claim to being the Son of God (verse 37).
- John 10—Jesus stated, "I and the Father are one" (verse 30).
- John 11—Martha declared, "You are the Messiah, the Son of God" (verse 27).
- John 12—To the Greeks, He said, "And I, when I am lifted up from the earth, will draw all people to myself" (verse 32).
- John 13—At the Last Supper, He said, "You call me 'Teacher' and 'Lord,' and rightly so, for that is what I am" (verse 13).
- John 14—He stated, "You believe in God; believe also in me" (verse 1).
- John 15—Likening us to branches on a vine, He said, "Apart from me you can do nothing" (verse 5).
- John 16—In promising the Holy Spirit, He said, "I will send him to you" (verse 7).
- John 17—He said, "Glorify your Son" (verse 1).
- John 18—During His trial, He stated, "You say that I am a king" (verse 37).

John

- John 19—In His atonement, He had the right to say, "It is finished" (verse 30).
- John 20—In his confession, Thomas the doubter exclaimed, "My Lord and my God!" (verse 28).
- John 21—In demanding obedience, He said, "You must follow me" (verse 22).

Seven Witnesses

John brings seven witnesses to the stand to prove that Jesus Christ was God. Turn to the Scriptures, and imagine each one making his or her own statement:

1. What do you say, John the Baptist? "This is God's Chosen One" (John 1:34).
2. What is your conclusion, Nathanael? "You are the Son of God" (John 1:49).
3. What do you know, Peter? "You are the Holy One of God" (John 6:69).
4. What do you think, Martha? "You are the Messiah, the Son of God" (John 11:27).
5. What is your verdict, Thomas? "My Lord and my God!" (John 20:28).
6. What is your statement, John? "Jesus is the Messiah, the Son of God" (John 20:31).
7. What do You say of Yourself, Christ? "I am God's Son" (John 10:36).

Seven Miracles

Besides the seven witnesses John calls on, he describes seven signs, or miracles, that prove Jesus was God. "For no one could perform the signs you are doing if God were not with him," were Nicodemus's words (John 3:2).

Look over these signs as they occur throughout the book:

1. Turning water into wine—John 2:1-11
2. Healing the nobleman's son—John 4:46-54

3. Healing the man at Bethesda—John 5:1-47
4. Feeding the five thousand—John 6:1-14
5. Walking on water—John 6:15-21
6. Healing the blind man—John 9:1-41
7. Raising Lazarus—John 11:1-57

Seven "I AM"s

There is yet another proof of Jesus' deity. Jesus reveals His God-nature in the "I am"s of this book:

1. "I am the bread of life"—John 6:35.
2. "I am the light of the world"—John 8:12.
3. "Before Abraham was born, I am"—John 8:58.
4. "I am the good shepherd"—John 10:11.
5. "I am the resurrection and the life"—John 11:25.
6. "I am the way and the truth and the life"—John 14:6.
7. "I am the true vine"—John 15:1.

John, only, records the triumphant shout, "It is finished" (John 19:30). The finished work of salvation is accomplished only by the Son of God.

JOHN 1:1-18: THE GREAT PROLOGUE

We open the book of John with this question in mind: "What do you think of Christ?" (see Matthew 22:42). Was He only the world's greatest teacher, or is He actually God? Was He one of the prophets, or is He the world's Savior whose coming was foretold by the prophets?

All of this prologue deals with Christ before His incarnation. God did not send Christ into the world so that He would become His Son. Christ *is* the eternal Son. He is the eternal Word. Jesus is none other than the Jehovah of the Old Testament, God manifest in the flesh. In Luke we see Christ going down to meet people's needs; in John we see Him drawing people up to Himself (see John 12:32).

John

All that John plans to discuss in his book is crowded into the first 18 verses. Let us study this Gospel with John's purpose clearly in mind, so read John 20:31 again. Let us see how the plan is developed and how the purpose is shown as we read the book.

The Son of God

Comparing the first verses of John with the beginning of the other three Gospels, we see how differently it opens, how exalted is its theme. Read John 1:1-18 carefully.

John does not open with the birth of Jesus (which connotes the Son of man) but before all worlds were formed. John begins, "In the beginning was the Word" (John 1:1). It opens like the book of Genesis opens! Jesus is portrayed as the Son of God before He became flesh and dwelled among us.

Our Lord had no beginning. He was in the beginning. He is eternal. Christ was before all things; therefore, Jesus is no part of creation—He *is* the Creator (see Colossians 1:16; Hebrews 1:2).

"The Word was with God" (John 1:1). Jesus is the Second Person of the Triune God (God the Father, God the Son, God the Holy Spirit). He is called "The Word." He came to declare God, to tell about God. As words give voice to thoughts, so Christ gives substance to God. Words reveal the heart and mind, so Christ expresses, manifests and shows God. Jesus said to Philip, "If you really know me, you will know my Father as well" (John 14:7).

Then comes the wonderful announcement that "through him all things were made; without him nothing was made that has been made. In him was life, and that life was the light of all mankind" (John 1:3-4). Yes, "The Word became flesh and made his dwelling among us" (John 1:14). The full claims of Christ are given here: truly God, light of life, declarer of God the Father, baptizer with the Holy Spirit.

Remember, John is writing to prove that Jesus is the Son of God.

The Son of Man

John's prologue points out the incarnation of Christ. Christ became what He was not previously—a man. But Christ did not cease to be God. He was God-Man. He lived in a tabernacle of flesh here in this world for 33 years. "Incarnation" comes from two Latin words, *in caro,* meaning "flesh." So Christ was God in the flesh.

People had sinned and no longer reflected the image of God, so Christ—"the image of the invisible God" (Colossians 1:15)—came to dwell with people. No person could see God; therefore, the only begotten Son who was "in the bosom of the Father" (John 1:18, *KJV*) came to literally embody Him for us.

Even the witness of John the Baptist is different in John's Gospel. According to Matthew, John the Baptist told of the coming Kingdom. According to Luke, he preached repentance. According to John, he was a witness to the light so that all people might believe (see John 1:7). John the Baptist pointed to "the Lamb of God" (John 1:36).

Jesus is God Himself in human form on earth. Jesus is the witness of the Father to humans. Jesus knows the Father. He lived with Him from the beginning. He came down to tell us what He knows. He wanted humans to know the Father as well as He knows Him.

And the way Jesus told us about God was through His words, His deeds, His character, His love and, most important of all, His dying on the cross and His rising on the third day. All this was an embodying, a witnessing, a telling.

How was Christ the Word received? Read John 1:11: "He came to that which was his own, but his own did not receive him." He presented Himself as Messiah and King to His people, but He was rejected. All through John's book, we see Jesus dividing the crowds. As He comes out and speaks the truth, the crowds listen. Some believe Him, and John presents the results of faith. Some in the crowd, however, reject what He has to say—tragedy indeed!

The Way of Salvation

John reveals to us the following about salvation:

- What must we do to receive salvation? Believe and receive.
- What will be the result? You will become a child of God (see John 1:12).
- What are you not to count on for salvation? Yourself.

John

Sometimes the way to better understand what something is, is to find out what it is not. In John 1:13, John tells us what salvation is not: being born "of natural descent . . . of human decision or a husband's will." All of these things are what too many people are counting on today for eternal life. It is our "new birth" that makes us "children of God" (John 1:12). In verse 13, John makes four points about God's children:

1. "Not of natural descent"—heredity; how much we depend on good birth! But not where salvation is concerned!
2. "Nor of human decision"—culture and education; it is not what we know but whom we believe that saves us.
3. "Nor of the will of man" (*KJV*)—prestige or influence; it is not by human determination that we are saved.
4. "But born of God"—by the power of the Holy Spirit of God; God comes down and redeems us, if we will only believe and receive Him as Savior and Lord.

JOHN 1:19-12: PUBLIC MINISTRY

When John the Baptist appears on the scene, the great drama of John's Gospel begins. "Among those born of women there has not risen anyone greater than John the Baptist," Jesus declared (Matthew 11:11; see also Luke 7:28). John was the forerunner of the Messiah. In this Gospel, John the Baptist is not described. He merely testifies that Jesus is the Messiah (see John 1:18-34).

A delegation of priests and Levites were sent to ask John who he claimed to be. He told them that he was not the Messiah, and he was not Elijah or any other prophet Moses spoke of; he was merely "the voice of one calling in the wilderness, 'Make straight the way for the Lord'" (John 1:23).

The next day, when he sees Jesus, John points to Him and says, "Look, the Lamb of God" (John 1:29).

Then John the Baptist indicates that he knew Jesus was the Messiah because he saw "the Spirit come down from heaven as a dove and remain on him" (John 1:32). So John adds, "I have seen and I testify that this is God's Chosen One" (John 1:34).

Jesus' Signs

Jesus' disciples were convinced of His deity by His first miracle: turning water into wine. He spoke, and it was so. This was one of the big factors that caused the disciples to have faith and believe in Jesus. This miraculous act was the first sign to prove that He was the Messiah (see John 2:11).

The next sign that Jesus gave occurred when He cleared the Temple. There was only one place where Jesus could start His ministry—in Jerusalem, the capital city. Just before the Passover, the Lord entered the Temple, and using a whip as a badge of His authority, He cleared the sanctuary, which He declared was His "Father's house" (John 2:16). By this act, He claimed to be the true Son of God.

After Jesus cleared the Temple and drove out the moneychangers, the rulers asked Jesus for a sign to prove His authority. Jesus answered, "Destroy this temple, and I will raise it again in three days" (John 2:19). The rulers were shocked, for it had taken 46 years to build the Temple. "But the temple he had spoken of was his body," John explains (John 2:21). The supreme proof of Christ's deity is the resurrection.

Jesus gave to Nicodemus the wonderful teachings about eternal life and His love (see John 3:16) and the new birth (see John 3:6). Nicodemus was a moral, upright man, yet Christ said to him, "You must be born again" (John 3:7). If Jesus had said this to the Samaritan woman, Nicodemus would have agreed with Him. She was not a Jew and could not expect anything on the grounds that she had been born a Samaritan. But Nicodemus was a Jew by birth, and he had a right to expect something on this basis alone. But it was to him Jesus said, "You must be born again" in order to enter the kingdom of heaven. (Have you been born again?)

Like the Jewish people of his day, Nicodemus knew God's law but nothing of God's love. He recognized Jesus as a teacher, but he did not know Him as the Savior. This is what too many people in the world do today. They put Jesus at the head of the list of the teachers of the world but do not worship Him as the one true God.

Jesus revealed to one woman the truth of His Messiahship. Jesus brought an immoral woman face to face with Himself and showed her what kind of life she was leading. Christ did not condemn her or pass judgment upon her, but He did reveal to her that He is the only One who could meet her needs. Christ revealed the wonderful truth to her that He is the water of life. He alone can satisfy. The wells of the world cannot provide satisfaction.

This woman's loose view of marriage is not unlike the view of marriage held by many people today. People try every kind of well—money, power, clothes, food, possessions, drugs—but they still are unhappy and unsatisfied.

Did the woman believe Christ? What did she do? Her actions spoke louder than any words could have. She went back to town, and by her simple testimony brought a whole town to Christ (see John 4:1-42). This story gives us Christ's estimate of a single soul.

By healing the son of a nobleman, Jesus gives another sign of His deity. During His interview with the centurion, Jesus brought him to an open confession of Christ as Lord—yes, and his whole household joined with him (see John 4:46-54).

The miracle of feeding five thousand was a parable in action rather than in words. Jesus Himself is the bread from heaven. He wanted to tell them that to all who put their trust in Him, He will give satisfaction and joy (see John 6:35).

The people wanted to make Christ their King because He could feed them. How like people today! They long for someone who can give them food and clothing. But Christ would not be King on their terms. He dismissed the excited multitude and went to a mountain. The people were disappointed that He would not be a political leader, so they "turned back and no longer followed him" (John 6:66).

The people were divided because of Jesus (see John 7:40-44). Unbelief was developing into actual hostility, but in His true followers, faith was growing. Some people said, "He is a good man." Others said, "Not so." We must say one or the other today as well. Either He is God or an impostor. There is no middle ground.

The healing of the blind man led Jesus to reveal to this fellow who He was. When "they threw him out" because of his confession of Christ (John 9:34), Jesus gave a great discourse on the Good Shepherd (see John 10). Read John 10:19-21 to learn the results produced by His words. Notice the accusations of blasphemy they made against Christ when He said, "I and the Father are one" (John 10:30). "Again his Jewish opponents picked up stones to stone him" (John 10:31). What happened in the face of all this criticism and opposition? Read John 10:42.

The raising of Lazarus is the final sign in John's Gospel. The other Gospel authors tell about the raising of Jairus's daughter and the son of the widow of Nain. But John tells about Lazarus, a man who had been dead four days. In reality, would it be any harder for God to raise one than the other? Nevertheless, it had a profound effect on the leaders (see John 11:47-48). The great claim Jesus made for Himself to Martha is recorded here: "I am the resurrection and the life. He who believes in me will live, even though they die; and whoever lives by believing in me will never die. Do you believe this?" (John 11:25-26).

This scene closes with Jesus' triumphant entry into Jerusalem. His public ministry had come to an end. It is recorded that many of the chief Jewish leaders believed in Him but did not make a public confession of faith.

Jesus' Startling Claims

Jesus claims to be equal with God. Jesus calls God "my Father" (John 5:17). The Jews knew what He meant. He made Himself equal with God, they said. They knew that He claimed God as His Father in a way that meant that He is not the Father of any other person.

Jesus claims to be the light of the world. Jesus said, "I am the light of the world. Whoever follows me will never walk in darkness, but will have the light of life" (John 8:12).

Jesus claims to be eternal with God. Jesus said, "Very truly I tell you . . . before Abraham was born, I am!" (John 8:58). This claim of eternity with God was unmistakable. He was either the Son of

God or a deceiver. Indeed, He uses the "I AM" of God's personal name, equating Himself with the Father (Exodus 3:14). No wonder the Jews "picked up stones to stone him" (John 8:59).

JOHN 13–17: PRIVATE MINISTRY

With the beginning of John 13, we leave the multitude behind and follow Jesus as He lived the last week of His life on earth before His crucifixion. We call it Passion Week:

Sunday—the triumphant entry into Jerusalem
Monday—the cleansing of the Temple
Tuesday—the conflicts in the Temple
Evening—the discourse on the Mount of Olives
Thursday—preparation for the Passover
Evening—the Last Supper with His disciples

Last words are always important. Jesus is leaving His disciples and is giving them His last instructions. These chapters, John 13–17, are called the holy of holies of the Scriptures. Prayerfully read them all at one sitting.

Christ's Last Meal with the Disciples

Jesus divided the Jewish people—some believed Him, others rejected Him completely. Now before He left them, He gathered His own around Him in the Upper Room and told them many secrets. He wanted to comfort His disciples, for He knew how hard it would be for them when He was gone. They would be sheep without a shepherd.

It is wonderful that Jesus selected and loved men like these. With the exception of Peter and John, they were all "nobodies." But they were "His own," and He loved them (John 13:1). One of Jesus' specialties is to make "somebodies" out of "nobodies." This is what He did with His first group of followers, and this is what He has continued to do through the centuries.

John

What a picture we have in John 13:1-11! Jesus, the Son of God, has a towel around His waist, has a basin of water in His blessed hands and is washing His disciples' feet! He wants us to serve others in the same spirit. He taught us that greatness is always measured by service. There is no loving others without living for others (see verses 16-17). Christ said, "The greatest among you will be your servant" (Matthew 23:11).

Jesus foretells His betrayal by Judas (see John 13:18-30), and Judas goes out into the night. It was night in Judas's heart, too. Fellowship brings light. Sin brings darkness. What a pitiable picture Judas is! He had such a wonderful opportunity to get to know Jesus, but he rejected the Lord. This is what unbelief can do. Belief means light and life, while unbelief means darkness and death.

After announcing that He will be leaving, the Lord gives His disciples a new commandment: "A new command I give you: Love one another. As I have loved you, so you must love one another. By this everyone will know that you are my disciples, if you love one another" (John 13:34-35). Discipleship is tested not by the creed you recite, not by the hymns you sing, not by the rituals you observe, but by the fact that you love one another. The degree to which Christians love one another is the degree to which the world believes them and believes in their Christ. It is the final test of discipleship. Jesus mentions this new commandment again in John 15:12.

Christ's Promise of a Comforter

"I am going there to prepare. . . . I will come back and take you to be with me" (John 14:2-3). This is Jesus' cure for heart troubles—faith in God. How many hearts have been put to rest and how many eyes have been dried by these words in John 14!

Jesus had spoken of His Father, but now He speaks of the other person of the Godhead, the Holy Spirit. If He (Christ) is to go away, He will send the Comforter, and He will stay with them. This is a wonderful promise for the child of God! Jesus repeats the promise in chapter 15 and again in 16. Look up John 15:26; 16:13-15. Few know of this presence in their lives, but it is by His power that we live. Never call the Holy Spirit "it." He is a person. He is one of three persons in the Triune God (the Trinity).

Let us look at the teaching about the Holy Spirit as given to us by John:

1. The incoming Spirit (John 3:5)—This is the beginning of the Christian life, the new birth by the Spirit. We are born by the Spirit into the family of God.

2. The indwelling Spirit (John 4:14)—The Holy Spirit fills us with His presence and brings us joy.

3. The overflowing Spirit (John 7:38-39)—"Rivers of living water will flow from within him." Not just little streams of blessing will flow but rivers—Mississippis and Amazons—if the Holy Spirit dwells within us.

4. The witnessing Spirit (John 14–16)—The Holy Spirit speaks through us. Testifying about Christ is a necessity that every Christian fulfills through the Holy Spirit.

"Peace I leave with you; my peace I give you" (John 14:27). This is Christ's legacy to us. The only peace we can enjoy in this world is His peace.

The Secret of Remaining

Jesus reveals the real secret of the Christian life to His disciples in John 15: "Remain in [Christ]" (John 15:4-10; "abide," *KJV*). He is the source of life. Remain in Christ as the branch remains in the vine. In order to bear fruit, the branch cannot sever itself from the vine and then reconnect itself at will to the trunk. It must remain in the vine if it wants to bear fruit. This is the picture of our lives in Christ. Live and walk in Christ and you will bear fruit. If you do not remain in Christ, the fruit will soon disappear.

After He ended His talk with the 11 disciples, Jesus spoke to the Father. The disciples listened to His loving and solemn words. How thrilled they must have been as He told the Father how much He loved them and how He cared for them! He mentioned everything about Himself that He had taught them. He would keep them (see John 17:11); He would sanctify them (see John 17:17); He would make them one (see John 17:21); and finally, He would let all His children share in His glory someday (see John 17:24).

If you truly want to experience the beauty and depth of these wonderful words, kneel and let the Son of God lead you in prayer as you read aloud this seventeenth chapter of John.

JOHN 18–19: SUFFERING AND DEATH

Immediately following His prayer, Jesus went to the Garden of Gethsemane, knowing full well what would happen to Him. The change from the scene in the Upper Room to the scene in the olive grove is like going from warmth to cold, from light to darkness. Only two hours had passed since Judas left the supper table. Now we see him betraying his best friend. Remember, Judas was not forced to betray his Lord—he personally chose to betray Christ, and this treacherous act fulfilled prophecy. God did not cause Judas to sin, but Judas's betrayal was prophesied because it was going to happen. No one has ever *had* to sin to carry out any of God's plan.

The final hours had come! The mission of our Lord on earth was ending. Only the greatest work of Christ remained to be done—His supreme, crowning act of His life on earth. It was not a crisis but a climax. He was to die so that He would glorify the Father and save the sinful world. He came to earth to "give his life as a ransom for many" (Matthew 20:28; Mark 10:45). Christ came into the world by the manger and left it by the door of the cross.

Jesus was now ready to give the Jews the real sign of His authority in answer to the question they had asked in chapter 2: "'What sign can you show us to prove your authority to do all this?' Jesus answered them, 'Destroy this temple, and I will raise it again in three days'" (John 2:18-19).

We see Jesus, still poised, still gentle. He knew His hour had come. He was not surprised when He heard the soldiers approach.

He stepped forward to meet them. The men retreated and fell before the majesty of His look.

A Willing Captive

Follow Him, bound as a captive, to the hall of the high priest. Jesus was the One in command of the situation all through this terrible drama. He went of His own accord, a voluntary sacrifice (see John 18:4). He deliberately tasted death for every person.

Almost as pathetic as Judas was Peter, the deserter in the hour of need, denying three times that he had any connection with his best friend! This is a lesson for us in overconfidence. Poor Peter is to be pitied, for he really loved the Master.

Peter did not know that the supreme trial of his life would come in the form of a question from a servant girl. This is often the case. We lock and bolt the main door, but the thief breaks in through a tiny window that we had not even thought of. We would die at the stake but deny Christ in our speech.

All the disciples but John deserted Jesus in the hour of His greatest need. (Peter denied Jesus, but he stayed close by.) Among those fleeing is James of the inner circle, Nathanael the guileless, and Andrew the personal worker. Yet, here they were, running as fast as they could down the road together, away from their friend. A sorry sight! But wait! Don't start blaming them. Look to see where you are. Are you following Jesus closely? Remember, the majority is not always right. Be sure you are right! Can Christ count on you?

The brief interval between Peter's denial and Jesus' climbing the hill to Golgotha was crowded with incidents. The night trial before Caiaphas and the Sanhedrin (a court of 70 religious rulers) probably preceded the last denial of Peter. Then came the awful scourging by the Romans, which was often so severe that prisoners died under the torturing blows. The crown of thorns that was thrust upon Jesus' holy brow was only another act of cruel torture. When He comes again, He will wear "many crowns" (Revelation 19:12).

Finally, Pilate led Him forth and said, "Here is the man!" (John 19:5). What a sight! To see the Creator of this universe, the light and life of the world, the holy One treated so! But Satan energized the religious rulers, and they cried, "Crucify! Crucify! . . . He claimed to be the Son of God" (John 19:6-7).

The Blackest Hour

Finally the make-believe trials are over. It is morning, yet it seems like night. It is the world's blackest hour. The courtyard is deserted. The fire at which Peter warmed himself is only gray ashes. The soldiers' jeers, Herod's sneers and Pilate's vacillation are over. At the cross, we have hate at its worst and love at its best. People so hated Christ that they put Him to death. God so loved the world that He gave people life.

Our religion is one of four letters instead of two. Other religions say "Do." Our religion says "Done." Our Savior has done all on the cross. He took on our sins; and when He gave up His life, He said, "It is finished" (John 19:30). This was the shout of a conqueror. He had finished humanity's redemption. Nothing was left for people to do. Has the work been done in your heart?

Jesus was crucified on Golgotha, "the place of the Skull" (John 19:17). He is crucified there today—in people's minds. They crucify Him afresh and put Him to an open shame. "Christ died for our sins" (1 Corinthians 15:3). Salvation is costly—it cost Jesus His life.

JOHN 20–21: VICTORY OVER DEATH

We have a Savior who is victorious over death. He "always lives" (Hebrews 7:25).

On the third day, the tomb was empty! The grave clothes were all in order. Jesus had risen from the dead but not as others had done. When Lazarus rose from the dead, he was still wrapped in his grave clothes. Jesus, however, came out in his natural body—he was not "a ghost" (Luke 24:39)—but His natural body had been changed into a spiritual body. The changed body came right out of its linen wrappings and left them behind in the same way that a butterfly leaves behind its chrysalis, or shell. Read what John says in 20:6-8.

Jesus' appearances, 11 in all after His resurrection, helped His disciples to believe that He was God. Read John 20:28, the

John

confession of the sixth witness, Thomas the doubter. Jesus wanted every doubt to be removed from each one of His disciples, because they must carry out His Great Commission to carry the gospel to all the world (see John 20:21).

Jesus gave the disciple who three times had denied Him, Peter, three opportunities to confess Him (see John 21:15-19). He restored Peter to full privileges of service again. Christ only wants those who love Him to serve Him. And if you love Him, you must serve Him. No one who loves Christ can help but serve.

What are Jesus' last words in this Gospel? "You must follow me" (John 21:22). This is His word to each one of us. May we all follow Him in loving obedience "until he comes" (1 Corinthians 11:26; see also Matthew 26:29).

A. J. Gordon, founder of Gordon College, once aptly summed up the Gospel of John in one sentence: "This Gospel opens with Christ in the bosom of the Father, and closes with John in the bosom of Christ."

WAYS TO REMEMBER THE BOOK OF JOHN

There are various ways of remembering the contents of the book of John. We will list only two here.

Use the Human Element

One way to remember the contents of John's Gospel is to memorize humanity's opinion of the Son of God:

- What individuals thought about Christ—John 1-5
- What Christ said about Himself—John 6-10
- What crowds thought of Christ—John 11-20

Use the Three Keys

Dr. S. D. Gordon, an American author, once suggested that three keys be used to unlock John's Gospel. *The back door key is John 20:31.* This key unlocks the whole book. It states the purpose of the Gospel.

The side door key is John 16:28. At the Last Supper with His disciples, Jesus reveals this truth to them: "I came from the Father and entered the world; now I am leaving the world and going back to the Father." He constantly thought that He used to be with the Father. He came down to earth on an errand and stayed for 33 years. He would go back again to His Father.

The front door key is John 1:12. This key hangs right at the very front, outside, low down, within every child's reach: "Yet to all who did receive him, to those who believed in his name, he gave the right to become children of God." This is the great key—the chief key to the whole house. Its use permits the front door to be flung wide open. Anyone who believes may enter.

John

History

of the New Testament

ACTS

Key Events of Acts

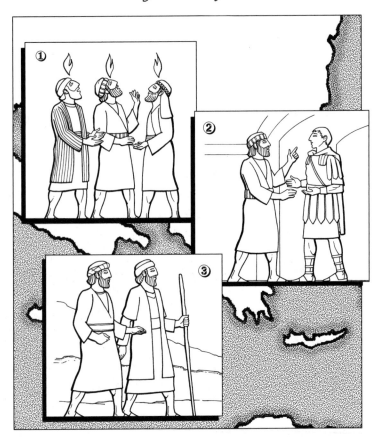

History: The Holy Spirit and the Beginning of the Church

The Holy Spirit comes with power ① at Pentecost, just as Jesus promised. Soon thousands of Jewish people believed that Jesus was in fact the Messiah, the "coming One" God had promised through the Law and prophets. After a few years of growth, the Jewish church decided that Gentiles ② can be full participants in salvation without having to submit to the Mosaic laws. This momentous decision enabled thousands of Gentiles from around the Mediterranean to freely come to Christ, thanks to missionary bands led by people such as Paul the apostle and Barnabas ③ .

31

Understanding Acts

Acts Portrays Jesus Christ, the Living Lord

 SELECTED BIBLE READINGS

DAY OF THE WEEK		MAIN TOPIC
Sunday: Acts 1–4	First Church in Jerusalem	
Monday: Acts 5–8:3	Witnessing in Jerusalem	
Tuesday: Acts 8:4–12	Witnessing in Judea and Samaria	
Wednesday: Acts 13–15:35	Establishment of Churches (First Tour)	
Thursday: Acts 15:36–18:21	Revisiting of the Churches (Second Tour)	
Friday: Acts 18:22–25:9	Encouragement of the Churches (Third Tour)	
Saturday: Acts 25:10–28	Going to Rome	

AUTHOR: The book of Acts does not specifically identify its author. From Luke 1:1-4 and Acts 1:1-3, it is clear that the same author wrote both Luke and Acts. The tradition from the earliest days of the Church has been that Luke, a companion of the apostle Paul, wrote both Luke and Acts (see Colossians 4:14; 2 Timothy 4:11).

DATE: The book was likely written in 63 AD or later.

PURPOSE AND SUMMARY: Addressed to a certain Theophilus, about whom nothing is known, the book of Acts records the early history of the Early Church (see Acts 1:1). Beginning with the Ascension of Jesus to heaven, Acts traces the explosive growth of messianic Jewish Christianity in Jerusalem and the land of Israel—with healing signs and wonders confirming the preaching of the gospel—and then its spread also to non-Jews (Gentiles) in Judea, Samaria, Syria, Asia Minor, Macedonia, Greece and, eventually, Rome. The leading figure in the first chapters is the apostle Peter, who delivered the anointed message on the day of Pentecost, explaining the powerful move of God's Spirit on the original 120 messianic Jewish believers (see Acts 2). The greater part of the book, however, is devoted to the experiences of the apostle Paul and his companions during their missionary journeys. The book of Acts provides a useful background for study of the letters in the remainder of the New Testament.

THE GOSPELS AND ACTS

- The Gospels set forth the Son of Man, who came to die for our sins—Acts shows the coming of the Son of God in the power of the Holy Spirit.
- The Gospels set forth what Christ began to do—Acts shows what He continued to do by the Holy Spirit, through His disciples.
- The Gospels tell of the crucified and risen Savior—Acts portrays Him as the ascended and exalted Lord and leader.
- In the Gospels we hear Christ's teachings—in Acts we see the effect of His teachings on the acts of the apostles.

Acts is not a record of the acts of the apostles, as no extensive accounts are given of any apostles except Peter and Paul. Instead, Acts records the acts of the Holy Spirit through the apostles. His name is mentioned more than 40 times. Look for some work of the Holy Spirit in every chapter of this book.

The word "witness" (in one form or another) is also used a great many times. "You will be my witnesses" (Acts 1:8) is the heart of the book of Acts. Salvation comes to this world through Christ alone (see Acts 4:12); therefore, people must know Him.

Christ's plan includes us. Christ told His disciples that He would send the Spirit, and "he will testify about me. And you also must testify, for you have been with me from the beginning" (John 15:26-27). Are you witnessing for Christ? If not, why not? It is true that Christ alone can save the world, but Christ cannot save this world alone. If you are not witnessing for Christ, look into your heart, "for the mouth speaks what the heart is full of" (Matthew 12:34).

Christ's promise to send the Spirit was fulfilled on the Day of Pentecost when He poured the Holy Spirit on the disciples (see Acts 2:16-17,33). From that moment on, as they testified about the Savior, the Holy Spirit testified at the same time in the hearts of their listeners; and multitudes began to believe in the Lord.

It is a wonderful thing to know that when the Spirit prompts you to speak to someone about Christ, He has been working in that person's heart and making it ready to receive your witness, or testimony. There is a perfect example of this in Acts 8 where Philip was sent to speak to the Ethiopian.

In Acts, we follow as the first church pursued a definite program in carrying out its missions plan. They chose for their base a great center of population from which they could go out to work and spread their message throughout the surrounding area. In each widening circle of influence, we find a marked outpouring of the Holy Spirit. Isn't it amazing that in one generation, the apostles had moved out in every direction and had preached in every nation of the then-known world (see Colossians 1:23)?

The infant Church was slow to realize the extent of their commission. At first, they confined their preaching to Jerusalem, the metropolis of the Jewish nation, until persecution drove them out. The blood of Stephen, the first Christian martyr, proved to be the seed of the growing Church. The book closes with the gospel in Rome, the true metropolis of world power.

In Acts 1–12, we find Peter witnessing primarily to the Jews. He said, "Repent" (Acts 2:38; see also verses 36-37). Why? Because they needed a definite change of mind about the Messiah.

In Acts 13–28, we find Paul witnessing primarily to the Gentiles. He said, "Believe" (Acts 16:31; see also verse 30). Why?

Acts

Because the Gentiles needed not to change their minds concerning the Messiah; they needed to believe in Him.

All through the Old Testament, we find God dealing with the Jewish people. In the New Testament, we find Him working among all nations.

No doubt Acts is the best guidebook to missions that has ever been written. We find in it the motive for missions. The only aim of the early believers was to bring people the saving knowledge of Jesus Christ. Jesus was their one theme; and the Word of God, their one weapon.

We follow as the first church pursued a definite program in carrying out its missions plan. They chose for their base a great center of population from which they could go out to work and spread their message throughout the surrounding area.

The disciples were simple, straightforward and successful. They depended entirely upon the power of God, through His Spirit. They moved with a zeal that could not be extinguished and a courage that was unflinching.

ACTS 1–2: WITNESSING WITH POWER

What a wonderful 40 days after the resurrection of Jesus the disciples spent with the Lord before His ascension! How anxious they were to hear His last words of instruction! He "spoke about the kingdom of God" (Acts 1:3). It was then that Jesus "gave this command: 'Do not leave Jerusalem, but wait for the gift my Father promised, which you have heard me speak about'" (Acts 1:4).

The first 26 verses of the first chapter are introductory to the rest of the book. They tell about several important things:

- The Great Commission—Acts 1:6-8
- The Ascension—Acts 1:2,9,11
- The promise of Christ's return—Acts 1:10-11

The disciples still were not satisfied regarding the time when Christ would set up His kingdom on earth. They still expected a kingdom that would give them political independence and establish them in a place of leadership in the world (see Acts 1:6). What was Jesus' answer? He told them their power was not to be political but spiritual. Read Acts 1:7-8 to learn what He said.

After He spoke His last words to His disciples, "he was taken up . . . and a cloud hid him from their sight" (Acts 1:9). Think of so great an event told in such few words! The Father took His Son back to glory.

Christ's Second Coming

"This same Jesus . . . will come back in the same way you have seen him go into heaven" (Acts 1:11). What does "come back" really mean? Does it mean when we die? Does it mean He'll come to dwell in our hearts? No. The promise is that He will come "in the same way." Since this is how He will come, we should examine how He went. Then we will know how He will come back. The Scriptures describe four characteristics that this Second Coming will have:

1.   Personal (see 1 Thessalonians 4:16)
2.   Visible (see Revelation 1:7)
3.   Bodily (see Matthew 24:30)
4.   Local (see Luke 24:50)

Picture the disciples as they returned from the Mount of Olives to Jerusalem. They went into an upper room (see Acts 1:13). It might have been the very same room where Jesus had eaten the Last Supper with them (see Luke 22:12). They "all joined together constantly in prayer" for 10 days (Acts 1:14). Jesus had told them to stay in Jerusalem until they should receive "power from on high" (Luke 24:49). Even though they had spent three years training with the Lord, they still needed the presence of the Holy Spirit, whom Jesus said He would send to empower them. They had proved themselves to be a weak group.

It would have been natural for them to flee from Jerusalem, the place where their Lord had been crucified, and to go back to

Galilee. But Christ had said to "stay in the city," because it was to become the center from which they would spread their message. We cannot always choose our place of service.

Pentecost

Next in importance to the coming of the Lord Jesus Christ to this earth is the coming of the Holy Spirit. The Church was born on the Day of Pentecost. Become familiar with the account given in Acts 2:1-13. Pentecost (also known as the Feast of Weeks, or the Feast of Harvest) was one of the most popular of the Jewish feasts, and Jerusalem would be crowded with pilgrims from everywhere. It was 50 days after the Crucifixion. This Pentecost was to be not just a Jewish feast but also the dawn of a new day, the birthday of the Church of Christ. At the ascension of Christ, our Lord went out of sight, but He stayed with the people in a far more real way.

The scene opens with the disciples assembled together, with their hearts fixed on Christ, waiting for His promise to be fulfilled. The Holy Spirit Himself descended that day. Luke does not say there was an actual "violent wind," but the sound of the wind was a symbol, as were the "tongues of fire" (Acts 2:2-3). The wind (see Acts 2:2) represented heavenly power. The fiery flames represented the power to witness. Fire was a symbol of God's presence. It not only brightens, but it also purifies. The Spirit came in to them and on them (see Acts 2:1-3). The Spirit "filled" them (Acts 2:4). The Spirit worked through them (see Acts 2:41-47). Read Acts 2:6,12 to learn what happened after they were filled with the Spirit.

Being filled with the Holy Spirit made the disciples able to perform special service. They not only were enabled to preach in power, but they also could speak in the different languages represented by the different people in Jerusalem that day (see Acts 2:2-4). Were those present able to understand and benefit? Read Acts 2:6.

The wonderful thing about Pentecost was not the "violent wind" or the "tongues of fire"; the wonderful thing was the disciples being filled with the Holy Spirit so that they could be wit-

Acts

nesses to all people. If we do not have the desire to tell others about Christ, it is evident that we do not know the fullness of the Holy Spirit.

Do not think that at this Pentecost the Holy Spirit came for the first time to the world. All through the Old Testament we see an account of how He had been guiding people and giving them strength. It's just that now the Spirit was to use a new instrument, the Church, which was born on that very day.

All the people were "amazed and perplexed" by what had happened (Acts 2:12). People by nature are unbelieving. Isn't it a great demonstration of God's grace when people come to truly believe God and really accept His word?

Some people made fun of what had happened: "They have had too much wine" (Acts 2:13). People always try to explain away the miracles of God on natural grounds. But rationalism can never give a reasonable explanation for anything that is divine. Also it was only nine in the morning, and no Jew could touch wine that early. Read Acts 2:14-21 to learn what Peter's defense was against this false charge.

Peter's Sermon

The real power of the Holy Spirit was shown when Peter, the humble fisherman, rose to speak and three thousand souls were saved! The theme of the first sermon in Acts was that Jesus is the Messiah, as shown by His resurrection. How can we account for cowardly Peter's boldness as he stood that day to preach before a multitude on the streets of Jerusalem? What was the secret of Peter's ministry?

It is a serious thing to charge men with murder, yet Peter did exactly that (see Acts 2:36). Will he get away with it? Will he be stoned? The last verses in chapter 2 answer the question (see Acts 2:37-47).

What a Church was this First Church of Jerusalem, organized with a membership of three thousand on the Day of Pentecost! What glorious days followed in "teaching" and "fellowship," and "wonders and signs," and, above all, salvation (Acts 2:42-43)!

Acts

"And the Lord added to their number daily those who were being saved" (Acts 2:47). This is the real objective of the Church—to increase the number of those saved. Are we seeing this today in our churches?

Just as marvelous as the gift of the Holy Spirit was the daily life of this first church. It is not surprising that they found "favor of all the people" and that additions were made "daily" (Acts 2:47).

These first Christians were "regular" Christians:

- Regular in church going—"All the believers were together" (Acts 2:44)
- Regular in church giving—Acts 2:44-45
- Regular in church missions—Acts 2:46-47

ACTS 3–8:3: WITNESSING IN JERUSALEM

Chapter 3 opens at the Beautiful Gate of the Temple. Peter healed a cripple considered incurable, a man who was lame from birth and who had been carried daily to this place to beg for his living. The miracle attracted the notice of the Jewish leaders and resulted in the first real opposition to the Church.

When a great crowd had gathered around the lame man who had been so miraculously healed, Peter took advantage of the circumstances to preach his second recorded sermon. He did not spare his countrymen. Again he told them that Christ, whom they had crucified, had been the long-promised Messiah. So powerful were the words of Peter and John that day that a total of five thousand men turned to Christ!

The leaders were upset because the apostles taught the people that Jesus, whom they had crucified, had risen from the dead and would appear again (see Acts 4:2). They commanded the apostles not to preach, but opposition made the Church thrive. Opposition should never be a matter of amazement, not even a matter of surprise to any Christian. The work of the Spirit is always a signal for Satan to work. Whenever the Spirit comes to bless, the adversary comes to curse. But martyrdom is an aid to the Church, and whenever the truth is faithfully preached, people *will* believe (see Acts 4:3-4).

As soon as the rulers released Peter and John, they sought their friends, reported their experiences and united in prayer and praise. The Church must expect opposition, but in all circumstances, we can find courage and help from God. "The place where they were meeting was shaken. And they were all filled with the Holy Spirit and spoke the word of God boldly" (Acts 4:31).

We find that bold preaching brought unity in the Church. They were of one heart and of one soul (see Acts 4:32). They went out "to testify to the resurrection of the Lord Jesus" (Acts 4:33). Let *us* tell about it! Dying people need to hear it; the day demands it!

Sharing and Surrender

In Peter's time, people were not compelled to part with their personal possessions. It was not expected of them. If they brought what they had to the Early Church, it was a purely voluntary act. Sharing property was voluntary, not obligatory; individual, not general; it was confined to Jerusalem, temporary and limited to the believers.

The Church became so unselfish that many sold all they had and gave it to the apostles to distribute "to anyone who had need" (Acts 2:45). But this act of love and generosity was open to abuse and deception. Barnabas's generosity was a demonstration of the spirit of love. Ananias and Sapphira were a demonstration of deception in that they deceived themselves and the apostles as well. But the Holy Spirit revealed the truth about what they had done. Ananias and Sapphira wanted glory without paying the price. They wanted honor without honesty. They were punished with instant death, for while claiming to give all to God, they had kept back part (see Acts 5:4-5).

As Christians, we claim to give all to Christ. Complete surrender is the condition Jesus sets down for discipleship. "Give up everything" and "follow me" are His conditions (see Luke 14:27,33). Do we hold back anything from Christ? Are we hypocrites in our testimony?

Acts

The power in the apostles' story was in the fact that their lives fitted in with the life of their risen Christ. "You've got to show me" is the attitude of the world today. Those early Christians did show the world. Do you show by how you conduct your life that you are a Christian?

Signs and Wonders

When signs and wonders were worked among the people, the crowds came to see. When the Holy Spirit was among them, the people saw the power of God. The same is true today. When churches present Christ in His humanity and the Holy Spirit in His power, the people will come. Christ attracts everyone. Thousands of articles have been written about how to put people to work in the Church. There will be plenty of service in the Church when we yield to the Holy Spirit. The Spirit-filled Church will be a serving Church.

Miracles commonly result in converts. When the miracle of fiery flames appeared, the people thronged to the place (see Acts 2). When Peter healed the man at the Beautiful Gate, "all the people were astonished and came running to them in the place called Solomon's Colonnade" (Acts 3:11). When the miracle of judgment came upon Ananias and Sapphira, "more and more men and women believed in the Lord and were added to their number" (Acts 5:14). There are many such instances throughout the book of Acts. Look for them.

Opposition and Influence

"Then the high priest and all his associates . . . arrested the apostles and put them in the public jail" (Acts 5:17-18). Again we see that the wonderful work of the apostles aroused the opposition of the Sanhedrin. A few unlearned fishermen had risen up to teach, and multitudes were listening and following them; so the religious leaders were disturbed. Even though the apostles were beaten with rods and prohibited from preaching, we find them rejoicing because they had been considered important enough to attract the attention of the Sanhedrin and had been considered

Acts

worthy enough to be punished for Jesus' name! "Day after day, in the temple courts and from house to house, they never stopped teaching and proclaiming the good news that Jesus is the Messiah" (Acts 5:42). We find their boldest words in this statement: "We must obey God rather than human beings!" (Acts 5:29). Is this the conviction of your life?

Let us have the spirit of these apostles! Let us not be discouraged when our opponents outnumber us.

A meeting of the Church was called, and seven members were elected as deacons (see Acts 6:1-7). There were two offices in the Church now: One was to equitably distribute food and care for the needy; the other office was to preach and pray.

The first two deacons named were Stephen and Philip (see Acts 6:5). These two men were mighty in their influence over the Church, perhaps more than any besides Peter and Paul.

There was, however, opposition centered around Stephen. Read the experiences recorded in Acts 6–7. Stephen was just a layman, but like thousands of other laymen since his time, he "did great wonders" because he was "full of grace and power" (Acts 6:8). We have a record of only one day of his life—the last (see Acts 7). What an account it is! It is not the length of time we live that counts but how we live. Someone once said, "A Christian is always on duty." This means that every minute of our lives is important and under God's direction.

The leaders in the synagogue "could not stand up against the wisdom the Spirit gave [Steven] as he spoke" (Acts 6:10). Their anger flared into murderous hatred. Stephen was the first martyr of the Christian Church. Stephen's life and death had an incalculable effect upon the history of the world because of his influence on Saul of Tarsus. Who can tell who you may influence in *your* life?

ACTS 8:4–12: WITNESSING IN JUDEA AND SAMARIA

The disciples witnessed in Jerusalem, but Jesus had told them they must also go into Judea and Samaria.

If you were quite sure that you would lose your life by remaining in your own hometown but would be safe in some nearby village, do you think you would go to that village? This is the very problem that faced the members of the Early Church in Jerusalem: preach where they were and face death, or move away to safety. There were religious leaders in Jerusalem who thought they were doing God's will when they tried to wipe out the new sect by killing and imprisoning Jewish believers in Jesus, followers of the way (see Acts 9:2). Paul said, "I too was convinced that I ought to do all that was possible to oppose the name of Jesus of Nazareth" (Acts 26:9).

Paul really began his work of spreading the gospel then, but he did not know it. Read Acts 8:3. He was stamping out what he considered to be a heretical and dangerous group. Instead, he was spreading it. Try laughing when you see anyone opposing the gospel. Persecution almost always has spread the gospel like wind spreads fire. This has been true throughout the centuries since our Lord lived on the earth.

See what kind of a Church this Early Church was: "Those who had been scattered preached the word wherever they went" (Acts 8:4). This is the reason the gospel spread at first. What commission did the disciples have? "Go into all the world and preach the gospel to all creation" (Mark 16:15). How many did Jesus train for His work? Just 12, and one of them had betrayed Him.

Well, here were the Twelve again (see Acts 1:26), sitting down at Jerusalem and all the world needing the gospel. Saul's persecution, like the confusion of languages at the tower of Babel, scattered the Christians throughout the world. Fear had not caused them to flee, for every place we find them preaching the gospel.

Philip, the Evangelist

Philip (not the apostle), one of the seven who had been chosen as a deacon (see Acts 6:5), was an evangelist. He had settled in Samaria as a result of the persecution. Jesus had said, "You will be my witnesses . . . in . . . Samaria" (Acts 1:8). Philip preached Christ. Multitudes were following him as he continued his evangelistic campaign. But God called him to leave his successful work and "go south to the road—the desert road—that goes down from Jerusalem to Gaza" (Acts 8:26). Philip obeyed and left, and on the way he met an Ethiopian. "By chance" you say? When you are in the will of God, things do not just happen. No friend crosses your path by accident. No joy or sorrow comes into your life except by God's permission. Read this thrilling story!

This story raises a question concerning which achieves larger results—preaching to great numbers of people about the Lord or telling people one at a time. Some people think that winning just one person at a time to Christ would be a slow process, but listen to this!

In 1953, there were a little more than 230 million people in the United States; in 1997, there were about 260 million. Today there are more than 300 million. Suppose you were the only Christian among the 300 million today. You win one soul of the 300 million today. Then tomorrow, each of the two of you win for Christ one soul each. On the following day, each one of the four of you do the same; the next day the eight of you win one apiece. Here is a startling fact. If each of these Christians and the newly won Christians were to each day win one soul to Christ, how long would it take to win 300 million? Just a little over one month from the day the first one began! Wouldn't it be a good thing for you and your friends or your Sunday School class or your church to form a G. O. Club? Each club member Get One. This is Christ's method of soul winning.

Philip's Ethiopian convert no doubt preached the gospel in Africa. There is nothing to show that Africa previously had any knowledge of the Son of God. The gospel was on its way "to the ends of the earth" (Acts 1:8).

Saul/Paul

At Stephen's death, we have the first mention of Saul. Stephen's martyrdom seemed to have inflamed this persecutor of the Church. Saul was struggling with a conscience recently awakened. He knew he was in the wrong, but he would not give up. This is

Acts

why Jesus told him in his vision that "it is hard for you to kick against the goads" (Acts 26:14).

Saul made havoc of the Church! The more moral and intelligent a person is, the more harm that person can do when controlled by Satan.

The story of Saul's conversion is one of the most thrilling accounts in history. Become familiar with this great story. He was a man "breathing out murderous threats against the Lord's disciples" (Acts 9:1). Then we find him preaching "in the synagogues that Jesus is the Son of God" (Acts 9:20).

At every step of his three great missionary journeys, Paul told about Christ's will with unmistakable clarity. There is no doubt that Paul holds the most important place of any man in the New Testament. He was converted and made an apostle by Christ Himself. It was to him that Christ gave first-hand revelations of truth and to him Christ committed the doctrine of the Church. What people were Paul especially sent to reach? He was the apostle to the Gentiles, as Peter had been to the Jews.

Peter

What had Peter done since Pentecost? It is not only what a person believes but what the person does about it that counts. Christ had told Peter that he was to be a witness. Peter helped start the first church, worked miracles and baptized thousands. His work had been among the Jewish people.

We find Peter now in the house of Simon the tanner (see Acts 10:5-6). God was going to show Peter that the gospel was for the Gentiles as well as the Jews (see Acts 10:9-16). The high wall of religious difference between Jew and Gentile must be broken down. Peter was the man God used to start leveling it. Christ was building a Church, and He wanted both Jews and Gentiles to be the living stones that formed it (see Ephesians 2:20-22).

At Pentecost, Peter had used "the keys of the kingdom" (Matthew 16:19) that had been entrusted to him to open the door of the gospel to the Jews. While Paul was in Tarsus, Peter in the house of Cornelius put the key into the lock of the door that had barred the Gentiles, and he opened it. Read this account in Acts 10. Do you think that what God told Peter to do was easy? Read verses 14-16. What is the Church doing today in regard to people who are different, whether the difference is because of race, nationality, disability or financial circumstances?

ACTS 13–28: WITNESSING TO THE ENDS OF THE EARTH

The death of Stephen was only the beginning of great persecution of the believers in Jesus, most of whom were Jewish. How did they ever get to Antioch? Read Acts 11:19-21. Someone has called the Church in the early days "A Tale of Two Cities"—Jerusalem and Antioch.

Up through Acts 12, we have seen the beginning of the Church, with Peter as its leader, in Jerusalem. From Acts 13 through 28, we are going to see Paul and the Church at Antioch. Antioch is the new base of operations. All the wonderful missionary journeys of Paul started from here, not from Jerusalem. It became the new center of the Church for carrying out Jesus' commission.

The Jewish believers in Jesus who had been compelled to leave Jerusalem because of persecution were naturally thrown in with all the Gentiles. They could not help but talk about the subject that interested them the most. The power of the Lord appeared so strongly that a great crowd joined the Church (see Acts 11:21).

It was here in this church in Antioch that a new name was given to Christ's disciples: "Christians" (see Acts 11:26).

It is interesting to note here that the Church had lost track of Paul. They apparently didn't care what had become of him, but Barnabas looked him up (see Acts 11:25). He had kept track of him over the years. If it had not been for Barnabas, Paul might have remained in obscurity all his life! Think of what the world would have missed had Paul not been discovered! Many a person is waiting to be discovered for God.

Acts

Foreign Missions

We see Paul and Barnabas, the first foreign missionaries, starting westward from Antioch (see Acts 13:2-3). The greatest enterprise in the world is foreign missions, and this is the very start of this great movement. The whole idea began just the way it should, at a prayer meeting.

While Paul and Barnabas were preaching the gospel and suffering persecution and all kinds of hardships, many in Jerusalem were stirring up the most troublesome question the Church had ever faced: "Must a Gentile become a Jew, accepting Jewish laws and ceremonies, in order to be saved?" (see Acts 15:1). Paul and Barnabas had said nothing about the law of Moses. They had simply stated, "Believe in the Lord Jesus, and you will be saved" (Acts 16:31). The law doesn't save anyone.

Luke now joined the missionary party (see Acts 16:10). The first convert in Europe was not a famous scholar or some mighty ruler but a businesswoman—Lydia, a seller of purple cloth (see Acts 16:14-15).

In Philippi, we find Paul and Silas in prison. Why do we find men like these locked behind iron bars? Read Acts 16:16-24. The second Christian in Europe was very different from the first. Lydia was converted in a prayer meeting, but it took an earthquake to awaken the next convert—a jailer. The jailer's question is one of the most important questions in all the world (see Acts 16:30).

Paul's experiences in the greatest cities of his day are filled with interesting and important occurrences, such as his founding a church at Thessalonica (see Acts 17:4).

In Athens, Paul preached his immortal sermon on the hill of Ares, where the Greek council met. This is one of the great scenes in history. What effect did Paul's sermon have on his listeners? Read Acts 17:32.

Paul was not only giving a wonderful message to the Athenians when he preached that day, but he was also speaking to you and to me. Paul tells us that God is near. He seems so far away to some people that they do not even try to reach Him, yet God hears our faintest whisper if we speak to Him.

Acts

Paul left Athens and arrived at Corinth, very much discouraged. We do not know whether he was successful in starting a church in Athens; but in Corinth, one of the most wicked cities of the ancient world, he founded a church and remained there 18 months to establish the people in the faith (see Acts 18:8). Here Paul met Aquila and his wife, Priscilla, who afterward became his loyal friends.

After an absence of three or four years, Paul returned to Antioch by way of Ephesus. In Antioch he reported his entrance into Europe.

Do you realize that we Americans might have been pagans living in spiritual darkness and superstition were it not for the European travels of these early Christian missionaries? Wouldn't you think that Americans, above every people, ought to believe in missions? Think of what our condition might have been today if missionaries had not brought Christ to us.

Paul's Third Missionary Tour

Now we find Paul spending three years in one of the greatest cities of his day. Next to Rome, Ephesus was perhaps the world's largest and most cosmopolitan city. Multitudes of Jews and Gentiles of Asia heard the gospel preached. Ephesus was notorious for its luxury and licentiousness and for the worship of the goddess Artemis (Diana, to the Romans).

The years Paul spent here are so crowded with interesting details that it is hard to choose the most important. Enthusiastic converts who had been practicing "sorcery" burned their scrolls (Acts 19:19), and others probably threw their silver idols of Artemis into the fire (see Acts 19:23-27). There was a great bonfire in Ephesus. It almost seems as though we can see the flames burning to this day. It represented the burning of old lives. Paul has taught us that every idol must be torn down from its place in our hearts, and the Lord alone must occupy the throne. Is there anything in our lives that calls for a bonfire? Don't be afraid of bringing yourself face to face with your own inner self.

Acts

Such blessings as these could not last long without opposition. When we read on to the end of chapter 19, we will see the results of Paul's work. The silversmiths stirred up a riot, and the apostles were rescued from danger only by the help of the city officials.

As Paul traveled, he wrote his wonderful letters, which we read today with great profit and interest. From Ephesus, Paul sent his First Epistle to the Corinthians (see 1 Corinthians 16:8). During this third journey, Paul also wrote 2 Corinthians, Galatians and Romans.

Paul's Farewell

Paul's last missionary journey must have been a heartbreaking experience. He had to say farewell at every stop. He knew it was a final farewell. Read Acts 20:37-38. All the elders of the church wept and "embraced him and kissed him," a universal expression of sorrow, knowing they would never see him again (Acts 20:37). Think of this sad experience repeated a dozen times over. Probably no man, except David, has ever inspired such intense personal love in so many hearts.

Sailing out of the harbor of Ephesus, Paul bids his friends a last farewell. He is headed for Jerusalem, and from now on he is seen as "a prisoner for the Lord" (Ephesians 4:1). Paul makes his last visit to Jerusalem, and here a swiftly formed mob rushes against the apostle and binds him, declaring that he is teaching the Jewish people to ignore Moses. No doubt he recalls the fact that outside that city he himself, 26 years before, had assisted in the murder of Stephen. After learning that Paul is a Roman citizen, the commander promises to arrange a fair trial. Paul makes his defense before the Roman governor Felix at Caesarea. After two years' imprisonment, Paul is tried a second time before the new governor, Festus, and then Paul appeals to Caesar, the emperor, himself (see Acts 21:27–26).

After a most exciting voyage, in which his ship was wrecked in a terrific storm off the coast of Malta, Paul arrived in Rome. Here he was kept a prisoner in his own hired house for two years.

Even as a prisoner, the great preacher and evangelist led to Christ the servants in Nero's own palace (see Acts 27–28:24). Service for the Master can brighten life's darkest hours. When we seek to lift others' burdens, we lighten our own.

During his confinement in Rome, Paul wrote several of his Epistles—Philemon, Colossians, Ephesians and Philippians. It was probably during his imprisonment in a dungeon in Rome, expecting at any hour to be beheaded, that he wrote his second Epistle to Timothy.

According to tradition, the beloved apostle was finally condemned and beheaded. His heroic soul was released and the feeble body buried in the catacombs.

Paul changed the Early Church from a sect of believers within Judaism to a worldwide movement. He tried to break down the barriers between Jew and Gentile and between slave and free.

Acts is the only unfinished book in the Bible. Notice how abruptly it closes! How else could it close? How could there be a complete account of a person's lifework as long as He lives? Our risen and ascended Lord still lives. From the center, Christ, the lines are seen radiating in every direction, but "the ends of the earth" are not yet reached. The book is evidently a fragment. The gospel of Christ moves on! You are still living the Acts.

Acts

Letters of Paul

of the New Testament

ROMANS • 1 CORINTHIANS

2 CORINTHIANS • GALATIANS

EPHESIANS • PHILIPPIANS • COLOSSIANS

1 THESSALONIANS • 2 THESSALONIANS

1 TIMOTHY • 2 TIMOTHY

TITUS • PHILEMON

Key Events of the Letters of Paul

Christ is over all and in all, has all authority in heaven and earth.
Colossians 1

Christ is head of His Church, saves by grace through faith, not works.
Ephesians 1; 2

Christ is coming back soon.
1, 2 Thessalonians

Letters of Paul: The Church Is the Body of Christ!

The apostle Paul vigorously pursued relationships with the churches he established on his three missionary journeys through the letters (Epistles) he wrote. These letters instruct us that: Christ is over all and in all; Christ has all authority in heaven and earth; Christ is the Head of His Church; Christ saves us by grace through faith, not by works of the law; through Christ's sacrifice on the cross we are reconciled to God and to one another; and Christ is coming back soon!

Understanding Romans

Romans Portrays Jesus Christ, Our Righteousness

SELECTED BIBLE READINGS

DAY OF THE WEEK		MAIN TOPIC
Sunday: Romans 1–3:20	What We Are by Nature	
Monday: Romans 3:21–5	How to Become a Christian	
Tuesday: Romans 6	How to Live a Christian Life	
Wednesday: Romans 7	What Our Struggle with Sin Is Like	
Thursday: Romans 8	How to Live a Spirit-Filled Life	
Friday: Romans 9:30–11:12	Why Israel Is Set Aside	
Saturday: Romans 12	How to Serve God	

AUTHOR: Romans 1:1 identifies the author of the book of Romans as the apostle Paul. Romans 16:22 indicates that Paul used a scribe named Tertius to write this letter.

DATE: The book was likely written AD 56-58.

PURPOSE AND SUMMARY: This letter, the first in canonical order but not the first of Paul's epistles, is the longest and the most influential of all the apostle Paul's letters. Writing to Christians at Rome, Paul presents to them his core teachings on faith in Christ: the universality of sin; the powerlessness of the law to make us righteous before God; the power of God's saving act in Christ's death and resurrection; and believers receiving that power and forgiveness of sins by faith in Christ.

We now begin a study of the Epistles (letters) in the New Testament. Paul wrote 13 of the 21; hence, they are called the Pauline epistles. He wrote his letters to the churches at Thessalonica, Galatia, Corinth and Rome during his missionary journeys. While he was a prisoner in Rome he wrote his letters to the church at Ephesus, one to the Colossians, one to Philemon and one to the Philippians. After his imprisonment, he wrote two letters to Timothy and one to Titus.

LIFE OF PAUL

Paul was born at Tarsus, "circumcised on the eighth day, of the people of Israel, of the tribe of Benjamin, a Hebrew of Hebrews; in regard to the law, a Pharisee" (Philippians 3:5). His teacher was Gamaliel, the great teacher of the Pharisees. Like all Hebrew boys, he learned a trade—he was a tentmaker. At Jerusalem, he was present at the stoning of Stephen, the first Christian martyr. No doubt this scene made a tremendous impression on the young Saul. On the way to Damascus, on a mission to persecute Christians, the young Pharisee had a head-on collision with Jesus Christ! After his miraculous conversion, he was baptized and received his commission to preach the gospel. He spent three years studying and preparing in Arabia.

After laboring for three years in Tarsus and one year in Antioch, Paul was directed by the Holy Spirit to become the great missionary to the Gentiles. On his three missionary journeys, he founded many churches and wrote his epistles. The combination of Roman citizenship, Greek education and Hebrew religion wonderfully qualified him for his great work, but you will find that he trusted alone in the "grace and apostleship" he received directly from Jesus Christ (Romans 1:5).

After a life filled with sacrifice and suffering, he sealed his testimony with his own life's blood. Tradition says he was beheaded at Rome, and his body buried in the catacombs.

THE CHURCH AT ROME

Who founded the church at Rome we do not know. Peter did not found it. Peter's ministry was to the Jewish people (see Galatians 2:9). Visitors from Rome, in Jerusalem for the Passover and converted at Pentecost, went back to the capital, carrying the seed of the gospel and established a new center in Rome. During the 28 intervening years, many Christians from all parts of the East had migrated to Rome, some of them Paul's own converts.

Paul was eager to visit this church, and sent them this letter from Corinth, from the home of Gaius, a wealthy Corinthian Christian, while he was on his third missionary journey. It was written in the fourth year of Nero, then the emperor of Rome. In this epistle, he sets forth his gospel (see Romans 1:16-17).

Paul, "a servant" (Romans 1:1), writes to the saints at Rome (see Romans 1:7), concerning the Savior (see Romans 1:3-4). As a servant, Paul reveals several things about himself:

- Set apart for the gospel—Romans 1:1
- Serving in the gospel—Romans 1:9
- Saved by the gospel—Romans 1:16

Is the gospel of Christ gripping you this way? Are you saved by it, set apart for it, and serving in it?

After Paul's greeting to the church, he thanks God for their faith (see Romans 1:8). Notice Paul's expression of obligation to this church (see Romans 1:14-15):

- "I am obligated"—Romans 1:14
- "I am so eager" to fulfill my obligation—Romans 1:15
- "I am not ashamed" of the message—Romans 1:16

Why was Paul not ashamed of the gospel of Christ? Because it reveals what the sinner needs and what the sinner may have on the ground of simple faith: "the righteousness of God"—the righteousness of Jesus Christ (Romans 1:17). The terrible sinfulness of humans, as pictured in Romans 1:18-32, had reached its climax in Rome.

The gospel has dynamic power. It is the power of God for salvation. Do you realize that nothing short of the power of God could make one Christian?

MESSAGE OF ROMANS

Paul spoke from the white-hot conviction that is born of experience. On the road to Damascus, he had in a single instant all the artificial props of works, race and character knocked out from under him. He caught a full glimpse of the glorified Christ. From then on, he had but one message: faith in the crucified and risen Lord. He would hear nothing else; he spoke nothing else; he lived nothing less. He proclaimed that from now on "the righteous will live by faith" (Romans 1:17). One must simply believe. There is only one salvation and that is by the acceptance of the gospel of Christ. When we believe in Christ, God gives us righteousness. We are not made righteous, but "declared righteous" (Romans 2:13). God gives to us the righteousness He demands of us. Why is God's righteousness necessary? Because we have none of our own.

After Paul states the subject of the book of Romans, in 1:16-17, he then reveals people's need of this righteousness. All people have sinned and all the world is guilty before God. From his elevated pulpit, Paul looks around and sees zealous Jews, proud Greeks, boastful Romans and a multitude of ordinary, common sinners like ourselves. What a terrible picture he presents in Romans 1:18-32! First the unrighteousness of the Gentiles is portrayed; then, that of the Jews.

Fortunately, Paul tells us how God makes guilty people good. The keys to this are found in Romans 1:16-17:

- The person of the gospel—Christ
- The power of the gospel—"power of God" (verse 16)

- The purpose of the gospel—"salvation" (verse 16)
- The people to whom sent—"to everyone" (verse 16)
- The plan of acceptance—"to everyone who believes" (verse 16)
- The particular result—"the righteous will live by faith" (verse 17)

Paul was proud of the gospel because he had proved its power in his own life and in the lives of all who would believe.

Good news! These words will command the attention of anyone. When you say to someone, "I have good news for you!" you can always get that person to listen. The real value of good news depends on the source—who said it. That is why the gospel Paul presents is so welcome. The news comes from God. Romans is Paul's shout of joy to a lost world.

The first three chapters describe the hell of sin. The last five chapters describe the heaven of holiness. The intervening chapters describe Christ, the Way. When you look at Jesus, you see the righteousness God requires.

ROMANS 1–3:20—WHAT WE ARE BY NATURE

Why do we need salvation? Because we are sinners. God has the human heart, and Paul shows us what God finds in all of us. I know your X-ray is the same because Paul says, "There is no one who does good, not even one" (Romans 3:12). Read every word of Romans 3, a picture of a person without God. You will believe then that the natural state of the human heart is desperately wicked. Have you ever asked the Holy Spirit to throw a searchlight on your own heart? If you have, you know today that you need a Savior.

Paul presents a courtroom scene: God, the judge of all the earth, summons Jews and Gentiles before the bar of justice. Prisoner after prisoner is brought up. Both Jews and Gentiles are given the opportunity for a hearing (see Romans 2:1-16; 2:17–3:8).

The general charge is stated: "All [are] under the power of sin" (Romans 3:9).

We get an awful picture of sin in these first three chapters of Romans. Remember, "sin" is a marksman's word. It means "missing the mark"—the standard God has set for us. God's Word says, "For all have sinned and fall short of the glory of God" (Romans 3:23). Fall short in our good deeds? No—of the glory of God. Do not measure your life by any other standard but this. Do not compare yourselves to others like you. Of course you may not have fallen as short as some others you know, but you are short as far as God is concerned.

We are all sinners because we were born into a sinful race. We are all children of Adam. Adam, the head of our race, was not created that way (see Genesis 1:26). He deliberately sinned and his sinful nature was passed on to us all. And we were not only born into sin, but we also have sinned ourselves, for "all have sinned." Remember this: We sin because we are sinners. This is our nature. A plum tree bears plums because it is a plum tree. The fruit is the result of its nature. Sin is the fruit of a sinful heart: "The heart is deceitful above all things" (Jeremiah 17:9).

The judge hears the prisoners' pleas of "not guilty," and these are carefully considered and answered, clearing the way for the final verdict pronounced by the judge. "The whole world [is] held accountable to God" (Romans 3:19). If this sort of announcement were to be made today, every media outlet would lead with this headline: "All the world found guilty!"

Against all this there is no defense. The judge says, "Is there anyone to plead the case of the prisoners?" No one answers. Every mouth is "silenced" (Romans 3:19). There is no room for excuse.

The condemnation of the world is settled. The next step in order will be to reveal the plan of God to save this lost world. (Remember, Paul tells us how God makes people good.)

Do not say, "God is love. He will not condemn me." Listen to God's words here: "The wrath of God is being revealed from heaven against all the godlessness" (Romans 1:18). He has already passed sentence on everyone. All are guilty. There is no chance of appeal. It is the decision of the Supreme Court of the universe. Sin is universal—all have sinned! Therefore, we need a world Savior. Because God is the God of love, He has provided just this One! Repeat aloud John 3:16. The judge on the bench says, "Is there anyone to appear for the prisoners?" Then the Son of God says, "Yes, I am here to represent these people. It is true that they committed these sins. It is true that they are guilty, but I bore their guilt on the cross. I died in their place so that they could go free. I am their righteousness." And the Judge sets them free.

Christ not only saves us from the penalty of sin, but He is also able to free us from the consciousness of guilt and the power of sin. Sin makes us feel guilty. A person who has broken the law feels guilty and seeks to hide. This is what the first man, Adam, did. A guilty conscience causes a fear of punishment. The sinner is always trying to flee from the consequences of the broken law. The person fears the judge and what he will pronounce. This is why a person's sins and guilty conscience banish him or her from the presence of God. God does not need to banish the sinner. The person flees of his or her own accord. This is what will happen on the day when the wrath of God will be revealed (see Revelation 6:15-16).

The first thing that is necessary for the sinner to be free is that the dreadful consequences of the person's guilt have to be taken away. The sinner needs more than pardon, for that would leave the person with his or her sense of guilt. A president or governor or king can pardon a criminal, but no human has the power to remove the sense of guilt. Proper punishment for the deed must be pronounced and carried out. This is what Christ accepted for us. "The wages of sin is death" (Romans 6:23) and because all of us "have sinned," Christ came to die and bear the penalty for the sins committed against a holy God.

ROMANS 3:21–5: HOW TO BECOME A CHRISTIAN

How does God save sinners? "Through the redemption that came by Christ Jesus" (Romans 3:24). God's plan of salvation runs through the entire Scriptures. It is like a thread that is an essential part of a cord, interwoven in such a way that its removal would destroy the cord. The thread of salvation can be seen very plainly in certain portions of the Bible. Romans 3 is one of them.

When God looks at us, He sees no righteousness (see Romans 3:10). When God looks at us "in Christ," He sees not only an improvement, but also perfection, for God sees only His own righteousness, Jesus Christ.

Salvation

You will find the stream of sin and the river of salvation running along together from Romans 1 through 16. "Where sin increased, grace increased all the more" (Romans 5:20). Paul shows sin in all its squalor and salvation in all its splendor. Some simple steps in these next paragraphs will show you how to become a Christian!

One does not have to be a sinner in the sight of people to be lost. Of course there is a difference in the degree of sin but not in the fact of sin and its result, death. We may drown in seven feet of water and be as dead as if we had been submerged in 70 feet of water. In our inability to save ourselves, we are all on the same level: "There is no difference" (Romans 3:22).

We are saved by Christ's righteousness. He has made it available for us by His death. We "are justified freely by his grace through the redemption that came by Christ Jesus. God presented Christ as a sacrifice of atonement, through the shedding of his blood—to be received by faith" (Romans 3:24-25).

I am a person condemned to die because of my sin, "for the wages of sin is death." But I can look on the cross and see that Christ has already died for me. I believe that He died for my sin. So in exchange for my poor, sinful, condemned life, I can accept His righteousness and His life (see 1 Peter 2:24).

"Whoever believes in the Son has eternal life" (John 3:36). "But now apart from the law the righteousness of God has been made known. . . . This righteousness is given through faith in Jesus Christ to all who believe" (Romans 3:21-22). Apart from a person's effort to be good, God has provided His righteousness, the Lord Jesus Christ. "All our righteous acts are like filthy rags" (Isaiah 64:6).

Your sins are on Christ. He bore them for you. Have you accepted Him as your Savior and "crossed over from death to life" (John 5:24)? If you have decided to let Christ be your sin bearer, you now have His salvation (see Romans 3:24).

Justification

You have become acquainted with one great word of Scripture, "salvation." Here is another: "justification"—"just-as-if-I'd . . ." Everything Christ did has been credited to my account. Justification buries all of my sins and guilt in the grace of Jesus Christ and then sets me in heavenly places with Christ our Savior. His righteousness is mine!

Justification happens when Christ's righteousness is looked at as ours—we are counted just (or righteous) before God: "The righteous will live by faith" (Romans 1:17). No one is considered just because of works, but rather because of a belief in Christ (see Romans 3:28). This great truth gave birth to the great Reformation of the sixteenth century, when believers were freed from the idea that people were saved by works, and believers recognized a life of faith and liberty in Christ. Not only are we saved by faith, but we must also live by faith, trusting in Christ.

Paul gives us illustrations of justification by faith from the Old Testament, especially emphasizing how Abraham's faith was "credited to him as righteousness" (Romans 4:3). Abraham received three things by faith: "righteousness," inheritance and posterity (Romans 4:3; see also verses 13,17).

We, too, have great benefits when we are justified by God's grace. Grace is unmerited favor. In this life, we find that faith is followed by peace, pardon, promise (see Romans 5:1-5) and, more than all, an assurance of salvation (see Romans 5:6-11).

How can a person be justified by God? Read Romans 3:24-28. God imparts His righteousness to people in the following six ways:

1. By grace—He is the source of it (see Romans 3:24).
2. By God—He is the giver of it (see Romans 3:26; 8:33).
3. By blood—He is the reason for it (see Romans 3:24; 5:9).

4. By faith—He is the means by which it is received (see Romans 3:22).
5. By works—He is the way it is shown (see James 2:21-23).
6. By experience—He is the blessing we enjoy from it (see Romans 5:1-4).

None of us like the idea of being called a "sinner," but we must face what we are. Read what Paul says in Romans 5:12-21. We were born sinners. We were not asked if we wished to come into this world. We woke up to the fact one day that we were subject to a sinful nature.

But over against Adam, the head of the natural race, we find Christ, the head of a spiritual race. When we believe in Him, we become a "new creation" (2 Corinthians 5:17). When I was born in this body, I was born a descendant of Adam. I have his nature, which is sinful. When I am born into the family of God, by Christ Jesus, I have Christ's nature, which is holy. In the words of Scripture, "For as in Adam all die, so in Christ all will be made alive" (1 Corinthians 15:22). I did not choose to be a descendant of Adam. I may choose to be a child of God. If one man's sin made it possible for all humankind to die, one man's righteousness made it possible for all humankind to get out of this condition (see Romans 5:15).

When I look into heaven and remember that God who sits on His throne has condemned me, I am in despair. But then I see Jesus sitting at His right, holding up wounded hands and presenting His pierced feet and side. With these wounds Christ pleads for me, and I have His own assurance that they are effective and sufficient to meet my needs.

Have you received "eternal life through Jesus Christ our Lord" (Romans 5:21)? Are you a sinner "in Adam," or are you a son or daughter "in Christ"?

ROMANS 6–8: HOW TO LIVE A CHRISTIAN LIFE

We have learned how to become a Christian. Now we must find out how to live like a Christian. It is one thing to accept what Christ has done for you. It is another thing to experience it as personal and real.

In Romans 6, there are three important words that you need to mark:

- "Know" that Christ died for you (Romans 6:3; see also verses 5,10); know that you died with Christ (see Romans 6:8).

- "Count" on this: You are "dead to sin but alive to God in Christ Jesus" (Romans 6:11). If a trustworthy uncle told you that he had put $5,000 in the bank for you for a trip and you could withdraw it any time you needed it, you would count on it, I am sure, though you never actually saw the money. If you were to question it and not withdraw it, the money would never be yours. If you count it as yours by signing and cashing a check, that which you have never seen becomes a reality. Counting on something makes it real! Because we are dead to sin and alive in God, how should we live? Read Romans 6:13.

- "Offer" yourself (Romans 6:13)! "Do not offer any part of yourself to sin as an instrument of wickedness, but rather offer yourselves to God as those who have been brought from death to life; and offer every part of yourself to him as an instrument of righteousness" (Romans 6:13).

This means let go of your life and *let God* live through you. This is the surrendered life. This is the right way to live a life of victory and blessing. Let Him work His will in you and through you.

Christians soon find a new standard for life. They do not try to live up to the Law, for they are no longer under it. They strive to please the One who dwells within them. "For to me to live is Christ," and I "do it all to the glory of God" (Philippians 1:21; 1 Corinthians 10:31).

The End of Self

In Romans 6, Paul reveals the secret of a life of victory: living in Christ—dead to sin but alive to God! This tells us how we can lead

Christian lives. Self, we have learned, was a condemned thing, unable to be good, never righteous (see Romans 3). Now when self becomes a Christian and tries to live a Christian life, it finds this to be impossible. But we are saved by faith; we cannot live by our own efforts.

This sad truth is revealed in Romans 7, which tells us why we cannot live a victorious life. Mark every "I" in this chapter, and you will find it is used more than 30 times in the 25 verses. Although "I" tries, it finds only defeat. Dr. W. H. Griffith Thomas, a famous New Testament scholar, said, "It is not hard to live a Christian life; it is impossible."

Paul said, "I have been crucified with Christ and I no longer live, but Christ lives in me" (Galatians 2:20). Listen to the words of the man who tries to live by his own effort. "What a wretched man I am! Who will rescue me from this body that is subject to death? Thanks be to God, who delivers me through Jesus Christ our Lord! So then, I myself in my mind am a slave to God's law, but in the sinful nature a slave to the law of sin" (Romans 7:24-25).

Finally, "I" finds that there is One who is sufficient. Struggling yields to power, defeat is changed to victory, misery is transformed into joy. When "I" goes out, Christ comes in.

A Life in Christ

The life "in Christ" is a wonderful thing. Paul says, "Because through Jesus Christ the law of the Spirit who gives life set you free from the law of sin and death" (Romans 8:2). This is what happens. When I am in an airplane, I am free from the law of gravity. The plane operates in such a way that it is able to lift itself above the clouds, although the law of gravity a few minutes before held me fast to the earth. The law of gravity is not destroyed but rendered inoperative. This is what happens in my life when I am in Christ. The law that operates by the Spirit in my life lifts me above the world and sin, and sin no longer has dominion over me. I am free. I am without condemnation. Are you in Christ? Are you living on a plane far above the evil principalities and powers?

Have you come to the end of self? Remember, "I" never brings anything but failure. It is the *i* in "sin" that must be removed. Put *o* in its place and you have "Son." He will give you victory!

Step out of the self-life into the Spirit-filled life. In Romans 8, instead of the word "I" we find the word "Spirit" used over and over again (more than 20 times). We must yield our lives to Him. This is our part. Then He will fill us with His Spirit. That is Christ's part.

This glorious chapter opens with "no condemnation," and ends with "no separation" (Romans 8:1). This is a picture of our life in Christ. Christians are safe: Christ is around them; the Spirit is within them; and God is for them.

ROMANS 9–11: WHY ISRAEL IS SET ASIDE

The story of the Jewish people being set aside and scattered throughout the world without a homeland and without a king is a warning for us (see Romans 9–11). God is a sovereign God, and He will do what He will. He has a perfect right to turn to the Gentiles, because most Jewish people would not seek the righteousness of God, which is "by faith" (Romans 9:32). They tried to set up their own righteousness. But people do not build up righteousness. They only receive it. If God will put aside His Chosen People, won't He put us aside if we are disobedient?

Let us be careful not to become self-willed and disobedient, not heeding God's commandments.

Ask Christ to take control of your life and guide you in His path. Wreckage awaits those who stray outside His divine course. The Old Testament story of the Hebrew people is a solemn lesson to us. Read the wonderful description of God's mercy in Romans 11:32-36.

ROMANS 12–16: HOW TO SERVE GOD

"Therefore, I urge you, brothers and sisters, in view of God's mercy, to offer your bodies as a living sacrifice, holy and pleasing to God—this is your true and proper worship" (Romans 12:1). In this appeal, Paul urges us to have our lives measure up to our beliefs. He shows that the doctrine of justification by faith will not allow laxity in life or conduct. We are saved to serve. The Christian life must be lived in its relation to God, self and others.

It may surprise you to find out that up to this point we have not had to do a thing but believe in Christ and yield ourselves to Him to use as He wills. Now we are to serve, and our Christian service may be in any of several places:

- Church—Romans 12:3-8
- Government—Romans 13:1-14
- Disputed things—Romans 14–15:3
- The whole world—Romans 15:4-13

Until we have been saved by His grace and transformed by His love, we can do little for God. Read 1 Corinthians 13. But when we present ourselves to Christ and become filled with His love, we can find a lot to do. Christ wants a "living sacrifice," not a dead one (Romans 12:1). Many will die for Christ. Few will live for Him. Many of you might rather be burned at a stake than face ridicule from the people you know. One definition of a modern Christian is "a person who will die for the church he or she will not attend." How many of us say nothing when Christ's name is brought into question or is used in vain!

Let others see Jesus in you! Live for Him. Then you will be ready to die for Him.

33

Understanding First Corinthians

First Corinthians Portrays Jesus Christ, Our Lord

DAY OF THE WEEK		MAIN TOPIC
Sunday: 1 Corinthians 1:10-31	Division in the Church	
Monday: 1 Corinthians 2	The Mind of Christ	
Tuesday: 1 Corinthians 3	Worldliness in the Church	
Wednesday: 1 Corinthians 5	Immorality in the Church	
Thursday: 1 Corinthians 11	Significance of the Lord's Supper	
Friday: 1 Corinthians 13	A Hymn of Love	
Saturday: 1 Corinthians 15	Resurrection of Christ	

AUTHOR: First Corinthians 1:1 identifies the author of the book of 1 Corinthians as the apostle Paul.

DATE: The book of 1 Corinthians was written in approximately AD 55.

PURPOSE AND SUMMARY: This letter to the church at Corinth discusses divisions at that church and their mishandling of the work, gifts and power of the Holy Spirit they had received. First Corinthians gives us a picture of the life of a local church in New Testament times. Writing from Ephesus, where he spent at least three years, Paul addresses the Corinthian church concerning the significance of their new life in Christ, which should be demonstrated within the Church through working for unity in the worship gatherings, in exercising the gifts of the Spirit, and not neglecting the poor in the Lord's Supper. Paul gives focused teaching to the Corinthians regarding spiritual gifts (see chapter 12), Christian love (see chapter 13), and the meaning of the resurrection of the dead (see chapter 15).

The name "Lord" is very prominent in 1 Corinthians. This is significant because much of the confusion that had crept into the church at Corinth had come because the believers failed to recognize Jesus Christ as Lord.

The archaeologist's spade is making ancient Corinth live again! Corinth was the most important city of all Greece in Paul's day and attracted great crowds of foreigners from the East and the West. Its wealth was fabulous and its cultural achievements and fine arts many. Men spent their days participating in tournaments and giving speeches, and the city had many places to study language and philosophy. However, dissipation and public immorality, reflecting the Greek gods of pleasure and lust, were rampant among Corinth's great industrial and seafaring population.

As in most cities, there was a large colony of Jews who had kept a strong moral standard and held to their religious beliefs. But the city itself was the center of a debased form of the worship of Venus.

Acts 18 describes how the gospel reached this wicked city. The apostle Paul, then a man about 50 years old and dressed as the working man that he was, entered the busy metropolis and went through its streets in search of a workshop where he might earn his own living as a tentmaker. This was a leading industry in that day, as construction is today. He went into business with the well-to-do tentmakers Aquila and Priscilla. (He was always able to support himself, making enough to carry on his missionary work.) A wonderful work was done in Corinth during the year and a half Paul was there. He began his evangelistic work by speaking in the synagogues to mixed congregations of Jews and Greeks.

First Corinthians is a difficult book to outline, for it takes up many wonderful subjects. "In him you have been enriched in every way" (1 Corinthians 1:5). In Romans, Paul told us that it was by Christ that "we have gained access by faith into this grace in which we now stand" (Romans 5:2). Now in 1 Corinthians, Paul deals with Christian conduct and the riches of grace in Christ Jesus, our all in all.

1 CORINTHIANS 1–11: CORRECTING CHRISTIAN CONDUCT

The wonderful church at Corinth, the brilliant jewel in the crown of Paul's labor, was failing. The worldliness (carnality) of the city had infected the fellowship of believers. It was all right for the church to be in Corinth, but it was fatal when Corinth got into the church. It is a glorious sight to see a ship launched into the sea, but it is a tragic sight when the sea gets into the ship. The Church of Christ should be a light in our dark world, but woe to the Church when the wickedness of the world invades it.

Wicked practices common in Corinth soon crept into the church. There were divisions among the believers; Christians were suing other Christians before heathen judges; behavior at the communion table was disgraceful; the women of the church no longer observed standards of modesty; the church membership was arguing over marriage and even spiritual gifts. Finally, the church wrote Paul about these things and asked his advice on these matters. Paul's two letters to the Corinthians were written in answer to their requests.

After the usual greeting, Paul refers to the coming again of our Lord Jesus Christ (see 1 Corinthians 1:1-3,7-8). Then he plunges right into the church failures about which he had been told. The source of his information he gives us in 1 Corinthians 1:11.

People had lost sight of God. Three kinds of selfishness had blinded them:

1. Self-admiration—their intellect had been perverted.
2. Self-will—their conscience had been darkened.
3. Self-indulgence—their passions had been given full rein.

The greatest danger to the Corinthian church was from within.

Divisions over Leaders

Paul speaks first of the divisions and cliques about which he had learned from friends and travelers. Nothing ruins a church like party politics.

In Corinth, Greek party politics had divided the church into four groups, each vying for supremacy. Their names of the leaders of each party are given in 1 Corinthians 1:12. Paul, Apollos and Cephas (Peter) were parties named for each group's favorite teacher. The Christ Party held to that name as if it did not belong to everyone in the church.

This dissension about religious leaders meant that the Christians at Corinth had slipped off center. There is only one leader at the center of every church. That leader and center is Christ. If the church gets off center here, it goes off all down the line. A correctly centered flywheel moves quietly; off center it shakes the machine to pieces. Christianity must be Christ-centered. If it is Christ centered, it is powerful. Christ Himself is the good news. He not only brought God's message, but He also was and is God's message. The Corinthians had slipped off center. Paul, Peter and Apollos were all good men, but they were not God-men. How many are following religious leaders today rather than Christ Himself! "For to me, to live is Christ" (Philippians 1:21).

Jesus Christ is the only cure for division (see 1 Corinthians 1:13). Every eye, every heart, every spirit must be turned to one object—Jesus Christ, our personal Savior. Paul said, in effect, "Your factional spirit is a sin. Can you follow a mere man, hoping that he can give you life? Was that man crucified for you? Trusting in what people have to say is foolish. People see nothing in the cross of Christ. Christ alone has all the power and wisdom of God."

Youth and the elderly alike follow Christ to the cross and then stumble at the blood of the sacrifice. This is what the Jews and Greeks of Paul's day did. Should we remove the cross from the gospel because people do not like it? If we do, we remove the world's only way of salvation. We must preach Christ crucified.

The Obstacle of the Cross

The cross was "a stumbling block to Jews," an obstacle they could not get over (1 Corinthians 1:23). They could not understand how such a display of weakness could be a source of power. A man dying on a cross did not look much like a world savior to them. The scribes and Pharisees scornfully turned from the cross. To them, the cross meant failure. The Jews needed signs of power. They demanded something they could see and grasp. The Messiah must be a world prince. Way too many Christians are like this today. They worship success as much as did the Jews. They despise weakness and admire force. These people tell us that scientists are apt to stumble at the cross because they cannot explain how the blood of one man could wash away the stain of sin.

The cross was "foolishness to Gentiles" (1 Corinthians 1:23). The Greek-influenced Gentiles regarded with contempt the unscientific religion first taught in Nazareth, an unschooled corner of the world, by the son of a carpenter who never studied in Athens or Rome. The Greeks idolized brains. But God has never despised the humble things.

Either the cross is the "power of God" or it is "foolishness" (1 Corinthians 1:23-24). If "foolishness," then you think it is unfit to do any good in your life. But listen! That condemns you, not the cross.

No one ever leaves the cross in exactly the same condition as he or she came to it. You must receive it or reject it. If you receive the cross, you become a child of God (see John 1:12); if you reject it, you are lost (see John 3:36). If you neglect it, you are in effect rejecting it.

Paul did not preach Christ the conqueror or Christ the philosopher, but Christ crucified, Christ the humble. Read Paul's words in 1 Corinthians 2:2. Paul remembers that his words will be tried by "fire" (1 Corinthians 3:13). To know Christ crucified is the ultimate knowledge.

The Minister as Servant

One objection to Paul was that his preaching was too simple. He answered that he could not preach any differently because they were mere babies in Christ. They could not tolerate anything but a milk diet. The proof of their childish state (carnality) was in the division among them (see 1 Corinthians 3:1-4).

Paul points out that the Christian minister is not the head of a school or a rival sect, as were the Greek philosophers. The Christian minister is the servant of God, not a master of people. Paul always called himself a servant of the Lord Jesus Christ. Christian service is only acceptable to God when it is done in the spirit of Christ and for His glory.

The Christian in Judgment

Everyone has four faces—one the world knows, one our friends know, one we know ourselves and one God knows. Paul describes this in 1 Corinthians 4. There are three courts before which we stand:

1. People—1 Corinthians 4:3
2. Our own conscience—1 Corinthians 4:3
3. Jesus Christ—1 Corinthians 4:4

Do not depend on human judgment. The world may use a single act of ours to judge our character. The voices of criticism may be loud, but if you go high up on the hilltop with God, you will see the bustle of the crowd without hearing it.

Beware of your friends' judgment because they may be too favorable in their opinion of you. We like to believe all the good things said about us and resent unfavorable criticism.

Paul says, "I do not even judge myself" (1 Corinthians 4:3). Beware when you stand at the bar of your own conscience. When your conscience says to you, "You may do it," it is always well to go to Jesus Christ and say, "May I?" It is hard to be fair with ourselves. No one, no matter how honest, is permitted to judge his or her own case.

Paul says there is one judgment to which he will submit—one that is always right. "It is the Lord who judges me" (1 Corinthians

4:4). I am Christ's steward and to Him only am I ultimately responsible. From His judgment there is no escape. His calm eyes are on me.

Seek praise from Him, which is praise indeed. If He says, "Well done, good and faithful servant," nothing else matters!

Vice in the Church

In Paul's letter to the Romans, his theme was the righteousness of God. In Corinthians, Paul enlarges this theme to the life of righteousness in the Christian. We, as Christians, must act out in our lives what we believe in our hearts. It is a serious thing to claim to live the life of a Christian. If we lower the standard Christ has set, we give the wrong testimony to the world. Each of us is an epistle open and read by all people. What kind of a gospel is "The Gospel According to You"? Do not let your life be so near the edge of questionable things that someday you will slide off. If you fall, others will fall with you. Watch your testimony, how you conduct your life. Righteousness comes from God, but it must be shown in our daily walk.

The Corinthians, living in the Hollywood of their day, needed admonition just as we do. Righteousness is from Christ and for Christ. "What would Jesus do?" should be asked of every questionable thing in life. Christ in you is the secret and the way of life.

In the church at Corinth, a member actually was having an incestuous affair with his own stepmother, which was considered immoral among the pagans to say nothing of Christians. Paul reproves them for being puffed up with pride while this scandal existed in the church. He urges them not to tolerate evil among them while calling themselves Christians. Just as yeast spreads through all the dough, so a bad person's spirit spreads through all a church. The church should exclude the wrongdoer in order to prove that it does not condone sin (see 1 Corinthians 5:13). Discipline in the Church should always, however, begin with mourning and sympathy, not anger or pride or revenge (see 1 Corinthians 5:2).

Paul also gives a practical and a personal application, useful in our own lives: "Therefore let us keep the Festival . . . with the unleavened bread of sincerity and truth" (1 Corinthians 5:8).

1 Corinthians

Self-examination is often the most difficult thing we do, but it is one of our most important personal tasks.

"Do you not know" ("Know ye," *KJV*) is one of Paul's favorite expressions in 1 Corinthians 6. His faith was built on facts. He wanted to know things. Underline every "know" in chapter 6. What are we supposed to know?

First, Paul declares that although it might be necessary at times for Christians to go to court, Christians never should quarrel with each other and then drag this quarrel before a worldly court. What a terrible impression of Christianity this gives to the world! When we do that, in effect we are saying, "We, as Christians, are just like everybody else. We want our way. We are as bad and as covetous and just as ambitious for our own rights as others are." Paul says, "Dare you do such a thing?"

Paul then gives us a picture of the Corinthians as he found them. Read 1 Corinthians 6:9-10. Then read verse 11 to find what grace has done!

The Dwelling Place of Christ

Christ has paid a great price to purchase us, and it is His purpose to make us like Himself (see 1 Corinthians 6:19-20). If the Lord Jesus Christ has redeemed our bodies, then they no longer belong to us. The One who purchased us with His precious blood owns us. "You were bought at a price" (1 Corinthians 6:20).

God used to have a Temple for His people; now He has a people for a temple. When a man steps into the church, he realizes he has stepped into the sanctuary. But has he forgotten that the real sanctuary in which Christ dwells is his body? We are taught as boys and girls not to be noisy or boisterous in the church, for it is the house in which we meet God. How much more important it is that we remember that each of our bodies is His dwelling place and that we should do nothing to grieve Him (see Ephesians 4:30).

Liberty Without Recklessness

The Scripture does not lay down little rules for our conduct and tell us just the things we ought to do or not do; rather, it states principles that should guide the Christian's actions. Someone has well said that Christian liberty does not mean the right to do as we like, but, rather, to do as we ought. Paul puts it this way: "'I have the right to do anything,' you say—but not everything is beneficial. 'I have the right to do anything'—but I will not be mastered by anything" (1 Corinthians 6:12).

A man was walking down the street swinging his arms out from his chest and, by mistake, struck a passerby in the face. The man struck was furious and started to strike the man back. "Hey, isn't this a free country? Can't a fellow do his exercises on the street if he wishes?"

"Yes," was the answer, "but remember that where my nose begins, your liberty ends."

Let this be constantly in your mind as far as your conduct is concerned. If your liberty harms another, then your liberty has gone too far.

Yes, I can do anything I want to, but I must be sure my desires are to please Christ. What I do is an example to others and may harm or bless them. I should not only ask, "Does my action harm weaker Christians?" but also ask, "Does my action glorify God?"

The Subject of Marriage

Controversy had arisen between the Jewish and Greek philosophers about the importance of marriage. Paul wanted to keep scandal from reaching the church, so in 1 Corinthians 7:2, he begins his advice regarding marriage. Some members of the church had tried to discourage marriage, and others thought that when one became a Christian, an unbelieving spouse should be divorced. But Paul was wise. He knew the evil conditions in Corinth and advised every man to have his own wife and every woman to have her own husband. He did not believe that a Christian should divorce an unbelieving partner. He told them that it was possible that the Christian would lead an unbelieving mate to Christ (see 1 Corinthians 7:16).

Mark 1 Corinthians 7:9,13 in your Bible. Think over these verses. They tell you what your Christian responsibility is toward those who are not Christians.

The Value of the Lord's Supper

Paul gives a careful account of the beginning of the Lord's Supper and then tells of its value.

- It was established on the night in which Christ was betrayed.
- It is celebrated in remembrance of His undying love for His followers.
- It is a symbol of His body, which was broken for them— 1 Corinthians 10:16.
- It was a new covenant in His blood.
- It is a pledge of His coming again—1 Corinthians 11:26.

We should be careful not to eat or drink in an unworthy manner. "Everyone ought to examine themselves" (1 Corinthians 11:28). And never eat without a self-critique and thankful love. "For whenever you eat," do it "in remembrance of me" (1 Corinthians 11:24-26). Christ wants us to remember Him! Think about Christ when you go to His table. He longs for your love!

It was the custom of the Corinthian church to eat a meal in connection with the Lord's Supper. They all brought food for themselves. Often this led to excesses among the rich, while the poor had nothing. What an unworthy observance of the supper itself this led to! Paul reminds them of the deep spiritual significance of this supper, and of the scandal of their behavior.

Paul closes this scene with these words: "And when I come I will give further directions" (see 1 Corinthians 11:34). Other things needed to be straightened out, but he would move to other instructions.

1 CORINTHIANS 12–16: USING GIFTS AND BELIEVING THE GOSPEL

In 1 Corinthians 12, we are told about the gifts that the Spirit gives to believers. In verses 1-3, Paul describes the change that had come into the lives of these Corinthian Christians when they turned from worshiping dead idols to the living Christ. So that they might develop in their Christian lives, Christ gave them the gifts of the Spirit (see 1 Corinthians 12:4-7). The Holy Spirit is the giver of spiritual gifts (see 1 Corinthians 12:8-11). One cannot teach the Scriptures unless the Spirit gives wisdom. One must pray "in the Spirit"; and for singing to be acceptable to God, it too must be done "in the Spirit." Sometimes when we look at a successful Christian man, we say, "Wow, he is a man of many talents," when in actuality he has received many gifts from the Spirit.

Many people in Paul's day made much of the spiritual gifts Paul mentions, but they were coveting the more showy gifts, such as speaking in tongues. And the Corinthian Christians were using these gifts as ends in themselves.

Many people today, like the Corinthians of old, pray constantly for the power of the Spirit. They forget that all the gifts that God bestows are given so that Christ might be exalted and others blessed. If God gives me any little gift at all, He gives it not so that I may gather people about myself, but so that it may through me be a blessing for others. God gave these nine gifts mentioned in 1 Corinthians 12 to assist in the founding of the new Church, but people were using them to gratify their pride. Paul points out that the purpose of the gifts is for building the Church (see 1 Corinthians 12), that they should be used in love (see 1 Corinthians 13); and that their value was to be measured by their usefulness to the Church.

God gave gifts such as healing, miracles and tongues, I believe, for "sign" gifts—to prove to the world that Jesus was the true Messiah and that the apostles were divinely appointed (see 2 Corinthians 12:12). These signs were given to put the stamp of authority on the apostles and their preaching. Today we are also to believe and walk by faith. If it is God's will for us to have any of these gifts, He will give them to us; otherwise, He will not. The Holy Spirit "distributes them to each one, just as he determines" (1 Corinthians 12:11).

The way to use these gifts the Spirit gives is beautifully described in 1 Corinthians 13. This chapter is often called the hymn of love. Gifts without love are poor things. People talk of love, but they do not live it. Until the love of Christ is in their hearts, it is impossible for people to love one another with any degree of permanency. People seem to worship force. But history has shown us that the victories won by force do not last.

The Resurrection of Christ

No doubt there was a group in the Corinthian church who did not believe in the resurrection of the dead. To deal with this, Paul starts out by giving a wonderful description of what the gospel is (see 1 Corinthians 15:1-11). Paul did not describe a new gospel. It was the old gospel given in Genesis, Exodus and Leviticus.

1. "Christ died for our sins according to the Scriptures"—1 Corinthians 15:3.
2. "He was buried"—1 Corinthians 15:4.
3. "He was raised on the third day according to the Scriptures"—1 Corinthians 15:4.
4. He was seen by many witnesses—1 Corinthians 15:5-6.

If we deny the Resurrection, we deny one of the greatest of all truths of the gospel. If the Resurrection is denied, all preaching is in vain; faith and hope are in vain. But more than all that, no Resurrection would mean no gospel at all, for we would be worshiping a dead Christ. There would be no "good news," for there would be no proof that God had accepted Christ's death as an atonement for our sins. If a sailor who jumps overboard to rescue a drowning man were drowned himself, then we would know that he did not save the man after whom he went. If Christ did not rise from the grave, then He could not bring anyone with Him from the grave. Christ's body died, and it was His body that was raised again. His soul was committed into the hands of the Father.

Because Christ lives, we will live also. "Where, O death, is your victory? Where, O death, is your sting?" (1 Corinthians 15:55).

Paul gives many proofs of the resurrection in 1 Corinthians 15, and his proofs also lend veracity to what the future holds:

1. Second coming of Christ
2. Resurrection of believers
3. Overthrow of Christ's enemies
4. Glorious reign of Christ
5. Immortality of our bodies

34

Understanding Second Corinthians

Second Corinthians Portrays Jesus Christ, Our Sufficiency

SELECTED BIBLE READINGS

DAY OF THE WEEK		MAIN TOPIC
Sunday: 2 Corinthians 1–2	Our Comfort	
Monday: 2 Corinthians 3–4	Living Epistles	
Tuesday: 2 Corinthians 5–6	Ambassadors for Christ	
Wednesday: 2 Corinthians 7–8:15	Paul's Heart	
Thursday: 2 Corinthians 8:16–9	Christian Giving	
Friday: 2 Corinthians 10:1–11:33	Paul's Apostleship	
Saturday: 2 Corinthians 12–13	God's Strength	

AUTHOR: Second Corinthians 1:1 identifies the author of the book of 2 Corinthians as the apostle Paul, possibly along with Timothy.

DATE: The book of 2 Corinthians was written in approximately AD 55 some time after 1 Corinthians was written and sent to Corinth.

PURPOSE AND SUMMARY: Often called "the hard letter," 2 Corinthians is an intensely personal letter. It recounts the difficulties and hardships Paul has endured in the service of Christ (see chapters 10-13). The apostle Paul regards the Corinthians as his children in Christ, because he brought most of them to faith and new birth in Christ (see Acts 18:1-18).

Paul apparently had worried somewhat about how the church at Corinth had received his first letter—how they had accepted his rebukes. So he sent Titus, and perhaps Timothy, to Corinth to find out the effect of his epistle. During Paul's third missionary journey, while he was in Philippi, Titus reported that the majority of the church had received the letter in the proper spirit. But there were those who doubted his motives and even denied his apostleship, saying that he did not have the proper credentials for an apostle. Perhaps they questioned this because he was not one of the original Twelve.

Under these circumstances he wrote his second epistle, to express his joy over the encouraging news of how his first epistle had been received and to defend his apostleship.

Paul gives more of his personal history in this letter than in any of his other epistles and only here does he tell us about some things that happened in his life:

- His unusual suffering—2 Corinthians 11:23-27
- His escape from Damascus in a basket—2 Corinthians 11:32-33
- His experience of being caught up to the third heaven— 2 Corinthians 12:1-4
- His thorn in the flesh—2 Corinthians 12:7

He told none of these until he was compelled to, to prove that if he wanted to boast, he had good reason. He reveals his courage and his self-sacrificing love, and he speaks of glorying, or boasting, 31 times because he was compelled to. Read 2 Corinthians 12:11.

The epistle begins with "comfort": "Praise be to the God and Father of our Lord Jesus Christ, the Father of compassion and the God of all comfort" (2 Corinthians 1:3). And it closes with comfort: "Finally, brothers and sisters, rejoice! Strive for full restoration, encourage one another, be of one mind, live in peace. And the God of love and peace will be with you" (2 Corinthians 13:11).

In the middle we find the reason for comfort: "And God is able to bless you abundantly, so that in all things at all times, having all that you need, you will abound in every good work" (2 Corinthians 9:8).

The source of this comfort? "My grace is sufficient for you" (2 Corinthians 12:9).

2 CORINTHIANS 1–7: PAUL'S MINISTRY

Paul opens this second epistle to the Corinthians with his usual greeting and thanksgiving (see 2 Corinthians 1:1-3). Everyone loves a true story. Paul tells so many personal experiences of his life in this letter that everyone loves to read it. He begins by telling of the great troubles that he recently had had. Through all of his trials, though, he had learned to know God better. God is always made more real to us in times of sorrow. That's when we find out for sure that God never fails.

Paul's sufferings in Asia were of a very serious nature. Very likely he went through a sickness dangerous enough to threaten his life (see 2 Corinthians 1:4-11). He appreciated the prayers of the Corinthians and now he was appealing to their love and sympathy. He wanted them to be ready for everything that he was going to write about concerning the defense of his apostleship.

Paul had a clear conscience about his sincerity and faithfulness while he worked to educate them. He explained that he had sent his first letter instead of coming himself so that when he did visit them, he might be able to praise and not scold them; and he calls on God as a witness to the truth of that statement (see 2 Corinthians 1:23–2:4).

The teachers of Jewish law of Paul's day carried letters of introduction with them. They were Paul's chief troublemakers. They tried in every way to fight him. We hear them asking, "Who is this Paul? What letters of recommendation from Jerusalem does he have?" How foolish this question was to Paul! Did he need a letter of recommendation to a church he himself had established?

He answers, "You yourselves are our letter, written on our hearts, known and read by everyone" (2 Corinthians 3:2).

The lives of the true Christians at Corinth served as letters to recommend both Paul the servant and Christ the Lord. Paul's gospel was a triumphant and transforming gospel (see 2 Corinthians 3:18). Living epistles are read when Bible Epistles are not. Remember that your life is an open letter as well. Christian lives are sometimes the only religious books the world "reads." The world may not study God's Word, but they *will* study God's people. This gives us a great opportunity for good, for we may lead people to Christ by our example.

Paul's Suffering

Paul's ministry was a triumphant one, but it was filled with suffering. Warfare always is full of illustrations of triumph through suffering. Victory costs! Paul tells us much about his ordeals (see 2 Corinthians 4; 6; 11). When Paul was so gloriously converted, the Lord said, "I will show him how much he must suffer for my name" (Acts 9:16). It seems as though the trials began immediately after his conversion and continued to dog his life for 30 years.

But Paul was always optimistic. As Winston Churchill once said, "The pessimist sees the difficulty in every opportunity. The optimist sees the opportunity in every difficulty." Paul could sing as he suffered because he knew the wonderful grace of God. He was always conscious of the presence of the Lord Jesus Christ. He knew that the greater the suffering in this present world, the greater the glory of eternity (see 2 Corinthians 4:8-18). Paul lived with his eye on the future!

Christ nowhere promises that a Christian will be free from suffering or sorrow. Rather, we are told that "in this world you will have trouble" (John 16:33). Christ allows troubles so that He may deliver us. He allowed Daniel to be put into the den of lions so that He could pull Daniel out. He allowed Shadrach, Meshach and Abednego to go into the fiery furnace so that He could deliver them. He allowed Paul to be shipwrecked so that He could save him. Our God is able to deliver!

Paul's Comfort

Through all his troubles, Paul finds his comfort in the fact of the resurrection that Christ promised. Paul lived inspired by the fact that one day he would have a changed, glorified body. Our suffering bodies will soon be exchanged for painless, glorified bodies. Whether we live or die, we must keep this reward in view (see 2 Corinthians 5:10).

The aim of Paul's ministry was to have people "reconciled to God" (2 Corinthians 5:20). People are God's greatest concern. As Christ's ambassador, he makes his appeal for reconciliation to the people of the world.

Paul follows this with an appeal for holy living. Holy living means wholly for God. Read 2 Corinthians 6:11-7—every verse! Paul appeals to his fellow workers, not to receive God's lovingkindness in vain, but to open their hearts to Him. God demands a clean and separated life. He wants Christians to separate themselves from unbelievers.

2 CORINTHIANS 8–9: LIBERAL GIVING

Paul tells the church at Corinth about the generosity of the churches of Macedonia. Although poor themselves, they had begged for an opportunity to give money to help the needy believers in Jerusalem, and they had given liberally because first they had given themselves to the Lord. Moneys were gathered from all the churches of Asia Minor and Greece.

A similar collection had been started the year before in Corinth but had not been finished (see 2 Corinthians 8:10). So Paul, who was in Macedonia at the time he wrote this and who had accepted no pay for his work from any of the churches except Philippi, suggests that the Corinthians follow Christ's example (see 2 Corinthians 8:9). The Lord knows that if He gets us, He will get our gifts and our service.

How did Paul say believers should give?

• Give out of poverty—2 Corinthians 8:2
• Give generously—2 Corinthians 8:3

- Give proportionately—2 Corinthians 8:12-14
- Give bountifully—2 Corinthians 9:6
- Give willingly—2 Corinthians 9:7
- Give cheerfully—2 Corinthians 9:7

God has always promised to reward the generous giver (see 2 Corinthians 9:6). He enriches us with spiritual graces as well as with material things. These gifts strengthened the ties of brotherhood between the Jewish and Gentile Christians. "Thanks be to God for his indescribable gift!" (2 Corinthians 9:15).

This is the reason for our giving: "For God so loved the world that he gave his one and only Son" (John 3:16). God Himself delights to give.

2 Corinthians

2 CORINTHIANS 10–13: PAUL'S APOSTLESHIP

The charge against Paul by some in the church was that he was a coward. He was bold in his writings, but was weak in character. However, to imagine that this man, who had turned city after city upside down, was weak is absurd. He was a powerful and dominating person. He was a man of outstanding gifts and had a keen and inquiring mind. Besides this, Christ lived in him and worked through him.

His enemies had said that no apostle would work with his own hands and support himself, and they had pointed to the other apostles as examples of this. But Paul explained that although he had the right to receive pay, he had refused it because he didn't want his example to be abused by these false teachers who wanted to commercialize the ministry. He declared that at least he had founded his own churches and did not go around troubling churches founded by others, as the false teachers were doing.

Paul also stated that if these false teachers could boast of their power and authority, then he would boast, too. In a dramatic manner, he challenged these critics to compare themselves with him in every way. He was a loyal Hebrew; he had worked more than all the rest of them put together; as a martyr he had suffered more than they all had, on land and on sea. He realized that it was in poor taste to boast about himself, and he disliked doing it, but his critics had forced him to do it. When Paul boasted, however, he did it for the glory of God.

We all have a tendency to use a wrong standard for measuring character. We compare ourselves to others like us, and we conclude that we are as good as the average person. But "when they measure themselves by themselves and compare themselves with themselves, they are not wise" (2 Corinthians 10:12). Average Christians are not what the Bible requires. Let us pray John Wesley's prayer, "Lord, make me an extraordinary Christian."

Experiencing Paradise

Paul saw paradise; he was even "caught up to the third heaven" (2 Corinthians 12:2). Recall that Jesus went to paradise at His death (see Luke 23:43). There, Paul was given marvelous visions and revelations, and he heard things that could not be put into words (see 2 Corinthians 12:4). No doubt no human language could describe the glory. It would have been like trying to describe a sunset to a person born blind. Paul had nothing to compare it with that we could understand.

It seemed that because of Paul's heavenly experiences, God allowed Paul to suffer "a thorn in [his] flesh" (2 Corinthians 12:7). The Lord knows the danger of boastful pride after such an experience, so He permitted "a messenger of Satan, to torment [him]"; Paul himself called his affliction "a thorn in my flesh" (2 Corinthians 12:7). There has been much speculation about what this "thorn" really was, but God has left us to wonder about it so that we would know that the grace that was sufficient for Paul in his trouble would be enough for any thorn given to any of us.

Understanding Thorns

Many people have wondered why God does not remove "thorns" from the flesh when we pray to Him. We must learn that God always answers prayer, but sometimes the answer is no. He knows it will be better for us to bear the thorn than be without it.

Some "thorns" in the flesh have caused the sufferers to lean on Christ. Sometimes a "thorn" is a warning to keep us from sin and failure. God proved to Paul that no matter what his weakness was, God's strength was sufficient for his needs.

Let me tell you about someone who more recently experienced this sufficiency. One day a minister buried his only child. The next day he went into his study to prepare his message for Sunday, but he couldn't, because his grief was too great. Then, through his tears, which continued to run down his cheeks, his eyes fell on these words: "My grace is sufficient" (2 Corinthians 12:9). To the minister, it seemed to say, "My grace *is* sufficient." He wrote it that way on a card and posted it so that he saw it whenever he sat at his desk. Because of this phrase, he learned to know that God is always present.

Understand that every word of 2 Corinthians 12:9 is important:

- "My"—means God.
- "Grace"—means unmerited favor. I bring Christ what I have—my sins. He brings me what He has—His righteousness. An exchange is made. He takes my sin and gives me His righteousness. This is grace, wonderful grace!
- "Is"—means present, always.
- "Sufficient"—means enough to satisfy. "Our sufficiency is of God" (2 Corinthians 3:5, *KJV*). Here is where Charles Haddon Spurgeon laughed out loud. "To think," he once said, "that our little cups could exhaust the ocean of His grace."

We are satisfied with Jesus. Is He your personal comfort? God gives us unusual strength for unusual tasks. Paul says, "For when I am weak, then I am strong" (2 Corinthians 12:10). When Christ dwells within us, we have the strength and courage to face whatever we need to.

Testing Oneself

"Examine yourselves to see whether you are in the faith; test yourselves" (2 Corinthians 13:5). In this second letter, Paul emphasizes that the Corinthians needed to know themselves spiritually—they needed to test themselves to make sure of their faith. He was anxious that none of them would be deceived. We too must use every means available to us to determine where we really stand spiritually.

Do not depend on a mere profession of religion. Do not rely on church membership. Joining a church saves no one. Joining Christ saves, so examine your standing with Him.

Do not trust a past experience. Live only for today. Trust only in a present love, a present faith and a present service. This gives you the test of your spiritual life in Jesus.

Do not rest on mere approved methods of conduct. You may go through the motions of religious worship but not be religious. Wax museum figures seem to wink and blink and breathe, but there is no actual life in them. Examine your motives for how you conduct your life. Is it to please God or people? What and who do you love? The adversary always tells us we are good enough, but Christ says we must be perfect. Here are some questions you need to ask yourself:

- *Do I love to think of Christ?*
- *Do I love to pray?*
- *Do I love to study God's Word?*
- *Do I love Christian friends?*
- *Do I love the Church?*
- *Do I love to serve Christ?*

Strive to make your answers always positive, and may you be blessed by the benediction in 2 Corinthians 13:14, which brings to a close many church services today.

Understanding Galatians

Galatians Portrays Jesus Christ, Our Liberty

AUTHOR: Galatians 1:1 clearly identifies the apostle Paul as the writer of the epistle to the Galatians.

DATE: Depending on where exactly the book of Galatians was sent and during which missionary journey Paul started the churches in that area, the book of Galatians was written somewhere between AD 51 and 57.

PURPOSE AND SUMMARY: Paul's letter addressed to the churches in Galatia, in modern Turkey, is an impassioned message on freedom in Christ. In Galatians Paul refutes the false teaching of those Jewish believers who claimed that one must be circumcised and keep Mosaic law to be saved and counted as followers of the Jewish Messiah, Jesus. This book's emphasis is similar to the theme of

Paul's letter to the Romans: Salvation is by faith in Christ alone, apart from keeping the Law (see chapters 1–4). Paul follows this with intensely practical teachings on walking in the Spirit and putting to death the sinful deeds of the flesh (see chapters 5–6).

Galatians shows that the believer is no longer under the law but is saved by faith alone. "It is for freedom that Christ has set us free. Stand firm, then" (Galatians 5:1). The Law is the first five books of God's Word (Genesis to Deuteronomy), written by Moses, by which every phase of Israel's life was to be guided.

During Paul's second missionary journey, he was delayed in Galatia by sickness (see Acts 16:6; Galatians 4:13). Though ill, this tireless servant of the Lord could not remain silent but kept on preaching the gospel. The theme of his sermon was Christ crucified (see Galatians 3:1), and he succeeded in founding the Christian churches in Galatia (see Galatians 1:6). They were scattered over a wide area and the people were mainly rural. Teachers of the Law had followed Paul, but they advocated salvation by works and claimed that even if Jesus were the Messiah, Christians should be circumcised and do all the works of the Law. These teachers explained that the reason Paul had not taught the Galatians this was that he was not a true apostle and had learned his doctrines from others. This news had upset the new converts.

Ceremonial Law

Circumcision was the initial rite of the Jewish religion. If people born Gentile wished to become Jewish, they had to observe this ceremonial law. It was much like immigrants to our country today must fulfill certain requirements in order to become US citizens, but once those requirements are met, although born on foreign soil, they are regarded as citizens just as those who are born here.

False teachers had "bewitched" the people by telling them they must keep all kinds of ceremonies (Galatians 3:1). Paul wanted them to know that nothing—no fetishes or works or ceremonies—could bring them to Christ. Salvation comes only by believing in Christ.

Being very fickle and loving something new, the Galatians were on the verge of accepting the views of these false teachers. When Paul heard about it, the matter seemed so urgent that, because no one was with him to write it, he wrote the letter himself (see Galatians 6:11).

Christ's Law

It has been said that Judaism was the cradle of Christianity and very nearly its grave. God raised up Paul as the Moses of the Christian church to deliver it from this bondage. This epistle has done more than any other book in the New Testament to free our Christian faith from Judaism and from the burden of salvation by works (taught by so many false cults), which has threatened the simple gospel of the Lord Jesus Christ. Many people want *to do* something to be saved. The question of the Philippian jailer, "What must I do to be saved?" is the question multitudes ask (Acts 16:30). And the answer is always the same: "Believe in the Lord Jesus, and you will be saved" (Acts 16:31).

A religion without the cross is not Christ's religion. Christ did not come merely to blaze a trail through a tangled forest or to give us an example of how we should live. He came to be our Savior. The cross has a great deal of power:

- To deliver from sin—Galatians 1:4; 2:21; 3:22
- To deliver from the curse of the law—Galatians 3:13
- To deliver from the self-life—Galatians 2:20; 5:24
- To deliver from the world—Galatians 6:14
- In the new birth—Galatians 4:4-7
- In receiving the Holy Spirit—Galatians 3:14
- In bringing forth the Spirit's fruit—Galatians 5:22-25

This epistle to the Galatians is the Christian's Declaration of Independence. Our battle hymn is "Christus Liberator." "So if the Son sets you free, you will be free indeed" (John 8:36). Many people think that restrictions destroy liberty, but the opposite is true. On entering a free public park, the first thing we usually see are a variety of signs: "Don't walk on the grass." "No dogs allowed." "Don't pick the flowers." But this is a free park! We do not, however, complain, because these laws preserve the park. If they were not enforced, the park would be the same as any neighborhood vacant lot. It is the same with society at large. If we revolt against God and His order, civilization will deteriorate into barbarism. This is what is happening in the world today. Liberty is not freedom from law—that is recklessness. Liberty is freedom from the Mosaic law system but obedience to "Christ's law" (1 Corinthians 9:21). Paul speaks of the liberty we have "in Christ" (Galatians 2:4): "Where the Spirit of the Lord is, there is freedom" (2 Corinthians 3:17). This is the one great secret of liberty.

This is the liberty that is discussed in this book, so get hold of Galatians and let Galatians get hold of you. In Galatians we are not servants working for a living, but daughters and sons working in our living. Learn what it is to be free in Christ! Christ said, "I no longer call you servants. . . . Instead, I have called you friends" (John 15:15).

In Romans we find our *standing*—in Galatians we take our *stand*:

- In Romans we are told to use our *heads* to grasp the great facts of Christianity.
- In 1 Corinthians we are told to put out our *hands* to grasp our privileges in Christ.
- In 2 Corinthians we are told to lift our *hearts* to receive the comforts that are ours.
- In Galatians we are told to stand on our feet in the liberty that Christ gives.

GALATIANS 1:1-10: ONE GOSPEL

The beginning of Galatians is the only time in all of Paul's writings when he does not express his thankfulness. Rather he says, "I am astonished" (Galatians 1:6). And this is the only church he does not ask to pray for him. How could he, seeing that they were dishonoring the Lord (see Galatians 1:6-9)?

Paul marvels that these new Christians could give up the gospel of liberty so quickly and accept a legalistic message that was no gospel at all. Twice he pronounced a curse on those causing the trouble. He says that if an angel from heaven were to preach any other gospel than the one he preached, "Let them be under God's curse!" (Galatians 1:8-9).

What was this gospel Paul preached? Paul's gospel shuts out all works. "Know that a man is not justified by the works of the law, but by faith in Jesus Christ . . . because by the works of the law no one will be justified" (Galatians 2:16). The difficulty about salvation is not that we should be good enough to be saved but that we should see that we are bad enough to need salvation. Christ can save only sinners. Grace cannot begin until the Law has proven that we are guilty, as the book of Romans shows each of us to be. Then Christ offers us His righteousness.

A gospel that is a mixture of law and grace has no power. The false teachers of this kind of gospel were "under God's curse" because they pervert (not deny) the gospel. They admitted that Christ had to die on the cross, but they denied that faith alone in His sacrifice was sufficient for salvation. They taught that to be saved, a person must keep at least some decrees of the Law. They thought that simple faith according to the gospel Paul preached was not sufficient for salvation. Some people still like this kind of preaching because they believe they can do something to look better before God.

Paul shows us the seriousness of our condition outside Christ. When a medical specialist says that your only hope is this or that, you know you must be in a critical and serious condition. Here the great gospel specialist, Paul, declares that our position is so serious that the gospel of the grace of God is our only hope. There is no other.

Paul introduced the atonement, a truth once so dear to the Galatians but now practically rejected: Christ gave Himself for our sins (see Galatians 1:4).

GALATIANS 1:11–2: PAUL'S APOSTLESHIP

God Himself authorized Paul's teaching (see Galatians 1:11-24). Paul proves that he received his gospel directly from the Lord. Only God could have changed him from a murderer to a preacher.

We can learn many things by experience, but that is not so with the things of God. To know them they must be revealed to us. Paul says, "I want you to know, brothers and sisters, that the gospel I preached is not of human origin. I did not receive it from any man, nor was I taught it; rather, I received it by revelation from Jesus Christ" (Galatians 1:11-12).

Paul did not consult any person about what he should preach; instead, he retired to the wilds of Arabia for three years and there listened to God. He was taught by the Spirit. He had been with Peter and James only 15 days after his three years in Arabia so he couldn't have learned much from them.

The authority behind Paul's gospel is shown by his rebuke of Peter (see Galatians 2:11-21). To prove that Peter was not a greater apostle than he, he points out how he had openly rebuked Peter for being two-faced about Jewish customs when he was in Antioch. Paul made no secret attempt to undermine Peter's authority, but he was not dominated by Peter's strength as an apostle to the Jewish people. Galatians 2:11 is an unanswerable argument against the supremacy of Peter. Fortunately, the friendship between Peter and Paul was so real that it withstood this severe test (see 2 Peter 3:15).

After Paul describes his confrontation of Peter, he writes a personal word of testimony, which gives us a complete picture of the Christian life both positively and negatively: "I have been crucified with Christ and I no longer live, but Christ lives in me. The life I now live in the body, I live by faith in the Son of God, who loved me and gave himself for me" (Galatians 2:20). This verse, describing a paradox, is true of every believer. We do not need to be crucified with Christ. We have already been crucified with Him. He died in our place. Now we live not by law but by faith. Christ was our sacrifice for sin and now is our sufficiency for the new life. The Christian life is a dying life—dying daily to self and sin. The crucified Savior lives in those who have shared His crucifixion.

GALATIANS 3–4: THE GOSPEL'S DEFENSE

"I've tried religion for the past five years and it hasn't worked. I gave it up." These were the words of a young man in answer to a preacher who had asked him to accept Christ.

"Why, I tried religion for 15 years and it did nothing for me. I gave it up too," the preacher said.

A pause followed. "Then why are you a minister?" the youth asked.

"Then I tried Christ, and He fully met my needs. It is not religion I am recommending to you, but a living, loving Savior."

Religion Versus Savior

"Religion," a word once so commonly used among Christians, is fast becoming out of vogue because it has been twisted and misapplied. A religious person now means someone who has accepted a creed or who observes certain ceremonies or who attends certain places of worship. But these things are not enough. There must be a living faith in the living Savior. It is possible to have a religion without the gospel. This was the peril that faced the Galatian Christians. Many people count on going to heaven based on their sincerity in believing some creed they have worked out to save themselves. They say, "The golden rule is my religion." But there is no salvation in that, for "without the shedding of blood there is no forgiveness" of sins (Hebrews 9:22).

People who do not believe that foreign missions have any value say that non-Christians have their own religions, so why try to change their thinking? Yes, they have so much religion that they are bowed down under the weight of the load, but they don't have the good news of the gospel. And we are commanded to preach the gospel to every creature.

Religion is the best some people can do. Christianity is the best God can do. See the results of people's best: "By the works of the law no one will be justified" (Galatians 2:16). How can a person be made just? "By faith in Christ and not by the works of the law" (Galatians 2:16). Christianity is God's best. Christ is no sheriff. He is "the Lamb of God, who takes away the sin of the world" (John 1:29). We are pronounced righteous not by works of the Law, but by faith in Him.

Free Salvation Versus Personal Effort

Paul defends the gospel of Christ. He describes his own preaching as having been so detailed that it was as if his listeners had actually seen Christ crucified (see Galatians 3:1). He shows that what the Law could not do grace did.

Paul puts a challenging question to these "foolish Galatians" (Galatians 3:1):

> You foolish Galatians, I have brought you the true gospel, and you received it with eagerness and gratitude. Now suddenly you drop the gospel. What has gotten into you? Come on now, my smart Galatians, you who all of a sudden have become professors while I seem to be your pupil, did you receive the Holy Spirit by the works of the law or by the preaching of the gospel? [This question was a challenge to them because their own experience proved the truth of Paul's preaching to them.] You cannot say you received the Holy Spirit because you kept the law. Nobody ever heard of such a thing. But as soon as the gospel came, you receive the Holy Spirit by the simple hearing of faith (see Galatians 3:1-6).

It is hard for us to believe that the priceless gift of forgiveness of sins and the gift of the Holy Spirit are not gained by real effort, but God offers them to us free of charge. Why not take them? Why worry about your own unworthiness? Why not accept them with thanks?

Immediately foolish reason says, "If people don't have to do a thing for their salvation or for an atonement for their wrongdoings, then they will become lazy and will not even try to do good." But we have found that when we have accepted the gospel with a thankful heart, then we get busy doing good works. We want to please God. Those who think we ought to be saved by our works think faith is an easy thing, but we know from personal experience how hard it is to simply believe.

Righteousness from Faith

"So also Abraham 'believed God, and it was credited to him as righteousness'" (Galatians 3:6). Abraham may have had a good reputation for his upright life, but not with God. In God's sight, Abraham was a condemned sinner. You see, righteousness had been given to Abraham because of his faith, not his works. If faith without works was sufficient for Abraham, why should we turn from faith to law? Abraham believed. That is faith. Faith says to God, "I believe what you say."

It must have startled the proud and troublesome legalists when Paul told them that those who believe in Christ Jesus are the true children of Abraham, not those born of Abraham's flesh and blood (see Galatians 3:26-29). Though born in obscurity, all who have had a new birth can sit down with Abraham as a child of the father of the faithful (see Galatians 3:14,29).

Civil Law Versus God's Law

Remember, the law Paul talks about is not civil law. Civil law has its place, but civil righteousness will never deliver a person from the condemnation of God's Law. Just because I am a law-abiding citizen does not mean I am a Christian. Governmental laws are blessings for this life only, not for the life hereafter. Otherwise, many unbelievers would be nearer to heaven than some Christians are, for unbelievers often excel in civil righteousness.

A guilty man would never appear in court and claim he is innocent because he is a good church member, a generous giver or a member of a Sunday School class. Neither can the same man as a sinner appear in the court of heaven and claim that because he serves as a public official, is a good citizen or is a moral man, God should accept him. The civil courts require that you keep the law. The court of heaven requires that you have faith in Jesus Christ.

The law cannot give righteousness but it does bring death to all who do not keep it (see Galatians 3:10). Law demands perfect obedience. Many think they should get a reward just for keeping the law. People really ought to keep the law and get nothing for doing so. Suppose you live in a city all your life, and during your lifetime, you obey all the laws of that city. Will the mayor present you with a gift because you have not broken any laws? Of course not. But suppose after 20 years of law keeping you then commit a crime. The authorities will then give you something—a jail sentence for breaking the law. The Bible tells us that a curse (a sentence) is on all who break the law, while a blessing is on all those who live by faith.

"Christ redeemed us from the curse of the law by becoming a curse for us" (Galatians 3:13). As all had broken the Law, all had come under its curse. But Christ redeemed us. "Don't turn back to the Law from which Christ redeemed us. You foolish Galatians, who has bewitched you, that you should turn from the blessing of faith to the curse of law?" (see Galatians 3:1-3,13-14).

Purposes of the Law

The Law deals with what we are and do, while grace deals with what Christ is and does. What good is the Law? We find the answer in Galatians 3:19-20. The Law restrains the wicked by giving punishment for crimes, just as civil laws restrain people by inducing fear of jail or the death penalty. These restraints do not make people righteous, but they do restrain them from crime.

Another purpose of the Law is spiritual. The law reveals to us our sins, our blindness and our contempt of God. As long as we are not murderers or thieves, we would swear we are righteous. As long as we think we are right, we are proud and despise God's grace. How does God show us what we really are? By the Law. Our monster of self-righteousness needs a big ax, and the Law is just that. When people see by the Law that they are under God's wrath, they begin to restrain themselves. When the conscience has been thoroughly frightened by the Law, it welcomes the gospel; and we are led to the way of grace.

Law reveals sin but does not remove it. The Law proves that we are all sinners by nature and directs us to Christ! We so often think that we become sinners when we commit some sinful act. But it is because we are already sinners that we commit the act. We lie because we are liars. We steal because we are thieves. We do not become liars when we utter the lie. The Law only proves we are liars.

The Law too was given to drive us to Christ by showing us our need. The gospel tells us that Christ is the only One who can meet that need (see Galatians 3:23–4:11). Paul says the law was our "guardian" to shock us into a sense of our need of Christ so that we could be justified by faith in Him (Galatians 3:24). God's Law is not like the cruel and tyrannical schoolmaster of the past. His Law is not meant to always torment us. God's Law is like the good teacher who trains children to find pleasure in doing the things they formerly detested.

The Law really has a place in leading us into a Christian experience. Did you ever see a woman trying to sew without a needle? She would never make anything with only a thread. This is like God's dealing with us. He puts the needle of the Law first, for we sleep so soundly in our own sins that we need to be aroused by something sharp. Then when He has the needle of the Law squarely in our hearts, He pulls through it a lifelong thread of gospel love and peace and joy.

Sons of God

Paul tells us that all people are not the children of God. It is faith in Christ—not works of the law or the Fatherhood of God or the brotherhood of people—that makes us children of God. "You are all children of God through faith [in Christ Jesus]" (Galatians 3:26). Faith, not works, puts us into the family of God.

Galatians

As long as an heir is underage there is no difference between that person and a slave, for the heir is under the control of a guardian just as a slave is under the control of a master. So Paul tells us in Galatians 4:5-6 that all believers are children of God, yet all children are not grown-up ones. Christ came to ransom us so that we would be no longer slaves under the law, but possess all the privileges of full-grown sons and daughters and heirs.

As another illustration of their state of freedom in Christ, Paul reminds the Galatians that Abraham had two sons—Ishmael, the child of Hagar (the bondwoman), and Isaac, the child of Sarai (the free woman). Ishmael did not enjoy the blessings of a son in Abraham's house but was left out in the cold, although he was the firstborn. Isaac was the one called. This is what happens to those who seek to be saved by keeping the Law. But Isaac, the child of promise and faith, was the heir of all things. So we are heirs of a spiritual promise.

GALATIANS 5–6: GOSPEL APPLICATIONS

Personal Freedom

The first application of the gospel pertains to one's own personal freedom from the Law. Paul wants the Galatians to hold fast to their personal liberty (see Galatians 5:1-12). The gospel of God's grace gives true liberty: "It is for freedom that Christ has set us free. Stand firm, then, and do not let yourselves be burdened again by a yoke of slavery" (Galatians 5:1). If the Galatians seek to be saved by keeping the Law, they are bound by the Law. Their liberty should be prized because it cost so much, the blood of Christ.

"Stand firm." This is one of Paul's favorite expressions. Maintain your position of being erect!

- In the faith—1 Corinthians 16:13
- In the liberty—Galatians 5:1
- In the Spirit—Philippians 1:27
- In the Lord—Philippians 4:1

The gospel of grace guards against recklessness (see Galatians 5:13-15). Many people are afraid to live under grace instead of the Law because they're afraid that it will lead others to live as they please and do as they like. But grace will always lead a person to live as God pleases and to like what He likes.

We abuse our liberty in two ways:

1. By lack of love—Galatians 5:13-14. "Serve one another humbly in love. For the entire law is fulfilled in keeping this one command: 'Love your neighbor as yourself.'" Use love!

2. By unclean living—Galatians 5:16-26. See how the flesh acts up. Read Galatians 5:19-21, a list of more than a dozen evil works of the flesh. These are sins of the mind as well as the body. This is what we are by nature and these are the things we do. Christ has given the Holy Spirit to make us free from these: "Walk by the Spirit, and you will not gratify the desires of the sinful nature" (verse 16). Let the Holy Spirit rule your life.

Children begin to walk by someone holding on to their hand. We begin our Christian walk by the Spirit holding on to us. But He is not only a help on the outside, as when an adult holds on to a child, but He also helps on the inside. Think of walking arm in arm with the Holy Spirit! This means no running ahead or lagging behind (see Galatians 5:16).

Spiritual Fruits

There are nine graces given to us by the Spirit, described in Galatians 5:22-23:

- Toward God—(1) love, (2) joy, (3) peace
- Toward others—(4) patience, (5) kindness, (6) goodness
- Toward self—(7) faithfulness, (8) gentleness, (9) self-control

These nine fruit of the Spirit are in stark contrast to the works of the sinful nature. But if we "remain" in Christ, we will be free to bear fruit with God (John 15:4-10). Are you showing this cluster of fruit in your life?

Sowing and Reaping

"A man reaps what he sows" (Galatians 6:7). If we sow the seeds of our life in the soil of the Spirit, we will reap a spiritual harvest and honor God. If we sow in the soil of the flesh (the baser appetites), we will reap moral weakness and corruption (see Galatians 6:7-8). The Spirit brings forth only good fruit; the flesh, only evil.

The harvest will not be according to how much we know but how much we sow. We may have a large supply of seed in the barn of the mind, but unless it is planted in suitable soil it will produce no harvest. Sow the seed of thoughts in word and deeds. God's Word always brings forth seed after its kind.

Many deceive themselves by saying, "It doesn't matter what I sow as long as I am sincere." Would that be good advice for a farmer? Self-life will never produce the fruit of the Spirit. "Sowing" and "reaping" are agricultural terms. The Christian worker is compared to a farmer, not to a salesman or a mechanic. Christian work—dealing with souls—is not about buying and selling or about repairing; we are to plant the living Word.

Ownership

Paul's body bore "the marks of Jesus" (Galatians 6:17). These marks showed three things about Paul.

First, they showed ownership—Paul belonged to another. The Greek word *stigma* means a brand or a mark applied to the face, body or arm of a slave or criminal. What were Paul's stigma? They were the scars he had received by enduring for Christ persecutions and hardships (see 2 Corinthians 6:4; 11:23). The rough hands of a laborer reveal that he or she is used to hard physical labor; the weather-beaten face of a sea captain, the wounds of a soldier, the lines in a mother's brow are all honorable. The slave marks of

Christ speak, first, of a changed character and, second, of a labor of love for Him.

Second, they showed devotion—Paul dedicated his life to God. What scars had the false teachers received for Christ? None. They saved themselves. But behold Paul!

Third, they showed commission—Paul's authorization came from God. The false teachers came armed with letters of authority. Paul was without letters of recommendation. But behold his scars! They constituted his commission.

In Christ, we are free to know the boundless life that is in Him. In Him, we are a "new creation" (Galatians 6:15). Being a new creation, we have a new life in Christ. No wonder Paul cries out, "May I never boast except in the cross of our Lord Jesus Christ, through which the world has been crucified to me, and I to the world" (Galatians 6:14). "Let the world go by! I have Christ, and having Him, I have all things," Paul is saying. "Oh, the joy of a free, full life in Christ Jesus!" Can you say the same?

POINTS TO REMEMBER

- The Law shows us our need—grace shows God's provision to meet that need.

- The Law says we must work for our salvation ("do")—grace says salvation is free, a gift ("done").

- Faith makes us receive salvation by believing—works keep us striving to earn it.

- The Spirit gives us daily victory over sin—the flesh makes us prone to sin.

- The *cross* means love and sacrifice—the *world* suggests force and selfishness.

36

Understanding Ephesians

Ephesians Portrays Jesus Christ, Our All in All

AUTHOR: Ephesians 1:1 identifies the author of the book of Ephesians as the apostle Paul.

DATE: The book was possibly written around AD 60 while Paul was under house arrest in Rome (see Acts 28:14-31).

PURPOSE AND SUMMARY: The letter to the Ephesians is one of the apostle Paul's four "Imprisonment Letters"—Ephesians, Philippians, Colossians and Philemon. Although addressed to the church in Ephesus, this letter is generally believed to have been a circular letter, to be read in other churches, describing the believers' exalted position through Christ, the Church as the Body of Christ, the Church's relationship to God, and practical implications of living as children of light through faith in Christ.

In this epistle, we enter the holy of holies in Paul's writings. Paul speaks in 2 Corinthians 12:2 of being "caught up to the third heaven." Here, as it were, he gives his report, and he seems to be carried away as he tells about it. It is the greatest revelation of truth that God has given to us, the revelation of a mystery that has been hidden from before the foundation of the world.

This book shows us the great mystery of the Church. The real Church is the Body of Christ, and believers are members of that sacred Body of which Christ is the head. The Father not only prepared a body in which Jesus Christ would suffer, but He also prepared a Body for Him in which He should be glorified. The Greek word for "church" is *ecclesia*, which means an assembly of called-out ones. Christ is choosing "a people for his name" (Acts 15:14). The Church is an organism. It is the Body of Christ.

Imagine for a moment that the Body is like a great building. The "stones" are redeemed human beings. Christ, the Head, occupies the great throne room. All the parts are like rooms in the building. With this picture in mind, it is easy to see the whole story of the mystery of the Church. The suffering of Christ in an earthly body is now to be made up for by erecting a spiritual body, or building. Come with Paul through this glorious structure as he outlines it in Ephesians:

A. The believer's position—Ephesians 1–3
    1. "In Christ"—Ephesians 1:1
    2. "In the heavenly realms"—Ephesians 1:3,20; 2:6; 3:10

B. The believer's walk—Ephesians 4–6
    1. Ecclesiastically—Ephesians 4
    2. Morally—Ephesians 5
    3. Socially—Ephesians 5:21–6:9
    4. Martially—Ephesians 6:10-24

Paul seems to present a picture of "Christ's Temple of Ephesus," which the Christian may enter. It is "a holy temple in the

Lord" (Ephesians 2:21). We approach in these chapters, one after another, six magnificent rooms in this great temple. They are all "in Christ." Let the scenes of this book be laid in each of these rooms successively.

EPHESIANS 1: THE ANTEROOM

Let us enter this sacred temple with hushed voices and bared heads. Christ is going to allow us to come before His holy presence. The door opens into the spacious anteroom, where we read on the walls our standing with God through Jesus Christ: "Blessed . . . with all spiritual blessings: chosen . . . in him before the foundation of the world: . . . holy and without blame before him in love: . . . accepted in the beloved" (Ephesians 1:3-6, *KJV*). These are some great wall mottoes for Christians. It will take all of our spiritual energy to live up to them.

Our Blessings

The blessings of the Christian are not only heavenly (eternal life with God) but also "in the heavenly realms." Go through this first chapter and mark all you find "in Christ." (And when you read the next two chapters, do the same thing.) You will find that our blessings are many:

- Saints in Christ Jesus—Ephesians 1:1
- Blessed in Christ—Ephesians 1:3
- Chosen in Christ—Ephesians 1:4
- Adopted by Christ—Ephesians 1:5
- Lavished with love in Christ, the One God loves—Ephesians 1:6
- Redeemed and forgiven in Christ—Ephesians 1:7
- His will revealed in Himself—Ephesians 1:9
- Everything centered in Christ—Ephesians 1:10
- Participants in God's good plan in Christ—Ephesians 1:11
- Glorified in Christ, sealed with the Holy Spirit—Ephesians 1:12-13

Ephesians

- Inheritance in Christ—Ephesians 1:14
- Faith in Christ—Ephesians 1:15
- Wisdom in Him—Ephesians 1:17
- Hope in Christ—Ephesians 1:18
- Power in Christ—Ephesians 1:19-20
- Made alive in Christ—Ephesians 2:5-6
- Created in Christ—Ephesians 2:10
- Brought near to God in Christ—Ephesians 2:13
- Growing in Christ—Ephesians 2:21
- Built in Christ—Ephesians 2:22
- Sharers in His promise in Christ—Ephesians 3:6
- Wisdom of God manifested in Christ—Ephesians 3:10-11
- Freedom and confidence through Christ—Ephesians 3:12

Did we always exist in this state? Read Ephesians 2:11-13. We learn on entering this temple that our calling and position have been planned and worked out by God the Father, the Son and the Holy Spirit "before the creation of the world" (Ephesians 1:4). All Christians should know their calling above everything else (see Ephesians 1:18). The true knowledge of it will govern their lives.

Our Redemption

- The Father planned it—Ephesians 1:4-6
- The Son paid for it—Ephesians 1:7-12
- The Spirit applied it—Ephesians 1:13-14

"In him we have redemption through his blood, the forgiveness of sins, in accordance with the riches of God's grace" (Ephesians 1:7).

Redemption is the most glorious work of God. It is far greater than His work of creation. He spoke a word and worlds were formed, but it cost Him the life of His beloved Son to redeem the world. Paul enjoyed dwelling on this theme, because he had experienced Christ's redeeming love. He had been redeemed from sin, from the curse and bondage of the law. He had been washed clean in the blood of Christ and anointed by the Holy Spirit. So it only makes sense for him to have gloried in his Redeemer.

"Redeem" means to buy back or to pay the ransom price. This is what Christ did for us when we were held captive to sin. Let us consider what the sinner is a captive to:

1. Sin—"Jesus replied, 'Very, truly, I tell you, everyone who sins is a slave to sin'" (John 8:34). We feel that bondage. We know sin rules our lives.

2. Satan—Paul speaks of sinners, recovering "from the trap of the devil, who has taken them captive to do his will" (2 Timothy 2:26).

3. Law—We have broken the Law, and for this reason "the whole world is a prisoner of sin" (Galatians 3:22). We are behind the bars of a prison. We have been put under arrest for violating the Law.

The captive is in a miserable state and needs to be redeemed.

- The provision for our redemption is Christ—Christ is our Redeemer! "In him we have redemption" (Ephesians 1:7).

- The means of our redemption is Christ—Christ voluntarily took our place. "In him we have redemption through his blood. . . . Not with perishable things such as silver or gold . . . but with the precious blood of Christ" (Ephesians 1:7; 1 Peter 1:18-19). He stood charged with our sins and paid the penalty with His blood.

- The fruit of our redemption is God's grace—Even "the forgiveness of sins" is the result of redeeming love, and this is "in accordance with the riches of God's grace" (Ephesians 1:7). Grace is unmerited favor. God's forgiveness is according to His unending favor, which is not limited by our faults.

God casts our sins behind His back. He blots them out of His book of remembrance. He sinks them into the depths of the sea. He removes them as far as the east is from the west. Yes, He forgives "in accordance with the riches of [his] grace."

We hear a great prayer in this anteroom. Imagine hearing Paul pray (see Ephesians 1:15-23)! Paul wants every one of us who is a believer to realize fully his or her privileges in Christ. He wants our understanding to "be enlightened" so that we will behold the glory of Christ (Ephesians 1:18). There is no use showing a gorgeous sunset to a blind person. So we cannot understand the greatness of God until the great physician has healed our spiritual eyes.

Each believer should know the three "whats" in this prayer. Do you know the answers?

1. What is the hope of His calling?

2. What are the riches of the glory of His inheritance in the saints? (Think of Christ's inheritance in us. He has suns and stars, but He wants sons and saints.)

3. What is the exceeding greatness of His power? (What the Church needs today is power. Her real strength has been cut away.)

EPHESIANS 2: THE AUDIENCE CHAMBER

Next we are conducted into the glorious audience chamber of the King, into the divine presence. "We . . . have access to the Father by one Spirit" (Ephesians 2:18). We would tremble as we enter if we did not hear the gracious words sound out, "You were dead in your transgressions and sins . . . but because of his great love for us . . . made us alive with Christ. . . . And seated us with him in the heavenly realms" (Ephesians 2:1-6). But best of all, there is a sweet Voice sounding through the corridors: "You are welcome here!" "Consequently, you are no longer foreigners and strangers, but fellow citizens with God's people and also members of his household" (Ephesians 2:19). All of this is in sharpest contrast to what we were "formerly" (Ephesians 2:11; see also verses 12-13). We once were far off. Now we are near.

In this audience chamber, we find that God has made both believing Jews and Gentiles one in Christ. This can be better understood by an illustration from Dr. Frank A. Keller.

Dr. Keller, who spent more than 25 years as a missionary in China, once told about a barber who was marvelously converted. He had been an opium addict and a moral degenerate. In desperation, he came to the missionaries, and their prayers for him were answered. His appetite for opium left and he became a living witness for Christ.

During the barber's stay in the mission, a young man of "the student class" came with questions to the mission, but seeing the barber, he refused to enter. (A barber's occupation was held in contempt in China.) One day, thinking the barber had gone, the student entered the mission and met the barber. Being too polite not to speak to him, he began to talk with him. The barber told him about the wonderful change that had come into his life through Christ. Suddenly, class barriers melted away. The barber soon was a guest in the student's home, surrounded with wealth and culture. Christ had made both of them new people, equal in His eyes.

This is what Christ will do with both Jew and Gentile, slave and free. Christ makes each one of us a new person and gives us access to the very audience chamber of the King. This new person has access to God through the blood of His Son (see Ephesians 2:13). He is our only mediator, and He says, "No one comes to the Father except through me" (John 14:6). When we have been redeemed, the Holy Spirit introduces each new person at the court of heaven. The Father rejoices in the new person and welcomes him or her into His presence.

The Planning and Production of the Masterpiece

God is producing a masterpiece, His Church. Paul says, "For we are God's handiwork" (Ephesians 2:10). "Handiwork" is translated from the Greek word *poiema*—poem or masterpiece.

In Ephesians 1, we find how God planned and worked to produce this masterpiece. We were "chosen in Christ" to be holy and blameless (see Ephesians 1:4-5). In the ages of past eternity, God was thinking about us, loving us and planning to bless us. You must understand that before Satan ever appeared to spoil the happiness of people on this earth, God made plans to make blameless all who would believe in Him.

Then in Ephesians 2:1-10 we find out how the masterpiece was produced. Look at the material God had to work with:

- What the nature of a person is—Ephesians 2:1-3
- What the walk of a natural person is—Ephesians 2:2

How does God produce a masterpiece out of such material? "But . . . God"—see God act! He changes all by His touch! "But . . . God" is the bridge that leads us out of our dark and hopeless condition (Ephesians 2:4). When all human strength is at an end, "But . . . God." Remember Christ comes to give life to the dead.

An old tale relates how a piece of marble once cried from a pile of material that was left as rubbish after a great building had been erected, "Glory, glory!" A passerby, hearing the cry, stopped. He learned from the marble, half-covered with dust and rubbish, that Michelangelo had just passed by and said, "I see an angel in that stone." Now he had gone to get his mallet and chisel.

Humanity was like that stone in the heap—broken and useless—but the great sculptor saw it and began His masterpiece. As Michelangelo saw the angel in the old stone, so God sees the image of His Son in wretched humanity. The greatest proof of Christianity is that it has produced a new person who is approved unto God. Only God could make a Paul out of Saul.

Destiny of the Masterpiece

What is the fate of this new production? What a destiny it has in store! What is a little suffering with a few trials here in comparison to the glory "in the coming ages" when God will "show the incomparable riches of his grace" (Ephesians 2:7)? He will tell the universe what He has accomplished.

Salvation is the gift of God: "For it is by grace you have been saved, through faith—and this not from yourselves, it is the gift of God" (Ephesians 2:8). Faith is a gift, too: "Faith comes from hearing the message" (Romans 10:17). Faith is the channel of salvation. It is the hand that receives the gift. It connects us with God.

EPHESIANS 3: THE THRONE ROOM

Standing at the doors of the throne room are the stalwart guards of Law. They demand: "Who goes there? Why do you come? What are your credentials?"

I answer feebly, "A sinner; I come to see the Lamb. I have nothing to recommend me for admittance."

Then I hear the voice of the Lamb from within, the call of the Son of Grace: "It is one of my sheep. Invite her in. My blood covers all. She needs no credentials." And grace brings me past the stern guards of Law into the throne room of His mercy.

"In him and through faith in him we may approach God with freedom and confidence" (Ephesians 3:12). What a piling up of words to convince us that our privilege and position as Christian believers are real! We are "accepted in the beloved" (Ephesians 1:6, *KJV*).

Here we behold the King! With Paul we bow our knee "before the Father, from whom every family in heaven and on earth derives its name" (Ephesians 3:14-15). Is posture a small thing? Kneeling is the attitude of humility, confession and entreaty. Remember that the holiest men in the Bible have approached God this way. David, Solomon and Daniel all went down on their knees. These men stooped to conquer but knelt to prevail.

Paul tells how God had held back from the Gentiles the secret that they should be heirs and shareholders of the gospel and have admission into the Church (His Body) on the same terms as the Jewish people (see Ephesians 3:8-10). But "to bring unity to all things in heaven and on earth under Christ" was God's plan (Ephesians 1:10).

The word "mystery," which occurs four times in this chapter, does not mean something mysterious. It merely refers to something that is hidden until the appropriate time comes for God to reveal it.

The mystery of the Church is that the Gentiles are to share equally with the Jewish people of God's promises (see Ephesians 3:6). All this was "by faith" (Galatians 3:8; see also Romans 15:9-10). That God would make the Gentiles co-heirs of Christ and co-members of His Church was radical.

Paul prays again and his prayer is recorded in Ephesians 3:13-21. Paul's first prayer gave us three whats (see Ephesians 1). This prayer gives us four thats and is steeped in the love of Christ:

1. That they should be strengthened by His Spirit
2. That they might have Christ dwelling in their hearts
3. That they might understand what is the breadth, length, depth and height of the love of Christ
4. That they might be filled with the fullness of God

Paul enjoys the "riches" of the gospel (Ephesians 3:8,16). Its gifts are abundant and its resources are inexhaustible.

If we are to enjoy this life in the Temple of God, we must be yielded in obedience to Him. If we as willing subjects yield to His plan for our lives, we will find that our lives will be filled with joy and beauty.

EPHESIANS 4: THE JEWEL AND DRESSING ROOMS

Here amid the flash of the jewel room, we will get our decorations and our garments of holiness—"Be completely humble and gentle; be patient, bearing with one another in love" (Ephesians 4:2). Here are our banners and emblems—"one Lord, one faith, one baptism" (Ephesians 4:5). Here are the brilliant gems of the graces as assigned—"But to each one of us grace has been given as Christ apportioned it" (Ephesians 4:7). We must lay aside the old life as we would lay aside an old garment, and we must now wear the new life as a new garment (see Ephesians 4:22-25).

We must be different, but how? In what respect? What are the things we should be very careful about? We must put away lying. Our speech shows our spirit. We must put away all bitterness and anger and harsh words. We must be kind to each other. We must not have anything to do with evils of any sort. Read Ephesians 4:31-32.

We must go into God's dressing room, not to make new garments, but to put them on. God is the tailor and He makes our clothing to conform to our position and purpose in life. God wants His sons and daughters to wear suitable garments.

We have discovered as we came into this temple what our riches are in the heavenlies (see Ephesians 1:18-21). Now we must "live a life worthy of the calling you have received" (Ephesians 4:1). The way we live must correspond to our creed. A heavenly calling demands a heavenly conduct.

We know that our spiritual lives affect our social lives. But many turn that around and attempt to create a social life that will in turn create a spiritual life. This cannot be. When we are in right relation to God, we will be in proper relation to people.

When God puts on us His jewels of grace, He seals us by His Spirit (see Ephesians 4:30). This seal is like the diamond a young man puts on the engagement finger of the one he has promised to marry. The Lord knows the ones that are His.

The seal is the mark of ownership. "They are mine." The seal is established for security. We are sealed for the day of redemption. Have you the seal? Then show it!

EPHESIANS 5: THE CHOIR AND ORATORY ROOMS

Now that we are sealed with the seal of ownership, we are to go out and be followers of God as dear children. A Christian is *I* following Christ—Christ-*I*-an.

What is a Christian "walk"? It is not a path or a way of moving about over the earth or even a sphere of work. A Christian's walk includes conduct, attitudes and commitment; it is, in short, a way of living before all people.

According to Ephesians 4:1-3, we are to walk:

- Humbly—"Be completely humble and gentle."
- Lovingly—"Be patient, bearing with one another in love."
- Peacefully—"Make every effort to keep the unity of the Spirit through the bond of peace."

The walk of a Christian requires us to do the following:

- Walk in love—Ephesians 5:1-2.
- Walk in light—Ephesians 5:8.
- Walk carefully—Ephesians 5:15-16.

The Lord not only tells us to walk carefully in the spiritual sphere of our lives, but also in every other field. How is your walk as a Christian before your family, your friends and your acquaintances? God demands a walk worthy of Him every place and everywhere. How practical all of this is! How simple yet how spiritual! Only men and women who believe that the Christian life "is not I but Christ" could fulfill such demands. Christ is the key to a life of victory in the Son of God. He teaches that a child of God can and must, under all circumstances, be a living witness to the power of Christ in his or her life.

"Do not get drunk on wine, which leads to debauchery. Instead, be filled with the Spirit" (Ephesians 5:18). The body, mind and spirit cannot function without outside stimulants. No one will think clearly or feel deeply unless something without excites him or her. But this is where the tragedy can occur. The world has plenty of powerful stimulants that can give quick and exciting highs to our systems. But the results are devastating. Our bodies and minds are not made for such ruinous jolts and are destroyed by them.

Our bodies are for God's altars. "Therefore, I urge you, brothers and sisters . . . to offer your bodies as a living sacrifice, holy and pleasing to God—this is your true and proper worship" (Romans 12:1). The Holy Spirit fires our bodies and spirits and sets them aglow, but He never destroys. Therefore God commands, "Do not get drunk on wine. . . . Instead, be filled [set aflame] with the Spirit" (Ephesians 5:18).

We can burn and never be consumed. We may live dangerously for God and never be in danger.

It is just as great a sin not to be filled with the Spirit of God as it is to be drunk with wine. Don't think that only ministers and missionaries need to be filled with God's blessed presence. Everyone has that need! God's Spirit is waiting to fill His temples (see Ephesians 5:19-20).

"[Speak] to one another with psalms, hymns, and songs from the Spirit. Sing and make music from your heart to the Lord" (Ephesians 5:19). Sing, Christian, sing! Christ wants you to. A singing heart guarantees a transformed life. When the Spirit fills the heart, the lips overflow with praise. We will walk the Christian life as we sing and talk about Christ.

This joyful praise heard during Christians' meetings is in contrast to the noisy drunken revelries of Ephesus. Singing is the most natural joyous expression of the Christian life. I hope your church takes part in making music in many ways in God's house. God does not delight in sighing and groaning or weeping but in songs of praise and adoration, in rejoicing and thanksgiving. He is the One who inspires the poet, the hymn writer, the artist in the world. The devil is the author of distress and discord.

There is social life in this great music room of God's temple. And we find it in relationship to everyone.

EPHESIANS 6: THE ARMORY

Now we stand in a room hung with the whole armor of God. The armor is His, not ours! But He tells us to put it on. We must put on all of it if we want to be safe. The armor is not for a museum where we can go and admire it for its strength; it is for the battle-field. Polished armor hanging up in the hall of our creed will not save us on the day of battle. What a relief to know that we do not have to provide the armor! How ignorant we are of the strength and schemes of the enemy! How inadequately we judge our own ability and weakness!

Paul says, "Finally, be strong in the Lord and in his mighty power" (Ephesians 6:10). You can be strong! You must be strong! But remember this: "Be strong in the Lord, and in the power of His might!" As soon as you are brought into communion with God, you need to be fitted for the fight of faith. All who belong to the kingdom of God's dear Son have the forces of the king-dom of Satan against them, so they need to be covered with the whole armor of God.

The Christian's walk includes a warfare. We need to know the tricks of the forces marshaled against us! We have been raised to the heavenly places of fellowship with Christ. Let us maintain the honor of our calling and the wealth of our high status. As good soldiers, let us stand and defend our interests. The crying need of our day is for strong people. In Ephesians 5, we were asked to put on clothing suited to the new person living in society. In Ephesians 6, we are told to put on armor necessary to the combat soldier—"the full armor of God" (Ephesians 6:11):

- "Belt of truth"—verse 14
- "Breastplate of righteousness"—verse 14
- "The readiness that comes from the gospel" on our feet—verse 15
- "Shield of faith"—verse 16
- "Helmet of salvation"—verse 17
- "Sword of the Spirit, which is the word of God"—verse 17
- "Prayers"—verse 18

We must go to Calvary for each piece of this wonderful ar-mor. When we put it on, we can see that our whole body is cov-ered. But you notice there is no armor for the back. The Christian is never supposed to run from the enemy but fight the good fight of faith, praying always! We are to "take [our] stand against" the enemy (Ephesians 6:11).

Stand, Christian, in the victory Christ wrought on Calvary!

37

Understanding Philippians

Philippians Portrays Jesus Christ, Our Joy

SELECTED BIBLE READINGS

DAY OF THE WEEK		MAIN TOPIC
Sunday: Philippians 1	Joy in the Midst of Suffering	
Monday: Philippians 2:1-11	Joy in Christ	
Tuesday: Philippians 2:12-30	Joy in Salvation	
Wednesday: Philippians 3:1-9	Joy in Christ's Righteousness	
Thursday: Philippians 3:10-21	Joy in Christ's Will	
Friday: Philippians 4:1-7	Joy in Christ's Strength	
Saturday: Philippians 4:8-23	Joy in Christ's Provision	

AUTHOR: Philippians 1:1 identifies the author of the book of Philippians as the apostle Paul and possibly also Timothy.

DATE: The book was written in approximately AD 61, when Paul was under house arrest in Rome (Acts 28:14-31).

PURPOSE AND SUMMARY: In this letter, which is a message of joy, the apostle Paul expresses his gratitude for the Philippians' love and material assistance. The epistle is uniquely significant because of its presentation of the humility of Jesus as a model for us. Its practicality is also observed in Paul's advice to Euodia and Syntyche to try to work out their differences and "to be of the same mind in the Lord" (Philippians 4:2).

The epistle to the Philippians was written to the first church founded in Europe. Paul was called there by the vision and the cry, "Come over to Macedonia and help us" (Acts 16:9).

Paul urges the Church to have Christian unity and joy. This letter shows how unity among Christians can be broken. Christ is the secret of joy. "Further, my brothers and sisters, rejoice in the Lord!" (Philippians 3:1). Then there is a pause. Paul tries to think of some better last word to speak, but he can't find it. Finally he cries out, "Rejoice in the Lord always. I will say it again: Rejoice!" (Philippians 4:4). This is joy in the midst of troubles and problems.

Paul and Silas, you remember, sang in the jail there at Philippi at midnight when their backs were bleeding and sore! Paul is rejoicing now as he writes this letter, in effect under house arrest, for he knows that his detention was helping him to spread the gospel. He could reach some in Caesar's household that he otherwise never could have brought to Christ. He urged his Philippian converts to rejoice because they were allowed to suffer for Christ (see Philippians 1:29).

"The joy of the LORD is your strength" (Nehemiah 8:10). The words "joy" and "rejoice" occur in this epistle more than a dozen times. Paul seems to laugh out loud for sheer joy in this letter. He is the rejoicing apostle. "Joy" and "rejoice" and "all" are the words to underline. "Be glad" is Paul's exhortation. We are commanded to rejoice. We break a commandment if we do not rejoice, for joy drives out discord. It helps in the midst of trials. As Charles Spurgeon once said, "Joy is a bird; let it fly in the open heavens, and let its music be heard of all men." Sinners, like Augustine, are attracted to Jesus by the joy of Christians.

This letter is the sweetest of all Paul's letters. There is no scolding. It is more of a love letter. His words seem to come from a light heart. It is evident that the soul of this great apostle is free!

Paul mentions the Savior's name some 40 times in this short epistle. Some of the most wonderful things concerning Christ and the Christian life are here. So that your life may be purified, dangers avoided and progress made, Christ must be your joy, your trust and your aim in life. Paul tells us of his own joyful triumph over trying circumstances because of his trust in Christ.

PHILIPPIANS 1: JOY IN LIVING

Paul loved to call himself the servant (really a bond servant) of Jesus Christ. Christ had made him free and now he wanted to serve Him as long as he was alive: "Paul and Timothy, servants of Jesus Christ" (Philippians 1:1). That is the reason he says, "For to me to live is Christ" (Philippians 1:21). Can you say this? Is Christ everything to you? Do you live for Him? Is your one aim and purpose to glorify Him?

Notice when Paul writes his letters that he puts his name first. How sensible this is, for the first thing you do in opening a letter is to turn to the end and find out who wrote it.

Although his movements were restricted, Paul could pray for his friends. "I thank my God every time I remember you. In all my prayers for all of you, I always pray with joy" (Philippians 1:3-4).

Paul lived to intercede for others. So should every true Sunday School teacher, Christian friend, father, mother, brother or sister. All Christians should always remember others in their prayers. Have you a prayer list? Do you talk with the Lord about your friends? Do you "always pray with joy" (Philippians 1:4)? Why can we rejoice in prayer? What is your answer?

Although Paul had to remain in his house, people came to hear him preach. The Roman guards were so interested in the gospel that they spread it around. This encouraged others to be bold in preaching, and many found Paul's Christ.

There is great power in the witness of a consistent life. You may be bound to unsympathetic companions, but by how you conduct your life you may win them for God. Your obstacle may become your pulpit. Christians who work for Christ when everything is against them encourage others to look at the Savior in a new light.

Listen to the cries of the people of this world. What are they? The successful businessperson cries, "To me to live is wealth." The scholar cries, "To me to live is knowledge." The soldier cries, "To me to live is victory." The young man cries, "To me to live is pleasure." The man desirous of recognition cries, "To me to live is fame." The high school student cries, "To me to live is recognition." We could go on and list all the voices of the world, but one is heard over them all: "To me to live is not wealth or knowledge or fame or glory but Christ. Christ first, last, in the middle of everything, and always Christ":

- Christ is the giver of life—"I have come that they may have life, and have it to the full" (John 10:10).
- Christ is life itself—"I no longer live, but Christ lives in me" (Galatians 2:20).
- Christ is the model of my life—"Be perfect, therefore, as your heavenly Father is perfect" (Matthew 5:48).
- Christ is the aim of my life—I desire to make known "the coming of our Lord Jesus Christ in power" (2 Peter 1:16).
- Christ is the reward of my life—"Thanks be to God for his indescribable gift!" (2 Corinthians 9:15).

Paul says:

- When I travel, it is on Christ's errands.
- When I suffer, it is in Christ's service.
- When I speak, the theme is Christ.
- When I write, Christ fills my letters.

PHILIPPIANS 2: JOY IN SERVICE

Paul says that the wonderful example of the Christian life that we must follow is Jesus Christ. We must imitate Christ, for although He is Lord of all, He became servant to all! Paul urges the Philippian church to complete his happiness by living together in love and unity. Is there anything more Christlike for Christians to do? "Make my joy complete by being like-minded" (Philippians 2:2). This is not an easy thing to do. It means love without compromise.

What is the most important social accomplishment? Elegant manners? The ability to always know what to say? No, it is courtesy of heart, not mere fashion. D. L. Moody once said, "Strife is knocking others down; vainglory is setting oneself up." "In humility value others above yourselves" is an astonishing phrase; in other words, "Be willing to be third" (Philippians 2:3).

We must always bear in our thoughts the example of Jesus Christ (see Philippians 2:5-11). Paul says, "Your attitude should be the same as that of Christ Jesus," which is self-forgetting love. Although Jesus was God, He humbled Himself. Christ took on not only the form of a man but also the form of a servant. Then He humbled Himself even more: He who was author of life became obedient to death. But even more than this, He faced death on a cross, a degrading way to die. This must be our spirit (see Matthew 16:25).

Paul is practical as well as profound. He never leaves us in the clouds. He never separates knowledge from action. Christianity is both creed and life. A creed without the right conduct amounts to little. After Paul has scaled the heights in Christ's exaltation, he does not plan to leave us there. "Therefore, my dear friends . . . continue to work out your salvation with fear and trembling" (Philippians 2:12). "Work out" means "live out"—not working for salvation, but showing the works of salvation. God has a plan for each of our lives as He had for Jesus. We must live out that plan. It is an entirely personal matter. No one can do it for somebody else. God plants in our hearts salvation in Christ—great, divine, wonderful and to be lived out. Happy is the person who finds God's plan for life and actively participates in it.

Christian experience is not something that is going on around you, but in you. "Christ lives in me" (Galatians 2:20)!

"Do everything without grumbling or arguing" (Philippians 2:14). Paul is saying, "Don't be grouchy! You can't glow if you are!" Having committed your life to the control of the Lord, you are under orders not to murmur or complain! "If God is supreme, why did He allow this thing to happen?" should never pass your lips. You cannot ask your commander in chief the why of anything He asks you to do.

Paul shows us, too, that there is a sacrificial side of the Christian life. That which costs nothing amounts to nothing. Paul feared his work might be "in vain" (Philippians 2:16). So much in life is done in vain. Are we running in vain, or working in vain? So many days are spent in vain! So many books are written in vain! So many sermons are printed in vain! So many gifts are given in vain! The Christian life should be a sacrifice if we are to follow Christ. Does your faith cost anything?

But if Christ is our example, then we see that there is no cross without a crown. If we suffer with Him, we will also reign with Him. We are God's lights in a dark age. No flame can shine brightly when it is filthy. The Christian who brings honor to the Lord must be faultless, innocent and not blameworthy.

PHILIPPIANS 3: JOY IN FELLOWSHIP

Paul tells the Philippians that the duty of all Christians is that they be joyful. A long-faced Christian is the worst advertisement for Christianity. The world doesn't want a greater burden; it wants a light heart. How can a Christian be joyful in a world so full of sorrow? Paul tells us in Philippians 3:1, "Rejoice in the Lord!"

Saul of Tarsus, a man rich in religious education, who had every honor and privilege, was an earnest searcher after truth and blameless as far as the Law was concerned. One day Christ found him on the way to Damascus, and his whole being was changed (see Acts 9). His eyes were opened. He discovered in Christ a store of spiritual wealth that made him count all that he had as trash (see Philippians 3:7). He became willing to gladly sacrifice everything and counted the treasures of this world as nothing in comparison with Christ. He became willing to lose everything to gain Christ. He had a new standard of values. He had a new reason for life.

Philippians

Christ had stepped in between Paul and his old ideals and made him change the headings at the top of his ledger page. He erased "gains" (credits) and wrote "losses" (debits). This was his choice in life. Paul had weighed both the world and Christ and remembered the words of the Lord Jesus: "What good will it be for someone to gain the whole world, yet forfeit their soul?" (Matthew 16:26).

In Philippians 3:12-14, Paul tells us that every person's life is a plan of God! If I only do one things in life, I should carry out this plan. Neither the successes nor failures of the past must keep me from pressing on today: "I am ready for anything and equal to anything through Him Who infuses inner strength into me; I am self-sufficient in Christ's sufficiency" (Philippians 4:13, *AMP*).

Here are some of the ambitions of Paul's heart. Mark these in your Bible.

- "That I may gain Christ" (Philippians 3:8). Christ had won him. Now he wished to win Him as a daily prize.

- "I want to know Christ" (Philippians 3:10). There are degrees of knowing Him.

- "And be found in him" (Philippians 3:9). To be found in Christ is to be blameless and complete.

- "I want to know Christ—yes, to know the power of his resurrection" (Philippians 3:10). The power of the gospel is in a risen Christ.

- "I want to know . . . partnership in his sufferings" (Philippians 3:10). This means a life consecrated to Him, even willing to die as He did.

- "I press on to take hold of that for which Christ Jesus took hold of me" (Philippians 3:12). He wanted to know Christ's purpose for seizing him on that road to Damascus.

- "I press on toward the goal to win the prize" (Philippians 3:14). The higher the calling, the greater the prize.

Do you know that your citizenship is in heaven, that you have been born from above? Read Philippians 3:20-21. We should live as citizens of a better country, a heavenly Kingdom. Don't love the world or the things of this world, but be loyal to Him who rules in the heavenly Jerusalem. When Christ comes, He will change these bodies of ours into bodies like His own—fit for His heavenly kingdom.

Christ's residence was for 33 years here on earth, but it did not naturalize Him as a citizen of earth. Let us not forget where our citizenship is. Remember Paul's advice in Romans 12:2: "Do not conform to the pattern of this world, but be transformed by the renewing of your mind."

PHILIPPIANS 4: JOY IN REWARDS

"Rejoice in the Lord always. I will say it again: Rejoice! Let your gentleness be evident to all. The Lord is near" (Philippians 4:4-5). This blessed hope of Christ's coming again casts its gracious influence over all of life. Paul prays that the Christian may have joy at all times and not be worried by cares. D. L. Moody said that Philippians 4:6 meant: "Be careful for nothing; be prayerful for everything; be thankful for anything!"

Yes, the way to be anxious about nothing is to be prayerful about everything. The prayer of faith must be a prayer of thanksgiving because faith knows how much it owes to God. Put your prayers into God's hands and go off and leave them there. Do not worry about them. If you do this, then the peace of God will stand guard over your heart and mind.

Guard your thoughts! Thoughts determine your life! "As [a man] thinketh in his heart, so is he" (Proverbs 23:7, *KJV*). Paul tells us what to think about and remember: "Whatever is true, whatever is noble, whatever is right, whatever is pure, whatever is lovely, whatever is admirable—if anything is excellent or praiseworthy, think about such things" (Philippians 4:8).

Paul expressed his gratitude for the loving thought that had prompted the church at Philippi to send him gifts. He was especially happy about their gifts, not because he needed them, for he had "learned to be content" in any circumstance with Christ (Philippians 4:11), and he could do all things through Christ who strengthened him. But their gifts meant "fruit that may abound to your account" (Philippians 4:17, *KJV*). He opened God's bank account to them: "And my God will meet all your needs according to the riches of his glory in Christ Jesus" (Philippians 4:19).

38

A Quick Look at

The New Testament: Matthew Through Philippians

 REVIEW QUIZ

Multiple Choice

1. The Gospel that portrays the manhood of Jesus is
   - (a) Matthew
   - (b) Mark
   - (c) Luke
   - (d) John

2. The Gospel that best presents the plan of salvation is
   - (a) Matthew
   - (b) Mark
   - (c) Luke
   - (d) John

3. The Sermon on the Mount is stated at greatest length in
   - (a) Matthew
   - (b) Mark
   - (c) Luke
   - (d) John

4. The genealogy of Jesus is given in
   (a) Matthew
   (b) Mark
   (c) Luke
   (d) John

5. Paul called the Galatians "foolish" because
   (a) They followed other leaders.
   (b) They turned back from their liberty in Christ to the bondage of the law.
   (c) They formed a new church.

6. A Christian's "works" count before God
   (a) For his or her salvation
   (b) For rewards
   (c) For escape of punishment

Short Essay
   1. Name five outstanding miracles of Jesus.
   2. Name three persons with whom Jesus had a personal interview.
   3. Describe Christian love as Paul explains it in 1 Corinthians 13.
   4. Describe how Jesus is portrayed in each of the four Gospels.
   5. Describe how Jesus is portrayed in each of the six of Paul's epistles we have studied so far.
   6. Trace the spread of Christianity from Jerusalem to Rome as given in the book of Acts.

Fill In the Blanks

   1. Matthew was written especially for the _____ _____.

   2. The only Gospel that tells the story of the wise men is _____.

3. The two greatest preachers in the book of Acts whose
    names begin with *P* are _____ and
    _____.

4. The greatest event in the book of Acts that begins with
    P is _____.

Understanding Colossians

Colossians Portrays Jesus Christ, Our Life

AUTHOR: The apostle Paul was the primary writer of the book of Colossians and possibly also Timothy according to Colossians 1:1.

DATE: The book was likely written in AD 60, when Paul was under house arrest in Rome (Acts 28:14-31).

PURPOSE AND SUMMARY: The Colossian letter is well known for its teaching about the treasure of "Christ in you, the hope of glory" through the indwelling Holy Spirit (Colossians 1:27; see also Romans 8:9-10). In the letter, Paul insists on the fact that Christ is Lord of all, the agent God used to create all things, and the agent through which God is reconciling all men and women and all creation to Himself by the peace that comes from the blood of Christ. Colossians emphasizes these truths partly to refute incipient Gnosticism, a growing heresy in the Church.

GENERAL CHARACTERISTICS

This letter begins, like 12 others, with the name of Paul and is addressed to Gentile believers. It was likely Epaphras who founded the church at Colosse, which was located about 100 miles east of Ephesus (see Colossians 1:7). It consisted of Gentile Christians. Philemon was a member. Paul kept in close touch with the people and was greatly beloved.

Epaphras went to Rome to tell Paul about the heresies that were creeping into the church. These false teachings took Christ off the throne and denied His being the headship of the Church. To help answer the heresies, Paul sent this letter back by Epaphras. He writes especially about the preeminence and deity of Christ, for Christ is truly God.

Ephesians and Colossians were written about the same time, while Paul was under house arrest in Rome. They both contain great doctrines of the gospel, and were meant to be read aloud in the churches. They are very similar in style, yet very different in emphasis.

- Ephesians talks about all believers, calling them the "body of Christ" (Ephesians 4:12). Colossians talks about the head of the body, Jesus Christ.
- In Ephesians, the Church of Christ is the main concern. In Colossians, the Christ of the Church is emphasized.

Both are needed. There cannot be a body without a head, nor a head without a body. Notice this all the way through Colossians—"Christ," "Christ," "Christ."

Heresy had broken out in the church at Colosse, misleading the young believers by calling for the worship of angels and a strict observance of Jewish ceremonies (see Colossians 2:16,18,21). This heresy actually involved a mixture of Jewish, Greek and Oriental religions, and necessitated this letter from Paul about the truth of the supreme Lordship of Christ. This epistle draws a faithful portrait of Christ in all His glory and dignity.

Christ Our Head

Christ is all in all. The basic failure of the Colossians was that they did not hold fast to the Lord. The place Christ holds in any religious teaching determines whether it is true or false. Some thought in Paul's day, as now, that Jesus was only a man and that Christ was the divine Spirit that came at Jesus' baptism and left Him at the cross. This meant that Christ did not die but that Jesus died.

You can see that this is the root error of many cults today. Many modern cults are based on this same old heresy and misrepresent the truth in regard to Christ and His person and work. It is good for us, in reading the Colossian letter, to examine our own belief and see that we always put Christ Jesus in His rightful place in our thinking and glorify this wonderful One.

Have you noticed that many of the Epistles were used to answer the heresies that crept into the early churches everywhere?

The gospel, by this time, had been taken "throughout the whole world" and had "been proclaimed to every creature" (Colossians 1:6,23). Thirty-two years after Christ's death, the gospel had reached the whole Roman world. It needed only one generation to establish the Church as a worldwide fact.

The Church's position "in Christ":

- United in Christ—Colossians 2:2
- Complete in Christ—Colossians 2:10
- Dead in Christ—Colossians 2:20
- Buried with Christ—Romans 6:4
- Risen with Christ—Colossians 3:1

Christ Our Life

"And your life is now hidden with Christ in God" (Colossians 3:3). This epistle tells us that Christ is our life and we are complete in Him (see Colossians 2:10).

The Christian life is not a creed or a system of teachable laws or a certain kind of worship but a life that is Christ's very own within you. Christ is all in all:

- In His deity—"the image of the invisible God" (Colossians 1:15)
- In creation—sovereign Creator of the universe (Colossians 1:15-16)
- In preeminence—before all things (Colossians 1:18)
- In redemption—reconciling the universe through His blood (Colossians 1:20-22)
- In headship—over all principalities and powers (Colossians 1:18; 2:14)
- In His Church—"the head of the body" (Colossians 1:18; see also 2:19)
- In His indwelling presence—the Christian's hope (Colossians 1:27)

God has given Christ preeminence in all things (see Colossians 1:18). We dare not give Him a lower place!

- In Romans we are justified in Christ.
- In 1 Corinthians we are enriched in Christ.
- In 2 Corinthians we are comforted in Christ.
- In Galatians we are free in Christ.
- In Ephesians we are made alive in Christ.
- In Philippians we are joyful in Christ.
- In Colossians we are complete in Christ.

Colossians presents the glorious culmination of it all: "In Christ you have been brought to fullness" (Colossians 2:10). We are "complete in him" (Colossians 2:10, *KJV*). We are "rooted and built up in him" (Colossians 2:7); we are in effect grounded and settled. We discover the facts of this building process in the four chapters of this book:

Colossians

- Building "downward"—rooted in Jesus, "established and firm" (Colossians 1:23). The deeper life is rooted in eternity. It begins in Him who was in the beginning with God. God gives eternal life.

- Building "upward"—"built up in him" (Colossians 2:7). The higher life is the life Jesus is living for us at the right hand of God, and living in us, for "I have been crucified with Christ and I no longer live, but Christ lives in me" (Galatians 2:20).

- Building "inward"—"hidden with Christ" (Colossians 3:3). The inner life is all the life we have as Christians. It is the life "hidden with Christ" in God. It is life real and sufficient, for we are "complete in him" (Colossians 3:3; 2:10).

- Building "outward"—"be wise in the way you act toward outsiders" (Colossians 4:5). The outer life is that expression of life that makes Christ known to others. As Emerson is known to have said: "What you do speaks so loudly that I [people] cannot hear what you say."

COLOSSIANS 1: THE DEEPER LIFE

Paul opens this letter as he opens so many: "We always thank God" (Colossians 1:3). He rejoices in the good news from the brethren scattered abroad in the various churches he founded.

Notice that Paul's favorite words to use are "faith," "love" and "hope" (Colossians 1:4-5). He wants everyone to have faith in Christ, love toward others and hope of heaven.

Paul tells us the secret of the deeper life that we as Christians should have in Christ: We are to become "established and firm" ("grounded and settled," *KJV*) in Christ (Colossians 1:23). Send the taproot of your Christian faith down deep into Christ's life, just as the great oak sends its root into the heart of the earth. We find that storms may beat against the solid oak, but it stands fast, for it is rooted deep. In sharp contrast is the California redwood. It may have acres of roots, but they are spread close to the surface of the earth. The giant redwood lifts its head several hundred feet into the air, but it has no taproot, so when the storm beats against it, it topples.

Send your roots down into Christ. The source of your life is in Him. Bonsai is the Japanese way of pruning the roots and branches of the trees of the forest and confining them in small containers. The tree maintains its life partially from water absorbed through small surface roots and grows to be only two or three feet high. Every soul is similarly stunted until it puts its taproot into God and begins to draw on Him.

Next, Paul presents a glowing description of the mighty Christ, the superior One. He is "all in all" (1 Corinthians 15:28).

We find in this first scene that not only are we in Christ but also Christ is in us: "Christ in you, the hope of glory" (Colossians 1:27). This is what it is to be a Christian: living in Him—this glorious, wonderful person, the Creator of this universe, in whom we have redemption through His blood—and having Him live in us.

In closing this scene, read Colossians 1:9-14, Paul's beautiful prayer for the Church. He expresses his desire for all Christian believers:

- That they might be filled with a knowledge of Christ's will. He wants us to know how to live a Christlike life, for the fullness of Christ's wisdom will keep us from error—verse 9
- That they might walk worthy of the Lord, fruitful in work, increasing in knowledge—verse 10
- That they might be strengthened with might so as to be able to withstand all temptations—verse 11
- That they might be thankful—verse 12

COLOSSIANS 2: THE HIGHER LIFE

"So then, just as you received Christ Jesus as Lord, continue to live your lives in him, rooted and built up in him" (Colossians 2:6-7). Paul is always practical. He says, "Act out what you believe.

You started out well. Now keep going! You've received Christ and have been grounded and settled in Him. So walk in Him" (see Colossians 1:23). Paul always wants our walk and life to correspond with our belief. It is sad when a Christian believes in Christ and acts like the devil—no one will accept such a faith as sincere. If we have received Christ, let us walk as He would have us walk. If we have been rooted in Him, let us grow up in Him. If we have been founded on Him, let us be built up on Him. All of these are proof of a changed heart. Walking expresses life. Growing signifies an inner power. Building up shows progress of character until the structure is complete.

We have to do a great deal more than just believe truths about Christ. We must *receive* Christ if we are to have life. We cannot earn God's grace or purchase it. It is a free gift (see Colossians 2:6). Then we are to build downward, "rooted . . . in Christ" (Colossians 2:7). Being rooted in Christ means that we draw our nourishment from Him, just as a plant can only grow if it is in life-giving material. We are built up in Him. We have our foundation in Him. Every structure needs a foundation.

Next we must build upward, "rooted and built up in him, strengthened in the faith" (Colossians 2:7). We must raise a stately structure to His praise and, of course, wholly by His grace. The Christian life starts with a foundation in Christ and then grows in His grace and gifts. We must be as dependent on Christ for our unswerving walk as we are for our assurance of salvation. This is the higher life.

The higher you go with the Lord, the steadier is your disposition, the less disturbing are temptations and the smoother is your everyday life.

Christ's Sufficiency

All the life we have as Christians—the real and satisfying eternal life—is the life "in Him":

- Walking in Him—Colossians 2:6
- Rooted in Him—Colossians 2:7

- Built up in Him—Colossians 2:7
- Brought to perfection in Him—Colossians 2:10
- Dead with Him—Colossians 2:20
- Risen with Him—Colossians 3:1
- Hidden with Him—Colossians 3:3

Paul tells us in Colossians 2 that Christ is all-sufficient: "For in Christ all the fullness of the Deity lives in bodily form" (Colossians 2:9). This is a tremendous truth for us to grasp. In this Jesus, who walked on the earth, dwelt the whole Godhead. But more than this—in Him was the fullness of the Godhead.

Read that again: "For in Christ all the fullness of the Deity lives in bodily form." This Jesus was actually God in all of His fullness. Neither angels nor prophets nor saints rank with Him—for He is the very embodiment of the divine!

Firm Beliefs

We also see in this chapter Paul's personal concern for the Church at Colosse. He longs for the Christians there to be secure and firm in their beliefs so that the shrewd philosophers and legalists of their day won't shake their faith. The best way to be protected from the snares of the world and its philosophy is an understanding of the perfection of Christ, for He is all and in all. Be rooted and grounded in the Word so that you won't be swept away by false teachers.

Some of the popular street-corner philosophers of Paul's day were teaching that people are unworthy to approach Christ directly and that they needed to approach Him by means of angels (see Colossians 2:18). But Christ said that He is the only mediator between God and people, adding, "I am the way. . . . No one comes to the Father except through me" (John 14:6). Paul rebukes the Colossians for their failure to recognize the supremacy of Christ as the only mediator between God and people.

Paul reminds us that when Jesus died on the cross, He freed us from the law. Therefore we need not let others judge us regarding food or drink or severe treatment of the body (see Colossians 2:16-23). The sacrifice God asks is a broken spirit, not a beaten body. A sinful heart can still dwell in a fasting body. Self-imposed hardships are of no value in offsetting the thoughts of a sinful heart. We like to think that when we have done something bad we can clear our record by doing something we think is good. But we must remember that only what Christ does is good, for "there is no one who does good, not even one" (Romans 3:12). If *God* is taken out of *good*, nothing—*o*—is left.

COLOSSIANS 3: THE INNER LIFE

Building our life cannot be only downward, "rooted . . . in [Christ]," but upward, "built up in him"; our building must also be inward (Colossians 2:7). Let the world know that Christ is your life. Many believe that Christ gave us life similar to the way a person would put a living seed into a flowerpot: The pot would hold a detached thing—life. But Christ is more than that. He Himself is in the believer. The life that is in Christ is in the believer: "I am the vine; you are the branches" (John 15:5).

We find that our new life in Christ makes us less interested in the things the world offers. We become "dead to the world" (see Colossians 2:20). We find ourselves "hidden with Christ"; and as we know Him, we discover, one by one, the beauties of the Lord Jesus: "compassion, kindness, humility, gentleness and patience" (Colossians 3:3,12). "Let the message of Christ dwell among you richly" (Colossians 3:16). It will make a difference.

The Brown family lived in a house that was an eyesore in the neighborhood. Weeds grew over the porch; the shades were always torn; the curtains were sagging and soiled. One day when we passed the house, we saw the grass cut, fresh white curtains hanging at the windows, and the broken steps mended. "When did the Browns move?" we asked.

"Why, they haven't moved," answered our neighbor.

"Oh yes, they have. The Browns don't live in that house anymore. A new family has moved in. We haven't seen the people yet, but we know by the house's appearance that a new owner is living there."

Yes, our outward life will be different. Others will see Christ living in us.

Because we are rooted in Christ and our life is in Him, we are not only identified with Him in His death, but we are also one with Him in His resurrection. In Christ's death we died to sin; in His resurrection we rose to walk in a new life. Because we "have been raised with Christ," we should seek those things that are above and should show to the best of our ability the goal of our lives (Colossians 3:1).

For example, the submarine is made to travel under the water, but every submarine is equipped with a periscope by which it seeks those things that are above. It travels in the water, but the wellbeing of those in it depends on a knowledge of what is above.

We live in the world, but we must set our minds (affections and thoughts) on things above, for we are citizens of a heavenly country. Look to Christ and He will draw you upward.

A New Self

First we must rid ourselves of the old nature. Paul tells us to put it to death (see Colossians 3:5-9). After we receive our new life in Christ Jesus, we must "put to death, therefore, whatever belongs to your earthly nature" (Colossians 3:5). It should not be necessary to tell Christians that they must stop doing things that are more like the devil than the Savior!

Any self-denial or asceticism not built on our union with Christ—whether practiced by the priests of India or the Buddhists of Thailand or the monks of Catholicism or laypeople of Protestantism—is condemned at the start.

Christianity is not about giving up a lot of things; it is a new life. Children do not give up playing jacks; they outgrow it. As we come to know Christ better, we find that some things no longer interest us. Christ adds so much to our lives that there is no room for our old interests. The first thing we know, we have lost interest in the old and are busy with the new in Christ.

Paul admonishes us to destroy our old nature and rid ourselves of all its vices. Read over Paul's black catalogue: immorality, impurity, passion and greed, rage and wrath and the many sins of speech. Let us forever give up these sins. It *is* possible to do now that we are in Christ.

Can you imagine how ridiculous you would look if you went to buy a new suit but refused to take off the one you had on, insisting that the new one should be tried on without getting rid of the old one! This is what many Christians try to do. They try to put the garment of a new life on over their old nature. It just doesn't fit. We must put aside sin first and then "put on the new person."

A Christian's conduct is what people see you do. As clothes can indicate what kind of a person you are—careful or careless, a soldier or a civilian, a king or a commoner—so outward expression will show "to whom [you] belong and whom [you] serve" (Acts 27:23).

Now Paul thinks of our new nature in Christ as putting "on the new self" (Colossians 3:10). This new nature we receive from Christ is always being renewed as we grow in the knowledge of our Lord and Savior. But we must not become so absorbed in our great privileges in Christ that we neglect our duty to our fellow humans. Our knowing Christ should make us much more thoughtful of others.

Thus the new Christian also puts on, or adds to, his or her life. Let us "put on" the virtues of this new life, such as tenderness, kindness, humility, patience, forgiveness and love (see Colossians 3:12-14). Yes, these are the things with which we are to adorn ourselves. If we lived clothed like this, we would find perfection on earth. Paul says that all these virtues are like pieces of clothing, all held in place by a belt of love. This fills our lives with the peace of God.

Did you know that Luther Burbank, an American horticulturist, took the little wild daisy and developed it into a bloom five to seven inches in diameter, and the little poppy was developed into a blossom 10 inches across? So our Christian graces must be cultivated and enlarged. Too often they perish for want of care. Too often the fruit of our lives looks only like the ordinary fruit of the world. We must grow into the full stature of the fullness of

Christ. As long as we live, there is something new for us to learn. We should never stop growing.

Write down all the commands given to you in this chapter.

All or Nothing

Yes, "Christ is all, and is in all" (Colossians 3:11). If Christ is not all in your life, He is nothing. No surer test can be given to any false teaching of today than this: Where does it put Jesus Christ? The Bible says: "Every spirit that acknowledges that Jesus Christ has come in the flesh is from God" (1 John 4:2). This is the test of every creed. Does it proclaim that "we have redemption, the forgiveness of sins" (Colossians 1:14)? If so, it is true; if not, it is false (see 1 John 4:1-3).

A Christian heart is a singing heart (see Colossians 3:16). Christ wants us to be taught in His Word, and then He wants us to express our joy in Him by singing hymns.

COLOSSIANS 4: THE OUTER LIFE

Colossians 4 introduces another phase of our life in Christ, the outer life. We found we must build within, cultivating the virtues of the new life in Christ, but we also want our new life to be seen and felt among others (see Colossians 4:5). This is the way we present Christ to the world. Remember, "Christians" mean "little Christs." Biographies of Christ are not written only by great authors such as John Paul Meier or fictionalized by such writers as Anne Rice. Christ's life did not end when the Gospels were completed. Christ is living in us. His life is told today in living epistles that are known and read by all people who see us.

Colossians

Understanding First Thessalonians

First Thessalonians Portrays Jesus Christ, the Coming One

AUTHOR: First Thessalonians 1:1 and 2 Thessalonians 1:1 indicate that the apostle Paul wrote these books, possibly along with Silas and Timothy.

DATE: The books were written in AD 51-52, soon after the founding of the Thessalonian church, and are among the earliest letters written by the apostle Paul.

PURPOSE AND SUMMARY: These letters give Paul's answers to some basic problems disturbing the Christians in Thessalonica. The major themes of these letters are living pure and holy lives in

Christ, the resurrection of the dead, and the events preceding and accompanying the return of Christ.

The second coming of the Lord Jesus Christ is the truth Paul presents in these two letters to the Thessalonians, and it would be missing the mark not to recognize this fact. The two epistles contain 20 different references to the coming of the Lord. This is the hope of the Church. It is mentioned in the closing of every chapter of 1 Thessalonians: "To wait for his Son from heaven" (1 Thessalonians 1:10); "in the presence of our Lord Jesus Christ when he comes" (1 Thessalonians 2:19); "in the presence of our God and Father when our Lord Jesus comes with all his holy ones" (1 Thessalonians 3:13); "caught up together with them in the clouds to meet the Lord in the air" (1 Thessalonians 4:17); "may your whole spirit, soul and body be kept blameless at the coming of our Lord Jesus Christ" (1 Thessalonians 5:23). In view of all this, should anyone bother to ask whether Christ will come again?

Christ's first coming was sudden and a surprise to the philosophers of His time. We learn that His second coming will be no less surprising.

Paul, accompanied by Timothy and Silas, had spent only three Sabbath days at Thessalonica on his second missionary journey (see Acts 17:2); but during that time he not only founded a church, but he also grounded it firmly in the faith. In the time he was there, Paul also created a great stir. His enemies accused him of having "caused trouble all over the world" (Acts 17:6). On account of this charge of treason, the brethren sent the apostle away. He went on to Berea and Athens and Corinth. It was from here that he wrote this first letter to the Thessalonians and sent it by way of Timothy. We know he had only been gone a short time, for he said he was "separated from you for a short time" (1 Thessalonians 2:17).

During Paul's stay in Thessalonica, a great number of Greeks and women came to believe in Jesus (see Acts 17:4), and the church grew to be composed mostly of Gentile rather than Jewish believers. Paul began at once to feed this church with the meat of the Word. He talked of the Holy Spirit (see 1 Thessalonians 1:6), of the Trinity (see 1 Thessalonians 1:6) and of the second coming of Christ (see 1 Thessalonians 1:10).

Being greatly concerned about the young converts, Paul sent Timothy from Athens to strengthen their faith and to bring him news of how they were getting along. Timothy brought back a favorable report that was a great comfort to the apostle-founder of the church. However, Timothy had discovered that some faults needed to be corrected. The church members at Thessalonica held some false views concerning the Lord's return. They were worried about some people who had died, fearing that they would not have any part in the rapture and glory of the Lord's return. Others were so overwhelmed by the expectation of Christ's return that they were neglecting their daily tasks (see 1 Thessalonians 4:10-12). Wishing to correct these wrong views and to inspire and comfort these new converts, Paul wrote this epistle.

First Thessalonians is an intimate epistle. The letter is a heart-to-heart talk. Paul gets very close to his brothers and sisters in the church and the words "brothers and sisters" occur more than a dozen times. It is a message of comfort and instruction to those who are in the midst of persecution.

There should be nothing doubtful or divisive about this "blessed hope" of our Lord's return (Titus 2:13). No one can read the Word without finding the teaching. Let us not quarrel with one another about so sweet a message as our Lord's "I will come back" (John 14:3). This is the Christian's hope. Let us rather be watchful, for we know not the day or the hour when the Son of man will come.

1 THESSALONIANS 1: INSPIRATION WHILE WAITING FOR CHRIST'S COMING

If you wish to know how to get on with other folks in Christian work, just go over the things Paul said and did under the guidance of the Spirit.

- Paul did not try to please others in ways that displeased God.
- Paul did not try to capture others by flattery.
- Paul was not covetous of what others had.
- Paul was not seeking glory for himself out of his work.
- Paul kept at his task day and night.
- Paul always encouraged others.

This is the kind of service the Lord Jesus would have *us* render in His name.

Loving as Paul Loved

In his greeting to the Thessalonians, Paul includes his friends and fellow workers, Silas and Timothy. Silas had been with him when he founded the church at Thessalonica, and Timothy had been his special messenger to them, carrying the good news of their progress and reporting their needs back to Paul at Corinth. Paul knew the secret of friendship so many of us would like to possess. The Bible tells us how to have friends: "There is a friend who sticks closer than a brother" (Proverbs 18:24). This is just what Paul did. He loved people, and he always acknowledged others in his service and expressed appreciation for their part in every work done.

Praying as Paul Prayed

"We always thank God for all of you and continually mention you in our prayers" (1 Thessalonians 1:2). Do we follow up our new converts as Paul did? Paul's converts were in more than a score of different cities, yet he carried all of them in his heart and kept in touch with them.

Do you have a prayer list? Do you pray for others by name? Do you mention your friends to God? If you find it difficult to speak to others about Christ, try speaking to Christ about others; soon you will be speaking to others about Him. All of us can do this, even the most timid.

Do we realize as Christians why we are in the world? How seriously do we take our task? Have we any evidence that we have been "approved by God" to be entrusted with the gospel (1 Thessalonians 2:4)? Paul sets forth in this letter the intensity of his ministry, his willingness to die for his new converts, and his dealing with each one.

But first Paul thanks God for this church. The beauty of this church did not consist of a gorgeous building of mortar and stone but a people who are "in God the Father and in the Lord Jesus Christ" (1 Thessalonians 1:1). Paul is very pleased about the wonderful growth these young converts had made. He holds them up as an example everywhere he goes: "You became a model to all the believers in Macedonia and Achaia" (1 Thessalonians 1:7). Already their zeal has made a profound impression all over Macedonia and Achaia (Greece), and everyone is talking about the wonderful way God is working in the young, vigorous church at Thessalonica.

This is what everyone in the world is looking for—Christians who live the Christian life, who act out what they believe. This is just what the Thessalonians did. Nothing was mentioned about the condition of their finances. But their faith in God was "known everywhere" (1 Thessalonians 1:8). Their missionary enthusiasm for making the Word of God known had been felt all through Greece. They were what every church should be.

Life in Three Tenses

In two verses, 1 Thessalonians 1:9-10, Paul tells us how to live:

- In the past tense
- In the present tense
- In the future tense

In the past tense, we are "turned to God" (1 Thessalonians 1:9). The believers at Thessalonica "turned to God from idols" (1 Thessalonians 1:9). There must be a personal turning to God from sin and unbelief if one is to become a child of God. The idols of our lives are numerous and varied. To turn to God we must forsake the numerous and varied idols of our lives—everything that would divide our affections or hinder us from following Him with our whole heart.

In the present tense, we are "to serve the living and true God" (1 Thessalonians 1:9). The Thessalonian believers "turned to God from idols to serve the living and true God" (1 Thessalonians 1:9). What a change! Serving a living God instead of going through a dead ritual that only mocked their needs by a dead silence!

In the future tense, we are "to wait for his Son from heaven" (1 Thessalonians 1:10). The believers at Thessalonica were serving and waiting! These early Christians believed that Christ would come again, as He had promised. This was called "the blessed hope" (Titus 2:13). The prophets of old waited for the coming of the Messiah for many generations before He came, but "when the set time had fully come," Christ did come (Galatians 4:4). The Church may have to wait a very long time for His promised second coming. Because of the wait, many have lost the vision and hope. But in the fullness of time, Christ will come again, as He had promised. Mark in your Bible these blessed promises: John 14:3; Acts 1:11; 1 Thessalonians 4:16; Revelation 1:7.

1 THESSALONIANS 2: SERVING WHILE WAITING FOR CHRIST'S COMING

Paul gives us these descriptions of his services at Thessalonica:

- "Not without results"—1 Thessalonians 2:1
- "We dared to tell you his gospel" in spite of contention—1 Thessalonians 2:2
- Not from "error or impure motives" or trickery—1 Thessalonians 2:3
- "Not trying to please people but God"—1 Thessalonians 2:4
- "Never used flattery"—1 Thessalonians 2:5
- For God's glory, not "for praise from people"—1 Thessalonians 2:6
- "Like young children"—1 Thessalonians 2:7
- Affectionate—1 Thessalonians 2:8
- "Worked night and day"—1 Thessalonians 2:9

- Backed by holy living—1 Thessalonians 2:10-12
- Successful in its results—1 Thessalonians 2:13-18

What a man Paul was! He preached to please God, and lived to convince people of the truth of his preaching. His conduct commended his preaching. He was not a flatterer, nor did he seek wealth. He came as simple as a child and as gentle as a nurse caring for little children. He was never idle but toiled night and day. Giving the Thessalonians this example of his own life, he pleaded with them to make their daily lives worthy of the name "Christian," urging them "to live lives worthy of God" (1 Thessalonians 2:12). A Christian's walk is a Christian's life. An Indian pastor who was worried about the inconsistent lives among some of his flock said to a missionary, "There is much crooked walk by those who make good talk." Our walk and our talk should be twins going along on the same trail.

It is so true for young people that this life holds such strong interests, such demanding problems, such vital experiences, that even this most blessed hope for the future is not the only teaching that must be found in God's Word. Paul's letter to the Thessalonians proves how well Paul knew this, for it is filled with plenty of things we should do right now while we wait for Christ to appear. All the way through, Paul enjoins us to work and be witnesses while we hope.

Paul looked forward during these trying days to the "Lord Jesus Christ at his coming" (1 Thessalonians 2:19). Paul's greatest reward, after he has seen his wonderful Savior's face, will be to present to Christ the young converts of his ministry, letting them share in the glory of His advent. They will be his "crown of rejoicing" (1 Thessalonians 2:19-20, *KJV*).

1 THESSALONIANS 3:1–4:12—HOPING WHILE WAITING FOR CHRIST'S COMING

First Thessalonians 3 describes Paul's labor of love among the brethren. Paul was aware of the strain under which the members of the church at Thessalonica were living. He sent Timothy from Athens to encourage them even though they suffered bitter persecution.

Timothy had brought back the good news of their "faith and love" (1 Thessalonians 3:6). This report filled Paul with unbounded joy. How glad Paul was to hear of their firm stand in the faith and to know that they thought kindly of him and his fellow workers and longed to see them! In the midst of their persecution and suffering, Paul flashed the light of that wonderful day when they would be made "blameless and holy," when they will be changed in a moment at the return of Christ and His holy ones (1 Thessalonians 3:13).

The test of any hope that a person has is what it does for that person *now*. Paul told the Thessalonians that the coming of the Lord should be an incentive for several things:

- Right living—1 Thessalonians 3:13
- Consistent walk—1 Thessalonians 4:1
- Purity—1 Thessalonians 4:3-7
- Love—1 Thessalonians 4:9-10

Paul urges personal purity and a life that is consistent with their testimony (see 1 Thessalonians 4:1). This is the place where most Christians fail. Let us strive to have our ideals beyond reproach. Our attitude toward each other should be one of love. Remember the two commandments Jesus gave: "Love the Lord your God," and "Love your neighbor as yourself" (Matthew 22:37-39; Mark 12:30-31; Luke 10:27). Paul charges us to "make your love increase and overflow for each other" (1 Thessalonians 3:12; see also 4:9-10).

Paul also urges us not to live a life of idleness while waiting for Christ's glorious appearing (see 1 Thessalonians 4:11-12). Looking for Christ never makes idle hands. If we were expecting a loved one to return home after a long absence, we would not just sit down as the day of his return approached. Rather, we would be busy getting everything ready, doing the things the loved one wanted done. Can you imagine a mother waiting for her son to come home from the service or from college just sitting down and letting everything go! She would be fixing up her son's room, making his favorite cake and preparing his favorite food as she listened for his footsteps. This is the true Christian's attitude concerning our blessed Lord's return.

1 THESSALONIANS 4:13-18: COMFORTED WHILE WAITING FOR CHRIST'S COMING

A little band of Native American converts in Canada came to a missionary with a strange demand: "We are always hearing what God has done. Now tell us what He is going to do."

Where would you find an answer to that wise order? We have it in our Bibles: He will come again (see 1 Thessalonians 4:16)! If one of your best friends was coming to see you, you would not rest until you found out when your friend was coming and how. But our wonderful Lord and Savior says that He is coming, and when He does, He will transform the whole world and glorify all humanity. Can it be possible that we would be less curious about His coming than we would be about the fleeting visit of an earthly friend?

The Dead Will Rise

There is so much comfort in these few verses that end with "therefore encourage one another with these words" (1 Thessalonians 4:18). There is comfort because of His sure return.

The Christians at Thessalonica were disturbed because of their mistaken ideas about Christ's return. They were under the impression that Christ's return would be soon, and they were worried about what would happen to those who had died. What part would they have in His glorious coming and kingdom?

When Christ returns to earth, He will not come alone: "God will bring with Jesus those who have fallen asleep in him" (1 Thessalonians 4:14). What a meeting that will be! Death does not end everything. Parents and children, husbands and wives, loved ones and friends will be united. How anxious we are to know that "ours" will be in that happy crowd.

Those who have Christian loved ones who have died should not give way to undue sorrow when they lay them in the grave, for they have a double assurance from Christ's Word. When Christ comes, He will greet the believers who are dead first and bring them with Him (see 1 Thessalonians 4:13-14). When the archangel sounds the trumpet call of God, announcing the Lord's coming, then "the dead in Christ will rise first" to meet Him (1 Thessalonians 4:16). Then those who are alive and remain will be "caught up" in the clouds to share with them the glory of His coming and to "be with the Lord forever" (1 Thessalonians 4:17-18).

"The Lord himself will come down from heaven" (1 Thessalonians 4:16). Christ does not say He is going to send the messenger of death to bring His Bride (the Church) home. He is coming Himself for her! "This same Jesus . . . will come back in the same way you have seen him go into heaven" (Acts 1:11). And "they [will] see the Son of Man coming on the clouds of heaven, with power and great glory" (Matthew 24:30). What a marvelous hope this is!

The second coming of Christ was the bright hope of the Early Church, just as it should be for us. The greatest fact of the past is that Christ came the first time, as a man, and died on the cross to free us from the penalty of sin. The greatest fact of the future is that He is coming again, as King, to free us from the presence of sin (see Matthew 24:42).

The Living Will Meet Him

"After that, we who are still alive and are left will be caught up together with them in the clouds to meet the Lord in the air" (1 Thessalonians 4:17). Paul assures us that all will not die before He comes. "We will not all sleep, but we will all be changed—in a flash, in the twinkling of an eye, at the last trumpet. For the trumpet will sound, the dead will be raised imperishable, and we will be changed" (1 Corinthians 15:51-52).

"And so we will be with the Lord forever" (1 Thessalonians 4:17). Made like Him, we will eternally be with Him. He has gone to prepare a place for us. "I will come back and take you to be with me that you also may be where I am" (John 14:3). Heaven is where Christ is now. There we will be. This is heaven's greatest honor conferred on mortals.

This is the order of these great events:

1. The Lord's descent from heaven
2. The dead in Christ raised
3. The living believers changed
4. The whole company caught up to meet the Lord in the air

The truth of Christ's return thrills us. He went away in the clouds (see Acts 1:9). He will come back in triumphal glory (see Revelation 1:7). The angels will be with Him (see Matthew 25:31). The believers of the past ages will be raised; those that are alive will be changed, and as Enoch and Elijah were taken into heaven, so will the whole Church be caught up, to give a joyful welcome to the returning Savior!

1 THESSALONIANS 5: WATCHFUL WHILE WAITING FOR CHRIST'S COMING

Christ's second coming will be like the coming of a thief in the night or like the flood in Noah's time. The world will know nothing of His return. They scoff at the idea. But Jesus said there would be signs before His coming so that watchful believers will know when the time is drawing near. Over and over again, Jesus told His disciples that His coming would be "like a thief in the night" (1 Thessalonians 5:2; see also Matthew 24:36,42; 25:13; Mark 13:32-37; Luke 12:40; 21:25-35). He warned His disciples to always be alert. This should be their duty and their attitude. Christians need have no fear of that glorious day.

Don't plan on a specific date! Live a watchful life. We should not live lives of sleepy indulgence, but "be awake and sober" (1 Thessalonians 5:6). The hope of Christ's return does not mean a life of idleness. Activity should be the theme of our lives, as Paul reminds us again in this chapter of 1 Thessalonians.

"You also must be ready, because the Son of Man will come at an hour when you do not expect him" (Luke 12:40). Every morning when we get up, we should say to ourselves, *Be ready for the Lord's return, for He may come today.* Every night our closing thought should be, *Will I be ready for my Lord if He comes before I wake up?* (see 1 Thessalonians 3:12-13). Don't live to be ready to die, but live so that you may be ready for Christ's coming (see 1 Thessalonians 5:4-8)!

Hope, a Great Melody

While you wait, Paul gives you a grand octave to use to play great melodies of hope:

- "Rejoice always"—1 Thessalonians 5:16
- "Pray continually"—1 Thessalonians 5:17
- "Give thanks in all circumstances"—1 Thessalonians 5:18
- "Do not quench the Spirit"—1 Thessalonians 5:19
- "Do not treat prophecies with contempt"—1 Thessalonians 5:20
- "Test [everything]"—1 Thessalonians 5:21
- "Hold on to what is good"—1 Thessalonians 5:21
- "Reject every kind of evil"—1 Thessalonians 5:22

Strike every note on this wonderful octave. If you do, your life will be rich.

Paul, a Human Example

Have you ever thought of Paul as a human example of what following Christ means? Paul was "as straight as an arrow" and "as clean as a hound's tooth." Paul could easily meet the challenge of a critical examination of his record as a Christian. Paul had a brilliant and highly cultured mind. We are apt to think that a highly intelligent man would find it difficult to remain loyal to his maker. But Paul humbly prostrated his wonderful intellect at the feet of his Master. The only explanation for such a life is that it was entirely yielded to Christ. You can't be perfect in this life, young people. But there is one thing you can do 100 percent. It is what Paul did. You can give yourselves totally and without reserve to the Master.

Understanding
Second Thessalonians

Second Thessalonians Portrays Jesus Christ,
Our Returning Lord

SELECTED BIBLE READINGS

<table>
<tr><td rowspan="8">DAY OF THE WEEK</td><td>Sunday: Ephesians 1:1-2; Philippians 1:1-4; Colossians 1:1-3; 1 Thessalonians 1:1-3; 2 Thessalonians 1:1-4</td><td>Greetings in Paul's Letters</td><td rowspan="8">MAIN TOPIC</td></tr>
<tr><td>Monday: 2 Thessalonians 1:5-12</td><td>Our Comfort in Christ's Coming</td></tr>
<tr><td>Tuesday: 2 Thessalonians 2:1-12</td><td>Events Before Christ's Coming</td></tr>
<tr><td>Wednesday: 2 Thessalonians 2:13-17</td><td>An Appeal to Sound Doctrine</td></tr>
<tr><td>Thursday: Matthew 24:13-31</td><td>The Close of the Age</td></tr>
<tr><td>Friday: Matthew 24:30-31; 2 Thessalonians: Mark 8:38; 2 Thessalonians 1:7-8; Jude 14-15; Revelation 1:7</td><td>Warnings to the Wicked</td></tr>
<tr><td>Saturday: 2 Thessalonians 3</td><td>Consistency in Christian Conduct</td></tr>
</table>

AUTHOR: First Thessalonians 1:1 and 2 Thessalonians 1:1 indicate that the apostle Paul wrote these books, possibly along with Silas and Timothy.

DATE: The books of 1 and 2 Thessalonians were written in AD 51-52, soon after the founding of the Thessalonian church, and are among the earliest letters written by the apostle Paul.

PURPOSE AND SUMMARY: These letters give Paul's answers to some basic problems disturbing the Christians in Thessalonica. The major themes of these letters are living pure and holy lives in Christ, the resurrection of the dead, and the events preceding and accompanying the return of Christ.

This is the second epistle about "the blessed hope," or the return of our Lord Jesus Christ. The Thessalonians were forward-looking people. Paul talks to them about what is uppermost in their minds and thoughts. The first epistle says, "He is surely coming again." The second epistle says, "But work and wait until He comes."

The second coming of Christ is mentioned 318 times in 260 chapters of the New Testament. Because of this, we see how important this subject is. We read the prophecies of the Old Testament with deepest interest, to find out about our Lord's first appearance on this earth. We should be just as interested to discover what the New Testament teaches regarding His second coming "in power and great glory." He said He was coming again: "And if I go and prepare a place for you, I will come back" (John 14:3). He intended for His disciples to understand that His second coming would be in as literal a sense as His going away.

First Thessalonians tells about Christ's coming for His Church. The coming of Christ should be cleared up a bit in our minds. One day Christ will come to take away His Bride, the Church. He will not be seen by the world at that time, but those who are His, including the dead in Christ, will be "caught up" to meet Him. This is the teaching of 1 Thessalonians. After a period of seven years of tribulation for those left on the earth, Christ will appear to the world with His Church to establish His throne on the earth; then all the people will see Him, and He will exact judgment on His enemies. This is the teaching of 2 Thessalonians. His coming, then, includes both of these two events, seven years apart. We as Christians are looking for the first event. The world will not see Him until the end of the seven years (2 Thessalonians).

Between the two events, the Jewish people will reoccupy their own land; the gathering of the Gentile nations against them will take place; the Antichrist will become the world ruler, and he will make a covenant with the Jewish people and break it. Following this will be the great tribulation (see Matthew 24:21-22). Then Christ will come with His saints and mighty angels and set up His kingdom on this earth with Jerusalem as the center.

This second letter was written almost immediately after 1 Thessalonians. In addition to their trials and persecutions, the Thessalonian Christians were "unsettled" and "alarmed" by deceivers who made some of them believe that they were already passing through the great tribulation and "that the day of the Lord has already come" (2 Thessalonians 2:2). Paul tries to clear up the difficulty. When war is threatening and sorrow seems to cover the earth, people always wonder if they are in the end times, or tribulation. This second epistle to the Thessalonians is good for all of us to read so that these errors in our thinking can be cleared up.

The church at Thessalonica was carried away with the expectation of Christ's glorious return. Who can help but be thrilled when thinking about His triumphant return? But we must keep our feet on the ground. We must work while we wait, and pray as we watch, for there is much to do while we wait for Christ to come back.

The message here is something like our Lord's word to His disciples in Acts 1:6. You remember their eager question, "Lord, are You at this time going to restore the kingdom?"

"Leave that with the Father," Jesus in effect replied. "Do your day's work and wait. The Kingdom is coming."

2 THESSALONIANS 1: THINK CLEARLY WHILE WAITING FOR CHRIST'S COMING

We find that Silas and Timothy are mentioned again in the salutation of this letter. From this we can gather that this letter followed the first rather quickly. These two aides were still with Paul. Paul warmly commends the young Christians at Thessalonica before he rebukes them. Let us always first look to see if we can find something to praise in those we plan to criticize. Paul did this so often. He noticed that the promise of the Lord's coming again had inspired the Thessalonians to a growth in faith and "perseverance" (2 Thessalonians 1:4; see also verse 3). They knew that when Christ came, wrongs would be righted and the Lord would deal with those who had oppressed them (see 2 Thessalonians 1:5-7).

How does Paul describe the coming of Christ? It will be sudden and startling. "This will happen when the Lord Jesus is revealed from heaven in blazing fire with his powerful angels" (2 Thessalonians 1:7). This is no mild appearing for "those who do not know God" (2 Thessalonians 1:8). It will be very different for His own. We read that unbelievers "will be punished with everlasting destruction and shut out from the presence of the Lord and from the glory of his might on the day he comes" but that Jesus will "be glorified in his holy people and to be marveled at among all those who have believed" (2 Thessalonians 1:9-10). What a wonderful day this will be for them! Yes, He is coming. Remember the promise of the two angels as Jesus went into heaven. Read Acts 1:11. What a sharp contrast is shown between the glorious destiny of believers when Christ comes and the punishment of the wicked (see 2 Thessalonians 1:7-12)!

Many believe that Christ will not come to set up His kingdom until all the world is converted, but verses 7-12 of this first chapter seem to destroy this view. Read them carefully and you will find that the emphasis is on the fact that the coming of the Lord will be a terror for the disobedient.

The world has not seen our Lord Jesus since it crucified Him. He has been hidden from its view. But one day He will appear to the whole world. In 1 Thessalonians 4, Paul says that at first Christ will descend from heaven and, with the shout of the archangel, the Church will be taken away to be forever with the Lord. At that time He will be seen only by His own, His Church. Paul says, "For the Lord himself will come down from heaven, with a loud command, with the voice of the archangel and with the trumpet call of God, and the dead in Christ will rise first. After that, we who are still alive and are left will be caught up together with them in the clouds to meet the Lord in the air. And so we will be with the Lord forever" (1 Thessalonians 4:16-17).

Here in 2 Thessalonians Paul says Jesus will appear to the world "in blazing fire with his powerful angels. He will punish those who do not know God" (2 Thessalonians 1:8). First He comes to take His own out of this world. They "will be caught up" to meet Him in the air (1 Thessalonians 4:17). Then He appears for judgment (see Jude 15). "Whoever does not have, even what they have will be taken from them. And throw that worthless servant outside, into the darkness, where there will be weeping and gnashing of teeth" (Matthew 25:29-30). Christ is coming in the air for His saints, and later He is coming to the earth with His saints to set up His kingdom: "When the Son of Man comes in his glory, and all the angels with him, he will sit on his glorious throne" (Matthew 25:31).

2 THESSALONIANS 2: IGNORE FALSE TEACHINGS WHILE WAITING FOR CHRIST'S COMING

The Thessalonian Christians were suffering great persecution, and some of them had begun to think that the day of the Lord was already present and that they were passing through the great tribulation that Christ had described as the terrible time that would precede His coming. They were confused and were listening to wrong views about how soon His return would be. The reason for this was that a forged report of some sort, supposed to have come from the apostle Paul, had reached the church and added fuel to the fire (see 2 Thessalonians 2:2). But Jesus had told the disciples, "See to it that no one misleads you" (Matthew 24:4, *NASB*).

I once traveled with friends up the western highway to Mount Rainier. The morning of the day we arrived, the air was clear. The vista was perfect. There was the majestic snow-covered mountain. It seemed so near that it would only be a few minutes until we would be climbing up its side. We ate our breakfast and started off in anticipation. We rode on and there it was, but we hadn't reached it. Every once in a while a low hill and a turn in the road would cut it off from our view, but though it would reappear in all its glory, we weren't there yet. For three hours we traveled. There it was, the greatest thing on our horizon. Other things became insignificant next to its grandeur and importance. Lunchtime came and still we had not arrived, but it kept beckoning us on. Finally we reached its base. We were there!

Christ's coming again in glory, similar to my view of Mount Rainier, has loomed big on the horizon of every Christian's life since the Early Church. It is "the blessed hope" of the Church. His coming is "at hand" because it is the greatest future event, but it may not be immediate because God must finish His plan before Christ comes (2 Thessalonians 2:2, *KJV*). Do not be anxious. God will take care of His own program of the ages. But know this: The "man of lawlessness" ("man of sin," *KJV*) must be revealed first and "the secret power of lawlessness" must work itself out (2 Thessalonians 2:3,7).

The "man of lawlessness" is the Antichrist mentioned by Daniel the prophet and by the Lord (see Daniel 7:25; 8:25; 11:36; Matthew 24:23-24). In Revelation 13:1-8, John tells about him.

The Antichrist is a counterfeit Christ. Satan in a last desperate effort will try to imitate Christ. The world would not have God's man; now they must have Satan's man.

Events Before the Day of the Lord's Judgment

The Lord's coming will be sudden, but "sudden" does not necessarily mean "immediate." The Thessalonians were to wait expectantly for the time when the Lord would gather His children to Himself. Christ tells us to always be ready. The "day of the LORD" is "at hand" but it will not come until certain things take place. God always follows a program. Paul warns the people against confusing the hope of Christ's coming for His Church with the day of the Lord's judgment. Before this "day of the Lord's judgment," Paul describes several things that must happen.

A great "falling away" from the faith will occur (2 Thessalonians 2:3, KJV). In fact, Christ asks, "When the Son of Man comes, will he find faith on the earth?" (Luke 18:8). This is the picture of the Church preceding Christ's return—a falling away, a great apostasy. Does Christ really mean this? We should judge so from His description of the end days described in Matthew 24:1-14,36-42.

How true this is today! People are leaving "the faith that was once for all entrusted to God's holy people" (Jude 3), "denying the sovereign Lord who bought them" with His own precious blood (2 Peter 2:1), and "crucifying the Son of God all over again and subjecting him to public disgrace" (Hebrews 6:6). The world acknowledges Christ to be a teacher, but not the Savior. "Because of the increase of wickedness, the love of most will grow cold" (Matthew 24:12). These are perilous times. Scoffers will arise and ridicule the idea of Christ's return.

The "lawless one" must be revealed (2 Thessalonians 2:8). The Antichrist will be revealed before Christ appears to the world. But not until the Lord has caught up His own will the lawless one come into public view (see 2 Thessalonians 2:8). This "lawless one," who will oppose God, is described in 2 Thessalonians 2:4.

The "man of lawlessness" will open his awful campaign against the Lord. When Christ comes, He will find the Antichrist ruling with great power and signs and lying wonders. It will be a time marked with strong delusions. This is Paul's prediction of the Antichrist: The sin of man has its final outcome in the man of sin. Read Matthew 24:24. Christ will destroy the Antichrist.

The Antichrist—"Christ's counterfeit":

- Will establish himself in Jerusalem—Matthew 24:15
- Will make war with the saints—Revelation 13:7
- Will be worshiped as God—2 Thessalonians 2:4
- Will do signs and lying wonders—2 Thessalonians 2:9
- Will work for only three and a half years—Revelation 13:5-6
- Will be cast into the lake of fire at Christ's coming—Revelation 19:20

God's Plan for the Present Age

Does Paul teach that the world is getting better? Is it true that the preaching of the gospel is going to win the whole world for Christ? If so, has the gospel failed? What is God's plan for this present age?

The gospel has not failed. It is accomplishing just what Christ intended it to accomplish—the gathering of His people around the world, the Church. On the other hand, there is this "mystery of lawlessness" working (2 Thessalonians 2:7, *NASB*), a development of anarchy among all classes of society. Don't be disheartened.

When Christ returns, He will find the Antichrist carrying out his satanic plans. From the description of the man of lawlessness in the Scriptures and his diabolical use of "signs and wonders that serve the lie," we do not see how that and the millennial glory could exist together (2 Thessalonians 2:9). But it is just as God said it would be. Indeed, the darkest clouds that are gathering are but harbingers of the golden day that is surely coming when our Lord Himself will return to take up the reins of government.

Instructions for the Faithful

The time of the glorious Second Coming is to be left with God. The delay in the Lord's coming gives us real opportunities for service. We might have two wrong views of the Lord's coming. Either we become restless and troubled because of having to wait so long, or we grow idle because we know that when He comes He will right every wrong and overthrow iniquity. But both of these attitudes are wrong. We are not just to stand and wait, but rather be prepared for service, making ready for the glorious day when He will come. Let us not abandon the work Christ has given us to do.

Paul gives some instructions to the Thessalonians:

- "Stand firm" and don't be influenced by false teaching—2 Thessalonians 2:15
- "Hold fast to the teachings we passed on to you"; in other words, don't lose any of your foundation truth—2 Thessalonians 2:15

- "Encourage your hearts"—2 Thessalonians 2:17
- "Strengthen you in every good deed and word"—2 Thessalonians 2:17

2 THESSALONIANS 3: BE DISCIPLINED WHILE WAITING FOR CHRIST'S COMING

After instructing the Thessalonians, Paul asks for their prayers (see 2 Thessalonians 3:1). His heart was burdened and he needed their fellowship. He had great confidence in their faith. Then Paul points out that our Lord's delay gives us several opportunities:

- Be loyal to Him—2 Thessalonians 2:15
- Evangelize the world—2 Thessalonians 3:1
- Pray for His servants—2 Thessalonians 3:1-2
- Patiently wait for Him—2 Thessalonians 3:5
- Live a holy life—2 Thessalonians 3:6-14

The hope of Christ's coming stimulates but doesn't excite; sobers but doesn't depress. It is a balanced doctrine.

Some thought that because Christ was coming they would just withdraw from business and not work, claiming the right to be supported by the brethren who had money. Paul was very drastic in his dealing with these lazy fellows. The attitude on the part of these men was absolutely wrong, and he asked them to look to him for an example. He never ceased to labor while he was preaching to them. He laid down a great principle of life: "The one who is unwilling to work shall not eat" (2 Thessalonians 3:10). Any view of Christianity that makes an individual neglect working for a living is not of God. Although Paul always advocated charity toward those in need and spent much time taking up offerings for the poor, he was very severe in condemning the able-bodied person who could but would not work. He forbade the Church to support these folks and even urged the Church to withdraw fellowship from such people.

Understanding First Timothy

First Timothy Portrays Jesus Christ, Our Teacher

SELECTED BIBLE READINGS

DAY OF THE WEEK		MAIN TOPIC
Sunday: 1 Timothy 1	Soundness in Life	
Monday: 1 Timothy 2	Prayers for Everyone	
Tuesday: 1 Timothy 3	Qualities for Church Leadership	
Wednesday: 1 Timothy 4	The Good Ministry of Jesus Christ	
Thursday: 1 Timothy 5	Deal Fairly with Everyone	
Friday: 1 Timothy 6	Warnings Against False Teachings and Love of Money	
Saturday: 1 Timothy 1–6	The Good Fight of Faith	

AUTHOR: The books of 1 and 2 Timothy were written by the apostle Paul according to 1 Timothy 1:1 and 2 Timothy 1:1.

DATE: The books were written in AD 63 and 66 respectively.

PURPOSE AND SUMMARY: Along with Paul's letter to Titus, 1 and 2 Timothy are known as the Pastoral epistles, which address the pastoral and leadership issues that Titus and Timothy oversaw in the churches of Crete and Ephesus. These letters cover such topics as the duties and qualifications of elders and deacon-ministers, the inspiration of Scripture, the treatment of widows, and the expectation of God's reward for obedience and endurance.

The key verse in 1 Timothy is 3:15: "You will know how people ought to conduct themselves in God's household, which is the church of the living God." Realizing that behavior is based on belief, Paul stresses sound doctrine.

First and 2 Timothy and Titus are the three Pastoral epistles, written to ministers in charge of important churches instead of to the churches themselves. Both Timothy and Titus were given explicit directions for shepherding the sheep, for guarding the churches after Paul should be called "home," as he knew he soon would be (see 2 Timothy 4:7-8). Timothy had been entrusted with the government and supervision of Ephesus; and Titus, of the church at Crete. How inadequate both of these young men felt!

Because Timothy was a young man, we expect to find in Paul's writings to him valuable suggestions for other young men who are living the Christian life, but we also find helpful suggestions for those who are older in years. Take time to select from the two letters to Timothy the admonitions that are still useful today. This exercise would especially be helpful for those who think the Bible is out of date.

Today with so much information available so easily, it is well to recommend to young people the faith of their fathers and to warn them against "what is falsely called knowledge" (1 Timothy 6:20). It is well worth it to tell them to "fight the battle well, holding on to faith and a good conscience" (1 Timothy 1:18-19). And when sports threaten to consume the major portion of a student's interest and time, it is good for young Christians to remind themselves that although "physical training is of some value . . . godliness has value for all things, holding promise for both the present life and the life to come" (1 Timothy 4:8). And who can hear Paul's words to his young associate without hearing him say across the years to today's young people that whatever it costs, "keep yourself pure" (1 Timothy 5:22).

It was a real honor for the young Timothy to enjoy the friendship of the apostle Paul. Among the most enthusiastic of Paul's converts of Lystra were Eunice and her son, Timothy, and Paul calls him "my son whom I love, who is faithful in the Lord" (1 Corinthians 4:17). During the impressionable days of Timothy's boyhood, while Paul was visiting Lystra, the people first tried to worship the apostle and then tried to take his life. How Timothy had listened to the gospel preached by Paul! He saw him heal the cripple, heard him as he appealed to the multitude and then saw him stoned and left for dead. But the next day, Paul got up and again went into the city.

When Paul came back to Lystra on his second missionary journey, he took Timothy along as his companion. What a wonderful thing for so young a man! After long years of training under this mighty man of God, Timothy was left in charge of the important church at Ephesus. Paul had won a vast multitude to Christ during his stay in Ephesus.

In the succeeding years, the number of converts increased tremendously. Within the next 50 years, so many of the non-Christians turned to Christ that their idolatrous temples were almost entirely abandoned. This brought the timid young man face to face with serious problems. Think of this inexperienced young fellow being left in that big church to take the place of a man like its founder Paul! How unworthy he must have felt! How he leaned on the apostle for advice and direction!

While Timothy was in charge at Ephesus, Paul wrote his two letters to Timothy—letters of instruction and guidance indeed to Timothy, but also as a handbook for Christian pastors for the centuries to come. Paul told Timothy to deal severely with false teachers, to direct public worship, to choose church officers and to work with all classes of peoples found in the church. But most important of all, Paul told him that he must lead a life that would be an example to all. Timothy had a hard task.

One of the things to remember about this time of the Early Church is that there were no church buildings. Groups of Christians met in homes. No churches were built until about 200 years after Paul's day and not until the Roman emperor Constantine the Great put an end to the persecution of Christians. This meant that there would be hundreds of small congregations, each with its own pastor. These pastors were called "elders" (Acts 20:17). In these letters to Timothy, each is called "an overseer" (1 Timothy 3:1; "a bishop," *KJV*). Timothy's work was with these various pastors. Remember, there were no seminaries to prepare leaders. Paul had to train his own men. Even though there were no buildings and no theological seminaries, and also in spite of continued persecution, the Church grew by leaps and bounds.

1 TIMOTHY 1: SOUNDNESS IN LIFE

Paul calls Timothy his "true son in the faith" (1 Timothy 1:2). It is clear that the boy was led to Christ by Paul and that he was an example of someone who accepts Christ as a child because he had been brought up in a home in which the Scriptures were taught. This is the kind of Christian experience we need to emphasize today as not only possible but also as the expected norm.

Warnings Against False Teaching

Even in that first-century Church, Paul was called on to warn his young co-worker Timothy against the false teachings that are much like the false doctrines of this century. When he left Ephesus seven years before, Paul had warned the church members that savage wolves would ravage the flock (see Acts 20:29-30). Now the wolves were there in full force, presenting young Timothy with his worst problem.

There has never been a day when the Church has been free from false teachers who present new and strange doctrines. They are hard to combat because they base their teachings on parts of God's Word, but do not "correctly [handle] the word of truth" (2 Timothy 2:15) and interpret it as a whole. What the Church needs today is instruction in the vital truths. Above the teaching of the Law and "myths and endless genealogies" (1 Timothy 1:4), Paul puts "the gospel concerning the glory of the blessed God" (1 Timothy 1:11). Therefore Timothy must safeguard against any other doctrine. Fables and legends should never be mixed with the gospel!

Paul warns Timothy to hold "on to faith and a good conscience" (1 Timothy 1:19), because these save people from spiritual shipwreck. It is a thrilling sight to see a ship loosened from her moorings and plunging into the ocean. But it is a solemn sight, too, considering the many storms she is likely to meet. If this is true of a ship, how much more so of a Christian starting out on the voyage of life.

Paul speaks plainly of some people who, having put away faith and a good conscience, have suffered both spiritual and temporal shipwrecks, ruining hopes for two worlds. Paul advocated soundness in life. Paul realized that a person may believe the Word of God completely and yet live a life far from its truth. It is sad when one's life and one's belief are poles apart! Let us pay heed to his warnings.

The Best Way to Fight Error

In this letter, Paul says that the best way of fighting error in life is to live up to the standards set down in God's Word. Remember, many of us are the only Bibles others ever read. Christians have to live better than other people in this world if their testimony is to count. How we live our lives either commends Christ to others or drives them away from Him. How often have we heard, "Well, if that's what Christianity does for a person, I don't want any of it!"

Paul wants Timothy to live a life that will demonstrate the truths he preaches. He challenges Timothy to be a good soldier for Jesus Christ. Let us remember that we will not fight very hard for a truth we do not live. As it was with Timothy, so it is with us: What Timothy preached was empowered and made mighty by how Timothy lived. Timothy is charged to "fight the battle well" (1 Timothy 1:18). This suggests a military campaign and all the responsibilities of the officer in command.

Paul humbly declares, "Here is a trustworthy saying that deserves full acceptance: Christ Jesus came into the world to save sinners—of whom I am the worst" (1 Timothy 1:15). This bold statement gives us a glimpse of the man who probably did more for Christ than any other throughout the ages since the world began. But here he is on his knees, struck with the feeling of his own unworthiness.

Although Paul was once a blasphemer, God in His grace had appointed him an apostle; and although Paul had persecuted Jesus' followers, now he proclaimed Jesus' love. The closer we get to the heart of Christ, the more we realize our own unworthiness. A singer may think he has a very good voice, but let him compare himself with the likes of Caruso or Pavarotti and he feels as if he should never sing again. The reason many people today do not have a sense of sin is that they are not near to Christ. Just to stand in Christ's presence is enough to make us feel condemned. Paul did not realize how sinful he was until he was brought face to face with his Lord and Savior. After their meeting, Paul felt that his miraculous conversion was intended to be an example of how God can save and use the chief of sinners. Read 1 Timothy 1:2-15.

1 TIMOTHY 2–3—DIRECTIONS FOR THE CHURCH

Prayers

The Church has a great calling. We are called on not only to plead with people to turn to God but also to plead with God the cause of people. Read what Paul says: "I urge, then, first of all, that petitions, prayers, intercession and thanksgiving be made for all people—for kings and all those in authority" (1 Timothy 2:1-2). Yes, he tells us to pray for rulers. It is well to remember that Nero was the emperor of Rome at this time! Under this wicked despot, Paul was imprisoned and soon would be beheaded. This proves to us that we must pray for bad rulers as well as good so "that we may live peaceful and quiet lives in all godliness and holiness" (1 Timothy 2:2).

Remember when we pray that God "wants all men to be saved and to come to a knowledge of the truth. For there is one God and one mediator between God and mankind, the man Christ Jesus" (1 Timothy 2:4-5). Paul makes clear that when we pray for someone, we can go straight to God for that person. Our blessed Lord Himself stands in God's presence pleading for us.

When we look to heaven and remember that God has condemned us because of our sin, despair would be a normal reaction for us. But we see Jesus sitting at the right hand of the throne on high, holding up His nail-pierced hands and presenting His pierced feet and wounded side, pleading for you and me.

Finally, let all who pray be clean in conduct and pure in character (see 1 Timothy 2:8-10). Let us lift up "holy hands" when we pray (1 Timothy 2:8). That means that we should come to the Lord with a heart that is cleansed, not filled with worthless pleasures or needless obsessions (see 1 John 1:9).

Church Leadership

When we think of church officers, we usually immediately think of the official church board or leadership committee. Paul tells us the kind of people that really ought to be holding positions of leadership. If the Church is to fulfill her mission of proclaiming the gospel and praying for all, then she must be governed properly and know the real reason for her existence. Paul describes two officers who should direct the church—the overseer ("bishop," *KJV*) and the deacon—and outlines the requirements for both offices, which were to be complementary to each other. (Note that different denominations often use different titles for these offices.)

We find as we look at 1 Timothy 3:2-7 that the overseer, or pastor, must be a man of blameless character, "faithful to his wife," not quarrelsome, not greedy for money. He must be a skillful teacher and make his own children obey. He must not be a new convert; otherwise, his head might be turned with pride. He must have a good reputation in his community. It is important that the Church have the right leadership. Good pastors lead a church forward. How we need good and faithful shepherds today![1]

Deacons must have the same moral qualifications as elders or pastors. This office is not inferior, just different. A deacon must be as carefully chosen as the pastor. A woman may also be appointed to this office.

Church Purpose

Paul gives us a beautiful description of the Church and states her purpose: "the church of the living God, the pillar and foundation of the truth" (1 Timothy 3:15). The Church upholds all truth in the sight of people. She is the only earthly institution to which Christ committed the preaching of the gospel. (Paul also tells us how Christians "ought to conduct themselves in God's household" [1 Timothy 3:15].)

1 TIMOTHY 4–6: DEALING WITH VARIOUS PEOPLE

Picture the young Timothy awed by his instructor, the 50-year-old apostle Paul, as he says, "In later times some will abandon the faith" and turn to spiritualism and all of its teachings (1 Timothy 4:1). Those false teachings will tell you that to be holy, you must not marry and not eat certain kinds of food. But let us not ban that which God has given to us for our good. Turn a deaf ear to foolish isms filled with "do this" and "don't do that." People are always trying to find what they can *do* to inherit eternal life (see 1 Timothy 4:2-5).

Paul goes on to say, "If you point [the following] things out to the brothers and sisters, you will be a good minister of Christ Jesus" (1 Timothy 4:6): Lead a godly life, for "godliness has value" (1 Timothy 4:8). True religion is an appeal to common sense. God says it pays, because in one way, Christianity is a business: It asks us to get out our account books, to study the current prices, to consider the possibilities of profit and loss, and decide the question, "What good is it for someone to gain the whole world, yet forfeit their soul?" (Mark 8:36). Paul, after "going over his books," found that what he had counted as "gain" was "loss."

Does it pay to invest in the Christian life? Does it pay from the standpoint of life right now? God says it does. Christ says, "Seek first his kingdom and his righteousness, and all these things will be given to you as well" (Matthew 6:33).

A noted Puritan once said that God had only one Son, and He made Him a minister.

For the Pastor

Paul says to young Timothy and to all those who may be ministers, "Don't think entirely in terms of the physical, how you can please your body." Everyone usually thinks in terms of having fun, of *doing* things. The body must be fed, clothed, entertained and pleased! Paul says that "physical training is of some value, but godliness has value for all things, holding promise for both the present life and the life to come" (1 Timothy 4:8). Start living for eternity!

"Set an example for the believers in speech, in conduct, in love, in faith and in purity" (1 Timothy 4:12). Carry conviction and command respect. In order to do this, give much attention to your reading and preaching and teaching. The best way to combat any error is by reiterating the simple gospel truth. The Bible itself will do the job, if only you give it a chance. "Give yourself wholly to" the Scriptures (1 Timothy 4:15). If a person is to succeed in the ministry, all of the person's strength must be poured into it. Ministry demands the whole person, the whole time. Godliness does not starve real living. You will not become a sissy if you are good. Godliness is not "goody-ness."

The way a minister treats his or her flock is of vital importance. Each church member must be dealt with wisely and fairly. Widows must be cared for. Elders must be honored and supported, but they must also be publicly admonished, if they are found guilty of sinning so that others may be warned by example. In other words, sin can never be allowed to get by in the Church, no matter who is guilty of that sin.

For Slaves

Paul even remembers the Christian slaves. They must be taught. Those who serve unbelieving masters are to let their service be a testimony to these unbelievers. Those who serve Christians should not take advantage of the relationship simply because they are fellow believers. Love should make us serve better.

For All Believers

"Fight the good fight of the faith" (1 Timothy 6:12). Christ appeals to all men and women to show courage. The Christian life is not a thing to be entered into lightly. We will not be carried into heaven on flowery beds of ease. We must fight if we intend to be conquerors. But it is a "good fight."

Note

1. Some evangelical scholars and Church leaders point to evidence from the New Testament and the Early Church that suggests that women, alongside men, served as elders (pastors) in the pre-fourth-century AD Church.

Understanding
Second Timothy

Second Timothy Portrays Jesus Christ, Our Example

SELECTED BIBLE READINGS

DAY OF THE WEEK		MAIN TOPIC
Sunday: 2 Timothy 1:1-9	Strengthen Your Faith	
Monday: 2 Timothy 1:10-18	Guard the Good Deposit	
Tuesday: 2 Timothy 2:1-15	Endure Hardship	
Wednesday: 2 Timothy 2:16-26	Follow Righteousness	
Thursday: 2 Timothy 3	Know the Scriptures	
Friday: 2 Timothy 4	Keep the Faith	
Saturday: 1 Corinthians 9:25; 2 Timothy 4:8; James 1:12; 1 Peter 5:4; Revelation 2:10; 3:11	Receive a Crown	

AUTHOR: The books of 1 and 2 Timothy were written by the apostle Paul according to 1 Timothy 1:1 and 2 Timothy 1:1.

DATE: The books were written in AD 63 and 66, respectively.

PURPOSE AND SUMMARY: Along with Paul's letter to Titus, 1 and 2 Timothy are known as the Pastoral epistles, which address the pastoral and leadership issues that Titus and Timothy oversaw in the churches of Crete and Ephesus. These letters cover such topics as the duties and qualifications of elders and deacon-ministers, the inspiration of Scripture, the treatment of widows, and the expectation of God's reward for obedience and endurance.

"Join with me in suffering, like a good soldier of Christ Jesus" (2 Timothy 2:3). Be loyal to Christ and His Word!

- In 1 Timothy, Paul advocates a straight gospel—in 2 Timothy, a straight life.

- In 1 Timothy, Paul in effect says, "Guard the doctrine, which is our message from God"—in 2 Timothy, Paul in effect says, "Guard the testimony, which is our life from God."

- In 1 Timothy, Paul seems to say, "Shoulder arms! Polish the metal! Ammunition ready!"—in 2 Timothy Paul seems to say, "Onward march! Face front, shoulders square, keep step with our leader, who is Christ!"

The walk is as necessary as the weapon. The sons of Samuel Wilberforce, a great nineteenth-century British pastor, said of their father, "After a while father gave up preparing his discourses and simply prepared himself." Diligently guard your witness.

Second Timothy is a letter of Paul's, written from his last imprisonment in Rome, in which he himself says his course is "finished" here on this earth (2 Timothy 4:7). What ground had he covered? In answer to this question, note every city and province and island that Paul visited (there are at least 30 of them). To how many thousands had he preached his Christ, do you suppose, in those different locations? In how many languages had he testified for Christ? How many of his letters have found a place in the Christian Bible? Are these letters still being read?

After writing his first epistle to Timothy, Paul was arrested again, in Greece or Asia Minor, and went back to Rome, this time as a criminal (see 2 Timothy 2:9). While waiting in the Roman dungeon for "the time for [his] departure" (2 Timothy 4:6), he wrote this last letter to his beloved son in the gospel, Timothy. His arrest had been so sudden and unexpected that he had had no time to collect his valuable books and parchments or even to take his warm cloak with him (see 2 Timothy 4:13).

This second imprisonment was very different from the first. Then he had his own rented house; now he was kept in close confinement. Before, he was the center of a large circle of friends, accessible to all; now he was alone (see 2 Timothy 4:10-12). Before, he had hoped for freedom; now he was expecting to die (see 2 Timothy 4:6). Paul had already appeared before the wicked Nero, but his case had been postponed (see 2 Timothy 4:16-17). He expected his case to be heard during the coming winter and wrote urging Timothy to come immediately and bring Mark with him. He asked Timothy to bring with him the things that Paul had had to leave behind (see 2 Timothy 4:9,11,13,21). Being uncertain whether Timothy could get there before his death (and he did not, for Paul's trial probably took place in June rather than the next winter), he wanted to give him his last words of warning and encouragement.

It is well to remember that this is Paul's last writing! His pen was to be dry forever after this. This epistle is very personal. He mentions 23 individuals. Although alone and facing death, he forgot himself in thinking of others. The Right Reverend Arthur Michael Ramsey, once the Archbishop of Canterbury, said, "I have often found it difficult deliberately to read these short chapters through, without finding something like a mist gathering in my eyes. The writer's heart beats in the writing."

2 TIMOTHY 1—A WORSHIPING HOME

Parental example is the greatest answer to the problem of juvenile delinquency. We must first guard our testimony in the home, which is the training center for Christian life. This is also the hardest place for a young person to begin, because many young people today do not have a strong Christian influence in their homes. The problem youth have today often has to do with their parents: Too many parents are missing from church; they never hear the Word preached or taught and the family altar is unheard of. This kind of a home produces spiritual and social illiterates.

Timothy had been reared in a Christian home with his mother, Eunice, and his grandmother Lois. Paul mentions these wonderful Christian women and commends Timothy for having had early religious training in a worshiping home (see 2 Timothy 3:15).

Paul remembers Timothy's pure faith that "first lived in your grandmother Lois and in your mother Eunice and, I am persuaded, now lives in you also" (2 Timothy 1:5). Someone has said, "When you want to make a great person, start with his grandmother." Whatever may be the value of that observation, one thing is sure—when you want to build a Timothy, you must begin while the child is still a toddler.

Paul calls Timothy "my true son" (1 Timothy 1:2). It seems clear that the youth was led to confess Christ by Paul during Paul's first missionary journey. Since Timothy was a Christian from childhood, it is no surprise that Paul saw in Timothy a lad of promise as a minister in the Early Church. He in fact became Paul's understudy.

Timothy possessed fine qualities, backed up by excellent training. He had a splendid reputation in his own church, and he was the constant companion of the great apostle Paul. He knew the Word of God and made use of it in his life and teachings (see 2 Timothy 3:14-16). He demonstrated a splendid spirit of unselfishness in his service. He was given great responsibilities by Paul, who at the end of his life turned over his work to Timothy. All of this to a large degree was the result of his early training in a Christian home (see 2 Timothy 1:3; 3:15; 4:6-12).

Rely on Sound Teaching

Timothy is addressed as a "man of God" (1 Timothy 6:11). What does that mean? Godliness comes from the Word and prayer, God speaking to us and our speaking to God. Manliness includes truth in the mind, love in the heart and righteousness in the life. Manliness is due to godliness. The grace of God makes a man godly and then proceeds to make him manly.

No man ever lived a life of such constant abiding in Christ as Paul. Now that he was about to leave the Church he had established, he is concerned about its future. He is warning the youthful and timid Timothy that from now on, he must stand alone in comforting and directing the Church. Paul's son in the gospel, now perhaps 35 years of age, must emphasize above all things a doctrine that is true and sound, for "savage wolves" had already begun to play havoc with the Church (Acts 20:29).

The key verse is 2 Timothy 1:13: "What you heard from me, keep as the pattern of sound teaching, with faith and love in Christ Jesus." Paul's life was characterized by an unceasing effort to guard in its purity the priceless treasure of the Christian faith. He wanted it kept untarnished. We live at a time when deeds are counted above doctrine, but Paul's teaching was that conduct must be based on creed: "As [a man] thinketh . . . so is he" (Proverbs 23:7, KJV). Wrong thinking makes for wrong acting. World War II was brought about by men who possessed wrong creeds. These creeds soon became conduct, and millions died to correct it.

Develop Your Gift

How easy it is for us not to make use of our gifts and natural talents! How many of us lose all initiative! How few people think! Timothy had one of the gifts of the Spirit (see 1 Corinthians 12), but Paul noticed that he seemed to have been neglecting to use it. In his first letter to Timothy, Paul says, "Do not neglect your gift" and in the second letter, Paul writes, "Fan into flame the gift of God" (1 Timothy 4:14; 2 Timothy 1:6).

How about your gift? Have you let God tell you what it is? Cultivate whatever God has given to you. Remember, everyone has some talent. To be sure, some have five talents, others two and others only one. But develop and use whatever gift(s) you have.

Two men had been discussing the possibility of permanently destroying weeds in a garden, but they failed to agree on how to do it. A third person who had been listening said, "You differ, my friends, concerning the possibility of utterly destroying the weeds in the garden. One thinks fire will permanently destroy the weeds, while the other is sure fire will only increase their next growth. But in one thing you will agree with me: We must all agree that no weeds will spring up in that garden as long as the fire is kept burning." Young people, stir up the fire in your heart. It is easy to let it die down. Keeping the fire going will keep down the weeds in your life. Keep your love constantly burning for Christ by serving Him.

We find in 2 Timothy 1 one of the apostle's "I know"s. It is a verse that gives us great assurance: "I know whom I have believed, and am convinced that he is able to guard what I have entrusted to him until that day" (2 Timothy 1:12).

What is your attitude? Will you say as swiftly and strongly as Paul did, "I know whom I have believed"? Make it very personal. Don't say, "I know *in* whom," as the verse is so often misquoted, but "I know *whom* I have believed."

I know the One who is able to keep my love. Put your life in His hands. He will hold you fast. The psalmist said, "Commit your way to the LORD; trust in him and he will do this" (Psalm 37:5). Second Timothy 1:12 is the natural follow-up.

2 TIMOTHY 2—A HERO'S SPIRIT

We must "join with [Paul] in suffering, like a good soldier"—in and away from home, in school, at the office—wherever we are (2 Timothy 2:3). This is our field of service and discipline. Here we are to stand the test as one who does "not [need] to be ashamed" (2 Timothy 2:15).

Paul says, as a faithful steward, "entrust to reliable people who will also be qualified to teach others" (2 Timothy 2:2). As a brave soldier, endure hardships. A soldier does not become entangled with ordinary affairs but strives to obey his superior officer. Let that be your attitude. The athlete, too, must observe certain rules to gain the wreath of victory. So should you. Just as the farmer works hard in order to enjoy the fruit of the harvest, so should it be with you. Avoid business entanglements that will keep you from rendering the best service. Be careful, too, that the comforts of life and the common enjoyments make you love ease too well (see 2 Timothy 2:3-7). Suffer your hardships courageously and with the spirit of a hero. Don't just endure!

For somebody who was a good man, Paul endured the cruelest of suffering. He was charged as a criminal and was put in chains. But he was glad to suffer anything, just so the gospel would not be chained. He reminds Timothy that he is worshiping a living Christ: "Remember Jesus Christ, raised from the dead, descended from David. This is my gospel" (2 Timothy 2:8). Even though his body was bound, Paul's mind was thinking of eternal glory.

Paul urged Timothy to keep away from foolish discussions, for these only breed quarrels, and a Christian should not quarrel (see 2 Timothy 2:24). Do not argue about the Christian life. Live it! Outlive the world—live better than they do—and they will soon listen to what you have to say. The best argument for Christ is a victorious life.

God gives us a sure foundation on which to build our lives—the foundation laid by God (see 2 Timothy 2:19). It "stands firm," for that foundation is Christ (2 Timothy 2:19). All who build on it are secure, because "the Lord knows those who are his" (2 Timothy 2:19). It is wonderful to know that we are known personally by Him. This is not true of any other religion under heaven. In Christianity we are God's children and He knows every one of us: "And even the very hairs of your head are all numbered" (Matthew 10:30). He calls us by name.

God's work needs proper conduct. It was said of the Messiah, "Your help has made me great" (Psalm 18:35). Courtesy and conviction in the ministry will break down hatred for the Church and give the Church its rightful place in the world. Take care how you conduct yourself. Don't be cruel and critical, for this only sends people away; draw them to Christ by your love.

2 TIMOTHY 3—THE ENDURING WORD

When the battle is on and our faith is assailed, stand firm and strong. Fight effectively by living "a godly life in Christ Jesus"

(2 Timothy 3:12). During every engagement, let us wield the Word that is the sword of the Spirit. Let us be soldiers "thoroughly equipped for every good work" (2 Timothy 3:17).

Paul's catalog of first-century vices sounds like a list of twentieth-century vices (3:2-5):

- "Lovers of themselves"—not lovers of God (verse 2)
- "Lovers of money"—those who will do anything to gain possession of what they want (verse 2)
- "Boastful [and] proud"—those who take pride in self (verse 2)
- "Blasphemers" (*KJV*)—those who take God's name in vain (verse 2)
- "Disobedient to their parents"—no respect in the home (verse 2)
- "Ungrateful"—no gratitude, taking everything for granted (verse 2)
- "Unholy"—those who care for neither God nor people (verse 2)
- "Without natural affection" (*KJV*)—mothers taking the lives of their own children; divorce courts full; pornography and homosexuality rampant (verse 3)
- "Trucebreakers" (*KJV*)—those who make meaningless promises (verse 3)
- "Lovers of pleasure"—those who pursue self-gratification (verse 4)
- "Having a form of godliness but denying its power"—shadow without the substance of Christ Jesus (verse 5)

There is only one way to be strengthened against all the vices that tempt us today. We find it in 2 Timothy 3:14-17. The Scriptures will make us "wise for salvation" (2 Timothy 3:15). Jesus met His temptations by the Word of God. We can do no better.

Have you ever heard anyone say, "I was a drunk, a disgrace to my family, a nuisance to the world, until I began to study mathematics and learned the multiplication table; but since then I have been as happy as the day is long. I feel like singing all the time, for my heart is at peace!" Have you ever heard a man say that he was saved from a life of addiction and sin by the multiplication table or science? Of course you haven't. But thousands have said, "I was unhappy and heartbroken. I had no reason for living until I heard God speak to me through His Word, and now I know the living Savior."

The Word of God is the only thing that will keep the Church alive in this terrible day. The church of Rome put aside the Word and the Dark Ages was the result. The Protestants brought it back into circulation, but Christians everywhere are neglecting it again. The ignorance of the Word today is appalling.

2 TIMOTHY 4—THE GOOD FIGHT

To endure to the end and look back over a hard and bitter fight and say, "I have won!"—that is enduring as a good soldier. Life's last hours for Paul were full of glory. He forgot that lions in the arena, flames at the stake or nails on a cross might end his earthly life at any moment. His good fight was ended, his long hard race was run, and now only the memories of a noble life gave him great peace.

Paul's Farewell

Paul closes this letter with a solemn farewell instruction to Timothy before God and Christ who will judge him and who will return to establish His kingdom on earth: "Preach the word; be prepared in season and out of season. . . . For the time will come when people will not put up with sound doctrine" (2 Timothy 4:2-3).

This is the grandest utterance of the grandest mortal who ever lived. Where can we match Paul's words that he wrote from his dungeon to Timothy, his own true son in the faith? Let us picture the old battle-scarred hero of the cross, standing in the gloomy dungeon, bound with chains and looking up through the one opening in the roof of his cell through which only a tiny shaft of light could enter but which reveals his countenance of perfect peace. His lips are moving, and we hear him say, "I have fought the good fight, I have finished the race, I have kept the faith. Now there is in store for me the crown of righteousness, which the Lord, the righteous Judge, will award to me on that day—and not only to me, but also to all who have longed for his appearing" (2 Timothy 4:7-8).

Ever since Jesus had laid His hand on him, Paul seemed to have been competing in the arena and running in the stadium. There had been scarcely a moment of rest. It had required intense training and strenuous wrestling all the way through. But within—inside his heart—peace reigned. His questions had been answered. His sins had been forgiven. His needs had been supplied. Peace within but an athlete's contest without—this is the true Christian life.

A Glorious Crown

"The crown of righteousness" that Paul will receive is also for us—"to all who have longed for his appearing" (2 Timothy 4:8). You and I, whose achievements are so much less than Paul's, may yet share in Paul's heaven.

Surely "the crown" that gleams before us should spur us on to a new and more diligent service in His name. Do we long for His appearing?

A Hero's Strength

The last verses of this letter give us a glimpse of the loneliness of this great wrestler and runner. Many were leaving him because of persecution. "But the Lord stood at my side and gave me strength, so that through me the message might be fully proclaimed" (2 Timothy 4:17). This is the secret of Paul's success. This is why he could fight a good fight and finish the course. His greatest opportunity seemed to be reserved for the end. He stood in Nero's courthouse, face to face with the lion (see 2 Timothy 4:17). He was alone as far as human help was concerned. The great basilica was crowded and every eye was fastened on the old man who had been abandoned at the bar. Did he lose heart? Was he afraid? No, indeed! He leaped to the height of the momentous occasion. He was not content in defending himself. That he did, but he did so much more. To the multitude, curious and hostile, he told clearly the gospel of Christ, and all the Gentiles heard.

Understanding Titus
and Philemon

Titus Portrays Jesus Christ, Our Pattern;
Philemon Portrays Jesus Christ, Our Lord and Master

SELECTED BIBLE READINGS

DAY OF THE WEEK		MAIN TOPIC
Sunday: Titus 1:1-9	Church Officers	
Monday: Titus 1:10-16	Church Enemies	
Tuesday: Titus 2:1-8	Church Influence	
Wednesday: Titus 2:9-15	Church Rule	
Thursday: Titus 3	Church Works	
Friday: Philemon 1-7	A Christian Gentleman	
Saturday: Philemon 8-25	A Prisoner's Plea	

UNDERSTANDING TITUS

AUTHOR: Titus identifies the apostle Paul as the author of the book of Titus.

DATE: The epistle to Titus was written in approximately AD 66. Paul's many journeys are well documented and reveal that he wrote to Titus from Nicopolis in Epirus. This letter may have been written between the first and the second letters to Timothy.

PURPOSE AND SUMMARY: This is a personal letter written by the apostle Paul to a young minister whom he had left on Crete. Like the Timothy correspondence, the letter to Titus is practical and discusses the everyday problems confronted by a young church leader.

The importance of good works is stressed in this epistle. Not that we are saved by good works, but that we are saved for good works. Here also God presents His ideal for the Church and its officers and members.

The epistle to Titus was written by Paul. Titus was bishop of Crete, a hard post (see Titus 1:12-13). Paul had given Titus a difficult task before, that of settling the differences at Corinth and tactfully persuading the Church to do the right thing in the matter of divisiveness. Paul's second letter to the Corinthians shows how successful Titus was in this mission.

Titus was a Gentile. No doubt he was one of Paul's converts during the early years of the apostle's ministry. He accompanied Paul and Barnabas to Jerusalem 17 years after Paul's conversion.

When Paul heard that Apollos was about to go to Crete, he took the opportunity to send this letter to Titus (see Titus 3:13). It is full of practical advice to the young pastor, giving him directions for church administration and warning him against the heretics of his day. He asks Titus to come to him and to report about the condition of the church on the island. Although this is a personal letter, it undoubtedly was meant to be read to the church also.

The letter is very much like Paul's first letter to Timothy, being written about the same time and dealing with the same subjects.

TITUS 1—WORKS FOR CHURCH OFFICERS

Paul presents himself in this scene as the "servant" of the Lord Jesus Christ and then as His "apostle" (Titus 1:1). Paul loves to refer to himself as someone bound to serve Christ. It is terrible to be a slave to most anyone or anything, but to be a slave of Jesus Christ—to be bought by Him—that is wonderful! It is a slavery of love.

"In grace," Charles Spurgeon once said, "you can be under bonds yet not in bondage. I am in bonds of wedlock but I feel no bondage. On the contrary it is joy to be so bound."

Paul kept his eyes steadfastly on heaven as he neared the end of his earthly life. Read what he says of his apostleship: "to further the faith of God's elect and their knowledge of the truth . . . in the hope of eternal life" (Titus 1:1-2).

Paul had left Titus in Crete to superintend the work of the church organization there. He was to set things in order and ordain elders in every city on the island (see Titus 1:5).

What kind of officers the church should have is carefully detailed. Only a man of character should even be considered for the position. He must be above reproach in his home life and in his personal life and also be true to the Word (see Titus 1:6-9).

How do you act at home? What kind of a Christian are you there? This is so often the test of your Christianity. Home life reflects what you really believe. The Christian household is the main evangelizing agency everywhere. When every home is Christian, the community is Christian. For this reason, the bishop (overseer or elder) and pastor are to set good examples for the people. He must have only one living wife, but he is not compelled to be married. Because a minister is judged by his family life, he must rule his own children well; if he cannot rule his own household well, he cannot rule the church of God (see 1 Timothy 3:5). He must be a man of moral courage and sympathy. He must be a good teacher and encourage others by his teaching.

The Cretan churches were being upset by outside teachers who, for the sake of making money, were wreaking havoc in "whole households" (Titus 1:11). This probably meant whole congregations, for the Early Church met in private homes. Paul calls these fellows "detestable, disobedient and unfit" and said they must be stopped in their teaching (Titus 1:16). He demands that they be dealt with severely. How much false teaching there is today everywhere! And more and more cults and sects based on false teachings are started by men and women only to make themselves rich.

During the 1906 California earthquake, an old saint in San Francisco remained in her room, joyously rocking back and forth in her chair, singing, while all around her people were running away to avoid death or injury. After all was over, someone asked her how she could have had such a feeling of joy. "Oh," replied the old saint, "I was so happy in the thought that my God was mighty enough to rock the world like that while He held me securely in His hand, I did not have time to be frightened."

Today, we hear so many confusing voices and opinions and "there are many rebellious people, full of meaningless talk and deception. . . . They must be silenced, because they are disrupting whole households by teaching things they ought not to teach—and that for the sake of dishonest gain," who "claim to know God, but by their actions they deny him" (Titus 1:10-11,16). So let us, I say, rest our faith, not on the arguments and opinions of people, but on the infallible Word of God. By this Word alone judge new and strange doctrines, and silence those who handle the Word of God deceitfully (see Titus 1:9-11).

TITUS 2–3—WORKS FOR CHURCH MEMBERS

Paul believed that doctrine must be expressed in life, so he had a word to Titus about the aged, the youth and the slaves:

- The Aged: *Older men* are "to be temperate, worthy of respect, self-controlled, and sound in faith, in love and in endurance" (Titus 2:2). *Older women* are "to be reverent in the way they live, not to be slanderers or addicted to much wine, but to teach what is good" (verse 3). They in turn are to train younger women to become good wives and mothers (verses 4-5).

- Youth: *The young* are to exercise self-control, and be examples of a noble life (verse 6).

- Slaves (Servants): *Servants* are to obey their masters, be diligent and faithful, and give satisfaction; they are to not contradict and not steal (verses 9-10).

True Life

In Titus 2:11-13, Paul gives us the three *L*s for life:

1. *L*eave the old life.
2. *L*ive the new life.
3. *L*ook for that blessed hope and glorious appearing of Christ.

How essential that this be our foundation! Then we can "make the teaching about God our Savior attractive" (Titus 2:10). To think that we in any way can beautify the wonderful gospel simply by how we live! But just as we put a frame on a picture to enhance its beauty and make it more conspicuous, so we must adorn and make more beautiful the gospel of Christ. A king in his royal robes is more easily recognized than a king in ordinary clothing.

How we can either make or mar the gospel! In everything you do, do good (see Titus 2:7). The test of fellowship is not warmth of devotion but holiness of life. One cannot live on strong feelings. Some mistake religious feeling for holiness, and good thoughts for good conduct. There is use and abuse in religious emotion.

Be so faithful in your attitudes and obligations in life that critics of your religion will be silenced (see Titus 2:8). Make others say, "If this is what Christ can do for you, there must be something to your religion."

Good Works

Paul says we are saved by "his mercy" and "justified by his grace" (Titus 3:5,7). But because we have been saved at such a cost, we should show it by good works.

God our Savior did not save us as a result of our good works but through His kindness and according to His mercy. He cleansed us by His blood and gave us a new life by His Holy Spirit. Because of that, we are to do good works:

- "Set . . . an example by doing what is good"—Titus 2:7
- "Eager to do what is good"—Titus 2:14
- "Ready to do what is good"—Titus 3:1

- "Careful to devote [ourselves] to doing what is good"—Titus 3:8
- "Doing what is good, in order to provide for urgent needs"—Titus 3:14

Paul urges citizens of the heavenly kingdom to be good citizens of the country under whose flag they live. Every Christian should obey their civil rulers and authorities (see Titus 3:1-2; Romans 13:1-7; 1 Peter 2:13-17).

"Don't say anything about a person if you can't say something good" is a wonderful admonition to follow. Paul said it long ago: "Slander no one" (Titus 3:2). Don't be quarrelsome. Be gentle in your dealing with others. Remember that "we too were foolish, disobedient, deceived and enslaved" (Titus 3:3). Yes, we had all the faults we hate in others. We must remember that the things we criticize in others are very apt to be our own weaknesses. We like to call attention to these faults in others to take eyes off ourselves. Test yourself and see whether you do this.

Avoid controversies and foolish discussions. They are always useless and futile. Often an argument only strengthens a person's previous beliefs. Do all you can to correct someone, but if the person persists in causing divisions among your church members, after being warned once or twice, say nothing more to that person and avoid him or her (see Titus 3:10). Devote your time in doing good.

UNDERSTANDING PHILEMON

AUTHOR: Philemon 1 reveals that the author of the book of Philemon was the apostle Paul.

DATE: The book was written in approximately AD 60.

PURPOSE AND SUMMARY: This shortest of all Paul's letters was addressed to Philemon (although two other persons are included in the salutation). Paul entreats Philemon, the master of Onesimus, a runaway slave, to receive him back as a brother in Christ (see Philemon 16-17). This very personal letter reveals not only the concern of the apostle for a converted slave but also a practical demonstration of brotherhood in Christ, where "there is . . . neither slave nor free" (Galatians 3:28).

Christian love and forgiveness are given prominence in the book of Philemon. The power of the gospel in winning a runaway thief and slave and in changing a master's mind is clearly shown here. This is a book in applied Christianity, a textbook of social service.

The Reverend Sir W. Robertson Nicoll, editor of the *Expositor's Bible*, once said, "If I were to covet any honor of authorship, it would be this: That some letters of mine might be found in the desks of my friends when their life struggle is ended." We don't know whether Paul coveted this honor or not, but tucked away in your New Testament, between Titus and Hebrews, you will find a model letter written by a master of letter writing. It is a personal letter from Paul to Philemon. Only one chapter—only 25 verses—but containing such strong and beautiful statements so well expressed that it stands out as a gem, even in the Book of books.

Notice the courtesy and tactfulness of Paul's letter. Letter writing seems to be a lost art these days, having given way to emails and text messages, but text of any sort can be a ministry for God, if we make it so. Some people who find it hard to speak to anyone about Christ might easily write about Him. Then, too, text is good for the one who receives it, for the person has a chance to read and reread it and think its contents over. Use the keyboard (or that old-fashioned pen) to witness to your friends. Remember that all that has been preserved to us of Paul's ministry has come mainly through his epistles—letters, even short ones. What a heritage his letters are for all Christians today! In order to appreciate what God thought of correspondence, see how many letters He kept for us in Holy Scripture.

In this letter, Paul intercedes with Philemon (who was an outstanding member of the church at Colosse) for his runaway slave Onesimus who had stolen from his master and made his way to Rome. There he had been providentially brought face to face with Paul and had found Christ as his Savior. He became endeared to the apostle by his devoted service. But Paul knew he was Philemon's lawful slave, so he could not think of keeping him permanently. So Paul sends him home and pleads with Philemon to take him back. He makes himself personally responsible for the debts that Onesimus owes, asking that they be charged to his (Paul's) account. He wished to save the runaway slave from the severe and cruel punishment he deserved according to Roman law. Paul sent his letter with the slave so that Onesimus would not encounter his outraged master alone.

This letter deals with the question of slavery, but Paul does not demand the abolition of slavery. Instead, he shows that slavery can never be a byproduct of Christianity. This beautiful letter from God's aged servant, bound to serve the gospel, foreshadows the time when the bonds of Christ's love will break the bonds of slavery.

PHILEMON—PAUL'S PLEA FOR ONESIMUS

Paul, the "old man," was not old so much from the passing of years as he was from work, anxiety and eagerness of spirit (Philemon 9). He was only about 60, but he was a prisoner, and as such he appealed to his friend Philemon on behalf of Onesimus.

Paul speaks of himself, not, as in the letter to the Colossians, with the authority of an apostle, but as a friend to a friend. He says of Philemon that he is "our dear friend and fellow worker" (Philemon 1). He does not say these kind things just to flatter his friend but because he always looked for the good in others.

This letter is addressed to a man, his wife and (possibly) his son in Colosse. A little meeting of Christians was held at their home, and Paul gives us a beautiful picture of a Christian home during the time of the Early Church. This family was the nucleus

Philemon

of that home-church and doubtless other believers in Colosse gathered there for worship.

Paul always begins his letters with commendations unless there is a reason for not doing it, as in Galatians. Here he speaks of love and faith and tells of the joy he finds in fellowship. Even though he was separated by a great distance from his friend Philemon, nevertheless this man's loving helpfulness to others had done Paul good in that far-off prison in Rome. He prays that Philemon's faith may continue to grow.

Work on a Sinner's Behalf

Paul was a wonderful student of human nature. The picture he portrays of himself as the bent and battered "prisoner of Christ Jesus" probably opened a well of sympathy in the heart of Philemon as he continued to read his friend's letter (Philemon 9).

Paul slowly approaches the main purpose of his letter and does not immediately blurt it out. He anticipates anger, so he uses the finest tact. He admits that Onesimus had been good for nothing in the past but, playfully alluding to Onesimus's name (which means "useful"), points out that the "useless" servant now will be "useful " (Philemon 11). Christ makes a person useful to others. Thus Paul hopes to put his reader in a favorable mood.

While Philemon's voice trembles as he continues to read aloud this letter, the mother, Apphia, is wiping her eyes on her robe and son Archippus is clearing his throat. Paul has his little joke and pun, and the faces of the trio break into smiles. Onesimus, meanwhile, nervously fumbles with his sash as he stands in the back of the room and then breaks into a broad grin. The tension is over.

Paul's action with regard to Onesimus is an illustration of the Lord's work on behalf of the sinner. Paul does not minimize the sin, but he pleads for forgiveness for the sinner on the grounds of his own merit in the eyes of Philemon, his friend. More than that, he makes himself personally responsible for the debts of Onesimus: "Charge it to me" (Philemon 18). This is the message of the gospel, for Christ took on our sins when He was crucified.

Philemon

The Practice of Slavery

This epistle gives a clear idea of the attitude of Christianity to the social organization of the world; but slavery, which was widespread in that day, is not dealt with directly. If slavery is wrong, why didn't Paul say so instead of apparently condoning it in this letter to the owner of a runaway slave?

If Paul had made slavery an issue, he might have torn society to shreds because the practice of slavery was so widespread. Instead he presents principles that would surely undermine slavery and in time actually did so. Brotherhood in Christ is, however, about more than emancipation. Christianity does not merely free the slaves but teaches them that they and their masters are one in Christ.

Has Christianity yet driven slavery from the world? Mighty attempts to vanquish this terrible menace have been made wherever there is brotherly love of Christ. But there are still portions of the world in which slavery is practiced, and even in some societies that no longer openly practice slavery, an underground slave trade exists. Sometimes it is disguised by other names, but wherever human life is sold, wherever forced labor is carried on, slavery exists. It takes changes in people's thinking to destroy slavery. Christ came to change people; He frees us from sin's slavery and sends us into the world to abolish slavery of every kind.

If Timothy or Tychicus took Paul's dictation of this letter, Paul took the stylus or quill and wrote in his big, near-sighted scrawl: "I, Paul, write it with my own hand, I promise to repay it [in full]—and that is to say nothing [of the fact] that you owe me your very self!" (Philemon 19, *AMP*).

Philemon

General Letters

of the New Testament

HEBREWS • JAMES • 1 PETER

2 PETER • 1 JOHN • 2 JOHN

3 JOHN • JUDE

Key Events of General Letters

Jesus is the pinnacle of God's revelation. True citizenship not in the world but heaven.

Hebrews 1; 11

God uses persecution to purify our faith. Following Jesus may bring hardship.

1 Peter

We can trust God to do right. Evil will be punished and faith rewarded.

2 Peter

General Letters: Our True Citizenship

The General Letters are letters of encouragement to believers, many of whom have suffered persecution for their faith. The General Letters remind us that Jesus Christ is the pinnacle of God's revelation to us; that our true citizenship is not in this world, but in heaven; that God uses persecution to purify our faith; that following Jesus may very well bring hardship upon us; and that we can trust God to do what is right because the day is coming when evil will be punished and faith rewarded.

Understanding Hebrews

Hebrews Portrays Jesus Christ,
Our Intercessor at the Throne

SELECTED BIBLE READINGS

DAY OF THE WEEK		MAIN TOPIC
Sunday: Hebrews 1	The Superiority of Christ to Prophets and Angels	
Monday: Hebrews 3	The Superiority of Christ to Moses	
Tuesday: Hebrews 5	The Superiority of Christ to Aaron	
Wednesday: Hebrews 8	The Superiority of Christ's Covenant	
Thursday: Hebrews 10:1-25	The Superiority of Christ's Atonement	
Friday: Hebrews 11	The Superiority of Christ's Faith Life	
Saturday: Hebrews 12–13	The Superiority of Christ's Privileges	

AUTHOR: Although some include the book of Hebrews among the apostle Paul's writings, the identity of the author remains unknown. Missing is Paul's customary salutation common to his other letters. In addition, the suggestion that the writer of this epistle relied upon knowledge and information provided by others who were actual eyewitnesses of Christ Jesus makes Pauline authorship doubtful (see Hebrews 2:3). Some suggest that Luke wrote this letter. Others suggest Hebrews may have been written by Apollos, Barnabas, Silas, Philip, or Aquila and Priscilla. Regardless of the human hand that held the pen, the Holy Spirit of God is the divine author of all Scripture, and the Early Church fathers recognized the letter to be divinely inspired (see 2 Timothy 3:16).

DATE: The Early Church father Clement quoted from the book of Hebrews in AD 95, showing that the letter had been written at least by that time. Furthermore, internal evidence such as the fact that Timothy was alive at the time the letter was written (see Hebrews 13:23) and the absence of any evidence in the letter showing that the Temple sacrificial system had come to an end (as it did when the Romans destroyed Jerusalem in AD 70) suggests that Hebrews was written before AD 70.

PURPOSE AND SUMMARY: The letter to the Hebrews portrays Jesus, who gave Himself up as the perfect sacrifice for the sins of the world, as the great high priest from the line of Melchizedek (see Genesis 14). One of the Bible's only extended definitions of faith occurs in Hebrews chapter 11 and is followed in chapter 12 by the description of the "great cloud of witnesses," the heroes of the faith from the pages of the Old Testament (Hebrews 12:1).

We as Christians have that which is better—better in every way. The keyword to the book of Hebrews is "better." It occurs more than 10 times.

Several particular words in this book help us in understanding it. Trace the words "eternal," "perfect," "once," "blood" (mark this one in red), "without," "better" ("superior," "greater"), "therefore," "sat down" and "heavenly."

This book has been called the fifth Gospel. The four Gospels describe Christ's ministry on earth; this one describes His ministry in heaven at God's right hand.

The glories of our Savior are exhibited in this epistle. Our eye is fixed on Jesus, "the pioneer and perfecter of faith" (Hebrews 12:2). "Crowned with glory and honor," He is set before us in the heavens (Hebrews 2:9).

This book was written to Jewish believers, probably in Jerusalem, who were wavering in their faith. Because of the taunts and jeers of their persecutors, the Jewish believers in Jesus were beginning to think that they had lost everything—altar, priests, sac-

Hebrews

rifices—by accepting Christ. The author of Hebrews proves that they had only lost the shadow but were given the substance (Jesus Christ). They were undervaluing their privileges in Christ and were engaged in self-pity and mutual discouragement. They were in danger of even giving up their faith (see Hebrews 5:11-12). They had started well but had not made any progress (see Hebrews 6:10-11). The writer tries to lead them from an elementary knowledge of their faith to a mature grasp of all it means. He urges them to be loyal to Christ, showing them the superiority of Christ over all they had previously known. The writer wanted to keep them from drifting back to their traditional rites and ceremonies, so he urges them to let go of everything else in order to hold fast to the faith and hope of the gospel.

The book is also a timely warning and a word of comfort to all, especially in this day when many people have little instruction in the things of Christ and are apt to be led astray by any fad or cult that comes along.

When you take a trip for the first time over a new road, how often do you drive straight along, anticipating your destination and any difficulties you may have along the way but not noticing much along the way. When you come back over the same road, however, you have time to look around and notice things. Do this as you study the book of Hebrews. Read it through, and don't worry about the things you don't understand. Then go back over what you read and take note of the many details along the way. You could spend months in Hebrews, because it presents so many wonderful truths.

At your first reading, you will be impressed by one fact above all others: Jesus Christ is prominent on every page. This is not true in all the other books of the New Testament. In Acts, the apostles, disciples, Jews and pagans are predominant. In Romans, a great doctrine attracts our attention. In the other letters, the Church and its problems are considered, but here it is our Lord Himself:

- Greater than prophets—Hebrews 1:1-3
- Greater than angels—Hebrews 1:4-2

- Greater than Moses—Hebrews 3
- Greater than Joshua—Hebrews 4
- Greater than Aaron—Hebrews 5–10:18

The reason the writer uses these comparisons is that each of these groups or people were of great importance in rabbinical Judaism. They were the framework of Jewish worship, and for their followers to transfer their allegiance, something or someone must be proven to be better to take their place.

Do we know the real difference between having Christ as a Savior and as a priest? Well, this book answers the question.

The book of Hebrews proves that we can never understand the Old Testament without the New, or the New without the Old.

HEBREWS 1–4:13: THE SUPERIORITY OF CHRIST THE PERSON

Nowhere are our Lord's deity and humanity so emphasized as in Hebrews 1 and 2. As our great high priest, Christ is able to understand all our needs, because He was a perfect man. He is able "to empathize with our weaknesses," because He "has been tempted in every way, just as we are—yet he did not sin" (Hebrews 4:15). He is able to meet all our needs, because He is perfect God. He *is able.*

The opening sentences of the book of Hebrews are some of the grandest in the Bible (see Hebrews 1:1-4). They rank with the opening words of Genesis and of John. We find Jesus there—His deity, His glory, a Creator, heir of all things, superior to all things, and our Savior.

Write down all you find about Christ in Hebrews 1 and 2. If you knew nothing more about Him than what you learn in these two chapters, you would know a great deal.

Two great truths are taken for granted by the author of Hebrews: the existence of God, and the fact that He reveals Himself to us. He revealed Himself before, "in the past . . . to our ancestors through the prophets . . . but in these last days he has spoken to

Hebrews

us by his Son" (Hebrews 1:1-2). The Bible records a series of stories about how God speaks to people and reveals His will and His plan to them. How marvelous to hear His only begotten Son speak!

Remember, this letter is written to correct the erroneous idea that the Jewish believers had lost some things because they had taken up Christianity. The letter is written to remove this misconception. Christianity is not about giving up but about receiving—receiving the greatest gifts of life, in fact Life itself, for Christ is Life.

Jesus and All Others

The Lord Jesus Christ is greater than any prophet:

- He is God's Son—Hebrews 1:2
- He is "heir of all things"—Hebrews 1:2
- He created the universe—Hebrews 1:2
- He is God—Hebrews 1:3
- He sustains all things by His word—Hebrews 1:3
- He cleansed us from sin—Hebrews 1:3
- "He sat down at the right hand of [God]"—Hebrews 1:3

The Lord Jesus Christ is greater than angels (Hebrews 1:4–2):

- He has the more excellent name of Son—Hebrews 1:4-5
- He is worshiped by angels—Hebrews 1:6
- He is the eternal God—Hebrews 1:7-12
- His throne is forever—Hebrews 1:8
- He is the ruler of the coming age—Hebrews 1:11-13

It is well to notice that angels and human spirits (of those who die) are not the same. Human life is a different order of creation from angels. We do not become angels when we die. Angels are our servants now, as they will be in heaven (see Hebrews 1:14). Angels worship Christ just as we do.

When God wanted to save us from our sins, He did not send an angel but His Son. And God did not come in the form of an angel but in the form of a man. He became a human to redeem humankind. He suffered as a man and died as a man so He would be our Redeemer (see Hebrews 2:10). Jesus tasted the bitterness of death for us so that He would make the devil (who has the power of death) powerless. He came up from the grave with the keys of hell and of death; no longer can the devil lock any of us in death.

The Lord Jesus Christ is also greater than Moses (Hebrews 3):

- Moses was a faithful servant—verses 2,5
- Christ is the Son over His own house—verses 3-6

The Lord Jesus Christ is greater than Joshua (Hebrews 4):

- Joshua was a great leader; he led the Hebrews into the Promised Land, but he did not lead the people into rest—verse 8
- Jesus is greater, for what Joshua failed to do, the Son accomplished; and He alone gives real rest—verses 9-10

The Lord Jesus Christ is greater than Aaron (Hebrews 5):

- Aaron was the high priest in charge of the Tabernacle and therefore in charge of sacrifices; he was the head of the hereditary priesthood.
- Christ sacrificed Himself to cleanse us from our sins and is in charge of the universe; He is the only One who can intercede for us with God.

Jesus and the Law

Our weakness is that we look to ourselves for answers to life's troubles, and what we find is our own weakness. "Fix your thoughts on Jesus" (Hebrews 3:1). Set your telescope to the heavens and gaze on Him.

Many Jewish believers in Jesus were confused about Christ's ministry on earth. They thought He had come to enforce the laws Moses had given. Moses was the lawgiver, so Christ must enforce those laws—or so they thought. But Christ is His own lawgiver.

The old Mosaic system was imperfect and weak (see Hebrews 7:11,18). It had served its purpose. Now Christ had a better way.

Canaan, the land that flowed with milk and honey, was the Promised Land into which Joshua had led the children of Israel. But this was only a suggestion, a taste, of the rest that faith in God provides for every Christian to enjoy. Saint Augustine said that no soul found rest until it found its rest in God. Joshua could not lead the children of Israel into this perfect rest and trust in God, but Jesus did. Stop self-effort and yield yourself to Christ (see Hebrews 4:10). Trust Jesus as your Joshua and enter into *His* land of promise. Cease struggling and place all in His hand. "Commit your way to the LORD" (Psalm 37:5).

Two Great Warnings

The first few chapters of Hebrews have two warnings that all Christians should heed:

1. Do not neglect the great salvation that is offered to us, not by angels, but by the Lord Himself. Listen to what the Son says (see Hebrews 2:1-4).
2. Do not "[turn] away from the living God" (Hebrews 3:12).

One Reminder

Hebrews 4:12 describes the power of God's Word. Let the Word search and try you! Let God's Word have its proper place in your life. It searches out every motive, desire and purpose of your life, and helps you evaluate them. Christ is the living Word of God. He is "alive" ("quick," *KJV*), powerful, all wise and all knowing (Hebrews 4:12).

HEBREWS 4:14–10:18: THE SUPERIORITY OF CHRIST THE PRIEST

Hebrews 4:14 is the beginning of the book's main theme, which is plainly expressed in Hebrews 8:1: "Now the main point of what we are saying is this: We do have such a high priest." Christ has been briefly compared with the prophets, angels, Moses, Joshua and Aaron; but because the most important comparison is with Aaron, the high priest, we will examine this in a bit more detail.

The author of Hebrews shows that the priesthood of Christ is greater than the priesthood of the Levitical law. The central point in the book is Christ's eternal priesthood and His sacrifice that atoned for the sins of the world. This epistle dwells on the supreme importance and power of the blood of Christ in obtaining redemption for us. He has purged our sins from us and has opened the way into the heavenly sanctuary and to the very throne of God.

Christ is Himself a priest: "Therefore, since we have a great high priest who has ascended into heaven, Jesus the Son of God, let us hold firmly to the faith we profess. For we do not have a high priest who is unable to empathize with our weaknesses, but we have one who has been tempted in every way, just as we are—yet he did not sin. Let us then approach God's throne of grace with confidence, so that we may receive mercy and find grace to help us in our time of need" (Hebrews 4:14-16).

Jesus Christ not only had the qualifications of a priest like Aaron, the earthly high priest, but He also is a high priest in the order of the eternal Melchizedek priesthood because this priesthood is continuous and will never end. The Aaronic priests could not make people perfect because they themselves were sinful, but Christ is eternal and sinless.

The Similarities of Christ's and Melchizedek's Priesthoods

Christ's priesthood is like Melchizedek's in several ways:

- A royal priesthood—both were kings of peace and righteousness.
- Was universal—it was not only for Jewish people.
- Had no human ancestry—both were "without father or mother" (Hebrews 7:3).
- Had no successor—when Melchizedek passed away, no one stepped in to take his place, so Christ is a priest forever.

Hebrews

Notice an important fact here: Christian ministers are nowhere called priests in the New Testament except as all Christians are called "a royal priesthood" (1 Peter 2:9). We have learned from Paul's letters that Christian ministers are called teachers and pastors.

The Superiority of Christ's Priesthood

The glories of our Savior are exhibited in Hebrews, and three great *betters* are connected with our high priest:

1. A better covenant (see Hebrews 8:13)—Jesus' new covenant is based on better promises. These promises are written on the heart, not on tablets of stone (see Hebrews 8:10).

2. A better Tabernacle (see Hebrews 9:1-12)—Christ officiates in heaven. The Tabernacle was earthly, and the high priest entered into the holy of holies once a year. But Christ has entered into the heavenly sanctuary "once for all" (Hebrews 9:12).

3. A better sacrifice (see Hebrews 10:18)—Jesus Himself is the sacrifice. He offered Himself as a lamb without blemish to cleanse us. The repeated sacrifices of the Old Testament were perfect animals. They could not take away sins. Jesus' sacrifice of His perfect self needed to be offered only once, and He *did* atone for our sins.

Christ is called our high priest. What does that mean? We are taught very plainly in the Word that sins cut people off from God. No sinner could approach God. The way had been closed since Adam and Eve. In the Old Testament, a representative, the high priest whom God appointed, could come into God's presence only once a year after sacrifice for the sins of the people had been made. He would offer the blood of calves and goats, not only for the sins of the people, but also for his own sins, for he, too, was a sinner. He then would go into the holy place and then on beyond the veil into the holy of holies where the Ark of the Covenant rested. Here was the mercy seat, and here God met people through the mediator, the high priest.

Our Approach to the Throne of Grace

How can we approach God today? Christ has made that possible. He is our high priest, our representative before the Father. He entered into the heavenly sanctuary, God's presence, bearing the blood of His own sacrifice to cleanse us from our sins and to give to us eternal salvation. His blood had to be shed, for "without the shedding of blood there is no forgiveness" (Hebrews 9:22). "But when this priest had offered for all time one sacrifice for sins, he sat down at the right hand of God" (Hebrews 10:12). "It is finished," He said on the cross (John 19:30). All His work of redemption had been completed, so we see Him sitting. We often find this picture of Christ in Hebrews.

Our high priest is at the right hand of the Father at this minute, making intercession for you and for me (see Hebrews 7:25; 8:1; 10:12). He has gone "now to appear for us in God's presence" (Hebrews 9:24). This is why we can boldly "enter the Most Holy Place by the blood of Jesus, by a new and living way" (Hebrews 10:19-20). Take advantage of this glorious privilege.

In Hebrews 9, our Lord's three great appearances stand out:

- Past—on the cross—"but he has appeared once for all at the culmination of the ages to do away with sin by the sacrifice of himself" (verse 26).

- Present—at the right hand of the throne—"now [He will] appear for us in God's presence" (verse 24).

- Future—in the clouds of glory—"and he will appear a second time, not to bear sin, but to bring salvation to those who are waiting for him" (verse 28).

The Great Advantage of Christian Fellowship

Let us not only approach the throne of grace, but let us also not neglect "meeting together, as some are in the habit of doing" (Hebrews 10:25). There is nothing like Christian fellowship to make us grow. D. L. Moody once visited a woman who had grown cold in her Christian life. She said that she had not been able to come to church and that she could not understand what had happened to make her feel as she did about spiritual things. Without saying a word, Mr. Moody got up and lifted out a live coal from the grate and placed it on the hearth. In a few moments the glow was gone and the coal was black. "I see it," she said. You cannot continue to glow in your Christian life alone. You need the warmth of fellowship with other Christians. This is a command to us.

HEBREWS 10:19–13: THE SUPERIORITY OF THE HIGHER REALM

Beginning in Hebrews 10:19, the writer of Hebrews tells us the kind of life we should live because of Christ's work as high priest for us.

After one has accepted Christ, there are several levels of Christian living. Some Christians live in the basement of Christian experience, inside the building but where it is dark, dismal and gloomy. Others live on the ground floor. They have moved beyond the foundation and some sunlight has entered their lives, but their outlook is limited to the circumstances that surround them. They live very close to the world. Still others live up higher. Sunlight and warmth flood the rooms. The noise and attractions of the worldly street do not disturb them. The air is pure. Their outlook is toward the blue skies and distant mountains. These Christians live above the world, hidden with Christ in God. God wishes us all to live continuously on this higher floor, in this higher realm.

Study the lives of a few men and women of God who lived in this higher realm; their names are given in Hebrews 11. The Holy Spirit tells us that the secret of each life was faith, yet it was not so much his or her faith as it was a reliance on our faithful God.

The Secret of Christian Living

The secret of Christian living is simply allowing Christ to meet our needs. Some say, "I have no faith; I can't believe." Yet we constantly place faith in our fellow humans. You want to go to New York from San Francisco. You buy your ticket and get on the airplane. In the course of your journey, a pilot will guide your plane. Without seeing the pilot or knowing a thing about his or her ability, you trust your life to this unknown person. Faith is just trusting God, believing Him. There is nothing mysterious about faith. It is a simple act of the will. Either we will believe God or we won't. We decide. It is as simple as turning on an electric light switch. This is not a difficult or baffling or mysterious thing to do. But the result? Light and power. When we decide to believe God absolutely, then supernatural life and power enter our lives. A miracle is wrought within us. One of the practical results of faith is that it makes weak people strong (see Hebrews 11:34).

The Hall of Faith

To live in the Hall of Faith forever we need to do two things. First, like anyone entering a race, "let us throw off everything that hinders" (Hebrews 12:1). Yield everything to Christ. Second, we are to truly believe that Jesus is trustworthy. When we do, we have given up the sin that so easily troubles us—the sin of unbelief. We give up that sin when we "[fix] our eyes on Jesus" (Hebrews 12:2).

Only one kind of human being in the world can please God. Who is it? Read Hebrews 11:6. It is not what we do for God but what God does for us that makes lives of power and strength. Our great God, rather than our great faith, is the thing to think most about. It may be fashionable or politically correct to be doubtful rather than sure about the great facts of God and Christ and salvation. But this does not please God. To please God:

    Forsaking
    All
    I
    Take
    Him

Christ is the belief that brings salvation.

Hebrews

Because of the great company of witnesses on the bleachers watching from heaven, let each of us run the race of life that God has set before us. As any athlete does when preparing for a race, let each of us:

- Lay aside every sinful habit and anything that would be a hindrance—Hebrews 12:1-2
- Have patience—Hebrews 12:1
- Endure chastening—Hebrews 12:11
- Follow peace and purity of heart—Hebrews 12:14
- Always look to Jesus, "the author and finisher of our faith"—Hebrews 12:2 (*KJV*)

A life well pleasing in His sight will be made possible by the Lord Himself: "May the God of peace, who through the blood of the eternal covenant brought back from the dead our Lord Jesus, that great Shepherd of the sheep, equip you with everything good for doing his will, and may he work in us what is pleasing to him, through Jesus Christ, to whom be glory for ever and ever. Amen" (Hebrews 13:20-21).

Understanding James

James Portrays Jesus Christ, Our Pattern

DAY OF THE WEEK		MAIN TOPIC
Sunday: James 1:1-21	Temptations	
Monday: James 1:22-27	Actions	
Tuesday: James 2:1-13	Brotherhood	
Wednesday: James 2:14-26	Deeds	
Thursday: James 3	Speech	
Friday: James 4	Worldliness	
Saturday: James 5	Prayer	

AUTHOR: The author of the book of James is James, also called James the Just, who is thought to be the brother of Jesus Christ (see Matthew 13:55; Mark 6:3). James was not a believer until after the resurrection (see John 7:3-5; Acts 1:14; 1 Corinthians 15:7; Galatians 1:19). He became the head of the Jerusalem church and is mentioned by Paul as a pillar of the church (see Galatians 2:9).

DATE: The book is probably the oldest book of the New Testament, written perhaps as early as AD 45, before the first council of Jerusalem in AD 50. James was martyred in approximately AD 62, according to the historian Josephus.

PURPOSE AND SUMMARY: James addresses the letter "to the twelve tribes scattered among the nations"—to Jewish messianic believers throughout the Mediterranean world—and is the most Jewish in style and form of any of the New Testament books (James 1:1). James is a practical letter dealing with Christian ethics and how to maintain a lifestyle of deeds that matches a confession of faith. James insists that good works, not empty words, are the mark of a person who has saving faith. James says that anyone who claims to have saving faith but whose life lacks any evidence of doing good in keeping with that claim actually has dead faith—which is not true saving faith at all. We can't say we believe in Jesus and then live like the devil; otherwise, we show that we really have no faith at all.

The law of Christ for daily life is found in the word "do": "Do not merely listen to the word, and so deceive yourselves. Do what it says" (James 1:22).

The author of the book is no doubt James, the brother of our Lord. He may well be called the practical apostle. He stands for efficiency and consistency in life and conduct.

Although James refers to his own brother Jesus only twice, he does it in a most reverent manner. Though he knew Him so well, there is no hint of that familiarity in the way James refers to Him, for he calls Him Lord and Christ. He associates his brother with God in such a way that it implies an equality with the Almighty. If Jesus were not deity, this would be blasphemous.

GENERAL CHARACTERISTICS OF JAMES

The book of James is the most practical of all the Epistles, and has been called "A Practical Guide to Christian Life and Conduct." This book is the Proverbs of the New Testament. It is filled with moral precepts. It states the ethics of Christian faith. It is full of figures and metaphors. It is often quite dramatic in style. It compels the reader to think. Hebrews presents doctrine; James presents deeds. They go together in vital Christian faith.

Paul and James

Some people have suggested that there is a conflict between what Paul and James have to say, but only superficial reading of both would warrant that accusation. Paul says, "Take the gospel in." James says, "Take it out." Paul saw Christ in the heavens, establishing our righteousness. James saw Him on the earth, telling us to be as perfect as His Father in heaven is perfect.

Paul dwells on the source of our faith. James tells about the fruit of our faith. One lays the foundations in Christ; the other builds the superstructure. Christ is both "pioneer and perfecter" (Hebrews 12:2) of our faith. Not only believe that fact, but live it! Although Paul lays great stress upon justification by faith, we have noticed in his epistles, especially in Titus, that he emphasizes good works. It is an astounding fact that while Paul uses the expression "rich in good deeds" (1 Timothy 6:18), James uses "rich in faith" (James 2:5).

It is good to notice, too, that when James seems to speak in a slighting way of faith, he means a faith that is mere intellectual belief that does not produce works, not a "saving faith" that is so essential. James exalts faith. He says that its trials produce patience in a person.

A Strong Prayer Life

James begins and ends with a strong encouragement to pray (see James 1:5-8; 5:13-18). Prayer is one of the easiest subjects to talk about but one of the hardest things to practice. Find all you can about this subject in this epistle. What was James's practice? Tradition tells us that because of his constant habit of prayer, his knees were as hard as a camel's.

God's Servant

James calls himself "a servant of God and of the Lord Jesus Christ" (James 1:1). He proudly accepts this title as a description of what his relationship was to Jesus. This reveals real humility, because nowhere does James refer to the fact of his earthly relationship to the Lord Jesus Christ, his brother.

James mentions the name of God 17 times, but he repeats the name of Jesus only twice. James was bitterly opposed to Jesus and His claims up to the time of Jesus' death; but after the Resurrection, he was converted by a special and private interview with the risen Lord (see 1 Corinthians 15:7). This adds value to James's testimony about the deity of our Lord. Immediately after the encounter, James became a man of prayer and was made bishop of the church at Jerusalem (see Acts 15:13-21). His life work was to win the Jewish people and to help them believe in Jesus as their Messiah. He was slain by the religious leaders in AD 62. Tradition says he was probably forced to the roof of the Temple by the high priest and rulers and commanded to blaspheme the name of Christ. Instead, he boldly proclaimed the fact that Jesus is the Son of God. James was then hurled from the roof.

Jewish Believers

James says his epistle is written "to the twelve tribes scattered among the nations" (James 1:1), to those who lived outside the holy land, those whose location was well known at the time. Like Hebrews, it is addressed to the Jewish believers in Jesus. The Jewish people to whom James wrote had not ceased to practice their religion, even though they had embraced Jesus as the Messiah. Many of them had believed on the Day of Pentecost but had carried home only a partial understanding of the gospel. In their enthusiasm at having found the true Messiah, they neglected the graces and virtues that should accompany faith in Christ. They thought and taught that all that was necessary to have salvation was to believe that Jesus was the true Messiah and Savior. They were in great danger of being discouraged in their faith, because they were persecuted by Jews who did not believe as they did.

JAMES 1:1-21: TEMPTATIONS BUILD CHARACTER

After the briefest of greetings, James plunges straight into his subject. Realizing that these Jewish believers scattered everywhere outside of the land of Israel were undergoing severe testing of their faith, he begins by telling them how they must meet temptation, and he tries to encourage and comfort them.

Spiritual arithmetic is of value, and the arithmetic of the Bible is important enough that none of us can afford to ignore it. James invites Christians to count: "Count it all joy when ye fall into divers temptations" (James 1:2, *KJV*). We usually count it joy when we escape temptation and sorrow. In addition, we should count testing as a glorious opportunity to prove our faith, just as the car manufacturer knows that the best proof of the car's worth is the road test. Why we must "count it all joy" is not because of the trial itself but because of what it will work out. In other words, use your trials.

What is the purpose of testing? God uses our trials to give us blessings (see James 1:3). Too often our trials result in our impatience, but God will give us grace so that His real purpose will be accomplished. Patience is necessary more than anything else in our faith life. We forget that time is nothing to God, for with Him a thousand years is as one day; and one day, as a thousand years (see 1 Peter 3:8). Christ's purpose for our lives is that we will be perfect and complete, wanting nothing.

Let us be careful where we lay the blame of temptation. Read James 1:14 carefully. Testings of character come from God (see Genesis 22:1), but temptations to do evil never come from Him; they come from the adversary through our own corrupt nature (see James 1:13), appealing for us to meet a proper desire in an improper way (see James 1:14). Instead of wrong things coming from God, we find that only good and perfect gifts come from above, from the Father of lights who never changes (see James 1:17). Our God is a God who loves to give. Alexander the Great supposedly said to one of his subjects who was overwhelmed by his generosity: "I give as a king!" Our Father in heaven gives to us as the infinite God.

It is hard to behave wisely, but God's wisdom will help you do it. Take notes as you read the teaching on wisdom in this short letter. Pray for wisdom to behave wisely in times of trouble. When you are wronged and insulted, ask God how you should act, what you should do: "If any of you lacks wisdom, you should ask God, who gives generously to all without finding fault, and it will be given to you" (James 1:5). What a sad need to have! What a mess such a need can lead us into. Does James say, "If you lack wisdom, sit down and think or study"? No, he says the wisdom we need is from God.

Did it ever occur to you to thank God for temptations? Do you think of your temptations as blessings? James says, "Consider it pure joy, my brothers and sisters, whenever you face trials of many kinds" (James 1:2). Do you look at troubles that way? Then he adds, "Blessed is the one who perseveres under trial" (James 1:12). How spineless and weak you would become without temptations. Character that is never tested has no value. There is joy in overcoming. There is no greater satisfaction than to know you have resisted temptation victoriously.

JAMES 1:22–2: OUR ACTIONS REFLECT OUR FAITH

Don't be merely listeners to God's Word, but put the gospel into practice. What is the good of people saying they have faith if they do not prove it by their actions? We must not be satisfied with only listening. We must be doing (see James 1:22). People who are listeners and not doers are like those who look at themselves in a mirror and then go away and forget what they looked like (see James 1:24).

James says we must keep looking into the mirror of God's Word to remember how we look, to find out the sins in our lives. Those who look carefully into the Scriptures and practice them will be blessed in what they do. The religion of those who think they are religious but don't control their tongues is vain. The religion that does not influence the tongue is not a true or vital one. An uncontrolled tongue in a Christian is a terrible thing—guard against it. And control your temper. It is dangerous. When you undergo a trial, be slow to speak. Close off the air to a fire and the flames will go out (see James 1:26).

What are we to do with the Word?

- Receive it—James 1:21
- Hear it—James 1:23
- Do it—James 1:22
- Examine it—James 1:25

Works Reveal Our Faith

Works do not save us, but they are pretty good evidence that we are saved. "Whatever you did for one of the least of these brothers and sisters of mine, you did for me" is not a "saving" text but a "sign" text (Matthew 25:40). What Jesus did is our salvation; what you do is proof of it. Keep faith and works in their proper place.

James says in effect, "The faith you have is the faith you show": "Religion that God our Father accepts as pure and faultless is this: to look after orphans and widows in their distress and to keep oneself from being polluted by the world" (James 1:27). Faith that does not express itself in works is of no value. Just as a body without a spirit is dead, so faith is dead without actions (see James 2:17).

Christianity Is a Brotherhood

Christianity is a brotherhood that has no "respect of persons" (James 2:1; see also verses 3-4, *KJV*). But how the world today ignores James's command not to show favoritism! The world worships the successful, strong and wealthy, and despises the person who is poor. A Christian must not show partiality to the person of wealth and position, however, because showing such favoritism is not only a breach of good manners and a discourtesy to the poor, but it also is a sin. Worshiping worldly success also breaks the law of God and is a sin. "Love your neighbor as yourself" (Leviticus 19:18). This law of love is a "royal law" (James 2:8). It comes from heaven's royalty. We are not only to admire and respect others but also to love them as we do our own selves (see James 2:1-13).

A Single Slip Is a Sin

To disobey God's law is a sin. It is natural to gloss over sin. To excuse herself for something she had done, a little girl was once heard to say, "I haven't broken the commandment, I only cracked it." James says that whosoever obeys the whole law but makes a single slip is guilty of everything (see James 2:10-11). That person is a lawbreaker. If you have to go to court for a traffic violation, you do not plead that you have kept all the other laws. The judge is interested only in the fact that you broke this particular law. You are classified as a lawbreaker. You may have a fine gold chain, but what good is it if all the links are good except one? That broken link makes the entire chain useless.

It is clear that although James here emphasizes one particular sin—showing favoritism to the wealthy—any one sin makes us guilty of everything (see James 2:9).

You Can Be God's Friend

Has the phrase "God's friend" ever gripped you (James 2:23)? God evidently needed a friend, and He found in Abraham the friendship He desired. What is essential to become a friend of God? Read James 2:23.

JAMES 3: OUR WORDS REVEAL OUR FAITH

Our speech reveals what we are and who we belong to. It expresses our personality more than anything else. Anyone who controls his or her tongue, James says, is a perfect person (see James 3:2). If a person has mastery over his or her tongue, the most difficult part of our being, the person will easily be able to control his or her whole nature. Just as we control a spirited horse by a firm hand on the bridle, so too the hand of Christ Jesus can grip and firmly use the bit and reins on our tongues. Just as a great ship is controlled by a very small rudder and turned in any direction the captain decides to go, so too the pierced hands of Jesus can firmly control and wisely use the helm of our lives—our tongue. The tongue, though small, is very powerful. It can determine the course of human life.

Remember, this same tongue can be used to testify for Christ and praise His holy name. It is the instrument the Holy Spirit uses to magnify the Lord (see James 3:9-10). We should not with the same tongue praise God and curse people who are made in His likeness! Cruel words have wrecked homes, broken friendships, divided churches and sent untold millions to ruin and despair. Many people who call themselves Christians don't seem to make the slightest effort to control their tongues, and this is wrong.

JAMES 4: SUBMISSION BUILDS FAITH

The world consists of all the things around us and the spirit within us that are blind and deaf to the value of spiritual things and care nothing about doing the will of God. The devil has organized this world on principles opposed to God in every way. They are principles of force, greed, ambition, selfishness and pleasure. The believer should be crucified to this world (see Galatians 6:14). We should regard its passing pleasures, its honors, its treasures as of little value; and we should remain unmoved by its attractions. Because we live in the world, surrounded by all its attractions and the things necessary for our daily living, we must be very careful to keep our affections and interests focused on what is above the world (see James 4:4).

People keep asking, "How can we end war?" James goes to the root of the problem and tells us the main cause of war: some nation's desire to get what does not belong to it. This has always been the cause of quarrels between nations and between individuals. Selfishness is the root of all conflicts.

Another cause of conflicts is the fact that people either fail to pray or pray with a wrong motive. God promises to answer prayer, but He will not give to those who would use it to satisfy their own pleasures instead of to glorify God (see James 4:1-3).

It is common to see worldly minded Christians praying for purely selfish reasons: "I don't believe in prayer. I prayed for a new car, and God didn't give it to me." "My husband was sick, and I prayed that God would heal him, but he died." In either case, the answer might easily have led the person farther away from God.

The car could have been driven to the beach and not to church. The family circle restored could make the wife find her joy in her husband rather than in her Lord.

Four times a form of the word "lust" is found in the first five verses of James 4 (*KJV*). Dr. Benjamin Jowett, a nineteenth-century British educator and theologian, defined "lust" as "anything that steams the windows of the soul and blurs our vision." This word "lust" can be translated "pleasures." This helps give meaning to these verses and furnishes the clue to the teaching they contain.

Overindulgence in pleasure is sinful:

1. There are "fights and quarrels among you" (James 4:1)—the media show horrible pictures of this every day.

2. Your desires "battle within you" (James 4:1)—if pleasure is allowed to have its own way in us, a war is on and we are mastered by it.

3. "When you ask, you do not receive, because you ask with wrong motives, that you may spend what you get on your pleasures" (James 4:3)—overindulgence in pleasure always affects our prayer life and causes stagnation in our Christian life.

4. "You adulterous people" (James 4:4)—how a pleasure lover degenerates in his or her Christian walk! He or she becomes a friend of the world and therefore an enemy of God.

What is the cure for all this? Examine James 4:6-10:

1. "Submit . . . to God" (James 4:7). Don't make a mess of your life; surrender to God.

2. "Come near to God and he will come near to you" (James 4:8). Come with clean hands and a pure heart.

3. "Humble yourselves before the Lord" (James 4:10). Remember you are a sinner and be unassuming. Then God "will lift you up" (James 4:10).

James

4. "Friendship with the world means enmity against God" (James 4:4). Jesus said, "You cannot serve both God and money" (Matthew 6:24). Do not be subject to the devil. When the devil is resisted by those who have surrendered themselves to God, the devil flees (see James 4:7).

How easy it is for us to plan without God, yet how futile! Let us submit all our plans to the Lord and see what His will is in every matter—"if it is the Lord's will" (James 4:15). One of the most amazing things in all of God's Word is that though He holds the whole universe in His hands, He has a definite plan for each one of our lives. Our lives are a series of surprises for us. We live just one day at a time. We don't know what tomorrow will bring, but God does (see 1 John 3:1-2). What a wonderful God we have!

JAMES 5: PRAYERS SHOW FAITH

Evidently, many of the humble people among the Jewish believers were being oppressed by the rich, and their hard earnings were being "kept back by fraud" (James 5:4, *KJV*). James warns the rich: "You have hoarded wealth in the last days" (James 5:3). How true this is today—the rich continue to amass billions of dollars, while millions of people stand in need. There *are* some great Christian souls among the rich, but for the most part, James's picture of wealth holds true for today. Remember that Jesus said it was easier for a camel to go through the eye of a needle than for a rich person to enter heaven (see Mark 10:25; Luke 18:25).

James again mentions the tongue. It is amazing how many Christians take the name of the Lord in vain in ordinary conversation (see James 5:12). God says, "The LORD will not hold anyone guiltless who misuses his name" (Exodus 20:7; Deuteronomy 5:11). This is a serious indictment.

Prayer is a golden key that, kept bright by constant use, will unlock the treasures of earth and heaven, and James gives us some good advice about it. Anyone in trouble should pray. Anyone sick should send for the elders of the church and be anointed with oil by them, and the elders should pray for the one sick (see James 5:13-14). "The prayer offered in faith will make the sick person well; the Lord will raise them up. If they have sinned, they will be forgiven" (James 5:15). Anyone who has wronged another should confess the fault to the one wronged (see James 5:16). The prayer of faith demands a confession of sin and a will surrendered to God. Elijah's mighty prayer that opened and closed the heavens is an example for us, for "the prayer of a righteous person is powerful and effective" (James 5:16).

This epistle closes abruptly but on a high note: James points out that a Christian who finds someone erring from the truth and restores that person, saves that person. Although only God can save a soul, He uses human instruments to accomplish it: "Whoever turns a sinner from the error of their way will save them from death and cover over a multitude of sins" (James 5:20).

Understanding First Peter

First Peter Portrays Jesus Christ, Precious Cornerstone of Our Faith

SELECTED BIBLE READINGS

<table>
<tbody>
<tr><td rowspan="7">DAY OF THE WEEK</td><td>Sunday: 1 Peter 1:1-12</td><td>Precious Faith</td><td rowspan="7">MAIN TOPIC</td></tr>
<tr><td>Monday: 1 Peter 1:13-25</td><td>Precious Blood</td></tr>
<tr><td>Tuesday: 1 Peter 2:1-10</td><td>Precious Cornerstone</td></tr>
<tr><td>Wednesday: 1 Peter 2:11-25</td><td>Precious Savior</td></tr>
<tr><td>Thursday: 1 Peter 3</td><td>Precious Spirit</td></tr>
<tr><td>Friday: 1 Peter 4</td><td>Precious Suffering</td></tr>
<tr><td>Saturday: 1 Peter 5</td><td>Precious Crowns</td></tr>
</tbody>
</table>

AUTHOR: First Peter 1:1 identifies the author of the book as "Peter an apostle of Jesus Christ," and there is no overriding reason to doubt the truth of his claim, although the beautiful Greek style employed in the letter suggests that the actual writing may have been the work of Silas, an associate of Peter, who was likely a trained scribe acting as secretary (see 1 Peter 5:12).

DATE: The book was likely written between AD 60 and 65.

PURPOSE AND SUMMARY: The themes of the letter bear Peter's imprint. His speeches recorded in Acts indicate a similar attitude toward persecution and suffering (see Acts 2:13-26; 3:12-26; 4:8-20; 5:29-32,41; 10:34-43; 15:7-11). The letter here reflects a time of suffering and trial. No doubt the widespread persecution of the Christians by the Roman authorities was the occasion of the "fiery ordeal" (1 Peter 4:12). The writer admonishes his readers to a life of purity and of godly living and exhorts them to steadfastness and faithfulness.

---

1 Peter

Jesus lived the kind of life described in this letter of Peter's and in 1 John: "Whoever claims to live in him must live as Jesus did" (1 John 2:6). We who have received Christ as Savior are "in God" (Colossians 3:3).

The secret of walking "in newness of life" (Romans 6:4, *KJV*), or living a Christian life victoriously, is simply to "remember Jesus Christ" (2 Timothy 2:8) and to rest on the blessed eternal fact of His ability to meet our needs.

"Now to you who believe, this stone is precious" (1 Peter 2:7). Peter talks about seven precious things. Mark these in your Bible:

1. "Genuineness of your faith"—1 Peter 1:7
2. "Blood"—1 Peter 1:19
3. "Cornerstone"—1 Peter 2:6
4. Christ—1 Peter 2:7
5. "Spirit"—1 Peter 3:4
6. "Faith"—2 Peter 1:1
7. "Promises"—2 Peter 1:4

Peter has been called the apostle of hope, as John was the apostle of love and Paul the apostle of faith. The word "hope" is found in 1 Peter 1:3,13,21; 3:5,15.

Another word (in one form or another) is used more than 15 times in this short epistle: "suffering"—the suffering of Christ and of Christians in following Him.

Try a complete reading at one sitting of this short five-chapter letter, preferably in *The New Testament in Modern English* by J. B. Phillips, the *New International Version* or another modern translation. Mark in one color each mention of "joy" and "grace" and "glory" (in red perhaps), and mark in another color every mention of "suffer" (in black). More than 20 times Peter mentions the joy and glory that are ours who have received God's grace; this number outweighs the number of times he mentions the suffering of Christ and of the Christians who follow Him.

Understand that Peter was enlarging on the statement, "Let us . . . [fix] our eyes on Jesus, the pioneer and perfecter of faith. For the joy set before him he endured the cross, scorning its shame, and sat down at the right hand of the throne of God" (Hebrews 12:1-2). Jesus knew the connection between suffering and joy and glory.

Peter's Life

Peter (or Silas) wrote this book toward the close of Peter's busy life. Peter had become a leader of the apostles and was their spokesman. He belonged to the inner circle of the three friends of Christ. He was the preacher at Pentecost. The first 12 chapters of Acts are centered around this apostle and his ministry to the Jewish people. He died a martyr's death, crucified under the Roman emperor Nero, sometime before AD 67. According to tradition, at his own request, he was crucified with his head downward, because he considered himself unworthy to resemble his master even in death.

The picture of Peter in the Gospels is amazingly different from that found in his own writings. In the Gospels we see Peter as an impulsive, restless soul, sometimes fearless but sometimes a coward, even going as far as to deny his Lord with a curse! In his own epistles, he seems patient, restful and loving, with a courage purified and strengthened by the indwelling Spirit. This is a wonderful illustration of the transforming work of God in a human life.

Peter's Audience Then

The Christians to whom Peter is writing were suffering a "fiery ordeal" from people who did not believe in Jesus (1 Peter 4:12). The Christians would not join their pagan neighbors in worshiping idols, drinking and seeking lustful pleasures, so they were called haters of the human race and were classed with thieves and murderers. Evidently this letter was written at a time when general dislike of Christians was threatening to pass into active persecution, developed particularly by Nero (see 1 Peter 2:15; 3:13-17; 4:12). Those Christians needed encouragement from one who knew what trial meant (see 1 Peter 1:6). Peter points away from the trials to the future glory that awaited them, to the example of Christ and the reward that would follow (see 1 Peter 1:7; 2:21; 4:13).

Christ's Return

A subject repeatedly mentioned is the reappearing of our Lord and Savior. Mark these instances as you read the letter. The influence of this "living hope" on the Christian's way of life cannot be minimized (1 Peter 1:3). This short epistle is full of golden nuggets of truth, all of which can be marked and memorized.

Peter's Audience Today

What specifically does this letter have for our lives today? After all, hostile emperors are not persecuting us. But on every side we *are* being assaulted by the temptations of that same adversary, the devil, who is seeking those whom he may win away from Christ, who endured all for us. Although we were not witnesses of Christ's suffering as was Peter, we are taught by the same Holy Spirit. Ask the Holy Spirit to teach you today!

Lives today are on the auction block, sold to the highest bidder. The devil in the world is bidding high. But remember that Christ already paid the price for us (see 1 Peter 1:18-19).

This book gives us good plain advice from Peter about how we ought to live. Read it and take heed! This letter, written some 12 or more years after the last record of Peter in Acts 15, shows how Peter has grown by his experiences. He wishes to encourage and give assurance to the believers, so he gives his own personal testimony; and his own experience proves all he was saying. There is power in personal testimony, and this personal note is heard all the way through the letter.

1 PETER 1–2:10: CHRISTIAN ENCOURAGEMENT

Peter, who is an apostle of jubilant hope, addresses this epistle to the "exiles" scattered everywhere (1 Peter 1:1). It is a letter to homesick Christians. He tells these persecuted and discouraged believers about the near and precious Savior. Let it lift you up and fill you with joy! This is the purpose of the book.

What are our privileges as Christians? First, we are redeemed by the precious blood of Christ. This is our position in Christ (see 1 Peter 1:18-19). Because of this relationship to Christ, we have everything in Him that God wants us to possess. If God has given us His Son, won't He freely give us all things with Him? Read Romans 8:32.

The Christian Life

The life of faith is described at the beginning of this letter. We are given a "new birth" by God (1 Peter 1:3). At the end, there is "an inheritance" for us; and to assure us of it, we are "shielded" by the power of God (1 Peter 1:4-5). What a life this is!

- Jesus Christ has given us a "new birth into a living hope"—1 Peter 1:3
- We have in reserve an imperishable inheritance— 1 Peter 1:4-5,10
- We are protected by the power of God—1 Peter 1:5
- We are being purified to make us fit to stand with Christ—1 Peter 1:7
- We have salvation for our souls—1 Peter 1:9
- We have a gospel that "even angels long to look into"— 1 Peter 1:12
- We have a great hope—1 Peter 1:13
- We have redemption through Jesus' blood— 1 Peter 1:18-19
- We are "born again . . . through the . . . word of God"— 1 Peter 1:23
- We are "built into a spiritual house"—1 Peter 2:5

- We "will never be put to shame"—1 Peter 2:6
- We "are a chosen people"—1 Peter 2:9
- We will have a "crown of glory"—1 Peter 5:4

Peter says that Christians exhibit characteristics of several different things:

- "Babies"—desire the milk of the Word (1 Peter 2:2)
- "Living stones"—built into the temple of life (1 Peter 2:5)
- "Priesthood, offering spiritual sacrifices" (1 Peter 2:5)
- "Foreigners"—keep themselves unspotted from the world (1 Peter 2:11)
- "Exiles" ("pilgrims," *KJV*)—good deeds along the way (1 Peter 2:11)
- Citizens—render obedience to rulers (1 Peter 2:13)
- People—honor all people in the fear of God (1 Peter 2:17-18)
- "Slaves" ("servants," *KJV*)—subject to Christ (1 Peter 2:18)
- Sufferers—patient, committing all to Christ (1 Peter 2:20-21)
- "Stewards" (1 Peter 4:10)
- "They . . . who [speak] the very words of God" (1 Peter 4:11)

Basic Advice

Peter's first piece of advice about how we ought to live concerns being alert and focused: "Therefore, with minds that are alert and fully sober, set your hope on the grace to be brought to you when Jesus Christ is revealed" (1 Peter 1:13). Fashion your life after the Lord Jesus Christ. Don't live your life after the old pattern. "Be holy, because I am holy" (1 Peter 1:16). "Love one another" (1 Peter 1:22). Since "you have been born again" (1 Peter 1:23), live like it. You are a new creature in Christ Jesus.

How can we put away all wickedness as Peter commands? Read 1 Peter 2. Not by effort! Not by trying! Not by practice! Not by setting our willpower against sin! Only by trusting that God through His grace can do it. The only people who can get rid of their sins are the ones who, having received Christ as Savior, know that Christ has already rid them of their sins.

We also must "rid" ourselves of several things (1 Peter 2:1). Peter tells us to abandon some ugly things: "all malice and all deceit, hypocrisy, envy, and slander of every kind" (1 Peter 2:1). All these noxious weeds spring from a root of wickedness. These must be eliminated from our hearts if we are to grow. Weeds always choke out a fruitful plant if they are allowed to spread. All that challenges the supremacy of the Lord Jesus Christ must be eliminated, whether it be our sin or our righteousness. Sometimes even good things keep us from God's best. "But seek first his kingdom and his righteousness, and all these things will be given to you as well" (Matthew 6:33). We must be careful about this. The choices we must make are not always between bad and good, right and wrong, but between good and best. "As for God, his way is perfect" (Psalm 18:30).

Infants' Milk

We are called "newborn babies" (1 Peter 2:2). Newborn babies have nothing in themselves. They are helpless and dependent 24 hours a day. They need food, clothing, shelter, the tireless care of a mother and the protection of a father. Similarly, Christians have nothing in themselves, but they have access to the untold riches of Christ and are filled with all the fullness of God. As new Christians, we have a new longing in our hearts, a new hunger. We are not self-sustained; we are God-sustained. We are newborn babes the whole way through. Peter describes the attitude as "craving pure spiritual milk" (1 Peter 2:2; "the sincere milk of the word," KJV). Food makes a difference; that's what we live on. Just as milk is a perfect food for children, containing all the elements for building up the body, so too the Word (spiritual milk) is perfect for building up the soul (see Jeremiah 15:16; Ezekiel 3:1-3).

"Word" in 1 Peter 2:2 (KJV) could very well mean Christ as well as His Word, for in the third verse we read that if you have once "tasted," you will find that He is gracious (1 Peter 2:3). He is the nourishment of our souls.

Christian Stones

In 1 Peter 2:4, Peter turned to another metaphor for Christ, calling Him "a living Stone—rejected by humans but . . . precious to [God]." Everyone in this world has to do something with this "Stone," Christ Jesus. He is in every person's path. We can put Him in as the chief cornerstone of our lives, which is God's will. If we do not, we must stumble headlong over Him, tragically, to our death. To many people in the first century, Jesus was a stumbling block and a rock of offense. To many today, He is that same thing. What have you done with this precious cornerstone? Is He in His rightful place in your life?

And we are stones, too, stacked on Christ, the foundation and cornerstone, to make a spiritual temple to God. This means that it is very important for each one of us to find our right place in God's plan and stay in it. The "spiritual house," built of believers, is the corporate temple of the Holy Spirit, as the individual Christian is the individual temple of the Holy Spirit (1 Peter 2:5; see also 1 Corinthians 6:19).

We are not only "living stones" in a spiritual temple, but each of us is also a priest in this temple (1 Peter 2:5). Priests represent God to people, and people to God. Christians are "a holy priesthood" (1 Peter 2:5). Are you faithfully representing God to others by how you live your life, and others to God by your intercessory prayer? As priests, we cannot sacrifice animals today, but Paul tells us to offer ourselves "as a living sacrifice" (Romans 12:1).

1 PETER 2:11–4:11: CHRISTIAN LIVING

Peter is giving us wise counsel by telling us how to behave in the game of life. Up to this point, he has been urging the Christians to walk worthy of their new calling. Now he compels them to glorify God in an ungodly and persecuting world. A greenhouse religion is of very little value to others, for no one sees it.

We need to justify our faith before our fellow humans.

Peter offers a simple program that anyone can follow. His first suggestion is that we remember that we are "foreigners and exiles" (1 Peter 2:11; "strangers and pilgrims," *KJV*). We are not permanently settled here; we are on our way to an eternal city. "Our citizenship is in heaven" (Philippians 3:20). We are in the world but not of it (see John 17:11,14). It is important that we keep this in mind; otherwise, we will be tying our lives to stakes that will be shaken loose some day.

But for Christians who follow Peter's plan, all is different. They have invested time and thought and money in the pursuit of Christ's plan for their lives. They find that life is sweeter as the years go by, and the end is the best of all!

The greatest satisfaction that can come to Christians is to please the Lord and Savior. In the power of the Lord, live for Christ during all stages of your life. Do not shut Him out of even the most insignificant parts. The devil will not allow this to be easy. He will use every weapon against you. But Christ has already won the victory over him, and that victory may be yours for the asking. Read again 1 Corinthians 15:57.

A Call for Purity

Peter makes an earnest appeal at this point. First there is a call for purity of life. Christians are warned against all fleshly appetites, for they are like an infection in our blood. If we once let them have a place in our lives, they will contaminate our souls and pollute our characters worse than any disease can harm our bodies. The body is the main channel through which debasing influences affect the soul. A Christian's life is to be true in the presence of those who are not yet Christian. This will disarm the opposition and glorify God. Peter says, "I urge you . . . to abstain from sinful desires" (1 Peter 2:11).

A Call for Excellent Behavior

We are to influence others by what we say and do: "Keep your behavior excellent among the Gentiles" (1 Peter 2:12, *NASB*). People are not reading much religious literature on paper or on their computer screen, but they are doing a lot of reading of religious (or antireligious) works by those professing Christ. It seems trite to say, but it is true that more people are won to Christ by the true Christian living of a believer than by any other means. If it is true that what you are speaks so loudly I cannot hear what you say, then it is equally true that your deeds speak so loudly that I cannot help but believe what you say.

Christians must live beyond reproach, "though [the pagans] accuse you of doing wrong" (1 Peter 2:12). The Christians were accused of horrible crimes. They were called atheists because they denied the Roman gods. They were regarded as unpatriotic because emperor worship was the official religion. To reject the state religion was considered an outrage against the state itself. The Christians would often be obliged to avoid social customs and often bore the stigma of evildoers. The only way to possibly avoid persecution was for every Christian to live a superior moral life.

Today some of you are subjected to severe tests. Your friends and the people you spend time with may do many things—in school, in business, for recreation—that you as a Christian cannot do. If you don't participate, you take the chance that your actions will be misunderstood and misrepresented. You will be called narrow or a killjoy or a wet blanket. The best way to meet all such criticism is not by assuming an air of superiority, playing the martyr or exhibiting a holier-than-thou attitude, but by accepting the position by smiling and trying to be helpful to those who are finding fault with you. Nothing cools opposition like a gentle laugh of love.

A Call to Live Free

"Live as free people, but do not use your freedom as a cover-up for evil" (1 Peter 2:16). I once heard an amusing story about the early days of the Russian Revolution. After the czar had abdicated, a stout old woman was seen walking leisurely down the middle of one of the busiest streets in Saint Petersburg, at no small peril to herself and to the great confusion of traffic. A policeman pointed out to her that there was a walkway for pedestrians and that the street was for wagons, automobiles and horsemen. But she was not to be convinced. "I am going to walk just where I like," she said. "We've got liberty now." When we declare that we have the right to do as we like, we are as thoughtless and foolish as the old woman. Freedom is not a question of doing as we like. It is rather a question of doing as we should.

Peter tells his readers how to live their lives (1 Peter 2:17):

- "Show proper respect to everyone"—honor others.
- "Love the family of believers"—actively care about every Christian (this would solve all of our social problems).
- "Fear God"—show God that you revere and stand in awe of Him; such "fear of the LORD is the beginning of wisdom" (Psalm 111:10).
- "Honor the emperor"—show respect for your government.

A Call for Patient Endurance

One of the most convincing and powerful demonstrations Christians can give that they have a newborn life is patiently enduring wrongs and injustices (see 1 Peter 2:19-20). That is when we manifest the grace of God. That is what Christ did while He was on earth, especially by His submitting to His crucifixion and death. This is what His followers are to do as we "follow in his steps" (1 Peter 2:21).

Being patient while undergoing undeserved punishment is one way of testifying for Christ. A wicked crowd in his regiment took a violent dislike to one Christian soldier because he wouldn't swear or gamble with them and he wouldn't disregard his moral principles. His days were made miserable. But he never lost his temper or gave in or tried to pay them back, and in the end he led one of the worst fellows to Christ.

Such suffering by Christians, without retaliation or defense, is a vicarious example of the atonement made by Christ on the cross (see 1 Peter 2:24). Suffering patiently is noble because it is Christlike (see 1 Peter 3:17-18; 4:12-16). The secret of patience is always found in divine grace (see James 1:3-4).

A Call for Thanks

"Christ suffered for you" (1 Peter 2:21). A lady was once visiting patients in a hospital. She went up to a bed on which lay a wounded soldier and said gently, "Thank you for being wounded for me." The young man's face brightened. That was a new thought for him. Looking at his injuries that way made his pain more bearable. Do you realize that many years ago there was someone who was wounded for you? And that One was the Son of God Himself? Yes, He was wounded for your sins and mine. "By his wounds you have been healed" (1 Peter 2:24).

Charles H. Spurgeon put it this way:

> The remedy for your sins and mine is found in the substitutionary suffering of the Lord Jesus Christ, and in this only. But if I say of a certain ointment that it heals, I do not deny that you need a bandage with which to apply it to the wound. Faith is the linen which binds the plaster of Christ's reconciliation to the sore of my sin. The linen does not heal; that is the work of the ointment. So faith does not heal; that is the work of the atonement of Christ.

A Call for Right Relationships

We find in 1 Peter 2–3 some instructions for the various relationships in our lives. First, there are some personal instructions (see 1 Peter 2:1-12). Next we find instructions for our social relationships. Servants should obey their masters with respect, not only those masters who are good and considerate, but also those who are arbitrary. In 1 Peter 3:1-7, relationships in our homes are described.

Naturally, relationships in the home begin with the marriage relationship. "Wives, in the same way submit yourselves to your husbands" (1 Peter 3:1). This means a wife should show unselfish devotion to her husband so that she wins his love and admiration. This might sound unreasonable—if we did not hear the injunction to husbands that they "be considerate as [they] live with [their] wives, and treat them with respect" (1 Peter 3:7). This makes a wife subject to love that acts with wisdom and not according to selfish desires. It is manly for a husband to be tender toward his wife. God's plan is that the love of husband and wife should be mutual. Each one is to consider the other. The result of all this will be a marriage relationship in which prayers are not hindered (see 1 Peter 3:7). And prayer is the surest secret of success in any married life.

A Call for Happiness

Peter tells us that we can be happy in a world that is wretched: "Whoever would love life and see good days must keep their tongue from evil and their lips from deceitful speech. They must turn from evil and do good; they must seek peace and pursue it. For the eyes of the Lord are on the righteous and his ears are attentive to their prayer, but the face of the Lord is against those who do evil" (1 Peter 3:10-12). He quotes Psalm 34:12-14. The best way of making this life happy and prosperous is to not do anything evil, to never speak slander and to always be ready to overcome evil with good. This is a remedy that works today as well as it worked in David's time.

A Call for Preparedness

Another important command is given in 1 Peter 3:15. This is for every one of us: "Always be prepared to give an answer to everyone who asks you to give the reason for the hope that you have." Do you have an intelligent answer to give to others about your trust in Christ? If not, stop right here and get one ready. What does Christ mean to you?

Christ's sufferings in the flesh were physical: "'He himself bore our sins' in his body on the tree" (1 Peter 2:24). Christians' sufferings, spoken of in 1 Peter 4:1, are spiritual. Christ suffered when He was put to death on the cross: "For Christ also suffered once for sins, the righteous for the unrighteous, to bring you to God" (1 Peter 3:18). Christians take up their cross and follow Christ, denying themselves (see Matthew 16:24). The phrase "arm yourselves also with the same attitude" means the same as the words "whoever wants to be my disciple must deny themselves and take up their cross and follow me" (1 Peter 4:1; Matthew 16:24). Such a noble purpose will involve a certain amount of actual suffering, for God's will may separate us from a desire to gratify some bodily craving. Very few in this world escape some sort of suffering, either mentally, physically or spiritually. And we cannot choose the way we will suffer.

Often God allows us to go through life denied the one thing we wish for more than anything else. But we should be comforted by the fact that whom God loves, He chastens. If He grinds down the surface of our lives, it is so that the stone may shine more brilliantly. The many facets of the diamond are what make it dazzling. Understand that the greater the suffering in this world, the greater the glory in heaven. This is what Peter means in 1 Peter 4:2.

The Christian sometimes has to forego the gratification of even right, or good, desires. The natural cravings of the body for food and drink, for example, are not to be considered merely as ends in themselves. They come to have a spiritual meaning because whether we eat or drink—whatever we do—we "do it all for the glory of God" (1 Corinthians 10:31). "Therefore, if what I eat causes my brother or sister to fall into sin, I will never eat meat again, so that I will not cause them to fall" (1 Corinthians 8:13). Sometimes we must refuse something for the sake of others. This is "the mind of Christ" (1 Corinthians 2:16).

Be careful not to follow the world, "doing what pagans choose to do" (1 Peter 4:3). What the heathen world wanted the Jewish believers in Jesus to do Peter names here. "Debauchery" is mentioned (1 Peter 4:3). The Greek word means "that which disgusts"; the English word, "anything which excites impure desire."

1 PETER 4:12–5: CHRISTIAN TRIALS

Trials resulting from loyalty to Christ are inevitable. Christ sits as a refiner before the fire. The metallurgist takes the most pains with the most precious metals as they are subjected to the heat. Such fires melt the metals and burn up the dross, the impurities. Christ allows us to be subjected to the heat until all of our impurities are burned up. And just as the metallurgist will eventually see his or her reflection in the finished pure metal, so too Christ can see His own face reflected in our lives.

Christians were burned every night in Nero's gardens. It looked as if the devil were about to devour the Church (see 1 Peter 5:8). It was a "fiery ordeal," but God would use its heat to burn up the dross and leave the pure gold (1 Peter 4:12; see also 1 Peter 1:7). History is filled with examples of the many persecutions of Christians. Some have been even more brutal than Nero's. Millions of Christians through the centuries have been subjected to every conceivable kind of torture. Peter's words have been for them, too. How ashamed we should be even to mention our little troubles in light of these!

Don't be surprised when you are tried in the fire, as if some strange thing were happening to you (see 1 Peter 4:12). Don't think that Christ has promised that just because we are Christians, we will be spared from pain or misfortunes or death. "Everyone who wants to live a godly life in Christ Jesus will be persecuted" (2 Timothy 3:12). This means that people *will* persecute Christians, because the world hates Christ and anything called by His name.

Peter exhorts the leaders of the Church to care for the flock, "not lording it over those entrusted to you" (1 Peter 5:3), but serving them. Jesus had told Peter to "feed my sheep" (John 21:17). Each assistant shepherd will receive a reward, an unfading "crown of glory," from the chief Shepherd when He appears (1 Peter 5:4).

The Christian life is like a jungle battle. Peter tells us who our enemy is: the devil. His work is opposed to all that is good in this world. He is pictured as a roaring lion, seeking his prey (see 1 Peter 5:8). This adversary is cagey, appearing sometimes as an angel of light, at other times as a serpent coiled for the strike. He always "prowls around like a roaring lion looking for someone to devour" (1 Peter 5:8). He is watching for the vulnerable spot, for the unguarded door to our hearts. Paul tells us what armor we should wear in Ephesians 6. But we need not be afraid, for "the God of all grace, who called you to his eternal glory in Christ, after you have suffered a little while, will himself restore you and make you strong, firm and steadfast" (1 Peter 5:10).

Understanding Second Peter

Second Peter Portrays Jesus Christ, Our Strength

SELECTED BIBLE READINGS

DAY OF THE WEEK		MAIN TOPIC
	Sunday: 2 Peter 1:1-14	Christian Virtues
	Monday: 2 Peter 1:15-21	God's Word
	Tuesday: 2 Peter 2:1-14	False Teachers
	Wednesday: 2 Peter 2:15-22	Punishable Heresy
	Thursday: 2 Peter 3:1-9	Future Scoffers
	Friday: 2 Peter 3:10-18	Christ's Assured Return
	Saturday: 2 Peter 1–3	Christian Watchfulness

AUTHOR: Second Peter 1:1 specifically states that the apostle Peter was the author of 2 Peter. Peter's authorship of 2 Peter has been challenged more than that of any other book in the New Testament. The very poor Greek style of this letter, in contrast to the good Greek style of 1 Peter, may indicate no more than the fact that Peter may have not used a Greek scribe to write this letter, as he apparently used Silas to write 1 Peter (see 1 Peter 5:12). In any case, the Early Church fathers found no good reason to reject Peter as the author of this letter.

DATE: Second Peter was written toward the end of Peter's life. Since Peter was martyred in Rome during the reign of Nero (AD 54-68), his death must have occurred prior to AD 68. It is likely that 2 Peter was written between AD 65 and 68.

PURPOSE AND SUMMARY: This letter was a reminder to the readers of the truth of the gospel, which they had received, and it was a warning against the attacks of false teachers who pervert the gospel. Peter urges believers to remain steadfast, even in persecution, and reminds them that the Lord will keep His promises to them. He speaks of the coming Day of the Lord and of the necessity of keeping themselves "spotless, blameless and at peace" (2 Peter 3:14).

Peter's first letter was to console; the second, to warn. In his first letter, Peter was trying to encourage Christians who were suffering terrible persecutions from without. In his second letter, he is warning them of dangers within the Church.

Christians need moral courage even more than physical courage. It is our duty to do right under all circumstances, with no qualification and no hesitation. A Christian is always on duty. To stand up for truth is often more difficult than to go into battle. Examples from the Bible of people who did exactly this are found in Joseph (see Genesis 39:9), Nehemiah (see Nehemiah 5:7; 6:1-16), Daniel (see Daniel 1:8) and Paul. History is full of instances, too: Polycarp (second-century bishop of Smyrna and martyr), Joan of Arc (martyred French national heroine and Catholic saint), Martin Luther (leader of the German Reformation), Hugh Latimer (British reformer and martyr) and John Wesley (founder of Methodism). They were never ashamed of Christ, because they knew Him.

Paul, in warning against the dangers from within the Church, urges the believers to grow strong "in the grace and knowledge" of Christ (2 Peter 3:18). Christian knowledge is the best way to overcome the false teaching that was creeping within the walls of belief. We obtain knowledge of Christ through His Word. Don't neglect the Word of God! It is indeed "a lamp for my feet, and a light on my path" (Psalm 119:105). In 1 Peter, we hear much about suffering. In 2 Peter, we hear much about knowledge. Shallow knowledge makes superficial Christians. Paul said, "I know whom I have believed" (2 Timothy 1:12). It is not what you believe that gives you strength but *whom* you believe.

Peter knew that heresy often leads to immoral living. Christianity must have a creed if right conduct is to be assured. Some leaders were using the Church strictly for money making. Other leaders in the Church were permitting wrongdoing of every sort. The false teachers were laughing at the Lord's coming, and the Church could easily have stopped looking for that "blessed hope."

Simon Peter, "a servant and an apostle of Jesus Christ," is the writer of this letter (2 Peter 1:1). The first name, "Simon," suggests his old, unstable nature. The name "Peter" (meaning "rock") suggests the new nature Christ had given him, strong and true. He calls himself "a servant." Slavery is the happiest life in the world when the slave has the right master. There is only one right master, and He is Jesus Christ. His slaves know the only true meaning of freedom.

Peter, the apostle of hope, speaks again to the younger Christians in the faith. He urges them to look toward heaven while dwelling for only a season in a very bad world. He says that he has written both letters "as reminders to stimulate you to wholesome thinking" (2 Peter 3:1). He talks about the readers as those who have obtained "a faith as precious as ours" (2 Peter 1:1). We remember how Peter's faith was kept through Christ's prayer for him: "But I have prayed for you, Simon, that your faith may not fail. And when you have turned back, strengthen your brothers" (Luke 22:32). This is how our faith can be preserved also.

2 PETER 1: CHRISTIAN VIRTUES

Do the days seem dark to you and does sin seem to be everywhere? That is the way the world looked to the young Christians of Peter's day. So they would not be discouraged by this outlook, he showed them how to escape "the corruption in the world caused by evil desires" (2 Peter 1:4): God has "given us everything we need for a godly life" (2 Peter 1:3).

Look at a criminal condemned to death. Suppose a messenger comes to him and says, "The governor has taken your case into consideration, and I have brought you a wallet filled with five thousand dollars."

The criminal will say, "What good will it do me? I am scheduled to die tomorrow."

"Well, I have another message. He has considered your case and sent you the deed to a multimillion-dollar estate."

The condemned man despairingly shakes his head and says, "What can I do with that? I must die tomorrow."

But the messenger goes on. "Stop! I have another offer to make. I have brought you the governor's own hand-tailored suit for you to wear."

The condemned man bursts into tears as he says, "Why do you continue to mock me? How would I look strapped to a table, wearing the governor's suit?"

Then the messenger says, "Wait, I have one more message. The governor has sent you a pardon. What do you say to that?"

The poor man looks at him and says he doesn't believe it. But the messenger hands him the pardon, signed by the governor, bearing the official stamp. Then the man leaps for joy while tears of gratitude run down his face.

Then the messenger says, "I am not through yet. I have brought you the pardon, the wallet filled with money, the deed to the mansion, and the hand-tailored suit, which are also yours." These are the "all things" God has given us in Christ, His Son. When we have these, nothing can defeat us, no matter what our age.

The way I can escape the awful sins in this world all day every day is by sharing His nature and letting Him live through me. Take hold of the "very great and precious promises, so that through them you may participate in the divine nature" (2 Peter 1:4). I am a sharer in the very nature of God. Everyone does not have the nature of God. The divine is not within human hearts. His image remains in us but not an atom of His life (see 1 Corinthians 11:7). We are dead and lifeless apart from Christ. "The divine nature" of God becomes ours only when the divine Savior becomes ours. This is a wonderful truth. We ought to have courage when we remember that with Christ in us, "the divine nature" also is within us. The "very great and precious promises" are before us. We ought to go straight ahead, fearing nothing.

"The divine nature" God has given us should be shown in the everyday practices of our Christian living. That is all Christian character is. It is no more or less than the practice of Christian virtues. And the Christian virtues are only the fruit of the Spirit (see Galatians 5:22-23).

Do others know you are a Christian by the way you look and act? Do you remember that night by the fire when a young girl recalled that Peter had been with Jesus, and Peter gave her some of the choice language of the Galilee fishing trade in order to try to prove otherwise? The crowd picked him out by his accent (see Mark 14:66-71). He gave himself away by a word. Later, the rulers picked him out as a companion of Jesus by his appearance and talk. The world recognizes us in exactly the same way. Something about a person's whole bearing proclaims him or her as a companion of Jesus Christ. As soon as we hear someone speak about Christ, we can tell what that person is.

Although God gives us a changed, divine nature, He wants us to do our part in developing this priceless gift (see 2 Peter 1:5-11). Because we are sharers in the very life of God, we should continue to learn and grow. God basically says, "Add one grace to another." In math terms:

- Multiplication—"Grace and peace be yours in abundance" (2 Peter 1:2)
- Addition—"Add to your faith" (2 Peter 1:5)
- Subtraction—"Cleansed from their past sins" (2 Peter 1:9)

A Full Life

Seven steps go up from faith, and the last one is love. These steps are the Christian virtues every Christian should have. Let's climb slowly and thoughtfully up this flight of stairs and see how far we have gone. To your faith add goodness, knowledge, self-control, perseverance, godliness, brotherly kindness and love (see 2 Peter 1:5-7). This is the result of our precious faith.

The fuller the measure of these virtues, the greater will be our knowledge of Jesus Christ our Lord. Know Christ, for to know Him is life eternal, and in none other is there salvation (see Acts 4:12).

Peter says that "whoever does not have [these virtues] is nearsighted and blind" (2 Peter 1:9). If we do not have these virtues, we will be nearsighted Christians, unfit for enlistment in God's army. Be sure of your position in Christ. Don't ever doubt your calling in Him. Make every effort to put God's call and choice beyond all doubt. Make every effort in prayer, in study and in talking with older Christians. Life is full of so much uncertainty, but you do not have to be uncertain in spiritual things. A spiritual certainty produces a stability in life; then "you will never stumble" (2 Peter 1:10).

Someone has said each Christian is a seven-story building with a strong foundation. Add story to story, but be sure to make faith your foundation. If you try to build without the proper base, the building will become top heavy. To be sure, faith is the foundation grace. But a foundation is of little use if no building follows. Peter, like Paul, warns Christians not to stand still. Don't remain babies in Christ, tripping over every teaching. Grow strong.

During especially tough economic times, it is not unusual to see the framework of a building standing stark and gaunt, weeds growing around it, abandoned by the workers who had begun a good work but because the economy became depressed, the work had stopped before the building was finished. The foundation was substantial and adequate, but for years it was entirely useless because nothing was added to make it habitable.

A Christian's ambition should be to have a full life. Then, Peter says, "you will receive a rich welcome into the eternal kingdom of our Lord and Savior Jesus Christ" (2 Peter 1:11).

Prophecy and Experience

Peter, like Paul, was conscious of his approaching death. He has a beautiful way of describing death: "I will soon put [this tent of my body] aside" (2 Peter 1:14). *Moffatt* says, "The folding up of my tent." Because he knew he was about to leave them, Peter wanted to stimulate them by reminding them of what he so well knew. His memory pictured before him the great Transfiguration. He had witnessed the glory of Christ, and at that moment, any doubt about Christ's reality or about Christ's coming again in power was forever banished from his mind. God Himself had borne testimony of His glory and honor, and Peter had heard the voice from above say, "This is my Son, whom I love; with him I am well pleased" (2 Peter 1:17). This is the testimony of deity. Then Peter knew *for sure*. Now he wanted the believers to know that he was not telling them fairy tales when he told them of the power and return of the Lord Jesus Christ. Peter had been an eyewitness of Jesus' majesty.

Remember, Peter suffered and died for this truth he was telling. At one time he said, "We cannot help speaking about what we have seen and heard" (Acts 4:20).

People depend too much on feelings instead of knowledge based on facts. Peter didn't want these Christians to rest on feelings. When the devil sees a poor soul in agony on the waves of sin and getting close to the Rock of Ages, he just holds out the plank of feeling to the person and says, "There, get on that. You feel more comfortable now, don't you?" And while the poor soul stands there getting back his or her breath, out goes the plank and the person is worse off than before.

Added to the evidence of the Transfiguration is "the prophetic message as something completely reliable"—prophecy made sure (2 Peter 1:19). This does not mean that Christian experience (the vision on the mount) is more reliable or better than prophecy; rather, it means that the word of prophecy is confirmed by experience. They go together. Peter sheds light on the inspiration of the Scriptures (see 1 Peter 1:10-12; 2 Peter 1:4,16-21; 3:15).

Remember the divine origin of the Scriptures. Dr. James M. Gray, a nineteenth-century evangelist and president of Moody Bible Institute, once said when referring to 2 Peter 1:21:

2 Peter

"Private interpretation means private origin. God is the One who has spoken."

A native in India, writing to a friend about a great revival they were having, said, "We are having a great 'rebible' here." Not a bad idea. The Church needs to be re-Bibled!

2 PETER 2: FALSE TEACHERS

Do the times in which we live have severe trials, strong temptations, and powerful opposition to the Christian message? Expect it and rise above it. We are warned that it will be this way. The world always has been and always will be full of antagonism to the truth and to those who speak it. But God will not let these troubles lead to anything of substance. In the meantime, "the Lord knows how to rescue the godly from trials" (2 Peter 2:9).

In 2 Peter 2, Peter tells of the dark and appalling coming, influence and doom of the false teachers. We need not be surprised at their coming, for Christ warned us of that (see Matthew 7:15; 24:11,24), and we have listened to Paul's words about them to Timothy (see 1 Timothy 4:1-3; 2 Timothy 3:1-9).

Deeds of False Teachers

What a black list Peter gives of the false teachers' deeds! There is no softening of the evil deeds from one end of the list to the other. It is a dark, dark picture indeed. Read it! No wonder Peter warned the Church about false prophets!

- "Secretly introduce destructive heresies"—2 Peter 2:1
- "[Deny] the sovereign Lord who bought them"—2 Peter 2:1
- "Bring the way of truth into disrepute"—2 Peter 2:2
- "Exploit you with fabricated stories"—2 Peter 2:3
- "Follow the corrupt desire of the flesh"—2 Peter 2:10
- "Despise authority"—2 Peter 2:10
- Are "bold and arrogant"—2 Peter 2:10
- "Not afraid to slander celestial beings"—2 Peter 2:10
- "Are like unreasoning animals"—2 Peter 2:12

- "Blaspheme in matters they do not understand"—
  2 Peter 2:12
- "Their . . . pleasure is to carouse in broad daylight"—
  2 Peter 2:13
- "Blots and blemishes" in society—2 Peter 2:13
- Revel in "their pleasures while they feast with you"—
  2 Peter 2:13
- "With eyes full of adultery . . . never stop sinning"—
  2 Peter 2:14
- "Seduce the unstable"—2 Peter 2:14
- "Are experts in greed"—2 Peter 2:14
- "Are . . . an accursed brood"—2 Peter 2:14
- "Have left the straight way and wandered off"—2 Peter 2:15
- "Are springs without water"—2 Peter 2:17
- "Are . . . mists driven by a storm"—2 Peter 2:17
- "Mouth empty, boastful words"—2 Peter 2:18
- "[Appeal] to the lustful desires of the flesh"—2 Peter 2:18
- "Are slaves of depravity"—2 Peter 2:19

The false teachers of today do the same things they did in Peter's day. First, they "secretly introduce destructive heresies" (2 Peter 2:1). They do this subtly. They don't believe in the deity of Christ—that Jesus, who was born of a virgin, was actually God. Peter says they "[deny] the sovereign Lord who bought them" (2 Peter 2:1). It does not say that they deny the Lord that *taught* them. Practically every false religion acknowledges Christ as a great teacher but will not accept Him as Savior, the One who *bought* us with His own precious blood. They deny the blood atonement.

Tests for False Teachers

The blood test is the first test of a false teacher. Ask for credentials of teachers who are active today. If a teacher does not put the cross at the center of his or her teaching, beware! Turn from that teacher. Our redemption is in the blood. Jesus bought us with His blood.

Another test for false teachers is the popularity test. These teachers are popular. "Many will follow their depraved conduct" (2 Peter

2:2). It's not unusual for false religions, of which there are many varieties, to attract a large following. Peter told us they would. People do not want to be told they need a Savior. That makes them admit they are sinners. They only want to be taught, not bought. The false teachers "will bring the way of truth into disrepute" (2 Peter 2:2). All these false teachings talk about "truth," but they forget that Christ said, "I am the way and the truth and the life. No one comes to the Father except through me" (John 14:6). He is not just a part of truth—He *is truth*. He does not show us the way—He *is the way*. He did not come to show us how to live. He *is life*.

The third test is the vocabulary test. "In their greed these teachers will exploit you with fabricated stories" (2 Peter 2:3). Words mean little in many of these false religions, and the teachers twist words for their own benefit. They say they believe in everything; but when we ask them what they mean by "everything," what we're told is far from what the Scripture says. They keep the form of words, but the meaning is wrung out. It is like an egg with holes in either end with the inside blown out. The form of the egg is there, but the substance is gone. Christ said that people would even say, "Lord, Lord"; but He would say, "I never knew you. Away from me, you evildoers!" (Matthew 7:22-23). Words mean nothing unless there is true understanding of their meaning. How these false religions prey upon the people for money, demanding more and more, saying no healing can take place until you pay. But God says we may come to Him "without money and without cost" (Isaiah 55:1).

God can only do one thing with these kinds of teachers, and that is destroy them. Peter declares with no uncertainty that that will be the end of false teachers who cover themselves with the cloak of the Church (see 2 Peter 2:3-9). As the English pastor John Henry Jowett wrote in *The Epistles of St. Peter,* "Light that is trifled with becomes lightning." God did not even spare the angels who sinned! He sent a flood upon the godless world in Noah's day. Sodom and Gomorrah were reduced to ashes. All these were as a warning to the godless of every generation of what God has in store for them. One thing we can be sure of: No matter how severe the judgment for the false teacher may be, the deliverance of God's people is promised. Leave to God the punishment of the wicked.

2 PETER 3: CHRIST'S RETURN

False teaching about Christ that denies His deity and power results in false thinking. The first thought that is questioned concerns the return of Christ. To help the Church about this subject, Peter reminds them of the things Jesus had said. People of Peter's time misunderstood what Jesus had said and thought His return might happen during their time. Peter tells them that time is nothing with God: "With the Lord a day is like a thousand years, and a thousand years are like a day" (2 Peter 3:8). He will keep His promise to return just as He has kept all His other promises, but He will do it according to His own time.

"The Lord is not slow in keeping his promise. . . . He is patient with you, not wanting anyone to perish, but everyone to come to repentance" (2 Peter 3:9). The last days are to be sad days, for scoffers will make fun of our beliefs and say, "Ha, ha! Where is the promise of Christ's return? As far as we can see, everything is going on, just as it has from the beginning of creation. Nature goes on in the same manner as always. There have been no signs of any radical change. The promise of His coming has failed." The scoffers during Peter's time were evil, but the sad truth is that good people even today scoff at the promise of His coming. They make light of the great hope of the Church: "How illogical is their reasoning about Christ's return! Here they are! He hasn't come, and He's not going to come. Nothing different has happened; therefore, nothing unusual is going to happen."

Because our Lord has not come as yet, will we give up hope? No, indeed. Rather, we will rejoice in the fact that His return comes nearer every day.

Floods and Fires
Peter reminds the skeptics that a mighty flood did drown the world once, and Christ likened His coming to the flood (see Matthew

(side tab) 2 Peter

24:37-38). No doubt Peter heard Him say it. But next time, God will destroy the earth by fire. Will it literally be a fire? Was the flood literal? Stored within the earth are enough gases, magma and other elements to burn it up. Erupting volcanoes release some of these elements. Scientists now tell us that we are sitting on a crust of earth that is only 20 to 30 miles thick. Beneath this is a mantle and a core, which is made up of molten matter. At a word, God could release a spout that would literally bury the earth with fire. The devastation caused by the atomic bomb proved the possibility of such a catastrophe. It's also possible that our earth may collide with some other heavenly body and worldwide fire would be the result.

We know that when God's clock strikes the hour, the earth will melt with a fervent heat. The earth will be burned up and in the great explosion, the heavens will pass away. Then "a new heaven and a new earth" will emerge (2 Peter 3:13).

Today people are tech savvy and have access to the "information highway." They think they know everything. But all this is to be expected. Satan will not give up his hold on this earth without protest. But his days of liberty are numbered and Jesus *will* reign: "Above all, you must understand that in the last days scoffers will come, scoffing and following their own evil desires. They will say, 'Where is this "coming" he promised? Ever since our ancestors died, everything goes on as it has since the beginning of creation.' But the day of the Lord will come like a thief" (2 Peter 3:3-4,10). Scorn and mockery did not hold back the flood when it was unloosed. The angel's mighty trumpet will make short work of the foolish "I don't believe it" and "I don't think it is true" and "I don't see it." Nevertheless, we, according to His promise, look for new heavens and a new earth where righteousness will dwell. It will not exactly be only destruction, for a new earth will be created. Look toward the east, for "the Sun of righteousness will rise with healing in its rays" (Malachi 4:2).

Cause and Effect

What effect should all this have on our lives? Read Peter's answer in verse 14. We are to be diligent in our service, striving always to be peaceable, spotless and blameless in character. We can't grow careless because according to us He is delaying, for one day the Lord will come suddenly. We are to be patient, knowing that He waits because He is long-suffering and wants to give the last man, woman and child a chance to accept Him.

Are you looking forward to His coming? What effect has this hope had on your life and conversation?

Peter's last word of warning is a notice for us to be cautious: "Be on your guard so that you may not be carried away by the error of the lawless and fall from your secure position" (2 Peter 3:17).

Knowledge and Growth

The remedy against falling back is to grow, or make progress. "Grow in the grace and in the knowledge of our Lord and Savior Jesus Christ" (2 Peter 3:18). Are you growing in your knowledge? Christian knowledge is an effective weapon against heresy. Christianity without a creed cannot stand against the attacks of the critics. If you are not growing, you may fall by the wayside, for we are living in a wicked world where many people are enemies of God and His truth. A living thing is meant to grow. When there is no growth, there is no life. The foundation of growth is the knowledge of Christ. As we grow in the knowledge of Christ, we grow in likeness to Him.

Understanding
First John, Second John,
Third John and Jude

*First John Portrays Jesus Christ, Our Life; Second John Portrays
Jesus Christ, the Truth; Third John Portrays Jesus Christ, the Way;
Jude Portrays Jesus Christ, Our Keeper*

SELECTED BIBLE READINGS

DAY OF THE WEEK		MAIN TOPIC
Sunday: 1 John 1–2:14	Walking in Fellowship	
Monday: 1 John 2:15–3:24	Walking as Children of God	
Tuesday: 1 John 4	Walking in Love	
Wednesday: 1 John 5	Walking in Knowledge	
Thursday: 2 John	Walking in Truth	
Friday: 3 John	Walking in the Way	
Saturday: Jude	Walking Without Falling	

UNDERSTANDING FIRST JOHN

AUTHOR: The books of 1, 2 and 3 John do not directly name their author. The author of 1 John is not named at all, and the author of 2 and 3 John is described as "the elder" but not named (2 John 1; 3 John 1). From earliest times, all three letters have been attributed to the apostle John, who also wrote the Gospel of John. The content, style and vocabulary suggest that these three epistles were addressed to the same readers as the Gospel of John.

DATE: The books were likely written at about the same time, between AD 85 and 95.

PURPOSE AND SUMMARY: First John is addressed to an unidentified group of believers. First John 5:13 indicates that the author writes in order that the readers might know the certainty of God's love and His promise of eternal life. Second John is addressed to an elect lady whose home is the meeting place of a house church. Third John is addressed to Gaius, a man commended for his hospitality.

It is believed that the aged apostle John wrote 1 John sometime between the years of AD 85 and 95, probably in Ephesus. Unlike the other apostles, he does not address this letter to any particular church or person. He writes to all Christians, old and young (see 1 John 2:12-14). He calls Christians by the tender Greek word *teknia*—which means "born ones" or "bairns." God is dealing with His very own born-again children.

John told us why he wrote his Gospel: so "that you may believe that Jesus is the Messiah, the Son of God, and that by believing you may have life in his name" (John 20:31). John wanted to show us how we might receive eternal life. He wrote this epistle so that those who believe in Christ would know, or be assured, that they have eternal life (see 1 John 5:13).

Turn to the Gospel of John 20:31 and read it along with 1 John 5:13. The epistle of 1 John appears to have been intended as a companion to the Gospel of John. Thus we find the word "believe" running all through the Gospel of John, and the word "know" running through this epistle. The word "know" is used more than 30 times in this short letter. Underline it each time you discover it.

John wrote to the believers for four reasons:

1. So that they might be happy—1 John 1:4
2. So that they won't sin—1 John 2:1
3. So that they will be on guard against error—1 John 2:26
4. So that they will *know*—1 John 5:13

Someone has well named this the "Really-and-truly Epistle." It has a confident, exultant tone all the way through. John was the disciple whom Jesus loved. He stood close to Him on the cross at Calvary. He looked into the empty tomb on that morning of the Resurrection. On Patmos, he was lifted up by the Spirit and saw a door opened into heaven. John gives us his witness, or testimony, of these facts. "We know," he says. "There is no possibility of doubt about it." "That which was from the beginning, which we have heard, which we have seen with our eyes, which we have looked at and our hands have touched—this we proclaim concerning the Word of life"—Jesus (1 John 1:1)! John even gives us proof that his knowledge is true and factual. He has heard and seen and handled the Word of life. He longs to bring his listeners into intimate fellowship with the Father and His Son so that their joy and His will be "complete" (1 John 1:4; see also 1 John 1:3,7; 2:13-14).

Christ, who was God, took on flesh and dwelt with people, so they could hear His voice, see His face and feel the touch of His loving hand. This brought God down to people so that we could "have fellowship" (1 John 1:7). To walk in fellowship is to live in agreement. God wants us to have fellowship with Him, and in Him to have fellowship with one another (see 1 John 1:3).

John says we not only must believe like Christians, but we also must act like Christians. In chapters 1-3, we find out whether we live like Christians. In chapters 4-5, we discover whether we believe like Christians. Striking lightning is accompanied by thunder. Similarly, "striking" faith is accompanied by life and testimony (see 1 John 2:3). Some people say they believe God, but they act more like the devil. This cannot be. We must be as orthodox in our behavior as we are in our belief. Do the truth and believe the truth: "If we claim to have fellowship with him and yet walk in the darkness, we lie and do not live out the truth" (1 John 1:6).

John exalts God in his epistles:

- "God is light"—1 John 1:5
- "God is love"—1 John 4:8,16
- God "is righteous"—1 John 2:29
- God is life—1 John 5:11-12
- God is truth—2 John
- God is good—3 John

1 JOHN 1-3: RIGHT BEHAVIOR

John gives us seven tests of Christian behavior, of our walk with God. Read these and figure out what your rating is as a Christian. The test is this: If we say one thing and do another, we are not living as Christ would want us to, in full fellowship with Himself. How much easier it is to talk than it is to do! As Dwight Moody said, "We talk cream and live skim milk." Because "our fellowship is with the Father and with his Son, Jesus Christ" (1 John 1:3), we are to walk together, talk together and live together. We are to eat at the same table (see Revelation 3:20). We are one family (see Ephesians 3:15). God is my Father because Jesus Christ, my elder Brother, has made me a child of the King; therefore, I must behave that way. Fellowship brings joy (see 1 John 1:4). There is no joy greater than fellowship with a friend.

I walk with a God of light: "God is light; in him there is no darkness at all" (1 John 1:5). If my walk is with Him, I will walk in the light of His love and grace.

Test #1—Walk in the Light

"If we claim to have fellowship with him [the God of light] and yet walk in darkness, we lie and do not live out the truth" (1 John 1:6).

Do you know of any sin in your life? If you do, you are not walking with Christ. His presence throws light on your conscience and heart and shows the presence of sin in your life (see Ephesians 5:13). A Christian who is walking in fellowship with God will enjoy fellowship with other Christians (see 1 John 1:7).

Have you ever picked up a stone that has been lying on the ground for a long time? The minute you lift it, loathsome things usually move in every direction to flee from the light. Light reveals sin. Your sins will keep you from fellowship with Christ, but fellowship with Christ will keep you from sinning. Do you ask Him to throw His searchlight on your heart?

Test #2—Admit You Are a Sinner

"If we claim to be without sin, we deceive ourselves and the truth is not in us" (1 John 1:8).

You cannot walk with God and practice sin in your life at the same time. God keeps showing us the sin in our lives. On the cross He redeemed us from the penalty of sin once and for all. But He let us know, too, that if we confess our sins, He keeps cleansing the sins that creep into our lives by our contact with this world.

When a farmer plows his field, he throws out every stone he finds. But the next year as the plow goes deep into the furrow, he finds other stones that had remained hidden the year before. He throws these aside as they turn up. Then the next year the same thing occurs. It is the same with sin in our lives! God will reveal by the plow of His Spirit the sins that are hidden in our lives, the ones we did not know were there. Don't be discouraged, but use His remedy of confession.

"If we confess our sins, he is faithful and just and will forgive us our sins and purify us from all unrighteousness" (1 John 1:9). Don't pray in general terms. Name your sins before God. Is it pride, lack of trust, anger, love of pleasure more than God? Well, whatever it is, put it out there before God and tell Him what it is. Call it by name. Then claim God's promise. "He is faithful and just," not only to "forgive us our sins," but also to "purify us from all unrighteousness." A human parent can forgive our misbehavior, but only God can cleanse us from our sins.

Test #3—Obey God's Will

"Whoever says, 'I know him,' but does not do what he commands is a liar, and the truth is not in that person" (1 John 2:4).

Obedience is a real test. God makes a very strong statement. If you say that you are a Christian and do not obey Him, you are a liar. The one who is a true Christian is the one who keeps God's commandments.

What are Christ's commandments? "Love the Lord your God with all your heart and with all your soul and with all your mind and with all your strength" (Mark 12:30; see also Luke 10:27). Do you love God that way? Ask yourself a few questions: *Do I spend more time watching television than I do with God?* Then you don't love Him with all your heart. *Am I ambitious to carry out some plan in my life that I hope will bring me fame, wealth or enjoyment?* Don't say you know God when you won't keep His commandments. *Do I know God's will for my life? Do I want to know it? Am I obedient to His Word? To His still, small voice?* Many times we do not want to let God talk to us. We will not listen to Him because we are afraid of what He'll say to us.

Youth looks for a career in the world. Look first to God who has a career for each one of us. He has a plan for every step of our lives, for "a person's steps are directed by the LORD" (Proverbs 20:24). We must obey in everything for "everything that does not come from faith is sin" (Romans 14:23). You will begin to know what God wishes as you grow to know Him better.

A group of fellows were going to a nightclub that had a reputation for being rowdy. They stopped to ask a young friend to go along. "I can't go," he said.

"Why not?" his associates asked.

"Well, because my mother wouldn't want me to."

"How do you know she wouldn't? She doesn't even know we're going."

"Because I know my mother," was his very wise reply.

This is true when you learn to know God—you will know what His desires are (see 1 John 3:24).

Christ says, "You are my friends if you do what I command" (John 15:14). Shortly after saying that, Jesus told His disciples His second command: "This is my command: Love each other" (John 15:17).

Test #4—Imitate Christ

"Whoever claims to live in him must live as Jesus did" (1 John 2:6).

We should be Christlike in all that we do in life. Christ says, "You are the salt of the earth" (Matthew 5:13). Salt preserves food from spoiling. Are you the preservative of your crowd? Do you keep your language clean? Do you refrain from using God's name in vain? Does your presence keep your friends from doing questionable things?

A little Chinese girl said, "I know why Christ said, 'You are the salt of the earth.' Because salt makes folks thirsty, and Christians should make others thirsty for Christ." Are you making folks thirsty?

Most people are too lazy to look up. Few try to find Christ. So Christ wants others to see Him reflected in us. In the famous Sistine Chapel in Rome, the beauty of the art is in the ceiling. As you enter, you are given a mirror. It seems strange to see people walking around looking down when the paintings are above them. But they see all the glory reflected in the mirrors they look down at, without breaking their necks. Be a reflector. Let the beauty of Jesus be seen in you.

Test #5—Love Others

"Anyone who claims to be in the light but hates a brother or sister is still in the darkness" (1 John 2:9).

Love changes a person. Love makes us have a concern for the welfare of others.

God speaks of our feelings toward others as personal attitudes. There are three chief attitudes toward others: (1) hatred, which is murder (see 1 John 3:15); (2) indifference, or no concern, which is akin to hate (see 1 John 4:20-21); and (3) love. Love shows itself in different ways (see 1 John 2:9-11; 3:14): physically, in concern for the welfare of others (see 1 John 3:16-18); and spiritually, in concern for the souls of others.

Test #6—Keep Apart from the World

"If anyone loves the world, love for the Father is not in them" (1 John 2:15).

We live in a "present evil age" (Galatians 1:4). The scheme of things as they exist today is not the standard for the Christian. Whenever you find Christians obeying the world's standards, they are walking on forbidden ground.

All sins may be put into three categories: (1) "lust of the flesh"; (2) "lust of the eyes"; (3) "pride of life" (1 John 2:16-17, *KJV*).

Lust of the flesh is the first category of sin. Temptations come through the body and its appetites and passions. The devil tempted Jesus in this way first. Jesus had been fasting 40 days, and every atom of His being cried for bread. How plausible was Satan's temptation! It was the same appeal to appetite that Satan had made to Eve. In all those thousands of years, the devil has invented no new weapons of attack. "Tell this stone to become bread" (Luke 4:3). The temptation for self-gratification is one of the strongest that can assail us. Our appetite is still one of the most vulnerable points when Satan attacks us. The necessity for bread and pleasure is supposed by some to justify any means to get them. But it is not necessary that we live at all! There is only one moral necessity: to trust God and keep His commandments.

Lust of the eyes is the second category of sin. Foiled with one weapon, Satan quickly drops it and tries another. Taking Jesus to a high mountain, he showed Him all the kingdoms of the world in a moment of time. "If you worship me, it will all be yours" (Luke 4:7). Satan was working his second trick.

How people worship at the altar of riches and honor because they long for what their eyes see of this world!

Your eyes can blacken your soul! Be careful what you look at. If you throw a white tennis ball against a sooty wall, a black mark will be left upon it. If your eye is thrown against impure objects, a mark will certainly be left on your mind and heart. Be careful what you look at!

Pride of life is the first category of sin. Everyone wants spectacular success and to be able to boast about what has been seen and done. The devil took Jesus to the pinnacle of the Temple and told Him to cast Himself down; if He was the Son of God, angels would save Him. It was a proposal to leap from the pinnacle of the Temple to immediate popularity. It is a temptation for any person to be popular; we all have the desire to succeed. But how many intelligent people have been led astray because the glittering prizes of wealth and popularity were held up before them! We want to win any prize with a single stroke. How strong is the temptation to take a shortcut for our ambition, whether of education, wealth, position or power! We are in danger of selling our very souls to gain our ends! Jesus saw the world spread before Him and recognized how short and alluring the step was that promised Him the world, but to become the subject of the prince of this world would have ended His mission as the Savior of the world.

Test #7—Prove Christ Is Righteous by How You Live

"If you know that he is righteous, you know that everyone who does what is right has been born of him" (1 John 2:29).

Do you acknowledge Christ by how you conduct your life? Others watch us to see if we "do righteousness." Those who are in Christ will bear the same fruit in their lives that Christ bears—and that is righteousness.

"Everyone who commits (practices) sin is guilty of lawlessness; for [that is what] sin is, lawlessness" (1 John 3:4, *AMP*). If we know Christ is God dwelling in our lives, we will not "practice sin." "No one who continues to sin has either seen him or known him. No one who is born of God will continue to sin, because God's seed remains in them; they cannot go on sinning, because they have been born of God" (1 John 3:6,9). It is possible that Christians who are strongly tempted will sin for a time, but they will not keep it up. If people continually practice sin, they may well doubt their conversion! We should consider sin as God does. Sin cost God His Son!

1 JOHN 4–5:11: RIGHT BELIEF

We need a creed by which to live. The word "creed" comes from the Latin word *credo*—"I believe." Is a creed necessary? Read John

3:16 and see if you think it is: "Whoever believes in him shall not perish but have eternal life." Christianity is Christ-centered. Christ out of Christianity leaves nothing. This means death. If we don't believe, we will die; but if we believe, we will live (see Romans 10:9-10).

You cannot believe things that are not true about Christ and at the same time have fellowship with Him. It is absurd to say that it doesn't make any difference what you believe as long as you are sincere. This statement is not logical. We cannot believe what is false, have it affect us and then go out and live lives that are true. This is not any more possible than believing that an eight-o'clock train leaves at nine o'clock and expecting to not miss the train. Neither can we sincerely believe a bottle containing poison actually holds a healing medicine and then expect anything but death if we drink it.

The false teachers of John's day denied the fact that Christ truly suffered and truly rose again. They said He was only a mystery man who appeared and vanished, but He was not God.

You cannot deny the death of Christ on the cross and expect a pardon for your sins. You cannot deny the resurrection of Christ and enjoy the privileges of Christianity that are found in a living Christ. You cannot deny that Christ is God and assume you'll receive access to the Father.

Your sins can start in your mind. What do you believe? Christ wants to be our only teacher. What we believe determines how we act.

Many Christians are spiritual babies in Christ. They are led astray by every new thing they hear. They are susceptible to everything around them. When doubt fills their minds, they sink in despair. Because of this, everyone needs to test every religion to see if it be true. This is especially necessary today when there are so many different religious beliefs. John states the test very clearly in 1 John 4:1-3:

> Dear friends, do not believe every spirit, but test the spirits to see whether they are from God, because many false

prophets have gone out into the world. This is how you can recognize the Spirit of God: Every spirit that acknowledges that Jesus Christ has come in the flesh is from God, but every spirit that does not acknowledge Jesus is not from God. This is the spirit of the antichrist, which you have heard is coming and even now is already in the world.

Four Basic Beliefs

First, we must believe "that Jesus Christ has come in the flesh" (1 John 4:2; see also 5:20-21). Jesus is the incarnate Lord. This is the first thing we must be sure of. We must believe that when Jesus walked this earth, He was God clothed in human flesh. As we often sing in "Hark the Herald Angels Sing": "Veiled in flesh the Godhead see; Hail th'incarnate Deity." He took upon Himself the form of a man so that He could die in our place, bearing our sins on His own body on the tree.

John records, "The Word became flesh and made his dwelling among us. We have seen his glory, the glory of the one and only Son, who came from the Father, full of grace and truth" (John 1:14). Christ's earthly life was 33 years, but that is not His whole existence. Christ was with the Father from the beginning. More than 2,000 years ago, this man of the ages came to this earth at His first advent. He did not begin life at the manger. He merely took upon Himself the form of a man at that time. Then He remained on this earth 33 years. He died and was buried and rose again. Then He went back to where He had come from.

Think how Christ was received on the earth the first time He came! "He came to that which was his own, but his own did not receive him" (John 1:11). Most people at the time did not think that this One "in the flesh" before their eyes was God. They called Him a blasphemer when He claimed to be equal with God: "I and the Father are one" (John 10:30). For this they put Him to death. They would not believe that Jesus Christ was God in the flesh!

Second, we must believe in the deity of Christ (see 1 John 4:15; 5:5). We must believe that Jesus is the Son of God—the *only* begotten

Son. The liar is the person who denies that Jesus is the Christ, the promised Messiah (see 1 John 2:22). The Old Testament prophets told us the Messiah was coming. The angel chorus said that the baby born in Bethlehem was the Messiah who had been prophesied. Simeon saw Christ in the baby (see Luke 2:25-35).

Third, we must believe that "God is love" (1 John 4:8). There is no force in the world to compare with Christian love. Its power is seen in the great fact that "God is love." All through this chapter in 1 John, it isn't our love that is the definition of love at its best but God's love that is the standard to meet. Listen! "Love comes from God. . . . God is love. . . . This is love: not that we loved God, but that he loved us and sent his Son as an atoning sacrifice for our sins. Dear friends, since God so loved us, we also ought to love one another" (1 John 4:7-11).

Love turns our hearts away from ourselves. We cannot really love God without loving others. So we become channels of blessing to those around us, because of what God is in us. Nothing could influence our lives as much as the love of God, for "God lives in us" (1 John 4:12).

A man went to a pastor and said, "Sir, I want to enter into your religion."

"My friend," said the pastor, "our religion must enter into you."

God's love was shown in the gift of His Son to be a sacrifice for our sins (see John 3:16; 1 John 4:9-10). When we look at the cross, we catch a glimpse of God's heart of love. The cross was the only way God had of showing us His heart. It is a picture of infinite love poured out in all its fullness. Christ did not die *to make* God love people. He died *because* God has loved people—always and with an everlasting love. "For God so loved . . ." Our salvation does not depend on what we are but on what God is, and God is love!

God's love is first directed toward the individual. Then the individual must affect society. God is unseen and there are many who need God's love. So we will show it to others when we love one another. And when we love, we are like God.

Fourth, we must believe that Christ is our Savior (see 1 John 5:10-12). Christ was sent to be "the atoning sacrifice [or propitiation] for our sins" (1 John 2:2; 4:10; see also Romans 3:25), because sin barred people from God's love, "for the wages of sin is death" (Romans 6:23). So Christ took the judgment of sin on His own body on the cross and made it possible for God to righteously show mercy. Propitiation is the satisfaction by Christ's death of the whole demand of the law on the sinner. Propitiation is the cause of life, for through the sacrifice of Christ we have everlasting life (see 1 John 4:10).

"Whoever believes in the Son of God accepts this testimony. Whoever does not believe God has made him out to be a liar, because they have not believed the testimony God has given about his Son. And this is the testimony: God has given us eternal life, and this life is in his Son. Whoever has the Son has life; whoever does not have the Son of God does not have life" (1 John 5:10-12).

Our Supreme Test

Love is the supreme test of our Christian faith. "We know that we have passed from death to life, because we love each other. Anyone who does not love remains in death" (1 John 3:14). The word "love" occurs more than 45 times in this first epistle of John. We find out how love acts in 1 Corinthians 13.

"Whoever does not love does not know God, because God is love" (1 John 4:8). Love is the first instinct of the renewed heart. Where do we get our love? From within? No, from above: "We love because he first loved us" (1 John 4:19). What if we do not love? Then we don't know God.

We should show our love to Him by loving one another (see 1 John 4:7). Those who have love in their hearts have fellowship with God (see 1 John 4:16). But where there is no love, there is no fellowship (see 1 John 4:19-21).

1 JOHN 5:12-21: RICH REWARDS

John states the rewards of life in the last verses of chapter 5:

- Assurance of eternal life—1 John 5:13
- Power of prayer—1 John 5:14-15

- Power of intercession—1 John 5:16
- Victory—1 John 5:18 (see also 1 John 5:4-5)

Underline the word "know" in verses 12-20. We can have confidence when we know Christ. John uses the word "know" more than 40 times in his epistles. True Christianity is more than a creed—it is something that can be known and felt. We *know* that Christ became a man to take away our sins. We *know* that we have passed from death to life. We *know* that whatever we ask for, we will receive. John assures us of these truths.

UNDERSTANDING SECOND JOHN

Second John is a good example of John's private correspondence to an individual. This letter was addressed to an unknown Christian woman. This is the only book in the Bible addressed to a woman.

The word "truth" is found five times in this short letter of 13 verses. It is the keyword. The word "love" occurs five times. Truth and love are inseparable.

We must test all the teachings in the world by the Scriptures "for the truth's sake" (2 John 2, *KJV*). Test your experience by the Word of God, but never test the Word of God by your experience!

The truth John speaks of is from above, the truth as it is in Christ Jesus. We are to walk in the truth, not just admire it. Then we will "love one another" (2 John 5). This love is genuine and not subject to change. "Christ's love compels us" (2 Corinthians 5:14). The proof of our love is in our walk: "And this is love: that we walk in obedience to his commands" (2 John 6).

John speaks of the teaching, or doctrine, of Christ: "Anyone who runs ahead and does not continue in the teaching of Christ does not have God" (2 John 9). This is the test of the gospel: Not what I think or what someone else has thought or said or done, but what has Christ said? What is He to you? Is He the Son of God?

Many false teachers who would not confess that Jesus Christ was here in the flesh were traveling to the churches (see 2 John 7-11). This "is the deceiver and the antichrist" (2 John 7; see also 1 John 4:1-2). They did not believe in the humanity of Christ and denied His incarnation. If you call Jesus Lord but deny His deity, you are a liar and an antichrist. John says this.

Apply this test to some of the popular religious movements of today—Christian Science, Spiritualism, Unity, Jehovah's Witnesses, Scientology, Transcendental Meditation, and so on. They deny all or at least parts of the Christ doctrine mentioned here (see "Four Basic Beliefs" above in the "Understanding First John" section).

Don't be friendly with or entertain any false teachers, John commands, for by doing so you share in their wicked work.

UNDERSTANDING THIRD JOHN

Do you remember what Christ said of Himself in John 14:6? "I am the way and the truth and the life." We find Jesus portrayed in 1, 2 and 3 John as those three:

- Jesus the Life—1 John
- Jesus the Truth—2 John
- Jesus the Way—3 John

Third John was written to John's generous and warmhearted friend Gaius. This man was the model of a true Christian layman who had dedicated his wealth and talents to the Lord. His purse strings were loose and his latchstring was out. All he had belonged to Christ. He was the picture of the man who had found Christ to be "the Way," and in his everyday life, he tried to show that gracious Way to others. Such people, scattered here and there, have through the years kept not only the Church alive in an unfriendly world, but also Christ's love burning brightly for God's people when all around seemed dark.

3 John

Gaius was noted for his hospitality, a manifestation of Christian love. John urges him to continue entertaining the traveling preachers in spite of the bitter opposition of an autocratic and blustering church official named Diotrephes.

You can be either a Gaius, helping in the Kingdom, or a Diotrephes, hindering the cause.

What a splendid thing to be rich and powerful and to choose to lay all of your gifts and talents at Jesus' feet, like Gaius and Demetrius!

UNDERSTANDING JUDE

AUTHOR: Jude 1 identifies the author of the book of Jude as Jude, a brother of James. This likely refers to Jesus' half-brother Jude, since Jesus also had a half-brother named James (see Matthew 13:55).

DATE: The book is closely related to the book of 2 Peter. The date of authorship for Jude depends on whether Jude used content from 2 Peter, or Peter used content from Jude when writing 2 Peter. The book of Jude was written somewhere between AD 60 and 80.

PURPOSE AND SUMMARY: Jude warns his readers against the dangers of falling away from the faith, and he points to the faithlessness of the Israelites in the wilderness as a reminder of how the Lord destroyed those who did not believe and obey Him. Surrounded as his readers were by moral corruption and evil influences, the author urges them to "contend for the faith" (Jude 3), and in a closing benediction he commends them to the One "who is able to keep you from stumbling" (Jude 24). Both the similarity of this letter to 2 Peter and the use of non-biblical Jewish religious literature have shown much about the Jewish character of the Early Church messianic leaders (see Jude 9,14-15).

Jude was a brother of the Lord. He knew Peter. They walked with the master and no doubt talked together after His departure. They evidently thought much alike about the great issues of the day. Second Peter and Jude are very similar in thought and language. Both men were dealing with the dangers confronting the doctrines of the Church.

No doubt certain persons who denied "Jesus Christ our only Sovereign and Lord" had joined the church (Jude 4). They were not outside but inside the church and evidently had crept in unbeknownst to the true believers.

Alas! What church is without them today? They are with us but not of us. Christ will judge these evil people as He did the fallen angels.

These intruders had begun to teach untruths in the Church. A leaven of evil was at work among the believers:

- "Ungodly people"—worldly (verse 4)
- "Pervert the grace of our God into a license for immorality"—carnal (verse 4)
- "Deny Jesus Christ our only Sovereign and Lord"—skeptical (verse 4)
- "Reject authority and heap abuse on celestial beings"—lawless (verse 8)
- "Grumblers and faultfinders"—critical (verse 16)
- "Flatter others for their own advantage"—flattering (verse 16)
- "Follow mere natural instincts and do not have the Spirit"—immoral (verse 19)

In contrast to these evil fellows, we find the true followers of the faith, lifting high the cross of Christ (see Jude 20-23). They were building on the foundation of Christ:

- "Praying in the Holy Spirit" (verse 20)
- Keeping "in God's love" (verse 21)

Jude

• Waiting for God's mercy (verse 21)
• Winning souls for Christ (verses 22-23)
• Resting on God's keeping power (verse 24)

Thank God for this noble army of faithful ones! Of these, God says that their reward will be that He will "keep you from stumbling and . . . present you before his glorious presence without fault and with great joy" (verse 24).

Prophecy

of the New Testament

REVELATION

Key Events of Prophecy

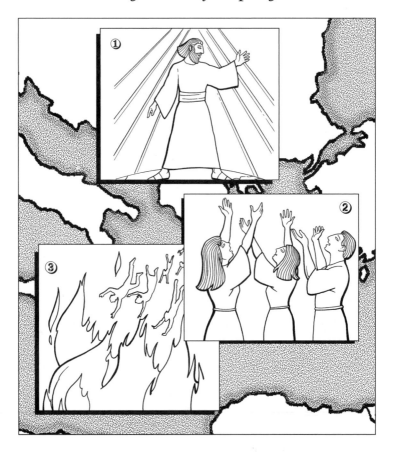

Prophecy: Jesus Christ Will Certainly Return!

The book of Revelation describes the end of human history. There will be severe trials and tribulations; Satan will deceive nations; he will viciously persecute believers. But those who believe will overcome Satan by the blood of the Lamb ①, the word of their testimony and the sacrifice of their lives (see Revelation 12:11). God will bring those who believe Him ② into His heavenly kingdom. Satan and all his demons and those who followed him will be thrown into the lake of fire ③ forever. But believers from among every people, tribe and tongue and language will worship the Lamb forever.

Understanding Revelation

Revelation Portrays Jesus Christ, Our Triumphant King

SELECTED BIBLE READINGS

DAY OF THE WEEK		MAIN TOPIC
Sunday: Revelation 1–3	Christ and the Churches	
Monday: Revelation 4–6	Christ's Throne and the Seven Seals	
Tuesday: Revelation 7–9	Christ's Trumpets	
Wednesday: Revelation 10–12	Christ and the Woes	
Thursday: Revelation 13–15	Christ and the Antichrist	
Friday: Revelation 16–18	Christ's Final Triumph	
Saturday: Revelation 19–22	Christ the Lord of All	

AUTHOR: Revelation 1:1,4,9; 22:8 specifically identifies the author of the book of Revelation as John, who is generally identified as the apostle John, the author of the Gospel of John.

DATE: The book was likely written between AD 90 and 95.

PURPOSE AND SUMMARY: This last book of the Bible identifies itself as "the revelation of Jesus Christ," and its author is designated "his servant John" who was exiled to the Greek island of Patmos because of his faith (Revelation 1:1). Addressed to seven historical churches in Asia Minor, the book of Revelation was written to warn against compromise and indifference to Jesus and to call for courage under persecution. Because of the extensive use of symbolism and picturesque imagery comprising the book's apocalyptic prophecies, the book's interpretation has posed many problems for students of the Bible. While recognizing the historical situation (Roman persecution) that gave rise to what is written in the book of Revelation, many scholars point to the fact that the book also depicts events that are to take place at the end of the age. The ultimate victory of Christ and His Body over satanic forces is the dominant theme.

Revelation is the only book of prophecy in the New Testament. It is the only book in the divine library that especially promises a blessing to those who read and hear it. "Blessed" is a strong word. "Blessed is the one who reads aloud the words of this prophecy" is what the book of Revelation says of itself (Revelation 1:3); but after reading the first chapters about the churches and the last chapters describing heaven, not many of us read much more in this book.

Revelation presents a glorious, reigning Christ. The Gospels present Him as a Savior, One who came to take the curse of sin; but in this last book we see no humiliation. In one way Revelation is the most remarkable book in the whole sacred canon. Revelation tells us about the reign of Christ on this earth, which Satan wants to control. It tells of Christ's complete and eternal victory over Satan. It describes Satan's defeat and punishment, first for a thousand years and then for eternity. It tells more about Satan's final doom than any other book. No wonder Satan doesn't want people to read it!

Does "revelation" mean a riddle? Most people, when speaking of this book, seem to think it does. No, it means just the opposite—"unveiling." Revelation was written using symbols. The hard of hearing have a sign language, each gesture of which is filled with meaning. So it is with every symbol in Revelation: Each of the 300 symbols in this book has a definite meaning and signifies a great truth.

This book was sent and signified by the angel to John, but it is the revelation of Jesus Christ, not the revelation of John. It is not the revelation of the growth of the Church and the gradual conversion of the world, but it is the revelation of Jesus Christ! It was given by Christ Himself to John (see Revelation 1:1-2). The book deals with the return of the Lord to this earth. It describes the readiness or unreadiness of the Church for this great happening (see Revelation 3:20). There are descriptions of the tremendous events on earth and in heaven just before, during and after His coming.

Christ is the theme of this wonderful book. Revelation gives an authentic portrait of the Lord Jesus as the triumphant One. More than 25 times in it we find Christ's sacrificial title "Lamb." In addition, we see a vision of the future of the Church and the world in relation to Christ—events yet to be fulfilled.

It has been said that the saving blood of Christ runs through the entire Bible like a red cord. It has also been said that the second coming of Christ runs through the Bible like a golden cord. We are saved and washed clean in His blood so that we may be ready and eager for His return.

What is meant by "the time is near" (Revelation 1:3)? Almost 2,000 years have passed since these words were written, but the idea is that this is the next thing on the agenda to fulfill God's plan. No matter how much time may intervene, the next thing after the day of grace is the Kingdom age to be ushered in by our Lord's return.

Few people who have any imagination have not sat down and thought, *I wonder how it would feel to be a king,* for Christ says that when He comes, He will make us reign as kings (see Revelation 1:6, *KJV*)!

Then "those who pierced him" will see Him (Revelation 1:7). Although that refers especially to the Jewish people, who at Christ's coming will turn to Him as a united people and be saved, at the same time it means that many others who have pierced Christ will see Him (see Romans 11:25-26). Have *you* pierced Him?

THE GREATEST DRAMA OF ALL TIME

Revelation is a wonderful way to finish the story that began in Genesis. All that was begun in the book of beginnings (Genesis) is consummated in Revelation:

- In Genesis the heaven and earth were created—in Revelation we see a new heaven and a new earth.
- In Genesis we see the sun and moon appear—in Revelation we read that there is no need of the sun or moon, for Christ is the light of the new heaven.
- In Genesis there is a garden—in Revelation there is a holy city.
- In Genesis there is the marriage of the first Adam—in Revelation there is the marriage supper of the second Adam, Jesus Christ.
- In Genesis we see the beginning of sin—in Revelation sin is done away with.
- In Genesis we see the appearance of the great adversary, Satan, and sorrow and pain and tears—in Revelation we see Satan, sorrow, pain and tears destroyed.

Things are very dismal in the world today. No one living has ever known such uncertainty about the future of human events. But things were dismal too when the apostle John, an old, old man, was exiled to the Isle of Patmos. He had been banished for his "testimony of Jesus" (Revelation 1:9). While on the island, John was forced to do hard labor in the mines and quarries. But his Commander-in-chief appeared to him and delivered a ringing message of ultimate glory.

God had determined from the beginning that His Son would be the ruler of this universe (see Isaiah 9:6-7).

Revelation is the greatest drama of all time. The plot is tense throughout; the final scene is glorious, for Christ comes into His own. The hero is our Lord Himself; the villain is the devil. The actors are the seven churches. The characters unloosed by the seals of chapters 6 and 7 are introduced by four different horsemen. Then those summoned by the trumpets in turn leave the scene of action; and we see the Antichrist, the world ruler, stalking across the stage (see Revelation 13). This incarnation of the devil himself is determined to set up his own kingdom and be worshiped by people. But Christ brings all of Satan's plans to nothing. This majestic actor, bringing His hosts with Him, comes forth—the long-looked-for King of kings and Lord of lords. He drives His enemies from the stage in utter defeat (see Revelation 19).

After all the struggle has ended and the beasts have been destroyed and the devil bound and "the old order of things has passed away. He who was seated on the throne said, 'I am making everything new!'" (Revelation 21:4-5). This book brings to a climax the great story commenced in Genesis, and as all good stories should, it ends "And they lived happily ever after."

Notice the sevens in this book:

- Seven churches
- Seven signs
- Seven seals
- Seven plagues
- Seven trumpets
- Seven dooms
- Seven new things

REVELATION 1:1-18: JESUS IN GLORY

Here is the last picture of Jesus Christ given in the New Testament. Many artists have tried to portray Him, but they have failed. Here is an authentic portrait (see Revelation 1:13-16). He is standing among seven golden lampstands representing the churches (see Revelation 20). The use of lampstands in this vision proves that the Church is to be a light bearer: "You are the light of the world" (Matthew 5:14). How many churches today—on the street, on the Internet or on TV—exist only to provide entertainment, to sell something or to promote money-making schemes, instead of to be lights that shine in a dark place!

Christ is likened to "a son of man," but it is clear from the vision that the One whom John saw was more than human (Revelation 1:13). He was the Son of Man. Everything symbolizes majesty and judgment, and this thought of judgment strikes the keynote of the book. Christ is presented to the whole world as its judge:

- "Dressed in a robe reaching down to his feet"—flowing robes are a token of His dignity and honor (Revelation 1:13).
- "Hair on his head was white like wool"—He is "the Ancient of Days" mentioned in Daniel (Revelation 1:14; Daniel 7:9,13,22).
- "Eyes were like blazing fire"—He exhibits an intelligence that brings hidden things to light (Revelation 1:14).
- "Feet were like bronze glowing in a furnace"—the metal symbolizes His judgment (Revelation 1:15).
- "Voice was like the sound of rushing waters"—His words reflect His power and majesty (Revelation 1:15).
- "Right hand . . . held seven stars"—He has guardian angels, or spirits, that do His bidding (Revelation 1:16).
- "Coming out of his mouth was a sharp, double-edged sword"—the sword is a symbol of His judgment (Revelation 1:16).
- "His face was like the sun shining in all its brilliance"—His look reveals His exalted glory status (Revelation 1:16).

John's vision was not of this age in which we are living but of a future day when people will appear before Christ to be judged (see John 5:27-29). Now, we may have all of God's grace, mercy and forgiveness for the taking. Now, Christ is before us to be judged. We can reject Him if we choose. In Revelation, Christ is pictured in judgment. The day of mercy will be past; then we will stand before the judge.

When John saw this glorious One, the vision was so overpowering that he fell at His feet as if he were dead (see Revelation 1:17). But Christ's words were reassuring. He said He was "the living One"; and though He had been dead, He was alive forevermore and held "the keys of death and Hades" (Revelation 1:17-18). Then follows the command to write what is found in this book (see Revelation 1:19). We do not have the usual picture of Christ as He existed as a man on earth. Here we see as He exists in heaven, as the crown and culmination of all.

Have you ever seen the Lord? Moses saw Him, and his face shone. Job saw Him and abhorred himself and repented in ashes. Isaiah saw Him and felt unclean. Thomas saw Him and said, "My Lord and my God." Saul (Paul) saw Him and fell down and worshiped Him as Savior. What would you do if you really saw the Lord?

REVELATION 1:19–3: JESUS AMONG THE SEVEN CHURCHES

In the second and third chapters of Revelation, we find Christ's love letters to His churches. Christ dictated each one to the specific angel who oversaw one of the seven churches to whom He addressed each letter. These letters are alike in pattern, so in each one, look for the speaker, praise, reproof, exhortation and promise.

The churches named were churches that actually existed in John's day. In dealing with them, Jesus gives us a brief history of the Church from the first century to today:

1. Ephesus—the Church of the first love, during the time of the apostolic Church (see Revelation 2:1-7)

2. Smyrna—the persecuted Church, during the time of Diocletian to Constantine (see Revelation 2:8-11)

3. Pergamum—the Church under imperial favor, during the time of Constantine (see Revelation 2:12-17)

4. Thyatira—the papal Church, during the Dark Ages (see Revelation 2:18-29)

5. Sardis—the Reformation Church, during the rise of Protestantism and spanning the sixteenth and seventeenth centuries (see Revelation 3:1-6)

6. Philadelphia—the missionary Church, during the period ushered in by the Puritan movement (see Revelation 3:7-13)

7. Laodicea—the rejected Church, during the final apostasy (see Revelation 3:14-19)

Where do you find Christ at the end of this Church age? "Here I am! I stand at the door and knock. If anyone hears my voice and opens the door, I will come in and eat with that person, and they with me" (Revelation 3:20). He is outside, knocking to get in. The Church will not let Him in, but He pleads with the individual: "If anyone . . . opens the door, I will come in." Have you opened your heart's door to Christ?

We need to heed such words as those found in this letter: "Yet I hold this against you. . . . Nevertheless, I have a few things against you. . . . Nevertheless, I have this against you" (Revelation 2:4, 14,20). These are the warnings of a faithful Savior.

Discover how Christ is set forth in these early chapters. Remember, this book is the Revelation of Jesus Christ. What are the promises to the overcomers, the believers who stand firm in their faith? See if you can find the seven promises given here.

REVELATION 4–22: JESUS ON HIS THRONE

The great revelation proper unfolds with the sound of trumpets and "a door standing open in heaven. And the voice . . . said, 'Come up here, and I will show you what must take place after this'" (Revelation 4:1).

First the throne of God comes into view (see Revelation 4:2-3). Revelation, in effect, becomes the "book of the throne," because this throne, which symbolizes judgment, pervades the book. The throne of grace is no more. The scene is a courtroom. The judge of all the earth is on the bench; the 24 elders, representing the 12 patriarchs of the Old Testament and the 12 apostles of the New Testament, are the jury (see Revelation 4:4). The seven spirits of God (see Revelation 4:5; 5:6) are the prosecutor, and the four living creatures are court attendants, ready to carry out the will of the judge.

Next in importance to the Lamb Himself is the sealed scroll (see Revelation 5:1). Who can open the scroll? None, save the One who "has triumphed. He is able to open the scroll and its seven seals" (verse 5). Christ prevailed in the wilderness after 40 days. He prevailed in Gethsemane. On Calvary He prevailed when He said, "It is finished" and dropped His divine head on His unmoving breast (John 19:30). On the third day He arose from the dead and conquered death, sin, hell and Satan. This same Christ now claims the kingdom of the world by right of conquest.

The day of tribulation begins with the opening of the seven seals (see Revelation 6). This describes the Great Tribulation period spoken of by the prophet Jeremiah in Jeremiah 30. Christ also referred to it as a great tribulation such as has never happened on the earth (see Matthew 24:21). During the Great Tribulation, God will allow sin to work its final and tragic results. God's hand will be lifted from humans and beasts. The earth will be filled with war, hunger, famine and pestilence. Judgment must come on those who have rejected the Son of God. We as Christians, however, do not have to fear this calamity. We can look forward to Christ's second coming, because our Savior is coming to receive us to Himself and free us from this world and its evil ways.

Four Horsemen and a Pause

In Revelation 6, we see the famous four horsemen (see Revelation 6:1-8). Restraint on forces of evil is removed as the seals on the scroll are broken. When the seals are torn away, war and destruction are set loose. People will reap what they have sown. The anguish and horror of the period will be the result of human ambition, hatred and cruelty.

First, we see the white horse of religious witness, which comes before the final catastrophe on the earth. Then comes the red horse, and universal war breaks out in the world when peace will be taken from it. The black horse of famine and scarcity follows the universal war. Lastly, the pale horse of pestilence and death treads mercilessly on those left on earth.

The sixth seal brings social chaos, the complete breakup of society and proud civilization (see Revelation 6:12-17). Darkness, falling stars, heavens rolled up as a scroll, islands moving—the picture presented here is grim. Then the most tragic prayer meeting on earth takes place: kings and priests, rich and poor, flee from God in a general stampede, praying for death, "for the great day of their wrath has come, and who can withstand it?" (Revelation 6:17).

There is a momentary pause while the saved of the tribulation period are presented at the throne (see Revelation 7). These are "a great multitude" with their garments washed and made white in the blood of the Lamb (Revelation 7:9). The "sealed" are all Israelites—whom God will gather to Himself (Revelation 7:4-5; see also Hosea 1:9-10; Romans 11:25-26). The "great multitude" is from all nations. This proves that the gospel preached in the tribulation period will be very effective.

Then there is silence in heaven for 30 minutes! Orchestras cease! Seraphim and cherubim fold their wings! All is still! It is as though all heaven waits in breathless expectation. This is the calm before the storm (see Revelation 8).

The Seven Trumpets

War, famine and pestilence devastate the earth. God's judgments take place; and Satan, knowing his time is short, is exceedingly wrathful. We find unprecedented demon activity, 200 million of them sweeping across the earth (see Revelation 9:16). Hell is let loose! Sin is allowed its full sway, and death becomes preferable to life (see Revelation 9:1-21). Satan does his last work on the earth.

Finally, Satan manifests himself in the Antichrist. His portrait is given in Revelation 13 (see also Daniel 12:11; Matthew 24:15; 2 Thessalonians 2:3). This Antichrist will be the political ruler of this world. He will demand the honors due to Christ Himself. The embodiment of wickedness, he will be shrewd and clever and a real leader of people. The Antichrist will be a Nero, a Stalin, a Hitler, a Pol Pot and a Saddam Hussein all in one. A person will not be able to "buy or sell unless they had the mark" (Revelation 13:17). The "mark" of the beast is like a trademark used to indicate ownership or a symbol of allegiance such as the swastika was. The number 666 is "the number of a man" (Revelation 13:18). Six is the number of evil, so three sixes express a trinity of wickedness.

The Seven Golden Bowls

When the seven trumpets sound, Satan releases his power to accomplish his objectives. The seven bowls are God's power released against Satan. Even though God has revealed Satan's utter evil, people still blaspheme God and do not repent (see Revelation 16:9,11). The bowls are God's answer to the devil, blasting his dominion with plagues such as those of Egypt—blood, hail, fire, locusts, darkness, famine, sores, earthquakes, war and death. Satan has dared to challenge God's power. God is now answering the challenge, unleashing the seven dooms of His wrath on a Christ-rejecting world:

1. Ecclesiastical—Revelation 17
2. Commercial—Revelation 18
3. Political—Revelation 19:11-19
4. The beast and the false prophet—Revelation 19:20-21
5. The nations—Revelation 20:7-9
6. The devil—Revelation 20:10
7. The lost—Revelation 20:11-15

Satan is forced into action. His kingdom is shaken to its foundations and he is undone. This ends in the battle of Armageddon (see Revelation 16:13-16), with Christ taking the leadership of His armies. This battle is fully described in chapters 17–19.

After the Battle of Armageddon, Christ, having subdued all His enemies, will take the Antichrist and the false prophet and cast them with a strong arm into the lake of fire (see Revelation 19:20). Then and there, Christ ends Satan and all of his evil. The name for this place where torment never ceases and from which none return is Hades. This Greek word *Hades* is used in the book of Revelation to refer to hell, just as the Greek word *Gehenna*, which is often translated "hell," is used in the Gospels of Matthew, Mark and Luke and in the book of James to refer to hell.

The Lamb's Marriage

The "Hallelujah Chorus" in Handel's *Messiah* announces the coming of the long-promised King, our Lord Jesus Christ, the heir of David's throne, here to meet His Church, His Bride (see 1 Thessalonians 4:17). Hell has been let loose on earth; Satan and his cohorts have done their worst; and Christ has finally triumphed. Righteousness, long on the scaffold, is now to mount the throne. "The wedding of the Lamb has come" (Revelation 19:7). The marriage supper of Christ will take place in the air. The saints will be rewarded in the air according to their works. This time of rejoicing will continue until Christ returns to the earth with His Bride to set up His millennial kingdom.

The Millennial Kingdom

This is the time when Christ, the Prince of Peace, will establish His kingdom on the earth for a thousand years. The devil is to be bound for a thousand years (see Revelation 20:3); the saints Christ brings with Him will reign with Him for a thousand years (see Revelation 20:4,6); the wicked dead will not rise until the end of the thousand years (see Revelation 20:5).

There will be a thousand years of peace and joy upon the earth, when "the earth will be filled with the knowledge of the glory of the LORD, as the waters cover the sea" (Habakkuk 2:14). It will be a glorious time to live. No wars, no weeds, no wild animals, no taxes, no heartache, no death! When this period has come to an end, then the devil will be released again. He will come to test the nations (see Revelation 20:7-9). We discover their real attitude and learn that they prefer Satan to Christ. We can hardly believe it, but read Revelation 20:7-8: "When the thousand years are over, Satan will be released from his prison and will go out to deceive the nations in the four corners of the earth—Gog and Magog—and to gather them for battle. In number they are like the sand on the seashore."

Satan is the author and instigator of war. After a thousand years of peace, Satan gathers "them for battle." Not a few gather, but a countless number, like "the sand on the seashore." But "fire came down from heaven and devoured them" (Revelation 20:9). Human rebellion against God seems almost unbelievable, but "the heart is deceitful above all things and beyond cure. Who can understand it?" (Jeremiah 17:9).

Satan and Final Judgment

Satan is treated too lightly by the average person. We forget that he is mighty! He is the deceiver of the whole world. He fell from the highest place, next to God Himself, to the lowest depths—"the lake of burning sulfur" (Revelation 20:10; "the lake of fire and brimstone," *KJV*). Christ described it as "the eternal fire prepared for the devil and his angels" (Matthew 25:41). The devil is given an eternal sentence (see Revelation 20:10).

The blazing white throne of the final judgment is set. The One sitting on it will judge all people. Read Revelation 20:11-15. All of the dead are brought before Him. The sea gives up its dead. The grave gives up its dead. Hades gives up its dead. The King judges the dead according to their works (see Revelation 20:13). Final doom is pronounced. The Savior is now the judge. "Anyone whose name was not found written in the book of life was thrown into the lake of fire" (Revelation 20:15). Judgment must come before the golden age of glory can be ushered in. Someone has called hell the penitentiary of the universe and the universal cemetery of the spiritually dead.

Eternal Victory

God says, "I am making everything new!" (Revelation 21:5), and John names the seven new things God will create:

1. A new heaven and earth—Revelation 21:1
2. A new people—Revelation 21:2-8
3. A new bride—Revelation 21:9
4. A new home—Revelation 21:10-21

5. A new temple—Revelation 21:22
6. A new light—Revelation 21:23-27
7. A new paradise—Revelation 22:1-5

Read the triumph of God in Revelation 21 and 22. Satan has not been victorious in his attempt to use sin to separate people from fellowship with God ever since his meeting with the first man and woman in the Garden of Eden. He has utterly failed, and we will be with Christ forever and ever! Yes, God's story ends, "And they lived happily ever after."

Don't try to overanalyze or interpret every little thing in the chapters of Revelation. Rather, meditate upon the contents of the chapters. This is heaven! How limited words are in explaining its glory! The fellowship between God and people is restored. God dwells with His people. Every purpose is realized and every promise is fulfilled. Heaven is the opposite of what we experience here. All is beautiful!

The last words of Christ in His Revelation are "Yes, I am coming soon" (Revelation 22:20). Our response should ever be, "Amen. Come, Lord Jesus" (Revelation 22:20).

A Quick Look at

The New Testament: Colossians Through Revelation

 OUTSTANDING TRUTHS

- The Second Coming of Christ
- False Religions in Our Time
- Christ, the Head of the Church
- The Power of a Christian Life
- The Word "Better" in Hebrews
- The Power of the Tongue

REVIEW QUIZ

1. Which Epistle is suggested by each of the following descriptions?

A. Righteousness _____

B. The unruly tongue _____

C. Christ's coming again _____

D. Christian love _____

E. The good fight (the wrestler) _____

2. What was the occasion for each of the following statements? In which book is each found?

   A. "I have fought the good fight, I have finished the race, I have kept the faith. Now there is in store for me the crown of righteousness, which the Lord, the righteous Judge, will award me."

   B. "For the Lord himself will come down from heaven, with a loud command, with the voice of the archangel and with the trumpet call of God, and the dead in Christ will rise first."

   C. "I am not ashamed of the gospel, because it is the power of God that brings salvation of everyone who believes."

   D. "We know that in all things God works for the good of those who love him."

   E. "Approach the throne of grace with confidence."

   F. "Blessed is the one who reads aloud the words of this prophecy, and blessed are those who hear it and take to heart what is written in it, because the time is near."

3. This is a list of the most notable sentences in the Epistles. Pick out the ones that seem most important to you, and tell why they are important. (Use a concordance if necessary.)

   A. "All Scripture is God-breathed."

   B. "Now faith is confidence in what we hope for and assurance about what we do not see."

   C. "Faith without deeds is useless."

   D. "Now to you who believe, this stone is precious."

   E. "Add to your faith goodness; and to goodness, knowledge."

   F. "If we confess our sins, he is faithful and just and will forgive us our sins and purify us from all unrighteousness."

4. What were the last words of each of the following?

   A. Christ (see Luke 24:46-53)
   B. Paul (see 2 Timothy 4:1-9)
   C. Peter (see 2 Peter 3:10-18)
   D. James (see James 5:10-20)
   E. Jude (see Jude 17-25)
   F. The Bible (see Revelation 22:8-21)

5. Circle the correct answer to complete each of the following sentences:

   A. Thessalonians tells about
      (1) the sin of the tongue.
      (2) Christ's second coming.
      (3) Christ, the High Priest.

   B. The heroes of the faith are found in
      (1) Timothy.
      (2) Hebrews.
      (3) Revelation.

   C. Timothy was
      (1) Paul's son.
      (2) an early missionary.
      (3) Paul's convert.

   D. God's future plans are revealed in
      (1) Hebrews.
      (2) Titus.
      (3) Revelation.

6. Briefly discuss the thoughts and habits we must cultivate in ourselves to make our lives count for Christ—physically, mentally and spiritually. Include the methods necessary for the cultivation.

PART THREE

Appendices

APPENDIX A
Teaching Suggestions

APPENDIX B
Becoming a Member of God's Family

APPENDIX C
A Glossary of Bible Words

APPENDIX D
Maps

APPENDIX E
Bible Reading Plans

Teaching Suggestions

Do your best to present yourself to God as one approved,
a workman who does not need to be ashamed and
who correctly handles the word of truth.
2 TIMOTHY 2:15

The primary purpose of this book is to give the Bible student a panoramic view of the Bible so that it is seen as a cohesive whole instead of a series of unrelated stories. The Bible is the story of what God is doing in history. Like any good story, it has a beginning and an ending. It starts with the Creation; conflict is introduced with the workings of Satan and the fall of humanity, introducing the dilemma. The rest of the story is God's solving that great dilemma and the final triumph of His purpose at the second coming of Christ. All the events in between fit into that story and contribute to the unfolding of the plot.

The Bible has one main theme—redemption—and many subthemes that run through the entire book. Redemption is hinted at in the beginning (see Genesis 3:15) and developed as the main theme, coming to a climax with the advent of Christ. The subthemes, interwoven into the narrative and all dependent upon the main theme of redemption, are all defined and illustrated in the events of the Bible. For instance, the innate rebelliousness of sinful humanity is played up and becomes a major chord in the story of the wandering in the wilderness and in Judges, as well as in other minor episodes. The mercy of God is portrayed in Hosea; the victory He gives, in Joshua.

GENERAL GUIDELINES

Fortunately, the general thirst for knowledge includes a wholesome curiosity about what the Bible teaches. In concert with traditional

Sunday School classes, home Bible-study groups are springing up and churches gladly respond to desires for weekday Bible-study classes.

For the use of small groups and individuals in either Sunday School or weekday Bible studies, *What the Bible Is All About Study Guides* are available as well as the *What the Bible Is All About: Life-Changing Visit to the Holy Land* DVD. These study aides are to be used with this parent volume, *What the Bible Is All About*. They may be purchased from Gospel Light, at your local Christian bookstore or over the Internet.

Teaching Principles

If you are teaching the Bible, remember that chances are good that your class members do not have any systematic knowledge of the Bible. Most of your students will not have attended Sunday School consistently enough to be really well informed. They probably see the Bible as a collection of unrelated stories with morals, interspersed with beautiful poetry and some outstanding verses, and a lot of long, dull passages they have never bothered to read. The pattern of the Bible will be new to them. The history will certainly be a hazy impression of dignified characters in flowing garments either wandering in the wilderness or tending sheep in the land of Israel. Keep this fact firmly in mind each time you teach, give your class a picture of the whole of God's pattern (emphasizing how the particular book that you are teaching fits into that whole), and drive home the major lessons of that book.

Application Principles

Ample material is provided for you to use any of several different approaches, but a few very broad principles apply no matter which method you use.

First, always keep the whole scope of the Bible in mind. To begin with, read through a particular Bible book for chief impressions and emphases—quickly, just picking out the main points. Details will come later, as you work on each chapter.

Second, begin preparing each lesson a week in advance. You may have had some issues raised during the last class session that need to be clarified. Write those down. It's better to work on the lesson a little bit each day and then put the final touches on it at the end of the preparation period. You will find that preparing a lesson this way is a little bit like making a pot of stew—the longer it simmers, the better it gets.

Third, do as much reading as you can about the book of the Bible you are teaching. This handbook has the most important passages listed. For instance, the chapter on Genesis has a list of the beginnings that are noted in that book, along with the Scriptures. In each chapter, the sections marked by subheadings cover the major themes, people and events of the book.

Fourth, constantly bring your thinking back to the central theme of each book. This is the thing you want to get across to your students! Other lessons may be drawn—other themes may be mentioned—but keep referring back to this *main* theme. "Cohesiveness" ought to be your watchword.

Fifth, bear in mind the character and needs of the students you are teaching. You may have a class of young adults, all wearing that brittle mask of self-sufficiency that cracks so easily to show the uncertainty underneath. They need absolutes, and they will respond to the absolutes of the Bible. They also need love and understanding, and they will open up like flowers to the understanding grace of God. Teach to those needs. A middle-aged group is another thing entirely. They may still have many of the same needs as the young adults, but added to this is the new dimension of attainment and power. It is up to the teacher to present the Bible in a manner suited to its importance. This age group especially needs to be shown that the persuasively presented philosophy that security is to be found in things is false. Stress that God's kingdom must always have priority.

Sixth, remember that you are teaching, not leading a devotional. Because we are all aware, as we ought to be, of the need to know Christ better and to love Him more, we tend to forget that one of the major means to achieve these ends is to teach what the Bible says. There is no substitute for real teaching. All kinds of inspirational meetings are designed to urge Christians to action, to move them out of their usual zone of operation, to help them with their devotional lives—but the purpose of Bible study is to give knowledge and direction to the believer's faith. Anything that makes your teaching clear and explicit, that clarifies and explains, is good. If you use stories and illustrations to bring out your point, be sure they do just that. If they have an emotional punch, well and good; but beware of mere sentimentality. You may move a class to the edge of tears with a touching little story of a dying child, but if that story doesn't relate to the real solid Bible truth of the book you're teaching, the effect will not last.

BASIC METHODS

There are three basic methods that can be used with this material:

1. Student preparation method
2. Class discussion method
3. Lecture method

Each method has some advantages and certain disadvantages; consider them, and see which one will best suit your class and its needs.

Student Preparation Method

Preparing for the lesson requires real work by the students. For instance, on the week preceding the study of the chapter on Genesis, you might assign sections to the students. Tell each one to read the section assigned, study the Scriptures and then, at the next session, give in his or her own words the lesson to be drawn from that story. Give each one a specified length of time to speak, allowing yourself at least 10 minutes to sum it all up and bring out the main theme of the book.

The main advantage of this method is obvious: It encourages interest and Bible study on the part of the students. Most students love to have an active part in whatever they're doing, so unless you have an entire class of introverts, you should be able to find enough members each week to participate. There are some drawbacks to this, however.

Your students must be dependable; otherwise, they may either prepare poorly or be absent from the class when they are supposed to give their presentations. This may be avoided by a phone call or email reminder during the week. Occasionally you'll have an original thinker who becomes so stuck on an obscure passage that he or she dwells on it to the exclusion of the main part of the story, sometimes drawing some very odd conclusions from the Scripture! The time can also get away from the speaker, and you may be left with one minute for summing up.

Experiment with this way of teaching. Perhaps you will want to modify it a bit or use it once in a while. It requires just as much preparation on the part of the teacher, for you must be on your toes to see that the lesson is correctly presented and be ready to supplement information as needed.

Class Discussion Method
Class discussion can be done in one of several ways. You might hand out discussion topics for the following week. These topics should be decided on from the lesson material you intend to cover. For example, for Genesis you might list the following topics for discussion: (1) God's answer to man's disobedience; (2) how sin entered the world; (3) how the Abrahamic Covenant illustrates the grace of God.

It is amazing how many people are seriously concerned about the origin of sin; they may ask some searching questions and want to go far beyond pointing out Satan as the tempter. They may well ask you, "Yes, but if Satan was originally created by God, how could he be evil? How can a good God create something evil?" Be prepared to treat such a question with respect. A quick answer is not always the best answer, and such a profound issue demands more than a simplistic reply. Sometimes it may be a good thing to tell the class that you will do some studying of your own and will bring the answer next week.

When you use this teaching method, be sure to keep the talk from wandering off topic. Remember, you have a point to get across, and you can't do justice to more than one major idea in the time you have. If the discussion starts to wander far afield, pull the class back to the main theme. One great secret in teaching is to know when an issue raised by the class is vital to their faith—something they've wondered about, puzzled over and need an answer to—or when an issue is merely an oddity to quibble over. If, in the course of the lesson, your students seem concerned about a point you are making, don't hesitate to take more time to clarify that point. You may have to skim lightly over the rest of the lesson because of it, but you are adhering to the fifth basic principle—you are *teaching to their needs*. As you can see, this kind of classroom method is a nice balance between concentrating on the main idea of your lesson and being flexible enough to allow for other themes to be covered. Such a method is very demanding on the teacher, but the rewards are great.

No matter which discussion method you use, there is one caution: You may have two or three very talkative students who are all too willing to speak at length on their ideas about the lesson. They may get a great deal of satisfaction from having everyone listen to them; but the rest of the class may lose interest, there may be others who want a chance to speak, and all discussion must be controlled, at least to a certain extent. Regardless of the brilliance of the few vocal ones, the others need to hear from someone with more authority and learning than simply "Joe, who always talks too much anyway." Frequently these extroverted students are the ones who linger after class with special questions or personal problems. They do need attention but not to the exclusion of the rest of the class and some of the quieter students who need to be gently coaxed into sharing their ideas.

Lecture Method

The lecture teaching method does not mean a strictly rigid, formal presentation. It can be as flexible as either of the other methods or used in combination with one of them. After you have established a good rapport with your class, they'll feel free to interrupt the lesson when they have questions.

Let's take the chapter on Genesis as our example again. Read over this chapter carefully. Read through the book of Genesis, not stopping for details, but simply reading to get the broad outline of the book. This can be done, remember, at the beginning of the week. Let the lesson build slowly in your thinking.

Now you are ready to begin thinking about the emphasis you want to give the chapter. There is enough written material in this handbook so that if you merely read through it, your class time would be filled. But what you have been provided with is the raw material of the lesson; it is up to you to shape it and give it emphasis.

First, think of the whole scope of the Bible as you want to present it. Beginnings are vitally important, and Genesis contains the germ of the whole story of the gospel. Read over the first portion of the chapter carefully, until it becomes your own.

Second, go over the rest of the material and decide where you want to stress a point and what you can cover lightly. Because all the stories are referred to as examples again and again in the Bible, they need to be well told. You may decide to dwell longer on one than on others in order to make a point. But remember that these should be related not as different stories but as parts of the whole. You have a double purpose in each lesson—to present the book in its proper relation to the entire scope of the Bible and to bring out one grand truth, one practical idea, from each book. Of course, you may cover several subthemes, but keep coming back to the main idea.

Third, go over your lesson, tie up any loose ends and decide how you are going to sum it all up. The closing of your lesson is of prime importance. Here is where many a good speaker goes wrong. There is, as you know, a kind of timing that effective speakers and teachers take advantage of. Some fortunate people have a built-in sense of timing—they know just how to build interest, when to hesitate the merest fraction of a second before uttering the punch line of a funny story, just when to move in fast for a climax and, most important of all, when to stop. There is a Spirit-chosen time to

stop—when you have made your point. *Don't embellish it.* After you
have said, in the most effective way you can, what you want the class
to remember, *that's all.* Resist the temptation to add just one more
effective little sentence; it will not be at all effective if it's said after
the psychological stopping time. Your audience has already mentally left, and you might as well leave too.

General Reminders

Now, here are some little tips to tuck away in the back of your mind.

It would be ideal if your students remembered everything you
gave them each week, but be realistic—they won't. Recapitulate a little—not in detail, which would bore you and them terribly, but *briefly*
go over the material covered the week before. Do this in a positive
way, so you won't make them conscious of their failure to remember. Say, "Of course you recall . . ." and then tell them what of course
they don't recall. Because none of us assimilates knowledge in huge
gulps, the teaching process consists largely of telling and retelling
the same truths in different ways so that gradually—very gradually—
those truths become a part of the lives of those who are learning them.

Because this is a discussion of methods, we have not mentioned
the very obvious things that underlie successful teaching—your desire to present Christ in a winning way, your constant dependence
on prayer and your utter reliance on the guidance of the Holy Spirit.

Beyond and above all the timeworn and timeless truths about
teaching—our duty to do it; the satisfaction it affords; and all the
reasons for devoting the time, work and energy necessary to do it effectively—lies the deep and abiding pleasure of having the Word of
God, to which we are all committed: be "a lamp for [our] feet, a light
on [our] path" (Psalm 119:105).

PRAYER TIME

Begin each class session with prayer. Prayer is the keynote of success. No individual, much less a class, can succeed in Christ without
it. Prayer is the breath of the Christian. We are commanded to "pray
continually" (1 Thessalonians 5:17). As natural as breathing is to a

natural person, so too should prayer be to a spiritual person. Does this describe you? Does prayer time in class have meaning, or is it just a part of the everyday agenda? It is true that the class will go no further spiritually than you as the teacher lead them.

What does prayer mean to you? To guide the time of prayer in class you must be completely sold on its necessity yourself. Make it a daily practice to ask the Lord for His guidance as you lead your students. Ask Him to give you a love and understanding of them that is like His love and understanding of you. Pray for the individuals by name, if possible. As you prepare your lesson, realize that prayer should be an important part of it.

Let your class know by your attitude that you are completely dependent on the Holy Spirit to guide your thoughts and words. Before you teach, ask that God will lead you. Do not rush through the opening prayer time, but do not prolong it unnecessarily. Give the students the opportunity to take part in it if they desire. Encourage, but do not force, participation. Be careful that no one monopolizes the prayer time. This is a time to talk to God, not the time to preach a sermon. When you pray, *really pray*.

VISUAL AIDS

Visual aids may be divided into four main types: electronic, boards, diagrams and charts, and maps. Use the aid (or combination of aids) that best illustrates or enhances a particular lesson. Visual teaching need not be elaborate to be effective, but it can be effectively used to impress great Bible truths on the minds of your students.

Electronics

Always preview any DVD, CD, slide or PowerPoint projections, Internet website or computer program before class. In this way you can prepare for the discussion that will follow the viewing and foresee any difficulties that may be created by the presentation. Electronic aids should not be looked upon as teaching crutches but should be used either to introduce the lesson or to summarize what has been taught.

Set up whatever electronic equipment is necessary well in advance of the presentation. Be sure that all is in good working order and that you know how to run the equipment or cue the various portions of the presentation. If necessary, practice ahead of time, or have someone help you. Whatever sort of electronics you use, make sure that the entire class can see and hear everything.

Boards

There are a wide variety of permanent and portable boards that can be used to enhance teaching. These include dry-erase boards (often called whiteboards), bulletin boards, felt boards, flip charts, and so on. Obviously, if you want to write things down for your class to see during the lesson, use a chalkboard or whiteboard. Bulletin boards can be used effectively to post a series of pictures or to post lists or quotes that you've written beforehand. Felt boards are usually used with figures to illustrate story action and are especially effective with young children.

A dry-erase board may be purchased, or you can make one yourself. One way to make an erasable board is to glue a piece of clear plastic over a piece of cardboard (covered with white paper), and write with a grease pencil. Or you can make your own whiteboard to be used with specially made pens; check the Internet for directions that fit your skill level. Choose a size that is appropriate for the size of the room you teach in.

If you would like to keep the material you write so that you can refer back to it in later lessons, use a flip chart. These too may be purchased, or make your own. Fasten several pieces of paper together at the top, fasten them to a cardboard sheet and then turn each piece as you complete the writing on it. Suit the size of the board to the size of your class. Often a small board is sufficient.

Some sort of visual aid is an indispensable part of teaching. It can capture student interest and serve to focus the students on the point under discussion. But, needless to say, if the board or chart is to be used successfully, it must be wisely and efficiently used. All material placed on it should be specific and serve an immediate purpose. To be easily readable, the material should be clearly and accurately reproduced with a minimum degree of artistry. And not too much material should be presented this way at any one time, because too much material clutters up the board and makes it less intelligible.

Generally speaking, it is a good idea to avoid distraction by turning the page on the flip chart or erasing material that is not needed.

When outlines, summaries or similar materials are to be used by the group at the beginning of class, they should be placed on the board before the class convenes. If the teacher writes on the board while the class waits, valuable time is lost and interest wanes. Do not be afraid, however, to use the board or chart as the lesson develops. Write down important points, list ideas that discussion brings up, or write the Bible reference for some Scripture that you are using.

Diagrams and Charts

A good diagram must meet several standards: (1) it must be technically correct; (2) it must be neatly drawn in proper proportion; (3) it must be completely labeled and explained (nothing should be left to the imagination); (4) it has to be artistic, because it must command the students' respect and thus encourage interest and understanding.

Various types of charts may be used. For example, a chronological chart that lists historical events in the proper sequence is often a help in getting an overall view of the book or topic under study. A genealogy chart may help to clarify family lines. A time-line chart may serve to keep specific events within the right general periods. A tree chart may be used effectively to show the relationship of one main thought to its several component parts.

Charts and diagrams may be prepared on poster board, on flannel boards or on erasable boards; or flip charts may be made in which each event or thought has its own specific representation.

Maps

As educational devices, maps can be indispensable because they can help students visualize and localize important geographical areas. But use maps only when appropriate: to answer questions, solve problems or supply information or data.

Explore the Internet as a source for whatever sort of map you decide to include in your lesson (see also the maps section in Appendix D). Although you're liable to find something you can use for free, you may also find that purchasing a map would allow you a greater choice of a size more appropriate for your room.[1]

Make sure that the students understand the purpose of the map. Is it supposed to show the distance between two places? The geography of a territory? The countries that existed during a certain time period? Paul's journeys?

If you have a blank map, trace the spread of the Church throughout the world by shading in areas on the map. Areas of non-Christian influence can be indicated also, perhaps with overlays of plastic. Or you can trace Paul's journeys as you discuss the places he visited.

Note

1. An additional resource to use is *Reproducible Maps, Charts, Timelines and Illustrations* (Ventura, CA: Gospel Light, 1997).

Becoming a Member of God's Family

This appendix can be used by any person who wishes to become a member of God's family or by anyone who wants to lead another person to Christ. If you're interested in becoming a member of God's family, simply read through and follow the steps below. If you want to help a friend, a relative or a student of any age become a member of God's family, use the material presented here as a guide to help a new believer declare his or her faith.

INTRODUCTION

In the Old Testament, God promised to send a Messiah, or Savior, to His people. The Messiah would save God's people from their sins, from the wrong things everyone has done. The people in Old Testament times knew about the promise of a Savior and looked for Him.

In the New Testament, God's promise came true! The Savior was born in Bethlehem, just where God had promised (see Micah 5:2). Jesus Christ was born, grew up and died for our sins.

God's Word always comes true. You can trust God's faithfulness, for He made it possible for you to become a member of His family. Just read through the five easy steps given here.

STEP ONE: GOD LOVES YOU

The Bible says in 1 John 4:8 that "God is love." He loves you very much. He loves you because He made you and He is concerned about you and your life today.

STEP TWO: YOU HAVE SINNED

The Bible also says that you and all other people have sinned. In Romans 3:23 we read, "For all have sinned and fall short of the glory of God."

We have all done wrong, and our sins keep us from being friends with God. As you read in the books of the Old Testament, sin always leads to trouble. Because you are a sinner, your sin will cause much trouble in your life. Romans 6:23 tells how bad this trouble will ultimately be: "The wages of sin is death."

God does not want you to ruin your life with sin. It makes Him sad when you sin and spoil your happiness and the happiness of other people. Because of sin, you cannot enjoy God's loving presence in your life, and can you can't live with God in heaven. Not one of us by even our very best efforts is able to remove sin from our lives or to earn God's forgiveness.

In the beginning of the Bible is the story of Adam and Eve, the first two people. Adam and Eve lived happily with God until they disobeyed Him. That was the first sin. One of the results of that sin was that Adam and Eve were separated from God, thereby robbing life of its greatest joy and ultimately bringing the penalty of death on themselves. All of us sin, so someday each of us will die, too.

However, the Bible is clear that there is another life after we die. The Bible is also clear that sin will continue to separate people from God's love forever. Because everybody has sinned, how does anybody get to go to heaven?

STEP THREE: GOD PAID THE PRICE

The Bible says in Romans 6:23, "The wages of sin is death, but the gift of God is eternal life in Christ Jesus our Lord." The result of sin is death. However, because God loves you so much, He offers eternal life as a free gift. You cannot work hard enough to earn eternal life. All you can do is accept it as a gift.

God gave His only Son to die for you on the cross. The Bible says in 1 Corinthians 15:3, "Christ died for our sins according to the Scriptures." Because Jesus was the perfect man (without sin) He accepted the results of sin (death) in your place. First John 4:14 says, "The Father has sent his Son to be the Savior of the world."

STEP FOUR: GOD WILL FORGIVE YOU

If you admit that you have sinned and believe that God gave His only Son to die in your place, God will forgive you and make you clean from all sin.

Tell God that you know you are a sinner.

Tell God that you believe Jesus Christ is the only way to have your sins forgiven.

Tell God that you want to learn to love and follow Christ in every area of your life.

Tell God that He is great and wonderful.

It is easy to talk to God. Jesus taught us to talk to Him as we would to a loving Father. He is ready to listen. What you are going to tell Him is something He has been waiting to hear.

If you believe and have told God you believe, you are now a child of God! God has forgiven all your sins. You are a Christian. And that makes you a member of God's family.

God has made everything right between you and Him. He has forgiven you and He looks on you as if you had never sinned!

STEP FIVE: YOU CAN LIVE AS GOD'S CHILD

The Bible says in John 1:12, "Yet to all who did receive him, to those who believed in his name, he gave the right to become children of God." As a child of God, you receive God's gift of everlasting life. God is with you now and forever.

Now that you are a member of God's family, God wants you to live as His child.

You Can Talk to God

Because God is your heavenly Father, He wants you to talk to Him in prayer. You can tell God how you feel, thank Him for His gifts to you and ask Him to help you obey and follow Him.

You can also talk to God when you sin. Ask God to forgive you and He will. The Bible says in 1 John 1:9, "If we confess our sins, he is faithful and just and will forgive us our sins and purify us from all unrighteousness." God will forgive you and help you do what He says.

You Can Read God's Word

God gave us His Word so that everyone can read about Him and His great love. Find out more about God by reading about Him in *your* Bible. As you read God's Word, you will stay close to Him. You'll get to know Him better and better, and He will help you to always do what is right. The Bible says, "I have hidden your word in my heart that I might not sin against you" (Psalm 119:11).

You Can Obey God

Your heavenly Father wants you to obey Him. He tells you in His Word how you should live. Jesus summed up God's law with two commandments (see Matthew 22:37-40):

1. "Love the Lord your God with all your heart and with all your soul and with all your mind" (Matthew 22:37).
2. "Love your neighbor as yourself" (Matthew 22:39).

God wants you to be an expression of His love in the world.

You Can Tell Others About Jesus

Jesus said in Acts 1:8, "You will be my witnesses." Jesus was talking to His disciples before He went back to His Father. Even though Jesus was talking to His disciples, He was saying these words to you, too. You can be a witness by telling others about Jesus and how His love has helped you. Ask God to give you opportunities each day to tell about—and to show—God's love.

A Glossary of Bible Words

Abba (AB-uh): An Aramaic word that means "Daddy." Aramaic was the language spoken by Jesus and other Jews living in Judea and Samaria.

admonition: Teaching or instruction, usually done as a warning.

adultery: Sexual union between a man and a woman when either or both of them are married to someone else. Adultery is a sin.

adversary: An enemy or someone who is against you. Can refer directly to Satan (see 1 Peter 5:8).

advocate: Someone who supports, comforts, gives help to or speaks up for another person. Jesus and the Holy Spirit are *advocates* for members of God's family (see John 14:16,26; 1 John 2:1).

affliction: Great trouble or pain.

alien: A person from another country; a foreigner.

altar: A place where sacrifices were made to worship God. An *altar* could be a pile of dirt or stones, or a raised platform of wood, marble, metal or other materials. The *bronze* or *brazen altar* was used for burnt offerings in the Tabernacle's courtyard. It was a large box, eight feet square and four-and-a-half feet high, made of wood covered with bronze. A much larger altar replaced it when Solomon built the Temple. The *altar of incense* (also called the *golden altar*) was smaller, covered with gold, and placed just in front of the veil to the holy of holies. Every day, both morning and evening, incense was burned here, symbolizing the prayers of the people.

Amalekites (uh-MAL-uh-kites): Nomadic, warlike people inhabiting the region southwest of the Dead Sea. Because of their vicious attack against the Israelites after the Exodus from Egypt, God pronounced judgment on them. Battles against the Amalekites were fought by Joshua, by several of the judges, by Saul and by David; they were finally destroyed in the days of Hezekiah.

amen: A Hebrew word that means "Let it be so!" or "This is the truth!" *Amen* is often said after a prayer to show that people agree with what has been said and believe that it will happen.

Ammonites: Descendants of Ben-Ammi, grandson of Abraham's nephew, Lot. They lived east of the Dead Sea, and were nomadic, idolatrous and vicious. The Ammonites often opposed Israel.

Amorites: Descendants of Canaan, a son of Ham, and grandson of Noah. Because of their wickedness, God told Abraham of future destruction He would bring. This punishment occurred under Moses and Joshua, and their land was given to the tribe of Reuben.

Ancient of Days: A name for God that describes Him as the everlasting ruler of heaven and earth (see Daniel 7:13-14).

angels: Heavenly beings created by God before He created Adam and Eve. *Angels* act as God's messengers to men and women. They also worship God.

anoint: To pour oil on a person or thing. A person was *anointed* to show that God had chosen him or her to do a special job. Samuel *anointed* David to show that God had chosen him to be king.

antediluvian (AN-tih-deh-LOO-vee-uhn): Before the Flood. The term is from Latin and is used in reference to the period and people before Genesis 7–9.

Antichrist (AN-tee-christ): The great enemy of Christ Jesus who pretends to be the Messiah. The Bible tells us that before the second coming of Christ, the *Antichrist* will rule over the world.

Antioch (AN-tee-ock): **(1)** The capital of Syria, site of the first Gentile church, which sent Paul and Barnabas on their first missionary journey. (2) A town in Asia Minor that Paul visited on his travels.

apostle: A person chosen and sent out as a messenger. In the New Testament, *apostle* usually refers to one of the 12 men Jesus chose to be His special disciples. Paul and some other leaders in the Early Church were also called *apostles.*

appeal to Caesar (SEE-zehr): If a Roman citizen accused of a crime thought that the trial or verdict was unfair, he could request that the emperor hear the case. Paul, a Roman citizen, once did this.

Arabia: The large area between the Persian Gulf to the east, the Indian Ocean to the south, the Red Sea to the west, and Israel, Syria and Mesopotamia to the north.

Aram (AIR-uhm): A son of Shem, grandson of Noah. The name is sometimes applied to all the land and people of the Fertile Crescent but usually is focused on the region that became known as Syria. The Aramaens were a Semitic people, and their history often intersects that of the Hebrews.

Aramaic (air-uh-MAY-ihk): The main language spoken by Jesus and other people who lived in Judea and Samaria when Jesus was alive. At least some parts of the books of Daniel and Ezra were written in Aramaic, as was most of the Talmud, a compilation of Jewish laws and traditions.

Ararat (AIR-uh-rat): A mountainous region of Armenia, between the Black Sea and the Caspian Sea where Noah's ark ran aground.

archangel: Chief angel. The term in the New Testament refers to Michael.

Ark of God, Ark of the Covenant: A special wooden chest that was covered with gold. God told Moses exactly how to make the Ark because it was to show the people of Israel that God was with them. The Ark was about four feet long, two feet tall and two feet wide. On top, two golden figures of angels faced each other. The two tablets of stone on which the Ten Commandments were written, a pot of manna and Aaron's rod that budded were kept inside the Ark. The Ark was placed in the most holy place in the Tabernacle.

Armenia (ar-MEEN-ee-uh): The area north of Assyria, containing the Ararat mountain region.

armor bearer: A person who carried the large shield and necessary weapons for a king or army officer.

Artemis (AR-tuh-mihs): A Greek goddess whose Roman name was Diana. Her most beautiful and influential temple was built in Ephesus.

ascend: To go up. Jesus *ascended* to heaven to return to God the Father.

Assyria (uh-SEER-ee-uh): A powerful and aggressive nation, the most powerful Middle Eastern empire from the tenth century BC through most of the seventh century. Nineveh was the capital city. Assyria conquered Israel and took its inhabitants captive.

Athens: A major Greek city, center of Greek art, science and learning. *Athens* was visited by Paul on his second missionary journey.

atonement: To make up for a wrong act; to become friends again. In the Bible, *atonement* usually means to become friends with God after sin has separated us from Him. In the Old Testament, the Israelites brought sacrifices to *atone* for their sins. The New Testament teaches that Jesus Christ made *atonement* for our sins when He died on the cross. Because Jesus died to "make up" for our sins, we can have peace with God.

Baal (bale), **Baalim** (BALE-uhm): A Hebrew word that means "master." *Baal* (plural, *Baalim*) was the name of many false gods worshiped by the people of Canaan. They thought the *Baalim* ruled their land, crops and animals. When the Israelites came to the Promised Land, each area of the land had its own *Baal* god. Names of places were often combined with the name *Baal* to indicate ownership (Baal-Hermon shows that Hermon belonged to *Baal*). Eventually, *Baal* became the name for the chief male god of the Canaanites. They believed that *Baal* brought the sun and the rain and made the crops grow. The Israelites were often tempted to worship *Baal*—something God had told them they were never to do.

Babel (BAB-uhl): The name popularly given to the tower built in a vain attempt by people to reach "the heavens" (Genesis 11:1-9). God blocked their effort by confusing their languages.

Babylon (BAB-eh-luhn), **Babylonia:** The capital city and the country that was one of the major political and cultural centers of the ancient world. The city of Babylon was located at the junction of the Euphrates River and major east-west caravan routes. For nearly 1,000 years, until the rise of Assyria in the ninth century BC, Babylon dominated much of the Middle East. Near the end of the seventh century BC, Babylon regained its independence and for nearly 100 years asserted its influence throughout the region and was a constant threat to the kingdom of Judah, finally resulting in the destruction of Jerusalem and the captivity of Judah's leading citizens. Babylon was captured by the Persians in 539 BC and then continued to decline, until it was destroyed by the Greek army under Alexander the Great.

balm: A sticky, sweet-smelling sap that was used as a medicine to heal sores or relieve pain. The plant or tree from which the sap was taken is unknown today.

balsam trees: Trees that grow in the Jericho Plain. The sweet-smelling sap of the trees and the oil from their fruit were used as medicine.

baptize: In the Old Testament, wash with water. But in the New Testament, when John the Baptist called the people to be *baptized,* he was using water to show that people were truly sorry for the wrong things they had done and that they were asking God to forgive their sins. Today, a person is baptized to show that he or she is a member of God's family.

barren: Unproductive. A woman who could not have children was *barren.* Fields that do not produce crops, or fruit trees that do not grow fruit, are *barren.*

Beelzebub, Beelzebul (bee-EL-zee-buhb): A god the Philistines worshiped. In the New Testament, *Beelzebub* is another name for Satan, the prince of the demons.

believe: To have faith or to trust that something is true. The Bible tells us that we can *believe* that Jesus Christ is God's Son and trust Him to keep His promise to forgive sins. We show that we *believe* that God loves us and wants what is best for us by obeying His commands.

Bethel: The site, located a few miles directly north of Jerusalem, where God confirmed to Jacob the covenant He had made with Abraham. Jacob named the place *Bethel,* meaning "House of God." It figures prominently in many biblical events, and for a time the Ark of the Covenant was kept there. After the division of Israel from Judah, Jereboam made Bethel one of two centers of idolatrous worship, which continued until Josiah's reforms.

betroth (bee-TROTHE): To promise to marry.

Bible: The writings of God's inspired words. The word *Bible* comes from the Greek word *biblos*, meaning book.

bier (bir): A stretcher or platform on which a dead body was carried to the place where it would be buried.

birthright: The special rights the oldest son in a Hebrew family enjoyed. When his father died, the oldest son received a double share of all that his father owned. He also received the right to make decisions for the entire family. Esau sold his *birthright* to Jacob for a bowl of stew.

bishop: Overseer, a leader in the Early Church.

bitter herbs (urbs): Unpleasant-tasting plants used for various purposes. A salad that includes *bitter herbs* is eaten at Passover to remind the Israelites of the sorrow, pain and bitter hardships they suffered as slaves in Egypt.

blaspheme: To say bad things against God, to swear using God's name, or to do actions that show disrespect to God. The Bible says that *blasphemy* is a sin. The Jews punished *blasphemers* by stoning them to death. Jesus and Stephen were falsely accused of *blasphemy*.

blemish: A spot or mark that makes something not perfect.

bless: To praise or make holy. The word *bless* is used in different ways in the Bible: (1) When God *blesses,* He brings salvation and prosperity and shows mercy and kindness to people. (2) When people *bless,* they (a) bring salvation and prosperity to other persons or groups; (b) they praise and worship and thank God; (c) they give good things or show kindness to others.

bondage: Being in slavery. In the Old Testament, the Israelites were in *bondage* to the Egyptians for many years. In the New Testament, *bondage* means slavery to sin. Jesus died and rose again to set people free from sin. Christians are no longer slaves to sin but are free to love and obey God and His Son, Jesus.

breastpiece: A square of colored linen cloth worn by the high priest when he entered the holy place. The *breastpiece* was decorated with 12 precious stones. Each stone represented one of the 12 tribes of Israel. The *breastpiece* reminded the priest to pray for each of the tribes of Israel.

breastplate: A piece of metal armor that protected a soldier's throat and chest.

burnt offering: A sacrifice, or gift, to God that was burned on an altar. The offering was a perfect animal, such as a goat, sheep, lamb or ram. *Burnt offerings* were always given for cleansing, or atonement, for sins.

Caesar (SEE-zehr): The family name of Julius Caesar, a famous Roman leader. Later the name *Caesar* was added to the name of each Roman ruler, so it became a title that meant the same as "emperor" or "king."

Calvary: A rugged bluff outside ancient Jerusalem. *Calvary* is from the Latin word for "skull," because the hill resembled a skull and/or because it was the site of executions.

Canaan (KAY-nuhn)**, Canaanites:** A son of Ham and a grandson of Noah. His descendants settled in and gave his name to the areas God promised to Abraham, which were later known as Judah (Judea) and Israel.

canon of Scripture (KAN-uhn): Measuring rod or standard. For Protestants, the 66 books of the Old and New Testaments have been widely and historically accepted as the *canon* because they have met the standard of being true and authoritative. Catholics, Orthodox Christians and some other denominations also regard the Apocrypha as part of the *canon*.

capstone: The stone that holds two walls together; the final most important stone that finishes a wall. When the Bible calls Jesus a *capstone*, it reminds us that He is the head of the Church and that He holds all Christians together.

captivity: The 70-year period when Jews were in exile in Babylon.

caravan: A group of people who traveled together, usually for protection from robbers and wild animals. When families moved, they often traveled in a *caravan*. Traders also traveled in *caravans*.

Carmel (KAR-mehl): A high ridge that juts into the Mediterranean Sea. Mount *Carmel* was the site of Elijah's contest with the prophets of Baal.

census: Counting the number of people living in an area or country.

centurion (sehn-TOUR-ee-un): An officer in the Roman army who was the leader of 100 men.

chaff: The worthless husks removed from grain. Farmers in Bible times got rid of *chaff* by throwing grain in the air on windy days. The light *chaff* blew away on the wind; the heavier grain fell to the ground. In the Bible, the word *chaff* often means something bad or worthless.

Chaldea (kahl-DEE-eh): The country of Babylon. The term is also used of the southern region of Babylonia. The Chaldeans overthrew the Assyrians in the late seventh century BC and established the regime that brought Babylon to its greatest power.

chariot: An open, two-wheeled cart pulled by horses.

cherub, cherubim: Heavenly beings, described as having multiple wings and both human and animal form. They are presented in Scripture as directly serving God. Carved representations of *cherubim* were placed on the Ark of the Covenant, and they were embroidered on the tabernacle's curtains. Solomon's Temple contained huge figures of *cherubim*.

chief priest. See **high priest.**

Chosen People: The Jews, as descendants of Abraham, were selected by God to be "a great and powerful nation, and all nations of earth will be blessed through him" (Genesis 18:18). The New Testament declares that the Church has also become the spiritual recipient of this blessing and responsibility (see 1 Peter 2:9).

Christ: The Greek word that means "God's Chosen One." "Messiah" is the Hebrew word meaning the same thing. Jesus was the *Christ*.

Christian (KRISH-chun): "Little Christ." People who believe Jesus Christ is God's Son and follow His teachings are called *Christians*.

church: An assembly or gathering. The word *church* is used to refer both to local groups of believers in Christ (*church*) as well as to all believers (*Church*).

circumcise: To cut an unneeded flap of skin, called the foreskin, from the penis. For the Israelites, *circumcision* was a sign of the special agreement (or covenant) they had with God: If they worshiped and obeyed Him, He would be their God and they would be His people. Abraham was the first Hebrew to be *circumcised*. After Abraham, Hebrew baby boys were *circumcised* when they were eight days old. Leaders in the Early Church said that it was not necessary for men or boys to be *circumcised* to become part of God's family.

cistern: A hole dug in the earth or a rock to collect and store water. Empty *cisterns* were sometimes used to store grain or as prisons.

City of David: (1) Another name for the town of Bethlehem where David was born. (2) Part of the city of Jerusalem. (3) The entire walled city of Jerusalem.

city of refuge: One of six cities set aside by Moses where a person who had accidentally killed someone could stay until a fair trial could be held. While the person was in a *city of refuge,* he or she would be safe from family or friends of the dead person who might want to kill him or her.

cloak: A long, loose fitting robe people in Bible times wore over their other clothing.

commandment: A rule or teaching that people are to follow. Moses received the Ten *Commandments* from God. The Bible gives *commandments* for Christians to follow because they love God and want to obey His Word.

conceive: (1) To become pregnant. (2) To think up or imagine something.

concubine: A slave woman in Bible times who lived with an Israelite family and had children by the father of the family. A *concubine* was considered an extra, or second-class, wife.

condemn: (1) To find someone guilty of doing something wrong and to declare or pronounce a punishment. (2) To be against or disapprove of something because it is wrong.

confess: Tell or agree about what is true. *Confess* sometimes means telling God your sins. *Confess* can also mean to say in front of other people that you believe that Jesus is God's Son and that He died and rose again to forgive you for your sins.

conscience (KON-shuns): A feeling about what is right and what is wrong; a sense of knowing what is good and what is bad.

consecrate: To set apart something or someone to serve God in a special way.

convert: A person who has changed from one belief or way of thinking to another. A person who decides to follow God's way instead of his or her own way has become a *convert*.

Corinth: A city in Greece. Always a commercial center, Corinth was made the capital city of the province by its Roman conquerors. Paul taught in Corinth for a year and a half.

cornerstone: A large stone in the foundation of a building at the corner of two walls, holding the two walls together. The *cornerstone* is the first and most important stone laid when a building is started. Jesus is called the *cornerstone* of a Christian's faith in God because He is the most important part of knowing who God is.

counselor: One who gives advice or help. Sometimes the Bible uses *Counselor* as another name for Jesus. In the New Testament, the Holy Spirit is also called the *Counselor* of Christians.

covenant (KUV-uh-nuhnt): An agreement. In the ancient Near East, sometimes *covenants* were made between two people or groups of people. Both sides decided what the agreement would be. However, in the Bible, the word usually refers to agreements between God and people, when God decides what will be done and the people agree to live by the *covenant*. The *Old Covenant* of law set standards of behavior in order to please God. The *New Covenant* of grace presents God's forgiveness based on faith in Jesus' death and resurrection.

covenant fathers: Abraham, Isaac and Jacob (father, son and grandson) who are often mentioned together in Scripture in reference to God's promises to His people.

covet (KUV-eht): Wanting very much to have something that belongs to someone else.

create: To cause something new to exist or to happen. God *created* everything that exists.

crucify: To nail or tie a person to a cross until he or she is dead. *Crucifixion* was a slow, painful punishment the Romans used for their enemies and the worst criminals.

cuneiform (ku-NEE-eh-form): Wedge-shaped form of writing used in ancient Sumeria, Babylon and Persia.

curse: (1) A request that harm come to someone; (2) blaspheme. In the Bible, *curse* does not mean to swear or to use bad language. When a person *cursed* something, he or she wished evil or harm to come to it. When God *cursed* something, He declared judgment on something.

Dan: (1) One of the 12 tribes of Israel, whose territory was directly north of Judah and west of Benjamin and Ephraim. (2) The northernmost city in Israel.

deacon: A helper or servant in the church. In the New Testament, men and women *deacons* were chosen to take care of the needs of people in the church. Today churches give their deacons many different jobs to do.

debt: Something a person owes someone else—usually money. In the Lord's Prayer, the word *debt* means sins or wrongdoing, and the word *debtor* means someone who sins against us.

decree: An order or law given by a king or ruler. A *decree* was often read in a public place so that many people would hear the new law.

dedicate: To set apart for a special purpose. In the Bible, the word usually means that a person or thing is given to God to serve Him in a special way.

demon: An evil spirit working for Satan (the devil). People can be tempted, harassed or possessed (controlled) by demons. Jesus has authority over all *demons* and in his earthly ministry ordered evil spirits to come out of many people.

denarius (duh-NAIR-ee-uhs)**:** Roman money. A *denarius,* which was a small silver coin, was the payment for about one day's work.

detest: To hate.

devote: To set apart for a special purpose or reason.

disciple: Someone who follows the teachings and example of another. In the New Testament, *disciple* usually refers to a person who believed that Jesus is God's Son and loved and obeyed Him. Sometimes *disciples* means the 12 men Jesus chose to be His special friends and helpers. At other times, it refers to all people who love Jesus and obey His teachings.

dispersion: The deportation of and emigration of Jews from the Promised Land. The term usually focuses on the Assyrians' forced relocation of people from the northern kingdom of Israel to distant locations throughout the Assyrian Empire. While large numbers of people from Judah who were exiled in Babylon did return, there was no similar restoration for the people of Israel.

doctrine: Teaching, or instruction, usually referring to the content of what is taught.

Eden: The perfect garden God created, between the Tigris and Euphrates rivers, in which Adam and Eve lived before they sinned.

edict (EE-dihkt)**:** A written law or order given by a king or ruler.

elder: (1) In the Old Testament, an older man in a family, tribe or town. (2) Also in the Old Testament, a member of a group of older men in a town. The town *elders* made major decisions for the town. (3) In the first four books of the New Testament, the Sanhedrin—the group of men who governed the Jewish people in Jesus' time. (4) In the Early Church, the church leaders.

enmity: Hatred or bad feelings that make two people or groups enemies.

envy: A strong feeling of jealousy caused by something someone else has or does well. *Envy* can cause a person to try to make him- or herself better than the other person. The Bible says *envy* is sin.

Ephesus (EF-uh-suhs): A city on the eastern coast of the Aegean Sea. *Ephesus* at one time was a commercial center but had fallen into decline by the first century AD. The city was the site of a large temple to the goddess Diana. Paul visited Ephesus on his missionary travels.

Epistles (ih-PIH-sehls): Letters sent to individuals or groups. Twenty-one New Testament books were letters, most of which were sent to specific churches or church leaders.

eternal: Lasting forever; without end. God is *eternal* and members of God's family have *eternal* life.

eunuch (YOO-nuhk): (1) A man who cannot have children because his sex organs are damaged, altered or defective. (2) A man who chooses not to marry but instead dedicates himself to serve God. Sometimes a man who was the most important helper or advisor to a king or queen was called a *eunuch*.

evangelism: The act of telling the good news of the gospel of Jesus Christ to others.

evangelist: Someone who tells the good news about Christ. The term is from the Greek word meaning "a messenger of good."

everlasting: Never-ending; forever.

exile (EG-zyl): Someone who has been made to leave his or her country and live somewhere else. The Jews were *exiles* in Babylon for 70 years.

faith: (1) To be certain about the things we cannot see or to trust someone because of who he or she is. For example, a Christian has *faith* that Jesus is God's Son. (2) The whole message about Jesus Christ—that He is God's Son and that He came to take the punishment for our sin so that we may become members of God's family. This describes the *faith* of a Christian.

faithful: Always loyal and trustworthy. God is *faithful*. We can always trust Him to do whatever He has promised. We are also to be *faithful* in doing what is right.

Fall: The original sin of Adam and Eve that broke the perfect relationship between people and God.

famine (FAM-ihn): A time when there is not enough food to keep people and animals alive. *Famines* can be caused by lack of rain, wars, insects that eat crops, and bad storms.

fear: To be afraid of something or someone. The Bible often uses the word *fear* to describe the sense of respect or awe that sinful people (and we are all sinful, according to Romans 3:23) should have for God because of His perfection, sovereignty and holiness.

feasts: (1) Dinners, celebrations and banquets. (2) Jewish religious holidays and celebrations.

fellowship: A time when friends who are interested in the same things come together. In the Bible, *fellowship* often means the friendship Christians share because they love God and His Son, Jesus.

fig: A brownish, pear-shaped fruit that grows on trees. *Figs* are plentiful in Israel. They can be eaten raw, cooked or dried.

firstborn: The first child born into a family. During Bible times, the *firstborn* son received special rights and power. He became head of the family after his father died, and he received twice as much money and property as his brothers.

firstfruits: An offering to God of the first vegetables, fruits and grains the Israelites picked from their fields. The people offered their *firstfruits* to God to thank Him for supplying their food.

flax: A useful plant grown in Israel. The seeds of the plant were used to make linseed oil, and the fibers of the plant were woven into linen cloth.

flint: A very hard stone that can be sharpened to a fine cutting edge.

flog: To beat with a whip or stick.

forefather: A person from whom one is descended—an ancestor. Your father, your grandfather, your great-grandfather and your great-great-grandfather are some of your *forefathers*.

foreigner: A person who is from another country.

forgive: A decision of the will to stop feeling angry and to stop blaming a person for something wrong he or she has done; to be friends again. God *forgives* everyone who repents of his or her sins and believes that Jesus died to take the punishment for his or her sins. When God *forgives* a person, God forgets the person's sins forever. God instructs Christians to *forgive* each other in the same way He has *forgiven* them.

forsake: To leave, to go away from; to leave completely alone.

frankincense (FRANK-ihn-sehns): A very expensive, hard gum made from the sap of a terebith tree. *Frankincense* was used to make sweet-smelling perfume. The Israelites used *frankincense* in religious ceremonies. One of the special gifts the wise men brought to Jesus was *frankincense*.

fruit: Evidence, outcomes, results. Although *fruit* is sometimes used in Scripture to refer to foods, it is commonly used to refer to the actions produced by good or evil in people's lives. The *fruit* of the Spirit refers to virtues produced in a Christian's life by the Holy Spirit (see Galatians 5:22-23).

Galilee (GAL-uh-lee): The northern part of the land of Israel in Jesus' day. Jesus grew up, preached and did most of His miracles in *Galilee*. *Galilee* is also the name of a large lake in this area.

gall (gol): A bitter, poisonous plant. The juice from the plant may have been used to make a painkiller. Jesus refused a drink of *gall* mixed with wine when He was dying on the cross.

Gaza (GAH-zuh): A major Philistine city. From the time of the judges until its destruction by Alexander the Great, Gaza was at times under the control of Israel or Egypt.

genealogy: A list of ancestors. Various such lists are included in the Scriptures to show lines of family descent.

generation: The length of time from birth until procreation. Grandparents, parents and children are three different *generations*.

Gentiles: All people who are not Jewish.

Gibeon (GIHB-ee-uhn): The only Canaanite city to make peace with Joshua, although done deceptively. The town, located a few miles northwest of Jerusalem, became an important place of worship, and Solomon had come to offer sacrifices at *Gibeon* when God spoke to him in a dream.

gifts: Abilities provided by God to believers that allow the accomplishment of good works.

Gilboa (gill-BOH-uh): A mountainous area south of Lake Galilee; the site of King Saul's final battle against the Philistines (both Saul and his son Jonathan died in this battle).

Gilead (GIL-ee-ad): The region of Israel west of the Jordan River.

Gilgal (GIL-gal): A town near Jericho; site of the Israelites' first camp after crossing the Jordan River. *Gilgal* was the site of Saul's confirmation as king and the place where he disobeyed Samuel's instructions, resulting in his being rejected by God as king.

glean: To pick fruits or grain that the harvesters missed. The Bible told farmers to leave some crops in the field for hungry people to *glean*.

glorification, glorify: (1) The act of being made perfect, as God is perfect. (2) To honor, praise and magnify God for His perfection.

glory: (1) Great beauty, splendor, honor or magnificence that can be seen or sensed. The Israelites saw the *glory* of the Lord in the cloud that filled the

Tabernacle. The shepherds saw the *glory* of the Lord when the angels told them Jesus had been born. (2) To praise; to be proud or happy; to boast.

Golgotha (GAHL-gah-thah): The place outside Jerusalem where Jesus was hung on a cross. In Aramaic, *Golgotha* means "the place of the skull."

Gomorrah (geh-MOR-uh): A city near the Dead Sea in the time of Abraham. *Gomorrah* and its neighbor Sodom were destroyed by fire from heaven because of the great wickedness of the people.

Goshen (GOH-shehn): The area of the Nile River delta where Jacob and his family settled under the protection of Joseph, Egypt's prime minister.

gospel: (1) Literally, "good news." The good news of the Bible is that God sent His Son, Jesus, to take the punishment for sin and then raised Him from the dead so that any person who believes may have new life. (2) The story of the life, death and resurrection of Jesus Christ told in the first four books of the New Testament. The books are also called the four *Gospels.*

grace: Love and kindness shown to someone who does not deserve it—especially the forgiveness God shows to us. We don't deserve God's *grace* because we sin against Him. God showed *grace* to all people by sending His Son, Jesus, to be our Savior. God's *grace* allows us to become members of His family (see Ephesians 2:8). God's *grace* also helps us live as God wants us to (see Acts 20:32). A person cannot earn God's *grace* by trying to be good; it is God's free gift.

Greece: A leading cultural, political and commercial center of the ancient world. In the fourth century BC, under Alexander the Great, Greece conquered much of the Mediterranean and Middle East, resulting in the spread of Greek culture throughout the region, even after Alexander's successors were defeated by the Romans.

Greek: The international language of the Mediterranean world in the time of Jesus. Most of the New Testament was originally written in common Greek, not in the classical language of ancient Greece.

guilty: Having done wrong or broken a law. A person who is *guilty* deserves to be blamed or punished.

Hades (HAY-dees): A Greek word that means "the place of the dead." Another word used in the Bible that means the same as *Hades* is "Sheol." *Hades* was thought to be a dark, shadowy place. Hell, or Gehenna, was a much more fearful place—it is not the same as *Hades.* If a person has asked Jesus to forgive his or her sins, that person does not need to fear either of these places, because he or she will live forever with Jesus.

hallelujah (ha-leh-LOO-yeh): A Hebrew word that means "praise the Lord!"

harlot: A prostitute; a woman who gets paid for having sexual relations with another person. The Bible says *harlotry* is a sin, but like other sins, it can be forgiven. Sometimes the Bible uses the word *harlot* to describe people who turn away from God to worship idols.

harvest: To gather ripe fruits, vegetables, grain and other crops from fields, vineyards and orchards.

heaven: (1) The sky or universe beyond earth. (2) The dwelling place of God, the angels and those granted salvation.

Hebrew: A name derived from Eber, a descendant of Noah's son Shem, and used to refer to the nation God chose to be His special people—the Israelites, later in history known as the Jewish people. *Hebrew* is also the name of any member of that nation, as well as the language they speak. Most of the Old Testament was originally written in the *Hebrew* language.

Hebron (HEE-bruhn): An ancient city less than 20 miles southwest of Jerusalem. Abraham lived there for a time, and David made it his capital during the seven and a half years he was king of Judah, before moving the capital to Jerusalem when he had also been accepted as king of Israel.

heir (air): Someone who has the right to receive the property or position of another person when that person dies. In Bible times, the *heir* was usually a son. The Bible says that anyone who is a member of God's family is His *heir*. God will never die, but because we are His children, God keeps on giving us great love, care and kindness.

herbs (urbs): Plants or parts of plants used to make teas and medicines and to flavor food.

Herod (HER-ehd): The family name of five kings appointed by the Roman emperor to rule Judea in New Testament times. Jesus was born during the rule of *Herod* the Great. The names of the other four kings are *Herod* Archelaus, *Herod* Antipas, *Herod* Agrippa I and *Herod* Agrippa II.

high place: Altars and locations for worship built on the tops of hills or mountains. Sometimes altars to God were built at *high places*. However, the *high places* were usually for the worship of idols. The Israelites were told to destroy the *high places* in their land where idols were worshiped.

high priest: The most important priest of all the priests, who served God in the Tabernacle and later in the Temple. In the Old Testament, the *high priest* offered the most important sacrifices to God for the people. In New Testament times, he was also a powerful political leader. He was the head of the Sanhedrin—the group of men who governed the Jewish people. He even had a small army. The *high priest* wore special clothing described in Exodus 28:1-39. Aaron was the first *high priest*. All other *high priests* were his descendants. The New Testament says that Jesus Christ is now our high priest, the One who offered Himself as the perfect sacrifice for our sins (see Hebrews 8–9).

Hivites (HI-vites): One of the Canaanite tribes defeated by Joshua.

holy: Pure; set apart; belonging to God. God is *holy*. He is perfect and without sin. Jesus is *holy*, too. He is without sin and dedicated to doing what God wants. Because Jesus died to take the punishment for sin and then rose again, people who believe in Him have the power to be *holy*, too. God helps them to become more and more pure and loving, like Jesus.

holy of holies: One of the two main areas in the Tabernacle and the Temple; it was separated by a large curtain (veil) and could only be entered once a year by the high priest on the Day of Atonement. The *holy of holies* was a smaller area than that of the holy place.

holy place: One of the two main areas in the Tabernacle and the Temple that could only be entered by the priests who were carrying out their sacred duties. The *holy place* was a larger area than that of the holy of holies.

Holy Spirit: The personal but unseen power and presence of God in the world. The book of Acts tells us that the *Holy Spirit* came to followers of Jesus in a special way after Jesus had gone back to heaven. The *Holy Spirit* lives within each person whose sins have been forgiven. Jesus said that the *Holy Spirit* is our helper and comforter. The *Holy Spirit* teaches us truth about God. He helps us understand the Bible and helps us pray in the right way. He gives us the power and strength to do what Jesus wants.

hosanna: A Hebrew word that means "save now!" The Hebrews shouted the word to praise someone important.

hypocrite (HIHP-eh-kriht): A person who pretends to be something different from what he or she really is. In the Old Testament, *hypocrite* means a godless person. In the New Testament, it means a phony. Jesus called the Pharisees *hypocrites* because they did many things to make themselves seem very religious, but they would not listen to God.

idol: A statue or other image of a god that is made by people and then worshiped as if it had the power of God. *Idols* are often made of wood, stone or metal. Sometimes the Bible calls anything that takes the place of God in a person's life an *idol*. God tells us not to worship *idols* but, rather, to worship only Him.

Immanuel: A name for Jesus that means "God with us."

incense: A mixture of spices held together with thick, sticky juice that comes from trees and plants. *Incense* is burned to make a sweet smell. In the Tabernacle and Temple, *incense* was burned on a small golden altar to worship God.

inheritance: Money, property or traditions received from another person. Often a person receives an *inheritance* after another person's death. The Bible tells us that everything that is God's belongs to Jesus Christ. By His death on the cross, Jesus made it possible for us to share His *inheritance* with Him.

inspiration: The process by which God communicated His word to the human writers of Scripture. *Inspiration* is from Hebrew and Greek words meaning "breathed," which conveys a vivid image of God imparting His truth to His people.

Israel: (1) The special name God gave to Jacob (meaning "Prince with God"). (2) Another name for the Hebrew nation—God's Chosen People. (3) The name of the nation ruled by the judges and the first three Hebrew kings—Saul, David and Solomon. (4) The name given to the northern kingdom after Jeroboam led 10 tribes to separate from Rehoboam and the two southern tribes. (The southern kingdom was called Judah.) (5) The name of the southern kingdom, after the northern kingdom of *Israel* was captured by the Assyrians. (6) A name used for the people of God. The Bible often uses "children of *Israel*" to mean that they were descendants of Jacob.

Israelite: A citizen of the country of Israel; a descendant of Jacob (Israel).

jealous: (1) To be careful to guard or keep what one has. This is the kind of *jealousy* the Bible is talking about when it says that God is a *jealous* God. He loves His people and wants them to turn away from sin and to love and worship only Him. (2) To be angry and unhappy when someone else has something you want. The Bible calls this kind of *jealousy* a sin. (3) To be afraid of losing someone's love or affection.

Jebusites (JEHB-yoo-sites)**:** A Canaanite tribe that controlled the hilly terrain of Jerusalem until they were defeated by David.

Jehovah: An English translation of one of the Hebrew names for God. A more accurate translation is "Yahweh." This name was considered to be very holy, and religious Jews would not say this name.

Jericho (JER-ih-koh)**:** A city several miles north of where the Jordan River enters the Dead Sea. *Jericho* was the first city conquered by the Israelites under Joshua's leadership. The city's walls and gates were rebuilt in the time of Ahab. *Jericho* was the home of Zaccheus, the infamous tax collector who reformed after meeting Jesus.

Jerusalem: The most important city of Bible times. *Jerusalem* was the capital of the united kingdom of Israel and the kingdom of Judah. The Temple was built in *Jerusalem,* so many people traveled to the city to worship God. In 587 BC, *Jerusalem* was captured and mostly destroyed by Babylonian armies. The city was rebuilt when the Jews returned after 70 years of exile in Babylon. Jesus taught in the city of *Jerusalem,* was crucified outside the city wall, was buried near the city and then rose again. The first Christian church began in *Jerusalem* after the Holy Spirit came to the believers there.

Jews: (1) At first in the Bible, anyone who was a member of the tribe of Judah. (2) By the return from exile in Babylon, anyone who was a descendant of Abraham or who was a follower of the Jewish religion.

Jordan River: The major river in Israel. The main part of the *Jordan River* flows from the Sea of Galilee southward into the Dead Sea. Numerous biblical events involved this famous waterway, including Jesus' baptism.

Josephus (joh-SEE-fehs): A Jewish historian. He wrote near the end of the first century AD, and his *Antiquities* contains the first non-Christian reference to Jesus.

Judah: (1) One of the sons of Jacob and Leah. (2) The descendants of Jacob and Leah's son of the same name, who became the tribe of *Judah*. (3) The southern kingdom when the Israelites divided into two separate countries after the death of King Solomon. (The northern kingdom was called Israel.)

Judaism (JOO-day-izm): The faith, laws, traditions and teachings of the Jewish religion. *Judaism* is based on worshiping the one true God, circumcision as a sign of being one of God's Chosen People, worship on the Sabbath (Saturday), obeying God's laws and following the traditions given from one generation to another.

Judaizers (JOO-day-ize-uhrs): People who claimed that a person must keep the Jewish laws in order to become a true believer in Jesus.

judge: A person who helps people settle their disagreements. When the Israelites were settling the Promised Land after the death of Joshua, God chose leaders called *judges* to rule the people. Often these *judges* led the people in battle against their enemies. Some of the *judges* were Deborah, Gideon and Samuel. After kings began to rule Israel, *judges* once again settled disagreements and took care of official business.

judgment: (1) In the Old Testament, God's laws of instructions. (2) Also in the Old Testament, God's punishment of a person or nation for disobeying Him. (3) In the New Testament, to criticize or disapprove of someone. The Bible says Christians are not to *judge* each other. (4) Also in the New Testament, the end of the world as we know it when God will *judge* sin and reward those people who have lived for Him.

justice: That which is right and fair. Most of the prophets in the Bible emphasized that God is just and that He wants His people to act justly. Many of the prophets' warnings were given because the leaders and people were guilty of injustice (such as cheating others, especially the poor).

justification, justify: God's action of declaring that sinners are made righteous by faith in Jesus Christ. God forgives their sins and becomes their friend. God also gives them the power to live right. *Justification* is possible because Jesus Christ died to take the punishment for sin.

Kadesh (KAY-dehsh): A location between the Sinai desert and the southern boundary of Canaan. From here, Moses sent 12 spies into Canaan, but the people rebelled, resulting in the Israelites spending an entire generation in the desert.

kingdom of God, kingdom of heaven: God's rule in the lives of His Chosen People and His creation. In the Old Testament, the people in the *kingdom of God* were the Israelites. In the New Testament and today, the people in God's kingdom are those who believe in and follow the Lord Jesus Christ. When Jesus comes again, then God's kingdom will become visible to all people.

kinsman: A relative.

Lamb of God: A name for Jesus that tells us that He died to take away our sins. During the times of the Old Testament, when a Jewish person had sinned, he or she offered a lamb as a sacrifice to God. Jesus became like one of those lambs when He gave Himself as a sacrifice to die so that our sins can be forgiven.

lampstand: A raised support for a light. The Tabernacle was furnished with one large, seven-branched golden *lampstand* (menorah), placed opposite the golden table. In the Temple, 10 golden *lampstands* were placed along the interior walls, five on each side.

law: (1) All the rules God gave to help people to know and love Him and to live happily with each other. The Ten Commandments are part of God's *law*. (2) The first five books of the Bible. These five books are often called the *Law*. (3) The entire Old Testament. Sometimes the Old Testament is referred to as the *Law*. (4) Any rule that must be obeyed, whether it was decided by God or by people. (5) God's rules in the Old Testament plus other rules added by Jewish religious leaders. (6) The conscience of an unbeliever who knows he or she has not followed his or her own moral code (see Romans 2:14-16).

leprosy (LEHP-reh-see): Serious skin diseases. People with *leprosy* were called *lepers*. The Jewish law said that *lepers* had to stay away from people who did not have the disease. *Lepers* lived outside their cities and towns, either by themselves or with other *lepers*, until the disease showed signs of healing.

Levites (LEE-vites): Descendants of Levi, one of the sons of Jacob and Leah. Some of the *Levites* were religious teachers. Others took care of the Tabernacle and, later, the Temple. Only *Levites* who were descendants of Moses' brother Aaron could become priests.

locusts: A large insect like a grasshopper. Sometimes *locusts* travel in huge swarms, eating all the plants they can find. In Bible times, *locusts* were sometimes eaten as food.

Lord's Supper: The Passover meal Jesus celebrated with His disciples the night of His arrest. Also the continuing observance in which Christ's followers gather to eat and drink in order to "proclaim the Lord's death until he comes" (1 Corinthians 11:26).

lute: A stringed musical instrument with a pear-shaped body and a neck, played by plucking the strings.

lyre (lier): A small harp with 3 to 12 strings. A *lyre* was held on the lap when it was played.

Magi (MAY-ji): Men who lived in the countries of Arabia and Persia and who studied the stars. People thought the *Magi* had the power to tell the meaning of dreams. Several of the *Magi* followed a star to Bethlehem and brought Jesus expensive gifts. The *Magi* honored Him as a newborn king.

manger: A food box for cattle, donkeys or other animals. When Jesus was born, His first bed was a *manger.*

manna: The special food God gave the Israelites for the 40 years they traveled in the desert. The Bible says that *manna* looked like white seeds or flakes and tasted sweet.

mantle: A loose fitting outer robe or coat.

master: (1) From a Latin word that means "teacher," a name for Jesus. (2) An overseer, boss or owner of a slave.

mediator: A person who settles differences or arguments between two or more people. Jonathan was a *mediator* between David and Saul. Moses was a *mediator* between God and Israel. By paying the punishment for sin, Jesus became the *mediator* who makes it possible for us to have peace with God.

mercy: Showing more love or kindness to people than they expect or deserve.

Mesopotamia (MEHS-oh-poh-TAY-mee-uh): The region between the Tigris and Euphrates Rivers. The term derives from two Greek words meaning "middle" and "river." The Assyrian nation developed in northern Mesopotamia, Babylon was in the central region, and Sumer (including Ur) was in the south.

Messiah: The Savior whom God promised to send. Jesus is the *Messiah.* In Hebrew, *Messiah* means "the Anointed One." In Greek, the word for "the Anointed One" is "Christos." Christ is the name used in the New Testament to show that Jesus is the Savior.

millennium: One thousand years. The term is used in reference to Revelation 20:1-15, which mentions a thousand-year period in which Satan is bound and Christ rules.

millstone: One of a pair of large stones used to grind grain into flour.

miracle: Some event or wonderful happening done by the power of God.

Moabite (MOH-uh-bite): A person from the country of Moab, located just east of the Dead Sea. Moab often fought against Israel and at times was under the control of Israel's kings. Ruth, an ancestor of David and of Jesus, was a *Moabite.*

Moriah (MOH-rye-uh): The hill in Jerusalem on which Solomon built the Temple. Jewish tradition claims this is the same Mount Moriah on which Abraham began to sacrifice Isaac.

mortal: Subject to death. All people, plants and animals are *mortal*. God is not *mortal;* He lives forever and will never die.

Mount of Olives, Mount Olivet: A hill just outside Jerusalem, and the site of many biblical events.

myrrh: The sap of the small bush, used to make anointing oil smell good, as a perfume, as a pain killer and to prepare a body for burial. The Magi brought Jesus a gift of *myrrh*.

mystery: A truth that is understood because of God's revelation. The term appears only in the New Testament (mostly in the letters of Paul) and refers to God's plan to redeem the world through Christ.

nard: A pleasant-smelling oil made from the roots and stems of a spikenard plant. This plant grew in India. Because the oil had to be brought from India, it was very expensive. Mary poured *nard* over Jesus' feet.

Nazarene (NAZ-uh-reen): A person who lived in the town of Nazareth. Because Jesus lived in Nazareth for almost 30 years, He was often called a *Nazarene*. Later, Christians were sometimes called *Nazarenes* because they were followers of Jesus.

Nazarite, Nazirite (NAZ-uh-rite): A Hebrew person who promised to serve God in a special way for a certain length of time (anywhere from 30 days to a lifetime). To show dedication to God, a *Nazirite* would not cut his or her hair, eat or drink anything made from grapes, or touch a dead body. At the end of the time, the person lived like other people. Samuel and Samson were *Nazirites* all their lives. Some scholars believe that John the Baptist was also a *Nazirite*.

Nebo (NEE-boh): A mountain adjacent to Mount Pisgah, overlooking the Dead Sea. Mount *Nebo* was one of the peaks from which Moses viewed the Promised Land.

New Covenant. See **Covenant**.

New Testament. See **Testament**.

nomad (NOH-mad): A person who moves from place to place. In the Middle East, *nomads* live in tents and usually move when seasons change or when they need to find grass for feeding their animals. Abraham was a *nomad* for much of his life.

northern kingdom: Israel, formed when Jereboam led the northern tribes in rebellion against Rehoboam. From the beginning, Israel's kings led the people in idolatrous practices, resulting in God's judgment in the form of Assyrian conquest. A series of massive relocations dispersed the Israelites throughout the Assyrian Empire and replaced them with people who became known as Samaritans.

oath: A serious promise that what a person says is true. In Bible times, people often made an *oath* by saying "God is my witness." The *oath* often asked for God's punishment if what was said was not true. Jesus taught that people who love and obey Him do not need to make *oaths,* because they should be known for saying only what is true.

offering: A gift of money, time or other possessions given to God by a person who loves Him. In Old Testament times, people brought food and animals to the Tabernacle or Temple as *offerings* to God. The *offerings* were often burned on the altar. Animal *offerings* were always killed. Their blood symbolized sins being forgiven by death. Christians believe that offering sacrifices for the forgiveness of sins is no longer necessary because Jesus' death was the once-for-all sacrifice through which our sins can be forgiven. See also **Sacrifice.**

offspring: (1) Sons and daughters of humans. (2) The young of animals.

oil: A smooth, greasy, thick liquid. In the Bible, *oil* almost always means olive *oil,* which was squeezed from olives and used in food, as a fuel for lamps, as a medicine for wounds and as a hair dressing and skin softener. Olive *oil* was used to anoint priests and kings. It was also used in religious ceremonies in the Tabernacle and later in the Temple.

ordain: (1) To cause to happen. Psalm 65:9 says that the streams are filled with water to provide people with food because God has *ordained*—or caused—it. (2) To appoint or set apart a person to do special work. Paul was *ordained* to be a missionary to the Gentiles. (3) To decide or command.

overseer: A person who watches over and takes care of others. Joseph was an *overseer;* he watched over and directed other people who worked for Potiphar. In the New Testament, leaders in the Early Church were sometimes called *overseers.* Paul told these leaders to take care of the people in the Church in the same way a good shepherd cares for his sheep.

ox, oxen: Strong male cattle. They were used for pulling plows, wagons and other heavy loads.

pagan: A person who does not worship the true God, especially a person who worships idols.

Palestine: The land of Israel that was earlier called the land of Canaan during the time of the biblical patriarchs. The land of Israel occupied territory along the southeastern coast of the Mediterranean Sea. These terms gradually came to refer to all of the land between Egypt and Syria. The name "Palestine" was used by the classical Greek historian Herodotus (440 BC) to refer to the land of Israel that the Babylonian empire (612–539 BC) and the subsequent Persian Empire (539–334 BC) referred to as the provinces of "Judea" and "Samaria." The name "Palestine" was derived from the word "Philistia" and referred to the enemies of Israel, the Philistines. The Romans attempted to wipe out the association of Jewish people with the land of Israel by changing the name of the Roman province of "Judea" ("Provincia Judaea") to "Syria Palaestina," because of the Jewish revolts against Roman rule in the first and second centuries AD.

parable: A story that teaches a special lesson or truth. Jesus often told *parables* to teach important lessons.

paradise: Heaven.

paralytic (PAIR-uh-lih-tihc): A person who has lost the ability to move one or more arms and/or legs.

Passover: One of the Jews' most important feasts. The Jews celebrate *Passover* every spring as a reminder that God freed them from slavery in Egypt. The word comes from the way the angel of death *passed over* the homes of Israelites on whose doorposts the blood of a lamb was sprinkled. In Egyptian homes, where there was no blood on the doorposts, all the firstborn sons died. This terrible disaster convinced the Egyptian pharaoh to let the Israelites leave Egypt. At the *Passover* feast, the Jews eat bread made without yeast (unleavened bread), bitter herbs and lamb. The unleavened bread reminds them that the Israelites left Egypt in a hurry; there was no time to let bread rise. The bitter herbs remind them of their suffering in Egypt. The lamb reminds them of the lamb they killed for the first *Passover.* The *Passover* feast was the last meal Jesus ate with His disciples before He was crucified.

Passover Lamb: The lamb killed at Passover as a sacrifice. The Bible says that Jesus is our *Passover Lamb.* He was sacrificed to deliver us from sin, just as the first *Passover Lamb* was sacrificed to deliver the firstborn sons of the Israelites from death and to provide them with escape from Egypt. See also **Passover.**

patriarch: A father, either of a family or a nation. The word usually refers to either Abraham, Isaac or Jacob—the founders of the Hebrew nation. Jacob's sons and David are also called *patriarchs.*

patriarchal period: The term refers to the time before Moses when the oldest male in a family or clan was the undisputed head of the group in both temporal and spiritual matters.

penitence: Repentance; expression of remorse for sins.

Pentateuch (PEHN-tah-took): The first five books of the Old Testament. The term is from the Greek word meaning "five scrolls." These five books are also referred to as the Books of the Law, the Books of Moses and the Torah (Hebrew).

Pentecost: A Jewish feast celebrated 50 days after Passover. Today the Christian Church remembers *Pentecost* because on the first *Pentecost* after Jesus' resurrection, the Lord sent the Holy Spirit to His followers as He had promised (see Acts 2).

Perizzites (PEAR-ih-zites): One of the Canaanite tribes defeated by Joshua.

persecute: To continually treat someone cruelly or unfairly, even though the person has done nothing wrong. The early Christians were *persecuted* for teaching that Jesus is God's Son.

Persia (PER-zhah): The territory between the Persian Gulf and the Caspian Sea, and the last of the Middle Eastern powers before the conquest by Alexander the Great. Until the mid-sixth century BC, the Persians were controlled by their northern neighbors, the Medes. Under Cyrus, the Persians became the dominant partners of the Babylonians to their west and then conquered Babylon. Cyrus then released the foreigners, including the Jews, who had been held captive by Babylon. Esther, as queen to one of Cyrus's successors, foiled an attempt to destroy the Jews remaining in Persia.

pharaoh: A title given to the rulers of ancient Egypt. *Pharaoh* was the top official of Egypt just as the president is the top official of the United States today.

Pharisee: In the time of Jesus, a Jew who tried very hard to obey every part of the Jewish law. Many *Pharisees* sincerely tried to please God and to be holy, but some of them worried more about keeping every little rule than about caring for people. Jesus commended the *Pharisees* for what they taught but often scolded them because of what they did. Speaking of those *Pharisees* and scribes who opposed Him, Jesus said on the outside they seemed very holy, but on the inside they were full of lies and hate (see Matthew 23). Saul of Tarsus (later called Paul) was a *Pharisee*. Many other *Pharisees* also ended up following Jesus.

Philippi: A city in Macedonia (today, northern Greece). *Philippi* was the first European city visited by Paul on his missionary journeys.

Philistines: The people of Philistia, a region along the southeastern coast of the Mediterranean Sea. During most of Old Testament history, the *Philistine*s were major competitors with Israel for territory and power. The *Philistines,* whose origins may be traced to Crete or Greece, were far ahead of the Hebrews in technology, having mastered skills in working with metal. They adopted at least some of the Canaanite gods and often controlled much of ancient Israel, until a series of decisive defeats at the hand of David. Still, battles with Judah and Israel continued for centuries.

Pisgah (PIZ-guh)**:** A mountain adjacent to Mount Nebo, at the northeastern end of the Dead Sea. Mount *Pisgah* was one of the peaks from which Moses viewed the Promised Land.

plague: (1) A very serious disease that spreads quickly among people in an area, often causing death. (2) Anything that causes great harm or suffering. Sometimes crops were destroyed by a *plague* of locusts. (3) The 10 great disasters God sent to the Egyptians to convince the pharaoh to free the Israelites (see Exodus 4–12).

plunder: (1) To loot or rob, especially during a war. (2) The property taken by such looting or robbery.

pomegranate (PAHM-uh-GRAN-ut)**:** A fruit about the size of an apple, with a tough, reddish skin. The fruit is ruby red, very juicy and filled with edible seeds. *Pomegranates* grow on small, bushy trees.

precepts: Commands, rules or laws.

predestined: Decided or chosen beforehand. In the Bible, the term refers to God's choice.

priest: Among the Jews, a man who offered prayers and sacrifices to God for the people. *Priests* led the public worship services at the Tabernacle and later at the Temple. Often the *priests* also taught the Law of God to the people. The *priests* of Israel were all descendants of Aaron's family. All Christians are also *priests* (see 1 Peter 2:9). We are to help others learn about and worship God.

proconsul (PRO-kon-suhl)**:** A ruler in the Roman government. The Roman Empire was divided into provinces or states. The highest Roman official in each province was called the *proconsul.*

prophecy: A message from God that a prophet spoke or wrote to people. Some *prophecies* told about what God would do in the future.

prophets: Men and women in the Old and New Testaments chosen by God to tell His messages to people. Also refers to the 17 Old Testament books written by prophets.

prostitute. See **harlot.**

proverb: A short, wise saying. The Bible book of *Proverbs* is made up of many wise sayings.

provoke: To make angry; to cause trouble on purpose.

psalm: A Hebrew song or poem. A *psalm* usually praises God or tells the deep feelings of God's people. The Bible book of *Psalms* is made up of many Hebrew songs and poems.

publican: A tax collector. In the New Testament, the tax collectors secured revenue for the Romans, earning bitter condemnation as traitors.

purge: To make clean and pure.

Purim (POOR-ihm)**:** A Jewish holiday to celebrate the victory of Queen Esther and the Jews over wicked Haman.

rams: Mature male sheep. *Rams* were used for sacrifices and food. Their wool was used to make warm cloth and their horns were often used to make musical instruments called rams' horn trumpets.

ransom: The price paid to buy the freedom of a captive or slave. The New Testament says that all people are held captives to sin and death. When Jesus died on the cross, He paid the price—the *ransom*—to rescue us from the powers of sin and death. See also **redeem.**

raven: A large, black bird.

reap: (1) To gather ripe grain and fruit. (2) The reward or punishment people receive for their actions (see Galatians 6:9).

rebuke: To correct someone sternly; to scold someone.

reconcile: To help people who have been enemies become friends. In the New Testament, the word usually refers to bringing God and people together again through Jesus' life, death and resurrection. Sin separates people from God, but by dying, Jesus took the punishment for sin. When a person comes to know and love Jesus, he or she learns to love God instead of being His enemy. When this happens, the person is *reconciled* to God.

Red Sea (sometimes translated from the Hebrew as "Sea of Reeds"): The Hebrew name for the body of water crossed by Moses and the Israelites when escaping from Egypt. Various bodies of water between the northern tip of the Red Sea's Gulf of Suez and the southern marshes of Lake Menzaleh in the Nile Delta have been suggested as possible sites for that miraculous crossing.

redeem, redemption: To buy back. In Bible times, a person could buy a slave and then set the slave free. The slave had been *redeemed* by the person who had paid the price and then given the slave freedom. The New Testament tells us that by dying, Jesus paid the price to buy us back and set us free from our slavery to sin. See also **ransom.**

redeemer: A person who buys back. The term is used in the Old Testament to refer to God and to the Messiah who was promised to come.

reeds: A variety of plants that grow in swamps or along the edges of water.

refuge: A place of safety, away from danger; a shelter. See also **city of refuge.**

remnant: A small part that is left. In the Old Testament, *remnant* usually refers to the few Israelite people who remained faithful worshipers of God after their exile in Babylon.

repent, repentance: To turn around and go in the opposite direction. In the Bible, *repent* means feeling sorrow for wrongdoing, stopping the wrong action and doing what God says is right. *Repentance* always involves making a change away from sin and toward God.

restore, restoration: (1) To bring back; to establish again. (2) To bring back to a former or original condition. (3) To return something lost, stolen or taken. The return of the Jews from being captives in Babylon is referred to as their *restoration*.

resurrection: (1) To come back to life after being dead. Jesus died, was buried and after three days He rose from the dead. That event is called the *Resurrection*. It shows Jesus' power over sin and death. (2) A future time when everyone who has ever lived will live again in new, spiritual bodies that will never die. Those who do not love God will be separated from Him forever.

retribution (re-truh-BYOU-shun): A payment that is deserved. The punishment that comes to a person because he or she has broken God's law is called *retribution*.

revelation: To make known something that was hidden or unknown. In Old Testament times, God *revealed* Himself through His mighty acts and through His words to the prophets and to other people such as Abraham, Moses and David. In the New Testament, God made Himself known by sending Jesus Christ. As Jesus lived on earth, He *revealed* God's love, His holiness and His power, helping us know what God is like. One of the ways God *reveals* Himself to us is through His Word, the Bible. The last book of the Bible is called the *Revelation* of Jesus Christ because it describes how Jesus will triumph over evil.

revenge: To avenge by retaliation; to inflict punishment, injury or harm as a payback in kind.

reverence: A feeling of deep love and respect. *Reverence* should be our feeling about God and His holiness, power and love.

righteous: Thinking and doing what is correct (or right) and holy. God is *righteous* because He does only what is perfect and holy. A person who has accepted Jesus as Savior is looked at by God as being free from the guilt of sin, so God sees that person as being *righteous.* People who are members of God's family show their love for Him by doing what is correct and holy, living in *righteous* ways.

Roman: (1) A person who lived in the city of Rome. (2) A person who was a citizen of the *Roman* Empire. A *Roman* citizen enjoyed special rights and protection during Jesus' time. For example, he or she could not be punished without a fair trial, nor could a citizen be crucified. The Romans defeated the remnants of Alexander the Great's empire and established control over most of the Mediterranean world, including Israel, in the first century BC. The spread of Christianity in the first centuries AD in spite of widespread, official persecution, was aided by the ability to travel freely throughout the Empire.

Rome: A city in Italy, the capital of the Roman Republic and Empire.

Sabbath: The weekly day of rest and worship that God set apart for all people. In the Old Testament, it is the seventh day of the week (Saturday); and today for many Jews and some Christians Saturday is still observed as the *Sabbath.* For Jews, *Sabbath* starts at sundown on Friday and lasts until sunset on Saturday. Because Jesus rose from the dead on a Sunday, most Christians set aside Sunday as the day of rest and worship (see Acts 20:7).

Sabeans (Suh-BEE-uhns): People of Sheba on the southern Arabian Peninsula. *Sabeans* are mentioned occasionally in the Old Testament in connection with their commercial activities, including slave trading.

sackcloth: A rough, dark material usually woven from goats' hair. When someone died, the person's friends and family wore clothes made of *sackcloth* to show that they were very sad. A person would also wear *sackcloth* to show that he or she was sorry for sinning.

sacred: Holy; belonging to God; set apart for God.

sacrifice: A gift or offering given to God. A *sacrifice* usually involved killing an animal to pay for sin. The New Testament tells us that Jesus died as the once-for-all *sacrifice* for sinners and that no further *sacrifices* for sin are necessary.

Sadducees (SAD-yoo-seez): A sect of Jewish religious leaders in New Testament times, to be distinguished from the Pharisees (see **Pharisees**). They said that only the laws in the first five books of the Old Testament had to be obeyed. They did not believe in the Resurrection or in angels or spirits. When the New Testament speaks of the chief priests, it is referring to the *Sadducees*.

saint: One of God's people. The New Testament says that all Christians are *saints*. Paul often addressed his letters "to the *saints*."

salvation: (1) To be rescued (or delivered) from evil. (2) To be kept from danger or death. In the New Testament, *salvation* usually means to be rescued from the guilt and power of sin. By His death and resurrection, Jesus brings *salvation* to people who believe in Him.

Samaritan (suh-MARE-eh-tuhn): A person who lived in or came from the area north of Judea known as Samaria. The *Samaritans* were only partly Jewish. They worshiped God differently from the other Jews. The Jews and *Samaritans* hated each other—perhaps because of the differences in the ways they worshiped, and most Jews avoided traveling in Samaria. By traveling through Samaria and teaching the *Samaritans* about God, Jesus showed that He loved the *Samaritans* as much as any other people. Jesus even told a story about the good *Samaritan*.

sanctification, sanctify: To be set apart for God's use. A Christian's *sanctification* is an ongoing process. When a person becomes a Christian, he or she is *sanctified*. The Holy Spirit continues helping him or her become more and more like Jesus, which is the process of *sanctification*.

sanctuary: A holy place; a place where God is worshiped. In the Bible, *sanctuary* usually refers to the Tabernacle or to the Temple.

Sanhedrin (san-HEE-druhn): The highest Jewish political and religious court. In New Testament times, the *Sanhedrin* was made up of 71 men who were experts in Jewish laws. The *Sanhedrin* included the high priest, members of wealthy or prominent Jewish families, and members of the Pharisee and Sadducee religious groups.

Satan: The most powerful enemy of God and all people. Other names for *Satan* include the devil, the evil one, the prince of this world, the father of lies, the enemy, the adversary, and Lucifer. *Satan* is the ruler of a kingdom made up of demons. He hates God and tries to destroy God's work. The Bible tells us that in the end, God will destroy *Satan* and the demons.

Savior: One who saves. The Old Testament almost always speaks of God as the *Savior* of His people. Sometimes God sent someone to help His people and that person was called a *savior*. In the New Testament, *Savior* refers to Jesus. He died and rose again to rescue, or save, us from our sins.

scepter (SEHP-tuhr): A short rod held by a king or queen to show that he or she is the person who has the most authority and power.

scorpion: A spiderlike small animal. A *scorpion* has a long tail with a poisonous stinger on the end. Its sting can kill a small animal and is very painful to humans.

scribe: (1) An expert in understanding the Jewish law. *Scribes* taught the people God's laws. They also copied the Old Testament writings onto scrolls. Ezra was a *scribe*. By New Testament times, the *scribes* often served as judges in Jewish courts because they knew so much about the law. (2) A writer or secretary who earned his living writing letters or important papers for other people.

Scripture, Scriptures: Literally, "writing." The Bible. Before the New Testament was written down, *Scripture* meant the Old Testament. After the New Testament was written down, Christians began calling both the Old and New Testaments *Scripture*.

scroll: A long strip of papyrus or parchment that has writing on it. A stick was attached to each end of the strip so that it could be rolled up to make it easier to read, store and carry.

seal (or **signet**): A small tool or ring that had a design cut into one side. The owner of each *seal* had his or her own special design. When the owner wanted to put his or her own special mark or brand on something, the person would press the *seal* into hot wax or soft clay. As the wax or clay hardened, it kept the design in it. *Seals* were used in many ways, including to show that two people had reached an agreement, to seal a letter, to show who owned something.

Second Coming: The promised return of Jesus Christ to rule the earth at the end of this present age.

seer (SEE-uhr): A prophet; a person who, with God's help, could see what would happen in the future. See also **prophet.**

Semites: Descendants of Shem, one of Noah's three sons. The term also refers to people who know languages belonging to the Semitic family of languages. In ancient times the Semites included the Canaanites, Hebrews, Arabs, Assyrians, Babylonians, Arameans (Syrians) and Ethiopians.

sensual (SEN-shoo-uhl): (1) Appealing to the body's senses. (2) Caring too much for physical pleasures.

seraph, seraphim: Heavenly beings mentioned only in Isaiah's vision of God (see Isaiah 6). *Seraphim* are similar to, or possibly the same as, the cherubim mentioned elsewhere in the Bible.

servant: A person who works for the comfort or protection of others. Jesus said He is a *servant*. He instructed His followers to be *servants* to each other instead of trying to have authority over each other. In the Bible, *servant* sometimes means slave.

sexual immorality: To use *sex* in ways that God says are wrong. Sexual union between two people who are not married to each other is an example of *sexual immorality* and is a sin.

sheaf, sheaves: A bundle or bundles of cut grain stalks.

Shechem (SHEE-kehm): An area and a city, west of the Jordan River, near Samaria. It is mentioned frequently in the Old Testament, and Jereboam made it the first capital of Israel when the northern kingdom split from Judah in the south.

sheep pen, sheepfold: A protected place for sheep to stay.

shekel (SHEHK-uhl): A small weight of silver or gold that was used as money in Bible times.

shepherd: A person who takes care of sheep. *Shepherds* find grass and water for their sheep, protect them from bad weather and wild animals, bring them safely into a sheepfold (or some other sheltered area) at night, and care for sick or hurt sheep.

Shiloh: A town in the hill country west of the Jordan River, between Bethel and Shechem. For about 400 years, from the time of Joshua until the building of Solomon's Temple, *Shiloh* was home to the Tabernacle. However, when the Ark of the Covenant was captured by the Philistines in the days of Samuel, *Shiloh* gradually faded in importance.

sickle: A tool with a sharp curved blade that is attached to a short handle. A *sickle* is used to cut stalks of grain.

siege (seej): Surrounding a city or town by an army so that nothing can go in or out. The purpose of a *siege* is to make the city or town surrender.

signet. See **seal**.

sin: Any act or thought that is against the way God wants us to act or think. The Bible says that all people have *sinned*. *Sin* separates us from God. God sent Jesus to die to take the punishment for our *sins*. Because Jesus died, our *sins* can be forgiven and the separation between God and us can be removed.

Sinai (SI-nie): (1) A desert peninsula between Israel and Egypt at the northern tip of the Red Sea. (2) A mountain on the peninsula where Moses received the Ten Commandments. *Sinai* is also used in reference to the Old Testament's covenant of law.

slander: Untrue things said about a person in order to hurt his or her reputation. The Bible says that *slander* is sin.

slave: A servant who is owned by his or her master and who could be bought or sold like property. People became *slaves* if they were defeated in battle by an enemy or if they were unable to pay their debts. A *slave* had to do whatever the master ordered.

Sodom (SAHD-uhm): A city near the Dead Sea in the time of Abraham. Fire from heaven destroyed *Sodom* along with its neighbor Gomorrah because of the great wickedness of the people.

Son of Man: A name for Jesus. The name means that Jesus was a real man and that He was the One God promised to send (see Daniel 7:13). Jesus called Himself the *Son of Man* many times. *Son of Man* is also the title by which God called the prophet Ezekiel.

soothsayer (SOOTH-say-ehr): A person who said he or she could tell what would happen in the future; a fortune-teller. Both the Old and New Testaments say that *soothsaying* is wrong.

sorcerer (SOR-sihr-ehr): A person who claimed to be able to make spirits work for him or her. The Bible says that *sorcery* is a sin.

soul: The unseen part of a person that controls what he or she thinks, feels and does; spirit. Sometimes *soul* means the whole living person. The words *soul* and "spirit" mean just about the same thing, but sometimes the two are distinguished from one another.

southern kingdom: The kingdom of Judah after Jereboam led the northern tribes to rebel against Rehoboam and form the northern kingdom of Israel. For more than two centuries, until the destruction of Israel by the Assyrians, the two kingdoms were contentious neighbors. The longer existence of Judah is attributed to the occasional godly kings who led the people in spiritual reforms.

sovereign (SAH-veh-rehn/SAHV-rehn): Having authority and power over everything. God is *sovereign*.

sow: To plant seeds. In Bible times, a farmer *sowed* seeds by scattering them by hand over a plowed field.

spirit: The unseen part of a person that controls what he or she thinks, feels and does; soul. The Bible says that God is a *spirit,* showing that He does not have a physical body. See also **soul.**

staff: (1) A strong stick used for support when walking or climbing. (2) A strong wooden rod that has a hook on the end, used by a shepherd as he cares for sheep.

statute: A law or command. In the Bible, *statutes* usually refer to God's laws.

stiff-necked: Stubborn, rebellious and unwilling to learn.

stone: To throw large stones and rocks at a person until he or she is dead. *Stoning* was the way people were punished for disobeying certain parts of the Jewish law. Stephen was *stoned* for teaching that Jesus is God's Son (see Acts 7).

submission, submit: To choose to work with or to obey another person in a thoughtful, gentle way. The Bible says that Christians are to *submit* to each other in the same way that Jesus *submitted* to God when Jesus came to earth.

synagogue: A place where Jews meet together to read and study the Old Testament and to worship God.

Syria: The region directly north of Israel, called Aram in the Hebrew Bible and some modern English translations. The name *Syria* was not widely used until after Alexander the Great.

Tabernacle: The portable tent where the Israelites worshiped God. They used it while they wandered in the desert after they left Egypt and for many years after they entered the Promised Land. Moses and the people built the *Tabernacle* by following God's instructions (see Exodus 25-27). The *Tabernacle* was used until it was replaced by a permanent place of worship called the Temple.

table: A piece of furniture with a flat slab supported by legs. The Tabernacle and Temple were furnished with a golden *table* on which 12 loaves of bread, one for each tribe of Israel, were placed each week, symbolizing the presence of God among His people.

talent: A large amount of silver or gold worth a huge amount of money. One *talent* was considered to be the amount of money a working man would earn in about 10 years.

Temple: The permanent place in Jerusalem where the Jews worshiped God. The first *Temple* was built by King Solomon and the people by following the instructions God had given Solomon's father, King David. The *Temple* was a very beautiful place. It was destroyed and rebuilt twice. In AD 64, the *Temple* was destroyed again but was not rebuilt.

tempt: (1) To test a person to improve his or her spiritual strength. (2) To try to get someone to do something wrong.

testament: An agreement; a covenant. The 39 books of the Hebrew Bible are called the Old *Testament*, referring to God's original covenant of law. The 27 books of the New *Testament* present the covenant of grace that came through Jesus Christ.

testimony: (1) In the Old Testament, the Law of God. (2) In the New Testament, proof given that something is true.

tetrarch (TEH-trark): The head of a part of a country the Roman Empire divided into four sections. In the New Testament, Herod Antipas is sometimes called a *tetrarch* and sometimes a king. He was the ruler of Galilee in the time of Jesus.

threshing floor: The place where grain was trampled by oxen or beaten with a stick to separate the heads of grain from the stalk. A *threshing floor* was usually a large, flat rock or a large area of clay that was packed hard. *Threshing* *floors* were usually built where wind would blow away the chaff and leave the heavier grain. See also **winnow** and **chaff**.

Tishbite: A person from Tishbe, a town somewhere in Gilead, the West Bank region, between the Jordan River and the desert. Elijah was a *Tishbite*.

tithe: To give God one-tenth of what you earn. For example, if you had 10 dimes, you would *tithe* by giving one dime to God.

tomb: A place where dead people were buried. In Bible times, *tombs* were often natural caves or caves dug into stone cliffs.

tongues: Languages. The New Testament records miraculous speaking in *tongues*, indicating that the Holy Spirit enabled believers to speak in languages they had never learned.

trance: A deep, dreamlike state. In the Bible, a person in a trance may receive a message from God. Peter was in a *trance* when God showed him the vision of the animals in a sheet (see Acts 10:10).

transfigured: To have been changed in appearance or form. The Bible tells us that Jesus' physical appearance was *transfigured* as three of His disciples watched. His face glowed and His clothes became shining white. Moses and Elijah appeared and Jesus talked with them about His coming death.

transgression: A sin; disobeying the law of God.

treaty: A formal agreement between people, groups or countries.

trespass: To go against the rights of someone else. We *trespass* against people when we do something unfair to them or when we break laws made to protect people. We *trespass* against God when we break His laws. In the Bible, another word for *trespass* is "sin."

tribe: A group of people related in some way; clan; family. Each of the 12 *tribes* of Israel was descended from one of the 12 sons of Jacob. The descendants of Levi were assigned the honor of caring for the Tabernacle and were not given a territory, as were the other 11 tribes. (They were given 48 towns in which to live.) The descendants of Joseph were divided into two half tribes named after Joseph's two sons, Manasseh and Ephraim.

tribulation: Trouble or affliction, sometimes as punishment for wrongdoing. The Great *Tribulation* refers to a period of extraordinary, worldwide suffering when the Antichrist is allowed temporary control of human affairs.

tribute: (1) Money or services a weaker nation was made to pay to a stronger nation. (2) A gift or service given to indicate respect, affection or thanks.

trumpet: A musical instrument that looks like a straight tube that is flared at one end. *Trumpets* were played at every Temple service. See also **trumpet of ram's horn**.

trumpet of ram's horn: A horn of a ram, naturally curved, used as a musical instrument. *Trumpets of rams' horns* were used in religious ceremonies and were blown as a signal in battle.

tunic: A loose shirt reaching to the knees. A *tunic* was usually worn as an undergarment.

turban: A head covering made by twisting cloth and wrapping it around the head.

unclean: (1) Dirty. (2) Any action, thought, food, person or place that God has said is displeasing to Him. A Jewish person can become *unclean* by eating food that God had said not to eat, by touching a dead body or by getting a skin disease called leprosy. A person can become clean again by going through certain ceremonies.

unleavened bread: Bread made without yeast. *Unleavened bread* is usually flat, like a pancake or cracker.

Ur of the Chaldees/Ur of the Chaldeans: A major cultural and commercial city in ancient Mesopotamia. Ur was the original home of Abraham.

vengeance: Punishment for wrongdoing. In the Old Testament, a person was told exactly how much he or she could do to punish someone for a wrong he or she had done. But the New Testament tells people not to punish those who have wronged them. Instead, they are told to trust God to take care of the punishment because He is the only one who is completely fair and just.

vile: Disgusting or evil.

violate: (1) To break the law. (2) To force someone to have sex; to rape. (3) To make something unholy.

viper: A poisonous snake.

virgin: A person who has never had sexual intercourse.

vision: Something seen during a trance or dream. A *vision* was a way God showed someone a truth that would otherwise not be known. Sometimes people were asleep when God gave them *visions* (see Ezekiel 8:1-4; Acts 10:9-29).

vow: A promise, usually made to God.

wail: A long, loud cry to show sorrow.

widow: A woman whose husband has died.

wilderness: A large area of land where few people live. Depending on the amount of rainfall, the land might be a barren desert or be lush with vegetation.

will: Purpose; intention; plan.

wineskin: A bag made from an animal skin. Wine, milk, water and grape juice were stored in *wineskins*.

winnow: To separate the kernels of grain from the worthless husks removed from the grain. *Winnowing* was done by tossing the grain into the air during a strong breeze. The breeze would blow away the light husks and the heavier kernels of grain would fall to the ground.

wisdom: Knowledge; understanding; the application of knowledge and insights to life situations. *Wisdom* in the Bible usually refers to a God-given ability rather than human common sense.

witness: (1) A person who tells what he or she has seen. (2) To tell others what has been seen. Jesus told His followers to be *witnesses.* We are to tell what we have seen Jesus Christ do in our own lives.

woe: Misery, sorrow or great suffering.

womb: The part of a woman's body where a baby grows until it is born.

wonder: A miracle; a thing or event that causes surprise and awe. God did many *wonders* to convince Pharaoh to let the Israelites leave Egypt.

works: Actions or deeds. Although the Bible encourages us to do good *works,* it clearly teaches that no *works* can earn enough merit to secure salvation.

world: (1) The planet Earth. (2) People who follow Satan. (3) Anything that belongs to life on earth instead of eternal life with God.

worldly: Attached and attracted to values and commitments that go against God rather than being attracted to the values and commitments of the eternal kingdom of God. The Bible warns against loving *worldly* things more than the things of God.

worship: Anything a person does to show love and respect. Some people *worship* idols. Some people *worship* the one true God.

wrath: Very great anger.

Yahweh: An English equivalent of the Hebrew word for God; also translated "Jehovah." This divine name is usually translated "LORD" in the *New International Version.*

yoke: (1) A wooden bar that goes over the necks of two animals, usually oxen. The *yoke* holds the animals together when they are pulling something such as a cart or plow. (2) Two oxen *yoked* together. (3) A word picture for any burden or demand. Slavery, imprisonment, taxes or unfair laws may be called *yokes.* (4) A partnership.

Zealot (Zehl-uht): A member of a Jewish group in the time of Jesus who wanted to fight against and overthrow the Roman rulers in Judea. Jesus' disciple Simon (not Peter) was a *Zealot.*

Zion (ZI-uhn): (1) One of the hills on which the city of Jerusalem was built (Mount *Zion*). (2) The entire city of Jerusalem. (3) Another name for the nation of Israel. 4. Another name for heaven.

Maps

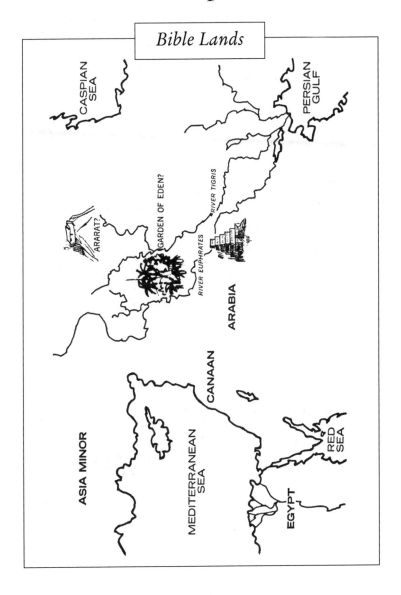

Bible Lands

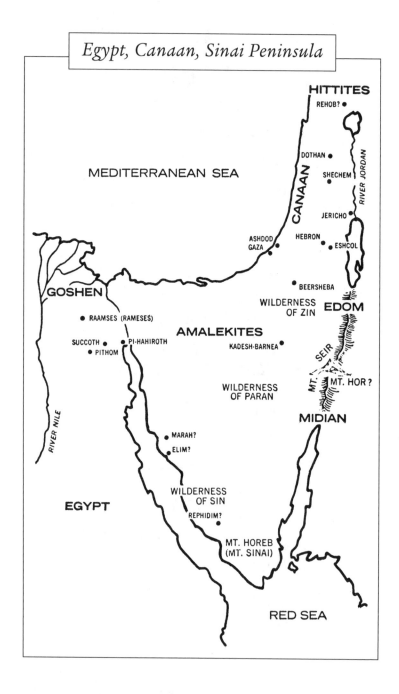

Egypt, Canaan, Sinai Peninsula

HITTITES

REHOB? •

MEDITERRANEAN SEA

DOTHAN •

CANAAN

SHECHEM •

RIVER JORDAN

JERICHO •

ASHDOD
GAZA •

HEBRON •

ESHCOL •

GOSHEN

BEERSHEBA •

• RAAMSES (RAMESES)

WILDERNESS
OF ZIN

EDOM

AMALEKITES

SUCCOTH •
• PITHOM

• PI-HAHIROTH

KADESH-BARNEA •

SEIR

WILDERNESS
OF PARAN

MT. HOR ?

MT.

MIDIAN

RIVER NILE

• MARAH?
• ELIM?

WILDERNESS
OF SIN

EGYPT

REPHIDIM?

MT. HOREB
(MT. SINAI)

RED SEA

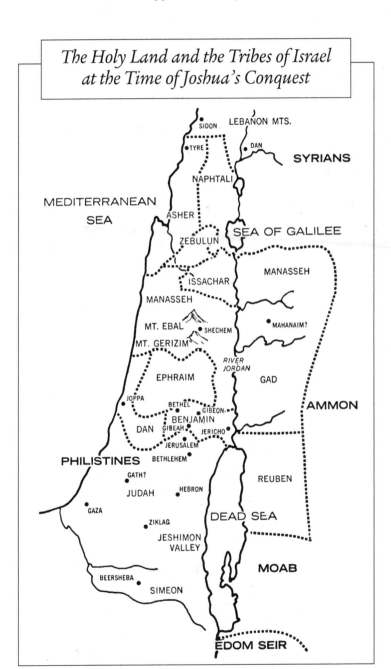

The Holy Land and the Tribes of Israel at the Time of Joshua's Conquest

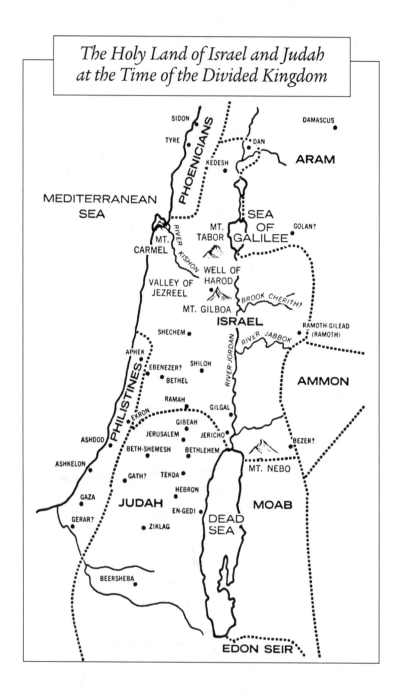

The Holy Land of Israel and Judah
at the Time of the Divided Kingdom

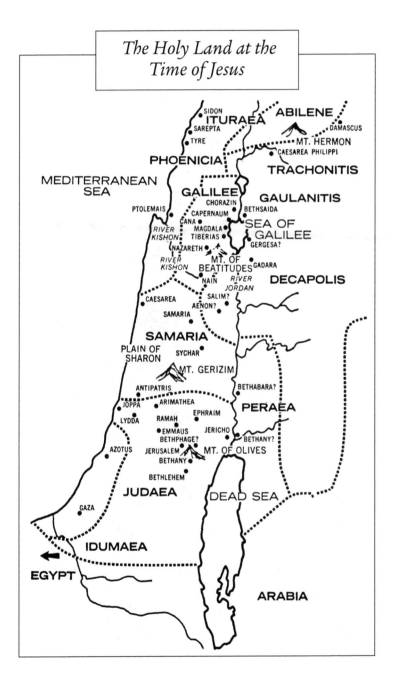

The Holy Land at the Time of Jesus

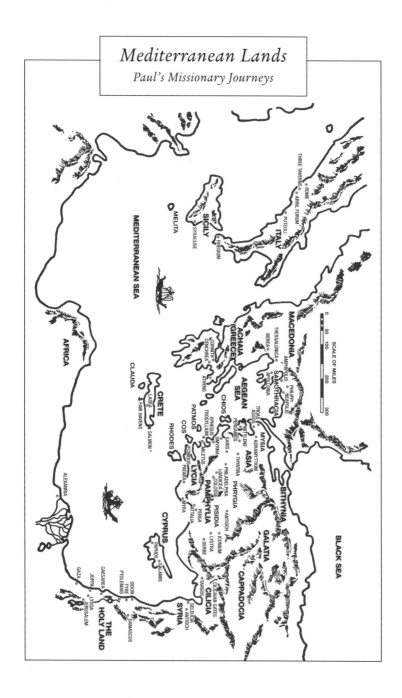

Mediterranean Lands
Paul's Missionary Journeys

Bible Reading Plans

1-YEAR PLAN
O.T. Books of Law and History

By the end of	Read Through	No. Pgs.
1st mo.	Genesis 37	
2nd mo.	Exodus 25	
3rd mo.	Leviticus 23	
4th mo.	Numbers 28	
5th mo.	Deuteronomy 30	
6th mo.	Judges 8	
7th mo.	1 Samuel 21	
8th mo.	1 Kings 2	
9th mo.	2 Kings 10	
10th mo.	1 Chronicles 17	
11th mo.	2 Chronicles 31	
12th mo.	Esther 10	

1-YEAR PLAN
O.T. Books of Poetry and Prophecy

By the end of	Read Through	No. Pgs.
1st mo.	Job 41	
2nd mo.	Psalm 62	
3rd mo.	Psalm 117	
4th mo.	Proverbs 18	
5th mo.	Isaiah 8	
6th mo.	Isaiah 43	
7th mo.	Jeremiah 6	
8th mo.	Jeremiah 38	
9th mo.	Ezekiel 15	
10th mo.	Ezekiel 45	
11th mo.	Amos 6	
12th mo.	Malachi 4	

1-YEAR PLAN
New Testament Books

By the end of	Read Through	No. Pgs.
1st mo.	Matthew 20	
2nd mo.	Mark 8	
3rd mo.	Luke 6	
4th mo.	Luke 23	
5th mo.	John 13	
6th mo.	Acts 11	
7th mo.	Romans 1	
8th mo.	1 Corinthians 11	
9th mo.	Ephesians 6	
10th mo.	Philemon	
11th mo.	2 Peter 3	
12th mo.	Revelation 22	

Bible Reading Plans

2-YEAR PLAN
New Testament Books

By the end of	Read Through	No. Pgs.
1st mo.	Matthew 11	
2nd mo.	Matthew 20	
3rd mo.	Matthew 27	
4th mo.	Mark 8	
5th mo.	Mark 16	
6th mo.	Luke 6	
7th mo.	Luke 13	
8th mo.	Luke 23	
9th mo.	John 6	
10th mo.	John 13	
11th mo.	Acts 2	
12th mo.	Acts 11	
13th mo.	Acts 20	
14th mo.	Romans 1	
15th mo.	Romans 14	
16th mo.	1 Corinthians 11	
17th mo.	2 Corinthians 10	
18th mo.	Ephesians 6	
19th mo.	1 Thessalonians 5	
20th mo.	Philemon	
21st mo.	Hebrews 13	
22nd mo.	2 Peter 3	
23rd mo.	Revelation 8	
24th mo.	Revelation 22	

2-YEAR PLAN
O.T. Books of Poetry and Prophecy

By the end of	Read Through	No. Pgs.
1st mo.	Job 20	
2nd mo.	Job 41	
3rd mo.	Psalm 33	
4th mo.	Psalm 62	
5th mo.	Psalm 88	
6th mo.	Psalm 117	
7th mo.	Psalm 150	
8th mo.	Proverbs 18	
9th mo.	Ecclesiastes 7	
10th mo.	Isaiah 8	
11th mo.	Isaiah 27	
12th mo.	Isaiah 43	
13th mo.	Isaiah 59	
14th mo.	Jeremiah 6	
15th mo.	Jeremiah 23	
16th mo.	Jeremiah 38	
17th mo.	Jeremiah 52	
18th mo.	Ezekiel 15	
19th mo.	Ezekiel 29	
20th mo.	Ezekiel 45	
21st mo.	Daniel 12	
22nd mo.	Amos 6	
23rd mo.	Habakkuk 2	
24th mo.	Malachi 4	

2-YEAR PLAN
O.T. Books of Law and History

By the end of	Read Through	No. Pgs.
1st mo.	Genesis 21	
2nd mo.	Genesis 37	
3rd mo.	Exodus 6	
4th mo.	Exodus 25	
5th mo.	Leviticus 5	
6th mo.	Leviticus 23	
7th mo.	Numbers 11	
8th mo.	Numbers 28	
9th mo.	Deuteronomy 9	
10th mo.	Deuteronomy 30	
11th mo.	Joshua 14	
12th mo.	Judges 8	
13th mo.	1 Samuel 2	
14th mo.	1 Samuel 21	
15th mo.	2 Samuel 12	
16th mo.	1 Kings 2	
17th mo.	1 Kings 16	
18th mo.	2 Kings 10	
19th mo.	1 Chronicles 1	
20th mo.	1 Chronicles 17	
21st mo.	2 Chronicles 8	
22nd mo.	2 Chronicles 31	
23rd mo.	Nehemiah 3	
24th mo.	Esther 10	

TAKE YOUR KIDS DEEPER

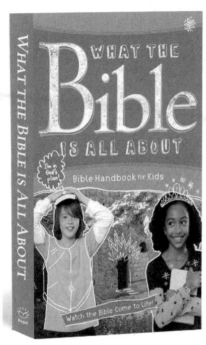

ISBN: 978-1-4964-1611-7

HELP KIDS DISCOVER JESUS ON EVERY PAGE OF THEIR BIBLE

- *Jesus Connection* helps kids find Jesus in every book of the Bible
- Engages kids in ways they can study and understand the Bible for themselves
- Includes kid-friendly visual and written resources that will help children believe, understand, know, love and follow Jesus

WHAT THE BIBLE IS ALL ABOUT
BIBLE STUDY SERIES

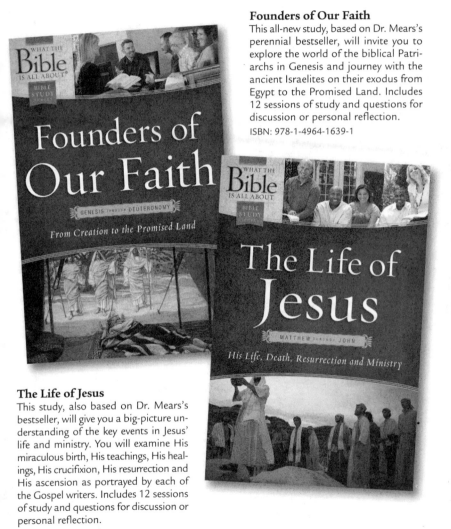

Founders of Our Faith

This all-new study, based on Dr. Mears's perennial bestseller, will invite you to explore the world of the biblical Patriarchs in Genesis and journey with the ancient Israelites on their exodus from Egypt to the Promised Land. Includes 12 sessions of study and questions for discussion or personal reflection.

ISBN: 978-1-4964-1639-1

The Life of Jesus

This study, also based on Dr. Mears's bestseller, will give you a big-picture understanding of the key events in Jesus' life and ministry. You will examine His miraculous birth, His teachings, His healings, His crucifixion, His resurrection and His ascension as portrayed by each of the Gospel writers. Includes 12 sessions of study and questions for discussion or personal reflection.

ISBN: 978-1-4964-1620-9

Available at Bookstores Everywhere!
www.whatthebibleisallabout.com